THE

WORKS OF THOMAS KYD

THE WORKS

OF

THOMAS KYD

EDITED FROM THE ORIGINAL TEXTS

WITH INTRODUCTION, NOTES, AND FACSIMILES

BY

FREDERICK S. BOAS

O.B.E., M.A., Hon. LL.D., Hon. D.Litt., F.R.S.L.

OXFORD
AT THE CLARENDON PRESS

Oxford University Press, Amen House, London E.C.4

GLASGOW NEW YORK TORONTO MELBOURNE WELLINGTON
BOMBAY CALCUTTA MADRAS KARACHI LAHORE DACCA
CAPE TOWN SALISBURY NAIROBI IBADAN ACCRA
KUALA LUMPUR HONG KONG

FIRST PUBLISHED 1901
REPRINTED LITHOGRAPHICALLY IN GREAT BRITAIN
AT THE UNIVERSITY PRESS, OXFORD
FROM CORRECTED SHEETS OF THE FIRST EDITION
WITH THE ADDITION OF A SUPPLEMENT, 1955
REPRINTED 1962

EDITOR'S NOTE TO NEW IMPRESSION

IT is more than half a century since this first attempt was made in 1901 to issue in one volume *The Works of Thomas Kyd* and a reprint has now become necessary. It was felt desirable that the opportunity should be used to take account of the chief corrections and additions to our knowledge that fifty years have provided. There has been no such single 'find' of the first importance as the Coroner's inquest in the case of Marlowe. But almost year by year contributions have been made by scholars in different countries which enable us to envisage Kyd and his work more clearly. These are arranged below, not chronologically, but under relevant heads. Particular interest has been shown in Kyd's letters to Sir J. Puckering attacking Marlowe, in the bibliography of *The Spanish Tragedie*, the problem of the 'Additions', and in the question of Kyd's authorship of the pre-Shakespearean *Hamlet*. The Malone Society's reprints of the 1602 and 1592 quartos of *The Spanish Tragedie* will act as checks on any textual inaccuracies in this edition.

It must, however, be borne in mind that the increased recognition of Kyd's dramatic importance is not confined to publications dealing specifically with him, but has coloured much recent comment on Elizabethan drama.

It may be claimed too that this edition of Kyd helped to lead in this same Clarendon Press series to R. Warwick Bond's *Lyly* and Churton Collins's *Greene*, and, more distantly, to the crowning achievement of C. H. Herford's and Dr. and Mrs. Simpson's *Ben Jonson*.

F. S. B.

February 1954

PREFACE

THIS attempt to issue, for the first time, an edition of Thomas Kyd's extant works, so far as they can be identified, will, I believe, need no lengthy justification. In the study of pre-Shakespearean literature, during the closing years of the past century, there has been no more marked feature, especially on the Continent, than the increased prominence given to Kyd. The growing realization of the unique popularity and influence of *The Spanish Tragedie* during the period between the defeat of the Armada and the outbreak of the Civil War, and the equally growing conviction that Kyd was a forerunner of Shakespeare in dramatizing the story of Hamlet, have combined to arouse the keenest interest in his personality and his writings. As the final section of my Introduction shows, monographs on different aspects of his career have, especially during the last dozen years, followed fast upon one another.

But hitherto the study of Kyd has been hampered by the lack of a complete and trustworthy text of his works. The best available substitute has been vol. v of Mr. Carew Hazlitt's edition of Dodsley's *Old Plays*, which contains *The Spanish Tragedie*, *Cornelia*, and *Soliman and Perseda*, preceded at the close of vol. iv by the anonymous *First Part of Ieronimo*. The volumes have been of much service to all students of Kyd; but texts with modernized spelling, and based upon an imperfect collation of the original Quartos, cannot satisfy the requirements of present-day scholarship. I have therefore, for the present work, collated in every case all the extant texts, and reproduced the original spelling. I had at one time thought of also keeping the original punctuation, but its chaotic state made this impossible.

In the case of *The Spanish Tragedie* I have aimed, as explained more fully in the Prefatory Note to the play, at indicating more clearly than has hitherto been done the exact relation of the Additions to the original work. And while including the *First Part of Ieronimo* in this volume as, in effect, another 'Addition' by a far inferior hand, I have, I venture to think, demonstrated more decisively than has hitherto been done, the impossibility of this fore-piece being from Kyd's pen. Nothing has interfered so much with the recognition of Kyd's dramatic powers as the ascription to him of this crude melodrama. But even some of the critics who have condemned it as spurious have not realized, as I think, adequately the merits of *The Spanish Tragedie*, when set free from this encumbrance. I have therefore sought, by a detailed examination of the play in my Introduction, to bring out the higher qualities of Kyd's art, and to show, by consequence, that the effective dramatization of the Hamlet-story was well within his range. Further, by a comparison of *The Spanish Tragedie* and the First Quarto of Shakespeare's *Hamlet*, I have tried to show that we have grounds for believing that in this Quarto we have traces of Kyd's style, and that *Hamlet*, in its final form, is due to the fusion of his inventive stagecraft, probably modified by some intermediate hand, with Shakespeare's philosophic and poetic genius.

In the discussion of the Hamlet problem an important factor is *The Housholders Philosophie*, an English version of Tasso's *Padre di Famiglia* by T. K. I have reprinted this for the first time from the Quarto of 1588, and have brought forward new internal evidence to support the identification of T. K. with Thomas Kyd, and of the work itself with one of the Italian translations produced, as Nash tells us, by the author of the *Ur-Hamlet*. I have also reprinted from the unique copy in Lambeth Palace Library the short prose tract, *The Murder of Iohn Brewen*, hitherto only accessible in vol. i of J. P. Collier's *Illustrations of English*

Popular Literature. I have further included the fragments
of lost works by Kyd preserved in Allott's *England's Parnassus*, as well as Ayrer's almost contemporary German
adaptation of *The Spanish Tragedie*.

I have also fortunately been able to make important
additions to our knowledge of Kyd's personal career from
manuscript sources. Mr. Sidney Lee, in his article on Kyd
in the *Dictionary of National Biography*, was the first to
give publicity to some brief notes by the antiquary, Thomas
Baker, transcribed by Hunter in his *Chorus Vatum*, on
charges of Atheism against Kyd, Marlowe, and others.
I succeeded in rediscovering among the Harleian Collection
the documents upon which Baker's notes were based,
and gave an account of them, with extracts, in *The Fortnightly Review* for February, 1899, but they now appear
in full for the first time. I have to thank the authorities
of the British Museum for permission to reproduce in
facsimile Kyd's letter to Sir T. Puckering and part of the
so-called 'Atheistic' treatise, which he states that he got
from Marlowe. I have also to thank Mr. J. A. Herbert of
the Department of MSS. at the British Museum for expert
help in transcribing some of the documents.

I have a number of other obligations to acknowledge.
To His Grace, the Archbishop of Canterbury, to the
Director of the British Museum, and to the Curators of
the Bodleian, I am indebted respectively for permission
to reproduce the title-pages of Kyd's various works.
Through the kind offices of Professor Morsbach, the
authorities of the University Library at Göttingen con-
ferred on me the favour of sending their unique copy of
the 1594 Quarto of *The Spanish Tragedie* to the British
Museum to enable me to collate it for the present volume.
Mr. S. Arthur Strong, Librarian to the House of Lords
and to the Duke of Devonshire, placed similarly at my
disposal the Chatsworth copies of the play, including the
unique specimen of the 1602-3 Quarto. Lord Ellesmere
very kindly gave me facilities for collating his unique copy
of the 1599 Quarto at Bridgwater House, and Mr. A. H.

Huth for examining at Ennismore Gardens his specimen
of the 1623 Quarto, which differs in its imprint from the
other extant copies of that year. The Head Master and
Secretary of Merchant Taylors' School kindly investigated,
at my request, their records for further possible light upon
Kyd's early years; and the Library Committee of the
Court of Common Council permitted me to make some
researches at the Guildhall in the hope of further eluci-
dating the circumstances of Kyd's arrest. But in neither
case was new material discovered. I have finally to
thank the staff of the Clarendon Press for many valuable
suggestions while the sheets were being printed; my wife
for help in compiling the Index; and, above all, Professor
F. York Powell for his ungrudging help and counsel at
every stage of the work.

In my Introduction and Notes I have aimed at acknow-
ledging my obligations to previous writers upon Kyd.
But two names need special mention, Professor G. Sarrazin,
the author of *Kyd und sein Kreis*, who has taken the lead
in vindicating Kyd's claim to the authorship of the pre-
Shakespearean *Hamlet*; and Professor J. Schick, whose
excellent edition of *The Spanish Tragedie* in the Temple
Dramatists is the forerunner of the larger German critical
edition of the play which he will very shortly publish, and
who has kindly supplied me with information on certain
points. But it is perhaps not unfitting that the first edition
of Kyd's writings on a comprehensive scale should appear
in the land of his birth; and though some of the issues
raised in this volume may not admit of final settlement,
I venture to hope that it may give fresh stimulus to the
study of Kyd's works, and do something to restore per-
manently to his rightful place a notable figure in the
history of the English drama.

                                                F. S. B.

CONTENTS

FACSIMILES

INTRODUCTION

I. THOMAS KYD'S EARLY LIFE AND EDUCATION.

THE fickleness of Fortune is the *Leitmotif* that runs through the writings of Thomas Kyd, and the goddess has taken a character-istic revenge upon her traducer by making him a victim of her most cruel caprice. For fifty years—the greatest years of the greatest dramatic movement the modern world has known—his chief work maintained a popularity, alike with theatre-goers and readers, probably unrivalled by that of any other single play. This popularity was not confined to England, but extended over a large part of the Continent, where, through adaptations in Dutch and German, *The Spanish Tragedie* achieved a vogue scarcely inferior to that it had won in the land of its birth. But with the triumph of Puritanism in the middle of the seventeenth century, and the closing of the theatres, came a sudden total eclipse of Kyd's fame; and the Restoration, with its new dramatic methods and ideals, knew not him nor his brethren of the 'race before the flood.' Thus, when, rather more than a hundred years after the issue of the last Quarto edition of *The Spanish Tragedie*, it was brought anew before the reading world of 1744, the very name of the author had been forgotten, and an attempted substi-tution (not endorsed, however, by Dodsley) had been made of the *nominis umbra*—Smith! As every one of the round dozen extant editions of the play is anonymous, the world might long have remained no wiser on the point, had not Hawkins, some time before 1773, fortunately lighted on the passage in *The Apology for Actors* where Heywood, in quoting three lines from *The Spanish Tragedie*, IV. i. 86–8, names Kyd as their author.

Yet even after this there remained obstacles in the way of an impartial judgement of the work. For within a decade after Kyd's death, it had attached to itself two alien elements of a strangely diverse kind. From 1602 onwards there were incor-porated in the text of the play certain 'Additions,' so steeped in passion and wild, sombre beauty, that they threw into harsh relief

Kyd's more old-fashioned technique and versification, and have prevented till this day the merits of his work in its original form being fairly recognized. On the other hand, there was published in 1605 a fore-piece to *The Spanish Tragedie* entitled *The First Part of Ieronimo*—an extravagant piece of melodrama, if indeed it be not an intentional burlesque—which has become traditionally associated with the name of Kyd, and which even some of his latest interpreters are ill-advised enough to claim as his. Fortune could scarcely have taken a more crushing revenge upon the dramatist than by doing her best to sink his reputation beneath this *damnosa hereditas*. But her malice has worked itself out in other, if possible, more ingenious ways. A punning allusion by Nash points to Kyd as having been the first of playwrights to dramatize the story of Hamlet, and to have thus laid down the lines of the world's most famous tragedy. Evidences of the most varied kind combine to support this conclusion. But as their cumulative force just falls short of complete scientific demonstration, a loophole for scepticism is left to those who either question the identification altogether, or deny the presence of Kyd's hand in any of the extant forms of the play.

And when at last, after more than two centuries of neglect or depreciation, his fame as a dramatist has begun to revive, Fortune has malevolently redressed the balance by taking the opportunity of exhibiting him, as a man, in a strangely sinister light. Till lately his life was a total blank; but now we know the main episodes of its closing years. We see him the victim of apparently unjust arrest, broken down by imprisonment and torture, pleading for the recognition of his innocence in suppliant tones. And, what is worse, we see him, in self-defence, blackening the name of the greatest of his fellows in pre-Shakespearean tragedy—the poet-dramatist round whom cluster the affections of generations of readers. It is hard to imagine any attitude more likely to repel from Kyd the sympathies of the modern world. But the revelation thus made, if not attractive, is invaluable to his biographer; and supplemented by other results of recent research, it enables us to sketch the outlines of his career.

The birth of Thomas Kyd may be fixed, beyond reasonable doubt, in the autumn of 1558. In the register of baptisms of the Church of St. Mary Woolnoth, Lombard Street, under the date

November 6, 1558, there is the entry, 'Thomas, son of Francis Kidd, Citizen and Writer of the Courte Letter of London[1].' This Thomas Kyd, as Mr. Gordon Goodwin was the first to point out (cf. *Notes and Queries*, 8th series, vol. v. pp. 305–6), may safely be identified with the dramatist. The name is not a common one, and the date fits well with the known facts of his career. His associations throughout his life, as far as we can trace them, are with the City of London. The atmosphere of his writings, apart from a few pretty but conventional rural touches added at the opening of Act III of his version of *Cornelie*, is essentially that of the town.

A few weeks after Kyd's baptism, John Morris, the rector of St. Mary Woolnoth, died, and was succeeded on November 30 by Miles Geard. During his incumbency a sister, Ann, was born to the dramatist, and baptized on September 24, 1561; and two years later the family lost a servant, Prudence Cooke, who was buried on September 2, 1563. It has been supposed that John Kyd, the stationer, who printed *The Murder of Iohn Brewen*, besides other sensational tracts and ballads, was a brother of Thomas; but as his name does not occur in the St. Mary Woolnoth registers, which go back to 1538, this can scarcely be the case; he was probably, however, a connexion.

There is no mention in the registers of the dramatist's mother; but from other sources we learn that she was called Agnes or Anna, which at the time were alternative spellings of the same name (cf. Lee's *Life of William Shakespeare*, p. 19). In a document recently discovered by Schick in *The Archdeaconry of London Probate and Administration Act Book*, fol. xi, and dated December 30, 1594, Anna Kyd, in the name of her husband Francis Kyd, 'renounces the administration' of the goods of their deceased son Thomas, of the parish of St. Mary Colchurch[2]. In the will of Francis Coldocke, the printer, proved on February 1, 1602–3, 'Francis Kyd, Scrivenour,' is named as one of the overseers, and twenty shillings are bequeathed to him, and a similar

[1] Cf. *The Transcript of the Registers of the United Parishes of St. Mary Woolnoth and St. Mary Woolchurch Haw*, by J. M. S. Brooke and A. W. C. Hallen, p. 9. 'A writer of the Courte Letter of London' was the usual designation of a scrivener prior to 1616.

[2] Cf. Schick's article, *Thomas Kyd's Todesjahr*, in the *Shakespeare-Jahrbuch* for 1899, pp. 277–80. The document is printed in full below, pp. lxxvi–lxxvii.

sum 'to Agnes Kyd, nowe the wief of Frauncis Kyd.' It is not probable that ' nowe ' implies that Agnes was a second wife.

Thus Francis Kyd was evidently a man of consideration among his neighbours ; and in 1575 and 1576, during the incumbency of Thomas Buckmaster, who succeeded Geard on October 17, 1572, he was a churchwarden of St. Mary Woolnoth, having as colleagues, first Hugh Keale, a goldsmith, and afterwards George Kevall (or Revall), a scrivener like himself (cf. *The Transcript of the Registers*, p. xxxvii). A man of this type would naturally be anxious to give his son a good education, and on October 26, 1565, we find that 'Thomas Kydd, son of Francis, scrivener,' was entered on the books of the newly-founded Merchant Taylors' School (cf. C. J. Robinson's *Register of Merchant Taylors' School*, i. p. 9, and *The Academy* for 1887, p. 346).

From the *History of Merchant Taylors' School* by H. B. Wilson, containing a reprint of the original statutes drawn up on September 24, 1561, we can gather a few facts about his early training. At the time of his admission 12*d*. had to be paid ' for writing in of his name,' and before being accepted as a scholar he must have shown that he knew ' the catechisme in English and Latyn,' and that he could ' read perfectly and write competently '—no mean accomplishments for a boy of seven. He had ' to come to the schoole in the morning at seven of the clock both winter and somer, and tarry there until eleaven, and returne againe at one of the clock, and departe at five.'

The new school, under the able headmastership of Richard Mulcaster, prospered rapidly. Soon after Kyd's admission on November 12, 1565, the Bishop of London and other ecclesiastical dignitaries held an examination of the boys ; and though he was doubtless too young to appear on this occasion, he may have had to go through the ordeal in a later year, when on June 10, 1572, the Bishop of Winchester, the Dean of St. Paul's, and others, tested the top scholars in Horace, Homer, and other subjects. Among his schoolfellows at Merchant Taylors' was Spenser, who entered the school probably about 1561, and left early in 1569. But among the poet's numerous references to his contemporaries in *The Teares of the Muses, Colin Clouts Come Home Againe*, and elsewhere, no mention is to be found of Kyd ; while the passages in *The Spanish Tragedie*, which have been supposed to show the influence of *The Faerie Queene*, are probably merely accidental parallels. Thomas Lodge, who entered Merchant Taylors' on March 23, 1570-1, and went up to Oxford in 1573, may perhaps have been a younger schoolfellow of Kyd. We do not know how long Kyd remained at Merchant Taylors', but he probably did not proceed to either of the Universities. His name cannot be found on their registers, or on that of any of the Colleges, and the scraps of Cambridge slang which occur in *The First Part of Ieronimo* (II. 3. 9) count for nothing as the piece is not by Kyd. The passage in *The Spanish Tragedie* (IV. 1. 76-7) where Hieronimo declares—

> When in *Tolledo* there I studied,
> It was my chance to write a Tragedie.

has often been taken as an autobiographical reference to a period of residence by the Isis or the Cam. But this interpretation, though plausible, cannot be accepted in default of any external evidence in its support. Kyd must have known the custom of producing plays in the halls of Colleges and other learned societies, especially as Mulcaster himself encouraged acting among his pupils. He thus naturally represented his hero, when called upon to furnish a piece for an amateur performance, as refurbishing a composition of his student days.

A careful examination of the extent and nature of the classical attainments displayed in Kyd's works tends to support the view that they are the fruit of a clever schoolboy's reading, reinforced by later private study, rather than of a methodical university training. He is familiar with a fairly wide range of Latin authors. He had Seneca's dramas at his fingers' ends. In *The Spanish Tragedie* almost every one of them is drawn upon. The beginning of the Induction is modelled upon the opening scene in the *Thyestes*. Quotations, sometimes in slightly mutilated form, are made from the *Octavia* (III. xiii. 1), the *Agamemnon* (III. xiii. 6), the *Troades* (III. xiii. 12-3), and the *Oedipus* (III. xiii. 34-5). The opening eleven lines of Act III are a paraphrase of seventeen lines in the *Agamemnon*, and in I. iii. 7, and III. xiii. 72, we have reminiscences of phrases in the *Phaedra* and the *Octavia*. Next to Seneca, Virgil appears to have been his favourite Latin writer. The main portion of the Induction is suggested by the *Aeneid*, Bk. VI. In I. iv. 20 we have a reminiscence of *Aeneid* II. 615-6, and in II. v. 78 the *Sic, sic iuuat ire sub umbras* of *Aeneid* IV. 660 is quoted as part of Hieronimo's dirge over his son. This dirge further contains echoes of Tibullus and Propertius. An adaptation of three lines of Claudian's *De Tertio Consulatu Honorii* occurs in I. ii. 12–4, and a half-line from the *Thebais* of Statius is quoted in I. ii. 55. Parts of the description of the battle in this scene are modelled on Lucan's *Pharsalia*, Bk. VII, but in this case the imitation is probably at second hand, from Garnier's reproduction of Lucan's lines in his *Cornelie*. In III. xiii. 19, however, a well-known line from the *Pharsalia* is paraphrased.

The *Letter to Puckering* contains two quotations from Cicero, from the *De Amicitia* and the *De Officiis*, besides three proverbial Latin phrases. In the *Cornelia*, in the lines added at the opening of Act III, we have an allusion to the legend of Clytie or the sunflower, taken from Ovid's *Metamorphoses*; and in III. ii. 39–44 Kyd substitutes a story from 'morall Esop' for the original passage in Garnier.

In *Soliman and Perseda*, I. iii. 140[1], we have a jocose version of the Ciceronian *O tempora, O mores*; and in IV. ii. 5 a translation of the proverbial *patria est ubicumque est bene*, quoted by Cicero in the *Tusculan Disputations*. Another proverbial phrase, in intentionally inaccurate form, occurs in II. i. 398, and a burlesque Latin line, perhaps suggested by Ovid, in IV. ii. 67. The allusion to the fate of Astyanax in V. ii. 126–8 is probably taken from Ovid's *Metamorphoses*, XVI. iv. 4.

The Housholders Philosophie gives opportunity for the display of some odds and ends of classical knowledge. The marginal notes added by Kyd include a line from Ovid's *De medicamine faciei* (p. 256) and several Scriptural texts in Latin (p. 281). In the translation itself he substitutes part of a line from Terence, though inaccurately quoted, for Tasso's Italian version of it (p. 249). In three places (pp. 246, 253, and 260) he shows his knowledge of the source of passages quoted from the *Aeneid*. But the last of these passages he mistranslates badly, while in another case (p. 266) he assigns to Bk. II of the *Aeneid* a couple of lines belonging to Bk. I; and in yet another (p. 276) he reproduces without comment a mistaken allusion of Tasso to some lines in Bk. VII, though with an added inaccuracy of his own.

Kyd, moreover, had a certain faculty of classical composition.

---

[1] Biographical data from this play, which is not an undisputed work of Kyd's, are only used to supplement the evidence from his unquestioned writings.

The Spanish Tragedie contains a number of Latin lines (I. iii.
15–7, II. v. 68–81, and III. x. 102–3) constructed mainly out
of familiar verse-tags.   Hieronimo's play in IV. iv, though in
the printed editions 'set down in English more largely for the
easier vnderstanding to euery publique reader,' was composed in
'vnknowne languages'—Balthazar, as Soliman, speaking Greek,
and Hieronimo, as the Bashaw, Latin.   The *Verses of Prayse
and Ioye*, if authentic, contain a dozen Latin elegiacs from his pen.

But in spite of Kyd's range of classical attainments, his knowledge of ancient history and legend was curiously inaccurate, as
appears from the numerous mistakes in his translations.   In *Cornelia*, III. iii. 196–200 he misses the point of an allusion to the
defeat of Hannibal by Scipio Africanus ; and in V. 410 he speaks
of the Carthaginian leader making Thrasymene 'so dezart,' evidently
not realizing that the battle took its name from a lake. In III. iii. 201
he renders *Marius, l'honneur d'Arpin* as 'Marius, Arpin's friend,'
apparently not knowing of Arpinum, and taking 'Arpin' to be
a person.   In IV. i. 91 he misunderstands an allusion to the
Campus Martius; in IV. ii. 57 he speaks of Pompey as Caesar's
brother-in-law instead of son-in-law ; while in III. iii. 88 he calls
Photinus, one of his murderers, Photis.   In numerous other
passages, as shown in the Notes, he misconceives the spirit of
Garnier's allusions to Roman history.   The *Housholders Philosophie* contains similar blunders.   Several passages from Tasso
are mistranslated, because Kyd did not understand the significance
of the term 'hero' in Greek mythology (pp. 245–6 and 260).
He twice shows his ignorance of important episodes in the story
of Ulysses (pp. 246 and 273).   He confuses the Roman Servile
War with one of the Civil Wars (p. 264), and speaks of the
Republican worthies as rising to be 'mightie men in Princes
Courts'!

Nor, judging by his allusions in Act I. v. of *The Spanish Tragedie*,
was his knowledge of modern history more accurate than that of
ancient.   He represents Robert of Gloucester in Stephen's reign
as having conquered Portugal, though he was never in that
country ; and he blunders grossly about the expeditions of
Edmund Langley to Portugal, and John of Gaunt to Spain, in
the time of Richard II.   And, as will be shown later, the historical
framework of *The Spanish Tragedie* itself is of the most unsub-
stantial kind.   Of Spanish geography he must have known even

less, for he speaks of the journey from Lisbon to Madrid being made by sea (*Sp. Tr.* III. xiv. 11). And it is doubtful if his acquaintance with the language went beyond a few current phrases, such as *pocas palabras* (*Sp. Tr.* III. xiv. 118) and *basolus manus* (*Sol. and Pers.* IV. ii. 34), an intentional corruption of *beso las manos.*

With French and Italian he was much more familiar. In the acting version of Hieronimo's play, Bel-imperia spoke in 'courtly French.' But though, like his heroine, Kyd had doubtless 'practised the French,' his translation of Garnier's *Cornelie* is full of mistakes. It is probable that he visited France, for Lorenzo speaks of having seen extempore performances 'in Paris, 'mongst the French Tragedians' (*Sp. Tr.* IV. i. 167), and the remark seems suggested by an experience of the author himself. But Kyd's journey could not have extended far south, or he would not have translated *dans le Loire* by 'at Loyre' (*Corn.* VI. ii. 45). Of Italian, as of French, his knowledge was serviceable rather than accurate. He twice quotes Italian couplets in *The Spanish Tragedie,* and makes Balthazar use that language as the Bashaw in Hieronimo's play. He puts sentiments into Lorenzo's mouth which seem borrowed from Machiavelli. But his English version of Tasso's *Padre di Famiglia* is crowded with blunders, and fully deserves Nash's sneer in the prefatory epistle to *Menaphon* at the 'home-born mediocritie' of the translator.

Indeed this fact, proved for the first time by the detailed comparisons between *The Housholders Philosophie* and Tasso's dialogue in the Notes to the present volume, is a powerful new argument in favour of applying Nash's famous piece of invective to Kyd. The passage bears upon so many points in his career that I reproduce it in full. The use of the plural throughout by Nash is evidently a mere rhetorical device, as so elaborate an indictment could only be aimed at a single personage.

'It is a common practise now a daies, amongst a sort of shifting companions, that runne through euery art and thriue by none to leaue the trade of *Nouerint*, whereto they were borne, and busie themselues with the indeuors of art, that could scarcelie latinise their neck-verse if they should haue neede; yet English Seneca read by candle-light yeeldes manie good sentences as "*bloud is a begger*" and so forth: and if you intreate him faire in a frostie morning, he will affoord you whole *Hamlets,* I should say handfulls of tragical speeches. But o griefe! *tempus edax rerum*; what's that will last alwaies? The sea exhaled by droppes will in continuance be drie, and Seneca let bloud line by line, and page by page, at length must needes die to our stage: which makes his famisht followers to imitate the Kidde in *Aesop*, who enamored with the Foxes newfangles, forsooke all hopes of life to leape into a new occupation; and these men renowncing all possibilities of credit or estimation, to intermeddle with Italian translations: wherein how poorelie they haue plodded (as those that are neither prouenzall men nor are able to distinguish of Articles) let all indifferent Gentlemen that haue trauailed in that tongue discerne by their twopenie pamphlets: and no meruaile though their home-born mediocritie be such in this matter; for what can be hoped of those that thrust *Elisium* into hell, and haue not learned, as long as they haue liued in the spheares, the iust measure of the Horizon without an hexameter. Sufficeth them to bodge vp a blanke verse with ifs and ands, and other while for recreation after their candle stuffe, hauing starched their beardes most curiouslie, to make a peripateticall path into the inner parts of the Citie, and spend two or three howers in turning ouer French *Doudie*, where they attract more infection in one minute than they can do eloquence all dayes of their life, by conuersing with anie Authors of like argument.'

Reserving for later discussion the main portion of the passage, and assuming that Nash in the allusion to 'the Kidde in *Aesop*' points, as it has been put, 'with his very finger to the person of Kyd,' we get from the opening words some light on the earlier stages of the dramatist's career. The 'trade of *Nouerint*' is the occupation of a scrivener, so termed derisively from the '*Nouerint uniuersi per praesentes*,' with which he began his documents. Kyd, the scrivener's son, was certainly 'borne' to the trade, and Nash seems to imply that he followed it for a time, before leaving it to 'busie' himself 'with the indeuors of art.' This would account for the frequent use of legal terms and technicalities in his works. In *The Spanish Tragedie*, III. xiii. 59–66, 'an action of Debt,' 'an action of the Case' and 'an *Eiectione firmae*' are mentioned, and the documents required by the respective plaintiffs—a declaration, a 'band,' and a lease—clearly distinguished. In I. iv. 85–6 Bel-imperia, in one of her repartees to Balthazar, borrows a metaphor from the procedure in the case of a loan. In I. iii. 47 the Viceroy, on the report that Balthazar, when a prisoner of war, had been slain for his father's fault, retorts that this would be 'a breach to common law of armes.' And throughout the play the negotiations between the Courts of Spain and Portugal, especially as to the articles of marriage between Balthazar and Bel-imperia, are conducted in the formal phraseology of international law. *Soliman and Perseda*, I. iv. 86–8, contains a jest by Piston at the lawyers who fleece their rich clients, while they let the poor go *sub forma pauperis*; and a few lines later the phrase 'consideration' seems to be used in its technical sense. In *The Murder of Iohn Brewen*, p. 288, in the account of Brewen's arrest of Anne Welles for the detention of his jewels, we have such bits of legal terminology as 'let the action fall,' 'released his prisoner on his owne perill.'

But if there is any truth in Nash's charge, that he was one of the 'shifting companions that runne through euery art and thriue by none,' he must soon have thrown up the paternal 'trade.' He may, as Sarrazin has suggested, have turned schoolmaster for a time. A didactic vein runs throughout his works, and his knowledge of languages would have been serviceable in this career. He was familiar, too, with the elements of mathematics. In *The Housholders Philosophie*, p. 269, he uses the learned synonym 'Algorisme' for arithmetic. In *Soliman and Perseda*, IV. i. 109–10, the thoughts of the Sultan and the heroine are compared to

> Lines parallel that neuer can be ioyned.

Earlier lines in the same play (I. ii. 75–6)—

> Yong slippes are neuer graft in windy daies ;
> Yong schollers neuer entered with the rod.

suggest that if Kyd was a teacher of youth, he was less ruthless in his methods than many Elizabethan pedagogues.

Literature, however, must from an early date have attracted him, and evidently with little material success. Hieronimo's lines in *The Spanish Tragedie*, IV. i. 70–3 :

> When I was yong, I gaue my minde
> And plide my selfe to fruitles Poetrie ;
> Which though it profite the professor naught,
> Yet is it passing pleasing to the world.

have the ring of bitter personal experience, the more so as they
are not specially appropriate either to the speaker or the situation.
And at a later date Kyd repeated this lament in the motto
appended to his *Cornelia*:

Non prosunt Domino, quae prosunt omnibus, Artes.

But though no record remains of these earlier years of authorship,
we can from various allusions in his works trace some of the
formative influences on him at this time. The theatre had
probably attracted him from his school-days, and his description
of the preparations for Hieronimo's play shows an intimate
familiarity with the details of stage arrangements. He refers
(*Sol. and Pers.* I. v. 5-8) to the flatterer, Aristippus, one of the
characters in Richard Edwardes' popular play, *Damon and
Pithias*, printed 1571. The allusion (*Sp. Tr.* IV. iv. 80) to
tragedies on the subject of 'Aiax or some Romaine peere'
probably covers, as shown in the Notes, a number of dramas
produced between 1570 and 1580. But it was not only in
English plays and players that Kyd was interested. His
reference to the extempore acting of the French tragedians in
Paris has already been mentioned; and he speaks also (*Sp. Tr.*
IV. i. 163-5) of similar performances by Italians—probably the
'comedians of Ravenna,' whose visit to England is mentioned
by Whetstone in 1582. About the time that Kyd attained his
majority, several books appeared which influenced him strongly
in various ways. In 1578 Francis Coldocke, his father's friend,
and Henry Binneman printed Henry Wotton's *Courtlie Controuersie of Cupids Cautels*, a translation of Jacques Yver's
Printemps d'Iver (1572). It is a collection of five stories
related to a company of ladies and gentlemen, the first of which
is that of Soliman and Perseda, introduced by Kyd into *The
Spanish Tragedie*, and worked up by him later, in all probability,
into separate dramatic form. In 1579 appeared his old schoolfellow Spenser's *Shepheardes Calender*, which he is likely to have
read with interest, and whence—not really from 'Aesop'—Nash
borrowed his satirical image of 'the Kidde . . . enamored with
the Foxes newfangles.' The other chief publication of this year,
Lyly's *Euphues*, affected him more powerfully. Some of the
features of style common to Kyd and Lyly—as the delight in
antitheses and plays upon words, the frequency of classical
allusions, and the artificial balancing of clauses—are due merely

to the general literary influences of the time. But we find the dramatist reproducing also distinctively Euphuistic mannerisms. Lyly is fond of making a statement and then contradicting it in a sentence beginning with ' Ay but.' This trick is carried to extremes in *The Spanish Tragedie*, II. i. 19–28. Lyly's similes from natural history, real or imaginary, have their counterpart in Kyd. Thus *Soliman and Perseda*, II. i. 130 and 199 introduce favourite Euphuistic comparisons (cf. *Notes*, and Sarrazin, p. 6). Lyly's curious transverse alliteration is also imitated. Sarrazin has illustrated this from *The Murder of Iohn Brewen*, p. 288, 11–2 : 'he had her fauours whosoeuer had her frowns : he sate and smiled when others sobbed.' And with this we may compare a couple of clauses from the *Letter to Puckering* : ' of whose consent if I had been, no question but I also shold haue been of their consort.'

In 1581 was published *Seneca his tenne Tragedies translated into Englysh*, the quarto in which Thomas Newton collected together the versions of the Roman dramatist's single plays which had been appearing at intervals since 1559. And though Nash grossly exaggerates Kyd's debt to ' English Seneca,' it had a strong influence upon his dramatic work. Important, too, was the influence of Watson's sonnet series, *Hecatompathia*, about 1582. The opening lines of Sonnet 47 are adapted in *The Spanish Tragedie*, II. i. 1–10, and Sonnet 21 possibly inspired *Soliman and Perseda* IV. i. 77–83. Tasso's *Padre di Famiglia* probably fell into his hands not very long after its composition in 1580, and he must have welcomed the publication of the first complete edition of R. Garnier's plays in 1585. It is from the text of this edition that his translation of the *Cornelie* was made.

We can thus trace the outlines of his intellectual development up to the time about which he probably began to make his reputation as a poet and dramatist. His *Letter to Puckering* supports the view that his powers, like those of Marlowe, matured rapidly, and that his chief works belong to a comparatively early stage in his career. The *Letter* was written after the death of Marlowe on June 1, 1593. In it Kyd speaks of having been in the service of a certain Lord ' almost theis three yeres.' This carries us back to the late summer or the autumn of 1590. During this period, his words seem to imply, he wrote little for the stage, for he emphasizes the contrast between his own relation to his patron and that of Marlowe, whose service ' his

Lordship neuer knewe . . . but in writing for his plaiers.' And this harmonizes well with the allegations of Nash in 1589 that Kyd had thrown up playwriting 'to leape into a new occupation' as a translator from the Italian. Hence we may plausibly infer that the bulk of Kyd's original work, especially as a playwright, belongs to the period before 1588, when *The Housholders Philosophie* appeared.

It is possible that the three fragments preserved in Allott's *England's Parnassus* (1600), and reprinted on p. 294, are from lost early dramas ; but Allott's extracts throughout his miscellany are mainly from poems, or tragedies like *Cornelia*, not intended for the stage [1]. That Kyd was a poet as well as a playwright we know from Meres, who, in drawing a parallel between two groups of English and Italian poets, names Kyd, absurdly enough, as parallel to Tasso. And there is still extant in the British Museum what may be a specimen of his non-dramatic hack work. It is a slim pamphlet printed by John Wolfe in 1586, and entitled *Verses of Prayse and Ioye* 'written vpon her Maiesties preseruation' from the conspiracy of Babington, Tychborne, and Salisbury. The pamphlet includes a copy of the 'elegie' written by Tychborne in the Tower before his execution, and 'an annswere to the same,' entitled *Hendecasyllabon T. K in Cygneam Cantionem Chidiochi Tychborne*. This *Hendecasyllabon* is an adaptation of Tychborne's verses, converting his self-reproaches into fierce invective ; and in the adapted lines there are phrases of which Kyd is fond. Thus in st. 1, l. 4, 'thy hope, thy hap and all' recalls 'the hopeles father of a hapless Sonne' (*Sp. Tr.* IV. iv. 84) and 'hopeles to hide them in a haples

---

[1] On the third fragment Schick thus comments (Preface to *Sp. Tr.* xliii): 'Thus to indulge in a last flight of fancy, we might even suppose that the third of the quotations may be taken from the *Ur-Hamlet*, say from a chorus towards the end of the play, denouncing the tyrant Claudius, whose "cursed court swells with blood and incest," and who "for a pastime, whets on the fury of his peers"—Laertes and Hamlet. We might go on to say that the lines are sufficiently wretched to account for the ridicule cast upon this lost *Hamlet*'! This flight of fancy is highly ingenious, though, as stated above, the lines come more probably from a poem than a play. But why does Schick call them 'wretched'? Torn from their context they cannot be fairly judged; and the description of a tyrant as

> An Owle that flyes the light of Parliaments
> And state assemblies,

is striking and suggestive.

tombe' (*Corn.* I. 214). St. 2. l. 1, 'Time trieth trueth and trueth
hath treason tript' is akin to the couplet (*Sp. Tr.* II. v. 58–9)—

> Time is the author both of truth and right,
> And time will bring this trecherie to light;

while in l. 3 the use of the uncommon word 'nipt' may be
paralleled from *The Spanish Tragedie*, I. i. 13. Probably
T. K. was the writer of the whole tract, not only of the
Hendecasyllabon—to which his initials are specially prefixed in
contrast to Tychborne's lines; and in some of the verses we find
phrases that may be matched from Kyd's works, e.g.—

> Raigne, liue and blissfull days enioy,
> Thou shining lampe of th' earth,

compared with—

> Perseda, blisfull lampe of Excellence.
> *The Spanish Tragedie*, IV. iv. 17.

The Latin elegiacs mingled with the English verses, might well
have been written by the dramatist, who, as has been shown,
introduced classical lines of his own composition into his chief
play.

But whether or not these *Verses of Prayse and Ioye* are to
be assigned to Kyd, it is unquestionable that about the date
when they appeared, the subject of conspiracies and murders
in royal households, and the nemesis they involved, was occupying
his mind, and was being worked up by him in plays which were
to have a far-reaching influence upon dramatic history in England
and abroad. Of these plays *The Spanish Tragedie*, whose
authenticity is beyond dispute, may be conveniently considered
first.

II. The Spanish Tragedie.

There are three extant editions of *The Spanish Tragedie* in
its original form, each represented by a single copy. They are
(1) The undated Quarto in the British Museum, with the title,
'THE | SPANISH TRAGE- | die containing the lament-
able | end of *Don Horatio* and *Bel-imperia* : | with the pittiful
death of olde *Hieronimo*. | Newly corrected and amended of
such grosse faults as | passed in the first impression | [woodcut]
AT LONDON | Printed by *Edward Allde*, for | Edward White.'
(2) The Quarto of 1594 in the University Library at Göttingen,

with the title, 'THE | SPANISH TRAGE- | die containing
the lamentable | END OF *DON HORATIO* AND | Bel-
imperia : with the pittiful death | of old *Hieronimo* | NEWLY
CORRECTED AND | amended of such grosse faults as passed
in | the first impression | LONDON | Printed by Abell
Ieffes, and are | to be sold by Edward White | 1594.'

(3) The Quarto of 1599 in the Earl of Ellesmere's Library at
Bridgewater House, with the title, 'The Spanish Tragedie|
containing the lamen | table ende of *Don Horatio*, and | *Bel-
imperia* : with the pittiful | death of old *Hieronimo* | *Newly
corrected and amended of such grosse* | faultes as passed in the
former impression. | At London | Printed by William White |
dwelling in Cow Lane | 1599.'

Of these three Quartos the undated one is, in my opinion, the
oldest. It is printed in beautifully clear type ; and though it
contains a sprinkling of mistakes, it presents the play to us, in the
main, faithfully, and in numerous passages it alone gives what is
obviously the right reading. Now a comparison of the variants
in all the extant issues—including those between 1602 and 1633
which contain Jonson's Additions [1]—establishes the practically
uniform rule, that each successive Quarto perpetuated the errors of
its predecessors and added further corruptions of its own. Thus
when we find that the 1599 Quarto agrees much more frequently
with that of 1594 than with the undated Quarto, we may conclude
that the last named represents the earlier, as it undoubtedly does
the purer text. But this undated Quarto, as the title-page tells,
was a second edition 'amended of such grosse faults as passed
in the first impression.' This first impression, of which no copy
is extant, is either that licensed for the press to Abel Jeffes on
Oct. 6, 1592, under the title of *The Spanishe tragedie of Don
HORATIO and BELLMIPEIA* ⟨sic⟩, *&c.* (Arber's *Transcript*,
II. 261), or a piratical edition issued by Edward White between
Oct. 6 and Dec. 18 [2].

---

[1] On the Quartos containing the Additions, see pp. lxxxv–lxxxvi.

[2] The question of the inter-relation of these early issues of the play is
complicated by proceedings of which we have only an imperfect record. A
writer in *The Athenæum* for Oct. 5, 1899, in a review of Schick's edition of
The Spanish Tragedie, argues in favour of the 1594 Quarto being the
earliest of the three extant texts, and the undated Quarto the latest, on
the following grounds. ' The copyright of the play remained in the possession of Jeffes from the date on which it was entered to him in the Stationers'

We are carried further back in the same year by the entries in Henslowe's *Diary*, beginning on February 19, 1591–2. Among his receipts from plays performed by Lord Strange's men Henslowe notes, 'At spanes comodye donne oracoe, the 23 of febreary, xiiis. vid.,' and 'At Ieronimo, the 14 of marche, £3. 6s.' The meaning of the earlier entry will be discussed later; the second, without doubt, refers to *The Spanish Tragedie*. Thus early in 1592 the play was in the full tide of its popularity. How much further back may we push the date of its composition? Ben Jonson in the Induction to *Bartholomew Fair*, 1614, declares: 'He that will swear *Ieronimo* or *Andronicus* are the best plays yet, shall pass unexcepted at here as a man whose judgment shows it is constant, and hath stood still these five and twenty or thirty years.' This fixes the date between 1584–9. It was in the latter year that Nash, in his attack upon Kyd, ridiculed those 'that thrust *Elisium* into hell and haue not learned so long as they haue liued in the spheares the iust measure of the Horizon

Registers, October 6, 1592, until August 13, 1599, when he transferred his right to William White, who accordingly printed an edition in that year. For Allde to have printed an edition between these dates would have been a gross invasion of Jeffes' rights. Unless, then, there were some very irregular proceedings in this business, the undated Quarto printed by Allde must have been issued at some time between Aug. 13, 1599 and Aug. 14, 1600, when *The Spanish Tragedie* was set over to Thomas Pavier, whose earliest extant edition, dated in 1602, gives for the first time the Jonsonian additions.' The writer, however, goes on to allow that 'there were some very irregular proceedings in connexion with this play and another, *Arden of Faversham*, in which both Jeffes and Edward White were concerned,' and that therefore the priority of the undated Quarto is possible. An incomplete record of these proceedings, transcribed from the lost Court Book of the Stationers' Company for 1576–1603, is preserved by Herbert in his edition of Ames' *Typographical Antiquities*, iii. 1160. We there learn that on Dec. 18, 1592, the Court ordered: 'Whereas Edw. White and Abell Jeffes have each of them offended, viz. E. W. in having printed the Spanish tragedie belonging to A. J. And A. J. in having printed the Tragedie of Arden of Kent, belonginge to E. W. It is agreed that all the books of each impression shalbe confiscated and forfayted according to thordonances to those of the poore of the company,' and 'that either of them shall pay for a fine 10s. a piece.' From this entry, coupled with the internal evidence of the Quarto, two alternative conclusions may, I think, be drawn. Either the undated Quarto is a stray copy of Edw. White's piratical edition (Allde having merely printed it to his order) which escaped confiscation, and the first faulty impression is that licensed to Jeffes; or this first impression was the confiscated one, and the undated Quarto is a copy of a second impression issued by Edw. White in 1593, by friendly arrangement with Jeffes. As Jeffes prints the Quarto of 1594 for White to sell, they must soon have come to terms.

without an hexameter. Sufficeth them to bodge vp a blanke
verse with ifs and ands.' The references here to striking passages
in *The Spanish Tragedie* are, I consider, unmistakable.   When
Nash speaks of 'thrusting Elisium into hell' he .is alluding to
The Spanish Tragedie, I. i. 73, where Kyd represents the 'faire
Elizian greene' as one of the regions in the nether world beyond
Acheron, and the abode of Pluto and Proserpine. The sneer at
those who 'haue not learned the iust measure of the Horizon
without (i. e. without the aid of) an hexameter' is directed (with
a probable pun upon the various senses of 'measure') at Kyd's
borrowing the details of his picture of the lower world from the
Sixth Book of the *Aeneid* (cf. Note on *Sp. Tr.* I. i. 18–85). The
reference to bodging up a blank verse 'with ifs and ands' is to
The Spanish Tragedie, II. i. 77, where Lorenzo cries to Pedringano
'What, Villaine, ifs and ands?' That the scene was a notorious
one is proved by the parody of it in Jonson's *Poetaster*, iii. 1,
where among the passages from *The Spanish Tragedie* declaimed
by the two *Pyrgoi* are the lines immediately preceding Lorenzo's
ejaculation.

But Nash, as shown above, implies that the writer at whom he
is aiming had given up writing tragedies to intermeddle with
Italian translations. Hence as Kyd's version of Tasso's *Il Padre
di Famiglia* was published in 1588, there is a strong presumption
that *The Spanish Tragedie* was produced before that date. On
the other hand, the play must be later than 1582, when Watson's
Hecatompathia, from which Kyd adapts a passage, was printed
(cf. Note on *Sp. Tr.* II. i. 1–10). In the same year the island of
Tersera, or 'Terceira,' mentioned in I. iii. 82, became prominent
from its prolonged resistance to Spanish attacks during the
Hispano-Portuguese war. Schick notes that the Spanish admiral,
the Marquis of Santa Cruz, wrote accounts of his expeditions,
which were translated into English about 1582 and 1584; and
Sarrazin (p. 51) points out that it became further known to literary
circles in London by Lodge's voyage to the Azores in 1585. It
was in 1585, too, that the collected edition of Garnier's works
was issued; and when Nash speaks of the authors who 'attract
infection' by spending 'two or three howers in turning ouer
French *Doudie*' he may be referring to Kyd's imitation in the
Lord General's narrative (*Sp. Tr.* I. ii. 22 ff.) of the Messenger's
account in *Cornelie*, Act V, of the battle of Thapsus.

Thus a series of evidences suggests 1585-7 as the period within which the play was written. This would be exactly midway between the limits fixed by Jonson's words in *Bartholomew Fair*. Internal tests, too, seem to support this conclusion. The 'end-stopt' blank verse, with its trifling percentage of double endings and its considerable admixture of rhyme, the excessive alliteration and the archaic vocabulary, in which Middle-English forms frequently survive, are all marks of early composition. And the allusions in Act I. sc. v to antiquated and partly mythical English victories in Spain and Portugal, are in keeping rather with the few years just before than after the splendid reality of the triumph over the Armada[1].

With the question of date that of source is partly involved. Schick has argued very plausibly that the political background of the play, dealing with the victory of Spain over Portugal, the capture of the Portuguese heir to the throne, and his proposed marriage to a Spanish lady of royal blood, is a dramatic perversion of incidents in the struggle between the two countries in 1580. The Viceroy would then be the Duke of Braganza, to whom Philip II promised 'that he should have Brazil in full sovereignty with the title of King, and that a marriage should be arranged between his daughter and the Prince of the Asturias.' Another competitor for the throne however appeared—Don Antonio, the prior of Crato, who was defeated by the Duke of Alva on Aug. 26, 1580, at Alcantara in a battle which Schick identifies with that described in Act I. sc. ii. And it seems

---

[1] These semi-historical allusions, however, taken by themselves do not help much towards fixing the date. They might have been penned after the Armada year, and Prof. Bang of Louvain has argued in *Englische Studien*, xxviii. 2. 229-34 that the line I. v. 54—

> That Spaine may not insult for her successe,

is a reference to the unsuccessful expedition of Drake and Norris to Portugal in 1589. In any case it must be noted that Peele in his *Farewell to Norris and Drake* does not mention *The Spanish Tragedie* when he appeals to the two 'Generalls' to—

> Bid theatres and proud tragedians,
> Bid Mahomet's Poo and Tamburlaine,
> King Charlemagne, Tom Stukely, and the rest,
> Adieu.

'The rest,' however, evidently covers well-known plays of the time, among which *The Spanish Tragedie* might easily be included. The argument therefore *ab silentio* cannot weigh against Nash's allusions, and the almost certain inference that the play preceded the translation from Tasso published in 1588.

a strong confirmation of his theory that Andrea, who was killed in this battle, should speak of having been slain 'in the late conflict with Portugal' (I. i. 15).

Yet, if such recent events are introduced, how can they have been woven into the texture of the main plot by 1585-7, or even earlier? For though no source of the story of Hieronimo has hitherto been found, it is probably drawn from some lost romance which preceded the play. It is antecedently improbable that an English dramatist would invent a plot concerned so entirely with incidents in the southern peninsula. And the play itself contains allusions to episodes outside the scope of its own action, and apparently narrated in the tale that formed its source. We learn that Andrea had gained Bel-imperia's love secretly, using Pedringano as a go-between, and that the discovery of their intrigue had aroused the heroine's father to violent wrath (cf. I. x, II. i. 45-50, III. x. 54-5, and III. xiv. 108-12). The incidents thus repeatedly referred to may have occurred (as will be shown later) in a fore-piece, but even so they give the impression of being taken from some work of fiction. Yet what romance writer would have ventured within a few years of 'the late conflict' between Portugal and Spain to make its well-known episodes, even in perverted form, the framework for the purely imaginary experiences of Hieronimo? This is one of the problems suggested by the play which has hitherto attracted little attention, and which cannot at present be satisfactorily solved.

But whatever the source from which Kyd drew, he succeeded in producing what was perhaps the most popular of Elizabethan plays. It achieved this distinction, be it said at once, because it was the work of a man who, though not a great poet, thinker, or moralist, was a born dramatist, with a genius for devising impressive situations and flamboyant phrases, and for exploiting to the full the technical resources of the contemporary stage. London-born and bred, versed from his earliest youth in the ideas, manners, and amusements of the citizens, and at the same time familiar with ancient and foreign literatures, he was exactly fitted to introduce a dramatic type which, while appealing to popular sympathies, would include loftier elements borrowed from classical tradition. Too many plays written in the opening decades of Elizabeth's reign have disappeared for us to be con-

fident that any single one is positively the first of its kind. But
none could exhibit more clearly, and on a broader scale, the
union of national and foreign elements than *The Spanish Tragedie*.
The Senecan machinery utilized by the authors of *Gorboduc* for an
academic, semi-political play is here adapted to a tale of elemental
human passion—the revenge, slow but sure, of Hieronimo, Marshal
of Spain, on the murderers of his only son.

But it is a mark of Kyd's originality and artistic perception,
not yet fully recognized, that he intermingles with the Senecan
elements in his tragedy strains from a purer, nobler muse. The
Induction to the play, in which the Ghost of Andrea appears
with Revenge, is suggested by the opening of Seneca's *Thyestes*.
But the first seventeen lines of the speech are sufficient for the
ordinary purposes of the classical prologue, which puts the
spectator in possession of past events necessary to the understanding of the action. The remaining sixty or seventy lines
are a flowing, vivid narrative of Andrea's descent into the
underworld, skilfully adapted and condensed from the Sixth
Book of the *Aeneid*. And though the melody of Kyd's blank
verse sounds thin beside the majestic roll of the Virgilian
hexameter, there are lines which have more than a touch of the
Mantuan's cadence with its 'dying fall' born of the poignant
sense of tears in human things. As the Ghost declaimed his
speech, an instructed auditor would realize that a greater than
Seneca stood in part sponsor to the play, and would bear with
him throughout its representation a sense of the unseen world
enfolding the solid earth, on which men hated, loved, slew and
were slain.

Another elaborate prologue precedes the opening of the action,
the narrative by the Spanish Lord General of the battle in which
Andrea met his death. The speeches of the Senecan messenger
are here Kyd's general model, but many details are borrowed
from Garnier's description of the battle of Thapsus—which in
its turn is modelled on Lucan's *Pharsalia*. Thus the Latin
epic, scarcely less than the Latin drama, has left its mark upon
The Spanish Tragedie.

Indeed, throughout the first Act the play is overweighted with
epic material. A third narrative is assigned to Horatio, who
retells the story of the battle to Bel-imperia; and yet a fourth
to Villuppo, who falsely announces the death of Balthazar on

the field at the hands of Alexandro. This superfluity of
narrative clogs the wheels of the action in the opening Scenes,
and the dramatic mechanism gets clumsily into motion. Thus it
is surprising that, before Horatio has found 'the place and hour'
to 'relate the circumstance of Don Andrea's death,' Balthazar
the captive prince should be already pleading for Bel-imperia's
hand. The swift transference of the heroine's affections from
Andrea to Horatio is inadequately motived, and her impatience
to revenge the death of her first lover, who has been slain in fair
fight, is wellnigh grotesque. The King of Spain and the Viceroy
of Portugal are, and remain throughout the play, wooden figures;
while Hieronimo is kept at first in the background, and fills no
more important rôle than that of presenter of a 'mask.' We only
realize later that this is an anticipation of the part he is to play
at the tragic crisis of the piece.

From the opening of the second Act, however, Kyd begins to
display effectively his dramatic powers. Horatio's part is too
passive, and too soon cut short, to give scope for much characterization, but the other personages are firmly drawn, and effectively
contrasted. The love-lorn, sentimental Prince Balthazar, doubly
captive to Spanish arms and Spanish beauty, is an admirable foil
to Lorenzo, the astute cold-blooded villain of quality. Lorenzo is
a remarkable figure, for in his person the Machiavellian 'politician'
makes his entry upon the Elizabethan stage. The maxims on
which he acts are those of the Florentine statesman, perverted
from public to private ends, and thus among the medley of
elements combined in *The Spanish Tragedie* he represents the
Italian Renaissance, on its sinister side. From the moment of
his confident cry (II. i. 35-6):

> I have already found a stratageme,
> To sound the bottome of this doubtfull theame,

his character is developed with unerring consistency. His attitude
in the interview with Pedringano is typical. When the latter
hesitates, though allured by the bait of 'golden coyne' to betray
his mistress' confidence, he threatens him with death for 'dallying';
and when even then Pedringano begins doubtfully,

> If Madam Bel-imperia be in love,

he cuts him short with the infuriated retort:

> What, Villaine, ifs and ands?

The phrase became notorious, but it is no mere expletive, as Nash insinuates, with which to ' bodge vp a blank verse ' : it is a revelation of the character of the man angrily tearing away figments and make-believes, bent on sounding the bottom of all doubtful themes.

Bel-imperia is Lorenzo's true sister.   With masculine strength of will and intellect, yet with a deep vein of affection in her nature, and with the polish and charm of a true *grande dame* she has her place amidst the band of tragedy heroines of whom Lady Macbeth is the supreme type.   In her opening dialogue with Balthazar (I. iv. 80 ff.) how admirable is the self-possession with which she parries his words of love, and how pithy are her rejoinders.   Kyd again shows his talent for transforming ancient devices by making the Senecan *stichomythia* the vehicle of this amorous fence.   And effectively contrasted with Bel-imperia's haughty reserve here is her passionate self-abandonment in the scenes with Horatio, wherein it is she who bids ' dangers goe,' and is forward in the war that ' breakes no bond of peace.'

To audiences on whose ears the music of the garden scenes in *Romeo and Juliet* and *The Merchant of Venice* had not yet fallen, the love-dialogue in the Marshal's 'pleasant bower,' with Flora, Cupid, Venus, and Mars shedding their influence on the scene, must have had an irresistible charm, though it is characteristic of Kyd's confused moral standard that his heroine is prepared to put no limits to her self-surrender ' when life in passion dies.'   And it is the instinct of the born dramatist that puts into her lips, in the moment of betrayal, the cry (II. iv. 56–7):

> O saue him, brother ; saue him, Balthazar,
> I loued Horatio, but he loued not me.

In the despairing effort to shield her wooer, the haughty maiden does not stop short at the most humiliating of confessions.   And how subtle is the insight which makes the love-lorn prince catch at this opportunity to reaffirm his own passion :

> But Balthazar loues Bel-imperia.

while Lorenzo, disdaining to notice the appeal, only makes the sardonic jest over his victim :

> Although his life were still ambituous proud,
> Yet he is at the highest now he is dead.

But though it is in such touches that Kyd shows his highest

dramatic faculty, his popularity with Elizabethan audiences was based mainly upon his genius for devising striking situations. The hurried entry of Hieronimo 'in his shirt,' and his discovery of his son's body waving in the wind, left an ineffaceable impression upon the Elizabethan imagination. The episode, so full of natural pathos, still keeps much of its affecting power, though our sympathy is checked by the Marshal's instant determination upon revenge.

This revenge *motif* is borrowed in part from the Senecan stage. But its tenacious grip upon pre-Shakesperean tragedy was due to its appeal to an aboriginal Teutonic instinct. The Senecan plays were founded upon tales drawn from the Greek heroic cycle, and reflecting its primitive code of ethics. But the early Northern epics and sagas, originating in similar social conditions, present kindred moral features. The feudal code of manners had hidden these primitive instincts beneath an attractive but half-unreal embroidery, which the Renaissance, with its realistic impulse, roughly bore away. There was thus something of an ethical 'reversion to type,' and the Senecan morality fell upon receptive soil. When Drake and Hawkins were emulating the deeds of the Vikings, it was natural for the drama to 'throw back' to Viking standards, and to glorify the 'wild justice' of revenge.

But it is not so much Hieronimo's deed of vengeance as his delay in accomplishing it that is the theme of the later Acts of *The Spanish Tragedie*. The cardinal weakness in the play, which prevents it ranking among dramatic masterpieces, is Kyd's failure in an adequate psychological analysis of the Marshal's motives for this delay. Inaction only becomes dramatic material when, as in the case of the Shakespearean *Hamlet*, it is shown to be rooted in some disease of character or will. But Hieronimo's procrastination is due at first merely to ignorance of who the murderers are, and afterwards to suspicion of Bel-imperia's designs. It is not till towards the close of the third Act that there is the suggestion, in the Marshal's self-reproaches, of infirmity of purpose as a contributory cause.

Yet, his mistrust of Bel-imperia's revelations in her 'bloudie writ' (III. ii. 26) is deftly made the starting-point of a grimly humorous underplot. For Lorenzo, alarmed by his inquiries, suspects Serberine, one of his tools, of having turned informer. He has him at once put out of the way by his confederate Pedringano, who is then trapped into the hands of the Watch. A delusive promise of pardon seals Pedringano's lips for the time, and nerves him to a jocular dialogue with the hangman at the foot of the gallows. But when he has been 'turned off,' a letter to Lorenzo found upon his body confirms the truth of Bel-imperia's disclosures—at the very moment when her brother, thinking the murder 'over-blown,' like 'a nine daies wonder,' releases her from the confinement in which he has 'clapt' her up.

Henceforward it is Hieronimo's own weakness of will that delays the execution of his revenge, and leads him instead to 'waste' his 'vnfruitfull words.' Kyd's art, however, is unequal to the handling of so subtle a dramatic problem; it sheds no steady, penetrating light on the tumult of the Marshal's soul. It is the art, in fact, of a playwright rather than of an introspective dramatist, and where it excels is in leading up skilfully to Hieronimo's half-frenzied outbursts. Thus in Scene xi the inquiry of the two 'Portingales' as to where Lorenzo is to be found inspires the agonized old man to the lurid description of the Inferno, wherein, with his mind's eye, he sees his arch-foe. In the following scene, when the Ambassador states that the Viceroy of Portugal has sent, on Balthazar's behalf,

His ransome due to *Don Horatio,*

Hieronimo, at the sound of the name, cries wildly,

Horatio, who cals *Horatio* ?

and appeals for justice on the murderers of his son, whom, unlike Balthazar, 'naught can ransome or redeeme.' The reaction from his agitation here to the brooding mood when he determines to seek revenge 'by a secret yet a certaine meane,' is naturally portrayed ; as is also his relapse into frenzied excitement, when his help is sought by other victims of injustice, among them the father of a murdered son. In his sympathy with this fellow-sufferer he offers him his 'handkercher' to wipe his eyes—and draws forth by mistake the one dyed in Horatio's blood. It is a notable instance of Kyd's command of striking stage effects, for the Marshal, thus suddenly confronted with the memorial of his unfulfilled revenge, breaks into fierce self-reproach, and tears distractedly the petitions in his hands as if they were the limbs of his foes. And when he is upbraided for this act of destruction, how fine is the insight which puts into his lips the retort :

> That can not be. I gaue it neuer a wound.
> Show me one drop of blood fall from the same.
> How is it possible I should slay it then?

But the delirious fit is again followed by reaction, and in the
episode of feigned reconciliation with Lorenzo the Marshal is
cool-headed enough to disarm the suspicions of his astute foe.

It is the pause before the catastrophe of the fourth Act, wherein
the Marshal, goaded at length to action by Bel-imperia's taunts,
works out the plot that is 'already in' his 'head.' In his handling
of the situation Kyd displays incontestable dramatic genius. It
has been shown above that he could press into the service of his
art purer classical models than Seneca, and in the closing Scenes
of his tragedy, not by conscious imitation, but by instinctive
affinity of method, he reproduces· something of that Sophoclean
dramatic irony which is among the crowning glories of the Attic
stage. Here Kyd is classic in a higher sense than he sought or
knew, and attains effects which were novel at the time, and have
remained rare throughout the history of the English theatre.

Hieronimo keeps the secret of his plot close, but from the
moment that Balthazar and Lorenzo ask him to help in enter-
taining the Viceroy of Portugal with a 'show,' we realize that it is
through this show that their doom is to fall upon them, and that
Hieronimo's apparently lightly dropped assent,

> Why then, ile fit you ; say no more,

has a sinister implication. Thus beneath the ripple of gay
discourse on so trivial a theme as the arrangements for an
amateur performance we catch the solemn undertone of an ever-
nearing catastrophe. When Hieronimo announces that he wishes
a tragedy of his own composition to be acted, Balthazar asks in
surprise, but without any idea of the grim significance of his
question,

> What? would you haue vs plaie a Tragedie?

And when the 'argument' of the piece has been described
Lorenzo cries approvingly, 'O excellent,' never suspecting that
the story of Soliman and Perseda has been chosen because it fits
the Marshal's bloody purposes. Nor does he scent danger even
when Hieronimo, in distributing the parts, declares meaningly

> Ile play the murderer, I warrant you,
> For I already haue conceited that,

and engages to 'furnish' the tragedy with the ransom sent by
the Viceroy to Horatio.   And though Balthazar repeats his
preference for a comedy, and objects to the performers using
'vnknowne languages' as certain to result in 'mere confusion,' he
divines nothing of the *double-entendre* in Hieronimo's assurance :

> It must be so ; for the conclusion
> Shall proue the intention, and all was good :
> And I my selfe in an Oration,
> And with a strange and wondrous shew besides,
> That I will haue there behinde a curtaine,
> Assure your selfe, shall make the matter knowne.

And, unlike his 'doomed victims,' we already with a shuddering
sense realize what that 'show' will be.

The nearer the moment of action comes, the more completely
does the Marshal seem absorbed in trifling details of stage-
management.   As he 'knocks up' the curtain for his piece he
chats with the Duke of Castile, begging him to give the King the
'copy' of the play, and to throw down the key of the gallery,
when the Court have taken their seats there.   He orders
Balthazar about unceremoniously, bidding him bring a chair and
a cushion for the King, and crying shame on him for his
dilatoriness in having his beard only half on.   Such are the
delusively common-place preliminaries to the fatal performance
in which Hieronimo, as the Bashaw, stabs Lorenzo representing
Erastus, and Bel-imperia, in the rôle of Perseda, kills Balthazar as
Solyman, and afterwards takes her own life.   And the tragic
irony culminates in the King's applauding cry (IV. iv. 68) :

> Well said.—Olde Marshall, this was brauely done,

followed by the Viceroy's smiling remonstrance,

> Were this in earnest, Bel-imperia,
> You would be better to my Sonne then so.

Nor will dramatic literature easily produce a more consummate
instance of an unforeseen περιπέτεια than when Hieronimo announces
to the horror-stricken Court that what they have beheld is not, as
they think, 'fabulously counterfeit,' and when in self-vindication
he unveils his 'show'—the murdered body of his son.

Up to this point the fourth Act is a masterly piece of work.
The criticism is strangely lacking in insight which denounces the
play as a tissue of horrors, because it abounds in episodes of

murder and suicide[1]. Tragedy is not to be distinguished from melodrama by comparative statistics about the number of violent deaths which either may legitimately introduce. The crucial point is whether such episodes are vital to the action or superfluous, and whether they have adequate psychological justification, or are dragged in from sheer lust after the horrible for its own sake. Until the close of Hieronimo's play *The Spanish Tragedie* abides the test successfully. But henceforth Kyd's finer instinct completely fails him. He shows us his hero biting off his own tongue, to ensure secrecy, and then plunging the knife, which he has obtained by a ruse, into his own breast and that of the innocent Duke of Castile, who has been throughout his friend. Thus the wild justice of revenge turns to mere massacre, and a situation inspired by the true genius of tragedy collapses into a series of blood-curdling incidents. Never has the maxim *finis coronat opus* been more disastrously violated. And the note of sheer savagery is prolonged in the epilogue where Andrea's Ghost gloats over the prospect of his enemies suffering eternal torment in hell. Yet even here echoes of Virgilian music temper the harsher strain, and glimpses are given us of Hieronimo and his loved ones amidst the Elysian fields—glimpses that help to make us less forlorn.

III. THE FIRST PART OF IERONIMO.

In passing to the discussion of the authenticity of *The First Part of Ieronimo* it is necessary to reproduce in full the entries relating to Kyd in Henslowe's *Diary*, from which a few extracts have been quoted in reference to the date of *The Spanish Tragedie*.

---

[1] Even a critic of the rank of J. A. Symonds (*Shakespeare's Predecessors in the English Drama*, p. 488) asserts that its plot contains ' the stock ingredients of a Tragedy of Blood,' because there are in it ' at least five murders, two suicides, two judicial executions, and one death in duel.' Symonds' whole discussion of *The Spanish Tragedie* is rhetorical and inaccurate. Thus he speaks of ' the ghost of Andrea crying out " Revenge! Vindicta " as it stalks about the stage.' It is Hieronimo, not the ghost, who utters the words here inexactly quoted (III. xiii. 1-2), and the ghost, so far from ' stalking,' sits down to watch the action of the play (I. i. 90). In describing the close of the drama Symonds says that Hieronimo ' bites out his tongue, and flings it on the stage ; stabs his enemy with a stiletto, and pierces his own heart.' The melodramatic touch about the Marshal flinging his tongue on the stage is a gratuitous addition, and the weapon with which he stabs Castile and himself is not a ' stiletto,' but a knife that he borrows to ' mend his pen.'

These entries, beginning on February 23, 1591–2, when Lord Strange's men were performing, are as follows :—

R(eceive)d at spanes comodye donne oracoe, the 23 of february.	xiiis vid
Rd at the comodey of done oracio, the 13 of marche 1591	xxixs
Rd at Ieronymo, the 14 of marche 1591	£iii vis
Rd at Ieronymo, the 20 of marche 1591	xxxviiis
Rd at done oracio, the 30 of marche 1591	xxxixs
Rd at Ieronymo, the 31 of marche 1591.	£iii
Rd at Ieronymo, the 7 of aprell 1591	xxvis
Rd at the comodey of Ieronymo, the 10 of aprell 1591	xxviiis
Rd at Ieronymo, the 14 of aprell 1591	xxxiiis
Rd at the comodey Ieronymo, the 22 of aprell 1591	xviis
Rd at Ieronymo, the 24 of aprell 1592	xxviiis
Rd at Ieronymo, the 2 of maye 1592	xxxivs
Rd at Ieronymo, the 9 of maye 1592	xxvis
Whittson-tyde. Rd at Ieronymo, the 13 of maye 1592.	£iii ivs
Rd at the comodey of Ieronymo, the 21 of maye 1592	xxviiis
Rd at Ieronymo, the 22 of maye 1592	xxviis
Rd at Ieronymo, the 27 of maye 1592	xxiiis
Rd at Ieronymo, the 9 of june 1592	xxviiis
Rd at Ieronymo, the 18 of june 1592	xxivs
Rd at the comodey of Ieronymo, the 20 of june 1592	xivs
* * * * *	
Rd at Ieronymo, the 30 of desembr 1592	£iii viiis
Rd at Ieronymo, the 8 of janewary 1593	xxiis
Rd at Ieronymo, the 22 of jeneway 1593	xxs

From January 23, 1593, there is no record by Henslowe of any representation of 'Ieronymo' or 'done oracio' till January 7, 1597, when the Lord Admiral's players were performing. During 1597 the following entries appear in the Diary :—

7 of jenewary 1597 Rd at Ioronymo			£iii
11 of jeneway 1597 Rd at Ioranymo			xxxxs
17 of jeneway 1597 Rd at Ioronymo			xxs
22 of jeneway 1597 Rd at Ioronymo			xixs
janeway 31, Rd at Ioronymo		01 04	01 15 06[1]
febreary 9, Rd at Ioronymo		00 17	04 15 02
marche 8, Rd at Ioronymo		01 01	00 03 04
aprille 21, Rd at Ieronymo		00 17	00 03 04
maye 4, Rd at Ioronymo		00 11	07 14 00
maye 25, Rd at Ioronymo		00 19	00 14 06
june 20, Rd at Ioronemo		00 14	00 00 00
july 19, Rd at Ieronemo		01 00	01 13 01
october 11, Rd at Ieroneymo		02 00	01 13 00

From a consideration of these entries, thus set out in full, there

---

[1] Henslowe here adopts a different system of entry. The figures to the left of the dividing line probably represent his receipts in pounds and shillings; the significance to the other figures is doubtful.

seems to me no doubt that Schick is right in concluding that by 'Ieronymo' Henslowe means *The Spanish Tragedie*[1]. It is by this title, it should be remembered, that he refers to the play in his record of the two payments on September 25, 1601, and June 24, 1602, to Ben Jonson for 'Additions' to it. It is the name, moreover, by which, as innumerable allusions prove, it was currently known during the Elizabethan age; and the large 'takings' on March 14 and 31, 1591-2, on May 13 and December 30, 1592, and on January 7, 1597, were evidently due to its exceptional popularity.

But what is to be made of the references to 'the comodey of done oracio' and 'the comodey of Ieronimo'? It is noteworthy that the play designated by one or other of these titles was performed, in almost every case, on the afternoon before *The Spanish Tragedie*, or but a few days earlier. The natural inference is that Henslowe is here mentioning some humorous fore-piece which it was customary to produce by way of introduction to the principal play. And in *The Spanish Tragedie* itself there are several allusions which seem to assume a knowledge in the audience of events prior to the opening of the action, and apparently handled in a preliminary piece. These, as shown in the note on Act I. i. 10, relate chiefly to the secret love of Andrea and Bel-imperia, and Castile's outburst of wrath at its discovery.

But allowing on these grounds that a fore-piece to *The Spanish Tragedie*, presumably from the hand of Kyd, probably existed in 1592, we have to inquire whether in the black-letter quarto of 1605, entitled *The First Part of Ieronimo or The Warres of Portugal*, this fore-piece has been preserved. The answer to this question must, in my opinion, be an unqualified negative. In the first place, as Henslowe does not mention the fore-piece after June, 1592, it would seem to have had a short stage life. Nor was it printed for the benefit of the reading public together with *The Spanish Tragedie* in any of the numerous editions of the latter play up to 1603. That it should have suddenly appeared

---

[1] Cf. *Archiv für neuere Sprachen*, xc. p. 185. Mr. Sidney Lee, in his article on Kyd in *The Dict. of Nat. Biography*, xxxi. p. 350, is mistaken, as Schick has shown, in identifying *donne oracoe* (or *done oracio*) and *the comodey of Ieronymo* with *The Spanish Tragedie*, and *Ieronymo* with *The First Part*. Hence his erroneous inference that 'contrary to expectation *The First Part* seems to have been usually played on the night succeeding that on which *The Spanish Tragedie* was represented.'

by itself in 1605 is therefore highly improbable. But apart from *a priori* presumptions, this quarto of 1605 contains internal proofs of having been written after the seventeenth century had begun. The allusion in Act I. i. 25–9 to the year of Jubilee in Rome is an evident reference to the Jubilee of 1600, and it is a purely arbitrary hypothesis that the passage is an interpolation. The constant jests, too, about Ieronimo's diminutive stature are probably suggested by the performance of *The Spanish Tragedie* by the Children of the Chapel at Blackfriars in 1604. These Children had misappropriated the play, and the King's Company had revenged themselves by performing Marston's *The Malcontent*, which belonged to their rivals. Hence in the Induction to *The Malcontent*, when Sly reproaches the King's men for acting Marston's piece, Condell retorts :

'Why not Malevole *in folio* with us, as Ieronimo *in decimo sexto* with them.

The natural inference from these considerations is that the quarto of 1605 does not represent the apparently short-lived sixteenth-century fore-piece mentioned by Henslowe ; but that it is the work of an anonymous playwright who took advantage of the excitement caused by the revival of *The Spanish Tragedie* in 1602 with Ben Jonson's Additions to bring out this so-called ' First Part '—a medley of farce and melodrama. The whole weight of internal evidence supports this view.

One important factor in the argument has, as far as I am aware, never been hitherto considered. It has been shown above that the episode of Andrea's and Bel-imperia's secret love and of Castile's explosion of wrath at its discovery must have been prominent in any fore-piece written by Kyd himself. But the plot of *The First Part of Ieronimo* contains nothing of this, and is indeed incompatible with it. The love between Andrea and Bel-imperia, so far from being secret, is known not only to the heroine's brother and to Horatio, but to a stranger like Lazarotto. She is courted also by Alcario, the Duke of Medina's son, whom Lazarotto murders in mistake for Andrea—incidents of which Kyd shows no knowledge. And when Lazarotto reveals the whole story in the presence of Castile, the Duke utters no word of surprise or anger (II. v. 23 ff.). In fact, Andrea and Bel-imperia are found in the next scene engaged in an amorous dialogue, as if nothing had happened. Moreover, the characters of Bel-imperia and her brother are quite differently portrayed in *The Spanish Tragedie* and *The First Part of Ieronimo*. In the latter, the proud, self-reliant heroine of Kyd's play is metamorphozed into a sentimental girl, 'a most weeping creature.' Lorenzo, who in the *Tragedie* is the typical aristocratic villain, disdaining to trifle words with ' base companions,' is here represented (I. iii) as indulging in undignified jocularity with a ' slave ' of the stamp of Lazarotto, and after-wards making to Alcario the childish proposal that he should win Bel-imperia's love by disguising himself in ' a suit iust of Andreas cullers.'

Still more remarkable is the transformation of the principal personage. Hieronimo in *The Spanish Tragedie* is throughout a dignified and pathetic figure; even his most extravagant utterances are inspired by a glowing, though turbid, imagination. In *The First Part of Ieronimo* he sinks into a buffoon. His opening words,

> My knee sings thanks vnto your highnes bountie ;
> Come hether, boy *Horatio* ; fould thy ioynts ;
> Kneele by thy fathers loynes, and thank my leedge

strike a grotesque note, which is repeated in every scene where he appears. The episode, for instance (I. v), of his dictation to Horatio of the letter of warning to Andrea is sheerly farcical, while his anger, as in the duel of abuse with Balthazar (III. i. 33–44), and his affectionate pride in his son find equally ludicrous expression.

Sarrazin (*Thomas Kyd und sein Kreis*, p. 56) has attempted to show that the differences in the character of the Marshal in the two plays are merely due to natural dramatic development, and he quotes a number of Shakesperean analogies, including Mercutio, Henry V, and the Fool in *King Lear*. But such modifications as these figures go through springs inevitably from the varying situations in which they are placed, and in essentials they remain always unchanged. The two Hieronimos have nothing in common but their name.

The love-lorn, moody, Balthazar, too, of *The Spanish Tragedie* is scarcely recognizable in the Portuguese Prince of *The First Part*, the hot-headed champion of his country's rights. For this the change in his circumstances might partly account, but the technique of the embassy and battle-scenes in which he appears is fundamentally different from the corresponding scenes in Kyd's play. Curt, cut-and-thrust repartee takes the place of carefully elaborated and frequently over-artificial dialogue, and feats of arms which Kyd, as has been shown, narrates in semi-epic fashion are here put upon the boards with the crudest spectacular realism. In so far as rhetorical effects are attempted, they are so extravagantly bombastic that it is hard to believe that they are not intentional burlesque. Such passages as Act III. ii. 14–7, 45–9, and 92–5. are in a vein of ludicrous hyperbole entirely foreign to the author of *The Spanish Tragedie*, and every page abounds in almost equally fantastic conceits. The anonymous playwright, amongst other singularities of diction, delights in giving prominence to the various parts of the human body. He dwells upon the joints, loins, ribs, veins, heart, and other organs of his *dramatis personae* with all the zest of an anatomical expert. He is fond too of using certain realistic verbs and adjectives, such as melt, sweat, bleeding, hot, purple. Of these strongly-marked peculiarities of vocabulary there is scarcely a trace in *The Spanish Tragedie*. The versification, also, of the two pieces is essentially dissimilar. Both are, it is true, alike in using blank verse interspersed with rhyming couplets. But the blank verse in the *First Part of Ieronimo* is distinguished from that in *The Spanish Tragedie* by the far more frequent introduction of *enjambements* and double endings. The rhythm of the couplet is less smooth than in Kyd's play, pauses being frequent in the middle of the line, and the construction harsh and elliptical. These are the metrical features that one would expect to find in a piece produced between 1600 and 1605, but not in one fifteen or twenty years earlier.

Thus on a review of all the evidence I have no hesitation in rejecting *The First Part of Ieronimo* as spurious, and in endorsing the conclusion of Rudolf Fischer that it is the work of a journey-man playwright who found in the Induction to *The Spanish Tragedie* hints from which he manufactured this crude melodrama, whose title served as a decoy to the theatre-going public, and which has had the effect, doubtless unforeseen by its author, of fatally injuring the fame of Kyd [1].

---

[1] See Fischer's able discussion of the piece in his *Zur Kunstentwicklung der Englischen Tragödie*, pp. 100–12. He notices that in one or two points it contradicts Kyd's play. Thus in Act III. sc. ii Lorenzo is made to kill Don Pedro, who is still alive in *The Spanish Tragedie*, and Andrea is slain, not by Balthazar, but by some 'Portugales.' Fischer does not allude to one

IV. THE UR-HAMLET[1].

But if Kyd's biographer can, as I hold, lift once and for all the incubus of *The First Part of Ieronimo* from off his reputation, he has a more difficult, if more alluring task in vindicating his claim to be the first playwright who put the story of Hamlet upon the stage. There is only one piece of external evidence in support of this claim, but it is very strong in itself, and is rendered practically conclusive by arguments from analogy. The external evidence is contained in the passage from Nash's prefatory Epistle to *Menaphon*, quoted on pp. xx–xxi. It has been shown there, and more fully on pp. xxviii–xxix, that, unless we are misled by a wellnigh incredible conspiracy of coincidences, Kyd must be the object of Nash's attack, and, consequently, the author of the early Hamlet-tragedy to which he derisively alludes.

One point only in Nash's invective, which has been somewhat overlooked, raises a difficulty. He talks of his enemy as being scarcely able to 'latinize' his neck-verse, and then continues : 'yet English Seneca read by candle-light yeeldes manie good sentences, as "bloud is a begger," and so forth : and if you intreate him faire in a frostie morning, he will affoord you whole *Hamlets*, I should say handfulls of tragical speeches.' It must be admitted that to say of Kyd that he could scarcely latinize his neck-verse is stretching a satirist's licence to its limits. The *alumnus* of Merchant Taylors' had, as has been shown, a fairly wide, if not very accurate knowledge of classical literature, and he knew his Seneca thoroughly in the original. But in a passage like Act III. i. 1–11 of *The Spanish Tragedie*, where lines 57–73 of the Roman dramatist's *Agamemnon* are adapted into English, an unfriendly eye might see the influence of a translation, and the *Ur-Hamlet* may have contained a number of these borrowings. In any case, the charge against its author of 'bleeding' English Seneca line by line, and page by page, must be exaggerated, for the play seems to have been in blank verse, while the translations

---

curious detail, the introduction in the stage-direction after Act III. iii. 27 of the two names Phillippo and Cassimero, which do not occur either in *The Spanish Tragedie* or elsewhere in *The First Part of Ieronimo*. It is just possible that the piece may have contained some scenes which have not come down to us, or that these names occur in the lost source of Hieronimo's story.

[1] I have adopted the convenient German title, which tersely distinguishes the *Ur*, or original, Hamlet-tragedy from Shakespeare's play.

of the 'Ten tragedies' were chiefly in rhymed fourteeners. Moreover, with a reckless disregard of consistency in his eagerness
to make damaging hits, Nash, having first taunted his enemy
with his lack of Latinity, afterwards accuses him of borrowing
his description of the lower world from Virgil, for this (cf. p. xxix)
is what is evidently meant by his learning 'the measure of the
Horizon' from 'an hexameter.' Thus the satirist's scurrilous depreciation of his rival's classical attainments may be largely discounted,
and cannot outweigh the cumulative argument from the entire
passage for identifying Kyd and the author of the *Ur-Hamlet*.

Can this identification be supported on other grounds, and
can we form any definite idea of the nature of the lost play?
To answer these questions, with their far-reaching consequences,
we must glance first at the Hamlet-story in its undramatized
form. As freely rendered by Belleforest in his *Histoires Tragiques*,
1571 (Bk. V. pp. 197–302), from the Latin of Saxo Grammaticus, it
is a primitive tale of lust, blood-feuds, and revenge. It embraces
the marriage of Horvvendille, governor of Diethmarsen, with
Geruthe, daughter of the King of Denmark, and the birth of
their son Amleth; the murder of Horvvendille by his brother
Fengon, and the latter's union with Geruthe, whom he had
previously seduced; Amleth's pretence of madness to compass
his revenge on his uncle; his interview with his mother in a closet,
and the murder of an eaves-dropping councillor; his dispatch by
Fengon to England with secret instructions for his assassination;
his discovery of the plot and return, followed by the execution of
his long-delayed vengeance; his ascent afterwards of the Danish
throne, his double marriage, and his death in battle at the hands
of his maternal uncle Wiglere.

The dramatization of this story was doubtless prompted by the
visit of English actors to the Court of Helsingör (Elsinore) in
1586. The troupe returned in the autumn of 1587, and it was
probably in the latter part of this year, or in 1588, that the piece
ridiculed by Nash was written. From his allusions we gather
that this first Hamlet-play was in Senecan style, and that it
contained elaborate 'tragicall speeches,' and phrases like 'bloud
is a begger,' which caught the popular ear. In all these points
its technique corresponded to that of *The Spanish Tragedie*.
One of its Senecan features was evidently the introduction of
the Ghost of Hamlet's father—of whom Belleforest knows nothing

—for Lodge in his *Wit's Miserie*, 1596, speaks of 'the ghost which cried so miserally at the Theator like an oister-wife, *Hamlet, reuenge.*' The parallelism with the Ghost of Andrea is obvious, but these bloodthirsty *Umbrae* haunt early Elizabethan Tragedy so assiduously that the presence of one of them does not count for much in deciding claims of authorship.

What is far more significant is the transformation in other, more unique, features which Belleforest's story seems to have undergone as soon as it was put upon the stage. For the First Quarto of the Shakespearean *Hamlet*, whatever view be taken of the problems which it raises in other ways, reproduces, it may be reasonably inferred, at least the broad outlines of the earlier play on the subject. And in it we find the original saga developed into a complex dramatic structure curiously analogous to *The Spanish Tragedie*. For as in that play the *Leitmotif* of Hieronimo's revenge is interwoven with a political intrigue and a love-romance, so the First Quarto contains a tripartite plot, on exactly parallel lines. Belleforest does not mention Norway except to say that Collere, its king, was killed in a duel with Horvvendille. But as in *The Spanish Tragedie* ambassadors pass to and fro, between Spain and Portugal, with 'articles' relating to the Viceroy's son, so in the First Quarto they come and go between Denmark and Norway with articles concerning the Norwegian king's nephew. Belleforest represents Hamlet, before his coronation, as indifferent to women. But as the Portuguese prince Balthazar has an ill-starred love for Bel-imperia, so Hamlet in the Quarto is found similarly circumstanced towards a lady, Ofelia. And as Bel-imperia's father and brother lecture her in turn on her behaviour, so Ofelia is treated in like manner by Leartes and Corambis. The parallel between the two brothers Leartes and Lorenzo is strikingly close, and it is noticeable that the latter, as well as the former, is represented as having been for a time in Paris (*Sp. Tr.* IV. i. 166–7). The contrast between Hamlet and Leartes in their pursuit of vengeance for a murdered father is akin to that between Hieronimo and Bazulto in their endeavours to obtain justice for a murdered son. Hamlet, like Hieronimo, makes use of a theatrical performance as a factor in his plan of revenge. This 'play-scene' in the Quarto, it is true, does not, as in *The Spanish Tragedie*, bring about the catastrophe of the piece. But the final episode of the fencing-match between Hamlet and Leartes, when (as the stage-direction puts it) they 'play' before the King, Queen, and Court, and when an apparently harmless diversion turns abruptly into a tragic *mêlée* involving performers and spectators in a common doom—does not all this, of which there is no hint in Belleforest, exactly reproduce the crowning situation at the close of *The Spanish Tragedie*?

Thus if the First Quarto of *Hamlet* preserves even the broadest outlines of the *Ur-Hamlet*, the strong external evidence in favour of Kyd's authorship thereof is confirmed by practically irresistible internal tests. But can we go even further and find in the First Quarto, or elsewhere, something more than mere outlines—actual traces of the early play? In the German piece *Der Bestrafte Brudermord*, known from a MS. dated 1710, and first printed by Reichard in 1781, critics like Latham (*Two Dissertations on Hamlet*, 1872) and Widgery (*Harness Prize Essay*, 1880) have seen an adaptation of the *Ur-Hamlet*, preserving features of it otherwise lost. But Tanger [1] has, I consider, conclusively proved that this piece is nothing more than a version of the First Quarto, with probably a few later additions due to actors familiar with Shakespeare's play in its later form. Its unique passages, instead of being survivals from a vanished original, are simply such accretions to the text as would naturally arise after its acclimatization on the German stage. Thus the poetical Prologue in which Night summons the Furies and dispatches them to their fell work might, with little change, be prefixed to any tragedy of lust and murder. Hamlet's anecdote (II. iv) of the cavalier in Anion who at night found his seemingly lovely bride a mere patchwork of paint and false features is met with in other German plays of the period. His reproof to the actors (II. vii), who call themselves *hochteutsche Comödianten*, exactly hits off the weak points in the German travelling companies of the time. His tale in the same Scene of the woman in Strassburg who, after murdering her husband, was moved to confess her crime by seeing a similar tragedy represented on the stage, is suggested by the lines,

> I have heard that guilty creatures sitting at a play
> Hath, by the very cunning of the scene, confest a murder.

[1] Cf. his article *Der bestrafte Brudermord oder Prinz Hamlet aus Dänemark und sein Verhältniss zu Shakespeare's Hamlet* in the *Shakespeare-Jahrbuch*, xxiii. 224–45.

There is only one of his utterances that presents difficulty. When the King tells him (III. 10) that he is going to send him to England he retorts, 'Ja, ja, König, schickt mich nur nach Portugall, auf dass ich nimmer wieder komme, das ist das beste.' Latham has detected here an allusion, retained from the *Ur-Hamlet*, to the disastrous English expedition to Portugal in 1589. But apart from the fact that the *Ur-Hamlet* was written probably in 1587 or 1588, the words blurted out by the Prince in a dialogue, where he talks arrant nonsense throughout, probably contain no historical reference whatever.

Thus, if traces of the old play survive at all, it is in the First Quarto only that they are to be found. It is needless to labour here the universally accepted conclusion that the text of this Quarto, however mutilated and imperfect, represents an earlier version of the tragedy than the definitive Quarto of 1604. The two Quartos diverge mainly in the later three Acts, and Messrs. Clark and Aldis Wright in their Clarendon Press edition of *Hamlet* (1871) conjectured that there was an old play in the story of Hamlet, some portions of which are still preserved in the Quarto of 1603; that about the year 1603 Shakespeare took this, and began to remodel it for the stage, as he had done with other plays; that the Quarto of 1603 represents the play after it had been retouched by him to a certain extent, but before his alterations were complete; and that in the Quarto of 1604 we have for the first time the *Hamlet* of Shakespeare. Since these words were written, the existence of the old play has been proved beyond dispute, and the evidences of Kyd's authorship of it have become practically conclusive. If then the First Quarto 'preserves portions' of the *Ur-Hamlet*, traces of Kyd's style should be found in it; and this, I hold, is the case. The bulk of the blank verse in the three later Acts is, in my opinion, unmistakably pre-Shakespearean. The vocabulary and the rhythm are not those of the master-dramatist at any stage of his career, while in Kyd's works they may be frequently paralleled [1].

---

[1] I regret to find my judgement here in direct conflict with that of Professor Dowden, who, in the Introduction to his edition of *Hamlet* (1899), writes thus (pp. xviii, xix): 'For my own part repeated perusals have satisfied me that Shakespeare's hand can be discerned throughout the whole of the truncated and travestied play of 1603. The Shakespearean irony of many passages is unlike anything we find in plays of 1588-9. With the exception of five lines beginning

Thus (First Quarto, III. 2) after the play-scene Hamlet cries:

> And if the King like not the tragedy,
> Why then, belike, he likes it not, perdy.

So (*Sp. Tr.* IV. i. 196–7) shortly before the play-scene, Hieronimo cries:

> And if the world like not this Tragedie, .
> Hard is the hap of olde *Hieronimo.*

When Hamlet proposes to his mother to help him in his revenge, she answers (First Quarto, III. 4):

> I will conceale, consent, and doe my best,
> What stratagem soere thou shalt deuise.

Compare the dialogue in a similar situation between Bel-imperia and Hieronimo:

> *Bel. Hieronimo,* I will consent, conceale,
> 　　And ought that may effect for thine auaile,
> 　　Ioyne with thee to reuenge Horatioes death.
> *Hier.* On then; whatsoeuer I deuise,
> 　　Let me entreat you, grace my practises.

After the King has sought to restrain Leartes' rage at his father's death, the young nobleman declares (First Quarto, IV. 5):

> You have preuailed, my Lord: a while Ile striue
> To bury grief within a tombe of wrath.

So when Horatio calms Bel-imperia's agitation, she murmurs (*Sp. Tr.* II. iv. 20)

> Thou hast preuailde; ile conquer my misdoubt,
> And in thy loue and councell drowne my feare.

The King, later, when proposing to Leartes the stratagem of the fencing-match, tells him that Hamlet has often wished (First Quarto, IV. 7)

> He might be once tasked for to try your cunning.

"Look you now, here is your husband," I find nothing that looks pre-Shakespearean, and I see much that is entirely unlike the work of Kyd. . . . The general style of the *Hamlet* of 1603 is much more like that of an ill-reported play of that date than like the style of a play of Kyd's and Marlowe's time.' I may be oversanguine in hoping that the parallels, which I proceed to quote, may lead Professor Dowden to reconsider his view. Some of them have been instanced already by Sarrazin (*Thomas Kyd,* &c. pp. 106–8), but I have added largely to their number and, I believe, to their cogency. But whether the hand of Kyd is or is not recognized in the First Quarto, I must reaffirm my conviction, that the last three Acts are almost entirely pre-Shakespearean, and that the Stratford dramatist found the *scenario* of Hamlet fully sketched out for him by an earlier playwright.

When Hieronimo suggests to Bel-imperia that she should act the part of Perseda in French, she replies in almost identical words (*Sp. Tr.* IV. i. 178):

> You meane to try my cunning then, Hieronimo.

Leartes, not understanding the purport of the King's suggestion, asks, 'And how for this?' and the latter begins his explanation with 'Marry, Leartes, thus.' Precisely in the same way, Lorenzo asks Hieronimo, when he is leading up to the mention of his 'tragedy' (*Sp. Tr.* IV. i. 74), 'And how for that?' to which the Marshal answers, 'Marrie, my good Lord thus,' and then discloses his project. And in either case, at the end of the explanation, there comes the applauding cry, ''Tis excellent' from Leartes, and 'O excellent' from Lorenzo.

Immediately after Leartes' ejaculation the Queen enters with the news of Ofelia's death by drowning, whereupon her brother exclaims:

> Too much of water hast thou, Ofelia,
> Therefore I will not drowne thee in my teares,
> Reuenge it is must yeeld this heart releefe
> For woe begets woe, and griefe hangs on griefe.

Hieronimo, gazing upon his murdered son, yearns 'to drowne' him 'with an ocean of' his 'teares' (*Sp. Tr.* II. v. 23), and cries fiercely:

> To know the author were some ease of greife,
> For in reuenge my hart would find releife.

And as Ofelia has 'A Dirge sung for her maiden soul' (First Quarto, V. 1), so over Horatio his father says his dirge, as 'singing fits not this case.'

Hamlet, in the same Scene, after asking Leartes why he wrongs him, protests, 'I neuer gaue you cause'; Lorenzo uses exactly the same words to the Marshal (*Sp. Tr.* III. xiv. 148). And as the King thereupon exclaims to Gertred:

> Wee'l haue Leartes and our sonne
> Made friends and Louers, as befittes them both;

so Castile cries to his son and to Hieronimo:

> But heere, before Prince Balthazar and me,
> Embrace each other, and be perfect freends.

In both cases, it may be added, the scene of feigned reconciliation is the prelude to the final catastrophe.

In Kyd's other works further parallels with the First Quarto occur. One of the most remarkable features of the plot in the Quarto, as contrasted with Belleforest's story, is the prominence given to the question of second marriage—a question in which Shakespeare nowhere else shows any interest. In the play-scene, especially, the dialogue on the topic is striking (First Quarto, III. 2):

> *Duke.* . . . Therefore, sweete, Nature must pay his due,
>   To heauen must I, and leaue the earth with you.
> *Dutchesse.* O say not so, lest that you kill my heart,
>   When death takes you, let life from me depart.
> *Duke.* Content thy selfe, when ended is my date,
>   Thou maist (perchance) haue a more noble mate . .
> *Dutchesse.* O speake no more, for then I am accurst,
>   None weds the second, but she kils the first:
>   A second time, I kill my Lord that's dead,
>   When second husband kisses me in bed.
> *Duke.* I doe beleeue you, sweete, what now you speake,
>   But what we doe determine oft we breake. . . .
> *Dutchesse.* Both here and there pursue me lasting strife,
>   If once a widdow, euer I be wife.
> *Duke.* 'Tis deepely sworne, sweete, leaue me here a while.

With the thought and, to a slighter degree, the phraseology of this passage, may be compared Cornelia's self-reproaches for having taken a second husband (*Corn.* II. 31–54)[1]. The same topic is discussed in *The Housholders Philosophie*, p. 253, 12–37, where second marriage is permitted only as a concession to human weakness. So, too, the King of Denmark's moralizings to Hamlet on the loss of fathers as a general law of nature (First Quarto, I. 2) are paralleled by Cicero's similar reflections addressed to Cornelia (*Corn.* II. 214–6 and 252–7). And his outburst of remorse after the play-scene (First Quarto, III. 3):

> The earth doth still crie out vpon my fact,
> Pay me the murder of a brother and a king.

recalls *The Murder of Iohn Brewen*, p. 287, 7–11, where of the first fratricidal sin it is said: 'Albeit there was none in the world to accuse *Caine* for so fowle a fact . . . yet the blood of the iust

---

[1] Cornelia returns to the subject of second marriage from a different point of view in V. 374–89. It is noteworthy that the line in the Quarto:
  Thou maist (perchance) haue a more noble mate
is very similar to *The Spanish Tragedie*, II. i. 26:
  I, but perhaps she hopes some nobler mate.

Abel cried most shrill in the eares of the righteous God for vengeance, and reuenge on the murderer.'

Even when we remember that Elizabethan writers were fond of ringing the changes on a stock of current phrases, and that verbal coincidences here and there may be purely accidental, the series of parallels quoted above point to the survival in the First Quarto of traces of Kyd's play. But it must be admitted, on the other hand, that we do not find in the Quarto some features of style characteristic of the author of *The Spanish Tragedie*. We miss the passages of semi-lyrical dialogue, the flights of rhetorical imagination, the 'handfuls of tragical speeches' which, as we know from Nash, must have been prominent in the *Ur-Hamlet*.

For so complex a problem, no short and simple solution is to be found. But the following theory of the evolution of the Hamlet-tragedy is the one I would propose as covering most satisfactorily all the known *data*. The *Ur-Hamlet* was written by Kyd, probably in the latter part of 1587, and resembled *The Spanish Tragedie* in style and technique. It did not, however, become as popular as its sister play. There is no record of its having been printed; and when it was revived by Henslowe on June 9, 1594, at Newington Butts, it brought in only eight shillings, and was not repeated under his management. But Lodge's allusion, quoted above, suggests a performance of it at the 'Theater' in 1596, and it would appear to have been brought out again about 1602 at Paris Garden, for Tucca in *Satiromastix* exclaims, ' My name's *Hamlet revenge* :— thou hast been at Parris garden, hast not ? '

We thus see the play keeping the stage in somewhat fitful fashion for fifteen years before Shakespeare began to handle it. During this period it probably underwent, in manuscript form, a certain amount of adaptation to suit the rapid changes of popular taste, or the circumstances of different companies. Thus, when Shakespeare, possibly stirred to emulation by the extraordinary success of Ben Jonson's expanded version of *The Spanish Tragedie*, began in 1602 to remodel the kindred *Ur-Hamlet*, he would appear to have had as his basis, not Kyd's play in its primitive form, but a popularized stage version of it [1]. Shakespeare himself, in his first

---

[1] Such a stage version would have had something of the same relation to the *Ur-Hamlet* as Ayrer's German adaptation of *The Spanish Tragedie* (printed as Appendix iii) has to the original. In it we find the Senecan features of Kyd's

revision, kept in the three last Acts considerable portions of this version. Evidences of Kyd's hand, though partly overlaid, are, as I have tried to show, scattered sufficiently through the text to vindicate his share in the creation of the modern world's most wonderful tragedy. Nor is there anything presumptuous or paradoxical in making such a claim on his behalf. Kyd, be it repeated, was not a great poet nor thinker, but he was a brilliant playwright. The elaboration of a complicated plot, the invention of striking situations and effective dialogue, the portraiture of aristocratic social types—all were well within his range. In so far as *Hamlet* still fascinates us by virtue of these qualities, the credit, I believe, belongs primarily to him. But, if untouched by Shakespeare, it would have remained a well-wrought stage-play, and nothing more. The master-dramatist transformed what was probably a flamboyant presentment of the Prince of Denmark's irresolution into the subtle study of diseased emotion and palsied will with which the world is familiar. He filled in the outlines of the other figures at the Court of Elsinore, till they formed a matchless picture of a corrupt, artificial society. He replaced monotonous and lack-lustre verse by dialogue, both in prose and poetry, so vivid and inexhaustibly suggestive, that *Hamlet* in its final form holds its unique position less as a play, in the strict sense, than as a marvellous literary creation thrown into dramatic form. Generations of critics have sought to find a completely satisfying interpretation of the work. They have failed to do so—even the greatest of them—and failed inevitably. For the *Hamlet* that we know is not a homogeneous product of genius. It is—unless evidences external and internal combine to mislead us—a fusion, with the intermediate stages in the process still partly recognizable, of the inventive dramatic craftsmanship of Thomas Kyd, and the majestic imagination, penetrating psychology, and rich verbal music of William Shakespeare.

V. Soliman and Perseda.

In the register of the Stationers' Company, on November 22, 1592, there is entered to Edward White 'vnder the[e h]andes of the Bisshop of LONDON and master warden Styrropp | *the tragedye* of

---

play, and its more poetic and imaginative elements almost entirely absent, while the theatrically effective and comic episodes have been elaborated.

SALAMON and PERCEDA' (Arber's *Transcript,* ii. 622).
The only dated copies, however, of the play that have come down
to us bear the imprint, 1599. There are two Quartos belonging
to that year. Both have exactly the same title-page :

THE | TRAGEDIE | QF *SOLIMON* AND *PERSEDA* |
Wherein is laide open, Loues | constancie, Fortunes incon- | stancie
and Deaths | Triumphs | AT LONDON | Printed by *Edward
Allde,* for | Edward White, and are to be solde at | the little North
doore of Paules Church, at the signe of the Gun.' They have also the
same colophon : 'Imprinted at London for *Edward* | White, and
are to be sold at his shop, at the | little North doore of S. Paules
Church | at the signe of the Gunne, 1599.'

But the text of one of these Quartos, represented by a single extant
copy in the British Museum (11773 c. 11), is printed in larger type
than that of the other, and varies from it in a number of readings. The
Quarto in smaller type is represented by two copies in the British
Museum (besides others elsewhere), and one of these (161 b. 4)
inserts on the title-page, in very minute lettering, under the word
'Triumphs,' the phrase 'Newly corrected and amended.' With what
earlier edition is a contrast thus challenged ? It can scarcely be
the other Quarto of 1599, as the differences between the two impressions are comparatively slight. Is it then the undated Quarto in
the British Museum (C 34 b. 44)? This has the following title-page:
'THE | TRAGEDYE OF | *SOLYMAN* AND | *PER-
SEDA* | wherein is laide open, Loues | constancy, Fortune's
incon- | stancy and Deaths | Triumphs | AT LONDON | Printed
by Edward Allde for | Edward White, and are to be solde at | the
little North doores of Paules | Church, at the signe of | the Gun.'
The colophon is identical with that of the 1599 Quartos, but for
the omission of the date. This edition contains one important
corruption of the text, peculiar to itself. It transfers III. i. 34
from the top of fol. E 3 to the top of fol. E 2, and thus inserts it
between II. ii. 75–6. Two passages are thereby rendered unintelligible ; and it may be to the correction of this blunder that
the words on the 1599 copy call attention. An additional argument
in favour of the undated Quarto being the earliest of those extant
is that, apart from this serious misprint, it represents, in the main,
the best text. It may possibly be a copy of the edition licensed
to Edward White in 1592, but its similarity in the ornamental
features of the title-page to the issues of 1599 suggests that it

appeared shortly before them. In any case, the entry in the Stationers' Register fixes November, 1592, as the downward limit for the composition of the play. The attempt to settle its date more precisely involves a discussion of wider questions.

Soliman and Perseda is anonymous in all three editions, and there is no external evidence to indicate its author. But there are weighty grounds for attributing it to Kyd, and, even if these are not accepted as conclusive, it still stands in unique relation to his dramatic work. For the story of Soliman and Perseda is the subject of Hieronimo's play in Act IV of *The Spanish Tragedie*. It must, therefore, have deeply interested Kyd, and been looked upon by him as suitable material for the stage. Could we be certain that the Marshal's words (*Sp. Tr.* IV. i. 76-7) :

> When in *Tolledo* there I studied
> It was my chance to write a Tragedie . . .
> Which long forgot, I found this other daie.

were thinly veiled autobiography, we should conclude that Kyd, while at one of the Universities, had composed a piece on this pathetic theme. But this is a very doubtful assumption (cf. p. xvii), and even if the tragic 'interlude' introduced into *The Spanish Tragedie* was a youthful production of Kyd's, it was little more than a skilful *tour de force* 'in vnknowne languages,' each of the characters speaking a different tongue. It is far more likely to have been written expressly for its function in *The Spanish Tragedie*, as the plot of the tale is modified to suit the peculiar exigencies of the situation in the main play. Wotton's *Courtlie Controuersie* (cf. p. xxiii) was probably the source of the Marshal's piece ; though in narrating its 'argument' he cites the 'Chronicles of Spaine,' and calls Perseda 'an Italian Dame,' though Wotton speaks of her as 'borne in the Isle of Rhodes.' But its *dénouement* is arranged to accomplish Hieronimo's purpose of revenge. Therefore Erastus (Lorenzo), instead of being beheaded on a false charge of treason (cf. Wotton, p. 60), is stabbed by the Bashaw (Hieronimo) ; and Perseda (Bel-imperia), instead of being slain by Turkish bullets (Wotton, p. 67), and buried by Soliman (Balthazar) in a magnificent tomb, kills the Sultan and afterwards herself. The Bashaw, too, instead of being hanged by Soliman (Wotton, p. 72), is the last survivor, because it was necessary for Hieronimo to address an *apologia* to the Court. Hence I cannot accept Sarrazin's theory that Kyd had written a youthful piece in

English on the subject of Soliman and Perseda before *The Spanish Tragedie*; that he drew upon this for Hieronimo's play; and that, in a later revised form, this is the drama licensed for the press in 1592, and known to us in the Quartos described above (cf. *Thomas Kyd und sein Kreis*, pp. 43–5). Kyd is much more likely to have first introduced the story episodically into *The Spanish Tragedie*, and afterwards to have elaborated it in an independent work. And the extant play in its metrical characteristics, such as the comparative frequency of double endings and run-on lines, and in its proportion of blank verse to rhyme, is more akin to *Cornelia* than *The Spanish Tragedie*. It was, we may conclude, written between the two, either towards the close of Kyd's chief dramatic period, about 1588, or possibly a few years later, when he had entered the service of his powerful patron (cf. pp. xxiv–xxv).

The play, especially in the first three Acts, follows the lines of Wotton's novel very closely, at times borrowing even from its phraseology. But it makes additions and changes which recall the technique of *The Spanish Tragedie*, and which, coupled with Kyd's known interest in the story, go far to prove his authorship of *Soliman and Perseda*. The introduction of a chorus consisting of the allegorical figures, Fortune, Love, and Death, is not in itself very significant; but it is noteworthy that the trio argue and quarrel at the end of each Act, like the Ghost of Andrea and Revenge in *The Spanish Tragedie*, and that, when all is over, the Ghost and Death respectively count up exultingly the numbers of the slain. Erastus' description to Perseda (I. ii. 53–61) of the combatants who have assembled for the tournament, is closely akin to the similar enumeration of national types in *Cornelia*, I. 59–63, and IV. ii. 44–51; while the next Scene, wherein the Prince of Cipris questions the knights about their exploits and mottoes, and they reply in turns, resembles *The Spanish Tragedie*, I. v. 13–56, where the King questions Hieronimo concerning the knights with their 'scutchions,' introduced into his masque, and he recounts the achievements of each of the three.

But more significant in its bearing on the problem of authorship is Act I, sc. v, to which there is nothing parallel in the novel. In this Scene Soliman is introduced with his two brothers Amurath and Haleb, of whom the former kills the latter as a traitor, for protesting against an attack on Rhodes, and is slain in retribution by Soliman himself. The episode has little relation to the main plot, and serves mainly to keep a balance between the scenes at Constantinople and on the island of Rhodes. It thus is remarkably parallel to Act I, sc. iii of *The Spanish Tragedie*, where, on similar grounds, the action is abruptly shifted from Spain to Portugal, and the Viceroy appears between two lords, one of whom, by a charge of treachery, nearly brings the other to his doom. As this Scene is followed by the first tender interview between Horatio and Bel-imperia, so the similar one at Constantinople precedes the opening love-dialogue between Ferdinando and Lucina, which is also an invention of the playwright's. Here Ferdinando's greeting—

> As fits the time, so now well fits the place,
> To coole affection with our words and lookes,
> If in our thoughts be semblant simpathie

recalls Horatio's address to his mistress (*Sp. Tr.* II. ii. 1–4)—

> Now, Madame, since by fauour of your loue
> Our hidden smoke is turned to open flame,
> And that with lookes and words we feed our thoughts,
> (Two chiefe contents, where more cannot be had).

And the dialogue between Erastus and Perseda (*Sol. and Pers.* II. i. 153–66), where the latter gives a mocking twist to her apparently faithless lover's pleadings, is akin in spirit and structure to that in which Bel-imperia parries ironically the addresses of Balthazar (*Sp. Tr.* I. iv. 77–89). Perseda again displays her powers of repartee, under graver circumstances, in her first interview with Soliman (*Sol. and Pers.* IV. i. 91–110). The episode that follows, where she is doomed to execution and delivered on the very stroke of death, is not found in the novel; but it has a counterpart in *The Spanish Tragedie*, III. i, where Alexandro similarly makes ready for martyrdom upon the stage, and is saved as if by miracle. The whole process, too, of Alexandro's condemnation on a false charge is paralleled by the arraignment of Erastus on perjured evidence, of which the novel gives only the barest hint (*Sol. and Pers.* V. ii). And the last interview between Soliman and Perseda, where the heroine, in man's disguise, declares (V. iv. 31):

> Then will I yeeld *Perseda* to thy hands,
> If that thy strength shall ouer match my right,
> To vse as to thy liking shall seeme best;

her death in single combat with the amorous Sultan, and her

crafty revenge upon him by granting him a kiss from her poisoned lips—all this is in the mingled vein of tragic irony and of crude melodrama, which marks the close of *The Spanish Tragedie*[1].

It is in these final episodes that the play diverges chiefly from the novel—where Perseda, as mentioned above, is slain by a volley of shot, and not by Soliman, who survives to mourn her loss and bury her and Erastus in a magnificent tomb. This, though appropriate in a sentimental tale, would have been an anti-climax on the boards, and is rightly altered by the dramatist. Nor are the differences between the finale here and in Hieronimo's play a proof of different authorship. For in the latter case the peculiar conditions made it inevitable that Perseda should kill Soliman, and then take her own life, and that the last survivor should be the Bashaw (Brusor) (cf. p. lvi). But in the independent drama the Sultan, not Brusor, is the dominant figure, and the *dénouement* had to be so managed that he should be the last left of the personages in the story, and utter the closing speech.

It has been objected, however, that the comic underplot of *Soliman and Perseda*, introducing Piston and Basilisco, is not in Kyd's manner. But the interweaving of humorous relief with the graver issues of the main theme is an essential feature of *The Spanish Tragedie*, though less prominent than in the present play. Thus the grimly jocular episode of the trial and execution of Pedringano, with its subordinate figures of the Hangman and the Boy, is elaborated into almost an independent little comedy. In *Soliman and Perseda* Piston, who, like Pedringano, is the servant of one of the principal characters, is a leading comic figure; and, though he is more of the conventional 'clown' than his fellow in *The Spanish Tragedie*, he might easily have been drawn by the same hand. Basilisco has no counterpart in Kyd's chief play, but the type of *miles gloriosus*, of which he is a notable variation, must have been so familiar to a man of the dramatist's classical

---

[1] I prefer to rest the main argument for Kyd's authorship of *Soliman and Perseda* on these similarities of technique between it and *The Spanish Tragedie*, rather than on resemblances of phraseology, which may be due to conscious imitation. But the latter are numerous and striking, as Sarrazin has shown (*Thomas Kyd*, &c., p. 3). I question, however, whether he is right in finding in IV. i. 77-83 an imitation of a sonnet of Watson's, parallel to that in *The Spanish Tragedie*, II. i. 10. The descriptions of Perseda and of Watson's mistress are both examples of a stock Renaissance catalogue of feminine charms, and they vary in a good many details (cf. *Thomas Kyd*, &c., p. 6).

attainments that its introduction into one of his works would be in no way surprising. Basilisco, of whom Wotton's tale knows nothing, owes his birth in a double sense to Latin comedy, for with the coxcombry of the braggart he unites much of the inflated verbiage of the pedant.

The recognition of Kyd as the author of *Soliman and Perseda* would certainly give us a higher estimate of his humorous powers ; but to deny his claim as Schroer has done[1], on the ground that it is a work of far greater merit than *The Spanish Tragedie*, is strangely uncritical. Though with more of lyrical grace and charm, and more even in workmanship, it has not the same stamp of genius as the more popular play. It contains no such titanic figure as Hieronimo, nor so strongly individualized a group of subordinate characters. It is less closely knit in structure, and has nothing to rival the wonderful situation of tragic 'suspense,' which precedes the performance of the Marshal's interlude. Nevertheless, it would be well worthy of Kyd. It transforms, as has been already partly shown, an over-sentimental and diffuse love-story into a well-balanced drama of diversified interest, and is particularly skilful in linking together the earlier and later episodes which in the novel are very loosely connected. Thus Brusor is introduced among the knights who take part in the tournament at Rhodes, and are overthrown by Erastus (I. iii). At the beginning of Act I. v, Soliman is eagerly expecting his return with the news 'how Rhodes is fenc'd'; and his account (III. i. 17–24) of Erastus' exploits on the tilting-field fittingly preludes the Knight's sudden entrance as a fugitive from his native isle. From this point Brusor plays much the same part as in the novel, but Lucina is made his accomplice in the betrayal of Erastus. Wotton only mentions her in the earlier part of the story as receiving from 'a gentleman of the town' the lost chain, which had been Perseda's gift to Erastus, and thereby producing the breach between the heroine and her lover. After the death of her suitor in a duel with Erastus she disappears from the tale. But in the drama she is brought with Perseda a prisoner to Constantinople, and for her share in Brusor's treachery towards the Rhodian knight his infuriated mistress stabs her dead. Thus her fortunes, instead of being merely an episode, are woven skilfully into the entire fabric of the plot.

[1] See his *Über Titus Andronicus*, pp. 51–3.

In the characterization of the principal figures less advance
upon the novel is shown. In fact, consistency is somewhat
sacrificed for the sake of heightened effect. Erastus remains the
type of chivalrous love and gallantry, crushed by adverse fate.
But a needless stain is thrown upon his honour by making him
win back the chain from Lucina by the use of false dice (II. i.
201-43). Perseda is more markedly changed. In the novel she
is a tender maiden, sentimentally impulsive, and quick to seek
suicide as a refuge from her woes. In Acts I-III of the play she
alters little, but when she is transported to Constantinople she
rises to tragic height. Instead of frantically attempting her own
life, she faces with heroic calm and fortitude the doom with which
Soliman threatens her. Better perhaps had she fallen beneath
his stroke then than later ; for her hypocritical method of vengeance
on him, more repellent far than her stabbing of Lucina, blurs
disastrously at the close the fair image of her womanhood. Yet
the Sultan's fate is the needful expiation of his crimes. For
though the drama borrows from the novel some of his traits of
quick sensibility and generous temper, it reveals much more fully
the barbarian nature underneath. Victim after victim, beginning
with his own brother, falls by his order or by his hand ; in his
crowning outburst of homicidal fury he kills, over Perseda's body,
Basilisco and Piston, and sends his faithful henchman, Brusor, to
the block. It is almost a repetition of the orgie of bloodshed
that ends *The Spanish Tragedie*, where Hieronimo extends his
vengeance to his well-wisher, the Duke of Castile. And though
internal evidence alone cannot establish beyond dispute the
authorship of an anonymous play, it may be affirmed without
doubt that *Soliman and Perseda* was either written by Kyd
himself, or—a less probable supposition—by some disciple who
elaborated in the master's manner a theme already handled by
him in brief upon the stage [1].

---

[1] I cannot therefore endorse Schick's suggestion (*Archiv für neuere Sprachen*,
xc) that *Soliman and Perseda*, in which he finds a ' weichere Hand ' than in *The
Spanish Tragedie*, may possibly be ascribed to a writer of such distinctive powers
as Peele. In the collection of anecdotes, *Peele's Merry Conceited Jests*, it is
stated that Peele once arranged at Bristol to give a performance ' of a certain
history of the Knight of Rhodes.' A play on the subject of *Soliman and Perseda*
is evidently alluded to, but it need not have been the present drama, nor, in any
case, written by Peele himself.

VI. Kyd's Translations and Last Years.

In 1588 Kyd appears to have given up, at least temporarily,
his work for the stage, and to have leapt into the 'new occupation'
of a translator from the Italian. It has already been pointed
out (pp. xx–xxi) that Nash's attack on him in this capacity was
prompted by the publication in that year of the slim 'twopenie
pamphlet' entitled ' *The Housholders Philosophie* . . . First written
in Italian by that excellent orator and poet, Signor Torquato Tasso,
and now translated by T. K.' A comparison between this version
of the *Padre di Famiglia* and Kyd's *Cornelia* supports strongly
the conclusion that they are from the same hand. The dedications, in the one case to 'the worshipfull and vertuous gentleman,
Maister Thomas Reade,' in the other to 'the vertuously noble
and rightly honoured lady, the Countesse of Sussex,' are curiously
alike in spirit, and even in phraseology. This is all the more
remarkable because the one is in verse, the other in prose. The
lines addressed to Reade run thus :

> Worth more then this digested thus in haste,
> Yet truely set according to the sence,
> Plaine and vnpollished for making waste
> Of that which *Tassos* pen so highly gracde,
> This worke I dedicat to your defence.
> Let others carpe, tis your discretion
> That must relieue myne imperfection.

In the opening words of his dedication to the Countess, Kyd
similarly apologizes for his hurried execution of 'a matter of this
moment: which both requireth cunning, rest, and oportunity.'
He applies to his work the epithets 'rough, vnpollished,' practically identical with those used of the Italian translation above;
and in either case he asks his patron to make allowance for
the loss of 'grace' which the original has suffered under his
hands. In both instances, too, he hints at detractors of his
work, who will either 'carpe' at it, or wonder at his undertaking
it without the necessary qualifications.

But more striking and important are some parallels in the text
of the translations themselves. The lines (*Corn.* II. 132–5)—

> When Isie Winter's past, then comes the Spring,
> Whom Sommers pride (with sultrie heate) pursues,
> To whom mylde Autumne doth earths treasure bring,
> The sweetest season that the wise can chuse.

are an expansion of Garnier's—

> Apres l'Hyuer glacé le beau Printemps fleuronne,
> L'Esté chaud vient apres, apres l'Esté Autonne.

Why does Kyd thus emphasize the fruitfulness of Autumn, and single it out as 'the sweetest season' of the year? He evidently has in mind the discussion in *The Housholders Philosophie* (pp. 247–9) on the comparative merits of the four seasons, where Autumn is declared to be 'the most noble and best,' because it 'most aboundeth' in fruits. Again, in *Corn.* I. 133 the early Romans are spoken of as—

> Ignobly issued from the Carte and Plough,

where Garnier has—

> Ignoblement issus de grands-peres champestres.

Here Kyd's phraseology is suggested by the passage in *The Housholders Philosophie* (p. 279, l. 6) where the Republican magistrates are spoken of as 'called from the Plough and Carte' (*dall' aratro*, Tasso). Other unusual phrases are common to both translations, as 'signiorize' and its derivatives (*Corn.* I. 55, III. 28, and *Hous. Phil.* 261, l. 34), and 'champant' (*Corn.* V. 176 and *Hous. Phil.* 270, l. 17). Another rare word, 'quadering' (*Hous. Phil.* 269, l. 20) occurs in Kyd's *Letter to Puckering*. Throughout the two versions, as a reference to the Notes will show, Kyd displays a love of out-of-the-way phrases. He at times reminds us of Spenser in his usage of Middle-English forms, and even of words coined apparently by himself, or to which he gives a unique meaning.

But apart from similarities of vocabulary *The Housholders Philosophie* resembles *Cornelia* in its relation to its original. The claim in the dedication that it is 'truely set according to the sence' is far from justified. Kyd repeatedly mangles Tasso's meaning, as he afterwards does that of Garnier. Yet in spite of gross blunders, the version in either case is spirited and vigorous. The Italian prose and the French verse are both somewhat expanded in their English rendering. The imagery becomes more concrete; more of realistic detail is introduced. Occasionally passages of some length are interpolated by the translator. Hence *The Housholders Philosophie* casts light on Kyd's views on certain subjects. Thus his emphatic elaboration (p. 256) of Tasso's protest against women painting their faces

shows that he shared Shakespeare's aversion to the practice.
But even more impassioned is his indictment, for which Tasso
gives little more than the hint, of the evils of usury as 'a corrupter of a Common wealth, a disobeyer of the Lawes of God,
a Rebell and resister of all humaine orders' (p. 280, ll. 34–5).
Not content with reproducing Dante's condemnation of it quoted
by Tasso, he adds marginal references to Scripture, and inserts
in the text an argument on the subject from Aristotle. It is
noteworthy that in the Induction to *The Spanish Tragedie* usurers
are placed in 'the deepest hell,' where they are 'choakt with
melting golde' (I. i. 67), and Kyd's detestation of their practices
may well have been the fruit of bitter personal experience.

His translation of the *Padre di Famiglia* not improbably
helped him to secure a position which improved his fortunes.
From his *Letter to Puckering* we learn that from about the
middle of 1590 to the early summer of 1593 he was in the
service of a certain Lord (cf. pp. xxiv–v), who may have been
pleased to give Kyd an opportunity of applying practically some
of the maxims of *The Housholders Philosophie*. We do not
know what his appointment was, but it would seem to have
been one, possibly of a tutorial kind, which involved his attendance at 'the forme of devyne praiers vsed duelie in his Lordship's
house.' Who was his Lordship? He may have been Robert
Radcliffe, Lord Fitzwalter, who became fifth Earl of Sussex on
December 14, 1593. It was to his wife that Kyd, early in 1594,
dedicated his translation of Garnier's *Cornelie*, on the ground that
he was 'well instructed in' her 'noble and heroyck dispositions,
and perfectly assur'd of' her 'honourable fauours past.' We
know, at any rate, of no other noble house with which Kyd
can be connected. But there is no record of Fitzwalter having
patronized Marlowe, who wrote plays for Kyd's employer (cf.
pp. xxiv–v). Possibly, therefore, when speaking of the Countess'
'honourable fauours past,' Kyd may be merely alluding to some
tokens of good-will which she extended to him as to other men
of letters, including Greene, who dedicated to her his *Philomela*.

But whoever Kyd's 'lord' may have been, the fact of his
holding a fixed appointment in his service makes his authorship
of *The Murder of Iohn Brewen* even more singular than it seemed
before. It was plausibly conjectured that this sensational tract had
been dashed off at a time when the dramatist was in sore need

of money. But on June 28, 1592, the date of John Parker and Anne Brewen's execution for the murder, and also of the licensing of the tract to the stationer, John Kid (cf. Arber's *Transcript*, ii. 289 b), its author had held for about two years a position where he was no longer merely a 'shifting companion,' dependent on literary hack-work for a livelihood. Yet its genuineness cannot be questioned. In the unique copy at Lambeth Kyd's name is written, in a contemporary hand, at the foot of the title-page, and at the close. The signatures are, however, probably not his own, for they vary considerably from the autograph in the *Letter to Puckering*. The pamphlet, hurriedly written to satisfy a debased popular taste, is, for the most part, bare of literary ornament, but here and there traces of Kyd's mannerisms may be found. His use of Lyly's transverse alliteration on p. 288, ll. 11–2 has been already noticed (cf. p. xxiv), and his fondness for words rare in themselves or in their application is illustrated by his introduction in peculiar senses of 'checkt,' 'shadow,' 'confection' and 'quibd' (cf. Notes, p. 406).

In justice to Kyd it should be said that the tract, sensational though it be, was probably intended, as the opening and closing passages show, to point a moral. The murder of the London goldsmith by his wife and her paramour had been successfully concealed for two years and a half, yet at last it had been revealed and avenged. That 'murder cannot be hid' is a doctrine which Kyd had emphasized in *The Spanish Tragedie*, and of which this sordid criminal case was a striking confirmation in contemporary life. He pushes home the lesson of the story—a lesson prominent in his writings since the time when, as is probable, he had taxed Tychborne with the disastrous consequences of his treasonable attempt against the Queen. But this somewhat *naïf* belief in the infallible workings of justice upon earth was soon to receive a rude shock from a singular series of incidents, which closely link Kyd's later fortunes with those of his most illustrious rival in pre-Shakespearean tragedy.

A full account of the relations, personal and literary, between Kyd and Marlowe would be of inestimable value to the historian of the drama, but we have to take on trust Kyd's statements made in his *Letter to Puckering* (cf. pp. cviii–cx) after Marlowe's death, and when it was of supreme moment to him to minimize the extent of their familiarity. Yet even this partial revelation is of the highest interest, and the broad outline of the facts, some of which might have been checked from independent sources, may be accepted as true.

'My first acquaintance,' writes Kyd to the Lord Keeper, 'with this Marlowe rose vpon his bearing name to serue my Lord, although his Lordship neuer knewe his seruice, but in writing for his plaiers.' The probable inference from this is that the two dramatists became associated in the latter part of 1590, soon after Kyd had entered his patron's household. Marlowe had by that time been for three or four years in London, and had taken the stage by storm with *Tamburlaine* and *Doctor Faustus*. The new playwright brought to the service of his art the splendours of a soaring imagination, the enchantments of a golden speech, to which Kyd could make no claim. But he had much to learn from the author of *The Spanish Tragedie* in dramatic technique and plot construction. The *Jew of Malta*, inferior in other ways to Marlowe's earlier works, shows advance in this direction, and it is noteworthy that it was written about the time when his acquaintance with Kyd began. Yet, if the latter's self-righteous protestations are to be believed, their intercourse was never close. 'That I shold loue or be familer frend with one so irreligious were verie rare . . . besides, he was intemperate and of a cruel hart, the verie contraries to which my greatest enemies will saie by me.' And without adopting Kyd's pharisaical standpoint, we can readily believe that his somewhat gloomy and rigid nature could never have been in full harmony with Marlowe's fiery and speculative temperament. Yet they must have come at times into intimate relations, for Kyd mentions to Puckering 'some occasion of our wrytinge in one chamber two years synce,' i. e. the summer of 1591, and declares that then 'some fragmentes of a disputation . . . affirmd by Marlowe to be his,' were 'shufled with some of myne (unknown to me).' These 'fragmentes' remained hidden among Kyd's papers till May 12, 1593, on which day he was arrested on suspicion of being guilty of a 'libell that concernd the State.' A search was made by the authorities for compromising documents, and 'amongst those waste and idle papers (which I carde not for) and which vnaskt I did deliuer up,' was found the mutilated 'disputation' (of. pp. cx–cxiii).

It is important to notice that Kyd, in writing to Puckering, always distinguishes clearly between the 'libell that concernd

the State,' of which he was originally suspected, and the further
more heinous charge of 'Atheism,' in which he was involved by
the discovery of the 'disputation' in his possession. What this
'libell that concernd the State' was we do not know for certain,
but it is probable that the following extract from the manuscript
Register of the Privy Council bears on the matter :—

At the Starr Chamber on Friday, being the 11th of May, 1593.

Present :

Lord Archbishop   Earl Derby
Lord Keper   Lord Buckhurst
Lord Thresorer   Sir Robert Cecil

Sir John Fortescue.

A letter to Sir Richard Martin, Anthonie Ashley, Mr. Alderman Buckle, &c.:
There haue bin of late diuers lewd and mutinous libells set up within the citie
of London, among the which there is some set uppon the wal of the Dutch
Churchyard that doth exceed the rest in lewdnes, and for the discouerie of the
author and publisher thereof hir Maiesties pleasure is that some extraordinarie
paines and care be taken by you commissioners appointed by the Lord Maior
for thexamining such persons as maie be in this case anie way suspected.

Theis shalbe therfore to require and aucthorize you to make search and
aprehend euerie person so to be suspected, and for that purpoze to enter into
al houses and places where anie such maie be remayning. And, uppon their
aprehencion, to make like search in anie the chambers, studies, chestes, or other
like places for al manner of writings or papers that may geue you light for the
discouerie of the libellers.

And after you shal haue examined the persons, if you shal finde them dulie
to be suspected, and they shal refuze to confesse the truth, you shal by auctho-
ritie hereof put them to the Torture in Bridewel, and by thextremitie thereof,
to be used at such times and as often as you shal think fit, draw them to
discouer their knowledge concerning the said libells. We praie you herein to
use your uttermost travel and endevour, to thend the aucthor of these seditious
libells maie be known, and they punished according to their desertes. And
this shalbe your sufficient warraunt.

This warrant of the Privy Council to the Commissioners
appointed by the Lord Mayor was issued on May 11, and it can
scarcely be a mere coincidence that Kyd, as we know from the
official endorsement on the 'Atheistic' pamphlet, was arrested the
following day. Moreover, there is no entry in the minutes of
the Council of an order for his apprehension individually, as in the
case, a week later, of Marlowe. He was, therefore, probably seized
and imprisoned under a general warrant, and if we compare the
phraseology of his letter to Puckering with that of the above transcript, the natural inference is that he was one of the victims of this
Order of May 11.

The Council in their preamble speak of 'diuers lewd and mutinous libells,' and afterwards of 'these seditious libells.' In almost identical terms the dramatist, in denying all responsibility for the 'libell laid unto my chardg,' alludes to it as 'that mutinous sedition toward the state.' Again, the passage in Kyd's letter in which he speaks of delivering up 'waste and idle papers' tallies exactly with the Council's order to the Commissioners to 'make search . . . for al manner of writings or papers that may geue you light for the discouerie of the libellers.' Further, the emphatic terms of the warrant illuminate only too vividly Kyd's brief reference to 'the paines and undeserued tortures' that he suffered after his arrest. He evidently 'refused to confesse the truth,' in the Council's sense of the words, for the good reason, apparently, that he was guiltless of the libel. He was consequently put to the torture in Bridewell, and underwent 'the extremitie thereof at such times and as often' as the Commissioners thought fit. To the depositions wrung from him under these circumstances he evidently alludes in his letter to the Lord Keeper, when he asserts : 'Of my religion and life I haue alredie geuen some instance to the late commissioners and of my reuerend meaning to the state.' The phrase 'late commissioners' is significant. It proves that Kyd's examination did not take place before the Council itself, or a permanent Board, like the Court of High Commission, but before a body appointed for a temporary purpose. The term would apply exactly to the Commission of Aldermen nominated by the Lord Mayor to investigate a particular series of offences.

It will be noticed that the Privy Council speaks of a libel 'set uppon the wal of the Dutch Churchyard' as exceeding the rest 'in lewdnes.' This Dutch Church was in Austin Friars, and was attended by the Flemish and other refugees who had settled in London. Now Strype, in his *Annals of Church and State under Elizabeth*, quoting from MSS. at that time in the possession of Charles, Lord Halifax, informs us that the rapid growth of the foreign colony in the City in the last decade of the sixteenth century aroused a strong feeling of hostility among the native traders, who complained that the strangers 'contented not themselves with manufactures and warehouses, but would keep shops and retail all manner of goods.' An inquiry was consequently made in May, 1593, into the number of foreigners resident in the capital, and while it was being held, 'to incense the populace

against them various libels were set out.' The one so severely
censured by the Council was, doubtless, what Strype describes as
' a rhyme set up upon the wall of the Dutch Churchyard, Thursday, May the 5th, between eleven and twelve at night, and there
found by some of the inhabitants of that place, and brought to
the Constable and the rest of the Watch, beginning—

> You Strangers, that inhabit in this land,
> Note this same writing, do it understand ;
> Conceive it well, for safe-guard of your lives,
> Your goods, your children, and your dearest wives.

The ' rhyme' doubtless went on to threaten the foreigners with
violence, if they remained in the City, and the Constable and his
fellows, knowing ' what belonged to a Watch,' must have handed
over the placard to the higher authorities.   It is evident that the
Council feared a serious outbreak, and strict disciplinary measures,
of which Strype gives details, were taken to prevent this.   But
from the fact of the libel affixed to the churchyard wall, and
very possibly others, being in verse, it seems to have been concluded that the malcontents had enlisted literary aid.   Hence the
stringent instructions in the warrant to the Commissioners ' to
take extraordinarie paines and care' for the discovery of the
author and publisher of the libel, and for this purpose ' to search
in chambers, studies, chestes, or other like places, for al manner
of writings or papers.'   The use of the word ' studies' shows that
it was not among the shopkeepers or their apprentices that the
libellers were expected to be found.

It was therefore probably in the search for the original of the
libel affixed to the Dutch Churchyard wall that Kyd's study was
visited by the authorities.   ' Some outcast Ismael,' to use his own
phrase, had evidently laid an information against him, and as he
belonged by birth and early association to the City, he may plausibly
enough have been suspected of sympathy with its grievances, and
of readiness to use his pen in its cause.   He was, however, apparently
guiltless in the matter, and the official visitation failed in its
immediate object.   But the discovery among his papers of the
fragmentary ' disputation' involved him in a new and yet more
formidable danger.   He stood accused of the ' deadlie thing,'
Atheism.

It is remarkable that while Kyd in his letter to Puckering
protests passionately his innocence of this charge, he yet admits

that his possession of the treatise was naturally regarded as *prima facie* evidence against him. But the incriminating document is endorsed as 'vile hereticall conceiptes denyinge the deity of Ihesus Christe our Sauiour,' and an examination of its contents proves that, so far from being Atheistic, it is a methodical defence, based on scriptural texts, of Theistic or Unitarian doctrines. The writer's attitude is summed up in the words, 'I call that true religion which instructeth man's minde with right faith and worthy opinions of God. And I call that right faith which doth creddit and beleue that of God which the Scriptures do testify.'

Can the writer be identified? Kyd's words, in their most natural interpretation, suggest that it was Marlowe. He speaks of the fragments of the 'disputation' as 'affirmed by Marlowe to be his.' The possessive pronoun here seems to imply authorship, and Vaughan in *The Golden Groue*, 1600, mentions a report that 'about fourteen years ago' the dramatist 'wrote a booke against the Trinitie.' This may be an inaccurate reminiscence of the 'disputation,' or of some longer work embodying the same views. On the other hand, 'his' may simply imply ownership, and this interpretation is perhaps supported by the official endorsement on the treatise; 'which he affirmethe that he had ffrom Marlowe.' Internal evidence points more strongly in the same direction. From autobiographical details in the third fragment, we learn that the writer was addressing, in 'vehement and vnthought on perturbation of mind,' a brief compendium of his views to a Bishop who had on earlier occasions admitted him 'to disputation before many witnesses, and then after to priuate and familier talk.' It is unlikely that Marlowe had gone through these experiences, and the 'disputation' is more probably from the pen of some heretical clergyman who was on the eve of suffering some drastic penalty for his opinions. The writer may possibly have been Francis Kett, formerly a Fellow of Marlowe's college at Cambridge, who was burnt to death at Norwich early in 1589. From the 'Articles of heretical pravity' objected against him by Edward Scambler, Bishop of Norwich, we know that the creed for which he went to the stake was a species of Unitarianism, mingled, however, with mystical doctrines to which there is no reference in the parts of the disputation that have been preserved.

But whoever the writer of the treatise may have been, Marlowe would scarcely have cared to possess it, unless he had been interested in the views that it set forth, and to some extent shared them.   The inference is that his opinions, though extremely heterodox and doubtless often expressed with the utmost licence of speech, were not of the blasphemous and revolting nature afterwards laid to his charge.   Nor were his chief associates, whom Kyd enumerates in his letter to Puckering, men of ribald and profane conversation.   They included Harriott, the distinguished mathematician, who had long been in Sir Walter Raleigh's service ; Warner, probably Walter Warner, a mathematical friend of Harriott; Matthew Royden, the poet; and 'some stationers in Paules Churchyard.'   Of the latter Kyd had doubtless in mind chiefly Edward Blount, who brought out Marlowe's *Hero and Leander* in 1598 with affectionate references to him in the dedication to Sir T. Walsingham, and whose shop was in the Churchyard, 'at the signe of the Blacke Beare.'   Kyd did not venture to introduce Raleigh's name into his letter, but Sir Walter was a friend and patron of Marlowe and his circle.   They doubtless belonged to that 'school of Atheism' which in 1592 Raleigh was accused by a Jesuit pamphleteer of keeping at his house. Reference is manifestly made to the same 'school' in the allegation somewhat later that Marlowe had read an 'Atheist lecture to Sir Walter Raleigh, and others.'   How loosely the term 'Atheism' was used has already been shown, and a clue to the real character of the discussions in the 'school' is now accessible, as will be seen below.

If Kyd's words are to be trusted, he was not himself a member of this circle.   In somewhat unctuous fashion he states that he has merely been 'geuen to vnderstand' who Marlowe's intimates were : 'whom,' as he cautiously adds, 'I in no sort can accuse nor will excuse by reson of his companie ; of whose consent if I had been, no question but I also shold haue been of their consort.' These assertions in his letter to Puckering are doubtless partly a recapitulation of his statements to the Commissioners under stress of ' paines and vndeserued tortures ' ; and it was in consequence probably of Kyd's allegations that on May 18, a week after his arrest, the Privy Council issued a warrant to Henry Maunder 'one of the messengers of Her Majesty's Chamber, to repair to the house of Mr. T. Walsingham in Kent, or to anie other place where he shall vnderstand Christopher Marlowe to be remayning, and by virtue hereof to bring him to the Court in his

companie, and in case of need to require ayd.' Maunder must
have executed the order at once, for in the *MS. Register of the
Privy Council* there is the following entry on May 20: 'This
day Ch. Marley of London, gent., being sent for by warrant
from their Lordships, hath entered his appearance accordinglie
for his idemnity therein, and is commanded to giue his daily
attendance on their Lordships till he shall be licensed to the
contrairie.'

The further proceedings against Marlowe and his associates do
not bear directly upon Kyd's biography, but a brief outline of them
in the fuller light recently obtained is needed to carry the complicated story to its conclusion. On Whitsun Eve, May 29, the
Council received from Richard Baines a 'Note' charging Marlowe
with the foulest blasphemies (cf. pp. cxiii–cxvi). What words may
have passed the dramatist's lips when the wine was red in the cup
one cannot tell, but against Baines' allegations we may fairly set the
fragments of the treatise found amongst Kyd's papers as being quite
as likely to approximate to Marlowe's real opinions. Kyd and
Baines agree in naming Harriott as one of his associates, but the
informer further mentions 'one Richard Cholmelie' as having
'confessed that he was perswaded by Marloes reasons to become an
Atheist.' An entry in the *MS. Register of the Privy Council* proves
that, on March 19, warrants had been issued against Chomeley
and a certain Richard Strange. From a paper entitled 'Remem-
brances of wordes and matter against Richard Cholmeley' (*Harl.
MS.* 6848, fol. 175), and from an unsigned letter by a Government
spy (*Harl. MS.* 6848, fol. 176 [1]), we learn that this Chomeley had
been at one time in the service of the Council, but had betrayed
their trust.. He had then organized a company of 'Atheists,'
professing apparently the most blasphemous opinions, and enter-
taining also revolutionary political designs. Marlowe may have
been concerned in these, for Baines accuses him of claiming 'as
good right to coyne as the Queen of England.' But this singular
conspiracy came to naught. Marlowe, while the Council were in-
vestigating his case, was stabbed to death at Deptford on June 1,
1593. Chomeley, as we learn from a letter of Justice Young to
Puckering (*Harl. MS.* 7002, fol. 10) was arrested on the twenty-

---

[1] I have reproduced the most important parts of these two documents, and
of Justice Young's letter mentioned below, in the *Fortnightly Review* for
February, 1899, pp. 223, 224.

eighth of the same month. The Government, however, were evidently much alarmed at the spread of 'Atheism,' and its possible consequences. Raleigh's connexion with the speculative side of the movement has been mentioned. He had been in London during the early months of 1593, attending the Session of Parliament, but before the arrest of Kyd and Marlowe in May he had returned to Sherborne. He was, however, kept under surveillance, and in consequence of reports that reached the ears of the authorities, the Court of High Commission ordered 'examinations' to be taken at Cerne in Dorsetshire on March 21, 1594. The record of these examinations is preserved in *Harl. MS.* 6842, fols. 183–190[1], and contains *inter alia* a 'relacion' by Ralph Ironside of a theological discussion between himself and Carew and Walter Raleigh at Sir George Trenchard's table in the summer of 1593. From Ironside's account it is plain that Raleigh's reputation for Atheism was gained by his keen and critical analysis of primary religious conceptions like 'God' and 'the soul.' These were doubtless the methods of controversy employed in his 'school,' and daring speculation on such lines may far more plausibly be attributed to Harriott and Marlowe than the crude profanities alleged by Baines. The examinations at Cerne do not seem to have been followed by any proceedings against Raleigh, but the discovery that even his private table-talk was not safe from espionage may well have helped to hasten him forth on his adventurous quest for an El Dorado across the southern main.

How long Kyd remained in custody after his arrest on May 12 we do not know. His letter to Puckering is not dated, but expressions in it prove that it was written after Marlowe's death on June 1. Whether or not his innocence was as complete as he protests, his condition after his release was pitiable in the extreme. His 'lord,' though, according to Kyd, not believing in his guilt, 'yet in his discreeter iudgment feared to offende in his reteyning' him in his service without the Lord Keeper's 'former priuitie,' (or in the more explicit statement that follows) 'he wold no waie' by such action 'moue the leste suspicion of

---

[1] An account of these documents, from different points of view, with extensive extracts, has been given by Mr. J. M. Stone in *The Month* for June, 1894, and by myself in *Literature*, Nos. 147 and 148, before I knew of Mr. Stone's article.

his loues and cares both towardes hir sacred Maiestie, ⟨their⟩
Lordships, and the lawes.' Kyd thus found himself 'vtterlie
vndon,' and sought a personal interview with Puckering 'to
entreate some speaches' on his behalf to his lord. But the
minister turned a deaf ear to the appeal, and as a last resource
the dramatist sent him the imploring letter which the caprice
of Fortune has preserved to be his permanent *Apologia*. Doubtless Puckering paid as little heed to it as to the previous verbal
entreaties, and Kyd found himself once more reduced to earning
a livelihood by his pen. Nor can this have been easy under the
circumstances, for his market as a dramatist had probably been
injured by his imprisonment and disgrace. It can scarcely be
a mere coincidence that after January 22, 1593, about three
months before Kyd's arrest, Henslowe records no performance
of *The Spanish Tragedie* till January 7, 1597 (cf. p. xl). He
therefore turned again to the 'occupation' of translator, though
now not from Italian, but French. The influence on him of
Garnier's dramas has been already noted. Their Senecan rhetoric
appealed strongly to the fashionable literary taste of the day,
and the Countess of Pembroke had made an English version of
the *Marc Antoine*, finished on November 26, 1590, at Ramsbury,
but not published till 1592. Her rendering, in spite of a few
mistakes, was accurate and close. She added only a single
couplet to the original, and showed remarkable skill and taste
in her choice of strophe-forms to reproduce Garnier's Choruses [1].
Inspired by her example Kyd, amidst the 'bitter times and priuie
broken passions' that he was enduring, devoted 'a winter's week'
at the close of 1593 or the beginning of 1594 to the translation
of another of Garnier's Roman plays, *Cornelie*. It was licensed
on January 26, 1594, 'as a book called *Cornelia*, Thomas Kydde
being the author,' and appeared in the same year with the simple
title-page, 'Cornelia | At London | Printed by James Roberts, for
N⟨icholas⟩ L⟨ing⟩ and Iohn Busbie | 1594.' It was thus at first
published anonymously, but the dedication to the Countess of
Sussex was signed with Kyd's initials. Of the terms of this dedication something has been already said (cf. pp. lxii and lxiv), and
if the Countess of Sussex was the wife of Kyd's patron, he may

---

[1] See Miss Alice Luce's Introduction to her edition of Lady Pembroke's
translation in *Literarhistorische Forschungen* (1897).

have had a lingering hope that it would be a passport back into his former service. His translation thus executed hurriedly with an ulterior motive, and amidst 'afflictions of the mind than which the world affoords no greater misery,' deserves partly his own strictures on it. It is a 'rough vnpolished work' in so far that its rendering of the original is (as shown in the Notes) often grossly inaccurate or obscure. Kyd's blunders are at times ludicrous, and Garnier's Alexandrines lose, as he confesses, much of their 'grace' by his 'defaulte.' Yet the vigour and swing of the versification are not unworthy of the author of *The Spanish Tragedie*. In fact the blank verse metre, with its considerably larger percentage of run-on lines and feminine endings, seems a more flexible instrument in his hands than in his period of independent dramatic activity. His versions, too, of Garnier's Choruses, though far from faithful to the original, show much skill in the manipulation of varied strophe-forms. Herein he resembles the Countess of Pembroke, but unlike her he has left a number of Garnier's lines untranslated, and has made some important additions of his own. These include the first eighteen lines of Act III, where he puts into the heroine's mouth a mournful reference to—

> Tyme past with me that am to teares conuerted,
> Whose mournfull passions dull the mornings ioyes,
> Whose sweeter sleepes are turnd to fearefull dreames,
> And whose first fortunes, fild with all distresse,
> Afford no hope of future happinesse.

The lines have the poignant ring of personal experience, and the gloomy prophecy of the last verse was almost certainly fulfilled. It is probable that the Countess did not appreciate the association of her name with the work of a writer who was still under a cloud, and that this was why Kyd did not carry out his promise of dedicating to her his 'next Somers better trauell' with Garnier's kindred drama of *Porcie*. Moreover, the reception given to *Cornelia* by the public was not encouraging, though scholars commended it highly. It is surprising to find its author, after his recent experiences, singled out in company with William Shakespeare, as the fitting elegist of Lady Helen Branch, wife of the Lord Mayor, who died on April 10, 1594. An *Epicedium* was composed to her memory by W. Har. (possibly Sir William Herbert), who thus addresses the two dramatists :—

You that haue writ of chaste *Lucretia*,
Whose death was witness of her spotless life,
Or pen'd the praise of sad *Cornelia*,
Whose blameless name hath made her fame so rife,
As noble Pompeys most renowned wife :
Hither vnto your home direct your eyes,
Whereas, vnthought on, much more matter lies.

In the following year William Clerke, author of *Polimanteia*, in an address to Oxford, Cambridge, and Lincoln's Inn, pictures an epoch of literary regeneration. 'Then,' he exclaims *inter alia*, 'should not tragicke *Garnier* have his poore *Cornelia* stand naked vpon euery poste: a work, howsoeuer not respected, yet excellently done by Th. Kyd.' It was probably in the hope of getting it more widely 'respected' that it was re-issued in 1595 with the more elaborate and alluring title-page, reproduced in the present volume, wherein Kyd's name as the translator for the first time appears. Its appearance, in violation of his seemingly lifelong practice of anonymity, was almost certainly due to the fact that he was now powerless to hinder this. Schick's discovery in *The Archdeaconry of London Probate and Administration Act Book* of the document already mentioned (cf. p. xv), wherein Francis and Anna Kyd on December 30, 1594, renounce the administration of the goods of their deceased son Thomas, of the parish of St. Mary Colchurch, proves beyond all reasonable doubt that the dramatist, worn out by his 'bitter times and priuie broken passions,' had died towards the close of the year. The document runs as follows :

Kydd Thome Administracionis
bonorum renunciacio.

'*Tricesimo die mensis Decembris Anno Domini* 1594, *in ecclesia Cath⟨edrali⟩ Sancti Pauli London⟨ensis⟩, coram venerabili viro Thoma Creak legum Doctore, Domini Archidiaconi London⟨ensis⟩ officiali &c., in praesencia mei Silvestri Hulett notarii publici, Deputati Registrarii &c. Comparuit personaliter Anna Kydd, vxor ffrancisci Kidd patris dicti Thome Kidd, dum vixit parochie sancte Marie Colchurch, defuncti, et nomine dicti mariti sui, tanquam coniuncta persona, realiter exhibuit Inventarium bonorum dicti defuncti pro vero &c., que hactenus &c., idemque penes Registrarium dimisit &c. Et pro diversis causis et consideracionibus Animum dicti mariti sui ⟨vt asseruit⟩ in hac parte iuste moventibus, onere Administracionis ac omni Iuri, titulo, et interesse dicti Mariti sui in bonis, iuribus, et creditis dicti defuncti competentibus seu in futurum competituris nomine mariti sui* (*ut supra*) *penitus et expresse renunciavit et refutavit. Et petiit eandem Renunciacionem admitti iuxta iuris exigenciam. Quam quidem Renunciacionem Dominus ad eius peticionem admisit, quatenus de Iure &c., et quatenus bona, iura, et credita &c., non extendant ultra summam xl s &c. Et decrevit litteras testimoniales fieri.'*

It would seem, from this formal renunciation, that Kyd's family were anxious to disassociate themselves completely from his memory, and doubtless the 'causes and considerations' which moved them thereto are to be found in the tragic record of his later days. This paternal repudiation after death forms a fittingly sombre climax to a career which seems to have been, in the main, that of a literary Ishmaelite. Whenever we have caught glimpses of him personally it has almost always been in an attitude of antagonism to his surroundings. Thomas Heywood, indeed, in his *Hierarchie of Blessed Angels*, 1635, when illustrating the custom among playwrights of familiarly abbreviating one another's names in token of good fellowship, tells us that 'Famous Kyd was called but Tom.' The dedications, too, to *The Housholders Philosophie* and *Cornelia*, prove that he was not without the power of making friends. Yet in both these dedications he hints at the existence of hostile critics, and Nash's scurrilous attack shows to what lengths they were ready to go. Other enemies, as we learn from his complaints to Puckering, were found to do him still deadlier injury; and that he could himself strike hard in self-defence is plain from his indictment of the 'reprobate' Marlowe. Yet he probably claimed justly not to be 'of a cruel hart.' He seems rather to have been a man of sombre, rigid temperament, curiously untouched by some of the distinctive influences of the English Renaissance. Its intoxication with the wild joys of living, its prodigal instinct for beauty in nature and in man, its ardent national feeling, have left scarcely a trace upon his work. But it gave him quickened sensibility of vision into the darker phases of human character and destiny. Round 'graves and worms and epitaphs,' round deeds of treachery and blood, his imagination played with morbidly fixed intensity. At the centre of the whirligig of existence he saw the figure of Fortune, cruel, capricious, yet exacting remorselessly the last doit of the penalties for sin. A nature gloomily absorbed in this spectacle, and soured by early struggle and adversity, stood inevitably somewhat apart from its fellows, and over Kyd's personal career may not unfitly be written the line, used originally of his schoolfellow Spenser,

Poorly—poore man—he liued, poorly—poore man—he died[1].

VII. KYD'S INFLUENCE AND REPUTATION.

The circumstances of Kyd's closing years forbade anything in the way of posthumous panegyric, yet a few tributes to his fame from men of the succeeding generations have been preserved. Meres, in his *Palladis Tamia*, 1598, mentions him twice. In his list of writers who are 'our best for Tragedie,' he names him between Watson and Shakespeare. In his parallel groups of six Italian and six English poets he places Kyd in the position corresponding to Tasso. Possibly he may have translated part of his verse, beside the *Padre di Famiglia*. Bodenham, in the preface to his poetical Miscellany *Belvedere* (1600), names him as one of 'the modern and extant poets' from whom he quotes. Bodenham's extracts, however, are all anonymous, and therefore those taken from Kyd's works cannot be identified. This is the more unfortunate as he chiefly selects pithy, sententious passages in Kyd's favourite vein, and his volume thus probably contains excerpts from lost or unrecognized writings of the dramatist. Robert Allott, in his more elaborate anthology, *England's Parnassus*, published in the same year as the *Belvedere*, differs from Bodenham in affixing the author's names to his extracts. Thus three fragments from otherwise unknown poems or plays of Kyd have been preserved (cf. pp. xxv and 294). But the bulk of his quotations are from the *Cornelia*, of which he evidently took as favourable a view as Clerke. Dekker, in *A Knights Coniuring* (1607), places 'industrious Kyd' with 'learned Watson,' 'ingenious Atchlow,' and others in the Elysian grove of bay-trees to which 'none resort but the children of Phoebus.'

But Kyd's true memorial is not to be found in these slender and detached references. We must look for it in the influence of his work upon his contemporaries and successors both at home and abroad. The most important and difficult section of this subject, the relation of the *Ur-Hamlet* to Shakespeare's play, has already been discussed. Another of Shakespeare's works, *Titus*

[1] Phineas Fletcher in *The Purple Island*, i. 39.

Andronicus, has a unique affinity to Kyd's writings, and was as early as 1614 coupled with *The Spanish Tragedie* by Ben Jonson as stock examples of a style which had already become *vieux jeu* (cf. p. xxviii). The two plays are akin in subject, technique, versification, and vocabulary. The *Leitmotif* of either is a father's revenge, and in both there are variations on the main theme. Thus in *Titus Andronicus*, the Gothic Queen Tamora's resolve to have retribution upon the Roman general for his sacrifice of her son Alarbus is the starting-point of the action. Hence she urges her other two sons to their hideous outrage upon Titus' daughter Lavinia, and procures the execution of Martius and Quintus on a false charge. The result is the madness of Titus, though, as with Hieronimo, there is method in it; his frenzied imagination plays round the project of revenge, and he is shrewd enough to see through the disguise of Tamora and her sons, and to turn their mummery to their own destruction, much as the Marshal makes an engine against his enemies of the performance which they had themselves proposed. Paternal feeling shows its power in even so loathsome a figure as Aaron the Moor, who saves his new-born babe from death, though its hue betrays the Queen's dishonour, and who, to save it a second time, unfolds to Lucius, Titus' son, the full record of his and his confederates' villainies.

Besides these kindred variations on the main theme of paternal love and anguish, *Titus Andronicus* and *The Spanish Tragedie* contain a number of parallel episodes. The feigned reconciliation between Saturninus and Titus, brought about by Tamora (I. 2. 365–98) to facilitate her scheme of revenge, reminds us of the similarly hypocritical scene between Hieronimo and Lorenzo—as also between Hamlet and Leartes in the First Quarto. When Titus arranges a hunt in honour of the Emperor's marriage (II. 2) he is playing something of the same part, as Schroer has pointed out (*Über Tit. And.* p. 85), as Hieronimo when he entertains the King and the Portuguese Ambassador with his Masque in Act I. The scene in II. 3, where Chiron and Demetrius in a forest murder Bassianus and drag off his bride Lavinia, resembles that in which Lorenzo and Balthazar murder Horatio in the bower and drag off his mistress Bel-imperia [1]. Even more strikingly similar

---

[1] Chiron interrupts Lavinia's protests with the words, 'Nay, then, Ile stop your mouth'; so Lorenzo cuts short Bel-imperia's cries for help with, 'Come, stop her mouth.'

are the lamentations of the two wronged fathers at the flight of justice from earth, and their conviction that she must be sought for underground. Thus Titus cries (IV. iii. 11–16):

> You must dig with mattock, and with spade,
> And pierce the inmost centre of the earth ;
> Then, when you come to Pluto's region,
> I pray you deliver him this petition ;
> Tell him it is for justice and for aid,
> And that it comes from old Andronicus.

and again (IV. iii. 43–4):

> I'll dive into the burning lake below,
> And pluck her out of Acheron by the heels.

With these lines may be compared the passage where Hieronimo speaks of finding a judge near the lake where Hell doth stand, who will do justice for his son's death (III. xii. 8–13); or the later scene where he exclaims (III. xiii. 107–9):

> Though on this earth iustice will not be found,
> Ile downe to hell, and in this passion
> Knock at the dismall gates of *Plutos* Court.

The similarities between the two plays in vocabulary have been often pointed out, and need not be enlarged upon. Emil Ritzenfeldt, for instance, has collected some of the most striking, and his list might be considerably increased[1]. The classical quotations strewn through *The Spanish Tragedie* may be paralleled in *Titus Andronicus*, which contains fragments from Seneca, Horace, and Ovid.

These considerations have led some modern critics, including Mr. Lee (*Life of Shakespeare*, p. 165), to regard with favour the theory that *Titus Andronicus* is a work of Kyd touched up by Shakespeare. Edward Ravenscroft, in 1678, stated that he had been told ' by some anciently conversant with the stage that it was not originally Shakespeare's, but bought by a private author to be acted, and he only gave some master-touches to one or two of the principal parts or characters.' This is, of course, a late and vague tradition, against which must be set the testimony of Meres in 1598, and the inclusion of *Titus Andronicus* in the First Folio. But with Shakespeare's fondness for refurbishing the work of other men there is no *a priori* improbability in Ravenscroft's state-

---

[1] See his Dissertation *Der Gebrauch des Pronomens, Artikels und Verbs bei Thomas Kyd, Anhang*, pp. 69, 70.

ment, and we know from Henslowe's *Diary* (p. 24) that a piece
'*tittus and vespacia*,' i.e. probably *Titus and Vespasian*, was performed by Lord Strange's men on April 11, 1592. This piece,
of which an early German version is still extant, may have formed
the basis of the *Titus Andronicus* which Henslowe mentions as
being acted for the first time by the Earl of Sussex's men on
January 23, 1593-4, and which was entered on the Stationers'
Register to Danter on February 6.

But was this *Titus Andronicus* the play that we know? Ben
Jonson's allusion in *Bartholomew Fair* suggests a date at least
five years earlier, and the internal evidence of style and versification supports this. If Shakespeare really adapted the play as late
as 1594, the 'master-touches' from his hand must have been
slight indeed.

But all this is very uncertain, and, in any case, I cannot accept
the theory that Kyd was 'the private author' (whatever Ravenscroft's curious phrase may mean) whose work Shakespeare is
supposed to have re-edited. To begin with, even accepting
January, 1594, as the date of the assumed adaptation, Kyd was
still alive and would scarcely have permitted this—still less the
entry of the revised version for publication. Secondly, in spite
of all the points of similarity between *Titus Andronicus* and *The
Spanish Tragedie*, there is a significant difference of atmosphere in
the two plays. Kyd's drama, it must be repeated, though full of
deeds of violence, does not, except in the culminating episode,
obtrude physical horrors, and never glances at the grosser side of
sexual relationships. The darker features of the plot are relieved
by polished and witty dialogue, by flashes of keen psychological
insight, and by the introduction of sustained tragic irony. Of all
this there is nothing in *Titus Andronicus*. It is a long-drawn tissue
of horrors, accentuating the most repulsive aspects of murder,
outrage, and mutilation. To speak of it being in the style of Kyd is
to ignore the highest elements of his art, and to do him an injury only
second to saddling him with *The First Part of Ieronimo*. Even the
redeeming merits of *Titus Andronicus* consist of qualities absent
from Kyd's works. There are fresh, first-hand touches of natural
description of which the 'Cockney' dramatist was incapable, and
the versification is more elastic and vigorous than that of *The
Spanish Tragedie*. The massively barbaric figure of Aaron the
Moor—a more powerful creation than Titus—is outlined with an

untutored strength somewhat beyond the scope of Kyd. Thus internal evidence suggests one of two conclusions as to the authorship of the play. Either it was written by the 'prentice hand of Shakespeare, fresh from Stratford, copying with crude exaggeration the superficial features of *The Spanish Tragedie*, but missing its finer spirit, though adding some new and distinctive traits; or, if Ravenscroft's statement is to be trusted, the 'private author' responsible for the original piece, perhaps the *tittus and vespacia* mentioned by Henslowe, was a clumsy follower of Kyd, to whose work Shakespeare may have added a few 'master-touches' as late as 1594.

The influence of Kyd on other early plays of Shakespeare is less definitely measurable, and parallels in expression and situation may be due to common literary tendencies of the age[1]. Yet the scene where Hieronimo dips his 'napkin' in the blood of the murdered Horatio may well have influenced the episode in 3 *Henry VI*, I. iv, where Queen Margaret offers to the Duke of York the napkin stained with the blood of his youthful son Rutland. And Margaret's lamentations in Act V. v over the body of her own son Edward, the 'sweet plant . . . untimely cropped,' echo the Marshal's wail for his 'sweet louely Rose ill pluckt before' its 'time.' In *Richard III* she haunts the background of the action, insatiate for revenge, till at last (IV. iv. 62) she is cloyed with beholding it, and like Andrea's Ghost counts with ghoulish glee the death-roll of her foes. *King John* contains a direct reference to a comic episode in *Soliman and Perseda* (cf. Note on *Sol. and Pers.* I. iii. 169–71), and Falstaff's ruminations on death and honour at Shrewsbury fight (1 *Henry IV*, V. i and 3) echo in part those of Basilisco at Rhodes (V. iii. 63–95). In 2 *Henry IV*, V. ii. 47–9, where the newly-ascended Henry V reassures his frightened brothers with the words:

> This is the English, not the Turkish court;
> Not Amurath an Amurath succeeds,
> But Harry Harry,

there may well be an allusion to Act I. v. 76–80 of the same play where Amurath kills his brother Haleb, and is slain in turn by his other brother Sultan Soliman. In the Roman history group traces

---

[1] Ritzenfeldt, in his 'Dissertation' mentioned above (p. lxxx n.), instances a number of passages as imitated by Shakespeare from Kyd, where the resemblance is merely accidental.

of Kyd's influence may also perhaps be found in a hitherto unsuspected quarter. Shakespeare, with his keen interest in the decline and fall of the Republic, is likely to have read *Cornelia*, and the dialogue in Act IV. i of that piece, between Cassius and Decimus Brutus, anticipates curiously in general spirit, and at times even in expression, that between Cassius and Marcus Brutus in *Julius Caesar*, I. ii. 25–177. The character of Cassius as revealed here, and in the interview with Casca, I. iii. 41–130— a character of which only the barest hints are suggested by Plutarch—has its exact prototype in the Cassius of Garnier-Kyd, fiery yet shrewd, envious of Caesar, yet full of a genuinely patriotic passion for liberty. When we add that in *Venus and Adonis*, 397, there is a reminiscence of Hieronimo's 'naked bed'; that Don Pedro in *Much Ado about Nothing* quotes *The Spanish Tragedie*, II. i. 3 (cf. Note on the line); and that the garden love-duets in *Romeo and Juliet* and *The Merchant of Venice* recall in glorified form the interview between Horatio and Bel-imperia in the 'pleasant bower': we realize that though Shakespeare in *The Taming of the Shrew* ridicules some notorious passages in *The Spanish Tragedie* (cf. Notes on II. v. 1–12; III. xii. 31; and III. xiv. 118), yet his debt to Kyd is scarcely, if at all, less than to Marlowe himself.

Ben Jonson probably recognized the kindred relation of the two dramatists to their great successor when in the verses pre-fixed to the First Folio he classed them together in a single line as far outshone by him. This is the only place where he mentions 'sporting Kyd' by name, but he repeatedly ridicules his style as altogether out of date. Even in *Every Man in his Humour* (1597-8), written within three or four years of Kyd's death, he takes up this 'superior' attitude towards *The Spanish Tragedie*, representing it as the favourite reading of the coxcomb Bobadill, and the Town Gull Master Mathew (I. iv)—

Bob. What new book have you there? What! '*Go by, Hieronymo.*'

Mat. Ay: did you ever see it acted? Is't not well penned?

Bob. Well penned! I would fain see all the poets of these times pen such another play as that was: they'll prate and swagger and keep a stir of art and devices, when, as I am a gentleman, read'em, they are the most shallow, pitiful, barren fellows, that live upon the face of the earth again.

[*While* Master Mathew *reads,* Bobadill *makes himself ready.*]

Mat. Indeed here are a number of fine speeches in this book. *O eies, no eies but fountains fraught with teares!* there's a conceit! *fountains fraught with teares! O life, no life, but liuely fourme of death!* another. *O world, no world, but masse of publique wrongs!* a third. *Confused and fillde with murder and misdeeds!* a fourth. O, the muses! Is't not excellent? Is't not simply the best that ever you heard, captain? Ha! how do you li ke it?

Bob. 'Tis good.

Bobadill and Mathew's critical peer is the theatrical *habitué* mocked at in the Induction to *Cynthia's Revels* (1600):

> Another whom it hath pleased nature to furnish with more beard than brain, prunes his mustaccio, lisps, and with some score of affected oaths, swears down all that sit about him, ' That the old *Hieronimo*, as it was first acted, was the only best and judiciously penn'd play of Europe.'

In *The Poetaster* (1601) several notable passages from *The Spanish Tragedie* are singled out for ridicule [1], and as late as 1614 Jonson returns to the attack in the Induction to *Bartholomew Fair* in the declaration already quoted that ' whoever will swear *Ieronimo* or *Andronicus* are the best plays yet, shall pass unexcepted at here as a man whose judgment shows it is constant and hath stood still these five and twenty or thirty years.' If Dekker is to be trusted—and there seems no reason for his inventing the statement—Jonson's familiarity with *The Spanish Tragedie* must have been gained by acting the hero's part in a company of strolling players. In *Satiromastix* (1602) Tucca cries to Horace, who represents Ben (*Dekker's Works* (1873) vol. i. p. 203), 'I ha' seene thy shoulders lapt in a Plaiers old cast Cloake, like a Slie Knave as thou art; and when thou ranst mad for the death of Horatio, thou borrowedst a gowne of Roscius the stager . . . and sentest it home lowsie didst not?' and similarly (p. 229), 'Thou has't forgot how thou ambled'st in a leather pilch by a play wagon in the high way, and took'st mad Ieronimoes part to get service among the mimicks.' Probably Jonson had this early experience in mind, when in *The Alchemist* (1610) he makes Face advise Drugger (IV. 4):

> Thou must borrow
> A Spanish suit: hast thou no credit with the players?
> Hieronimo's old cloak, ruff, and hat will serve.

---

[1] See Notes on II. i. 1–12; II. i. 67–75; and II. v. 1–12. Lines and phrases from the play are introduced in other of Jonson's dramas. In *The Alchemist*, III. ii, Dol cries in mock-heroic fashion to Face, ' Say, Lord Generall, how fares our Campe' (I. ii. 1). In *A Tale of a Tub*, III. iv, Hugh quotes ' In time the stately ox,' an inaccurate version of the first half of II. i. 3. In *The New Inn*, II. ii, Fly uses the notorious ' Go by, Hieronimo,' in its stock application as an expression of impatience (cf. Note on III. xii. 31).

Jonson's impersonation of the Marshal may have suggested to Henslowe the idea of getting him to make additions to Kyd's play. The transaction is recorded in his *Diary* (pp. 201 and 223) in two entries, referring apparently to earlier and later sets of additions :

Lent unto Mr. Alleyn, the 25 of Septembr, 1601, to lend unto Bengemen Johnson, upon his writtinge of his adicions in Geronymo, the some of xxxx^s.

Lent unto bengemy Johnsone, at the apoyntment of E. Alleyn and W^m. Birde, the 24 of June, 1602, in earneste of a boocke called Richard crockbacke, and for new adicyons for Iernonymo, the some of x^l.

In the same year as this second entry an enlarged edition of *The Spanish Tragedie* appeared, with the title-page : 'THE | Spanish Tragedie | containing the lamen- | table end of *Don Horatio* and *Bel-imperia* : | with the pittiful death of olde | *Hieronimo* | Newly corrected, amended, and enlarged with | new additions of the Painters part, and | others, as it hath of late been | diuers times acted | | Imprinted at London by W⟨illiam⟩ W⟨hite⟩ for | T. *Pauier*, and are to be solde at the | signe of the Catte and Parrats | neare the Exchange | 1602.'

The play in its revised form at once obtained a new lease of public favour, and editions poured rapidly from the press. The 1602 quarto was soon followed by another, with an identical title-page, but with numerous variants in the text, and with the colophon, 'Imprinted by *W. W.* for *T. Pauier* | 1603.' The discrepancy in the dates of the title-page and colophon is probably due to the quarto having been begun almost at the close of 1602 and not finished till the early part of the following year.

A similar discrepancy occurs in the next issue. The title is : 'THE | Spanish Tragedie | containing the lament- | able end of *Don Horatio*, and *Bel-imperia* | with the pittiful death of old | *Hieronemo* | Newly corrected, amended, and enlarged with | new additions of the Painter's part and | other ⟨*sic*⟩, as it hath of late been | divers times acted. | | Imprinted at London by W. White, 1610.' The colophon runs, 'At London printed for Thomas Pauier | 1611.' The discrepancy in this case seems to be due to the quarto having been printed in two sections at different times, for sheets H and following, from Act III. xii. 23 to the end of the play, are distinguished by inferior type and paper.

By 1615 the copyright had changed hands, and the title-page

of the issue in that year is for the first time embellished with a woodcut illustrating Horatio's murder, and runs in this somewhat modified form: 'The Spanish Tragedie | OR | Hieronimo is mad againe | containing the lamentable end of *Don Horatio*, and | *Belimperia*; with the pittiful death of *Hieronimo* | Newly corrected, amended, and enlarged with new | Additions of the *Painters* part and others, as | it hath of late been diuers times acted. | ⟨Woodcut⟩ LONDON | Printed by W. White for I. White and T. Langley, | and are to be sold at their Shop ouer against the | Sarazens head without New-gate, 1615.

Another edition appeared in 1618, the only change in the title being the substitution of John for William White as the printer 'for T. Langley.' In 1623 there was a further issue, with two alternative title-pages, one stating that copies are 'Printed by *Augustine Mathewes* and are to bee sold by | *Thomas Langley*, at his Shop ouer against the Sarazens head without Newgate, 1623'; the other that they are 'Printed by Augustine Mathewes, and are to be sold by | John Grismand, at his Shop in Pauls Alley, at the Signe | of the Gunne, 1623.' The last of this long series of Quartos appeared in 1633, printed again by Augustine Mathewes, but now for Francis Grove, and 'to bee sold at his Shoppe neere the Sarazens Head | vpon Snow-hill, 1633 [1].'

---

[1] The only extant copy of the 1602 Quarto is in the Bodleian. Sheets M and M 2 (Act IV. iv. 186 to the end of the play) are missing, and have been replaced by an exceedingly close MS. imitation of type, though not necessarily of the original text of this Quarto. Of the 1602–3 Quarto there is also only one accessible copy, in the Duke of Devonshire's library at Chatsworth, though mention is made of another copy, not now discoverable, 'wanting the title-page, and sheet F torn, with the autograph of Owen Feltham.' Of the 1610–11 Quarto there are copies in the British Museum, the Bodleian, and at Chatsworth, besides a fourth copy with the imprint cut off (cf. Hazlitt's *Bibl. Collections and Notes*, 3rd series, p. 134). Of the 1615 Quarto there are copies in the British Museum and at Chatsworth, and another in the library of Trinity College, Cambridge, which for the imprint, 'Printed by W. White for I. White and T. Langley, and are to be sold,' &c., substitutes, 'Printed by W. White, and are to bee sold by I. White and T. Langley,' &c. Of the 1618 Quarto there are copies in the Bodleian, at Chatsworth, at South Kensington (Dyce Collection), and in the Town Library at Danzig. Of Langley's issue of the 1623 Quarto there is a unique copy in Mr. Alfred Huth's library, and of Grismand's there are two, in the British Museum and at Chatsworth. Of the 1633 Quarto there are numerous copies, in the British Museum, the Bodleian, and other libraries. For some of these details I am

This rapid succession of editions proves the popularity of the play in its revised form, and Henslowe's entries seem decisive as to Ben Jonson's authorship of the interpolations. Yet this has been doubted on purely internal evidence. Charles Lamb, who printed some of the 'Additions' in his *Specimens of English Dramatic Writers* (1808), declared that they were 'the very salt of the old play.' 'There is nothing,' he continues, 'in the undoubted plays of Jonson, which would authorize us to suppose that he could have supplied the scenes in question. I should suspect the agency of some more potent spirit. Webster might have furnished them. They are full of that wild, solemn, preternatural cast of grief which bewilders us in *The Duchess of Malfi.*' At a later date Edward Fitzgerald wrote in a similar strain, 'Nobody knows who wrote this one scene ⟨III. xii. A⟩ : it was thought Ben Jonson, who could no more have written it than I who read it : for what else of his is it like? Whereas, Webster one fancies might have done it [1].' Coleridge looked to an even higher source, when he declared (*Table Talk*, p. 191) that 'the parts pointed out in "Hieronimo" as Ben Jonson's bear no traces of his style, but are very like Shakespeare's.' That the 'Additions' are unlike Jonson's other work cannot be denied, and it is possible that having contracted with Henslowe to revise Kyd's play he may have sub-let the task to some fellow dramatist. Yet his reiterated and splenetic attacks upon the style of *The Spanish Tragedie,* 'as it was first acted,' suggest a personal motive for belittling it, which his authorship of the 'Additions' would supply. And as J. A. Symonds has pointed out (*Ben Jonson* (1886), p. 15), the scenes may have been written before Jonson had settled down to his distinctively classical manner.

They consist of II. v. 46–97 ; III. ii. 65–74 ; III. xi. 2–50 ; III. 12 A ; IV. iv. 168–217, and whoever they are by, they fully deserved their great popularity. But to call them, as Lamb has done, 'the very salt' of the play is to apply a fundamentally wrong canon of criticism to a dramatic work. The salt of *The Spanish Tragedie* is not to be found in specimen passages, but in

---

indebted to Schick's list in his Preface to *The Spanish Tragedy*, pp. xxx-xxxiii, and to W. W. Greg's *A List of English Plays*, pp. 60–1 (1900).

[1] *Letters of Edward Fitzgerald to Fanny Kemble* (1895), p. 63. Quoted by Dr. A. W. Ward in his *History of English Dramatic Literature* (2nd edition 1899), p. 305, note.

the evolution of its elaborate and admirably devised plot. Hence the 'Additions,' striking as they are in themselves, are excrescences on an organic structure. Thus the lines inserted in Act II, which represent Hieronimo as going mad immediately after he finds his son's murdered body, are a sop to a debased theatrical taste. Kyd shows a finer instinct when he makes the Marshal's frenzy the result of his long-drawn agony and baffled yearning for revenge. In III. ii Hieronimo's answer to Lorenzo's proffer of service :

> In troth, my lord, it is a thing of nothing :
> The murder of a son, or so—
> A thing of nothing, my lord ;

is a fine piece of irony—though entirely unlike the Sophoclean irony of Kyd—but it is dramatically inappropriate, as the Marshal's scheme of vengeance would be frustrated by any such premature revelation of his suspicions to his arch-foe. Even in III. xi his outburst to the two 'Portingals' is a barefaced inter-polation, unlike his original riot of sombre fancy in the same Scene concerning Lorenzo's abode in Hell, which is directly prompted by the stranger's inquiry as to his whereabouts. Yet in itself this Addition is perhaps the most masterly abstract of a prodigal son's progress ever penned, against which Horatio's model career stands out in luminous relief. But it was in Scene xii A of this Act that the reviser, whether Jonson or another, reached his highest level. The peculiar imaginative irony of which he has the secret is here used with consummate art. We see Hieronimo at midnight revisiting the fatal bower with attendant torch-bearers, whom yet he rates for not lighting their torches—

> At the mid of noone
> When as the Sun-God rides in all his glorie.
> . . . . . . Night is a murderous slut,
> That would not haue her treasons to be seene.

We hear him tell his wife that he is 'very merry, very merry' beside the tree which he 'set . . . of a kernel,' and sprinkled with fountain-water, so that—

> It grew and grew, and bore and bore,
> Till at the length
> It grew a gallows, and did bear our son :
> It bore thy fruit and mine.

Then comes the climax in the dialogue with the Painter, which figures in all the seventeenth-century title-pages as a particular attraction. Yet this dialogue is, in conception, a replica of that between the Marshal and old Bazulto in the next Scene, and the latter episode has far greater dramatic plausibility. For while Bazulto comes, with other petitioners, to Hieronimo's house to beg for justice on his son's murderers, the Painter, Bazardo, is grotesquely introduced on a similar errand at midnight in the blood-stained bower[1]. But all this is forgotten as we read Hieronimo's instructions to his visitor for the painting of Horatio's murder and its discovery by himself. In the design for this unparalleled 'night-piece,' Elizabethan romantic art achieves one of its supreme triumphs. And Kyd must so far share the glory of it with his reviser that the details are plainly inspired by memories of the murder-scene itself upon the stage. It is hard to believe that the same hand was responsible for this magnificent interpolation, and for the very inferior 'Additions' in Act IV. iv, where Hieronimo at the close of his long Apologia, instead of preserving 'harmless silence,' flings undignified and heartless taunts at his foes.

Apart from his relation to the two protagonists of Elizabethan drama, abundant traces remain of the familiarity of playwrights, great and small, with Kyd's writings. The first among these to show incontestable evidence of his influence is the anonymous author of *Arden of Feversham*, printed in 1592, the same year as Kyd's *Murder of Iohn Brewen*, which deals with a not dissimilar *bourgeois* tragedy. This fact, and the similarity of certain lines and phrases in the play and in *The Spanish Tragedie*, have even suggested the conjecture that *Arden of Feversham* is from Kyd's pen. .Such a theory would need far more convincing arguments than these for its support, and the piece is, as a whole, too nakedly realistic, too free, as the Epilogue claims, from 'filed points' to be in his distinctive vein. Yet in the cadence and diction of many passages, and in the combination of lyrically

---

[1] The writer in *The Athenaeum* mentioned above (p. xxvii, note) finds in the inclusion of both these interviews a proof that the 1602 and later Quartos 'received but very slight editorial care, if any. . . . It is certain that both should not be given; but they are there. The play thus becomes an unintelligent mingle-mangle.' Of the 'mingle-mangle' there is no doubt, but as the Additions were intended chiefly to satisfy the popular craving to see more of Hieronimo in his lunacy, I have little doubt that both Scenes were acted.

elaborate verse-structure with colloquial directness of speech, *Arden of Feversham* recalls the manner of Kyd far more nearly than that of Shakespeare, to whom it has been often groundlessly attributed. And one episode in it at least is palpably inspired by *The Spanish Tragedie*. When Michael, Arden's servant, is waiting at night to betray his master to the villains Black Will and Shakebag, he is overcome by horrible anticipations of how they will murder himself as well, and he suddenly shrieks (III. i. 85–6):

> Ah, Master Franklin, help!
> Call on the neighbours, or we are but dead.

Thereupon Franklin and Arden, who have been abed, rush in:

> *Frank.* What dismal outcry calls me from my rest?
> *Arden.* What hath occasioned such a fearful cry?
> Speak, Michael: hath any injured thee?

The imitation here of *The Spanish Tragedie*, II. iv. 62–3 and v. 1–4 is so transparent that it is almost sufficient of itself to prove that Kyd could not have written the anonymous play.

In the Induction to another piece of the same *genre*, *A Warning for Faire Women* (1599), there is a satirical catalogue of the stock incidents in dramas of Kyd's semi-Senecan type:

> How some damn'd tyrant to obtaine a crowne,
> Stabs, hangs, impoysons, smothers, cutteth throats,
> And then a Chorus too comes howling in,
> And tells us of the worrying of a cat.
> Then ... a filthie whining ghost
> Lapt in some fowle sheete, or a leather pilch,
> Comes skreaming like a piggie halfe stickt,
> And cries *Vindicta*, reuenge, reuenge.

A species rather than a single play is ridiculed here, but the lines would fit the *Ur-Hamlet*, where, as we know from Lodge, the Ghost cried 'reuenge.' Possibly, however, there is a confused reminiscence of *The Spanish Tragedie*, where the Ghost never cries '*Vindicta*,' nor even 'reuenge,' but where Hieronimo uses the Latin phrase (III. xiii. 1). Ben Jonson, perhaps intentionally, commits the same error in *The Poetaster*, where, when burlesquing a number of passages in *The Spanish Tragedie*, he makes Tucca order the two Pyrgoi to act the Ghost, whereupon they cry alternately, '*Vindicta! Timoria! Vindicta! Timoria!*' And, oddly enough, Jonson's enemy, Dekker, carries on the mistake when, in his tract *The Seuen Deadly Sinnes of London* (1606), he speaks of the

'Ghost in *Ieronimo* crying "Reuenge."' Dekker's mention of
'industrious Kyd' in another tract, *A Knight's Coniuring*, has
already been noticed, and also his allusions in *Satiromastix* to
Jonson's performance of Hieronimo. This play contains some
other interesting references to Kyd's works. Tucca (*Dekker's
Works* (1873), vol. i. p. 218) calls Widow Miniver 'my smug-
Bel-imperia,' and later (p. 229) he almost certainly alludes to the
Ur-Hamlet, when he says, 'My name's *Hamlet Revenge*; thou hast
been at Parris garden, hast not?' Horace answers, 'Yes, Captaine,
I ha' plaide Zulziman there;' a reference, as Ward points out
(*English Dram. Lit.*, vol. i. p. 311, note), to *Soliman and
Perseda*. A more unmistakeable reference occurs later, when
Tucca salutes the king as 'great Sultane Soliman.' Some
instances of the way in which Dekker uses the catchwords 'Go
by, Hieronimo' are given in the Note on *The Spanish Tragedie*,
III. xii. 31. Other Notes illustrate the familiarity of Beaumont
and Fletcher, Nathaniel Field, Thomas Heywood, and James
Shirley with notable passages in the play (cf. Notes on I. i. 1–5,
II. i. 1–10, II. v. 1–12, and III. ii. 24–5). Less conspicuous
Jacobean dramatists show equal readiness to make theatrical
capital by travestying or imitating episodes in Kyd's masterpiece.
Thus Frederick Barry in *Ram Alley* (1611), v. 1, weaves into his
plot a grotesque reproduction of the famous scene at the close of
the second Act. A disappointed suitor, Boutcher, hearing that the
rich widow Taffata is to marry his rival Sir Oliver Small-Shanks,
hangs himself up outside her door. His true-love, Constantia, who
is with him in a page's disguise, calls 'help, help, murther, murther!'
Hereupon William Small-Shanks, Sir Oliver's son, rushes out with
ll. 1 and 4 of *The Spanish Tragedie*, II. v on his lips. He then
quotes ll. 9–12, garbled as follows :

> What's here?
> A man hanged vp, and all the murtherers gone.
> And at my door, to lay the guilt on me.
> This place was made to pleasure citizens' wiues,
> And not to hang vp honest gentlemen.

When Taffata comes forth he addresses her with ll. 36–7, and on
Constantia calling out that Boutcher 'stirs' and wants 'breath,'
he cries :

> Is there yet life, Horatio, my dear boy?

and continues with a slightly adapted version of ll. 28–9.

Other situations from *The Spanish Tragedie* are reproduced in W. Smith's *The Hector of Germanie* (1613), though here incidents rather than dialogue are borrowed. Thus in imitation of II. i. 40 ff. old Fitzwaters bids his steward reveal with whom his son is in love, and when he hesitates 'offers to kill' him. He then learns that it is Florimell, Lord Clynton's daughter, whom he wishes to win himself. Afterwards there is a dialogue between the lovers in a garden, and the two fathers steal in and overhear them. This is a blending of features from Act II, Scenes 1 and 4, while young Fitzwaters, on discovering the intruders, echoes Bel-imperia's cry (II. iv. 50) in the words, 'Sweet, we are betraid.'

Besides London playwriters and playgoers there was another section of society in which Kyd's works attracted special attention. Some 'wit' reared at Cambridge was responsible for *The First Part of Ieronimo* (cf. Note on II. iii. 9), and a few years earlier a resident member of that University, a humorist of rare gifts, had parodied Kyd's mannerisms in the happiest style. In the Hall of St. John's College, at dates ranging from 1598 to 1603, was produced in successive parts the *Parnassus* Trilogy, a 'comical satire' on contemporary academic and literary life, woven round the main thread of the adventures of the scholars Philomusus and Studioso, on their way to and from Parnassus Hill. The two pilgrims discourse chiefly in verse, and the utterances of Studioso are throughout in the distinctively sententious *larmoyant* vein of Kyd and his school. Sarrazin, to whom belongs the credit of first emphasizing the importance of the *Parnassus* Trilogy in its relation to Kyd, has collected a large number of parallels between Studioso's speeches and passages in the dramatist's works (cf. *Th. Kyd und sein Kreis* pp. 89-91); additions might be made to his list. Thus in Part II of the Trilogy, II. i. 783 (Macray's edition, 1886), 'when ragged pedants haue their passports sealde,' is a partial echo of *The Spanish Tragedie*, I. i. 54, as is IV. i. 1373, 'Come, let us caste our cards before wee goe,' of *The Spanish Tragedie*, I. ii. 140. Nor could Kyd's platitudinarian strain of moralizing be more skilfully travestied than in II. i. 620 ff. :

Phil. What shall wee doe in this adversitie?
Stud. We must make profit of necessitie.
Phil. When thinkest thou better fortune will begin?
Stud. I nere sawe winter but a springe came in.

Phil. Get I my pence by digginge of the earthe?
Stud. Ey! so the planets raigned at thy birthe.

. . . .

Phil. I' faith, Studioso, this dull patience of thine angers mee! Why, can a man be galde by povertie, free spirits subjected to base fortune, and put it up like a Stoick?

It is thus highly fitting that when, in Part III, IV. iii. 1842 ff., Burbage is testing Studioso's capacities for the stage, he should tell him, 'I think your voice would serue for *Hieronimo*, obserue how I act it and then imitate mee.' Whereupon the scholar begins:

Who calls *Hieronimo* from his naked bed?

and is told he 'will do well after a while.' But while thus recognizing Studioso as a mouthpiece of Kyd's distinctive ideas and style, we may stop considerably short of identifying him, as Sarrazin has done (*Th. Kyd*, &c., p. 92) with the dramatist himself. His chief argument in favour of this, besides the points mentioned above, is the striking similarity between some speeches of Studioso and portions of Nash's attack on the author of the *Ur-Hamlet*. Thus Nash's sneer at Seneca's 'famisht followers' who, if intreated fair 'in a frostie morning,' will supply 'hand-fulls of tragical speeches,' seems echoed in Studioso's lament (Part II, I. i. 89 ff.):

Fie coosninge árts! is this the meede you yelde
To your leane followers, your palied ghosts . . .
We, foolish wee, have sacrificed our youth
At youre coulde altars everie winters morne
Our barcking stomacks have had slender fare.

Nash's further flout at the 'candle-stuff' of these worthies may similarly be responsible for Studioso's lament (Part III, IV. iii. 1930 ff.) that so many 'actiueable wits'—

Sits now immur'd within their priuate cells,
Drinking a long lank watching candles smoke,
Spending the marrow of their flowring age,
In fruitelesse poring on some worme eate leafe.

Again, in Part I. v. 643–5, Ingenioso who, as Professor Hales was the first to point out (*The Academy*, 1887, I. p. 193), often talks in phrases drawn from Nash's works, counsels the pilgrims thus:

Turne home again, unless you meane to be *vacui viatores*, and to curse your wittless heades in youre oulde age for taking themselves to no better trades in there youthe.

Here again there might well be a reminiscence of Nash's gibe at the 'companions, that runne through euery art and thriue by none, who leaue the trade of *Nouerint*, whereto they were borne, and busie themselues with the indeuors of art.' Studioso in fact says of himself and his friend, in Nash's words, that they run 'through euery trade, yet thriue by none' (Part III, II. i. 567). The expression is, however, proverbial, and recurs later on the lips of Philomusus (V. iv. 2132). When again Studioso says of Fortune, Part II (IV. i. 1294), that she hath 'more whipps in store' for him, he may be merely using another phrase that had become current; but its source is, almost certainly, the *Ur-Hamlet* (cf. *Sp. Tr.* III. ii. 43, Note). Finally, when Studioso cries (Part III, I. iv. 404):

> Ile scorne the world that scorneth me againe,

and Philomusus retorts:

> Thy lame reuenging power the world well weenes.

the sarcasm seems aimed at the creator of Hamlet or Hieronimo.

All this is certainly remarkable, and may count as one of the many links in the chain of evidence that connects Kyd with the authorship of the *Ur-Hamlet*. But it is far from warranting the actual identification of Studioso with Kyd, or the attempt to extract from the *Parnassus* Trilogy materials for his biography. There is no evidence that he had ever been at Cambridge, much less at Rome' or 'Rhemes' (Part III, I. iv. 398); and the closing episodes of his career, which were unknown when Sarrazin worked out his able argument, make personal references to him in these 'Christmas toys' in the highest degree improbable.

If the author of the *Parnassus* Trilogy used his intimate knowledge of Kyd's writings to give a skilful burlesque of his style, another contemporary Cambridge playwright paid him the less equivocal tribute of lavish and undisguised imitation. For *Wily Beguiled*, printed in 1606, but written some years earlier, is evidently the work of an enthusiastic Cantab, and was primarily addressed to an academic audience. Its hero, Sophos, is a breezy representative of a type dear to the University imagination—the poor scholar who defeats a wealthy rival in the struggle for a maiden's hand and heart. The two dramatists for whom the author had evidently a whole-hearted admiration were Shakespeare and Kyd. He imitates closely episodes and speeches in *The Merchant of Venice* and *Romeo and Juliet*, while the influence of *The Spanish Tragedie* is patent on every page of the work. Once only does he seek to parody a passage from Kyd's play. It is in Robin Goodfellow's account of his mother's experiences—a counterpart to those of Andrea—in the underworld (Dodsley-Hazlitt's *Old Plays*, IX. p. 308):

> As she liv'd, at length she likewise died,
> And for her good deeds went unto the devil.
> But hell not wont to harbour such a guest,
> Her fellow-fiends do daily make complaint
> Unto grim Pluto and his lady queen
> Of her unruly misbehaviour,
> Entreating that a passport might be drawn
> For her to wander, till the day of doom,
> On earth again, to vex the minds of men.
> To this intent her passport straight was drawn.

With this exception Kyd's play is not travestied, but is used as a quarry for dialogue and plot by his admirer. A number of these borrowings are illustrated by Sarrazin (*Thomas Kyd*, &c., pp. 76-7), and the list might be increased. But the noticeable point is that they come chiefly from the sentimental, not the tragic, scenes of the earlier piece. The wooing of Sophos and Lelia, with its nocturnal elopement, is closely modelled on that of Horatio and Bel-imperia, though here it is necessary for Sophos to take the part of Balthazar as eavesdropper at an interview between his mistress and a rival suitor, Churms. Thus *Wily Beguiled*, like *The Hector of Germanie*, suggests that the popularity of *The Spanish Tragedie* was due more to the love-intrigue in the earlier Acts than has been hitherto recognized.

A later University playwright to make capital out of Kyd's play, though merely in the way of parody, was J. Tomkis, author of *Albumazar*, a comedy performed before James I, at Cambridge, on March 9, 1614-5, by 'the gentlemen of Trinitie College.' One of his allusions gives the names of the London theatres, at one or both of which *The Spanish Tragedie* was to be seen. For Trincalo, a farmer, about to plead for the favour of the maid, Armellina, declares (II. 1.):

I will confound her with complements drawn from the plaies I see at the Fortune and Red Bull, where I learne all the words I speake and understand not.

He then, after some high-flown phrases of compliment, recites (cf. *Sp. Tr.* III. ii. 1-3):

> O lips, no lips, but leaues besmear'd with mel-dew;
> O dew, no dew, but drops of Honey combs;
> O combes, no combes, but fountaines full of teares.

Later in the piece, when Trincalo to serve his landlord's purposes has adopted the disguise of Don Antonio and therein gone through various adventures, he adds another to the copious parodies of the Ghost's opening lines (*Albumazar*, V. 6):

> When this transformed substance of my carcass
> Did liue imprison'd in a wanton hogshead,
> My name was Don Antonio, and that title
> Preseru'd my life and chang'd my suit of clothes.

And that fifteen years afterwards another famous episode in *The Spanish Tragedie* was familiar to Cambridge audiences is plain from Randolph's allusion in his *Conceited Pedlar* (cf. *Sp. Tr.* II. v. 1–12, note), which forms part of a University 'show.'

But it is not only in plays, whether by professional or amateur dramatists, that signs of Kyd's influence are to be found. There is extant a singular poem, printed in 1604, *The Vnmasking of a feminine Machiavell*, by one Thomas Andrewe, who relates his own experiences under the thin disguise of 'hapless Andrea.' In one part of his long lament he describes a battle at Nauport on January 22, 1600, between the Duke of Brabant's forces and the Dutch. This contest, in which he took part, is narrated in phrases borrowed in the main from the Lord General's speech in *The Spanish Tragedie*, I. ii. 22–84. Compare, for instance, with ll. 22–5 the following lines:

> When now both armies on the euen sands
> Were come in sight, and proudly tooke their stands,
> Then all the Regiments of either side
> Were rang'd in order, neere the surly tide,
> Both furnisht well, both rich in their array;

or with ll. 57–8 and 63–4:

> Souldiers some slaine outright, some deadly torne,
> From the thick prease confusedly are borne.
> In th' Armies both was hope, whilst vnto neyther
> Proud Victory enclin'd but fauour'd eyther:
> With various fortunes, full three bloudy howers
> Endur'de the stern rage of these warlike powers.

In a later part of the work he introduces a picture of the underworld, for which he borrows suggestions from the Induction to the play.

A humbler poetic effort inspired by *The Spanish Tragedie* is the ballad reprinted as Appendix II to the present volume. At least seven editions of it appeared between 1599 and 1638 (cf. Mr. Lee's Article on Kyd in *Dict. of Nat. Biography*, xxxi, p. 350). The edition of which copies remain is undated, but as it is illustrated by the woodcut which figures for the first time on the title-page of the 1615 quarto, it was doubtless printed later than this. So bald a production, even when sung to the tune of Queen Dido, can scarcely, one imagines, have worked on its hearers so powerfully as the performances referred to in 1620 by Thomas May in the opening scene of *The Heir* (cf. Dodsley-Hazlitt's *Old Plays*, xi. p. 514):

> *Roscio.* Has not your lordship seen
> A player personate *Hieronimo*?
> *Polymetes.* By th' mass 'tis true. I have seen the knave paint grief
> In such a lively colour that for false
> And acted passion he has drawn true tears
> From the spectators. Ladies in the boxes
> Kept time with sighs and tears to his sad accents
> As he had truly been the man he seemed.

It must have been one of these ladies, a person 'of good rank,' concerning whom Braithwaite, in his *English Gentlewoman* (1631), tells the shocking anecdote that on her deathbed she refused all spiritual consolations, and kept crying out, 'Hieronimo, Hieronimo, O let me see Hieronimo acted!' Such a scandalous example of unregeneracy *in extremis* was not wasted on Prynne, who retailed the story with unction in *Histriomastix* (1633), fol. 556 a. But that Prynne's warnings fell on deaf ears is plain from the familiarity with the play presupposed by Thomas Rawlins in *The Rebellion* (1640), v. 1, where in a scene, perhaps inspired by *A Midsummer Night's Dream*, four tailors discuss what play to act before the King of Spain:

> 1. What say you to our Spanish Bilbo?
> 3. Who? Ieronimo?
> 1. I.
> 3. That he was a mad rascall to stab himselfe.
> 1. But shall wee act him?
> 2. I, let us doe him.
> 3. Doe againe, ha.
> 2. No no, let us act him.
> 3. I am content.

1. Who shall act the Ghost?

3. Why marry that will I—I Virmine.

1. Thou dost not looke like a Ghost.

3. A little Players deceite ⟨and⟩ flower will doe't. Marke me: I can rehearse, marke me rehearse some:

> ' When this eternall substance of the soule
> Did liue imprison'd in my wanton flesh
> I was a Tayler in the Court of Spaine.'

2. Courtier Virmine in the Court of Spaine.

3. I, there's a great many Courtiers Virmine indeed: those are they beg poore mens livings. But I say, Tailer Vermine is a Court Tailer.

2. Who shall act Ieronimo?

3. That will I! Marke if I doe not gape wider than the widest-mouth'd Fowler of them all, hang me.

> ' Who calls Ieronimo from his naked bed?' haugh!

Now for the passionate part—

> ' Alas, it is my sonne Horatio!'

1. Very fine: but who shall act Horatio?

2. I, who shall doe your sonne?

3. What doe, doe againe? Well, I will act Horatio.

2. Why, you are his father.

3. Pray who is fitter to act the sonne, than the father that begot him.

1. Who shall act Prince Belthazar and the King?

3. I will doe Prince Belthazar too: and for the King, who but I? which of you all has such a face for a King, or such a leg to trip up the heeles of a Traytor?

2. You will doe all, I thinke.

3. Yes, marry will I; who but Virmine? yet I will leaue all to play the King. ' Passe by, Ieronimo.'

2. Then you are for the King?

3. I, truly, I.

1. Lets goe seeke our fellowes and to this geere.

3. Come on then.

How odd to find Bottom ' translated' afresh into the shape of Vermine, ready with Protean genius to play every part in *The Spanish Tragedie*, king and prince, father and son! And the last of the many links between Kyd and Shakespeare is found in the same year 1640, in some verses by Richard Goodridge, which run :

> Were thy story of as much direful woe
> As that of Juliet and Hieronimo,
> Here's that would cure you.

But in the November of this year the Long Parliament met, and amidst the stern realities of the political, and later the armed, conflict, men forgot for a time the woes of heroes and heroines of

the stage. And with a new Stuart king came new literary and
dramatic ideals, and the generation that found it needful to
adapt Shakespeare forgot almost the very names of Marlowe and
of Kyd.

Yet here and there, even in the Restoration age, there were
critics of antiquated taste who could proclaim like Charles Cotton
in the Prologue to his *The Scoffer Scoffed* (1675):

> Old tales and songs and an old jest
> Our stomach easily digest,
> And of all plays *Hieronimo* 's the best.

But Edward Phillips, Milton's nephew, who in the same year
published his *Theatrum Poetarum*, did not know that Kyd was
author of the play which he ascribed to an imaginary William
(really Wentworth) Smith. Of Kyd himself he writes somewhat
vaguely (*Theatrum Poetarum*, vol. i, edited by Sir Egerton
Brydges, 1800, pp. 205-6), that 'he seems to have been of pretty
good esteem for versifying in former times. . . There is particularly remembered his tragedy *Cornelia*.' William Winstanley, in
his *Lives of the English Poets* (1687), repeated the views of
Phillips; and Langbaine, though he speaks of Phillips and
Winstanley as mistaken in ascribing *Hieronymo* to Smith, 'it being
an anonymous play' (*Dramatick Poets*, 1691, p. 489), only refers
to it briefly (p. 535) as having been 'diuers times acted,' and
a source of quotations to several authors. He calls Kyd (p. 316)
'an Ancient writer, or rather, Translator, in the time of Queen
Elizabeth,' who wrote *Cornelia*, of which he gives a brief account.

But it was the peculiar fortune of *The Spanish Tragedie* that
when banished from its native stage it retained its popularity
undiminished in other lands. Within a few years of its production in London it had been carried across the seas by the
travelling companies of English actors. We hear of a performance of the *erschröckliche Spanische tragoedia* at Frankfurt-on-the-
Main in 1601 (cf. *Anglia*, 1883, II. p. 15). At Dresden, on
June 6 and 19, 1626, an English company played a *Comoedia vom
König in Spanien vnd dem Viceroy in Portugal* (i.e. probably a lost
fore-piece to *The Spanish Tragedie*, or the extant *First Part of
Ieronimo*), and on June 28 a *Tragoedia von Hieronymo Marschall
in Spanien*. In 1651 in the répertoire of the Court Company at
Prague was included a piece *Von dem jämmerlichen und niemals*

erhörten Mord in Hispania; and at Lüneburg (1660) we hear
of one called *Von Don Hieronimo Marschalk in Spanien*. On
another list of plays belonging to the first years of the eighteenth
century is found *Der tolle marschalk aus Spanien* (cf. Creizenach,
Die Schauspiele der Englischen Komödianten, pp. xxxv ff.).

One of the earliest copies of the play brought to Germany must
have fallen into the hands of Jacob Ayrer of Nürnberg, whose
dramatic activity extends from 1593 till his death in 1605. It
was probably about midway between these dates that Ayrer
wrote his adaptation of *The Spanish Tragedie*, the *Tragoedia von
dem Griegischen Keyser zu Constantinopel und seiner Tochter
Pelimperia mit dem gehengten Horatio*, which is printed as
Appendix III to this volume. It was at any rate based upon the
unrevised text of the play without the 'Additions,' and perhaps the
higher qualities of Kyd's art are most fully revealed by a comparison of the adaptation with its original. For in Ayrer's version,
while the melodramatic episodes of *The Spanish Tragedie* are
retained, the skilful portraiture, the poetic embellishment, the
pathos, the irony, all disappear. The Senecan machinery of
Andrea's Ghost and Revenge is summarily swept away, as is also
the narrative speech of the Lord General who, however, as
'Ernestus der Hauptman,' winds up the play with a moralizing
Epilogue. The *venue* of the action is shifted to Constantinople,
perhaps, as has been suggested, not to implicate the Spanish
Court, so closely related to the House of Hapsburg, in such
sanguinary proceedings. Yet with frank inconsistency the incidents of the Portuguese war are retained, though the 'Vice-
Roy,' and the scenes at his Court disappear. The Duke of
Castile, too, necessarily vanishes, and thus Laurentzius and
Pelimperia become the children of the 'Keyser' or (as he is
called throughout the play) 'König' Amurates. Pelimperia is
given a *confidante* in Philomena, and the relative importance of
the princely actors in the story is greatly increased. Thus the
Marshal, Malignus, as he is rechristened, is thrust into a subordinate place, and in the first three of the six short Acts in
Ayrer's version his appearances are few and short, while his wife
Isabella vanishes altogether. Even in the later Acts his frenzied
agony is so feebly rendered that he is scarcely recognizable as the
hero of Kyd's tragedy. The conversations that precede the performance of the Marshal's play are narrowly curtailed and shorn

of all their ironic significance. But the play itself is elaborated and modified. Balthazar is still the Turkish Soldan, and Laurentzius the Knight of Rhodes, but Pelimperia becomes the Soldan's sister and the Marshal the ' König aus Babylonia.' The King wants to marry the Soldan's sister, who is wooed also by the Knight. The royal suitor stabs his rival, and then lends the lady his dagger to use against her brother who has thwarted her plans of marriage. All this is worked out on somewhat independent lines, and there are other parts of the play in which Ayrer shows some inventive faculty, as in the introduction of ' Jahn, der Narr,' and of some novel details in the episodes of 'the Watch,' and of the 'drey Supplicanten.' But not even the harshest critic of Kyd is likely to dissent from a modern German scholar's verdict : 'Wie ein schales Puppenspiel steht Ayrer's Tragödie neben der englischen.'

A later German version of *The Spanish Tragedie* is Kasper Stieler's *Bellemperie*, printed at Jena in 1680. It is in prose, except the Choruses at the end of the Acts, in one of which the figures of Venus, Alekto, Tisifone and Megära appear. Comic Scenes are interpolated introducing the figures of Skaramutza and Gillette. There is an Epilogue, with Nemesis as the ' Schluss-Sängerin.' Stieler's piece, however, is of minor interest, as it is not adapted from *The Spanish Tragedie* direct, but from a Dutch version of the play, for in Holland Kyd's drama gained a popularity even greater than in Germany, and more enduring than in the very land of its birth.

The earliest manifestation of this must be counted amongst the most remarkable of the 'curiosities of literature.' In 1615 there was published at Antwerp, by one Everaert Syceram of Brussels, a translation in *ottava rima* of the first twenty-three Cantos of Ariosto's *Orlando Furioso*. But Syceram, as he tells his readers, omitted certain portions not likely to interest them, and replaced them by 'something of his own,' in which elastic phrase he included a narrative version of the main part of *The Spanish Tragedie*. It is interpolated in sections, of which the first begins at stanza 31 of Canto III, and occupies about thirty stanzas, which cover the incidents of Act I, scenes i–iv. The later sections occur in Canto VII, stanzas 51–7 ; XIII, 60–74 ; XIV, 3–37 ; XV, 18–36 ; XIX, 107–124 ; XXI, 69–94. They carry on the story of the plot till the opening of Act III, sc. x, and further sections seem to have been included in a second unpublished part of Syceram's work [1].

Six years later appeared the first Dutch dramatic version of Kyd's play, written by Adriaen van den Bergh, and published under the title of *Ieronimo* at Utrecht on May 6, 1621. Van den Bergh, who also adapted the kindred piece, *Titus Andronicus*, must have had before him one of the enlarged Quartos of *The Spanish Tragedie*, as he introduces the dialogue between Hieronimo and the Painter. Like Ayrer he uses rhymed couplets, and like him he omits the Induction and the Lord General's speech. On the other hand, he introduces a novel Senecan feature of his own in the shape of Horatio's ghost, which appears in Act III. A different addition is an interlude containing the Flemish figures of Marri Slot-toffels and Kees Achterlam.

But Van den Bergh's piece was supplanted in popular favour by a later anonymous version of *The Spanish Tragedie*, entitled *Don Ieronimo, Marschalk von Spanje*, of which the first edition dates from 1638. Its author must have known Van den Bergh's play, for he follows him in altering Lorenzo's name to Don Pedro, though he complicates matters by calling the Prince of Portugal Don Lorenzo instead of Balthazar. He also, like his predecessor, omits the Induction [2] and the Lord General's speech, and brings in the ghost of Horatio, of which he ingeniously makes use to get round the weakest point in Kyd's plot-construction. For in *The Spanish Tragedie*, III. ii. 23, there is no explanation of how the imprisoned Bel-imperia contrives to send to Hieronimo the letter written with her own blood. But in the Dutch play Horatio's ghost appears to her while she is writing, receives the letter, and afterwards drops it beside the Marshal while he is asleep. On waking, Hieronimo finds the letter, reads it, and utters a long soliloquy. In the length and frequency of such soliloquies

---

[1] See J. A. Worp's interesting article *Die Fabel der ' Spanish Tragedy' in einer niederländischen Uebersetzung des Orlando Furioso* (1615), in the *Shakespeare-Jahrbuch*, xxix–xxx, pp. 183–191. He points out that as Syceram speaks of 'gaten van Hor' he must have used the undated Quarto, which contains this misprint, I. i. 83 (or, I may add, the 1594 Quarto, which also contains it). The slight variations in places between this version and the original scarcely warrant, I think, Worp's suggestion, that Syceram may have also had before him the source of the play.

[2] *Wraeck* (Revenge) is, however, introduced later with another allegorical figure, *Bedrog* (Fraud).

Don Ieronimo exceeds even its original, but it is loyal to its main outlines, and in the murder scene it even puts into Isabella's mouth the words—

Ieronimo, help, help, help, help, Ieronimo.

Thus in mangled form one of Kyd's own lines (III. iv. 62) was to sound in Dutch ears for a century to come; for so popular was the anonymous play that no less than nine editions were called for, of which the last appeared in 1729[1]. These editions almost completely bridge over the interval of more than a hundred years between the publication of the final Quarto of *The Spanish Tragedie* in 1633, and its reprint for the first time in modern form.

VIII. Modern Editions and Criticism of Kyd's Works.

In 1744 Robert Dodsley issued *A Select Collection of Old English Plays* in twelve volumes, of which the second included *The Spanish Tragedie*. In a short introduction he says, 'I know not who was the Author of this Play, nor exactly what Age it is.' He mentions the conjecture of Phillips and Winstanley, that it was the work of 'William Smith,' but rejects it on the ground that its 'Stile and Manner' differ from those of *The Hector of Germanie*. Dodsley knew only the 1633 Quarto, so that he reprinted this in modernized spelling, with some ingenious conjectural emendations of his own, but with no notes of any kind. How little was thought of the play at this time is plain from an incidental criticism of it by Peter Whalley in *An Enquiry into the Learning of Shakespeare* (1748), who dismisses it curtly as 'little else but a continued String of Quibbles and Conceits even in the most passionate and affecting Parts,' though he excepts II. ii. 45–51 as 'about six good Lines, describing the time of an Assignation appointed by two Lovers, which are tender and natural enough.' Dodsley also included in the eleventh volume of his collection the first reprint of *Cornelia* since the Quarto of 1595.

---

[1] For a list of these editions, and of the extant copies of them in the Libraries of Holland and elsewhere, see Schick's Preface to his edition of *The Spanish Tragedie* (Temple Dramatists), p. xxxvi. This list is the joint compilation of Prof. Schick and Herr R. Schönwerth, the latter of whom is bringing out a critical edition of the Dutch versions of the play.

In 1773 Thomas Hawkins published *The Origin of the English Drama* in three volumes, which were intended to supplement Dodsley's series. But he 'could not,' he tells us, 'consistently with his plan, omit *The Spanish Tragedy* which, as it stands in vol. ii. of the present collection, cleared of the many gross errors in the former edition, appears almost a different work.' The claim is excessive, but is so far justified that Hawkins based his text upon the earliest extant Quarto, that printed by Allde, instead of the latest. He added footnotes giving the variants in Quartos 1618, 1623, and 1633, and thus produced the first critical edition of the play, though it was marred by many inaccuracies. He proved from an allusion by Thomas Heywood (cf. *Sp. Tr.* IV. i. 86–8, Note) that Kyd was the author, but thought that the 'Additions' had been 'foisted in by the players,' and printed them at the foot of the page. Hawkins included in the same volume a reprint of *Soliman and Perseda* from a copy of the 'amended' Quarto of 1599, and assigned it conjecturally to Kyd.

In 1780 Isaac Reed reissued Dodsley's *Collection of Old Plays*, reprinting, however, *The Spanish Tragedie*, not from Dodsley's text, but from that of Hawkins with some slight changes. Reed, besides reprinting Hawkins' textual notes, the accuracy of which he exaggerated, added a number of explanatory notes in verbal and other difficulties. He added similar notes to the reprint of *Cornelia*, and included in the reissue *The First Part of Ieronimo*, reproduced in a somewhat slipshod way from the Quarto of 1605.

The editor of the *Ancient British Drama* (1810) simply reprinted (vol. i.) Reed's editions of *The Spanish Tragedie* and *The First Part of Ieronimo*; and J. P. Collier did little more than follow suit in respect of both these plays, as well as of *Cornelia*, in the second reissue of Dodsley's *Collection* (1825). He, however, added slightly to the number of the explanatory notes, and in 1863 he reprinted in his *Illustrations of Early English Popular Literature* (vol. i.) Kyd's prose tract *The Murder of Iohn Brewen*.

Mr. W. Carew Hazlitt, in the third reissue of Dodsley's *Collection* (1874), again took Reed's edition of *The Spanish Tragedie* as his basis, but personally collated, for the first time since Hawkins, the undated Quarto in the British Museum. He thus made numerous valuable emendations, though a good many errors were still left in the text, and conjectural readings were too often introduced without comment. The arrangement of the 'Additions' too was inconsistent and confusing[1]. He omitted some of Reed and Collier's explanatory notes, but added fresh illustrative matter of his own. Similarly with *Cornelia* and *The First Part of Ieronimo* he made some, though fewer, changes in his predecessors' text and notes. He also included in Dodsley's *Collection*, for the first time, *Soliman and Perseda*, which had not been reprinted since Hawkins' edition a century before, and the text of which he slightly emended (cf. p. 162). It is thus in Mr. Hazlitt's edition that the four plays indispensable to students of Kyd have been mainly accessible, and, whatever its shortcomings, it has contributed largely to the revival of interest in the dramatist's work.

That revival dates from the last twenty or twenty-five years. The 'Romantic' critical movement in England and Germany during the earlier decades of the nineteenth century, which renewed the fame of so many of the Elizabethans, did little for Kyd. Schlegel, in his *Lectures on Dramatic Art and Literature* (1817), compared *The Spanish Tragedie* to a child's drawing, scribbled down without regard to perspective or proportion. Lamb, in his *Specimens of English Dramatic Writers* (1808), spoke of it (apart from the 'Additions') still more harshly as 'but a *caput mortuum*, such another piece of flatness as *Locrine*.' J. P. Collier, however, in his *History of English Dramatic Poetry* (1831), took a more appreciative view, asserting that 'Kyd was a poet of considerable mind, and deserves, in some respects, to be ranked above more notorious contemporaries.' Collier, too, was the first to urge, in 1863, the publication of a collected edition of Kyd's works, and at the time that Mr. Hazlitt was partially satisfying this demand, F. Kreyssig, in his *Vorlesungen über Shakespeare* (1874), and Dr. Ward, in his *History of English Dramatic Literature* (1875), were showing something of the newly quickened interest in the long neglected dramatist.

In 1880 Mr. Widgery, in his Cambridge Prize Essay on the First Quarto of *Hamlet*, revived the theory of Malone that Kyd was the author of the *Ur-Hamlet*, and thus raised the problem whose development has been traced in Section IV of this *Introduction*. A further stimulus to the study of Kyd was given by Dr. Mark-

---

[1] On the arrangement of these 'Additions' by the successive editors of the play see p. 2.

scheffel's two dissertations on his 'Tragedies' in the *Jahresbericht des Realgymnasiums zu Weimar* for 1886 and 1887. This was an able and original piece of investigation, though Markscheffel erroneously maintained the authenticity of *The First Part of Ieronimo*. The perpetuation of this mischievous view is the blot on the otherwise brilliant work of Sarrazin, who, in his articles in *Englische Studien*, XV, and *Anglia*, XII and XIII, and especially in his monograph *Thomas Kyd und sein Kreis* (1892), brought illuminating criticism to bear on the authorship of *Soliman and Perseda* and the *Ur-Hamlet*, and on other important questions. The problems raised by Markscheffel and Sarrazin have been discussed from different points of view by Koeppel in *Englische Studien*, XVI and XVIII, Brandl in *Göttingische gelehrte Anzeigen* (1891), and Schroer in *Über Titus Andronicus* (1891). Careful monographs have been compiled by Anton Doleschal on *Eigenthümlichkeiten der Sprache in Thomas Kyd's Dramen* (1888) and *Der Versbau in Thomas Kyd's Dramen* (1891), and by Emil Ritzenfeldt on *Der Gebrauch des Pronomens, Artikels und Verbs bei Thomas Kyd*. But the value of these essays is impaired by their being founded on imperfect texts, and their inclusion of *The First Part of Ieronimo* as one of Kyd's works. Rudolf Fischer's *Zur Kunstentwicklung der Englischen Tragödie* (1893) contains an interesting study of the *technique* of *The Spanish Tragedie* and *Soliman and Perseda*, and a convincing demonstration of the spuriousness of *The First Part of Ieronimo*. Dr. H. Gassner has published (1894) a useful reprint of the text of *Cornelia*, retaining the original spelling, and adding brief notes on passages where Kyd varies from or mistranslates Garnier. G. O. Fleischer, in his *Bemerkungen über Thomas Kyd's Spanish Tragedy* (1896), gives the results of a careful personal collation of the undated Quarto, and the Quartos of 1602, 1610, 1615, 1618, 1623, and 1633, as well as of the modern editions of the play from Dodsley to Hazlitt. Professor Schick of Munich has been engaged for a number of years in the preparation of a critical edition of *The Spanish Tragedie*, for which he has collated all the extant texts. He has already made public the first-fruits of his ripe scholarship and research in his excellent small edition of the play in 'The Temple Dramatists' series (1898), as well as in articles in the *Archiv für neuere Sprachen*, XC and the *Shakespeare-Jahrbuch* for 1899. So constant indeed is the flow of essays on the dramatist in German periodicals that it is almost a case of '*Kyd und kein Ende.*'

In England Mr. Fleay has been amongst the first to recognize Kyd's importance in stage-history. But his account of him in *A Biographical Chronicle of the English Drama* (1891), vol. ii, is largely vitiated by reckless theorizing and by the ascription to him not only of *The First Part of Ieronimo*, but of plays so radically unlike as *The Rare Triumphs of Loue and Fortune*, *Arden of Feversham*, and *The Taming of a Shrew*. The important additions to our knowledge of Kyd's life by Mr. Gordon Goodwin and Mr. C. J. Robinson have been already mentioned (cf. pp. xv and xvi). But the most valuable contribution of English scholarship to the study of Kyd has been Mr. S. Lee's article on him in the *Dictionary of National Biography*, XXXI (1892), which not only focussed the results of previous criticism, but drew attention to Thomas Baker's memoranda (*MS. Harl.* f. 401) on contemporary documents then in his possession relating to Marlowe and Kyd. These documents I succeeded in re-discovering, and they are printed below.

The last decade of the nineteenth century has thus done much to give a renewal of youth to the 'name and fame' of Thomas Kyd. It may be, if report speaks true, that the first decade of the twentieth will even set *The Spanish Tragedie* again upon the stage; and though a modern audience is not likely to incur Jonson's censure by acclaiming it as 'the only best and judiciously penn'd play of Europe,' it might still be moved by the spectacle of the Marshal 'plucked' from his 'naked bed,' or slinking back with the muttered aside, '*Hieronimo*, beware; goe by, goe by.'

CONTEMPORARY DOCUMENTS RELATING TO THE
CHARGES OF ATHEISM AGAINST KYD
AND MARLOWE.

I. LETTER OF THOMAS KYD TO SIR JOHN PUCKERING,
THE LORD KEEPER.

⟨THIS Letter, in Kyd's autograph, forms ff. 218–9 of *Harleian*
MSS. 6849, and is reproduced in the frontispiece to the present
volume. It is addressed on f. 219 b.

'To the R. honorable Sr John
Puckering Knight Lord Keeper of
the great seale of Englande.'

The circumstances under which it was written are explained
in Section VI of the *Introduction*, pp. lxv–lxxiv.⟩

[fol. 218] At my last being wth yor L^p to entreate some speaches
from you in my favor to my Lorde, whoe (though I thinke he rest
not doubtfull of myne inocence) hath yet in his discreeter iudgm^t
feared to offende in his reteyning me w^thout yor hono^rs former
pryvitie; So is it nowe R⟨ight⟩ Ho⟨nourable⟩ that the denyall
of that favo^r (to my thought resonable) hath movde me to coniecture some suspicion, that yor L^p holds me in concerning
Atheisme, a deadlie thing wch I was vndeserved chargd w^thall,
and therfore have I thought it requisite, aswell in duetie to
yor L^p and the lawes, as also in the feare of god, and freedom
of my conscience, therein to satisfie the world and you.

The first and most (thoughe insufficient) surmize that euer
⟨as⟩ [1] therein might be raisde of me, grewe thus.   When I was
first suspected for that libell that concern'd the state, amongst
those waste and idle papers (wh^ch I carde not for) & wch vnaskt
I did deliuer vp, were founde some fragments of a disputation,
toching that opinion, affirmd by Marlowe to be his, and shufled
wth some of myne (vnknown to me) by some occasion of o^r
wrytinge in one chamber twoe yeares synce.

My first acquaintance wth this Marlowe, rose vpon his bearing

---

[1] A word partly illegible in MS.

name to serve my Lo : although his L^p never knewe his service, but in writing for his plaiers, ffor never cold my L. endure his name or sight, when he had heard of his conditions, nor wold indeed the forme of devyne praiers vsed duelie in his L^{ps} house, haue quadred wth such reprobates.

That I shold loue or be familer frend, wth one so irreligious, were verie rare, when *Tullie* saith *Digni sunt amicitia quib⁹ in ipsis inest causa cur diligantur* ,wch neither was in him, for p⟨er⟩son, quallities, or honestie, besides he was intemp⟨er⟩ate & of a cruel hart, the verie contraries to w^{ch}, my greatest enemies will saie by me.

It is not to be nombred amongst the best conditions of men, to taxe or to opbraide the deade *Quia mortui non mordent.* But thus muche haue I (wth yor L^{rs} favo^r) dared in the greatest cause, wch is to cleere my self of being thought an *Atheist*, which some will sweare he was.

ffor more assurance that I was not of that vile opinion, Lett it but please yor L^p to enquire of such as he conversd wthall, that is (as I am geven to vnderstand) wth *Harriot, Warner, Royden* and some stationers in Paules churchyard, whom I in no sort can accuse nor will excuse by reson of his companie ; of whose consent if I had been, no question but I also shold haue been of their consort, for *ex minimo vestigio artifex agnoscit artificem.*

Of my religion & life I haue alredie geven some instance to the late comission^{rs} & of my reverend meaning to the state, although p⟨er⟩haps my paines and vndeserved tortures felt by some, wold haue ingendred more impatience when lesse by farr hath dryven so manye *imo extra caulas* wch it shall never do wth me.

But whatsoeu^r I haue felt R⟨ight⟩ Ho⟨nourable⟩ this is my request not for reward but in regard of my trewe inocence that it wold please yor L^{ps} so t⟨o⟩ . . . s . . .[1] the same & me, as I maie still reteyne the favo^{rs} of my Lord, whom I haue servd almost theis iij. yeres nowe, in credit vntill nowe, & nowe am vtterlie vndon wthout herein be somewhat donn for my recoverie, ffor I do knowe his L^p holdes yor honor^{rs} & the state in that dewe reverence, as he wold no waie move the leste suspicion of his loves and cares both towards hir

---

[1] A word illegible in MS.

sacred Matie yor L^{ps} and the lawes wherof when tyme shall serve I shall geue greater instance wch I haue observd.

As for the libel laide vnto my chardg I am resolued wth receyving of ye sacram^t to satisfie yor L^{ps} & the world that I was neither agent nor consenting thervnto [**fol. 218 b**] Howbeit if some outcast *Ismael* for want or of his owne dispose to lewdnes, haue wth pretext of duetie or religion, or to reduce himself to that he was not borne vnto by enie waie incensd yor L^{ps} to suspect me, I shall besech in all humillitie & in the feare of god that it will please yor L^{ps} but to censure me as I shall prove my self, and to repute them as they ar in deed *Cum totius iniustitiæ nulla capitalior sit quam eorū, qui tum cum maximè fallunt id agunt vt viri boni esse videant^r?* ffor doubtles even then yor L^{ps} shalbe sure to breake ⟨thro⟩[1] their lewde designes and see into the truthe, when but their lyues that herein haue accused me shalbe examined & rypped vp effectually, soe maie I chaunce wth Paul to liue & shake the vyper of my hand into the fier for wch the ignorant suspect me guiltie of the former shipwrack. And thus (for nowe I feare me I growe teadious) assuring yor good L^{ps} that if I knewe eny whom I cold iustlie accuse of that damnable offence to the awefull Matie of god or of that other mutinous sedition tow'rd the state I wold as willinglie reveale them as I wold request yor L^{ps} better thoughts of me that neuer haue offended you.

Yo^r L^{ps} most humble in all duties,

TH. KYDDE

II. FRAGMENTS OF THE THEOLOGICAL DISPUTATION REFERRED TO IN THE ABOVE LETTER.

⟨These fragments form fols. 187–9 of *Harleian* MSS. 6848. On fol. 189 b there is this endorsement :

'12 May 1593
vile hereticall Conceiptes
denyinge the deity of Jhesus
Christe o^r Savio^r fownd
emongest the pap^{rs} of Thos
Kydd prisoner

[1] A word erased in MS.

to which is added in differently coloured ink, apparently on a later occasion,

'wch he affirmethe that he
had from Marlowe ')

[fol. 187] . . . for how may it be thought tru religion which vniteth in one subiect contraries as visibilitie & inuisibilitie, mortallitie & imortallitie &c. cet?

It is lawfull by many wayes to se the infirmitie of Jhesus Christ whom Paul in the last chapter to the Corinthiās of the second Epistle denieth not to be crucified through infirmitie. And the whole course & consent of the Euangelicall history doth make him subiect to the passions of man as hunger thirst wearines & fear. To the same end ar swete anxietie continuall praier the consolation of the Angell again spitting whipping rebukes or checks. His corps wrap^t in the linen cloth vnburied. And to beleue forsooth that this nature subiect to theis infirmities & passions is God or any part of the diuine essence what is it other but to make God mightie & of power of thone part weak & impotent of thother part which thing to think it wer madness and follie To persuade others impieties.

The Nature diuine is single comunicable to no creature comprehensible of no creat vnderstanding explicable w^t no speche. But as Paul saith in the first of the Romains by the visible structure of the world we deprehend the inuisible power sapience & goodnes of God wher it is by the Scriptures euident That ther is one God. As in the sixt of Deut: yor God is one God yet the vocable is transferred to other & therfore it is written in the eighteenth Psalme of Dauid God stood in the sinagog of Gods which place Christ in the tenth of John declareth to agree to the Prophetts whiles he studieth to auoid the crime of Blasphemie for that the calling of God Father had signified himselfe to be the Sonn of God. And Paul the first to the Corinthians 8 Chapter And though there be which are called Gods whether in heauen or in earth as there be Gods many and Lords many yet vnto me ther is but one God which is the father of whom ar all things and we in him and saith Paul ther be to whom their bellie is God But to many Idols. According to that saying all the Gods of gentils Idols. And Paul in the second to the Corinthians fourth Cap: doth call Satan the God of this world. To men it is applied but seldom yet somtime it is And then we vnderstand it as a name of mean power & not of the euerlasting power. Exodus two & twentie Thow shalt not detract the Gods And Moises be he a God to Pharao. Again Paul to the Romains Ninth calleth Christ God blessed foreuer, And in the Gospell of John Chap: twentie Thomas Didimus doth acknowledge him God thorough the feling of the wound. Many times that I remember I do not finde ...

. . . .

[fol. 188] ... will say throughly to one and the same perpetuall tenor & consent.

What the scriptures do witness of God it is clere &͘ manifest innogh for first Paul to the Romains declareth that he is euerlasting And to Timothi im̄ortal & inuisible To the Thessalonians liuing & true. James teacheth also that he is incom̄utable which things in the old law and prophets likwise are thought infixed inculcate so often that they cannot escape the Reader. And yf we think the epithetons not vainly put but truly & proffitably adiect And that they agree to God And that we must not beleue him to be God to whom the same agree not we therfor call God which onlie is worthie this name &c appellation, Euerlasting, Inuisible, Incom̄utable Incomprehensible Im̄ortall &c.

What the Scriptures do witness of God it is clere & manifest inough & so forth as is aboue rehearced.

And if Jhesus Christ euen he which was borne of Marie was God so shall he be a visible God comprehensible & mortall which is not compted God wᵗ me quoth great Athanasius of Allexandriae &c.

For yf we be not able to comprehend nor the Angels nor our own sowles which ar things creat To wrongfully then & absurdly we mak the creator of them comprehensible especiallie contrary to so manifest testimonies of the Scriptures & cet.

. . . .

[fol. 189] Albeit in this vehemēt &c vnthought on perturbation of mind reuerend father w⟨hen⟩[1] Labour is odious writing difficult & hard comentatiō vnpleasant & grieuos vnto me yet in the defence of my caus being required to write for the reuerence I ow to your Lordshipp Aboue other I haue purposed brefely & compendiosly to com̄it in writing what I think touching Tharticles.

---

[1] The word partly illegible in MS.

Albeit in this vehement & unthought on perturbation of
mind reuerend father a labor is odious writing difficult
& hard comentatio unpleasant & grieuos unto me yet in
the defence of my cause being required to write for the reuer=
ence I ow to your lordshipp Aboue other I haue purposed
brefely & compendiosly to comit in writing what I think
touching Tharticles.

W[i]th mine opinion by the comunication before had w[i]t your
Lordshipp might haue bin euident inough & sufficiently
known without writing for first at the beginning when yo[u]r
Lordshipp admitted me to disputation before many witnesses

FACSIMILE OF A PART OF THE HERETICAL DISPUTATION FOUND AMONGST THE PAPERS OF THOMAS KYD, 12 MAY, 1593, AND AFFIRMED BY HIM TO HAVE BEEN MARLOWE'S.—*Harleian MSS.* 6848, fol. 174.

W^{ch} thine opinion by the communication before had w^t your Lordshipp might haue bēn euident inough & sufficiently known withowt writing for first at the beginning when yor Lordshipp admitted me to disputation before many witnesses And then after to priuate & familier talk I did plainly say all that then came into my mind verilie I haue not dissembled my opinion which I got not or borrowed owt of Sarcerius Conradus Pellican & such garbages or rather sinks or gutters but owt of the sacred fountain.

To wch sacred fountain iust and right faith ought to cleaue & lean in all controuersies touching religion chefly in this point wch seemeth to be the piller & stay of our religion. Wher it is called in question concerning the inuocation of sainctes or expiation of sowles A man may err without great danger in this point being the ground & foundation of our faith we may not err without daṁage to owr religion. I call that true religion which instructeth mans minde w^t right faith & worthy opinion of God And I call that right faith which doth creddit & beleue that of God wch the scriptures do testify not in a few places & the same depraued & detort to wrong sense B⟨ut⟩ . . .

III. RICHARD BAINES' NOTE ACCUSING MARLOWE OF BLASPHEMY.

⟨This document forms fols. 185-6 of *Harleian* MSS. 6848. I have included here such portions of it as it is possible to reproduce, as the contrast between the above 'disputation' which passed to Kyd from Marlowe, and the blasphemies here alleged against the latter, is striking. Moreover, the Note proves how comprehensive the allegations under the head of 'Atheism' might be, and why Kyd was so eager to repudiate the charge.

This Note is here printed for the first time from the original document, the endorsement of which is partly illegible, but which appears to be

'Baynes Marley
of his blasphemeyes'

Its contents, however, have been long known from f. 320 of *Harleian* MSS. 6853, which is the official replica laid before Queen Elizabeth, as is proved by the endorsement:

'Copye of Marloes blasphemeyes
as sent to her H⟨ighness⟩

This copy, however, contains a number of slight variants from the original, which (excepting mere differences of spelling) I give in footnotes marked ' *C.*')

[fol. 185]   A NOTE

Containing the opinion of on Christopher Marly, concerning his damnable iudgment[1] of religion and scorn of Gods word[2].

That the Indians and many Authors of antiquity haue assuredly writen of aboue 16 thowsande yeers agone, wheras[3] Adam is proued to haue lived within 6 thowsand yeares.

He affirmeth[4] that Moyses was but a Iugler, and that one Heriots being Sir W. Raleighs man[5], can do more than he.

That Moyses made the Iewes to travell xl yeers in the wildernes (which iorney might haue bin don in lesse then one yeare) ere they came to the promised lande, to thintent that those who were privy to most of his subtilties might perish and so an everlastinge superstition remain in the hartes of the people.

That the first beginning of Religionn was only to keep men in awe.

That it was an easy matter for Moyses being broght vp in all the artes of the Egiptians, to abuse the Iewes being a rude and grosse people.

.   .   .   .

That ⟨Christ⟩ was the sonne of a carpenter, and that, yf the Iewes amonge whome he was borne did crucify him, theie best knew him and whence he came.

That Christ deserved better to dy than Barrabas, and that the Jewes made a good choise, though Barrabas were both a theif and a murtherer.

That if ther be any God or good Religion then it is the Papistes, because the service of God is performed wth more ceremonies, as

---

[1] opinions and iudgment *C*

[2] *In the Copy this title is scored through and altered to* A Note deliuered on Whitsun eve last of the most horrible blasphemes utteryd by Cristofer Marly who within 111 dayes after came to a soden and fearfull end of his life.

[3] wher *C*   [4] He affirmeth *scored through in C*

[5] being Sir W. Raleighs man *omitted in C*

elevation of the masse, organs, singing men, shaven crownes [1], &c. That all protestantes are Hypocriticall asses.

That if he were put to write a new religion, he would vndertake both a more exellent and Admirable [2] methode. . . .

That the woman of Samaria and her sister [3]. . . .
[fol. 185 b] . . . .

That all thei that loue not Tobacco . . . were [4] fooles [5].

That all the apostles were fishermen and base fellowes, neyther of wit nor worth, that Paull only had witt, but [6] he was a timerous fellow in biddinge men to be subiect to magistrates against his conscience.

That he had as good right to coine as the Queen of Englande, and that he was aquainted with one Poole, a prisoner in newgate, who hath great skill in mixture of mettalls, and hauing learned some [7] thinges of him, he ment, through help of a cunninge stamp-maker to coin French crownes, pistolets, and English shillinges [8].

That if Christ would haue [9] instituted the Sacrament [10] with more cerymoniall reverence, it would haue bin had in more admiration . . .

. . . .

That on Ric⟨hard⟩ Chomeley [11] hath confessed that he was per-swaded by Marloes reasons to become an Atheist.

These things, with many other, shall by good and honest witnes [12] be aproued [13] to be his opinions and comon speeches and that this Marlow doth not only hould them himself, but almost into [14] every company he cometh he [15] perswadeth men to Atheism willing them not to be afeard [16] of bugbeares and hobgoblines and vtterly scorning both God and his ministers as I Richard Baines [17] will Iustify and approue [18] both by mine [19] oth and the testimony of many honest men, and almost al men with whome he hath con-versed any time will testify the same, and as I think, all men in

---

[1] shaven crownes *scored out in C*   [2] more admirable *C*
[3] That the women of Samaria *C*   [4] are *C*
[5] That . . . fooles *scored out in C*
[6] that *C*   [7] such *C*   [8] *This paragraph scored through in C*
[9] had *C*   [10] Sacramentes *C*
[11] *In the margin of C, opposite Chomelei's name, is written in a different hand* he is layd for.
[12] men *C*   [13] proued *C*   [14] in *C*
[15] he *omitted in C*   [16] afrayed *C*   [17] Bome *C*
[18] and approue *omitted in C*   [19] my *C*

christianity ought to indevor that the mouth of [fol. 186] so dangerous a member may be stopped.

He saith likewise[1] that he hath quoted[2] a number of contrarieties oute of the Scriptures which he hath giuen to some great men who in convenient time shalbe named. When these thinges shalbe called in question, the witness[3] shalbe produced[4].

RICHARD BAINES[5].

[1] moreover *C*　　　　　　　[2] coated *C*　　　　　　　[3] witnesses *C*
[4] *This and the preceding paragraph are scored through in C*
[5] Bame *C*

SUPPLEMENT

CORRECTIONS AND ADDITIONS
1902–54

I

Abbreviations

T. K. = Thomas Kyd.
M.L.N. = Modern Language Notes.
N. and Q. = Notes and Queries.
R.E.S. = Review of English Studies.

T.L.S. = Times Literary Supplement.
Sp. Trag. = The Spanish Tragedie.
Y.W.E.S. = The Year's Work in English Studies.

II

General

In the *Cambridge History of English Literature*, vol. v, chap. vii (1910), G. Gregory Smith wrote on *Marlowe and Kyd*. Among the points in his section on Kyd were the rejection of his authorship of the *First Part of Ieronimo*; his acceptance as ' more than a plausible inference ' of Kyd's authorship of the early *Hamlet*; and his doubt whether *Soliman and Perseda* should be assigned to him. Gregory Smith summed up : ' Kyd is the first to discover the bearing of episode and of the " movement " of the story on characterization, and the first to give the audience and reader the hint of the development of character which follows from this interaction. In other words he is the first English dramatist who writes dramatically.'

Charles Crawford contributed a *Concordance to the Works of T. K.* to W. Bang's *Materialen* (1906–7).

Signs of the growing interest in Kyd's work on the Continent were J. de Smet's *Thomas Kyd: l'homme, l'œuvre, le milieu*, followed by a translation of *Sp. Trag.* into French prose (Brussels, 1925); and F. Carrère's *Le théâtre de Thomas Kyd* (Toulouse, 1951).

III

Biographical—Francis Kyd

Bernard M. Wagner in *N. and Q.*, Dec. 15, 1928, showed from the records of the Scriveners' Company (Bodl. MS. Rawlinson D. 51) that the dramatist's father, Francis Kyd, was admitted to the freedom of the Company in 1557, and in 1580 became one of its two Wardens.   There are entries concerning his apprentices in 1557, 1578, and 1591.

Kyd's Letters to Puckering

J. W. Baldwin in *The Chronology of Thomas Kyd's Plays* (*M.L.N.*, Jan. 1925) corrected a mistake in my transcript of Kyd's letter to Sir J. Puckering (Harl. MSS. 6849, f. 218). Kyd there speaks of ' my Lord whom I have served almost these vj yeres now '. Owing to the ' v ' being slightly blobbed the figure was wrongly transcribed as ' iij '. As Kyd's letter was written in the summer of 1593, his service with his lord must have begun in the latter part of 1587. But in noting this correction in *Y.W.E.S.*, vi. 155–6, I dissented from Baldwin's inference that Kyd's plays were written before he entered the household of his lord, for whose company Marlowe was providing plays, and Kyd may well have done likewise. There is thus no warrant for stating that Kyd ' had ceased writing for the stage before Marlowe, Greene and Shakespeare began '. Baldwin made a better case for Kyd's early beginning as a dramatist in *Thomas Kyd's Early Company Connections* (*Phil. Quarterly*, July 1927). He there quoted from Dekker's *A Knight's Conjuring* the following sentence : ' In another companie sat learned Watson, industrious Kyd, ingenious Atchelow, and (tho hee had been a player molded out of there pennes) inimitable Bentley.' Bentley was a member of Queen Elizabeth's Company on March 10, 1583, and remained with them till his death in August 1585. Dekker's words therefore imply that ' industrious Kyd ' had written plays presumably for the Queen's Company before August 1585.

In this letter to Puckering Kyd affirmed that some fragments of a heretical treatise, belonging to Marlowe, had got shuffled among his papers, when they were writing in the same chamber ' two yeares since ', i.e. in the early summer of 1591. These fragments (Harl. MSS. 6848, ff. 187–9, and 6849, f. 218) have been proved by W. Dinsmore Briggs (*Studies in Philology*, April 1923) to be parts of an anonymous treatise quoted in full for purposes of confutation by John Proctor in a book called *The Fal of the Late Arrian* (1549). The treatise had brought its author into trouble with Henry VIII's Privy Council, and now more than forty years later was to bring Kyd into suspicion of atheism, though the views in it are Socinian. Briggs has shown what is the right order of the fragments.   Owing to a change in pagination the wording under the facsimile between pp. cxii and cxiii should now be Harl. MSS., fol. 187, instead of fol. 174.

George T. Buckley in *Who was the Late Arrian?* (*M.L.N.*, Dec. 1934) argued plausibly that he was John Assheton, a parish priest, one of three persons examined by the Archbishop of Canterbury in 1549 on charges of heresy.   He recanted his opinions which were similar to those in the treatise.

Another letter of Kyd to Puckering concerning Marlowe was identified by Ford K. Brown, a Rhodes scholar at Exeter College, Oxford, in *T.L.S.*, June 2, 1921.   It is Harl. MSS. 6848, f. 184, and though it is unsigned and unendorsed, it is undoubtedly in the same hand as the signed letter.   It contains further charges against Marlowe's ' monstruous opinions ', and states that he would persuade men of quality to go unto the King of Scots, ' where if he had liud he told me when I sawe him last he meant to be '.   In welcoming this discovery in *T.L.S.*, June 30, 1921, I pointed out some minor inaccuracies.   The letter is transcribed with a facsimile by W. W. Greg in *English Literary Autographs, 1550–1650*. Part I, Dramatists, no. 15 (b) (1925).

IV

The Spanish Tragedie.   Early Editions

The most complete list of early editions, with full bibliographical details, will be found in W. W. (now Sir Walter) Greg's *Bibliography of the English Printed Drama to the Restoration*. Vol. I. *Stationers' Records. Plays to 1616*, no. 110. (Printed for the Bibliographical Society at the Oxford University Press, 1939.)

Abel Jeffes was licensed to publish the play on October 6, 1592, and it is probable that he had already issued the edition with a corrupt text, and that he only entered the copy by way of precaution when he heard that Edward White was intending to publish a corrected edition.   This appeared with no date or author's name, but it must have been before December 18, 1592, when it was ' Ordered in full Court that whereas E. White has printed The Spanish Tragedy belonging to A. Jeffes, and Jeffes has printed the tragedy of Arden of Kent, belonging to White, all copies be confiscated to the use of the poor of the Company, that each pay a fine of 10s., and that the question of their imprisonment be referred to the Master, Warden, and Assistants '.

These proceedings outlined in a note to my edition (pp. xxvii–xxviii) have been confirmed and explained further by entries now made available in the Stationers' Registers. They imply that Edward White's undated edition was issued in the later part of 1592, and was the first of which a copy is extant. White and Jeffes must have later come to terms for the 1594 edition, of which Göttingen University Library has the only copy, has the imprint ' Printed by Abell Jeffes and are to be sold by Edward White '. Of the 1599 edition there is also only one copy, which in 1901 was in the Earl of Ellesmere's Library in Bridgewater House but is now in the Huntington Library, California. It had been printed and published by William White, who on August 14, 1600, passed the rights in it to Thomas Pavier, though he printed for him the first edition with the Additions in 1602. Of this edition the only copy available in 1901 [when I listed the extant copies of early editions (p. lxxxvi)] was that in the Bodleian, which lacked the two leaves of signature M, which had been supplied by a transcript from a later edition. It has since been found that there is another imperfect copy of this edition in the Eton College Library, which, however, contains the passage missing in the Bodleian copy. In 1904 a hitherto unknown perfect copy of this edition appeared in the auction room and was acquired by the British Museum.

Of the next edition only one copy is known. Formerly in the Duke of Devonshire's Library at Chatsworth, it is now in the Huntington Library. The colophon has the date 1603 and the title-page 1602. But this is identical with that of the 1602 quarto, and does not seem to belong to the book, but to have been used as a repair. The edition 1602 A in my list (p. 2) may therefore be probably dated 1603.

Eight years later another edition appeared with a double date. The title-page stated, ' Imprinted at London by W White, 1610 '; while the colophon ran ' At London printed for Thomas Pavier, 1611 '. Sheets A–G and H–M differ greatly in typography, and W. W. Greg concluded that ' White must have ignored the transfer of ten years ago and tried to issue an edition for his own benefit ; Pavier, advertised of his intention, interfered, obtained possession of the seven sheets already printed (together with the copy), and had the impression completed for himself by another printer '. The former Chatsworth copy is now in the Huntington Library, as are also those of 1615, 1618, and a copy of 1623 (with

Grismand's imprint as seller). A 1623 copy (with Langley's imprint as seller), formerly in the Huth collection, is now in the Chapin Library, Williams College, Williamstown, U.S.A.

V

The Spanish Tragedie. Modern Editions. Malone Society Reprints

Most of the bibliographical details in the above section have been based upon the Introductions to the Malone Society Reprints of *Sp. Trag.*, and it will therefore be convenient to notice them first.

The Malone Society in 1925 included in its Reprints the 1602 edition of *Sp. Trag.* prepared under the direction of W. W. Greg in consultation with myself. In his Introduction Greg took the view that the ' additions ' which here first appeared were not those for which Henslowe paid Jonson about £5 in 1601 and 1602, but earlier anonymous additions which entitled the play to be entered as new in his *Diary*, when it was revived on January 7, 1597, though the record of this has since been erased. The Introduction also set forth the bibliographical history of the play, on which Greg wrote further in *The Library*, June 1925, ' *The Spanish Tragedy* '—*A Leading Case?*

The text of this reprint took advantage of the collations by Schick and myself, but a long list of variants (pp. xxiii–xxix of the Introduction) embodied the results of a new and independent comparison of the 1602 text with the undated one, now known as 1592. It was proposed that with a division of Act III, running to nearly half the play, it should properly occupy not four Acts but five.

The Malone Society in 1949 issued a reprint, edited by W. W. Greg and D. Nichol Smith, of Edward White's original 1592 text from the unique copy in the British Museum. In the Introduction they gave a fuller account of new entries in the Stationers' Registers, which had become available since 1925, of the relations described above between White and Jeffes concerning the publication of the play. Collotype plates reproduced the title-page and first page of this edition and the title-pages of the 1594 and 1599 editions.

There is a long list of irregular, doubtful, and variant readings, in which the 1592 text is collated with those of 1594, 1599, and

1602 (pp. xvii–xxv of the Introduction). The corrections are confined to obvious errors and typographical faults, and some new errors are introduced.

Opportunity was taken by the editors to qualify the view taken in the 1925 Reprint that the Additions in the 1602 quarto were not those for which Jonson was paid. It has been suggested that these were not printed from an authoritative copy, but were supplied by a reporter relying on his memory. As the entries show that Jonson supplied two distinct sets of Additions, the reporters might have had access only to the earlier one. But the problem of style would still remain.· Another possibility was suggested by Herford and Simpson in their *Ben Jonson*, vol. ii, pp. 237–45 (1925). ' Both entries indicate transactions not simply between Henslowe and Jonson but through the mediation of third persons.' The work undertaken by Jonson but not yet handed in may have been carried out by someone else.

VI

The Spanish Tragedie. Other Editions and Commentaries

To the editions of *Sp. Trag.* in the reissues of Dodsley's *Old Plays* should be added W. C. Hazlitt's in vol. v (1874).

To J. Schick's Temple edition has now to be added his edition with introduction and apparatus in German (Berlin, 1901).

An edition in J. M. Manly's *Specimens of Pre-Shakespearean Drama* is included in the new edition, vol. ii (Boston, 1903).

R. Schoenwerth wrote on *Die niederländische und deutschen Bearbeitungen T. K.'s ' Sp. Trag.'* (Berlin, 1903). A. O. Michael discussed *Der Stil in T. K.'s Originaldramen* (Berlin, 1905).· J. Le G. Brereton had *Notes on the Text of Kyd* (*Engl. Studien*, 1907).

R. S. Forsyte (*Philological Quarterly*, Jan. 1926) had *Notes on ' Sp. Trag.'* Among them were imitations of, or parallels with, the passages beginning, ' O eies, no eies ' (III. ii) and ' In time the sauage Bull ' (II. i). In the same number W. P. Mustard had other *Notes,* chiefly on the Classical sources of lines and phrases.

H. W. Crundell in *N. and Q.*, Mar. 4, 1933, on account of some resemblances in situation and verbal repetitions between the Additions to *Sp. Trag.* and *The Honest Whore* argued in favour of Dekker's authorship. He repeated the claim on further grounds in *N. and Q.*, Jan. 1941, but he has not found support.

Peter W. Biesterfeldt's *Die Dramatische Technik Thomas Kyd's* (Niemeyer, Halle, 1936) dealt only, but exhaustively, with *Sp. Trag.*, of which he gives a searching analysis, as combining features of Senecan drama and the popular stage. Plot, scenic arrangement, psychology, and characterization are in turn discussed. In the quartos the play is divided into four Acts but Biesterfeldt argues that this should be five. He holds that Act III ended with scene vii, and that viii–xv formed Act IV. The printer may have been misled by the absence of a Chorus after scene vii, but its place was taken, in Biesterfeldt's opinion, by Hieronimo's lengthy soliloquy.

Levin L. Schücking in *T.L.S.*, June 12, 1937, in the light of recent investigations into the average length of Elizabethan plays, pointed out that the 1602 Additions to *Sp. Trag.* made it 2,900 lines in all. He held that the whole of the revised text of the play cannot have been performed, and in especial after the ' passion ' of the Painter's scene (III. xii b) the repetition of a similar situation in III. xiii in more antiquated style must have fallen flat. He therefore maintained that the Additions were intended to replace, not to enlarge, the corresponding original scenes.

In *T.L.S.*, June 30, I pointed out that in my 1901 volume it was indicated that two of the Additions in Act III. ii. 67 ff. and Act II. ii. 169 ff. were evidently intended to replace the original lines, but that it was difficult to take this view about the Additions in the scene (II. vi) where Hieronimo finds Horatio's body, and about the Painter's scene.

In 1938 Schücking enlarged his English article into a German monograph (Hirtzel, Leipzig), *Die Zusätze der ' Spanish Tragedy '*. He maintained his position, and claimed that the Additions were all by one hand, not Ben Jonson's, nor any other's that can be identified. The only exception is Act IV. iv. 169–92, which is of inferior quality. Whether Schücking's views are accepted or not, his interpretation of the Additions in their psychological bearing is valuable.

A. K. McIlwraith included *Sp. Trag.* in his volume of *Five Elizabethan Tragedies* in the World's Classics series (1938, O.U.P.). The play was reprinted in modernized spelling from the 1592 edition, the 1602 additions following separately in an appendix. McIlwraith gives explanatory footnotes, and in discussing Kyd in his Introduction, claims that it is his grasp of human character and his portrayal of it that make good his claim to greatness.

In *Elizabethan Revenge Tragedy* (Princeton Univ. Press and O.U.P., 1940) Fredson Bowers singled out *Sp. Trag.* as the pure type of the revenge play, which was a subdivision of the tragedy of blood. He gave an analysis of the play, in which he found a combination of Senecan, Teutonic, and Italian elements.

VII

The Pre-Shakespearean (Ur-) 'Hamlet'

The claim for Kyd of this vanished play has found its most serious challenge from Ronald B. McKerrow. In his edition of *The Works of Thomas Nashe* (1910), vol. iii, pp. 315–16, he printed the relevant passage from Nashe's preface to Greene's *Menaphon*, and in vol. iv, pp. 448–52, he had a lengthy note on it, in which he contravened point by point the evidence which I had drawn from it in favour of Kyd's authorship, and which had also satisfied G. Sarrazin and J. Schick. McKerrow summed up : ' Nashe is, I think, speaking not of one writer, but of a group— probably, but not certainly, of dramatists. He did know of a Hamlet play, but the passage throws no light upon its authorship. There is no reason for supposing either Kyd or *The Spanish Tragedy* to be referred to.'

Where it is a question of interpreting tantalizing allusions there can be no completely convincing proof, but I retain my view (p. liv) that ' unless we are misled by a wellnigh incredible con-spiracy of coincidences ' Kyd must be the object of Nashe's attack. In the same year as McKerrow's volumes appeared Gregory Smith, as mentioned above, supported Kyd's claim to be the author of the vanished play, and in *The Westminster Review*, 1908, J. Allen had discussed *The Lost 'Hamlet' of Kyd*. Further independent support has been given by the Danish scholar V. Osterberg in his *Studier over Hamlet-Teksterna* (1920). The section of this book dealing with the pre-Shakespearean *Hamlet* was paraphrased by J. Dover Wilson in *R.E.S.*, Oct. 1942, under the title *Nashe's ' Kid in Æsop '*. Nashe after alluding to ' whole Hamlets, I should say handfuls of tragical speeches ', says that Seneca's famished followers have ' to imitate the Kid in Æsop, who enamoured with the Foxes newfangles forsooke all hopes of life to leape into a newe occupation '. Osterberg points out that there is no relevant story in Æsop's *Fables*. Nashe in all probability is thinking of the May eclogue of Spenser's *The Shepheardes Calender*, where a Kid attracted by a ' newell ' in the basket of the Fox, disguised as a pedlar, is trapped and carried off to be eaten. As Osterberg points out, ' the Kid forsakes safety and comes to destruction, while the famished writers are driven to seek a way of escape from indigence . . . Seeing then that there is no plausible connexion between Seneca's followers and the Kid, that a violent distortion is required to apply the pseudo-Æsopian illustration, and in any case that the phrase in question affords no meaning apart from a personal allusion—we are in a position to claim it for certain as pointing to Thomas Kyd '.

William Montgomerie in *Sporting Kid* (*Life and Letters*, Jan. 1943) also held that Nashe was referring to Spenser's May eclogue, but drew some far-fetched parallels between it and features in *Hamlet*.

In his *Elizabethan Revenge Tragedy*, noticed above, Bowers also attached the early *Hamlet* to Kyd, and on the basis of the first Quarto and of *Der bestrafte Brudermord* he made a speculative reconstruction of the main lines of the lost piece.

VIII
Soliman and Perseda

The British Museum 1599 quarto which I listed on p. 152 has now proved to be one of the facsimiles made about 1815 by J. Smeeton, Printer, St. Martin's Lane. The Museum has now a genuine copy (C. 34 b. 45). There are to be added seven copies in U.S.A. libraries.

Of the copies with *Newly corrected and amended* stamped on the title-pages (1599 A) there are to be added those in the Folger and Huntington libraries.

IX
The Murder of John Brewen

The unique copy of this pamphlet in the Lambeth Palace Library is anonymous but it has on it two manuscript signatures. One of these, on the title-page, is ' Ihō Kyde ', the publisher, John Kyd, which I incorrectly interpreted as Thomas Kyd. The other ' Thō Kydde ', the author, is at the end, and it has therefore been attributed to him.

R. M. Gorrell in *M.L.N.* (June 1942) pointed out that in S. R. Maitland's catalogue of English books in the Lambeth Palace Library the pamphlet was listed as anonymous. It was first claimed for Kyd by John Payne Collier in *N. and Q.*, Mar. 29, 1862, the year before he issued a reprint of it, asserting in the preface that the Lambeth copy was ' clearly that transmitted to one of the licensers who had written on it the two signatures '. Gorrell has found that in Collier's own copy of the reprint, now in the Huntington Library, signatures like those in the Lambeth copy have been queried on it. There is little doubt that these were written by Collier, and Gorrell is suspicious of the genuineness of those in the Lambeth copy.

X

Stage-Revivals

In conclusion it has to be recorded that *The Spanish Tragedie* has been revived on the stage, in London (at Birkbeck College), in Oxford (at Christ Church), and in Edinburgh (at a Dramatic Festival), and still retains something of its power to thrill an audience.

THE

WORKS OF THOMAS KYD

The Spanish Tragedie:

OR,

Hieronimo is mad againe.

Containing the lamentable end of *Don Horatio*, and
Belimperia; with the pittifull death of *Hieronimo*.

Newly corrected, amended, and enlarged with new
Additions of the *Painters* part, and others, as
it hath of late been diuers times acted.

LONDON,
Printed by W. White, for I. White and T. Langley,
and are to be sold at their Shop ouer against the
Sarazens head without New-gate. 1615.

EDITOR'S NOTE

THE text adopted is that of the undated Quarto in the British Museum (C. 34 d. 7), printed by Edward Allde for Edward White, which internal evidence, in my opinion, proves to be the earliest extant edition, and which has certainly the best text. The adoption of any reading other than that of this Quarto is indicated in the footnotes. I give all variants from the Quartos of 1594, -99, 1602 (Bodleian copy), 1602, with colophon 1603 (Duke of Devonshire's copy), 1610, -15, -18, -23, -33.

In the 'Additions' the text is that of the Bodleian Quarto of 1602; but after Act IV, Scene iv, *186*, where MS. replaces in this copy the missing leaves of print, it is that of the Duke of Devonshire's Quarto. I have aimed at indicating more clearly than has hitherto been done the relation of these Additions to Kyd's text. Dodsley, the first editor, having seen only the Quarto of 1633, did not know that they were not in the original play. Hawkins, who collated the undated Quarto and the Quartos of 1618, -23, -33, placed the Additions in his notes; but his arrangement, though more consistent than that of any of his successors, does not make the complicated changes in Act IV, Scene iv, 167 ff. sufficiently clear. Reed and Collier printed the Additions, distinguished by italics, in the text; and in Act III, Scene ii, and Act IV, Scene iv, where these Additions replace parts of the original, they transferred Kyd's lines to the notes. Hazlitt printed the Additions, except in Act III, Scene ii, in the text, distinguished merely by square brackets; which, however, he omitted in Act III, Scene xii A, while in Act IV, Scene iv, he gave a 'contamination' of the original and the revised versions. Schick, by printing the Additions in Act II, Scene v, and Act III, Scenes xi and xii A, in the text, while in Act III, Scene ii, he transfers them wholly, and in Act IV, Scene iv, partly, to the foot of the page, produces a numbering of the lines which is neither that of Kyd nor of the reviser. I have therefore printed all the Additions in the text, distinguished by smaller type and special numbering, and have further used a double numbering to mark the contrast between the Scenes in their original and their extended form.

The references in the notes are :—

Allde = undated Quarto printed by Allde
1594 -99 = Quartos of 1594 and 1599
1602 = Bodleian Quarto of 1602 } covered, when in agree-
1602 A = Duke of Devonshire's Quarto of 1602-3 } ment, by single figure, *1602*
1610 -15 -18 -23 -33 = Quartos of 1610, 1615, 1618, 1623, and 1633
Dodsley = R. Dodsley's edition in *Old Plays*, vol. ii (1744)
Hazlitt = W. C. Hazlitt's edition in his reissue of Dodsley's *Old Plays*, vol. v (1874)
Reed = I. Reed's edition in his reissue of Dodsley's *Old Plays*, vol. iii (1780)
Collier = J. P. Collier's ed. in reissue of Dodsley's *Old Plays*, vol. iii (1825)
Fleischer = G. Fleischer's *Bemerkungen üb. T. Kyd's 'Spanish Tragedy'* (1896)
Schick = Professor J. Schick's edition in the *Temple Dramatists* (1898)

Details about the Quartos and the later editions are given in the *Introduction*.

⟨DRAMATIS PERSONAE[1]

Ghost of Andrea, *a Spanish Courtier*⎫
Revenge   ⎬ In Induction and Chorus.

King of Spain.
Don Cyprian, Duke of Castile, *his brother*.
Lorenzo, *the Duke's son*.
Bel-imperia, *Lorenzo's sister*.
Pedringano, *Bel-imperia's servant*.
Lorenzo's Page.

Viceroy of Portugal.
Don Pedro, *his brother*.
Balthazar, *the Viceroy's son*.
Serberine, *Balthazar's servant*.

Hieronimo, *Marshal of Spain*.
Isabella, *his wife*.
Horatio, *their son*.
Isabella's maid.

Spanish General.
Deputy.
Portugese Ambassador.
Alexandro ⎱
Viluppo   ⎰ *Portugese Noblemen.*

Bazulto, *an old man*.
Christophil, *Bel-imperia's Janitor*.
Hangman.
Messenger.
Three Watchmen.
Two Portugese.

Soliman, Sultan of Turkey (*by Balthazar*)⎫
Erastus, Knight of Rhodes (*by Lorenzo*) ⎬ In Hieronimo's Play.
The Bashaw (*by Hieronimo*)   ⎪
Perseda (*by Bel-imperia*)   ⎭

Three Kings   ⎱ In First Dumb Show.
Three Knights⎰

Hymen   ⎱ In Second Dumb Show.
Two Torch Bearers⎰

Bazardo, *a Painter*   ⎫
Pedro ⎱ *Hieronimo's servants* ⎬ In the Additions to the play.
Jacques⎰

Army, Royal Suites, Nobles, Officers, Halberdiers, Servants, &c.⟩

No early Quarto contains *Dramatis Personae*. Dodsley's list of 1744 was copied by later editors till Schick, from whose list the above varies in some details, and in adding the characters in Hieronimo's play.

E 2

THE SPANISH TRAGEDIE

ACTVS PRIMVS.

⟨Scene I : Induction.⟩

Enter the Ghoast of Andrea, *and with him* Revenge.

Ghoast. When this eternall substance of my soule
  Did liue imprisond in my wanton flesh,
  Ech in their function seruing others need,
  I was a Courtier in the Spanish Court.
  My name was *Don Andrea*; my discent,   5
  Though not ignoble, yet inferiour far
  To gratious fortunes of my tender youth :
  For there in prime and pride of all my yeeres,
  By duteous seruice and deseruing love,
  In secret I possest a worthy dame,   10
  Which hight sweet *Bel-imperia* by name.
  But in the haruest of my sommer ioyes,
  Deaths winter nipt the blossomes of my blisse,
  Forcing diuorce betwixt my loue and me.
  For in the late conflict with Portingale   15
  My valour drew me into dangers mouth,
  Till life to death made passage through my wounds.
  When I was slaine, my soule descended straight,
  To passe the flowing streame of Acheron ;

---

2 wanton] wonted *1615 -18 -23 -33*   3 other *1623 -33*   8 For *om.*
1623 -33   in the prime and pride *1623* : in the pride and prime *1633*
12 summers *1623 -33*

But churlish *Charon*, only boatman there,   20
Said that my rites of buriall not performde,
I might not sit amongst his passengers.
Ere *Sol* had slept three nights in *Thetis* lap,
And slakte his smoaking charriot in her floud,
By *Don Horatio*, our Knight Marshals sonne,   25
My funerals and obsequies were done.
Then was the Feriman of Hell content
To passe me ouer to the slimie strond
That leades to fell *Auernus* ougly waues.
There, pleasing *Cerberus* with honied speech,   ·   30
I past the perils of the formost porch.
Not farre from hence, amidst ten thousand soules,
Sate *Minos*, *Eacus*, and *Rhadamant*,
To whome no sooner gan I make approch,
To craue a pasport for my wandring Ghost,   35
But *Minos*, in grauen leaues of Lotterie,
Drew forth the manner of my life and death.
This Knight (quoth he) both liu'd and died in loue,
And for his loue tried fortune of the warres,
And, by warres fortune, lost both loue and life.   40
Why then, said *Eacus*, conuay him hence,
To walke with louers in our fieldes of loue,
And spend the course of euerlasting time
Vnder greene mirtle trees and Cipresse shades.
No, no, said *Rhadamant*, it were not well   45
With louing soules to place a Martialist:
He died in warre, and must to Martiall fields,
Where wounded *Hector* liues in lasting paine,
And *Achilles* Mermedons do scoure the plaine.
Then *Minos*, mildest censor of the three,   50
Made this deuice to end the difference:
Send him (quoth he) to our infernall King,
To dome him as best seemes his Maiestie.
To this effect my pasport straight was drawne.
In keeping on my way to *Plutos* Court,   55

---

24 slackt *1610 -15 -18*   30 homed *1599, 1610 -15 -23 -33*   33 *Ninos,*
Eucus 1602 A   35 wondring *1610*   44 Cypres *1594, 1623 -33*: Cypers
1599, 1602 -10 -15 -18   49 do] to *1599*   50 censoret *1610 -15*: censorer
1618: censurer *1623 -33*   54 straight] strainge *1610*

Through dreadfull shades of euer glooming night,
I saw more sights then thousand tongues can tell,
Or pennes can write, or mortall harts can think.
Three waies there were: that on the right hand side
Was ready way vnto the foresaid fields,   60
Where louers liue and bloudie Martialists;
But either sort contain within his bounds.
The left hand path, declining fearefully,
Was ready dounfall to the deepest hell,
Where bloudie furies shakes their whips of steele,   65
And poore *Ixion* turnes an endles wheele;
Where vsurers are choakt with melting golde,
And wantons are imbraste with ouglie Snakes,
And murderers grone with neuer killing wounds,
And periurde wightes scalded in boyling lead,   70
And all foule sinnes with torments ouerwhelmd.
Twixt these two waies I trod the middle path,
Which brought me to the faire Elizian greene,
In midst whereof there standes a stately Towre,
The walles of brasse, the gates of adamant.   75
Heere finding *Pluto* with his *Proserpine*,
I shewed my passport humbled on my knee;
Whereat faire *Proserpine* began to smile,
And begd that onely she might give my doome.
Pluto was pleasd, and sealde it with a kisse.   80
Forthwith, *Revenge,* she rounded thee in th' eare,
And bad thee lead me through the gates of Horn,
Where dreames haue passage in the silent night.
No sooner had she spoke, but we were heere,
I wot not how, in twinkling of an eye.   85
Revenge. Then know, *Andrea,* that thou art ariu'd
Where thou shalt see the author of thy death,
Don Balthazar, the Prince of *Portingale,*
Depriu'd of life by *Bel-imperia.*

---

56 shapes of euer-blooming *1615-18* : shades of euer blooming *1623-33*
60 field *1615 -18 -23 -33*   64 fall downe *1618 -23 -33*   69 grone]
greeue *1594 -99, 1602 -10 -15 -18* : greene *1623 -33*   euerkilling *1599, 1602*
-10 -15 -18 -23 -33 : euerstilling *1602 A*   79 And] I *1615 -18 -23 -33*   my]
me *1602 A*   82 Horn *Hawkins and later editors* : Hor *Allde, 1594* : Horror
1599. 1602 -10 -23 -33 : Horrour *1615 -18*

Heere sit we downe to see the misterie,   90
And serue for *Chorus* in this Tragedie.

⟨SCENE II.⟩

Enter Spanish King, Generall, Castile, Hieronimo.

King. Now say, L⟨ord⟩ Generall, how fares our Campe ?
Gen. All wel, my soueraigne Liege, except some few
　That are deceast by fortune of the warre.
King. But what portends thy cheerful countenance,
　And posting to our presence thus in hast ?   5
　Speak, man, hath fortune giuen vs victorie ?
Gen. Victorie, my Liege, and that with little losse.
King. Our Portingals will pay vs tribute then ?
Gen. Tribute and wonted homage therewithall.
King. Then blest be heauen, and guider of the heauens,   10
　From whose faire influence such iustice flowes.
Cast. *O multum dilecte Deo, tibi militat aether,*
　Et coniuratae curuato poplite gentes
　Succumbunt: recti soror est victoria iuris.
King. Thanks to my louing brother of Castile.   15
　But, Generall, vnfolde in breefe discourse
　Your forme of battell, and your warres successe,
　That, adding all the pleasure of thy newes
　Vnto the height of former happines,
　With deeper wage and greater dignitie,   20
　We may reward thy blissfull chiualrie.
Gen. Where Spaine and Portingale do ioyntly knit
　Their frontiers, leaning on each others bound,
　There met our armies in their proud aray :
　Both furnisht well, both full of hope and feare,   25
　Both menacing alike with daring showes,
　Both vaunting sundry colours of deuice,
　Both cheerly sounding trumpets, drums, and fifes,
　Both raising dreadfull clamors to the skie,
　That vallies, hills, and riuers made rebound,   30
　And heauen it selfe was frighted with the sound.

---

4 pretends *1618 -23 -33*   10 be] the *1615*   12 *dilecto 1618*   *aethur*
1615 -18 -23 -33   13 *poplito Qq. exc. 1633*   14 *succumbant : 1615 -18*
-23 -33   21 may] will *1633*   23 bounds *1623 -33*   29 skies *1633*

Our battels both were pitcht in squadron forme,
Each corner strongly fenst with wings of shot;
But ere we ioynd and came to push of Pike,
I brought a squadron of our readiest shot   35
From out our rearward to begin the fight :
They brought another wing to incounter us.
Meane-while, our Ordinance plaied on either side,
And Captaines stroue to haue their valours tride.
Don Pedro, their chiefe Horsemens Corlonell,   40
Did with his Cornet brauely make attempt
To breake the order of our battell rankes :
But *Don Rogero*, worthy man of warre,
Marcht forth against him with our Musketiers,
And stopt the malice of his fell approch.   45
While they maintaine hot skirmish too and fro,
Both battailes ioyne and fall to handie blowes,
Their violent shot resembling th' oceans rage,
When, roaring lowde, and with a swelling tide,
It beats upon the rampiers of huge rocks,   50
And gapes to swallow neighbour bounding landes.
Now while *Bellona* rageth heere and there,
Thicke stormes of bullets ran like winters haile,
And shiuered Launces darke the troubled aire.
        Pede pes et cuspide cuspis,   55
    Arma sonant armis vir petiturque viro.
On euery side drop Captaines to the ground,
And Souldiers, some ill maimde, some slaine outright :
Heere falles a body scindred from his head,
There legs and armes lye bleeding on the grasse,   60
Mingled with weapons and vnboweld steedes,
That scattering ouer spread the purple plaine.
In all this turmoyle, three long houres and more,
The victory to neither part inclinde,

---

35 our] the *1618-23-33*   37 t' *1623-33*   39 valour *1618-23-33*   40 Colonell
1594-99 : Coronell *1602-10-15-18-23-33*   41 Coronet *1602-15-18-23-33*
44 Musketires *1594-99* : Muskatires *1610-15-18*   45 stops *1615-18-23-33*
50 rawpiers *1610* : rampires *1602 A-15-18-23-33*   52 while] when *1618-23-33*
54 darkt *1594-99, 1602-10* : dark'd *1618-23-33*   56 *Arma sonant armis 1633* :
Anni sonant annis other Qq.   57 dropt *1618-23-33*   58 souldiers lie
maimde *1602-10-15-18-23-33*   59 sundered *1602-15-18* : sundedred *1610* :
sundred *1623-33*   61 vnbowed *Qq. exc. Allde*

Till *Don Andrea* with his braue Launciers   65
In their maine battell made so great a breach
That, halfe dismaid, the multitude retirde :
But *Balthazar*, the Portingales young Prince,
Brought rescue and encouragde them to stay.
Heere-hence the fight was eagerly renewd,   70
And in that conflict was *Andrea* slaine,
Braue man at armes, but weake to *Balthazar*.
Yet while the Prince, insulting ouer him,
Breathd out proud vauntes, sounding to our reproch,
Friendship and hardie valour, ioynd in one,   75
Prickt forth *Horatio*, our Knight-Marshals sonne,
To challenge forth that Prince in single fight :
Not long betweene these twaine the fight indurde,
But straight the Prince was beaten from his horse,
And forcst to yeelde him prisoner to his foe.   80
When he was taken, all the rest they fled,
And our Carbines pursued them to the death,
Till, *Phoebus* wauing to the western deepe,
Our Trumpeters were chargde to sound retreat.
King. Thanks, good L⟨ord⟩ Generall for these good newes ;   85
And for some argument of more to come,
Take this, and weare it for thy Soueraignes sake.

> *Give him his Chaine.*

But tell me now, hast thou confirmd a peace ?
Gen. No peace, my Liege, but peace conditionall,
That, if with homage tribute be well paide,   90
The fury of your forces wil be staide :
And to this peace their *Vice-roy* hath subscribde,

> *Give the* King *a paper.*

And made a solemne vow that, during life,
His tribute shal be truly paide to Spaine.
King. These words, these deeds, become thy person well.   95
But now, Knight Marshall, frolicke with thy King,
For tis thy Sonne that winnes this battels prize.

---

66 their] this *1615 -18*   76 pickt *1618*   77 in] to *1594, 1602 -10 -15
-23 -33*   82 the *om. 1615 -18 -23 -33*   87 it *om. 1623 -33*   90 tribute
may be payde *1615 -18 -23 -33*   91 your] our *1615 -18 -23 -33*   92 this] that
1615 -18 -23 -33   94 His] This *1618 -23 -33*   96 frolicks *1602*   thy] the
Qq. exc. Allde   97 this] that *1594 -99, 1602 -10 -15 -18 -23* : the *1602 A -33*

Hier. Long may he liue to serue my Soureraigne liege,
And soone decay vnlesse he serue my liege.

                                        A tucket a farre off.

King. Nor thou nor he shall dye without reward :   100
    What meanes this warning of this trumpets sound ?
Gen. This tels me that your graces men of warre,
    Such as warres fortune hath reseru'd from death,
    Come marching on towards your royall seate,
    To shew themselues before your Maiestie ;   105
    For so I gaue in charge at my depart.
    Whereby by demonstration shall appeare,
    That all (except three hundred or few more)
    Are safe returnd, and by their foes inricht.

The Armie enters ; Balthazar, *betweene* Lorenzo *and* Horatio, *captive.*

King. A gladsome sight : I long to see them heere.   110

                                        They enter and passe by.

    Was that the war-like Prince of *Portingale*
    That by our Nephew was in triumph led ?
Gen. It was, my Liege, the Prince of *Portingale.*
King. But what was he that on the other side
    Held him by th' arme, as partner of the prize ?   115
Hier. That was my sonne, my gratious soueraigne ;
    Of whome, though from his tender infancie
    My louing thoughts did neuer hope but well,
    He neuer pleasd his fathers eyes till now,
    Nor fild my hart with ouercloying ioyes.   120
King. Goe, let them march once more about these walles,
    That, staying them, we may conferre and talke
    With our braue prisoner and his double guard.
    Hieronimo, it greatly pleaseth vs
    That in our victorie thou haue a share,   125
    By vertue of thy worthy sonnes exploit.

                                        Enter againe.

    Bring hether the young Prince of *Portingale* :
    The rest martch on, but ere they be dismist,

---

98 my *om. 1618*   S.D. *Trumpet 1599, 1602 -10 -15 -18 -23 -33*   101 this
Trumpet *1602 -10* : the Trumpet *1615 -18* : the Trumpets *1623 -33*   106 in]
them *1602 -10 -15 -18 -23 -33* : in *1602 A*   107 by *om. 1602 A*   S.D.
enters] *meetes 1615 -18 -23 -33*

We will bestow on euery souldier
Two duckets and on euery leader ten,　　　　　　　　130
That they may know our largesse welcomes them.

　　　　　　　　　　　　Exeunt all but Bal., Lor., Hor.

Welcome *Don Balthazar*; welcome Nephew;
And thou, *Horatio*, thou art welcome too.
Young prince, although thy fathers hard misdeedes,
In keeping back the tribute that he owes,　　　　　135
Deserue but euill measure at our hands,
Yet shalt thou know that Spaine is honorable.

Bal. The trespasse that my father made in peace
Is now controlde by fortune of the warres;
And cards once dealt, it bootes not aske, why so?　　140
His men are slaine, a weakening to his Realme;
His colours ceaz'd, a blot vnto his name;
His Sonne distrest, a corsiue to his hart:
These punishments may cleare his late offence.

King. I, *Balthazar*, if he obserue this truce,　　　　145
Our peace will grow the stronger for these warres.
Meane while liue thou, though not in libertie,
Yet free from bearing any seruile yoake;
For in our hearing thy deserts were great,
And in our sight thy selfe art gratious.　　　　　　150

Bal. And I shall studie to deserue this grace.

King. But tell me (for their holding makes me doubt)
　To which of these twaine art thou prisoner?

Lor. To me, my Liege.

Hor.　　　　　　　　To me, my Soueraigne.

Lor. This hand first tooke his courser by the raines.　155

Hor. But first my launce did put him from his horse.

Lor. I ceaz'd his weapon and enioyde it first.

Hor. But first I forc'd him lay his weapons downe.

King. Let goe his arme, vpon our priuiledge.

　　　　　　　　　　　　　　　Let him goe.

129-131 We . . . duckets | And . . . know | Our . . . them *Qq.*　　　131
welcome *1618*　　141 to his] to the *1610 -15 -18 -23 -33*　　145 obserues
Qq. exc. Allde　　147 though] as though *1599, 1602 -10 -15 -18*　　148 free
om. 1594 -99, 1602 -10 -15 -18　　154 Liege] lord *1618 -23 -33*　　155 his]
the *Qq. exc. Allde*

Say, worthy Prince, to whether didst thou yield?   160
Bal. To him in curtesie, to this perforce:
   He spake me faire, this other gaue me strokes;
   He promisde life, this other threatned death;
   He wan my loue, this other conquered me:
   And truth to say, I yeeld myselfe to both.   165
Hier. But that I know your grace for just and wise,
   And might seeme partiall in this difference,
   Inforct by nature and by law of armes
   My tongue should plead for young *Horatios* right.
   He hunted well that was a Lyons death,   170
   Not he that in a garment wore his skin:
   So Hares may pull dead Lyons by the beard.
King. Content thee, Marshall, thou shalt haue no wrong;
   And, for thy sake, thy Sonne shall want no right.
   Will both abide the censure of my doome?   175
Lor. I craue no better then your grace awards.
Hor. Nor I, although I sit beside my right.
King. Then by my iudgement thus your strife shall end:
   You both deserue, and both shall haue reward.
   Nephew, thou tookst his weapon and his horse: 180
   His weapons and his horse are thy reward.
   Horatio, thou didst force him first to yeeld:
   His ransome therefore is thy valours fee;
   Appoint the sum, as you shall both agree.
   But, Nephew, thou shalt haue the Prince in guard,   185
   For thine estate best fitteth such a guest.
   Horatios house were small for all his traine;
   Yet, in regarde thy substance passeth his,
   And that just guerdon may befall desert,
   To him we yeeld the armour of the Prince.   190
   How likes *Don Balthazar* of this deuice?
Bal. Right well, my Liege, if this prouizo were,
   That *Don Horatio* beare us company,
   Whome I admire and loue for chiualrie.
King. *Horatio,* leaue him not that loues thee so.   195
   Now let us hence to see our souldiers paide,
   And feast our prisoner as our friendly guest.   *Exeunt.*

---

160 Say] So *Qq. exc. Allde*   166 knaw *Allde*   180 weapons *1615*
-18 -23 -33   183 fee] feet *1599*

⟨Scene III.⟩

Enter Viceroy, Alexandro, Villuppo.

Vice. Is our embassadour dispatcht for Spaine?
Alex. Two daies, my Liege, are past since his depart.
Vice. And tribute paiment gone along with him?
Alex. I, my good Lord.
Vice. Then rest we heere a while in our unrest,　　　　5
　　And feed our sorrowes with some inward sighes,
　　For deepest cares break neuer into teares.
　　But wherefore sit I in a Regall throne?
　　This better fits a wretches endles moane:
　　Yet this is higher then my fortunes reach,　　　　10
　　And therefore better then my state deserues.
　　　　　　　　　　　　　　　　Falles to the ground.
　　I, I, this earth, Image of mellancholly,
　　Seeks him whome fates adiuge to miserie:
　　Heere let me lye; now am I at the lowest.
　　　　Qui iacet in terra non habet vnde cadat.　　　15
　　In me consumpsit vires fortuna nocendo,
　　　　Nil superest ut iam possit obesse magis.
　　Yes, Fortune may bereaue me of my Crowne:
　　Heere, take it now; let Fortune doe her worst,
　　She will not rob me of this sable weed.　　　　20
　　O no, she enuies none but pleasant things.
　　Such is the folly of dispightfull chance.
　　Fortune is blinde, and sees not my deserts;
　　So is she deafe, and heares not my laments;
　　And could she heare, yet is she wilfull mad,　　　25
　　And therefore will not pittie my distresse.
　　Suppose that she could pittie me, what then?
　　What helpe can be expected at her hands,
　　Whose foote ⟨is⟩ standing on a rowling stone,
　　And minde more mutable then fickle windes?　　　30
　　Why waile I then, wheres hope of no redresse?
　　O yes, complaining makes my greefe seeme lesse.

---

3 *Vice. om. 1594*　　8 a *om. 1594 -99, 1602 -10 -15*: this *1618 -23 -33*　　9 This]
It *1618*　　S.D. *Falles . . . ground after 9, 1623 -33*　　13 adiuged *Qq. exc.*
Allde　　14 I am *1633*　　17 *Nihil 1633*　　29 is *add. Dodsley*

My late ambition hath distaind my faith ;
My breach of faith occasiond bloudie warres ;
Those bloudie warres haue spent my treasure ;   35
And with my treasure my peoples blood ;
And with their blood, my ioy and best beloued,
My best beloued, my sweete and onely Sonne.
O wherefore went I not to warre my selfe ?
The cause was mine ; I might haue died for both :   40
My yeeres were mellow, his but young and greene,
My death were naturall, but his was forced.

Alex. No doubt, my Liege, but still the prince suruiues.

Vice. Suruiues ? I, where ?

Alex. In Spaine, a prisoner by mischance of warre.   45

Vice. Then they haue slaine him for his fathers fault.

Alex. That were a breach to common law of armes.

Vice. They recke no lawes that meditate reuenge.

Alex. His ransomes worth will stay from foule reuenge.

Vice. No ; if he liued the newes would soone be heere.   50

Alex. Nay, euill newes flie faster still than good.

Vice. Tell me no more of newes, for he is dead.

Vill. My Soueraign, pardon the author of ill newes,
And Ile bewray the fortune of thy Sonne.

Vice. Speak on. Ile guerdon thee what ere it be :   55
Mine eare is readie to receiue ill newes,
My hart growne hard gainst mischiefes battery.
Stand vp, I say, and tell thy tale at large.

Vill. Then heare that truth which these mine eyes haue seene.
When both the armies were in battell ioynd,   60
Don Balthazar, amidst the thickest troupes,
To winne renowne did wondrous feats of armes :
Amongst the rest I saw him, hand to hand,
In single fight with their Lord Generall ;
Till *Alexandro,* that here counterfeits   65
Vnder the colour of a duteous friend,
Discharged his Pistoll at the Princes back,
As though he would haue slaine their Generall :
And therewithall *Don Balthazar* fell doune ;

---

35 These *1623-33*   hath *1602 A*   41 but his *1623-33*   44 I but
where *1615-18-23-33*   51 will flie *Qq. exc. Allde*   57 Mine *1594,*
· *1602-10-15-18*   59 that] the *Qq. exc. Allde*

And when he fell, then we began to flie:　　70
　But, had he liued, the day had sure bene ours.
Alex. O wicked forgerie: O traiterous miscreant.
Vice. Holde thou thy peace. But now, *Villuppo*, say,
　Where then became the carkasse of my Sonne?
Vill. I saw them drag it to the Spanish tents.　　75
Vice. I, I, my nightly dreames haue tolde me this.
　Thou false, unkinde, unthankfull, traiterous beast,
　Wherein had *Balthazar* offended thee,
　That thou shouldst thus betray him to our foes?
　Wast Spanish gold that bleared so thine eyes,　　80
　That thou couldst see no part of our deserts?
　Perchance, because thou art *Terseraes* Lord,
　Thou hadst some hope to .weere this Diadome,
　If first my Sonne and then my selfe were slaine.
　But thy ambitious thought shall breake thy necke.　　85
　I, this was it that made thee spill his bloud,

Take the crowne and put it on againe.

　But Ile now weare it till thy bloud be spilt.
Alex. Vouchsafe, dread Soueraigne, to heare me speake.
Vice. Away with him; his sight is second hell.
　Keepe him till we determine of his death:　　90
　If *Balthazar* be dead, he shall not liue.
　Villuppo, follow us for thy reward.

Exit Vice.

Vill. Thus haue I with an enuious, forged tale
　Deceiued the King, betraid mine enemy,
　And hope for guerdon of my villany.　　95

Exit.

⟨Scene IV.⟩

Enter Horatio *and* Bel-imperia.

Bel. Signior *Horatio*, this is the place and houre,
　Wherein I must intreat thee to relate
　The circumstance of *Don Andreas* death,

---

70 began we *1594 -99, 1602*　　83 hast *1623 -33*　　85 thoughts *1618 -23 -33*
87 now Ile *1615 -18 -23 -33*　　88 dread] deare *1618 -23 -33*　　S.D. *Exit*
Vice. *om. 1602 -10 -15 -18 -23 -33*

Who, liuing, was my garlands sweetest flower,
And in his death hath buried my delights.   5
Hor. For loue of him, and seruice to your selfe,
I nill refuse this heauie dolefull charge;
Yet teares and sighes, I feare, will hinder me.
When both our Armies were enioynd in fight,
Your worthy chiualier amidst the thikst,   10
For glorious cause still aiming at the fairest,
Was at the last by yong *Don Balthazar*
Encountred hand to hand: their fight was long,
Their harts were great, their clamours menacing,
Their strength alike, their strokes both dangerous.   15
But wrathfull *Nemesis,* that wicked power,
Enuying at *Andreas* praise and worth,
Cut short his life to end his praise and woorth.
She, she her selfe, disguisde in armours maske,
(As *Pallas* was before proud *Pergamus*)   20
Brought in a fresh supply of Halberdiers,
Which paunckt his horse and dingd him to the ground.
Then yong *Don Balthazar* with ruthles rage,
Taking aduantage of his foes distresse,
Did finish what his Halberdiers begun,   25
And left not till *Andreas* life was done.
Then, though too late, incenst with iust remorce,
I with my hand set foorth against the Prince,
And brought him prisoner from his Halberdiers.
Bel. Would thou hadst slaine him that so slew my loue.   30
But then was *Don Andreas* carkasse lost?
Hor. No, that was it for which I cheefly stroue,
Nor stept I back till I recouerd him:
I tooke him up, and wound him in mine armes;
And welding him unto my priuate tent,   35
There laid him downe, and dewd him with my teares,
And sighed and sorrowed as became a freend.

---

4 sweetest] chiefest *1623-33*   7 I nil *1594*: I will *1602*: Ile not *1610-15-18*
-23-33   dolefull, heauy *1618-23-33*   8 sightes, *1610*   9 in] to
1618-23-33   10 chauilier *1594-99, 1602 A* : chauiller *1602*: chauilire
1610-15 : chauiliere *1618* : cauilier *1623-33*   thickest, *1610-15-18-23-33*
21 a *om. 1594-99, 1602-10-15-18-23*   30 so *om. 1610-15-18-23-33*
34 my *1602-10-15*   35 wilding *1602 A*

But neither freendly sorrow, sighes, nor teares,
Could win pale death from his vsurped right.
Yet this I did, and lesse I could not doe :   40
I saw him honoured with due funerall.
This scarfe I pluckt from off his liueles arme,
And weare it in remembrance of my freend.

Bel. I know the scarfe : would he had kept it still ;
For had he liued he would haue kept it still,   45
And worne it for his *Bel-imperias* sake :
For twas my fauour at his last depart.
But now weare thou it both for him and me,
For after him thou hast deserued it best.
But for thy kindnes in his life and death,   50
Be sure while *Bel-imperias* life endures,
She will be *Don Horatios* thankfull freend.

Hor. And (Madame) *Don Horatio* will not slacke
Humbly to serue faire *Bel-imperia*.
But now, if your good liking stand thereto,   55
Ile craue your pardon to goe seeke the Prince,
For so the Duke, your father, gaue me charge.

                                                     Exit.

Bel. I, goe, *Horatio*, leaue me heere alone,
For sollitude best fits my cheereles mood.
Yet what auailes to waile *Andreas* death,   60
From whence *Horatio* proues my second loue ?
Had he not loued *Andrea* as he did,
He could not sit in *Bel-imperias* thoughts.
But how can loue find harbour in my brest,
Till I reuenge the death of my beloued ?   65
Yes, second loue shall further my reuenge :
Ile loue *Horatio*, my *Andreas* freend,
The more to spight the Prince that wrought his end.
And where *Don Balthazar* that slew my loue,
Himselfe now pleades for fauour at my hands,   70
He shall, in rigour of my iust disdaine,
Reape long repentance for his murderous deed :

---

38 sorrowes *1602 -10 -15 -18 -23 -33*   42 I *om. Qq. exc. Allde*   off
from *Qq. exc. Allde*   48 thou *om. 1602 -10 -15 -18 -23 -33*   72 for] of *Qq.*
exc. Allde

KYD : BOAS   C

For what wast els but murderous cowardise,
So many to oppresse one valiant knight,
Without respect of honour in the fight?   75
And heere he comes that murdred my delight.

Enter Lorenzo *and* Balthazar.

Lor. Sister, what meanes this melancholie walke?
Bel. That for a while I wish no company.
Lor. But heere the Prince is come to visite you.
Bel. That argues that he liues in libertie.   80
Bal. No, Madame, but in pleasing seruitude.
Bel. Your prison then, belike, is your conceit.
Bal. I, by conceit my freedome is enthralde.
Bel. Then with conceite enlarge your selfe againe.
Bal. What, if conceite haue laid my hart to gage?   85
Bel, Pay that you borrowed and recouer it.
Bal. I die, if it returne from whence it lyes.
Bel. A hartles man and liue? A miracle.
Bal. I, Lady, loue can worke such miracles.
Lor. Tush, tush, my Lord, let goe these ambages,   90
    And in plaine tearmes acquaint her with your loue.
Bel. What bootes complaint, when thers no remedy?
Bal. Yes, to your gratious selfe must I complaine,
    In whose faire answere lyes my remedy;
    On whose perfection all my thoughts attend;   95
    On whose aspect mine eyes finde beauties bowre;
    In whose translucent brest my hart is lodgde.
Bel. Alas, my Lord, these are but words of course,
    And but deuise to driue me from this place.

She in going in, lets fall her glove which Horatio
coming out takes up.

Hor. Madame, your Gloue.   100
Bel. Thanks, good *Horatio*, take it for thy paines.
Bal. Signior *Horatio* stoopt in happie time.
Hor. I reapt more grace then I deseru'd or hop'd.
Lor. My Lord, be not dismaid for what is past;
    You know that women oft are humerous: 105

8o in] at *1615 -18 -23 -33*   88 lives *1602 -10 -15 -23 -33*   97 brestes
1602 -10 -15 -18 -23 -33   99 deuisde *1599, 1602 -10 -15 -23 -33*   S.D. *She*
going 1599, 1602 -10 -15 -23 -33   *takes it up 1618 -23 -33*

These clouds will ouerblow with litle winde; ·
Let me alone, Ile scatter them my selfe.
Meanewhile let vs deuise to spend the time
In some delightfull sports and reuelling.
Hor. The King, my Lords, is comming hither straight,   110
To feast the Portingall Embassadour ;
Things were in readines before I came.
Bal. Then heere it fits vs to attend the King,
To welcome hither our Embassadour,
And learne my Father and my Countries health.   115

⟨Scene V.⟩

Enter the banquet, Trumpets, the King, and Embassadour.

King. See, Lord Embassadour, how Spaine intreats
Their prisoner *Balthazar*, thy Viceroyes sonne :
We pleasure more in kindenes then in warres.
Emb. Sad is our King, and Portingale laments,
Supposing that *Don Balthazar* is slaine.   5
Bal. So am I slaine, by beauties tirannie.
You see, my Lord, how *Balthazar* is slaine :
I frolike with the Duke of *Castiles* Sonne,
Wrapt euery houre in pleasures of the Court,
And graste with fauours of his Maiestie.   10
King. Put off your greetings, till our feast be done ;
Now come and sit with vs, and taste our cheere.

Sit to the Banquet.

Sit downe, young Prince, you are our second guest :
Brother, sit downe ; and, Nephew, take your place.
Signior *Horatio*, waite thou vpon our Cup,   15
For well thou hast deserued to be honored.
Now, Lordings, fall too ; Spaine is Portugall
And Portugall is Spaine ; we both are freends ;
Tribute is paid, and we enioy our right.
But where is olde *Hieronimo*, our Marshall ?   20
He promised vs, in honor of our guest,
To grace our banquet with some pompous iest.

---

109 delightsome *1610 -15 -18 -23 -33*   reuellings *1618 -23 -33*   110 Lord
1599, 1602 -10 -15 -23 -33

Enter Hieronimo *with a Drum, three Knightes, each his Scutchin: then*
    he fetches three Kinges, they take their Crownes and them captive.

Hieronimo, this maske contentes mine eye,
Although I sound not well the misterie.
Hier. The first arm'd knight that hung his Scutchin vp,   25

                        He takes the Scutchin, and gives it to the King.

Was English *Robert*, Earle of Gloster,
Who, when King *Stephen* bore sway in Albion,
Arriued with fiue and twenty thousand men
In Portingale, and by successe of warre
Enforced the King, then but a Sarasin,   30
To beare the yoake of the English Monarchie.
King. My Lord of Portingale, by this you see
That which may comfort both your King and you,
And make your late discomfort seeme the lesse.
But say, *Hieronimo*, what was the next?   35
Hier. The second knight that hung his Scutchin vp,

                                He doth as he did before.

Was *Edmund*, Earle of Kent in Albion,
When English *Richard* wore the Diadem.
He came likewise, and razed Lisbon walles,
And tooke the King of Portingale in fight;   40
For which, and other such like seruice done,
He after was created Duke of Yorke.
King. This is another speciall argument,
That Portingale may daine to beare our yoake,
When it by little England hath been yoakt: 45
But now, *Hieronimo*, what were the last?
Hier. The third and last, not least in our account,

                                Dooing as before.

Was, as the rest, a valiant Englishman,
Braue *John of Gaunt*, the Duke of Lancaster,
As by his Scutchin plainely may appeare.   50
He with a puissant armie came to Spaine,
And tooke our King of Castile prisoner.
Emb. This is an argument for our Viceroy
That Spaine may not insult for her successe,

----

28 fiue and *om.* 1623-33

Since Englisb warriours likewise conquered Spaine,　　55
And made them bow their knees to Albion.
King. Hieronimo, I drinke to thee for this deuise,
Which hath pleasde both the Embassador and me.
Pledge me, *Hieronimo*, if thou loue the King.

Takes the Cup of Horatio.

My Lord, I feare we sit but ouer long,　　60
Vnless our dainties were more delicate :
But welcome are you to the best we haue.
Now let vs in, that you may be dispatcht :
I think our councell is already set.

Exeunt omnes.

⟨Scene VI.⟩

Andrea. Come we for this from depth of vnder ground,
To see him feast that gaue me my deaths wound ?
These pleasant sights are sorrow to my soule :
Nothing but league, and loue and banqueting.
Revenge. Be still, *Andrea* ; ere we go from hence,　　5
Ile turne their freendship into fell despight ;
Their loue to mortall hate, their day to night ;
Their hope into dispaire, their peace to warre ;
Their ioyes to paine, their blisse to miserie.

ACTVS SECVNDVS.

⟨Scene I.⟩

Enter Lorenzo *and* Balthazar.

Lor. My Lord, though *Bel-imperia* seeme thus coy,
Let reason holde you in your wonted ioy :
In time the sauuage Bull sustaines the yoake,
In time all haggard Hawkes will stoope to lure,
In time small wedges cleaue the hardest Oake,　　5
In time the Flint is pearst with softest shower,
And she in time will fall from her disdaine,
And rue the sufferance of your freendly paine.

---

59 the] thy *Schick*　　63 you] we *1610 -15 -18 -23 -33*　　II. 6 the hardest
flint *1610 -15 -18 -23 -33*　　8 rue] rule *1610 -15 -18 -23 -33*　　sufferance]
difference *1602 A*

Bal. No, she is wilder, and more hard withall,
  Then beast, or bird, or tree, or stony wall.   10
  But wherefore blot I *Bel-imperias* name?
  It is my fault, not she that merites blame.
  My feature is not to content her sight,
  My wordes are rude, and worke her no delight.
  The lines I send her are but harsh and ill,   15
  Such as doe drop from *Pan* and *Marsias* quill.
  My presents are not of sufficient cost,
  And being worthles, all my labours lost.
  Yet might she loue me for my valiancie :
  I, but thats slaundred by captiuitie.   20
  Yet might she loue me to content her sire :
  I, but her reason masters his desire.
  Yet might she loue me as her brother's freend :
  I, but her hopes aime at some other end.
  Yet might she loue me to upreare her state :   25
  I, but perhaps she hopes some nobler mate.
  Yet might she loue me as her beauties thrall :
  I, but I feare she cannot loue at all.
Lor. My Lord, for my sake leaue this extasie,
  And doubt not but weele finde some remedie.   30
  Some cause there is that lets you not be loued :
  First that must needs be knowne, and then remoued.
  What, if my Sister loue some other Knight ?
Bal. My sommers day will turne to winters night.
Lor. I have already found a stratageme,   35
  To sound the bottome of this doubtfull theame.
  My Lord, for once you shall be rulde by me ;
  Hinder me not what ere you heare or see.
  By force, or faire meanes will I cast about,
  To finde the truth of all this question out.   40
  Ho, *Pedringano.*
Ped.   *Signior.*
Lor.   *Vien qui presto.*
                                          Enter Pedringano.
Ped. Hath your Lordship any seruice to command me ?

---

    22 his] her *1602 A*, *1610-15-18-23-33*   26 hopes] loues *1623-33*   27
beauteous *Allde, 1594-99, 1602-10*   29 this extasie *Schick* : these extasies *Qq.*
S.D. *Enter* Ped. *after* Ho, *Pedringano 1615-18-23-33*

Lor. I, *Pedringano*, seruice of import :
  And not to spend the time in trifling words,
  Thus stands the case : it is not long, thou knowst,   45
  Since I did shield thee from my fathers wrath,
  For thy conueiance in *Andreas* loue,
  For which thou wert adiudg'd to punishment :
  I stood betwixt thee and thy punishment ;
  And since, thou knowest how I haue fauoured thee.   50
  Now to these fauours will I adde reward,
  Not with faire words, but store of golden coyne,
  And lands and liuing ioynd with dignities,
  If thou but satisfie my iust demaund :
  Tell truth, and haue me for thy lasting freend.   55
Ped. What ere it be your Lordship shall demaund,
  My bounden duety bids me tell the truth,
  If case it lye in me to tell the truth.
Lor. Then, *Pedringano*, this is my demaund :
  Whome loues my sister *Bel-imperia* ?   60
  For she reposeth all her trust in thee.
  Speake, man, and gaine both freendship and reward :
  I meane, whome loues she in *Andreas* place ?
Ped. Alas, my Lord, since *Don Andreas* death,
  I haue no credit with her as before,   65
  And therefore know not if she loue or no.
Lor. Nay, if thou dally, then I am thy foe,

                       Drawes his sword.

  And feare shall force what freendship cannot winne :
  Thy death shall bury what thy life conceales ;
  Thou dyest for more esteeming her then me.   70
Ped. Oh stay, my Lord.
Lor. Yet speake the truth, and I will guerdon thee,
  And shield thee from what euer can ensue,
  And will conceale what ere proceeds from thee ;
  But if thou dally once againe, thou diest.   75
Ped. If Madame *Bel-imperia* be in loue—
Lor. What, Villaine, ifs and ands ?   *Offer to kill him.*

---

45 knowest *Qq. exc. Allde*   53 liuings *1602 -10 -15 -23 -33*   58 it lies in mee
1610 : in me it lies *1615 -18 -23 -33*   S.D. *Drawes his sword add. 1602 -10
-15 -18 -23 -33*   S.D. *Offer . . . him. add. 1602 -10.*

Ped. Oh stay, my Lord, she loues *Horatio.*

Balthazar *starts back.*

Lor. What, *Don Horatio,* our Knight Marshals sonne?

Ped. Euen him, my Lord.   80

Lor. Now say but how knowest thou he is her loue,
And thou shalt finde me kinde and liberall:
Stand up, I say, and feareles tell the truth.

Ped. She sent him letters which my selfe perusde,
Full fraught with lines and arguments of loue,   85
Preferring him before Prince *Balthazar.*

Lor. Sweare on this crosse that what thou saiest is true,
And that thou wilt conceale what thou hast tolde.

Ped. I sweare to both, by him that made us all.

Lor. In hope thine oath is true, heeres thy reward: 90
But if I prooue thee periurde and uniust,
This very sword whereon thou tookst thine oath,
Shall be the worker of thy tragedie.

Ped. What I have said is true, and shall, for me,
Be still conceald from *Bel-imperia.*   95
Besides, your Honors liberalitie
Deserues my duteous seruice, euen till death.

Lor. Let this be all that thou shalt doe for me:
Be watchfull when and where these louers meete,
And giue me notice in some secret sort.   100

Ped. I will, my Lord.

Lor. Then shalt thou finde that I am liberall:
Thou knowst that I can more aduance thy state
Then she; be therefore wise, and faile me not.
Goe and attend her, as thy custome is,   105
Least absence make her thinke thou dost amisse.

Exit Pedringano.

Why so: *Tam armis quam ingenio:*
Where words preuaile not, violence preuailes;
But golde doth more then either of them both.
How likes Prince *Balthazar* this stratageme?   110

Bal. Both well and ill: it makes me glad and sad:
Glad, that I know the hinderer of my loue;

---

81 knowest thou that he *1615 -18 -23 -33*   108 preuailes *1602*   110 of this
1618 -23 -33

Sad, that I feare she hates me whome I loue:
Glad, that I know on whom to be reueng'd;
Sad, that sheele flie me, if I take reuenge. 115
Yet must I take reuenge, or dye my selfe,
For loue resisted growes impatient.
I thinke *Horatio* be my destinde plague:
First, in his hand he brandished a sword,
And with that sword he fiercely waged warre, 120
And in that warre he gaue me dangerous wounds,
And by those wounds he forced me to yeeld,
And by my yeelding I became his slaue:
Now, in his mouth he carries pleasing words,
Which pleasing wordes doe harbour sweet conceits, 125
Which sweet conceits are lim'de with slie deceits,
Which slie deceits smooth *Bel-imperias* eares,
And through her eares diue downe into her hart,
And in her hart set him where I should stand.
Thus hath he tane my body by his force, 130
And now by sleight would captiuate my soule:
But in his fall ile tempt the destinies,
And either loose my life, or winne my loue.
Lor. Lets goe, my Lord; your staying staies reuenge.
Doe you but follow me, and gaine your loue: 135
Her fauour must be wonne by his remooue.

Exeunt.

⟨SCENE II.⟩

Enter Horatio *and* Bel-imperia.

Hor. Now, Madame, since by fauour of your loue
Our hidden smoke is turned to open flame,
And that with lookes and words we feed our thoughts
(Two chiefe contents, where more cannot be had);
Thus in the midst of loues faire blandishments, 5
Why shew you signe of inward languishments?

Pedringano *sheweth all to the* Prince *and* Lorenzo, *placing them in secret.*

---

126 *om.* 1615 -18 -23 -33 127 slie deceits] sweete conceits 1615 -18 -23 -33
129 sets 1615 -18 -23 -33 134 your] our 1633

Bel. My hart (sweet freend) is like a ship at sea :
　　She wisheth port, where riding all at ease
　　She may repaire what stormie times haue worne,
　　And leaning on the shore may sing with ioy　　　　10
　　That pleasure followes paine, and blisse annoy.
　　Possession of thy loue is th' onely port,
　　Wherein my hart, with feares and hopes long tost,
　　Each howre doth wish and long to make resort,
　　There to repaire the ioyes that it hath lost,　　　　15
　　And, sitting safe, to sing in Cupids Quire
　　That sweetest blisse is crowne of loues desire.

　　　　　　　　　　Balthazar *and* Lorenzo *aboue.*

Bal. O sleepe, mine eyes, see not my loue prophande ;
　　Be deafe, my eares, heare not my discontent ;
　　Dye, hart : another ioyes what thou deseruest.　　　20
Lor. Watch still, mine eyes, to see this loue disioynd ;
　　Heare still, mine eares, to heare them both lament ;
　　Liue, hart, to ioy at fond *Horatios* fall.
Bel. Why stands *Horatio* speecheles all this while ?
Hor. The lesse I speak, the more I meditate.　　　　25
Bel. But whereon doost thou chiefly meditate ?
Hor. On dangers past, and pleasures to ensue.
Bal. On pleasures past, and dangers to ensue.
Bel. What dangers, and what pleasures doost thou mean ?
Hor. Dangers of warre, and pleasures of our loue.　　30
Lor. Dangers of death, but pleasures none at all.
Bel. Let dangers goe, thy warre shall be with me,
　　But such a warre, as breakes no bond of peace.
　　Speak thou faire words, ile crosse them with faire words ;
　　Send thou sweet looks, ile meete them with sweete lookes ;
　　Write louing lines, ile answere louing lines ;　　　　36
　　Giue me a kisse, ile counterchecke thy kisse :
　　Be this our warring peace, or peacefull warre

---

9 may *1602 and later Qq.*: mad *Allde* : made *1594 -99*　　11 follow *1599,
1602 -10 -15 -18 -23*　　12 the *1615 -18 -23 -33*　　15 thereon *Qq. exc. Allde*
S.D. Balthazar *aboue Allde, 1594 -99, 1602* : Balthazar *and* Lorenzo *alone
1610 -15 -18 -23 -33* : Balthazar *and* Lorenzo *aside Dodsley, Hawkins, Reed,
Collier, Hazlitt* ; *See Note*　　19 mine *1615 -18 -23 -33*　　21 this] the *Qq.
exc. Allde*　　23 Leaue *1599, 1602 -10 -15 -18 -23 -33*　　26 chiefly doest
thou *1615 -18 -23 -33*　　27 pleasure *1594 -99*　　28 pleasure *1602 -10* :
pleasures *1602 A*　　31 at *om. 1602, but in 1602 A*　　33 warre *Schick* :
warring *Qq.*

Hor. But, gratious Madame, then appoint the field,
  Where triall of this warre shall first be made.   40
Bal. Ambitious villaine, how his boldenes growes.
Bel. Then be thy fathers pleasant bower the field,
  Where first we vowd a mutuall amitie :
  The Court were dangerous, that place is safe.
  Our howre shall be when *Vesper* ginnes to rise,   45
  That summons home distresfull trauellers.
  There none shall heare us but the harmeless birds ;
  Happelie the gentle Nightingale
  Shall carroll us asleepe, ere we be ware,
  And, singing with the prickle at her breast,   50
  Tell our delight and mirthfull dalliance :
  Till then each houre will seeme a yeere and more.
Hor. But, honie sweet and honorable loue,
  Returne we now into your fathers sight :
  Dangerous suspition waits on our delight.   55
Lor. I, danger mixt with iealous dispite
  Shall send thy soule into eternall night.

                                   Exeunt.

⟨Scene III.⟩

Enter King of Spaine, Portingale Embassadour, Don Ciprian, *&c.*

King. Brother of Castile, to the Princes loue
  What saies your daughter *Bel-imperia* ?
Cip. Although she coy it as becomes her kinde,
  And yet dissemble that she loues the Prince,
  I doubt not, I, but she will stoope in time.   5
  And were she froward, which she will not be,
  Yet heerein shall she follow my aduice,
  Which is to loue him, or forgoe my loue.
King. Then, Lord Embassadour of Portingale,
  Aduise thy King to make this marriage vp,   10
  For strengthening of our late confirmed league ;
  I know no better meanes to make vs freends.
  Her dowry shall be large and liberall :

---

42 be] by *Qq. exc. Allde*   43 a] our *1602 -10 -15 -18 -23 -33*   46 dis-
tressed *1623 -33*   travailers *1623 -33*   51 sportfull *1623 -33*

Besides that she is daughter and halfe heire
Vnto our brother heere, *Don Ciprian*,   15
And shall enioy the moitie of his land,
Ile grace her marriage with an vnckles gift;
And this it is: in case the match goe forward,
The tribute which you pay shall be releast,
And if by *Balthazar* she haue a Sonne,   20
He shall enioy the kingdome after vs.
Emb. Ile make the motion to my soueraigne liege,
And worke it if my counsaile may preuaile.
King. Doe so, my Lord, and if he giue consent,
I hope his presence heere will honour vs,   25
In celebration of the nuptiall day;
And let himselfe determine of the time.
Emb. Wilt please your grace command me ought beside?
King. Commend me to the king, and so farewell.
But wheres Prince *Balthazar* to take his leaue?   30
Emb. That is perfourmd alreadie, my good Lord.
King. Amongst the rest of what you haue in charge,
The Princes raunsome must not be forgot:
Thats none of mine, but his that tooke him prisoner,
And well his forwardnes deserues reward.   35
It was *Horatio*, our Knight Marshals Sonne.
Emb. Between us theres a price already pitcht,
And shall be sent with all conuenient speed.
King. Then once againe farewell, my Lord.
Emb. Farewell, my Lord of Castile, and the rest.   40
                                                    Exit.

King. Now, brother, you must take some little paines
To winne faire *Bel-imperia* from her will:
Yong virgins must be ruled by their freends.
The Prince is amiable and loues her well;
If she neglect him and forgoe his loue,   45
She both will wrong her owne estate and ours.
Therefore, whiles I doe entertaine the Prince
With greatest pleasure that our Court affords,

---

22 my] our *1599, 1602 -10 -15 -18*   27 him *1633*   28 to command *1594
-99, 1602 -10 -15 -18*   30 where *1594*   39 againe *om. 1602 A*   41 paine *1602
-10 -15 -18 -23 -33*   47 while *1615 -18 -23 -33*   48 pleasures *1602 -10 -15 -18 -23 -33*

Endeauour you to winne your daughters thought :
If she giue back, all this will come to naught.   50

Exeunt.

⟨SCENE IV.⟩

Enter Horatio, Bel-imperia, *and* Pedringano.

Hor. Now that the night begins with sable wings
　　To ouer-cloud the brightnes of the Sunne,
　　And that in darkenes pleasures may be done,
　　Come, *Bel-imperia*, let vs to the bower,
　　And there in safetie passe a pleasant hower.   5
Bel. I follow thee, my loue, and will not backe,
　　Although my fainting hart controles my soule.
Hor. Why, make you doubt of *Pedringanos* faith?
Bel. No, he is as trustie as my second selfe.
　　Goe, *Pedringano*, watch without the gate,   10
　　And let vs know if any make approch.
Ped. In steed of watching, ile deserue more golde
　　By fetching *Don Lorenzo* to this match.

Exit Ped.

Hor. What meanes my loue?
Bel.　　　　　　　　　I know not what my selfe:
　　And yet my hart foretels me some mischaunce.   15
Hor. Sweet, say not so ; faire fortune is our freend,
　　And heauens haue shut vp day to pleasure vs.
　　The starres, thou seest, hold backe their twinckling shine,
　　And *Luna* hides her selfe to pleasure vs.
Bel. Thou hast preuailde ; ile conquer my misdoubt,   20
　　And in thy loue and councell drowne my feare :
　　I feare no more ; loue now is all my thoughts.
　　Why sit we not? for pleasure asketh ease.
Hor. The more thou sitst within these leauy bowers,
　　The more will *Flora* decke it with her flowers.   25
Bel. I, but if *Flora* spie *Horatio* heere,
　　Her iealous eye will thinke I sit too neere.
Hor. Harke, Madame, how the birds record by night,
　　For ioy that *Bel-imperia* sits in sight.

---

49 thoughts *Allde, 1594 -99, 1602 -10*　　11 reproch *1602 -15*　　17 heauen
hath *1618 -23 -33*　　24 sits *1610*

Bel. No, *Cupid* counterfeits the Nightingale,   30
  To frame sweet musick to *Horatios* tale.
Hor. If *Cupid* sing, then *Venus* is not farre ;
  I, thou art *Venus*, or some fairer starre.
Bel. If I be *Venus*, thou must needs be *Mars* ;
  And where *Mars* raigneth there must needs be warres.   35
Hor. Then thus begin our wars : put forth thy hand,
  That it may combate with my ruder hand.
Bel. Set forth thy foot to try the push of mine.
Hor. But first my lookes shall combat against thine.
Bel. Then ward thy selfe : I dart this kisse at thee.   40
Hor. Thus I retort the dart thou threwst at me.
Bel. Nay then, to gaine the glory of the field,
  My twining armes shall yoake and make thee yeeld.
Hor. Nay then, my armes are large and strong withall :
  Thus Elmes by vines are compast till they fall.   45
Bel. O let me goe, for in my troubled eyes
  Now maist thou read that life in passion dies.
Hor. O stay a while, and I will die with thee ;
  So shalt thou yeeld, and yet haue conquerd me.
Bel. Whose there, *Pedringano* ? We are betraide.   50

    Enter Lorenzo, Balthazar, Cerberine, Pedringano *disguised.*

Lor. My Lord away with her, take her aside.
  O sir, forbeare : your valour is already tride.
  Quickly dispatch, my maisters.

              They hang him in the Arbor.

Hor. What, will you murder me ?
Lor. I thus, and thus : these are the fruits of loue.   55

                 They stab him.

Bel. O, saue his life, and let me dye for him.
  O, saue him, brother ; saue him, *Balthazar* :
  I loued *Horatio*, but he loued not me.
Bal. But *Balthazar* loues *Bel-imperia*.

---

  35 warre *Qq.*   36 warre *1610*   41 returne *1602 A, 1615* -*18* -*23* -*33*
44 mine *1623* -*33*   50 Who's there ? Ped. ? *Hazlitt* : Who's there ? Ped. !
Schick   51 take her aside *as Stage-direction in 1602 A, 1610* -*15* -*18* -*23* -*33*
54 ye *1602* -*10* -*15* -*18* -*23* -*33*

Lor. Although his life were still ambituous proud, 60
  Yet is he at the highest now he is dead.
Bel. Murder, murder : helpe, *Hieronimo*, helpe.
Lor. Come, stop her mouth ; away with her.

Exeunt.

⟨SCENE V.⟩

Enter Hieronimo *in his shirt, &c.*

Hier. What out-cries pluck me from my naked bed,
  And chill my throbbing hart with trembling feare,
  Which neuer danger yet could daunt before ?
  Who cals *Hieronimo*? speak, heere I am.
  I did not slumber ; therefore twas no dreame. 5
  No, no, it was some woman cride for helpe,
  And heere within this garden did she crie,
  And in this garden must I rescue her.
  But stay, what murdrous spectacle is this ?
  A man hangd vp and all the murderers gone : 10
  And in my bower, to lay the guilt on me.
  This place was made for pleasure, not for death.

He cuts him downe.

  Those garments that he weares I oft haue seen :
  Alas, it is *Horatio*, my sweet sonne.
  O no, but he that whilome was my sonne. 15
  O was it thou that call'dst me from my bed ?
  O speak, if any sparke of life remaine.
  I am thy Father ; who hath slaine my sonne ?
  What sauadge monster, not of humane kinde,
  Hath heere beene glutted with thy harmeles blood, 20
  And left thy bloudie corpes dishonoured heere,
  For me amidst these darke and deathfull shades,
  To drowne thee with an ocean of my teares ?
  O heauens, why made you night to couer sinne ?
  By day this deede of darkenes had not beene. 25
  O earth, why didst thou not in time deuoure

---

60 still *om. Qq. exc. Allde*   S.D. *&c. om.* 1602 -10 -15 -18 -23 -33   1 out-
crie cals 1602 -10 -15 -18 -23 -33   2 chils 1602 *A*, 1610 -15 -18 -23 -33   7 this]
the 1599, 1602 -10 -15 -18 -23 -33   15 that] that who 1615 -18   20 eere
hath *Qq. exc. Allde*   22 these] this *Qq.*

The vilde prophaner of this sacred bower?
O poore *Horatio*, what hadst thou misdonne,
. To leese thy life ere life was new begun?
O wicked butcher, what so ere thou wert, 30
How could thou strangle vertue and desert?
Ay me most wretched, that haue lost my ioy,
In leesing my *Horatio*, my sweet boy.

Enter Isabella.

Isa. My husbands absence makes my heart to throb :—
Hieronimo. 35
Hier. Heere, *Isabella*, helpe me to lament;
For sighes are stopt, and all my teares are spent.
Isa. What world of griefe; my sonne *Horatio*!
O, wheres the author of this endles woe?
Hier. To know the author were some ease of greife, 40
For in reuenge my hart would find releife.
Isa. Then is he gone? and is my sonne gone too?
O, gush out teares, fountaines and flouds of teares ;
Blow sighes, and raise an euerlasting storme;
For outrage fits our cursed wretchednes. 45

⟨First Passage of Additions.⟩

Aye me, *Hieronimo*, sweet husband, speake.
Hier. He supt with us to-night, frolicke and mery,
And said he would goe visit *Balthazar*
At the Dukes Palace: there the Prince doth lodge.
He had no custome to stay out so late : (50)
He may be in his chamber; some go see.
Roderigo, ho.

Enter Pedro *and* Iaques.

Isa. Aye me, he raues, sweet *Hieronimo*.
Hier. True, all *Spaine* takes note of it.
Besides, he is so generally beloued; (55)
His Maiestie the other day did grace him
With waiting on his cup: these be fauours
Which doe assure me he cannot be short liued.
Isa. Sweet *Hieronimo*.

---

27 vile *1602 -10 -15 -18 -23 -33*   29 lose *1623 -33*   31 could'st *1602 -10
-15 -18 -23 -33*   58 he cannot *1602 A* : he *om. 1602 -10* : that he cannot
1618 -23 -33

Hier. I wonder how this fellow got his clothes: (60)
  Syrha, sirha, Ile know the trueth of all:
  Iaques, runne to the Duke of Castiles presently,
  And bid my sonne *Horatio* to come home.
  I and his mother haue had strange dreames to night.
  Doe ye heare me, sir?
Iaques.   I, sir.
Hier.   Well sir, begon.   (65)
  Pedro, come hither; knowest thou who this is?
Ped. Too well, sir.
Hier. Too well, who? who is it? Peace, *Isabella*:
  Nay, blush not, man.
Ped.   It is my Lord *Horatio.*
Hier. Ha, ha, Saint *Iames,* but this doth make me laugh,   (70)
  That there are more deluded then my selfe.
Ped. Deluded?
Hier.   I:
  I would haue sworne my selfe, within this houre,
  That this had beene my soone *Horatio*:
  His garments are so like. Ha, are they not great perswasions?
Isa. O would to God it were not so.   (76)
Hier. Were not, *Isabella*? doest thou dreame it is?
  Can thy soft bosome intertaine a thought,
  That such a blacke deede of mischiefe should be done
  On one so pure and spotles as our sonne?   (80)
  Away, I am ashamed.
Isa.   Deare *Hieronimo,*
  Cast a more serious eye vpon thy griefe:
  Weake apprehension giues but weake beleife.
Hier. It was a man, sure, that was hanged vp here;
  A youth, as I remember. I cut him downe.   (85)
  If it should prooue my sonne now after all.
  Say you? say you? Light, lend me a Taper;
  Let me looke againe. O God,
  Confusion, mischiefe, torment, death and hell,
  Drop all your stinges at once in my cold bosome,   (90)
  That now is stiffe with horror; kill me quickely:
  Be gracious to me, thou infective night,
  And drop this deede of murder downe on me;
  Gird in my wast of griefe with thy large darkenesse,
  And let me not suruiue, to see the light   (95)

---

  65 you *1618-23-33*   me, sir] me, sira *1610*   65-67 Doe . . . sir | I sir |
Well . . . hither | Knowest . . . sir *Qq.*   72 I *beg.* 73 *Qq.*   80 pure] poore
1602-10   81 Deare *Hieronimo beg.* 81 *Qq.*   88 O God *beg.*
89 *Qq.*

  KYD: BOAS   D

May put me in the minde I had a sonne.
Isa. O sweet *Horatio*, O my dearest sonne.
Hier. How strangly had I lost my way to griefe.

Hier. Sweet louely Rose, ill pluckt before thy time ;   47 (*99*)
    Faire worthy sonne, not conquerd, but betraid ;
    Ile kisse thee now, for words with teares are staide.
Isa. And ile close vp the glasses of his sight,   50 (*102*)
    For once these eyes were onely my delight.
Hier. Seest thou this handkercher besmerd with blood ?
    It shall not from me, till I take reuenge.
    Seest thou those wounds that yet are bleeding fresh ?
    .Ile not intombe them, till I haue reueng'd.   55 (*107*)
    Then will I ioy amidst my discontent ;
    Till then my sorrow neuer shalbe spent.
Isa. The heauens are iust, murder cannot be hid :
    Time is the author both of truth and right,
    And time will bring this trecherie to light.   60 (*112*)
Hier. Meane while, good *Isabella*, cease thy plaints,
    Or, at the least, dissemblè them awhile :
    So shall we sooner finde the practise out,
    And learne by whom all this was brought about.
    Come *Isabell*, now let us take him vp,   65 (*117*)

                              They take him vp.

And beare him in from out this cursed place.
Ile say his dirge, singing fits not this case.
O aliquis mihi quas pulchrum ver educat herbas,

                Hieronimo *sets his brest vnto his sword.*

Misceat, & nostro detur medicina dolori :
Aut si qui faciunt annorum obliuia, succos   70 (*122*)
Prebeat ; ipse metam magnum quaecunque per orbem
Gramina Sol pulchras effert in luminis oras ;
Ipse bibam quicquid meditatur saga veneni,

---

   49 staide *1602 A* -*10* -*15* -*18* -*23* -*33* : stainde *Allde, 1594* -*99, 1602*   51
chiefly *1623* -*33*   54 these *1602* -*10* -*15* -*18* -*23* -*33*   55 reuenge
1623 -*33*   57 sorrowes *1618* -*23* -*33*   65 *Isabella 1602* -*10* -*15* -*18* -*23*
-*33*   lets *1602* -*10* -*15* -*18* -*23* -*33*   68 *var Allde*   educet *Allde, 1594* -*99,*
1602 -*10*   69 *medician 1599, 1602* -*10* -*15* -*18* -*23*   70 *annum oblimia Qq.*
71 *metum Qq.*   magnam *Allde, 1623* -*33*   72 *effert . . . oras Schick :*
effecit . . . oras Qq. : *eiecit lucis in oras Hawkins, Reed, Collier, Hazlitt*

Quicquid & herbarum vi caeca nenia nectit:
Omnia perpetiar, lethum quoque, dum semel omnis　　　75 (*127*)
Noster in extincto moriatur pectore sensus.
Ergo tuos oculos nunquam (mea vita) videbo,
Et tua perpetuus sepeliuit lumina somnus?
Emoriar tecum: sic, sic iuuat ire sub umbras.
At tamen absistam properato cedere letho,　　　　　80 (*132*)
Ne mortem vindicta tuam tam nulla sequatur.

　　　Here he throwes it from him and beares the body away.

⟨SCENE VI.⟩

Andrea. Broughtst thou me hether to encrease my paine?
　I lookt that *Balthazar* should haue beene slaine :
　But tis my freend *Horatio* that is slaine,
　And they abuse fair *Bel-imperia*,
　On whom I doted more then all the world,　　　　　5
　Because she lou'd me more then all the world.
Reuenge. Thou talkest of haruest, when the corne is greene :
　The end is crowne of euery worke well done ;
　The Sickle comes not, till the corne be ripe.
　Be still ; and ere I lead thee from this place ;　　　10
　Ile shew thee *Balthazar* in heauy case. ·

---

74 *herbarum ... nenia Schick: irarum ...nenia Hawkins, Reed, Collier,*
Hazlitt: irraui euecaeca menia Qq.　　76 *pectora Allde, 1594*　　79 *Emor*
ira 1610 -15 -23 -33　　*iuua 1615 -18 -23 -33*　　80 *credere 1610*　　81 *vindista*
1610　　*tam Qq., Schick: tum other editors*　　*nalla 1594, 1602 -10 -15 -18 -23 -33*
5 Or *Allde* 7 the haruest *1618 -23 -33*　　8 growne *1599, 1602 -10 -15 -18 -23 -33*

ACTVS TERCIVS.

⟨SCENE I.⟩

Enter Viceroy of Portingale, Nobles, Alexandro, Villuppo.

Vice. Infortunate condition of Kings,
Seated amidst so many helpeles doubts.
First we are plast vpon extreamest height,
And oft supplanted with exceeding hate ;
But euer subiect to the wheele of chance ;   5
And at our highest neuer ioy we so,
As we both doubt and dread our ouerthrow.
So striueth not the waues with sundry winds,
As Fortune toyleth in the affaires of Kings,
That would be feard, yet feare to be beloued,   10
Sith feare or loue to Kings is flatterie :
For instance, Lordings, look vpon your King,   .
By hate depriued of his dearest sonne,
The onely hope of our successiue line.

Nob. I had not thought that *Alexandros* hart   15
Had beene enuenomde with such extreame hate :
But now I see that words haue seuerall workes,
And theres no credit in the countenance.

Vill. No ; for, my Lord, had you behelde the traine,
That fained loue had coloured in his lookes,   20
When he in Campe consorted *Balthazar*,
Farre more inconstant had you thought the Sunne,
That howerly coastes the center of the earth,
Then *Alexandros* purpose to the Prince.

Vice. No more, *Villuppo*, thou hast said enough,   25
And with thy words thou staiest our wounded thoughts ;
Nor shall I longer dally with the world,
Procrastinating *Alexandros* death :
Goe, some of you, and fetch the traitor forth,
That, as he is condemned, he may dye.   30

Enter Alexandro *with a* Noble man *and Halberts.*

Nob. In such extreames will nought but patience serue.

Alex. But in extreames what patience shall I vse?
  Nor discontents it me to leaue the world,
  With whome there nothing can preuaile but wrong.
Nob. Yet hope the best.
Alex.   Tis heauen is my hope.   35
  As for the earth, it is too much infect
  To yield me hope of any of her mould.
Vice. Why linger ye? bring forth that daring feend,
  And let him die for his accursed deed.
Alex. Not that I feare the extremitie of death,   40
  (For Nobles cannot stoop to seruile feare)
  Doo I (O King) thus discontented liue.
  But this, O this, tormentes my labouring soule,
  That thus I die suspected of a sinne,
  Whereof, as heauens haue knowne my secret thoughts,   45
  So am I free from this suggestion.
Vice. No more, I say: to the tortures, when!
  Binde him, and burne his body in those flames,

                              They binde him to the stake.

  That shall prefigure those vnquenched fiers,
  Of Phlegithon prepared for his soule.   50
Alex. My guiltles death will be aueng'd on thee,
  On thee, *Villuppo*, that hath malisde thus,
  Or for thy meed hast falsely me accusde.
Vill. Nay, *Alexandro*, if thou menace me,
  Ile lend a hand to send thee to the lake,   55
  Where those thy words shall perish with thy workes:
  Iniurious traytour, monstrous homicide.

                    Enter Embassadour.

Emb. Stay, hold a while,
  And here, with pardon of his Maiestie,
  Lay handes vpon *Villuppo*.   60
Vice.   Embassadour,
            What news hath vrg'd this sodain entrance?

---

36 infected *1610 -15 -18 -23 -33*   38 frind *1594* : friend *1599, 1602 -10*
-15   47 when] with him *Dodsley, Reed, Collier, Hazlitt   See Note*   50
Phlegiton *1594*: Phlegion *1599, 1602*: Peligon *1602 A*: Phlegeton *1610 -15 -18*
-23 -33   53 for] of *1615 -18 -23 -33*   60 Stay . . . *Villuppo* one line, *Qq.*
Embassadour, . . . entrance *one line, Qq.*

Emb. Know, Soueraigne L⟨ord⟩, that *Balthazar* doth liue.
Vice. What saiest thou? liueth *Balthazar* our sonne?
Emb. Your highnes sonne, L⟨ord⟩ *Balthazar* doth liue;
    And, well intreated in the Court of Spaine,   65
    Humbly commends him to your Maiestie.
    These eies beheld, and these my followers;
    With these, the letters of the Kings commends

                           Giues him Letters.

    Are happie witnesses of his highnes health.

           The King lookes on the Letters, and proceeds.

Vice. *Thy sonne doth liue, your tribute is receiu'd;*   70
Thy peace is made, and we are satisfied.
The rest resolue vpon as things proposde
For both our honors and thy benefite.
Emb. These are his highnes farther articles.

                     He giues him more Letters.

Vice. Accursed wretch, to intimate these ills   75
    Against the life and reputation
    Of noble *Alexandro.* Come, my Lord, vnbinde him:
    Let him vnbinde thee that is bound to death,
    To make a quitall for thy discontent.

                        They vnbinde him.

Alex. Dread Lord, in kindnes you could do no lesse,   80
    Vpon report of such a damned fact:
    But thus we see our innocence hath sau'd
    The hopeles life which thou, *Villuppo,* sought
    By thy suggestions to have massacred.
Vice. Say, false *Villuppo,* wherefore didst thou thus   85
    Falsly betray Lord *Alexandros* life?
    Him, whom thou knowest that no vnkindnes els,
    But euen the slaughter of our deerest sonne,
    Could once haue moued vs to haue misconceaued.
Alex. Say, trecherous *Villuppo,* tell the King: 90
    Wherein hath *Alexandro* vsed thee ill?
Vill. Rent with remembrance of so foule a deed,

My guiltie soule submits me to thy doome :
For not for *Alexandros* iniuries,
But for reward and hope to be preferd,   95
Thus haue I shamelessly hazarded his life.
Vice. Which, villaine, shalbe ransomed with thy deeth,
And not so meane a torment as we heere
Deuisde for him, who thou saidst slew our Sonne,
But with the bitterest torments and extreames   100
That may be yet inuented for thine end.

                    Alexandro *seemes to intreat.*
Intreate me not ; go, take the traytor hence.
                                        Exit Vill.
And, *Alexandro*, let vs honor thee
With publique notise of thy loyaltie.
To end those thinges articulated heere   105
By our great L⟨ord⟩ the mightie King of Spaine,
We with our Councell will deliberate.
Come, *Alexandro*, keepe vs companie.

                                        Exeunt.

                    ⟨SCENE II.⟩

                    Enter Hieronimo.
Hier. Oh eies, no eies, but fountains fraught with teares ;
Oh life, no life, but liuely fourme of death ;
O world, no world, but masse of publique wrongs,
Confusde and filde with murder and misdeeds.
O sacred heauens, if this vnhallowed deed,
If this inhumane and barberous attempt,
If this incomparable murder thus
Of mine, but now no more my sonne,
Shall vnreueald and vnreuenged passe,
How should we tearme your dealings to be iust,   10
If you vniustly deale with those, that in your iustice trust ?
The night, sad secretary to my mones,
With direfull visions wake my vexed soule,

93 guiltlesse *1602*: guiltfull *1610 -15 -18 -23 -33* : gultie *1602 A*   5 Heauen
1618 -23 -33   13 wake] make *1594 -99* : wakes *editors exc. Hawkins*
See Note

And with the wounds of my distresfull sonne
Solicite me for notice of his death.   15
The ougly feends do sally forth of hell,
And frame my steps to vnfrequented paths,
And feare my hart with fierce inflamed thoughts.
The cloudie day my discontents records,
Early begins to regester my dreames,   20
And driue me forthe to seeke the murtherer.
Eies, life, world, heauens, hel, night and day,
See, search, shew, send some man, some meane, that may—

                                            A Letter falleth.

Whats heere? a letter? tush, it is not so:
A letter written to *Hieronimo*.   25
                                            Red incke.

> *For want of incke receiue this bloudie writ :*
> *Me hath my haples brother hid from thee ;*
> *Reuenge thy selfe on* Balthazar *and him,*
> *For these were they that murd⟨e⟩red thy sonne.*
> Hieronimo, *reuenge* Horatios *death,*   30
> *And better fare then* Bel-imperia *doth.*

What meanes this vnexpected miracle?
My Sonne slaine by *Lorenzo* and the Prince.
What cause had they *Horatio* to maligne?
Or what might mooue thee, *Bel-imperia*,   35
To accuse thy brother, had he beene the meane?
Hieronimo, beware, thou art betraide,
And to intrap thy life this traine is laide.
Aduise thee therefore, be not credulous:
This is deuised to endanger thee,   40
That thou by this *Lorenzo* shouldst accuse,
And he, for thy dishonour done, should draw
Thy life in question and thy name in hate.
Deare was the life of my beloued Sonne,
And of his death behoues me be reueng'd: 45
Then hazard not thine owne, *Hieronimo*,
But liue t'effect thy resolution.
I therefore will by circumstances trie,

---

19 discontent *1618 -23 -33*   23 Some meane, that may *sep. line Qq.*
29 *these*] *those 1615 -18 -23 -33*   31 *farre 1602 -10 -15 -18*: *far 1633*
47 to *1618 -23 -33*

What I can gather, to confirme this writ;
And harkening neere the Duke of Castiles house,   50
Close, if I can, with *Bel-imperia*,
To listen more, but nothing to bewray.

                   Enter Pedringano.

Hier. Now, *Pedringano.*
Ped.   Now, *Hieronimo.*
Hier. Wheres thy Lady?
Ped.   I know not; heers my lord.

               Enter Lorenzo.

Lor. How now, whose this? *Hieronimo?*
Hier.   My Lord.   55
Ped. He asketh for my Lady *Bel-imperia.*
Lor. What to doo, *Hieronimo?* The Duke, my father, hath
Upon some disgrace a while remoou'd her hence;
But if it be ought I may inform her of,
Tell me, *Hieronimo*, and ile let her know it.   60
Hier. Nay, nay, my Lord, I thank you, it shall not need.
I had a sute vnto her, but too late,
And her disgrace makes me vnfortunate.
Lor. Why so, *Hieronimo*, use me.
Hier. O no, my Lord; I dare not; it must not be: 65
I humbly thank your Lordship.

   ⟨Second Passage of Additions, replacing lines 65 and
               first part of 66.⟩

Who? you, my Lord?   (*65*)
I reserue your fauour for a greater honor;
This is a very toy, my Lord, a toy.
Lor. All's one, *Hieronimo*, acquaint me with it.
Hier. Y' fayth my Lord, tis an idle thing I must confesse,
I ha' been too slacke, too tardie, too remisse vnto your honor. (*70*)
Lor. How now, *Hieronimo?*
Hier. In troth, my Lord, it is a thing of nothing:
The murder of a Sonne, or so—
A thing of nothing, my Lord.

Lor.   Why then, farewell.
Hier. My griefe no hart, my thoughts no tung can tell.

                      Exit.

---

50 harken *1610 -15 -18 -23 -33*   54 thy] my *1602 A*   73 *om. 1602 A*

Lor. Come hither, *Pedringano,* seest thou this?

Ped. My Lord, I see it, and suspect it too.

Lor: This is that damned villain *Serberine,*   70 (79)
     That hath, I feare, reuealde *Horatios* death.

Ped. My lord, he could not, twas so lately done ;
     And since he hath not left my company.

Lor. Admit he haue not, his conditions such,
     As feare or flattering words may make him false.   75 (84)
     I know his humour, and therewith repent
     That ere I vsde him in this enterprise.
     But, *Pedringano,* to preuent the worst,
     And cause I know thee secret as my soule,
     Heere, for thy further satisfaction, take thou this.   80 (89)

                              Giues him more gold.

And harken to me, thus it is deuisde :
This night thou must, and prethee so resolue,
Meet *Serberine* at S. *Luigis* Parke—
Thou knowest tis heere hard by behinde the house—
There take thy stand, and see thou strike him sure ;   85 (94)
For dye he must, if we do meane to liue.

Ped. But how shall *Serberine* be there, my Lord?

Lor. Let me alone ; ile send to him to meet
     The Prince and me, where thou must doe this deed.

Ped. It shalbe done my L⟨ord⟩, it shall be done ;   90 (99)
     And ile goe arme my selfe to meet him there.

Lor. When thinges shall alter, as I hope they wil,
     Then shalt thou mount for this ; thou knowest my minde.

                                  Exit Pedringano.

Che le Ieron.

                     Enter Page.

Page.   My Lord.

Lor.   Goe, sirra, to *Serberine,*

---

80 thou] thee *1623-33*   81 thus it is disguisde *1594-99, 1602*: thus it is, disguisde *1610*: thus it is : disguis'd *1615 -18 -23 -33*: thus it is deuisde *1602 A*
83 S. *Luigis Schick*: S. *Liugis Allde, 1594 -99, 1602*: S. *Leugis 1610*: S.
Leuges 1615 : S. *Luges 1618 -23 -33*   93 knowst *Qq. exc. Allde*   94
leron 1623-33 : *before* S.D. *Exit* Ped. *1615 -18 -23 -33. See Note*   94-97
Che le Ieron | My Lord | Goe ... forthwith | Meet ... Parke | Behinde ...
boy | I ... Lord *Qq.*

And bid him forthwith meet the Prince and me   95 (*104*)
At S. *Luigis* Parke, behinde the house;
This euening, boy.
Page.   I goe, my Lord.
Lor. But, sirra, let the houre be eight a clocke:
Bid him not faile.
Page.   I fly, my Lord.

                                              Exit.

Lor. Now to confirme the complot thou hast cast   100 (*109*)
Of all these practises, Ile spread the *Watch*,
Upon precise commandement from the King,
Strongly to guard the place where *Pedringano*
This night shall murder hapless *Serberine.*
Thus must we worke that will auoide distrust;   105 (*114*)
Thus must we practise to preuent mishap,
And thus one ill another must expulse.
This slie inquiry of *Hieronimo*
For *Bel-imperia* breeds suspition,
And this suspition boads a further ill.   110 (*119*)
As for my selfe, I know my secret fault,
And so doe they; but I have dealt for them.
They that for coine their soules endangered,
To saue my life, for coyne shall venture theirs:
And better its that base companions dye,   115 (*124*)
Then by their life to hazard our good haps.
Nor shall they liue, for me to feare their faith:
Ile trust my selfe, my selfe shall be my freend;
For dye they shall, slaues are ordeind to no other end.

                                              Exit.

⟨SCENE III.⟩

Enter Pedringano *with a Pistoll.*

Ped. Now, *Pedringano*, bid thy Pistoll holde;
And holde on, Fortune, once more fauour me,
Giue but successe to mine attempting spirit,

---

98 *Lor. om.* 1594 -99·   99 I . . . Lord. *sep. line Qq.*   105 This
1594 -99, 1602 -10 -15 -18   108 *and* 109 *Qq. one line*   115 tis 1599,
1602 -10 -15 -18 -23 -33   119 to] *for Qq. exc. Allde*

And let me shift for taking of mine aime.
Heere is the golde, this is the golde proposde;   5
It is no dreame that I aduenture for,
But *Pedringano* is possest thereof.
And he that would not straine his conscience
For him that thus his liberall purse hath stretcht,
Vnworthy such a fauour may he faile,   10
And, wishing, want, when such as I preuaile.
As for the feare of apprehension,
I know, if needs should be, my noble Lord
Will stand betweene me and ensuing harmes :
Besides, this place is free from all suspect.   15
Heere therefore will I stay, and take my stand.

Enter the Watch.

1. I wonder much to what intent it is
   That we are thus expressly chargde to watch.
2. Tis by commandement in the Kings own name.
3. But we were neuer wont to watch and ward   20
   So neare the Duke his brothers house before.
2. Content your selfe, stand close, theres somewhat in 't.

Enter Serberine.

Ser. Heere, *Serberine*, attend and stay thy pace,
For heere did *Don Lorenzos* Page appoint
That thou by his command shouldst meet with him.   25
How fit a place, if one were so disposde,
Me thinks this corner is to close with one.
Ped. Heere comes the bird that I must ceaze upon ;
Now, *Pedringano*, or neuer play the man.
Ser. I wonder that his Lordship staies so long,   30
Or wherefore should he send for me so late ?
Ped. For this, *Serberine*, and thou shalt ha' t.

Shootes the Dagge.

So, there he lyes ; my promise is performde.

The Watch.

1. Harke, Gentlemen, this is a Pistol shot.
2. And heeres one slaine; stay the murderer.   35

---

20 and] nor *Qq. exc. Allde*   21 brothers *om. 1602 -10 -15 -18 -23 -33* :
his brothers house *om. 1602 A*

Ped. Now by the sorrowes of the soules in hell,

He striues with the Watch.

Who first laies hand on me, ile be his Priest.

3. Sirra, confesse, and therein play the Priest,
　　Why hast thou thus vnkindely kild the man?

Ped. Why? because he walkt abroad so late.　　　　40

3. Come sir, you had bene better kept your bed,
　　Then haue committed this misdeed so late.

2. Come to the Marshals with the murderer.

1. On to *Hieronimos*: helpe me here
　　To bring the murdred body with vs too.　　　　45

Ped. Hieronimo? carry me before whom you will:
　　What ere he be, ile answere him and you;
　　And doe your worst, for I defie you all.

Exeunt.

⟨SCENE IV.⟩

Enter Lorenzo *and* Balthazar.

Bal. How now, my Lord, what makes you rise so soone?

Lor. Feare of preuenting our mishaps too late.

Bal. What mischiefe is it that we not mistrust?

Lor. Our greatest ils we least mistrust, my Lord,
　　And inexpected harmes do hurt vs most.　　　　5

Bal. Why tell me, *Don Lorenzo*, tell me, man,
　　If ought concernes our honour and your owne?

Lor. Nor you, nor me, my Lord, but both in one:
　　For I suspect, and the presumptions great,
　　That by those base confederates in our fault,　　　10
　　Touching the death of *Don Horatio*,
　　We are betraide to old *Hieronimo*.

Bal. Betraide, *Lorenzo?* tush, it cannot be.

Lor. A guiltie conscience, vrged with the thought
　　Of former euils, easily cannot erre:　　　　15
　　I am perswaded, and diswade me not,
　　That als reuealed to *Hieronimo*.
　　And therefore know that I haue cast it thus—

Enter Page.

---

37 hands *1610*: hold *1615 -18 -23 -33*　　　43 Marshall *1618 -23 -33*
44 *Hieronimo 1610 -15 -18 -23 -33*　　5 in expected *Allde, 1594, 1610 -15 -18 -23*
-33　　8 Nor you] Not you *1602 -10 -15 -18 -23 -33*　　S.D. *Enter* Page *add.*
1615, but after 19

But heeres the *Page*—how now, what newes with thee?

Page. My Lord, *Serberine* is slaine.   20

Bal. Who? *Serberine*, my man?

Page. Your Highnes man, my Lord.

Lor. Speake, *Page*, who murdered him?

Page. He that is apprehended for the fact.

Lor. Who?   25

Page. Pedringano.

Bal. Is *Serberine* slaine, that lou'd his Lord so well?

    Iniurious villaine, murderer of his freend.

Lor. Hath *Pedringano* murdered *Serberine*?

    My Lord, let me entreat you to take the paines   30

    To exasperate and hasten his reuenge

    With your complaintes vnto my L⟨ord⟩ the King.

    This their dissention breeds a greater doubt.

Bal. Assure thee, *Don Lorenzo*, he shall dye,

    Or els his Highnes hardly shall deny.   35

    Meane while ile haste the Marshall Sessions:

    For die he shall for this his damned deed.

                                     Exit Bal.

Lor. Why so, this fits our former pollicie,

    And thus experience bids the wise to deale.

    I lay the plot: he prosecutes the point;   40

    I set the trap: he breakes the worthles twigs,

    And sees not that wherewith the bird was limde.

    Thus hopefull men, that meane to holde their owne,

    Must look like fowlers to their dearest freends.

    He runnes to kill whome I haue holpe to catch,   45

    And no man knowes it was my reaching fatch.

    Tis hard to trust vnto a multitude,

    Or any one, in mine opinion,

    When men themselues their secrets will reueale.

           Enter a Messenger *with a Letter.*

Lor. Boy.   50

Page. My Lord.

Lor. Whats he?

Mes.   I haue a letter to your Lordship.

Lor. From whence?

Mes.   From *Pedringano* thats imprisoned.

Lor. So he is in prison then?

Mes.   I, my good Lord.

Lor. What would he with vs? He writes vs heere,   55
To stand good L⟨ord⟩ and help him in distres.
Tell him, I haue his letters, know his minde;
And what we may, let him assure him of.
Fellow, be gone; my boy shall follow thee.

                                            Exit Mes.

This works like waxe; yet once more try thy wits.   60
Boy, goe, conuay this purse to *Pedringano*;
Thou knowest the prison, closely giue it him,
And be aduisde that none be there about:
Bid him be merry still, but secret;
And though the Marshall Sessions be to day,   65
Bid him not doubt of his deliuerie.
Tell him his pardon is already signde,
And thereon bid him boldely be resolued:
For were he ready to be turned off—
As tis my will the vttermost be tride—   70
Thou with his pardon shalt attend him still.
Shew him this boxe, tell him his pardons in 't;
But open 't not, and if thou louest thy life;
But let him wisely keepe his hopes unknowne:
He shall not want while *Don Lorenzo* liues: 75
Away.

Page.   I goe, my Lord, I runne.

Lor. But, Sirra, see that this be cleanely done.

                                            Exit Page.

Now stands our fortune on a tickle point,
And now or neuer ends *Lorenzos* doubts.
One onely thing is vneffected yet,   80
And thats to see the Executioner,
But to what end? I list not trust the Aire
With vtterance of our pretence therein,

---

54 imprisoned *1602 -10 -15 -18 -23 -33*   55 He writes us heere *beg.*
56 *Qq.*   65 Marshals *1602 -10 -23 -33* : Marshials *1615 -18*   76 Away
end 75 *Qq.*   S.D. *Exit* Page *after* 76, *1623 -33*   82 I *om.*
1618 -23 -33   not to trust *1623 -33*

For feare the priuie whispring of the winde
Conuay our words amongst vnfreendly eares,   85
That lye too open to aduantages.

> *Et quel che voglio io, nessun lo sa;*
> *Intendo io: quel mi basterà.*

Exit.

⟨SCENE V.⟩

Enter Boy with the Boxe.

My Maister hath forbidden me to looke in this box; and by
my troth tis likely, if he had not warned me, I should not haue
had so much idle time: for wee mens-kinde, in our minoritie,
are like women in their vncertaintie: that, they are most forbidden, they will soonest attempt: so I now.—By my bare 5
honesty, heeres nothing but the bare emptie box: were it
not sin against secrecie, I would say it were a peece of
gentleman-like knauery. I must go to *Pedringano*, and tell
him his pardon is in this boxe; nay, I would haue sworne
it, had I not seene the contrary. I cannot choose but smile 10
to thinke how the villain will flout the gallowes, scorne the
audience, and descant on the hangman; and al presuming of
his pardon from hence. Wilt not be an odde iest for me
to stand and grace euery iest he makes, pointing my finger
at this boxe, as who would say, Mock on, heers thy warrant? 15
Ist not a scuruie iest that a man should iest himselfe to death?
Alas, poore *Pedringano*, I am in a sorte sorie for thee; but if
I should be hanged with thee, I cannot weep.

Exit.

⟨SCENE VI.⟩

Enter Hieronimo *and the* Deputie.

Hier. Thus must we toyle in other mens extreames,
That know not how to remedie our owne;
And doe them iustice, when uniustly we,
For all our wrongs, can compasse no redresse.

---

87 *io editors*: *Ii Allde*: *Il 1594 -99, 1602 -10 -15 -18 -23 -33*   88 *basterà*
Schick: *bassara Allde, 1594 -99, 1602 -15 -18 -23 -33*: *bessara 1610*   2 troth]
honesty *1615 -18 -23 -33*   3 menkinde *1618 -23 -33*   5-6 me bare honesty
1602 -10: my bare credite *1615 -18 -23 -33*: my bare honesty *1602 A*   15
should *1602 -10 -15 -18 -23 -33*   18 could not *1615 -18 -23 -33*

But shall I neuer liue to see the day,   5
That I may come (by iustice of the heauens)
To know the cause that may my cares allay?
This toyles my body, this consumeth age,
That onely I to all men iust must be,
And neither Gods nor men be iust to me.   10
Dep. Worthy *Hieronimo*, your office askes
  A care to punish such as doe transgresse.
Hier. So ist my duety to regarde his death,
Who, when he liued, deserued my dearest blood:
But come, for that we came for: lets begin,   15
For heere lyes that which bids me to be gone.

Enter Officers, Boy, *and* Pedringano, *with a letter in his hand, bound.*

Dep. Bring forth the Prisoner, for the Court is set.
Ped. Gramercy, boy, but it was time to come;
  For I had written to my Lord anew
  A neerer matter that concerneth him,   20
  For feare his Lordship had forgotten me.
  But sith he hath remembred me so well,
Come, come, come on, when shall we to this geere?
Hier. Stand forth, thou monster, murderer of men,
And heere, for satisfaction of the world,   25
Confesse thy folly, and repent thy fault;
For ther's thy place of execution.
Ped. This is short worke: well, to your marshallship
First I confesse, nor feare I death therfore,
I am the man, twas I slew *Serberine*.   30
But, sir, then you thinke this shalbe the place,
Where we shall satisfie you for this geare?
Dep. I, *Pedringano*.
Ped.   Now I think not so.
Hier. Peace, impudent, for thou shalt finde it so:
For blood with blood shall, while I sit as iudge, 35
Be satisfied, and the law dischargde.
And though my selfe cannot receiue the like,
Yet will I see that others have their right.

Dispatch : the faults approued and confest,
And by our law he is condemnd to die.   40

Hang. Come on, sir, are you ready ?

Ped. To doo what, my fine officious knaue ?

Hang. To goe to this geere.

Ped. O sir, you are to forward : thou wouldst faine furnish me
with a halter, to disfurnish me of my habit. So I should
goe out of this geere, my raiment, into that geere, the rope.
But, Hang-man, nowe I spy your knauery, Ile not change
without boot, thats flat.

Hang. Come, sir.

Ped. So, then, I must vp ?   50

Hang. No remedie.

Ped. Yes, but there shalbe for my comming downe.

Hang. Indeed, heers a remedie for that.

Ped. How ? be turnd off ?   54

Hang. I truely ; come, are you ready ? I pray, sir, dispatch ; the
day goes away.

Ped. What, doe you hang by the howre ? if you doo, I may
chance to break your olde custome.

Hang. Faith, you haue reason; for I am like to break your
yong necke.   60

Ped. Dost thou mock me, hang-man ? pray God, I be not preserued to breake your knaues pate for this.

Hang. Alas, sir, you are a foot too low to reach it, and I hope
you will neuer grow so high while I am in the office.

Ped. Sirra, dost see yonder boy with the box in his hand ? 65

Hang. What, he that points to it with his finger ?

Ped. I, that companion.

Hang. I know him not; but what of him ?

Ped. Doost thou think to liue till his olde doublet will make
thee a new trusse ?   70

Hang. I, and many a faire yeere after, to trusse vp many an
honester man then either thou or he.

Ped. What hath he in his boxe, as thou thinkst?

39 fault *1602 -10 -15 -18 -23 -33*   40 *Enter* Hangman *as S.D. after this
line add. 1615 -18 -23 -33*   52 my *om. Qq. exc. Allde*   54 be] to be
1615 -18 -23 -33   55 I pray you sir *Qq. exc. Allde*   59 haue
no reason *1599, 1602 -10 -15 -18 -23 -33*   64 whils *1615* : whiles
1623 -33

Hang. Faith, I cannot tell, nor I care not greatly.　Methinks
　you should rather hearken to your soules health.　　　75
Ped. Why, sirra Hangman, I take it that that is good for the
　body is likewise good for the soule : and it may be, in that
　box is balme for both.
Hang. Wel, thou art euen the meriest peece of mans flesh that
　ere gronde at my office doore.　　　　　　　　　　80
Ped. Is your roaguerie become an office with a knaues name?
Hang. I, and that shall all they witnes that see you seale it
　with a theeues name.
Ped. I prethee, request this good company to pray with me.
Hang. I, mary, sir, this is a good motion : my maisters, you see
　heers a good fellow.　　　　　　　　　　　　86
Ped. Nay, nay, now I remember me, let them alone till some
　other time ; for now I haue no great need.
Hier. I haue not seen a wretch so impudent.
　　O monstrous times, where murders set so light,　　　90
　　And where the soule, that shoulde be shrinde in heauen,
　　Solelie delights in interdicted things,
　　Still wandring in the thornie passages
　　That intercepts it selfe of hapines.
　　Murder, O bloudy monster, God forbid　　　　　　95
　　A fault so foule should scape vnpunished.
　　Dispatch, and see this execution done :—
　　This makes me to remember thee, my sonne.
　　　　　　　　　　　　　　　　　Exit Hier.
Ped. Nay, soft, no hast.
Dep. Why, wherefore stay you? haue you hope of life?　　100
Ped. Why, I.
Hang. As how?
Ped. Why, Rascall, by my pardon from the King.
Hang. Stand you on that? then you shall off with this.
　　　　　　　　　　　　　　　He turnes him off.
Dep. So, Executioner ; conuay him hence :　　　　　105
　　But let his body be vnburied :
　　Let not the earth be choked or infect
　　With that which heauen contemnes, and men neglect.　*Exeunt.*

---

　74 Me thinke *1599, 1602*: Methinks *1602 A*　　　82 they] the *1594 -99*
84 with] for *1602 -10 -15 -18 -23 -33*　　　97 this] the *Qq. exc. Allde*
108 heauen contemnes *1594 -99, 1602 -10 -15 -18 -33*: heauens contemnes
Allde: heauen contemne *1623*

⟨SCENE VII.⟩

Enter Hieronimo.

Where shall I run to breath abroad my woes,
My woes, whose weight hath wearied the earth?
Or mine exclaimes, that haue surcharged the aire
With ceasles plaints for my deceased sonne?
The blustring winds, conspiring with my words,   5
At my lament haue moued the leaueles trees,
Disroabde the medowes of their flowred greene,
Made mountains marsh with spring tides of my teares,
And broken through the brazen gates of hell.
Yet still tormented is my tortured soule   10
With broken sighes and restles passions,
That winged mount, and, houering in the aire,
Beat at the windowes of the brightest heauens,
Solliciting for iustice and reuenge:
But they are plac't in those empyreal heights,   15
Where, countermurde with walles of diamond,
I finde the place impregnable; and they
Resist my woes, and giue my words no way.

Enter Hang-man, *with a letter.*

Hang. O Lord, sir: God blesse you, sir: the man, sir, *Petergade*,
sir, he that was so full of merrie conceits—   20
Hier. Wel, what of him?
Hang. O Lord, sir, he went the wrong way; the fellow had
a faire commission to the contrary. Sir, heere is his pasport;
I pray you, sir, we haue done him wrong.
Hier. I warrant thee, giue it me.   25
Hang. You will stand between the gallowes and me?
Hier. I, I.
Hang. I thanke your L⟨ord⟩ worship.

Exit Hang-man.

Hier. And yet, though somewhat neerer me concernes,
I will, to ease the greefe that I sustaine,   30
Take truce with sorrow while I read on this.

---

8 spring-tide *Qq. exc. Allde*   13 Beat] But *Qq. exc. Allde*   15 empyreal
Schick: imperiall *Qq.*

My Lord, I write as mine extreames requirde,
That you would labour my deliuerie;
If you neglect, my life is desperate,
And in my death I shall reueale the troth.   35
You know, my Lord, I slew him for your sake,
And was confederate with the Prince and you;
Wonne by rewards and hopefull promises,
I holpe to murder Don Horatio *too.*
Holpe he to murder mine *Horatio*?   40
And actors in th'accursed Tragedie
Wast thou, *Lorenzo, Balthazar* and thou,
Of whom my Sonne, my Sonne deserued so well?
What haue I heard, what haue mine eies behelde?
O sacred heauens, may it come to passe   45
That such a monstrous and detested deed,
So closely smootherd, and so long conceald,
Shall thus by this be venged or reueald?
Now see I what I durst not then suspect,
That *Bel-imperias* Letter was not fainde,   50
Nor fained she, though falsly they haue wrongd
Both her, my selfe, *Horatio*, and themselues.
Now may I make compare twixt hers and this,
Of euerie accident I neere could finde
Till now, and now I feelingly perceiue   55
They did what heauen vnpunisht would not leaue.
O false *Lorenzo*, are these thy flattering lookes?
Is this the honour that thou didst my Sonne?
And *Balthazar*, bane to thy soule and me,
Was this the ransome he reseru'd thee for?   60
Woe to the cause of these constrained warres:
Woe to thy basenes and captiuitie:
Woe to thy birth, thy body, and thy soule,
Thy cursed father, and thy conquered selfe:
And band with bitter execrations be   65
The day and place where he did pittie thee.
But wherefore waste I mine vnfruitfull words,
When naught but blood will satisfie my woes?

---

32 *my* 1602 -10 -15 -18 -23 -33   *require* 1623   35 *truth* 1623 -33
48 Shall thus be this reuenged 1610 -15 -18: Shall thus be thus reuenged
1623 -33   56 should 1615 -18 -23 -33   60 for thee 1610 -15 -18 -23 -33

I will go plaine me to my Lord the King,
And cry aloud for iustice through the Court,   70
Wearing the flints with these my withered feet;
And either purchace iustice by intreats,
Or tyre them all with my reuenging threats.

Exit.

⟨SCENE VIII.⟩

Enter Isabell⟨a⟩ *and her* maid.

Isa. So that you say, this hearbe will purge the eye,
    And this the head?
Ah, but none of them wil purge the hart.
No, thers no medicine left for my disease,
Nor any phisick to recure the dead.   5

She runnes lunaticke.

    Horatio, O, wheres *Horatio*?
Maid. Good Madam, affright not thus yourselfe
    With outrage for your sonne *Horatio*:
    He sleepes in quiet in the *Elizian* fields.
Isa. Why, did I not giue you gownes and goodly things,   10
    Bought you a whistle and a whipstalke too,
    To be reuenged on their villanies?
Maid. Madame, these humors doe torment my soule.
Isa. My soule—poore soule, thou talkes of things
    Thou knowst not what—my soule hath siluer wings,   15
    That mounts me up vnto the highest heauens;
    To heauen: I, there sits my *Horatio*,
    Backt with a troup of fiery Cherubins,
    Dauncing about his newly healed wounds,
    Singing sweet hymnes and chanting heauenly notes: 20
    Rare hermonie to greet his innocence,
    That dyde, I, dyde a mirrour in our daies.
    But say, where shall I finde the men, the murderers,
    That slew *Horatio*? whether shall I runne
    To finde them out that murdered my Sonne?   25

Exeunt.

---

1 eyes *1615 -18 -23 -33*   2–3 *one line Qq.*   14 talkst *1623 -33*
15 knowest *Qq. exc. Allde*   21 innocencie *Qq. exc. Allde*   23 That
dyde] That liu'd *Qq. exc. Allde*   23 man *1618 -23 -33*

⟨Scene IX.⟩

Bel-imperia, *at a window.*

Bel. What meanes this outrage that is offered me?
  Why am I thus sequestred from the Court?
  No notice:—Shall I not know the cause
  Of these my secret and suspitious ils?
  Accursed brother, vnkinde murderer,   5
  Why bends thou thus thy minde to martir me?
  Hieronimo, why writ I of thy wrongs?
  Or why art thou so slacke in thy reuenge?
  Andrea, O *Andrea*, that thou sawest,
  Me for thy freend *Horatio* handled thus,   10
  And him for me thus causeles murdered.
  Well, force perforce, I must constraine my selfe
  To patience, and apply me to the time,
  Till heauen, as I haue hoped, shall set me free.

Enter Christophill.

Chris. Come, Madame *Bel-imperia*, this may not be.   15
                                        Exeunt.

⟨Scene X.⟩

Enter Lorenzo, Balthazar, *and the* Page.

Lor. Boy, talke no further; thus farre things goe well.
  Thou art assurde that thou sawest him dead?
Page. Or els, my Lord, I liue not.
Lor.   Thats enough.
  As for his resolution in his end,
  Leaue that to him with whom he soiourns now.   5
  Heere, take my Ring, and giue it *Christophill*,
  And bid him let my Sister be enlarg'd,
  And bring her hither straight.

                                Exit Page.

  This that I did was for a policie,
  To smooth and keepe the murder secret,   10
  Which, as a nine daies wonder, being ore-blowne,
  My gentle Sister will I now inlarge.

4 these *1633*: this *other Qq.*   6 bendst *1623 -33*   7 write *1599, 1602*
-10 -15 -18 -23 -33   15 may] must *1618 -23 -33*   S.D. *Exit* Page *om.*
1618 -23 -33   11 as] at *1594 -99, 1602 -10* : as *1602 A*

Bal. And time, *Lorenzo* : for my Lord the Duke,
You heard, enquired for her yester-night.

Lor. Why, and my Lord, I hope you heard me say 15
Sufficient reason why she kept away.
 But that's all one. My Lord, you loue her ?

Bal.   I.

Lor. Then in your loue beware, deale cunningly ;
Salue all suspitions, onely sooth me vp ;
And if she hap to stand on tearmes with vs, 20
As for her sweet hart, and concealment so,
Iest with her gently: vnder fained iest
Are things concealde that els would breed vnrest.—
But heere she comes.

            Enter Bel-imperia.

     Now, Sister—

Bel.   Sister ? no ;
Thou art no brother, but an enemy ; 25
Els wouldst thou not haue vsed thy Sister so:
First, to affright me with thy weapons drawne,
And with extreames abuse my company ;
And then to hurry me, like whirlewinds rage,
Amidst a crue of thy confederates, 30
And clap me vp where none might come at me,
Nor I at any, to reueale my wrongs.
What madding furie did possesse thy wits ?
Or wherein ist that I offended thee ?

Lor. Aduise you better, *Bel-imperia*, 35
For I haue done you no disparagement ;
Vnlesse, by more discretion then diseṛu'd,
I sought to saue your honour and mine owne.

Bel. Mine honour ? why, *Lorenzo*, wherein ist
That I neglect my reputation so, 40
As you, or any, need to rescue it ?

Lor. His highnes and my father were resolu'd
To come conferre with olde *Hieronimo*,
Concerning certaine matters of estate,
That by the Vice-roy was determined. 45

Bel. And wherein was mine honour toucht in that ?

 24–25 But . . . comes | Now Sister | Sister . . . enemy | *Qq.* 31 clapt
1610 -15 -18 -23 -33   33 wit *1610* -23 -33 : witte *1615* -18

Bal. Haue patience, *Bel-imperia* ; heare the rest.
Lor. Me, next in sight, as messenger they sent,
  To giue him notice that they were so nigh :
  Now when I came, consorted with the Prince,   50
  And vnexpected, in an arbour there,
  Found *Bel-imperia* with *Horatio*—
Bel. How than ?
Lor. Why, then, remembring that olde disgrace
  Which you for *Don Andrea* had indurde,   55
  And now were likely longer to sustaine,
  By being found so meanely accompanied,
  Thought rather, for I knew no readier meane,
  To thrust *Horatio* forth my fathers way.
Bal. And carry you obscurely some where els,   60
  Least that his highnes should haue found you there.
Bel. Euen so, my Lord ? and you are witnesse,
  That this is true which he entreateth of?
  You (gentle brother) forged this for my sake,
  And you, my Lord, were made his instruement :   65
  A worke of worth, worthy the noting too.
  But whats the cause that you concealde me since ?
Lor. Your melancholly, Sister, since the newes
  Of your first fauourite *Don Andreas* death,
  My Fathers olde wrath hath exasperate.   70
Bal. And better wast for you, being in disgrace,
  To absent your selfe, and giue his fury place.
Bel. But why had I no notice of his ire ?
Lor. That were to adde more fewell to your fire,
  Who burnt like *Ætne* for *Andreas* losse.   75
Bel. Hath not my Father then enquirde for me ?
Lor. Sister, he hath, and thus excusde I thee.

                              He whispereth in her eare.

  But, *Bel-imperia*, see the gentle Prince ;
  Looke on thy loue, behold yong *Balthazar*,
  Whose passions by thy presence are increast ;   80
  And in whose melanchollie thou maiest see
  Thy hate, his loue ; thy flight, his following thee.

---

58 know *1599, 1602 -10 -15 -18 -23 -33*   74 your] the *1602 -10 -15 -18 -23 -33*
82 his loue] is loue *1618*

Bel. Brother, you are become an Oratour—
   I know not, I, by what experience—
   Too pollitick for me, past all compare,   85
   Since last I saw you ; but content your selfe :
   The Prince is meditating higher things.
Bal. Tis of thy beautie, then, that conquers Kings ;
   Of those thy tresses, *Ariadnes* twines,
   Wherewith my libertie thou hast surprisde ;   90
   Of that thine iuorie front, my sorrowes map,
   Wherein I see no hauen to rest my hope.
Bel. To loue and feare, and both at once, my Lord,
   In my conceipt, are things of more import
   Then womens wits are to be busied with.   95
Bal. Tis I that loue.
Bel.   Whome ?
Bal.   *Bel-imperia.*
Bel. But I that feare.
Bal.   Whome ?
Bel.   *Bel-imperia.*
Lor. Feare your selfe ?
Bel.   I, Brother.
Lor.   How ?
Bel   As those,
   That what they loue, are loath, and feare to loose.
Bal. Then, faire, let *Balthazar* your keeper be.   100
Bel. No, *Balthazar* doth feare as well as we.
     Et tremulo metui pauidum iunxere timorem,
      Et vanum stolidae proditionis opus.

                                 Exit.

Lor. Nay, and. you argue things so cunningly,
   Weele goe continue this discourse at Court.   105
Bal. Led by the loadstar of her heauenly lookes,
   Wends poore, oppressed *Balthazar,*
   As ore the mountaines walkes the wanderer,
   Incertain to effect his Pilgrimage.

                                 Exeunt.

96–98 *Qq. begin a new line with each speaker*   98–99 As those ...
to loose *one line Qq.*   99 what] when *Qq. exc. Allde*   101 No
om. 1599, 1602 -10 -15 -18 -23 -33   102 *Et Hazlitt* : *Est Qq.*   *pauidem*
Qq. exc. Allde   103 *Et Qq.* : *Est Schick*

⟨SCENE XI.⟩

Enter two Portingales, *and* Hieronimo *meets them.*

1. By your leaue, Sir.

⟨THIRD PASSAGE OF ADDITIONS.⟩

Hier. Tis neither as you thinke, nor as you thinke,
  Nor as you thinke ; you 'r wide all :
  These slippers are not mine, they were my sonne *Horatios.*
  My sonne—and what's a sonne? A thing begot   (5)
  Within a paire of minutes, thereabout,
  A lump bred up in darkenesse, and doth serue
  To ballace these light creatures we call Women ;
  And at nine moneths ende, creepes foorth to light.
  What is there yet in a sonne,   (10)
  To make a father dote, raue, or runne mad ?
  Being borne, it poutes, cryes, and breeds teeth.
  What is there yet in a sonne? He must be fed,
  Be taught to goe, and speake. I, or yet ?
  Why might not a man loue a Calfe as well ?   (15)
  Or melt in passion ore a frisking Kid,
  As for a Sonne? methinks, a young Bacon,
  Or a fine little smooth Horse-colt
  Should mooue a man, as much as doth a sonne.
  For one of these, in very little time,   (20)
  Will grow to some good vse ; where as a sonne,
  The more he growes in stature and in yeeres,
  The more vnsquard, vnbeuelled he appeares ;
  Reccons his parents among the rancke of fooles ;
  Strikes care vpon their heads with his mad ryots ;   (25)
  Makes them looke olde, before they meet with age.
  This is a sonne :—
  And what a losse were this, considered truly ?—
  O, but my *Horatio*
  Grew out of reach of these insatiate humours :   (30)
  He loued his louing parents ;
  He was my comfort, and his mothers ioy,
  The very arme that did hold vp our house :

---

5 A thing begot *beg.* 6 *Qq.*   8 ballance *1618 -23 -33*   23 un-
leauelled *1623 -33*   25 cares *1623 -33*   27-28 *one line*
Qq.   29-31 O ... these | Insatiate ... parents *Qq.*   30 those
1615

Our hopes were stored vp in him.
None but a damned murderer could hate him.   (*35*)
He had not seene the backe of nineteene yeere,
When his strong arme vnhorsd the proud Prince *Balthazar,*
And his great minde, too ful of Honour,
Tooke him vnto mercy,
That valiant, but ignoble Portingale.   (*40*)
Well, heauen is heauen still,
And there is *Nemesis,* and Furies,
And things called whippes,
And they sometimes doe meete with murderers :
They doe not alwayes scape, that is some comfort.   (*45*)
I, I, I ; and then time steales on,
And steales, and steales,
Till violence leapes foorth like thunder
Wrapt in a ball of fire,
And so doth bring confusion to them all.   (*50*)

Hier. Good leaue haue you : nay, I pray you goe,
  For ile leaue you, if you can leaue me so.
2. Pray you, which is the next way to my L⟨ord⟩ the Dukes ?
Hier. The next way from me.
1.   .   To his house, we meane.   5 (*54*)
Hier. O, hard by : tis yon house that you see.
2. You could not tell vs, if his Sonne were there ?
Hier. Who, my Lord *Lorenzo* ?
1.   I, Sir.

          He goeth in at one doore and comes out at another.

Hier.   Oh, forbeare,
  For other talke for vs far fitter were.
  But if you be importunate to know   10 (*59*)
  The way to him, and where to finde him out,
  Then list to me, and Ile resolue your doubt.
  There is a path vpon your left hand side,
  That leadeth from a guiltie Conscience

---

39 Tooke him vnto mercy *ed.*: tooke him vs to mercy *Qq.*: took to
mercy *Dodsley*: took him to mercy *Hazlitt*: took him to his mercy
Schick. See Note   *39–40 one line Qq.*   *45* 's *Qq.*   *46–47*
one line Qq.   2 nay *om.* 1610 *-15 -18 -23 -33*   3 you *om.*
1610 *-15 -18 -23 -33*   4 next *om. Qq. exc. Allde*   6 ye *1602 -10*
-15 -18   8–9 Who ... *Lorenzo* | I sir | Oh ... were *Qq.*   10
importune *1610 -15 -18 -23*

Vnto a forrest of distrust and feare,   15 (*64*)
A darkesome place and dangerous to passe :
There shall you meet with melancholly thoughts,
Whose balefull humours if you but vpholde,
It will conduct you to dispaire and death :
Whose rockie cliffes when you haue once behelde,   20 (*69*)
Within a hugie dale of lasting night,
That, kindled with the worlds iniquities,
Dost cast vp filthy and detested fumes : —
Not far from thence, where murderers haue built
A habitation for their cursed soules,   25 (*74*)
There, in a brazen Caldron fixt by *Joue*,
In his fell wrath, vpon a sulpher flame,
Your selues shall finde *Lorenzo* bathing him
In boyling lead and blood of innocents.

1. Ha, ha, ha.

Hier.   Ha, ha, ha.   30 (*79*)
Why, ha, ha, ha.   Farewell, good ha, ha, ha.

                                                   Exit.

2. Doubtles this man is passing lunaticke,
Or imperfection of his age doth make him dote.
Come, lets away to seek my Lord the Duke.

                                                   Exeunt.

                    ⟨Scene XII.⟩

    Enter Hieronimo *with a Ponyard in one hand, and a Rope
                    in the other.*

Hier. Now, Sir, perhaps I come and see the King ;
    The King sees me, and faine would heare my sute :
    Why, is not this a strange, and seld seene thing,
    That standers by with toyes should strike me mute ?
    Goe too, I see their shifts, and say no more.   5
    Hieronimo, tis time for thee to trudge :
    Downe by the dale that flowes with purple gore,
    Standeth a firie Tower ; there sits a iudge
    Vpon a seat of steele and molten brasse,

---

18 palefull humours if you but behold *1618 -23 -33*   22 That's
1618 -23 -33   25 soule *1602 -10 -15*   30 *Hier.* Ha, ha, ha *beg.*
31 Q*q.*

And twixt his teeth he holdes a fire-brand,   10
That leades vnto the lake where hell doth stand.
Away, *Hieronimo* ; to him be gone :
Heele doe thee iustice for *Horatios* death.
Turne downe this path : thou shalt be with him straite ;
Or this, and then thou needst not take thy breth :   15
This way, or that way :—soft and faire, not so :
For if I hang or kill my selfe, lets know
Who will reuenge *Horatios* murther then ?
No, no ; fie, no : pardon me, ile none of that.

> *He flings away the dagger and halter.*

This way ile take, and this way comes the King,   20

> *He takes them vp againe.*

And heere Ile haue a fling at him, thats flat.
And *Balthazar*, Ile be with thee to bring,
And thee, *Lorenzo*.   Heeres the King—nay, stay,
And heere, I heere—there goes the hare away.

Enter King, Embassador, Castile, *and* Lorenzo.

King. Now shew, *Embassadour*, what our Viceroy saith :   25
    Hath hee receiu'd the articles we sent?
Hier. Iustice, O, iustice to *Hieronimo*.
Lor. Back, seest thou not the King is busie?
Hier. O, is he so?
King. Who is he that interrupts our busines?   30
Hier. Not I.   *Hieronimo* beware ; goe by, goe by.
Embas. Renowned King, he hath receiued and read
    Thy kingly proffers, and thy promist league ;
    And as a man extreamely ouer-ioyd
    To heare his Sonne so princelie entertainde,   35
    Whose death he had so solemnely bewailde,
    This for thy further satisfaction,
    And kingly loue, he kindely lets thee know :
    First, for the marriage of his Princely Sonne
    With *Bel-imperia*, thy beloued Neece,   40
    The newes are more delightfull to his soule,
    Then myrrh or incense to the offended heauens.

---

15 needs *1615 -18*

In person, therefore, will he come himselfe,
To see the marriage rites solemnized,
And in the presence of the Court of Spaine,   45
To knit a sure inextricable band
Of kingly loue and euerlasting league
Betwixt the Crownes of Spaine and Portingale.
There will he giue his Crowne to *Balthazar*,
And make a Queene of *Bel-imperia*.   50

King. Brother, how like you this our Vice-roies loue?

Cast. No doubt, my Lord, it is an argument
Of honorable care to keepe his freend,
And wondrous zeale to *Balthazar* his sonne;
Nor am I least indebted to his grace,   55
That bends his liking to my daughter thus.

Embas. Now last (dread Lord) heere hath his highnes sent,
Although he send not that his Sonne returne,
His ransome due to *Don Horatio*.

Hier. Horatio, who cals *Horatio*?   60

King. And well remembred: thank his Maiestie.
Heere, see it giuen to *Horatio*.

Hier. Iustice, O, iustice, iustice, gentle King.

King. Who is that? *Hieronimo*?

Hier. Iustice, O iustice: O my sonne, my sonne,   65
My Sonne, whom naught can ransome or redeeme.

Lor. Hieronimo, you are not well aduisde.

Hier. Away, *Lorenzo*, hinder me no more;
For thou hast made me bankrupt of my blisse.
Giue me my sonne; you shall not ransome him.   70
Away, Ile rip the bowels of the earth,

                                    He diggeth with his dagger.

And Ferrie ouer to th' Elizian plaines,
And bring my Sonne to shew his deadly wounds.
Stand from about me;
Ile make a pickaxe of my poniard,   75
And heere surrender vp my Marshalship;
For Ile goe marshall vp the feendes in hell,

---

46 inextricable *Hawkins and later editors*: inexecrable *Allde*: inexplicable
other Qq.   66 who *1623 -33*   74-75 *one line Qq.*   77 the]
my *1615 -18 -23 -33*

To be auenged on you all for this.

King. What meanes this outrage?
Will none of you restraine his fury? 80

Hier. Nay, soft and faire; you shall not need to strive:
Needes must he goe that the diuels driue.

- *Exit.*

King. What accident hath hapt *Hieronimo?*
I haue not seene him to demeane him so.

Lor. My gratious Lord, he is with extreame pride 85
Conceiued of yong *Horatio* his Sonne,
And couetous of hauing to himselfe
The ransome of the yong Prince *Balthazar,*
Distract, and in a manner lunatick.

King. Beleeue me, Nephew, we are sorie fort: 90
This is the loue that Fathers beare their Sonnes.
But gentle brother, goe giue to him this golde,
The Princes raunsome; let him haue his due.
For what he hath, *Horatio* shall not want;
Happily *Hieronimo* hath need thereof. 95

Lor. But if he be thus helplessly distract,
Tis requisite his office be resignde,
And giuen to one of more discretion.

King. We shall encrease his melanchollie so.
Tis best that we see further in it first: 100
Till when, our selfe will exempt ⟨him⟩ the place.
And, Brother, now bring in the *Embassador,*
That he may be a witnes of the match
Twixt *Balthazar* and *Bel-imperia,*
And that we may prefixe a certaine time, 105
Wherein the marriage shalbe solemnized,
That we may haue thy Lord the Vice-roy heere.

Embas. Therein your highnes highly shall content
His Maiestie, that longs to heare from hence.

King. On then, and heare you, Lord Embassadour. 110

- *Exeunt.*

79-80 *one line Qq.*   82 For needes *Schick*   83 hapt to *1599,*
1602 -10 -15 -18 -23 -33   91 is *om. 1594*   96 haplesslie *Qq. exc.*
Allde   100 that *om. 1599, 1602 -10 -15 -18 -23 -33*   101 exempt
him *ed.* : exempt *Qq.* : hold exempt *Hazlitt, Schick* : execute *Collier. See Note*
110 them *1599*   your, *1602 -10 -15 -18 -23 -33*

⟨FOURTH PASSAGE OF ADDITIONS.⟩

⟨SCENE XII A.⟩

Enter Iaques *and* Pedro.

Iaq. I wonder, *Pedro*, why our Maister thus
  At midnight sendes vs with our Torches light,
  When man and bird and beast are all at rest,
  Saue those that watch for rape and bloody murder.
Ped. O *Iaques*, know thou that our Maisters minde   (*5*)
  Is much distraught, since his *Horatio* dyed,
  And—now his aged yeeres should sleepe in rest,
  His hart in quiet—like a desperat man,
  Growes lunaticke and childish for his Sonne.
  Sometimes, as he doth at his table sit,   (*10*)
  He speakes as if *Horatio* stood by him;
  Then starting in a rage, falles on the earth,
  Cryes out: *Horatio*, Where is my *Horatio*?
  So that with extreame griefe and cutting sorrow,
  There is not left in him one ynch of man: (*15*)
  See where he comes.

Enter Hieronimo.

Hier. I prie through euery creuice of each wall,
  Looke on each tree, and search through euery brake,
  Beat at the bushes, stampe our grandam earth,
  Diue in the water, and stare vp to heauen,   (*20*)
  Yet cannot I behold my sonne *Horatio*.
  How now, Who's there, sprits, sprits?
Ped. We are your seruants that attend you, sir.
Hier. What make you with your torches in the darke?
Ped. You bid vs light them, and attend you here.   (*25*)
Hier. No, no, you are deceiu'd—not I, you are deceiu'd.
  Was I so mad to bid you light your torches now?
  Light me your torches at the mid of noone,
  When as the Sun-God rides in all his glorie:
  Light me your torches then.
Ped.   Then we burne day light.   (*30*)
Hier. Let it be burnt; night is a murderous slut,
  That would not haue her treasons to be seene,
  And yonder pale faced Hee-cat there, the Moone,
  Doth giue consent to that is done in darkenesse;

---

12 staring *1610*   *16* heere *1615 -18 -23 -33*   *18* on] at *1615 -18 -23 -33*
19 at] on *1615 -18 -23 -33*

And all those Starres that gaze vpon her face,   (35)
Are agglots on her sleeue, pins on her traine;
And those that should be powerfull and diuine,
Doe sleepe in darkenes when they most should shine.
Ped. Prouoke them not, faire sir, with tempting words;
The heauens are gracious, and your miseries   (40)
And sorow makes you speake, you know not what.
Hier. Villaine, thou liest, and thou doest nought
But tell me I am mad: thou liest, I am not mad.
I know thee to be *Pedro*, and he *Iaques*.
Ile prooue it to thee; and were I mad, how could I?   (45)
Where was she that same night when my *Horatio*
Was murdered? She should haue shone: Search thou the booke.
Had the Moone shone, in my boyes face there was a kind of grace,
That I know—nay, I doe know—had the murderer seene him,
His weapon would haue fall'n and cut the earth,   (50)
Had he been framed of naught but blood and death.
Alacke, when mischiefe doth it knowes not what,
What shall we say to mischiefe?

Enter Isabella.

Isa. Deare *Hieronimo*, come in a doores;
O, seeke not meanes so to encrease thy sorrow.   (55)
Hier. Indeed, *Isabella*, we doe nothing heere;
I doe not cry: aske *Pedro*, and aske *Iaques*;
Not I, indeed; we are very merrie, very merrie.
Isa. How? be merrie heere, be merrie heere?
Is not this the place, and this the very tree,   (60)
Where my *Horatio* dyed, where he was murdered?
Hier. Was—doe not say what: let her weepe it out.
This was the tree; I set it of a kiernnell:
And when our hot Spaine coulde not let it grow,
But that the infant and the humaine sap   (65)
Began to wither, duly twice a morning
Would I be sprinkling it with fountaine water.
At last it grewe, and grewe, and bore, and bore,
Till at the length
It grew a gallowes, and did beare our sonne,   (70)
It bore thy fruit and mine: O wicked, wicked plant.

One knockes within at the doore.

---

36 agglots *1610*: aglots *1615 -18 -23 -33*: aggots *1602. See Note   41* And
sorow *at end of 40, Qq.   46* that] the *1615 -18 -23 -33   47* Was murdered
at end of 46, Qq.   49 murderers *1618 -23 -33   50* fall'd *1615 -18 -23 -33
57* aske *Iaques*] aske *om. 1618 -23 -33   61* dyed *1602 A*: hied *1602   69-70*
one line, Qq.   71 The second wicked *om. 1602 A*

See who knocks there.
Ped.   It is a painter, sir.
Hier. Bid him come in, and paint some comfort,
For surely there's none liues but painted comfort.
Let him come in.   One knowes not what may chance: (*75*)
Gods will that I should set this tree—but euen so
Masters vngratefull seruants reare from nought,
And then they hate them that did bring them vp.

Enter the Painter.

Paint. God blesse you, sir.
Hier.   Wherefore, why, thou scornefull villaine?
How, where, or by what meanes should I be blest?   (*80*)
Isa. What wouldst thou haue, good fellow?
Paint.   Iustice, Madame.
Hier. O ambitious begger, wouldest thou haue that
That liues not in the world?
Why, all the undelued mynes cannot buy
An ounce of iustice; tis a iewel so inestimable.   (*85*)
I tell thee, God hath engrossed all iustice in his hands,
And there is none but what comes from him.
Paint.   O then I see
That God must right me for my murdred sonne.
Hier. How, was thy sonne murdered?
Paint. I, sir; no man did hold a sonne so deere.   (*90*)
Hier. What, not as thine? that's a lie
As massie as the earth: I had a sonne,
Whose least vnuallued haire did waigh
A thousand of thy sonnes: and he was murdered.
Paint. Alas, sir, I had no more but he.   (*95*)
Hier. Nor I, nor I: but this same one of mine
Was worth a legion.   But all is one.
Pedro, Iaques, goe in a doores; *Isabella,* goe,
And this good fellow heere and I
Will range this hidious orchard vp and downe,   (*100*)
Like to two Lyons reaued of their yong.
Goe in a doores, I say.

                                        Exeunt.

The Painter *and he sits downe.*

Come, let's talke wisely now.   Was thy Sonne murdered?
Paint. I, sir.

---

72 knocks *1602 A* : knocke *1602*   76 but euen so *beg.* 77, *Qq.*
77 reard *1602 A -10 -15 -18 -23 -33*   87 O then I see *beg. 88, Qq.*   *102* at
doores *1602 A*   *103–157 This prose dialogue between Hier. and the Painter*
Qq. print partly in doggrel

Hier. So was mine. How doo'st take it? art thou not sometimes *(105*
mad? Is there no trickes that comes before thine eies?

Paint. O Lord, yes, Sir.

Hier. Art a Painter? canst paint me a teare, or a wound, a groane
or a sigh? canst paint me such a tree as this?

Paint. Sir, I am sure you haue heard of my painting: my name's *(110*
Bazardo.

Hier. Bazardo, afore-god, an excellent fellow. Look you, sir, doe
you see? I'de haue you paint me ⟨for⟩ my Gallirie in your oile
colours matted, and draw me fiue yeeres yonger then I am—doe
ye see, sir, let fiue yeeres goe, let them goe like the Marshall of *(115*
Spaine—my wife *Isabella* standing by me, with a speaking looke to
my sonne *Horatio,* which should entend to this, or some such like
purpose: 'God blesse thee, my sweet sonne,' and my hand leaning
vpon his head, thus, sir. Doe you see? may it be done?

Paint. Very well, sir.   *(120*

Hier. Nay, I pray marke me, sir: then, sir, would I haue you paint
me this tree, this very tree. Canst paint a dolefull crie?

Paint. Seemingly, sir.

Hier. Nay, it should crie; but all is one. Well, sir, paint me.
a youth run thorow and thorow with villaines swords, hanging *(125*
vpon this tree. Canst thou draw a murderer?

Paint. Ile warrant you, sir; I haue the patterne of the most notorious
villaines that euer liued in all Spaine.

Hier. O let them be worse, worse: stretch thine Arte, and let their
beardes be of *Iudas* his owne collour, and let their eie-browes *(130*
iuttie ouer: in any case obserue that. Then, sir, after some violent
noyse, bring me foorth in my shirt, and my gowne vnder myne
arme, with my torch in my hand, and my sword reared vp thus:
and with these wordes:

> ' *What noyse is this? Who calls Hieronimo?* '

May it be done?   *(135*

Paint. Yea, sir.

Hier. Well, sir, then bring me foorth, bring me thorow allie and
allye, still with a distracted countenance going a long, and let my
haire heaue vp my night-cap. Let the Clowdes scowle, make the
Moone darke, the Starres extinct, the Windes blowing, the Belles
towling, the Owle shriking, the Toades croking, the Minutes ierring, *(140*
and the Clocke striking twelue. And then at last, sir, starting,
behold a man hanging, and tottering, and tottering, as you know
the winde will waue a man, and I with a trice to cut him downe.
And looking vpon him by the aduantage of my torch, finde it

---

105 dost thou *1623 -33*   *109* tree] teare *1602 A, perhaps rightly. See* ·
Note   *113* for my Gallirie *Schick*: my Gallirie *Qq.*: in my Gallirie *Fleischer*
115 yeeres agoe *1610 -18 -23 -33*   *143* waue *1602 A*: weaue *1602 -10 -15 -18 -23 -33*

to be my sonne *Horatio*. There you may ⟨shew⟩ a passion, there (*145*)
you may shew a passion.   Drawe me like old *Priam* of *Troy*, crying: 'the house is a fire, the house is a fire, as the torch ouer
my head.' Make me curse, make me raue, make me cry, make
me mad, make me well againe, make me curse hell, inuocate
heauen, and in the ende leaue me in a traunce—and so foorth. (*150*)
Paint. And is this the end?
Hier. O no, there is no end : the end is death and madnesse. As
I am neuer better then when I am mad : then methinkes I am
a braue fellow ; then I doe wonders : but reason abuseth me, and
there's the torment, there's the hell.   At the last, sir, bringe me (*155*)
to one of the murderers ; were he as strong as *Hector*, thus would
I teare and drage him vp and downe.

He beates the Painter *in, then comes out againe, with a Booke in his hand.*

⟨SCENE XIII.⟩

Enter Hieronimo, *with a book in his hand.*

Vindicta mihi.

I, heauen will be reuenged of euery ill ;
Nor will they suffer murder vnrepaide.
Then stay, *Hieronimo*, attend their will :
For mortall men may not appoint their time.   5
     Per scelus semper tutum est sceleribus iter.
Strike, and strike home, where wrong is offred thee ;
For euils vnto ils conductors be,
And death's the worst of resolution.
For he that thinks with patience to contend   10
To quiet life, his life shall easily end.
     Fata si miseros iuuant, habes salutem :
     Fata si vitam negant, habes sepulchrum.
If destinie thy miseries doe ease,
Then hast thou health, and happy shalt thou be :   15
If destinie denie thee life, *Hieronimo*,
Yet shalt thou be assured of a tombe :
If neither, yet let this thy comfort be,
Heauen couereth him that hath no buriall.

---

145 shew *add Schick*   *148* my] thy *1610 -15 -23 -33 and editors exc.*
Schick. See Note   *150* heauen *om. 1610 -15 -18 -23 -33*   5 their] a *1602*
-10 -15 -18 -23 -33   17 thou shalt *1623 -33*

And to conclude, I will reuenge his death,   20
But how? not as the vulgare wits of men,
With open, but ineuitable ils,
As by a secret, yet a certaine meane,
Which vnder kindeship wilbe cloked best.
Wise men will take their oportunitie,   25
Closely and safely fitting things to time.
But in extreames aduantage hath no time;
And therefore all times fit not for reuenge
Thus therefore will I rest me in vnrest,
Dissembling quiet in vnquietnes,   30
Not seeming that I know their villanies,
That my simplicitie may make them think
That ignorantly I will let all slip:
For ignorance, I wot, and well they know,
    Remedium malorum iners est.   35
Nor ought auailes it me to menace them
Who, as a wintrie storme vpon a plaine,
Will beare me downe with their nobilitie.
No, no, *Hieronimo,* thou must enioyne
Thine eies to obseruation, and thy tung   40
To milder speeches then thy spirit affords;
Thy hart to patience, and thy hands to rest,
Thy Cappe to curtesie, and thy knee to bow,
Till to reuenge thou know when, where, and how.

A noise within.

How now, what noise? what coile is that you keepe?   45

Enter a Seruant.

Ser. Heere are a sort of poore Petitioners,
    That are importunate, and it shall please you, sir,
    That you should plead their cases to the King.
Hier. That I should plead their seuerall actions?
    Why, let them enter, and let me see them.   50

Enter three Cittizens, *and an* olde Man.

---

27 **vantage** *1602 -10 -15 -18 -23 -33*   **no**] on *1610 -15*   32 **my** *om. 1610*
33 **all**] it *1602 -10 -15 -23 -33*   35 *iners*] *mers 1610* : *mors 1633 and editors exc.
Schick. See Note*   41 **spirits affoords** *1594 -99* : **spirits afforde** *1605 -10 -15
-18 -23 -33*   S. D. *A noise within, after* 45, *Allde, 1594 -99*   48 **causes**
1623 -33

1. So, I tell you this : for learning and for law,
   There is not any Aduocate in Spaine
   That can preuaile, or will take halfe the paine
   That he will in pursuit of equitie.

Hier. Come neere, you men, that thus importune me.—   55
   Now must I beare a face of grauitie,
   For thus I vsde, before my Marshalship,
   To plead in causes as Corrigidor.—
   Come on, sirs, whats the matter?

2.   Sir, an Action.

Hier. Of Batterie?

1.   Mine of Debt.

Hier.   Giue place.   60

2. No, sir, mine is an action of the Case.

3. Mine an *Eiectione firmae* by a Lease.

Hier. Content you, sirs ; are you determined
   That I should plead your seuerall actions?

1. I, sir, and heeres my declaration.   65

2. And heere is my band.

3.   And heere is my lease.
                              They giue him papers.

Hier. But wherefore stands yon silly man so mute,
   With mournefull eyes and hands to heauen vpreard?
   Come hether, father, let me know thy cause.

Senex. O worthy sir, my cause, but slightly knowne,   70
   May mooue the harts of warlike Myrmydons,
   And melt the Corsicke rockes with ruthfull teares.

Hier. Say, Father, tell me what's thy sute?

Senex. No, sir ; could my woes
   Giue way vnto my most distresfull, words,   75
   Then should I not in paper, as you see,
   With incke bewray what blood began in me.

Hier. Whats heere? 'The humble supplication
   Of *Don Bazulto* for his murdred Sonne.'

---

57 this *Qq. exc. Allde*   58 Corrigidor *Hazlitt and later editors* : Corrigedor *Allde, 1594 -99, 1602* : Corriegdor *1610 -15 -18 -23 -33*   60 *three lines Qq.*   62 *Eiectione firmae Fleischer, Schick* : *Eiectione firma Allde, 1623 -33* : *eiection firma 1594 -99, 1602 -10 -15 -18. See Note*   a *om. 1610 -15 -18 -23 -33*   66 *first* is *om. 1610*   67 stand you *1602 -10 -15 -18 -23 -33* 72 ruefull *1618 -23 -33*

Senex. I, sir.

Hier.   No, sir, it was my murdred Sonne,   80
Oh my Sonne, my Sonne, oh my Sonne *Horatio.*
But mine, or thine, *Bazulto,* be content.
Heere, take my handkercher, and wipe thine eies,
Whiles wretched I in thy mishaps may see
The liuely portraict of my dying selfe.   85

                              He draweth out a bloudie Napkin.

O no, not this ; *Horatio,* this was thine ;
And when I dyde it in thy deerest blood,
This was a token twixt thy soule and me,
That of thy death reuenged I should be.
But heere, take this, and this—what, my purse ?—   90
I, this, and that, and all of them are thine ;
For all as one are our extremeties.

1. Oh, see the kindenes of *Hieronimo.*
2. This gentlenes shewes him a Gentleman.

Hier. See, see, oh see thy shame, *Hieronimo* ;   95
See heere a louing Father to his sonne :
Behold the sorrowes and the sad laments
That he deliuereth for his Sonnes diceasse.
If loues effects so striues in lesser things,
If loue enforce such moodes in meaner wits,   100
If loue expresse such power in poore estates :
Hieronimo, when, as a raging Sea,
Tost with the winde and tide, ore turnest then
The vpper billowes course of waues to keep,
Whilest lesser waters labour in the deepe :   105
Then shamest thou not, *Hieronimo,* to neglect
The sweet reuenge of thy *Horatio* ?
Though on this earth iustice will not be found,
Ile downe to hell, and in this passion
Knock at the dismall gates of *Plutos* Court,   110

80–81 I sir | No . . . oh my Sonne | my Sonne . . . *Horatio Qq.*   81 my]
oh my *1602 -10 -15 -18 -23 -33*   82 *Bazulto*] *Balthazar 1599*   90 what, my
purse ? *Qq.* : *Sen.* What, thy purse ? *Hazlitt*   98 deliuered *1599, 1602 -10*
-15 -18 -23 -33   99 loue *1602 -10 -15 -18*   101 expresse] enforce *1618 -23*
-33 estate *1610*   103 oreturnest *Allde, 1594 -99, 1602 -10 -15* : ore-turned *1618*
-23 -33 : o'erturneth *Hawkins, Reed, Collier, Hazlitt. See Note*   107 swift
1602 -10 -15 -18 -23 -33

Getting by force, as once *Alcides* did,
A troupe of furies and tormenting hagges,
To torture *Don Lorenzo* and the rest.
Yet least the triple headed porter should
Denye my passage to the slimy strond,   115
The *Thracian* Poet thou shalt counterfeite.
Come on, olde Father, be my *Orpheus*,
And if thou canst no notes vpon the Harpe,
Then sound the burden of thy sore harts greife,
Till we do gaine that *Proserpine* may grant   120
Reuenge on them that murd⟨e⟩red my Sonne.
Then will I rent and teare them, thus, and thus,
Shiuering their limmes in peeces with my teeth.

Teare the Papers.

1. Oh, sir, my declaration.

Exit Hieronimo, *and they after.*

2. Saue my bond.   125
Enter Hieronimo.

2. Saue my bond.

3. Alas, my lease, it cost me ten pound, and you, my Lord,
   haue torne the same.

Hier. That can not be, I gaue it neuer a wound;
Shew me one drop of bloud fall from the same:
How is it possible I should slay it then?   130
Tushe, no; run after, catch me if you can.

Exeunt all but the olde man.

Bazulto *remains till* Hieronimo *enters againe, who, staring him
in the face, speakes.*

Hier. And art thou come, *Horatio*, from the deapth,
To aske for iustice in this vpper earth,
To tell thy father thou art vnreueng'd,
To wring more teares from *Isabellas* eies,   135
Whose lights are dimd with ouer-long laments?
Goe backe, my sonne, complaine to *Eacus*,
For heeres no iustice; gentle boy, be gone,
For iustice is exiled from the earth:

---

111 did *om.* 1594 -99, 1618   117 on *om.* 1599, 1602 -10 -15 -18 -23 -33
119 thy] the 1594 -99, 1602 -10 -15 -18   128 it] them 1602 -10 -15 -18 -23 -33

    Hieronimo will beare thee company.   140

    Thy mother cries on righteous *Radamant*

    For iust reuenge against the murderers.

Senex. Alas, my L⟨ord⟩, whence springs this troubled speech?

Hier. But let me looke on my *Horatio* :

    Sweet boy, how art thou chang'd in deaths black shade. 145

    Had *Prosperine* no pittie on thy youth,

    But suffered thy faire crimson coloured spring

    With withered winter to be blasted thus?

    Horatio, thou art older then thy Father :

    Ah, ruthlesse fate, that fauour thus transformes.   150

Baz. Ah, my good Lord, I am not your yong Sonne.

Hier. What, not my Sonne? thou then a furie art,

    Sent from the emptie Kingdome of blacke night,

    To sommon me to make appearance

    Before grim *Mynos* and iust *Radamant*,   155

    To plague *Hieronimo* that is remisse,

    And seekes not vengeance for *Horatioes* death.

Baz. I am a greeued man, and not a Ghost,

    That came for iustice for my murdered Sonne.

Hier. I, now I know thee, now thou namest thy Sonne : 160

    Thou art the liuely image of my griefe ;

    Within thy face my sorrowes I may see.

    Thy eies are gum'd with teares, thy cheekes are wan,

    Thy forehead troubled, and thy muttring lips

    Murmure sad words abruptly broken off   165

    By force of windie sighes thy spirit breathes ;

    And all this sorrow riseth for thy Sonne :

    And selfe same sorrow feele I for my Sonne.

    Come in, old man, thou shalt to *Izabell* ;

    Leane on my arme : I thee, thou me shalt stay,   170

    And thou, and I, and she will sing a song,

    Three parts in one, but all of discords fram'd :—

    Talke not of cords, but let us now be gone,

    For with a cord *Horatio* was slaine.

                                         Exeunt.

---

    145 how *om. 1594 -99, 1602 -10 -15 -18*   thou art *1623 -33*   147 suffer
1602 A   149 elder *1615 -18 -23 -33*   150 fate *Dodsley, Reed, Collier,*
Schick : Father *Qq., Hawkins, Hazlitt*   152 then thou *1633*   160 thy
1623 -33 : my *other Qq.*   163 grum'd *1610* : dim'd *1602 A, 1615 -18 -23 -33*

⟨SCENE XIV.⟩

Enter King of Spain, *the* Duke, Vice-roy, *and* Lorenzo, Balthazar,
Don Pedro, *and* Bel-imperia.

King. Go, Brother, it is the Duke of *Castiles* cause;
  Salute the *Vice-roy* in our name.
Cast.   I go.
Vice. Go forth, *Don Pedro*, for thy Nephews sake,
  And greet the Duke of *Castile*.
Pedr.   It shall be so.
King. And now to meet these Portaguise: 5
  For, as we now are, so sometimes were these,
  Kings and commanders of the westerne Indies.
  Welcome, braue *Vice-roy*, to the Court of Spaine,
  And welcome all his honorable traine:
  Tis not vnknowne to vs, for why you come,   10
  Or haue so kingly crost the seas.
  Suffiseth it, in this we note the troth
  And more then common loue you lend to vs.
  So is it that mine honorable Neece
  (For it beseemes vs now that it be knowne)   15
  Already is betroth'd to *Balthazar*:
  And by appointment and our condiscent
  To morrow are they to be married.
  To this intent we entertaine thy selfe,
  Thy followers, their pleasure, and our peace: 20
  Speak, men of Portingale, shall it be so?
  If I, say so; if not, say flatly no.
Vice. Renowmed King, I come not as thou thinkst,
  With doubtfull followers, vnresolued men,
  But such as haue vpon thine articles   25
  Confirmed thy motion, and contented me.
  Know, Soueraigne, I come to solemnize
  The marriage of thy beloued Neece,
  Faire *Bel-imperia*, with my *Balthazar*—

---

1 't is *1610 -15 -18 -23 -33*   4 be sir *1599, 1602 -10 -15 -18*: be done sir *1623*
-33   5 the *1602 -10 -15 -18 -23 -33*   Portagues *1602*: Portingales *1602 A*,
1610 -15 -18 -23 -33   10 ye *1602*   11 the raging seas *1623 -33*   12 sufficed
1610 -15 -18 -23 -33   18 they are *1633*   20 pleasures *1623*   25 as
om. 1594   mine *1610*   28 welbeloued *1623 -33*

With thee, my Sonne; whom sith I liue to see,   30
Heere take my Crowne, I give it her and thee;
And let me liue a solitarie life,
In ceaselesse praiers,
To thinke how strangely heauen hath thee preserued.
King. See, brother, see, how nature striues in him.   35
Come, worthy *Vice-roy*, and accompany
Thy friend with thine extremities:
A place more priuate fits this princely mood.
Vice. Or heere, or where your highnes thinks it good.

Exeunt all but Castile and Lorenzo.

Cast. Nay, stay, *Lorenzo*, let me talke with you.   40
Seest thou this entertainement of these Kings?
Lor. I doe, my Lord, and ioy to see the same.
Cast. And knowest thou why this meeting is?
Lor. For her, my Lord, whom *Balthazar* doth loue,
And to confirme their promised marriage.   45
Cast. She is thy Sister?
Lor.   Who, *Bel-imperia?* I,
My gracious Lord, and this is the day
That I haue longd so happely to see.
Cast. Thou wouldst be loath that any fault of thine
Should intercept her in her happines?   50
Lor. Heauens will not let *Lorenzo* erre so much.
Cast. Why then, *Lorenzo*, listen to my words:
It is suspected, and reported too,
That thou, *Lorenzo*, wrongst *Hieronimo*,
And in his sutes towards his Maiestie   55
Still keepst him back, and seeks to crosse his sute.
Lor. That I, my Lord?
Cast. I tell thee, Sonne, my selfe haue heard it said,
When, to my sorrow, I haue been ashamed
To answere for thee, though thou art my Sonne.   60
Lorenzo, knowest thou not the common loue
And kindnes that *Hieronimo* hath wone
By his deserts within the Court of Spaine?

---

31 Gowne *1615*   39 thinke *1615-23-33*   45 the *1623-33*   46 She...
Sister | Who . . . Lord | And this . . . to see *Qq.*   54 wrongd *1602 A*
56 keepes *1602-10-23*: keeps *1615-18*   60 art] wert *1618-23-33*

Or seest thou not the K⟨ing⟩ my brothers care
In his behalfe, and to procure his health?   65
Lorenzo, shouldst thou thwart his passions,
And he exclaime against thee to the King,
What honour wert in this assemblie,
Or what a scandale wert among the Kings,
To heare *Hieronimo* exclaime on thee?   70
Tell me, and looke thou tell me truely too,
Whence growes the ground of this report in Court?
Lor. My L⟨ord⟩, it lyes not in *Lorenzos* power
   To stop the vulgar, liberall of their tongues :
   A small aduantage makes a water breach,   75
   And no man liues that long contenteth all.
Cast. My selfe haue seene thee busie to keepe back
   Him and his supplications from the King.
Lor. Your selfe, my L⟨ord⟩, hath seene his passions
   That ill beseemde the presence of a King ;   80
   And, for I pittied him in his distresse,
   I helde him thence with kind and curteous wordes,
   As free from malice to *Hieronimo*
   As to my soule, my Lord.
Cast. Hieronimo, my sonne, mistakes thee then.   85
Lor. My gracious father, beleeue me, so he doth.
   But whats a silly man, distract in minde
   To thinke vpon the murder of his sonne?
   Alas, how easie is it for him to erre.
   But for his satisfaction and the worlds,   · 90
   Twere good, my L⟨ord⟩, that *Hieronimo* and I
   Were reconcilde, if he misconster me.
Cast. Lorenzo, thou hast said ; it shalbe so.
   Goe one of you, and call *Hieronimo*.

                         Enter Balthazar *and* Bel-imperia.

Bal. Come, *Bel-imperia*, *Balthazars* content,   95
   My sorrowes ease and soueraigne of my blisse,
   Sith heauen hath ordainde thee to be mine :
   Disperce those cloudes and melanchollie lookes,

And cleare them vp with those thy sunne bright eyes,
Wherein my hope and heauens faire beautie lies.   100
Bel. My lookes, my Lord, are fitting for my loue,
Which, new begun, can shew no brighter yet.
Bal. New kindled flames should burne as morning sun.
Bel. But not too fast, least heate and all be done.
I see my Lord, my father.
Bal.   Truce, my loue ;   105
I will goe salute him.
Cast.   Welcome, *Balthazar*,
Welcome, braue Prince, the pledge of Castiles peace ;
And welcome, *Bel-imperia*. How now, girle ?
Why commest thou sadly to salute vs thus ?
Content thy selfe, for I am satisfied :   110
It is not now as when *Andrea* liu'd ;
We haue forgotten and forgiuen that,
And thou art graced with a happier Loue.
But, *Balthazar*, heere comes *Hieronimo* ;
Ile haue a word with him.   115

                    Enter Hieronimo *and a* Seruant.
Hier. And where's the Duke ?
Ser.   Yonder.
Hier.   Euen so :—
What new deuice haue they deuised, tro ?
Pocas Palabras, milde as the Lambe :
Ist I will be reuengde ? no, I am not the man.
Cast. Welcome, *Hieronimo*.   120
Lor. Welcome, *Hieronimo*.
Bal. Welcome, *Hieronimo*.
Hier. My Lords, I thanke you for *Horatio*.
Cast. Hieronimo, the reason that I sent
To speake with you, is this.
Hier.   What, so short ?   125
Then Ile be gone, I thank you fort.
Cast. Nay, stay, *Hieronimo*—goe, call him, sonne.
Lor. Hieronimo, my father craues a word with you.

---

99 cheare *1615 -18 -23 -33*   102 no *om. Allde*   105–107 I see . . .
father | Truce . . . salute him | Welcome . . . Prince | The . . . peace *Qq.*
116–117 And . . . Duke | Yonder | Euen . . . tro *Qq.*   119 Ist] H st *1633* :
Hist *Dodsley*   125 What, so short *sep. line Qq.*

Hier. With me, sir? why, my L⟨ord⟩, I thought you had done.
Lor. No; would he had.
Cast.   *Hieronimo,* I hear   130
  You find your selfe agrieued at my Sonne,
  Because you haue not accesse vnto the King;
  And say tis he that interceptes your sutes.
Hier. Why, is not this a miserable thing, my Lord?
Cast. Hieronimo, I hope you haue no cause,   135
  And would be loth that one of your deserts
  Should once haue reason to suspect my sonne,
  Considering how I think of you my selfe.
Hier. Your sonne *Lorenzo*? whome, my noble Lord?
  The hope of Spaine, mine honorable freend?   140
  Graunt me the combat of them, if they dare.

                               Drawes out his sword.

  Ile meet him face to face, to tell me so.
  These be the scandalous reports of such
  As loue not me, and hate my Lord too much.
  Should I suspect *Lorenzo* would preuent   145
  Or crosse my sute, that loued my Sonne so well?
  My Lord, I am ashamed it should be said.
Lor. Hieronimo, I neuer gaue you cause.
Hier. My good Lord, I know you did not.
Cast.   There then pause;
  And for the satisfaction of the world,   150
  Hieronimo, frequent my homely house,
  The Duke of Castile, *Ciprians* ancient seat;
  And when thou wilt, use me, my sonne, and it:
  But heere, before Prince *Balthazar* and me,
  Embrace each other, and be perfect freends.   155
Hier. I marry, my Lord, and shall.
  Freends, quoth he? see, Ile be freends with you all:
  Specially with you, my louely Lord;
  For diuers causes it is fit for vs
  That we be freends: the world is suspitious,   160
  And men may think what we imagine not.
Bal. Why, this is friendly done, *Hieronimo.*

---

  130 *Hieronimo,* I hear *beg.* 131, *Qq.*   149 There then pause *beg.* 150, *Qq.*:
then *om.* 1602 *A*, 1615 -18 -23 -33

Lor. And that, I hope, olde grudges are forgot.

Hier. What els ? it were a shame it should not be so.

Cast. Come on, *Hieronimo*, at my request ;   165
    Let us entreat your company to day.   *Exeunt.*

Hier. Your Lordships to commaund. Pah : keepe your way.
         Chi mi fa più carezze che non suole,
         Tradito mi ha, o tradir mi vuole.

                                                  Exit.

⟨Scene XV.⟩

Enter Ghoast *and* Reuenge.

Ghoast. Awake, *Erichtho* ; *Cerberus*, awake.
    Solicite *Pluto*, gentle *Proserpine*[4],
    To combate, *Acheron* and *Erebus*.
    For neere, by *Stix* and *Phlegeton* in hell,
    O'er-ferried *Caron* to the fierie lakes   5
    Such fearefull sights, as poore *Andrea* sees.
    Reuenge, awake.

Reuenge. Awake? for why?

Ghoast. Awake, *Reuenge* ; for thou art ill aduisde
    To sleepe away what thou art warnd to watch.   10

Reuenge. Content thy selfe, and doe not trouble me.

Ghoast. Awake, *Reuenge*, if loue, as loue hath had,
    Haue yet the power or preuailance in hell.
    Hieronimo with *Lorenzo* is ioynde in league,
    And intercepts our passage to reuenge :   15
    Awake, *Reuenge*, or we are woe begone.

Reuenge. Thus worldlings ground, what they haue dreamd, vpon.
    Content thy selfe, *Andrea* ; though I sleepe,

---

167 Pah *Schick: Pha Qq.*   168–9 *Mi chi mi fa ? Pui Correzza che non
sule | Tradito viha otrade vule Allde : later Qq. more corrupt*   1 *Erichta
Qq.* : Alecto *Hazlitt. See Note*   3–5 *emend. Schick* : To combate *Achinon*
and *Erichus* in hell | For neere (neerd *1594 -99, 1602 -10 -15 -18*) by *Stix* and
Phlegeton | Nor ferried *Caron* to the fierie lakes *Qq. See Note*   6 see *Allde,
1594 -99*   8 Awake? for why? *om. 1618 -23 -33*   10 Th sleepe, away,
what, thou art warnd to watch. *Allde* : To sleepe, awaie, what thou art warned
to watch. *1594* : To sleepe ; away, what, thou art warnde to watch. *1599* : To
sleepe ; away what thou art warnde to watch. *1602* : To sleepe, away ; what?
thou art warnde to watch. *1602 A* : To sleepe, away ; what, thou art warn'd to
watch. *1610* : To sleepe, away: what art warn'd to watch. *1615 -18* : To sleepe,
away : what, art warn'd to watch ? *1623* : To sleepe, awake : what, art warn'd to
watch ? *1633* : To sleep—awake : what thou art warn'd to watch ! *editors*

Yet is my mood soliciting their soules.
Sufficeth thee that poore *Hieronimo*   20
Cannot forget his sonne *Horatio*.
Nor dies *Reuenge*, although he sleepe awhile ;
For in vnquiet quietnes is faind,
And slumbring is a common worldly wile.
Beholde, *Andrea*, for an instance, how   25
Reuenge hath slept, and then imagine thou
What tis to be subiect to destinie.

Enter a dumme shew.

Ghoast. Awake, *Reuenge* ; reueale this misterie.
Reuenge. The two first the nuptiall torches boare
As brightly burning as the mid-daies sunne :   30
But after them doth *Himen* hie as fast,
Clothed in Sable and a Saffron robe,
And blowes them out, and quencheth them with blood,
As discontent that things continue so.
Ghoast. Sufficeth me ; thy meanings vnderstood,   35
And thanks to thee and those infernall powers
That will not tollerate a Louers woe.
Rest thee, for I will sit to see the rest.
Reuenge. Then argue not, for thou hast thy request.

Exeunt.

ACTVS QVARTVS.

⟨SCENE I.⟩

Enter Bel-imperia *and* Hieronimo.

Bel. Is this the loue thou bearst *Horatio* ?
Is this the kindnes that thou counterfeits ?
Are these the fruits of thine incessant teares ?
Hieronimo, are these thy passions,
Thy protestations, and thy deepe lamentes,   5
That thou wert wont to wearie men withall.
O vnkind father, O deceitfull world,

---

19 is] in *1618 -23 -33*   23 found *1599, 1602 -10 -15 -18 -23 -33*   29 Lo ! the
two *Schick, unnecessarily*   boare *Qq.* : beare *Fleischer. See Note*   30 bright
Qq. exc. Allde   36 to] vnto *1610 -15 -18 -23 -33*   38 to] and *1618 -23 -33*
39 Then] Thus *1610 -15 -18*

KYD : BOAS   G

With what excuses canst thou shew thy selfe,
†With what dishonour and the hate of men,†
From this dishonour and the hate of men ?   10
Thus to neglect the losse and life of him,
Whom both my letters and thine own beliefe
Assures thee to be causeles slaughtered.
Hieronimo, for shame, *Hieronimo*,
Be not a historie to after times   15
Of such ingratitude vnto thy Sonne :
Vnhappy Mothers of such children then,
But monstrous Fathers to forget so soone
The death of those, whom they with care and cost
Haue tendred so, thus careles should be lost.   20
My selfe, a stranger in respect of thee,
So loued his life, as still I wish their deathes.
Nor shall his death be vnreuengd by me,
Although I beare it out for fashions sake :
For heere I sweare, in sight of heauen and earth,   25
Shouldst thou neglect the loue thou shouldst retaine,
And giue it ouer, and deuise no more,
My selfe should send their hatefull soules to hell,
That wrought his downfall with extreamest death.
Hier. But may it be that *Bel-imperia*,   30
Vowes such reuenge as she hath daind to say?
Why then I see that heauen applies our drift,
And all the Saintes doe sit soliciting
For vengeance on those cursed murtherers.
Madame, tis true, and now I find it so,   35
I found a letter, written in your name,
And in that Letter how *Horatio* died.
Pardon, O pardon, *Bel-imperia*,
My feare and care in not beleeuing it ;
Nor thinke I thoughtles thinke vpon a meane   40
To let his death be vnreueng'd at full :
And heere I vow—so you but giue consent,

---

9 *om. editors exc. Hazlitt* : *query,* dishonour . . . men *misprint for* deuices
seek thy selfe to saue *or similar phrase* ?   10 *om. Hazlitt*   11 life and
losse *Qq. exc. Allde*   17 mother *1599, 1602 -10 -15 -18 -23 -33*   18 Father
1602 -10 -15 -18 -23 -33   24 fashion *1623 -33*   32 applies *Qq.* : applauds
Collier. See Note

And will conceale my resolution—
I will ere long determine of their deathes
That causles thus haue murdered my sonne.   45
Bel. Hieronimo, I will consent, conceale,
And ought that may effect for thine auaile,
Ioyne with thee to reuenge *Horatioes* death.
Hier. On then; whatsoeuer I deuise,
Let me entreat you, grace my practises :   50
For why the plots already in mine head.
Heere they are.

                Enter Balthazar *and* Lorenzo.

Bal. How now, *Hieronimo* ? what, courting *Bel-imperia* ?
Hier. I, my Lord; such courting as, I promise you,
She hath my hart, but you, my Lord, haue hers.   55
Lor. But now, *Hieronimo*, or neuer, wee
Are to entreate your helpe.
Hier.   My helpe ?
Why, my good Lords, assure your selues of me ;
For you haue giuen me cause ; I, by my faith, haue you.
Bal. It pleasd you, at the entertainement of the Embassadour,
To grace the King so much as with a shew :   61
Now, were your studie so well furnished,
As for the passing of the first nights sport
To entertaine my father with the like,
Or any such like pleasing motion,   65
Assure your selfe, it would content them well.
Hier. Is this all ?
Bal. I, this is all.
Hier. Why then, ile fit you ; say no more.
When I was yong, I gaue my minde   70
And plide my selfe to fruitles Poetrie ;
Which though it profite the professor naught,
Yet is it passing pleasing to the world.
Lor. And how for that ?
Hier.   Marrie, my good Lord, thus :
(And yet me thinks you are too quicke with vs) :—   75

47 that] what *1633*   49 On] Oh *1610 -15 -18 -23 -33*   and whatsoeuer *Schick*
51 my *1602 -15 -18 -23 -33*   56–58 But now . . . your helpe | My helpe . . . of
me *Qq.*   59 faith] honour *1615 -18 -23 -33*   60 at th' *1618 -23 -33*   73 it
is *1633*   passing] passion *1618*   75 think *1599, 1602 -10*

When in *Tolledo* there I studied
It was my chance to write a Tragedie,
See heere, my Lords.—   *He shewes them a booke.*
Which, long forgot, I found this other day.
Now would your Lordships fauour me so much   80
As but to grace me with your acting it—
I meane, each one of you to play a part—
Assure you it will prooue most passing strange,
And wondrous plausible to that assembly.
Bal. What? would you haue us plaie a Tragedie?   85
Hier. Why, Nero thought it no disparagement,
    And Kings and Emperours haue tane delight
    To make experience of their wits in plaies.
Lor. Nay, be not angrie, good *Hieronimo*;
    The Prince but asked a question.   90
Bal. In faith, *Hieronimo*, and you be in earnest,
    Ile make one.
Lor. And I, another.
Hier. Now, my good Lord, could you entreat
    Your sister *Bel-imperia* to make one?   95
    For whats a plaie without a woman in it?
Bel. Little intreaty shall serue me, *Hieronimo*;
    For I must needes be imployed in your play.
Hier. Why this is well; I tell you, Lordings,
    It was determined to haue been acted   100
    By Gentlemen and schollers too,
    Such as could tell what to speak.
Bal. And now it shall be plaide by Princes and Courtiers,
    Such as can tell how to speake:
    If, as it is our Country maner,   105
    You will but let us know the Argument.
Hier. That shall I roundly.   The Chronicles of Spaine
    Record this written of a Knight of Rodes:
    He was betrothed, and wedded at the length,
    To one *Perseda*, an Italian Dame,   110
    Whose beauty rauished all that her behelde,

---

76 Tolado *1610*   78 See heere my Lords *beg. stage-direction,* 1594
84 plausible *Qq*: pleasurable *Hazlitt, unnecessarily*   87 *second* and *om. 1610*
90 asked you *1623 -33*   96 in't? *1602 -10 -15 -18 -23 -33*   103 plaide] said
1599, 1602 -10 -15 -18 -23 -33   108 of the Rhodes *1618*

Especially the soule of *Soliman*,
Who at the marriage was the cheefest guest.
By sundry meanes sought *Soliman* to winne
Persedas loue, and could not gaine the same.   115
Then gan he break his passions to a freend,
One of his Bashawes whom he held full deere;
Her had this Bashaw long solicited,
And saw she was not otherwise to be wonne,
But by her husbands death, this Knight of Rodes,   120
Whom presently by trecherie he slew.
She, stirde with an exceeding hate therefore,
As cause of this, slew *Soliman*,
And, to escape the Bashawes tirannie,
Did stab herselfe, and this the Tragedie.   125
Lor. O, excellent !
Bel.   But say, *Hieronimo*,
What then became of him that was the Bashaw ?
Hier. Marrie, thus : mooued with remorse of his misdeeds,
Ran to a mountaine top and hung himselfe.
Bal. But which of us is to performe that parte ?   130
Hier. O, that will I, my Lords, make no doubt of it :
Ile play the murderer, I warrant you,
For I already haue conceited that.
Bal. And what shall I ?
Hier. Great *Soliman*, the Turkish Emperour.   135
Lor. And I ?
Hier. *Erastus*, the Knight of Rhodes.
Bel. And I ?
Hier. *Perseda*, chaste and resolute.
And heere, my Lords, are seuerall abstracts drawne,   140
For each of you to note your partes,
And act it as occasion's offred you.
You must prouide a Turkish cappe,
A black mustacio, and a Fauchion.

                                        Giues a paper to Bal.

---

125 this is the *1602 -10 -15 -18 -23 -33*   126 O, excellent *Qq.* : Ay, sir,
Hawkins, Reed, Collier, Hazlitt   126–7 O, excellent | But . . . him |
That . . . Bashaw *Qq.*   129 hang *1602* : hang'd *1602 A, 1610 -15 -18 -23 -33*
135 that *1615 -18*

You, with a Crosse, like to a Knight of Rhodes.   145

Giues another to Lor.

And, Madame, you must attire your selfe

He giueth Bel. *another.*

Like *Phoebe, Flora,* or the huntresse,
Which to your discretion shall seeme best.
And as for me, my Lords, Ile looke to one,
And with the ransome that the *Vice-roy* sent,   150
So furnish and performe this Tragedie,
As all the world shall say, *Hieronimo*
Was liberall in gracing of it so.

Bal. Hieronimo, methinkes a Comedie were better.

Hier. A Comedie?   155
Fie, Comedies are fit for common wits:
But to present a Kingly troupe withall,
Giue me a stately written Tragedie;
Tragedia cothurnata, fitting Kings,
Containing matter, and not common things.   160
My Lords, all this must be perfourmed,
As fitting for the first nights reuelling.
The Italian Tragedians were so sharpe of wit
That in one houres meditation
They would performe any thing in action.   165

Lor. And well it may; for I haue seene the like
In *Paris,* mongst the French Tragedians.

Hier. In *Paris*? mas, and well rememb⟨e⟩red.
Theres one thing more that rests for us to doe.

Bal. Whats that, *Hieronimo*? forget not any thing.   170

Hier. Each one of us must act his parte
In vnknowne languages,
That it may breed the more varietie:
As you, my Lord, in Latin; I in Greeke;
You in Italian; and, for because I know   175
That *Bel-imperia* hath practised the French,
In courtly French shall all her phraises be.

Bel. You meane to try my cunning then, *Hieronimo*?

---

145 to *om. 1599, 1602 -10 -15 -18*   S. D. *giueth*] *giues 1602 -10 -15 -18 -23 -33*
152 As] That *1615 -23 -33*   155–6 A Comedie ... wits *one line Qq.*   159
cother nato Allde, 1599, 1618 -23: *cothornato 1602 -10 -15*   173 the *om.*
1618 -23 -33

Bal. But this will be a meere confusion,
　And hardly shall we all be vnderstood.　　　　　　　180
Hier. It must be so; for the conclusion
　Shall proue the intention, and all was good :
　And I my selfe in an Oration,
　And with a strange and wondrous shew besides,
　That I will haue there behinde a curtaine,　　　　　185
　Assure your selfe, shall make the matter knowne:
　And all shalbe concluded in one Scene,
　For there's no pleasure tane in tediousness.
Bal. How like you this?
Lor. Why thus, my Lord, we must resolue　　　　　190
　To soothe his humors vp.
Bal. On, then, *Hieronimo* ; farewell till soone.
Hier. Youle ply this geere?
Lor.　　　　　　　　　I warrant you.

　　　　　Exeunt all but Hieronimo.

Hier.　　　　.　　　　　　　　　Why so :
　Now shall I see the fall of Babylon,
　Wrought by the heauens in this confusion.　　　　　195
　And if the world like not this Tragedie,
　Hard is the hap of olde *Hieronimo*.

　　　　　　　　　　　　　　　　　　　Exit.

　　　　　　　　　　⟨SCENE II.⟩

　　　　　Enter Isabella *with a weapon.*

Isab. Tell me no more :—O monstrous homicides.
　Since neither pietie nor pittie mooues
　The King to iustice or compasion,
　I will reuenge my selfe vpon this place,
　Where thus they murdered my beloued sonne.　　　5

　　　　　　　She cuts downe the Arbour.

　Doune with these branches and these loathsome bowes

　184–5 *so, 1602 and later Qq.* : *but* 185–4, *Allde, 1594* -99　　186 your] thy
1618 -23 -33　192 On] O *1633*　　193 I, why so *Qq. exc. Allde*　193–4 Youle
. . . geere | I warrant you | Why so . . . Babylon *Qq.*　　5 thus *om. 1602 -10*
-15 -18 -23 -33　　they haue murdered *1633*　　6 *first* these] those *1602* : *but*
these *1602 A*

Of this vnfortunate and fatall Pine :
Downe with them, *Isabella*; rent them vp,
And burn the roots from whence the rest is sprung.
I will not leaue a roote, a stalke, a tree,   10
A bough, a branch, a blossome, nor a leafe,
No, not an herb within this garden Plot—
Accursed complot of my miserie.
Fruitlesse for euer may this garden be,
Barren the earth, and bliselesse whosoeuer   15
Immagines not to keepe it unmanurde.
An Easterne winde, commixt with noisome aires,
Shall blast the plants and the yong saplings ;
The earth with Serpents shall be pestered,
And passengers, for feare to be infect,   20
Shall stand aloofe and looking at it, tell :
'There, murdred, dide the sonne of *Isabell*.'
I, heere he dide, and heere I him imbrace :
See, where his Ghoast solicites with his wounds
Reuenge on her that should reuenge his death.   25
Hieronimo, make haste to see thy sonne ;
For sorrow and dispaire hath scited me
To heare *Horatio* plead with *Radamant* :
Make haste, *Hieronimo*, to hold excusde
Thy negligence in pursute of their deaths   30
Whose hatefull wrath bereu'd him of his breath.
Ah nay, thou doest delay their deaths,
Forgiues the murderers of thy noble sonne,
And none but I bestirre me—to no ende.
And as I curse this tree from further fruite,   35
So shall my wombe be cursed for his sake ;
And with this weapon will I wound the brest,
The haplesse brest, that gaue *Horatio* suck.

                                She stabs herselfe.

---

8 rend *1618 -23 -33*   15 blesselesse *1610 -15 -18 -23 -33*   24 solicited
1618 -23 -33   second his *om. 1633*   29 to holde exclude *1615 -18 -23 -33 :*
or hold accused *Hazlitt*   32 nay] na *1594 -99* : ha *1602 -10 -15 -18 -23 -33*
S. D. *She stabs herselfe after* 37, *Allde, 1594 -99*

⟨SCENE III.⟩

Enter Hieronimo ; *he knocks up the curtaine.*
Enter the Duke of Castile.

Cast. How now, *Hieronimo*, where's your fellows,
　That you take all this paine?
Hier. O sir, it is for the authors credit
　To look that all things may goe well.
　But, good my Lord, let me entreate your grace　　　5
　To giue the King the coppie of the plaie :
　This is the argument of what we shew.
Cast. I will, *Hieronimo.*
Hier. One thing more, my good Lord.
Cast. What's that?　　　　　　　　　　　　　　10
Hier. Let me entreat your grace
　That, when the traine are past into the gallerie,
　You would vouchsafe to throw me downe the key.
Cast. I will, *Hieronimo.*
　　　　　　　　　　　　　　　　Exit Cast.

Hier. What, are you ready, *Balthazar*?　　　　　15
　Bring a chaire and a cushion for the King.

　　　　Enter Balthazar, *with a Chaire.*

Well doon, *Balthazar*, hang up the Title :
Our scene is Rhodes :—what, is your beard on?
Bal. Halfe on ; the other is in my hand.
Hier. Dispatch, for shame ; are you so long?　　　20
　　　　　　　　　　　　　　　Exit Balthazar.
Bethink thy selfe, *Hieronimo*,
Recall thy wits, recompt thy former wrongs
Thou hast receiued by murder of thy sonne.
And lastly, not least, how *Isabell*,
Once his mother and thy deerest wife,　　　　　25
All woe begone for him, hath slaine her selfe.
Behooues thee then, *Hieronimo*, to be reueng'd.
The plot is laide of dire reuenge :
On, then, *Hieronimo*, pursue reuenge,
For nothing wants but acting of reuenge.　　　30
　　　　　　　　　　　　　　　Exit Hieronimo.

---

1 your] thy *1618 -23 -33*　9 good my Lord *1633*　12 are] is *1618 -23 -33*
13 You *end of* 12, *1618 -23 -33*　17 Tilt *1610*　20 you are *1610*　25 thy]
my *1623 -33*　29 them *1618 -23 -33*

⟨SCENE IV.⟩

Enter Spanish King, Vice-Roy, Duke of Castile,
and their traine.

King. Now, *Vice-roy*, shall we see the Tragedie
Of *Soliman*, the Turkish Emperour,
Performde of pleasure by your Sonne the Prince,
My Nephew *Don Lorenzo*, and my Neece?
Vice. Who? *Bel-imperia*?   5
King. I, and *Hieronimo* our Marshall,
At whose request they deine to doo't themselues.
These be our pastimes in the Court of Spaine:
Heere, brother, you shall be the booke-keeper:
This is the argument of that they shew.   10

                                     He giueth him a booke.

Gentlemen, this Play of Hieronimo, *in sundrie languages, was thought*
    good to be set downe in English, more largely, for the easier
    vnderstanding to euery publique Reader.

         Enter Balthazar, Bel-imperia, and Hieronimo.

Bal. Bashaw, *that Rhodes is ours, yield heauens the honour,*
  And holy Mahomet, *our sacred Prophet:*
  And be thou grac't with euery excelence
  That Soliman *can giue, or thou desire.*
  But thy desert in conquering Rhodes is lesse   15
  Then in reseruing this faire Christian Nimph,
  Perseda, *blisfull lampe of Excellence,*
  Whose eies compell, like powrefull Adamant,
  The warlike heart of Soliman *to wait.*

King. See, *Vice-roy*, that is *Balthazar*, your sonne,   20
  That represents the Emperour *Solyman*:
  How well he acts his amourous passion.
Vice. I, *Bel-imperia* hath taught him that.
Cast. That's because his minde runs all on *Bel-imperia*.

Hier. What euer ioy earth yields, betide your Maiestie.   25
Bal. Earth yields no ioy without Persedaes *loue,*
Hier. Let then Perseda *on your grace attend.*

---

  3 our *1623 -33*   7 denie *1618*   S. D. *giues 1602 -10 -15 -18 -23 -33*
16 *Christian om. 1633*   27 *Then let 1602 -10 -15 -18 -23 -33*

Bal. *She shall not wait on me, but I on her:*
  Drawne by the influence of .her lights, I yield.
  But let my friend, the Rhodian Knight, come foorth,   30
  Erasto, *dearer than my life to me,*
  That he may see Perseda *my beloued.*

Enter Erasto.

King. Here comes *Lorenzo* : looke upon the plot,
  And tell me, brother, what part plaies he?

Bel. *Ah, my* Erasto, *welcome to* Perseda.   35
Era. *Thrice happie is* Erasto, *that thou liuest ;*
  Rhodes losse is nothing to Erastoes *ioy :*
  Sith his Perseda *liues, his life suruiues.*
Bal. *Ah,* Bashaw, *heere is loue betwixt* Erasto
  And faire Perseda, *soueraigne of my soule.*   40
Hier. *Remooue* Erasto, *mighty* Solyman,
  And then Perseda *will be quickly wonne.*
Bal. Erasto *is my friend; and while he liues,*
  Perseda *neuer will remooue her loue.*
Hier. *Let not* Erasto *liue to grieue great* Soliman.   45
Bal. *Deare is* Erasto *in our princly eye.*
Hier. *But if he be your riuall, let him die.*
Bal. *Why, let him die ; so loue commaundeth me,*
  Yet greeue I that Erasto *should so die.*
Hier. Erasto, Solyman *saluteth thee,*   50
  And lets thee wit by me his highnes will,
  Which is, thou shouldest be thus imploid.

                                        Stab him.

Bel. *Ay me,* Erasto *; see,* Solyman, Erastoes *slaine.*
Bal. *Yet liueth* Solyman *to comfort thee.*
  Faire Queene of beautie, let not fauour die,   55
  But with a gratious eye behold his griefe,
  That with Persedaes *beautie is encreast,*
  If by Perseda *his grief be not releast.*
Bel. *Tyrant, desist soliciting vaine sutes ;*
  Relentless are mine eares to thy laments,   60
  As thy butcher is pittilesse and base,
  Which seazd on my Erasto, *harmelesse Knight.*

Yet by thy power thou thinkest to commaund,
And to thy power Perseda *doth obey :*
But, were she able, thus she would reuenge   65
Thy treacheries on thee, ignoble Prince :

                                    Stab him.
And on herselfe she would be thus reueng'd.

                                    Stab her selfe.
King. Well said.—Olde Marshall, this was brauely done.
Hier. But *Bel-imperia* plaies *Perseda* well.
Vice. Were this in earnest, *Bel-imperia,*   70
   You would be better to my Sonne then so.
King. But now what followes for *Hieronimo* ?
Hier. Marrie, this followes for *Hieronimo* :
   Heere breake we off our sundrie languages,
   And thus conclude I in our vulgar tung.   75
   Happely you thinke (but booteles are your thoughts)
   That this is fabulously counterfeit,
   And that we doo as all Tragedians doo :
   To die to day for fashioning our Scene—
   The death of *Aiax* or some Romaine peere—   80
   And in a minute starting vp againe,
   Reuiue to please too morrowes audience.
   No, Princes ; know I am *Hieronimo,*
   The hopeles father of a hapless Sonne,
   Whose tongue is tun'd to tell his latest tale,   85
   Not to excuse grosse errors in the play.
   I see your lookes vrge instance of these wordes ;
   Beholde the reason vrging me to this :

                                    Shewes his dead Sonne.
   See heere my shew, looke on this spectacle :
   Heere lay my hope, and heere my hope hath ende :   90
   Heere lay my hart, and heere my hart was slaine :
   Heere lay my treasure, heere my treasure lost :
   Heere lay my blisse, and heere my blisse bereft :
   But hope, hart, treasure, ioy, and blisse,
   All fled, faild, died, yea, all decaide with this.   95
   From forth these wounds came breath that gaue me life ;
   They murdred me that made these fatall markes.

S. D. *Let her stab him* 1602 -10 -15 -18 -23 -33   72 for *om.* 1618 -23 -33
76 are] be 1602 -10 -15 -18 -23 -33   85 turn'd 1615 -18   87 those 1618 -23 -33
S. D. *He shewes* 1602 -10 -15 -18 -23 -33

The cause was loue, whence grew this mortall hate ;
The hate : *Lorenzo*, and yong *Balthazar* :
The loue : my sonne to *Bel-imperia*.   100
But night, the couerer of accursed crimes,
With pitchie silence husht these traitors harmes,
And lent them leaue, for they had sorted leasure,
To take aduantage in my Garden plot
Upon my Sonne, my deere *Horatio* :   105
There mercilesse they butcherd vp my boy,
In black darke night, to pale dim cruel death.
He shrikes : I heard, and yet, me thinks, I heare
His dismall out-cry eccho in the aire.
With soonest speed I hasted to the noise,   110
Where hanging on a tree I found my sonne,
Through girt with wounds, and slaughtred as you see.
And greeued I (think you) at this spectacle ?
Speake, Portaguise, whose losse resembles mine :
If thou canst weepe vpon thy *Balthazar*,   115
Tis like I wailde for my *Horatio*.
And you, my L⟨ord⟩, whose reconciled sonne
Marcht in a net, and thought himselfe vnseene,
And rated me for brainsicke lunacie,
With *God amende that mad Hieronimo*,   120
How can you brook our plaies Catastrophe ?
And heere beholde this bloudie hand-kercher,
Which at *Horatios* death I weeping dipt
Within the riuer of his bleeding wounds :
It as propitious, see, I haue reserued,   125
And neuer hath it left my bloody hart,
Soliciting remembrance of my vow
With these, O, these accursed murderers :
Which now perform'd, my hart is satisfied.
And to this end the *Bashaw* I became,   130
That might reuenge me on *Lorenzos* life,
Who therefore was appointed to the part,

101 the coueter *1610* : the a couerer *1615*   102 the *Qq. exc. Allde*
trayterous *1623 -33*   108 shrikt *1610*   114 Portagues *1602* : Portingules
1602 A, -10 -15 -18 -23 -33   resemble *1599, 1615 -18 -23*   116 waile *1633*
120 With] Which *Qq. exc. Allde*   125 It] Is *1615 -18 -23 -33*   preserued
1618 -23 -33   126 haue *1610*   bleeding *1623 -33*

And was to represent the Knight of Rhodes,
That I might kill him more conueniently.
So, *Vice-roy*, was this *Balthazar*, thy Sonne,   135
That *Soliman* which *Bel-imperia*,
In person of *Perseda*, murdered:
Solie appointed to that tragicke part
That she might slay him that offended her.
Poore *Bel-imperia* mist her part in this,   140
For though the story saith she should haue died,
Yet I of kindnes, and of care to her,
Did otherwise determine of her end;
But loue of him, whom they did hate too much,
Did vrge her resolution to be such.   145
And, Princes, now beholde *Hieronimo*,
Author and actor in this Tragedie,
Bearing his latest fortune in his fist;
And will as resolute conclude his parte
As any of the Actors gone before.   150
And, Gentles, thus I end my play;
Vrge no more wordes: I haue no more to say.

He runs to hange himselfe.

King. O hearken, *Vice-roy*—holde, *Hieronimo.*
Brother, my Nephew and thy sonne are slaine.
Vice. We are betraide; my *Balthazar* is slaine.   155
Breake ope the doores; runne, saue *Hieronimo.*

They breake in, and hold Hieronimo.

Hieronimo, doe but enforme the King of these euents;
Upon mine honour, thou shalt haue no harme.
Hier. *Vice-roy*, I will not trust thee with my life,
Which I this day haue offered to my Sonne.   160
Accursed wretch,
Why staiest thou him that was resolud to die?
King. Speake, traitour; damned, bloudy murderer, speak.
For now I haue thee, I will make thee speak.
Why hast thou done this vndeseruing deed?   165
Vice. Why hast thou murdered my *Balthazar*?
Cast. Why hast thou butchered both my children thus?

---

133 present *1610*   144 too] so *1623-33*   151 Gentiles *1594, 1623-33*
S. D. *runneth 1623-33*   S. D. *They* . . . Hier. *om. Allde, 1594-99*   161-2
one line Qq.   162 staidst *1623-33*

Hier. O, good words : as deare to me was my *Horatio*,
　　As yours, or yours, or yours, my L⟨ord⟩, to you.
　　My guiltles Sonne was by *Lorenzo* slaine,　　　　　170
　　And by *Lorenzo* and that *Balthazar*
　　Am I at last reuenged thorowly,
　　Vpon whose soules may heauens be yet auenged
　　With greater far than these afflictions.
Cast. But who were thy confederates in this ?　　　175
Vice. That was thy daughter *Bel-imperia* ;
　　For by her hand my *Balthazar* was slaine :
　　I saw her stab him.
King.　　　　　　　Why speakest thou not ?
Hier. What lesser libertie can Kings affoord
　　Then harmeles silence ? then affoord it me.　　　180
　　Sufficeth, I may not, nor I will not tell thee.
King. Fetch forth the tortures.
　　Traitor as thou art, ile make thee tell.
Hier. Indeed thou maiest torment me, as his wretched Sonne
　　Hath done in murdring my *Horatio* :　　　185
　　But neuer shalt thou force me to reueale
　　The thing which I haue vowd inuiolate.
　　And therefore in despight of all thy threats,
　　Pleasde with their deaths, and easde with their reuenge,
　　First take my tung, and afterwards my hart.　　　190

⟨FIFTH PASSAGE OF ADDITIONS, REPLACING 168–90, BUT IN-
CORPORATING, IN TRANSPOSED ORDER, 168–78 (. . . STAB HIM)
AND 190 OF ORIGINAL TEXT.⟩

Hier. But are you sure they are dead ?
Cast. I, slaue, too sure.
Hier. What, and yours too ?　　　　　(*170*)
Vice. I, all are dead ; not one of them suruiue.
Hier. Nay, then I care not ; come, and we shall be friends ;
　　Let us lay our heades together :
　　See, here's a goodly nowse will hold them all.
Vice. O damned Deuill, how secure he is.　　　(*175*)
Hier. Secure ? why doest thou wonder at it ?
　　I tell thee, *Vice-roy*, this day I haue seene reuenge,

---

179 can] our *1594 -99*　　*169* slaine *1602 A -15 -18 -23 -33*　　*177* reuenge
1602 A : reuengd *1602 -10 -15 -18 -23 -33*

And in that sight am growne a prowder Monarch
Than euer sate vnder the Crowne of Spaine.
Had I as many liues as there be Starres,   (*180*)
As many Heauens to go to, as those liues,
Ide giue them all, I, and my soule to boote,
But I would see thee ride in this red poole.
Cast. Speake, who were thy confederates in this?
Vice. That was thy daughter *Bel-imperia*;   (*185*)
For by her hand my *Balthazar* was slaine:
I saw her stab him.
Hier. O, good words : as deare to me was my *Horatio*,
As yours, or yours, or yours, my L⟨ord⟩, to you.
My guiltles Sonne was by *Lorenzo* slaine,   (*190*)
And by *Lorenzo* and that *Balthazar*
Am I at last reuenged thorowly,
Vpon whose soules may heauens be yet reuenged
With greater far then these afflictions.
Mee thinkes, since I grew inward with *Reuenge*,   (*195*)
I can not looke with scorne enough on Death.
King. What, dost thou mocke us, slaue? bring torturs forth.
Hier. Doe, doe, doe; and meane time Ile torture you.
You had a Sonne (as I take it), and your Sonne
Shuld ha'e been married to your daughter : ha, wast not so? (*200*)
You had a Sonne too, hee was my Liege's Nephew;
Hee was proud and politicke. Had he liued,
Hee might a come to weare the crowne of *Spaine*—
I thinke twas so : twas I that killed him;
Looke you, this same hand twas it that stab'd   (*205*)
His hart—doe ye see? this hand—
For one *Horatio*, if you euer knew him :
A youth, one that they hanged vp in his father's garden,
One that did force your valiant Sonne to yeeld,
While your more valiant Sonne did take him prisoner.   (*210*)
Vice. Be deafe, my senses, I can heare no more.
King. Fall, heauen, and couer vs with thy sad ruines.
Cast. Rowle all the world within thy pitchie cloud.
Hier. Now do I applaud what I haue acted.
              Nunc iners cadat manus.   (*215*)
Now to expresse the rupture of my part,
First take my tongue, and afterward my heart.

                                    He bites out his tongue.

---

184 Speake (*instead of original* But) *1602 and later Qq.*   *193* reuenged
(*instead of original* auenged) *1602 and later Qq.*   *197* thou *om. 1623 -33*
205 was it *1618 -23 -33*   *206* you *1610 -15 -18 -23 -33*   *210* more *om. 1615*
-18 -23 -33   *215* iners cadat manus *emend. Schick* : mors caede manus *1602* :
mers cadae manus *1602 A -10 -15 -18* : mens cadae manus *1623 -33*   *216*
rapture *Dodsley, Reed, Collier*

King. O monstrous resolution of a wretch.
　See, *Vice-roy,* he hath bitten foorth his tung
　.Rather then to reueale what we requirde.
Cast. Yet can he write.
King. And if in this he satisfie us not,　　　　　　　195 *(222)*
　We will deuise the 'xtremest kinde of death
　That euer was inuented for a wretch.

　　　　　Then he makes signes for a knife to mend his pen.

Cast. O, he would haue a knife to mend his pen.
Vice. Heere, and aduise thee that thou write the troth.
King. Looke to my brother, saue *Hieronimo.*　　　200 *(227)*

　　　　　He with a knife stabs the Duke and himselfe.

　What age hath euer heard such monstrous deeds?
　My brother, and the whole succeeding hope
　That Spaine expected after my discease.
　Go, beare his body hence, that we may mourne
　The losse of our beloued brothers death;　　　　205 *(232)*
　That he may bee entom'd, what ere befall.
　I am the next, the neerest, last of all.
Vice. And thou, *Don Pedro,* do the like for vs:
　Take up our haples sonne, vntimelie slaine:
　Set me with him, and he with wofull me,　　　　210 *(237)*
　Vpon the maine mast of a ship vnmand,
　And let the winde and tide hall me along
　To *Silla's* barking and vntamed gulfe,
　Or to the loathsome pool of *Acheron,*
　To weepe my want for my sweet *Balthazar*:　　215 *(242)*
　Spaine hath no refuge for a Portingale.

The Trumpets sound a dead march, the King of Spaine *mourning
　after his brothers body, and the* King of Portingale *bearing the
　body of his sonne.*

〈SCENE V.〉

Enter Ghoast *and* Reuenge.

Ghoast. I, now my hopes haue end in their effects,

　S.D. *Then om. 1602 and later Qq.*　　200 *King. before* 201, *Qq.* *See Note*
S.D. *a*} *the 1602 and later Qq.*　　203 That] Of *1615 -18 -23 -33*　　212 hale
1599, 1602 -10 -15 -18 -23 -33　　213 gulfe *1623 -33*: greefe *Allde, 1594 -99,
1602 -10 -15 -18*　　215 for] of *1623 -33*

When blood and sorrow finnish my desires :
Horatio murdered in his Fathers bower ;
Vilde *Serberine* by *Pedringano* slaine ;
False *Pedringano* hangd by quaint deuice ;   5
Faire *Isabella* by her selfe misdone ;
Prince *Balthazar* by *Bel-imperia* stabd ;
The Duke of *Castile* and his wicked Sonne
Both done to death by olde *Hieronimo* ;
My *Bel-imperia* falne as *Dido* fell,   10
And good *Hieronimo* slaine by himselfe :
I, these were spectacles to please my soule.
Now will I beg at louely *Proserpine*,
That, by the vertue of her Princely doome,
I may consort my freends in pleasing sort,   15
And on my foes worke iust and sharp reuenge.
Ile lead my freend *Horatio* through those feeldes,
Where neuer dying warres are still inurde ;
Ile lead faire *Isabella* to that traine,
Where pittie weepes, but neuer feeleth paine ;   20
Ile lead my *Bel-imperia* to those ioyes
That vestall Virgins and faire Queenes possesse ;
Ile lead *Hieronimo* where *Orpheus* plaies,
Adding sweet pleasure to eternall daies.
But say, *Reuenge*, for thou must helpe or none,   25
Against the rest how shall my hate be showne ?
Reuenge. This hand shall hale them downe to deepest hell,
Where none but furies, bugs, and tortures dwell.
Ghoast. Then, sweet *Reuenge*, doe this at my request :
Let me be iudge, and doome them to vnrest.   30
Let loose poore *Titius* from the Vultures gripe,
And let *Don Ciprian* supply his roome ;
Place *Don Lorenzo* on *Ixions* Wheele,
And let the louers endles paines surcease
(*Iuno* forgets olde wrath, and graunts him ease) ;   35
Hang *Balthazar* about *Chimeras* neck,
And let him there bewaile his bloudy loue,
Repining at our ioyes that are aboue ;
Let *Serberine* goe roule the fatall stone,

---

17 my] me *1594*   28 none] nought *Qq. exc. Allde*

And take from *Siciphus* his endles mone ;   40
False *Pedringano*, for his trecherie,
Let him be dragde through boyling *Acheron*,
And there liue, dying still in endles flames,
Blaspheming Gods and all their holy names.
Reuenge. Then haste we doune to meet thy freends and foes :   45
To place thy freends in ease, the rest in woes ;
For heere, though death hath end their miserie,
Ile there begin their endles Tragedie.
                                                    Exeunt.

---

47 hath] doth *1623 -33*

FINIS.

H 2

Pompey the Great,

his faire
Corneliaes Tragedie:

Effected by her Father and Huſ-
bandes downe-caſt, death,
and fortune.

Written in French, by that excellent
Poet Ro: Garnier; and tran
ſlated into Engliſh by Thomͦ
Kid.

AT LONDON
Printed for Nicholas Ling.
1595.

TO

THE VERTVOVSLY NOBLE, AND RIGHTLY HONOVRED LADY,

THE COVNTESSE OF SVSSEX

Hauing no leysure (most noble Lady) but such as euermore is traueld with th' afflictions of the minde, then which the world affoords no greater misery, it may bee wondred at by some, how I durst vndertake a matter of this moment : which both requireth cunning, rest and oportunity ; but chiefely, that I would attempt the dedication of so rough, vnpollished a worke to the suruey of your so worthy selfe.

But beeing well instructed in your noble and heroick dispositions, and perfectly assur'd of your honourable fauours past (though neyther making needles glozes of the one, nor spoyling paper with the others Pharisaical embroiderie), I haue presum'd vpon your true conceit and entertainement of these small endeuours, that thus I purposed to make known my memory of you and them to be immortall.

A fitter present for a Patronesse so well accomplished I could not finde then this faire president of honour, magnamitie, and loue. Wherein, what grace that excellent GARNIER hath lost by my defaulte, I shall beseech your Honour to repaire with the regarde of those so bitter times and priuie broken passions that I endured in the writing it.

And so vouchsafing but the passing of a Winters weeke with desolate *Cornelia*, I will assure your Ladiship my next Sommers better trauell with the Tragedy of *Portia*. And euer spend one howre of the day in some kind seruice to your Honour, and another of the night in wishing you all happines. Perpetually thus deuoting my poore selfe

Yours Honors in

all humblenes

T. K.

THE ARGVMENT

CORNELIA, the daughter of *Metellus Scipio*, a young Romaine Lady
(as much accomplisht with the graces of the bodie, and the vertues of
the minde as euer any was), was first married to young *Crassus*, who
died with his Father in the disconfiture of the Romains against the
Parthians ; Afterward she tooke to second husbande *Pompey* the great, 5
who (three yeeres after) vpon the first fiers of the ciuill warres betwixt
him and *Caesar*, sent her fro thence to *Mitilen*, there to attende the
incertaine successe of those affaires. And when he sawe that hee was
vanquisht at *Pharsalia*, returnd to find her out, and carrie her with
him into Egipt, where his purpose was to have reenforc'd a newe 10
Armie, and give a second assault to *Caesar*.

In this voyage hee was murdred by *Achillas* and *Septimius* the
Romaine before her eyes, and in the presence of his young Sonne
Sextus, and some other Senators his friends. After which, shee retyred
herselfe to Rome. But *Scipio* her Father (beeing made Generall of 15
those that suruiued after the battaile) assembled new forces, and occupied the greater part of Afrique, allying himselfe to *Iuba* King of
Numidia. Against all whom *Caesar* (after he had ordred the affayres
of Egipt and the state of Rome) in the end of Winter marched. And
there (after many light encounters) was a fierce and furious battaile 20
giuen amongst them, neere the walls of *Tapsus*. Where *Scipio* seeing
himselfe subdued and his Armie scattered, he betooke himselfe, with
some small troope, to certaine shippes which he had caused to stay for
him. Thence he sailed towarde *Spayne*, where *Pompeys* Faction
commaunded, and where a suddaine tempest tooke him on the Sea, 25
that draue him backe to *Hippon*, a Towne in Affrique at the deuotion
of *Caesar*, where (lying at anchor) he was assailed, beaten and assaulted by the aduerse Fleete; And for hee woulde not fall aliue into the
hands of his so mightie Enemie, hee stabd himselfe, and suddainly
leapt ouer boord into the Sea, and there dyed. 30

Caesar (hauing finished these warres, and quietly reduc'd the Townes
and places there-about to his obedience) return'd to Rome in tryumph
for his victories; Where this most faire and miserable Ladie, hauing
ouer-mourn'd the death of her deere husband, and vnderstanding of
these crosse euents and haples newes of Affrique, together with the 35
pitteous manner of her Fathers ende, shee tooke (as shee had cause)
occasion to redouble both her teares and lamentations : wherewith she
closeth the Catastrophe of this theyr Tragedie.

34 ouer-mour'd *Qq*.

EDITOR'S NOTE

THE text adopted is that of the Quartos of 1594 and 1595, which are identical except in the title-page (cf. *Introduction*). This text is perfect, except for some trifling misprints, given in the notes. I have retained the inverted commas which Kyd, following Garnier, places before a number of moralizing passages, to emphasize their importance.

Other references are as follow :—

Dodsley = Dodsley's edition in his *Old Plays*, vol. xi (1744)

Reed = Reed's edition in his reissue of Dodsley's *Old Plays*, vol. ii (1780)

Collier = Collier's edition in his reissue of Dodsley's *Old Plays*, vol. ii (1825)

Hazlitt = W. C. Hazlitt's edition in his reissue of Dodsley's *Old Plays*, vol. v (1874)

Gassner = Dr. H. Gassner's edition (1894)

Details about these editions are given in the *Introduction*.

INTERLOCVTORES

M. Cicero.	Cornelia.
Phillip.	C. Cassius.
Deci⟨mus⟩ Brutus.	Julius Caesar.
M. Anthony.	The Messenger.

Chorus.

CORNELIA

ACTVS PRIMVS.

Cic. Vouchsafe Immortals, and (aboue the rest)
  Great *Iupiter*, our Citties sole Protector,
  That if (prouok'd against vs by our euils)
  You needs wil plague vs with your ceasles wroth,
  At least to chuse those forth that are in fault,   5
  And saue the rest in these tempestious broiles :
  Els let the mischiefe that should them befall
  Be pour'd on me, that one may die for all.
  Oft hath such sacrafice appeas'd your ires,
  And oft yee haue your heauie hands with-held   10
  From this poore people, when (with one mans losse)
  Your pittie hath preseru'd the rest vntucht :
  But we, disloiall to our owne defence,
  Faint-harted do those liberties enthrall,
  Which to preserue (vnto our after good)   15
  Our fathers hazarded their derest blood.
  Yet *Brutus Manlius*, hardie *Scevola*,
  And stout *Camillus*, are returnd fro *Stix*,
  Desiring Armes to ayde our Capitoll.
  Yea, come they are, and, fiery as before,   20
  Vnder a Tyrant see our bastard harts
  Lye idely sighing, while our shamefull soules
  Endure a million of base controls.
  Poysoned Ambition (rooted in high mindes),
  T'is thou that train'st vs into all these errors :   25
  Thy mortall couetize peruerts our lawes,
  And teares our freedom from our franchiz'd harts.

Our fathers found thee at their former walls;
And humbled to theyr of-spring left thee dying.
Yet thou, reuiuing, soyl'dst our Infant Towne   30
With guiltles blood by brothers hands out-lanched;
And hongst (O Hell) upon a Forte halfe finisht
Thy monstrous murder for a thing to marke.
'But faith continues not where men command.
'Equals are euer bandying for the best: 35
'A state deuided cannot firmely stand.
'Two kings within one realme could neuer rest.
Thys day, we see, the father and the sonne
Haue fought like foes Pharsalias miserie;
And with their blood made marsh the parched plaines, 40
While th' earth, that gron'd to beare theyr carkasses,
Bewail'd th' insatiat humors of them both,
That as much blood in wilfull follie spent,
As were to tame the world sufficient.
Now, Parthia, feare no more, for *Crassus* death   45
That we will come thy borders to besiege:
Nor feare the darts of our couragious troopes.
For those braue souldiers, that were (sometime) wont
To terrifie thee with their names, are dead.
And ciuill furie, fiercer then thine hosts,   50
Hath in a manner this great Towne oreturn'd,
That whilom was the terror of the world,
Of whom so many Nations stood in feare,
To whom so many Nations prostrate stoopt,
Ore whom (saue heauen) nought could signorize,   55
And whom (saue heauen) nothing could afright;
Impregnable, immortall, and whose power,
Could neuer haue beene curb'd, but by it selfe.
For neither could the flaxen-haird high Dutch
(A martiall people madding after Armes),   60
Nor yet the fierce and fiery humor'd French,
The More that trauels to the Lybian sands,
The Greek, Th' Arabian, Macedons or Medes,
Once dare t'assault it, or attempt to lift

---

30 soyld'st *editors*: foyl'dst *Qq*.   46 we *Qq*.: he *Hazlitt, wrongly*:
cf. Nous allions rassaillir *Garnier*

Theyr humbled heads, in presence of proud Rome :   65
But, by our Lawes from libertie restraynd,
Like Captiues lyu'd eternally enchaynd.
But Rome (alas) what helps it that thou ty'dst
The former World to thee in vassalage?
What helps thee now t'haue tam'd both land and Sea?   70
What helps it thee that vnder thy controll
The Morne and Mid-day both by East and West,
And that the golden Sunne, where ere he driue
His glittring Chariot, findes our Ensignes spred,
Sith it contents not thy posteritie ;   75
But as a bayte for pride (which spoiles vs all,)
Embarques vs in so perilous a way,
As menaceth our death and thy decay?
For, Rome, thou now resemblest a ship,
At random wandring in a boistrous Sea,   80
When foming billowes feele the Northern blasts:
Thou toyl'st in perrill, and the windie storme
Doth topside-turuey tosse thee as thou flotest :
Thy Mast is shyuer'd, and thy maine-saile torne ;
Thy sides sore beaten, and thy hatches broke;   85
Thou want'st thy tackling, and a Ship vnrig'd
Can make no shift to combat with the Sea.
See how the Rocks do heaue their heads at thee,
Which if thou sholdst but touch, thou straight becomst
A spoyle to *Neptune*, and a sportfull praie   90
To th' Glauc's and Trytons, pleasd with thy decay.
Thou vaunt'st not of thine Auncestors in vaine,
But vainely count'st thine owne victorious deeds.
What helpeth vs the things that they did then,
Now we are hated both of Gods and men?   95
' Hatred accompanies prosperitie,
' For one man grieueth at anothers good,
' And so much more we thinke our miserie,
' The more that Fortune hath with others stood :
' So that we sild are seene, as wisedom would,   100
' To brydle time with reason as we should.

---

72 Morne] North *Gassner.   See Note*

'For we are proude, when Fortune fauours vs,
'As if inconstant Chaunce were alwaies one,
'Or, standing now, she would continue thus.
'O fooles, looke back and see the roling stone,   105
'Whereon she blindly lighting sets her foote,
'And slightly sowes that sildom taketh roote.
Heauen heretofore (enclinde to do vs good)
Did fauour vs with conquering our foes,
When iealous Italie (exasperate   110
With our vp-rising) sought our Cittjes fall.
But we, soone tickled with such flattring hopes,
Wag'd further warre with an insatiate hart,
And tyerd our neighbour Countries so with charge,
As with their losse we did our bounds enlarge.   115
Carthage and Sicily we haue subdude,
And almost yoked all the world beside :
And, soly through desire of publique rule,
Rome and the earth are waxen all as one :
Yet now we liue despoild and robd by one   120
Of th' ancient freedom wherein we were borne.
And euen that yoke, that wont to tame all others,
Is heauily return'd vpon our selues—
A note of Chaunce that may the proude controle,
And shew Gods wrath against a cruell soule.   125
'For heauen delights not in vs, when we doe
'That to another, which our selues dysdaine :
'Iudge others, as thou wouldst be iudg'd againe,
'And do but as thou wouldst be done vnto.
'For, sooth to say, (in reason) we deserue   130
'To haue the selfe-same measure that we serue.
What right had our ambitious auncestors
(Ignobly issued from the Carte and Plough)
To enter Asia ? What, were they the heires
To Persia or the Medes, first Monarchies ?   135
What interest had they to Afferique ?
To Gaule or Spaine ? Or what did *Neptune* owe vs
Within the bounds of further Brittanie ?
Are we not thieues and robbers of those Realmes
That ought vs nothing but reuenge for wrongs ?   140
What toucheth vs the treasure or the hopes,

The lyues or lyberties of all those Nations,
Whom we by force haue held in seruitude;
Whose mournfull cryes and shreekes to heauen ascend,
Importuning both vengeance and defence   145
Against this Citty, ritch of violence?
'Tis not enough (alas) our power t'extend,
'Or ouer-runne the world from East to West,
'Or that our hands the Earth can comprehend,
'Or that we proudly doe what lyke vs best.   150
'He lyues more quietly whose rest is made,
'And can with reason chasten his desire,
'Then he that blindly toyleth for a shade,
'And is with others Empyre set on fire.
'Our blysse consists not in possessions,   155
'But in commaunding our affections,
'In vertues choyse, and vices needfull chace
'Farre from our harts, for stayning of our face.

Chor. Vpon thy backe (where miserie doth sit),
   O *Rome*, the heauens with their wrathful hand   160
Reuenge the crymes thy fathers did commit.
But if (their further furie to withstand,
Which ore thy walls thy wrack sets menacing)
Thou dost not seeke to calme heauens ireful king,
A further plague will pester all the land.   165

'The wrath of heauen (though vrg'd) we see is slow
'In punishing the euils we haue done:
'For what the Father hath deseru'd, we know,
'Is spar'd in him, and punisht in the sonne.
'But to forgiue the apter that they be,   170
'They are the more displeased, when they see
'That we continue our offence begunne.

'Then from her lothsome Caue doth Plague repaire,
'That breaths her heauie poisons downe to hell:
'Which with their noisome fall corrupt the ayre,   175
'Or maigre famin, which the weake foretell,
'Or bloody warre (of other woes the worst)
'Which, where it lights, doth show the Land accurst,
And nere did good, where euer it befell.

Warre, that hath sought Th' Ausonian fame to reare 180
In warlike *Emonye* (now growne so great
With Souldiers bodies that were buried there);
Which yet, to sack vs, toyles in bloody sweat
T'enlarge the bounds of conquering *Thessalie*,
Through murder, discord, wrath, and enmitie, 185
Euen to the peacefull Indians pearled seate.

Whose entrails fyerd with rancor, wrath and rage,
The former petty combats did displace,
And Campe to Campe did endlesse battailes wage;
Which, on the Mountaine tops of warlike *Thrace*, 190
Made thundring *Mars* (Dissentions common friend)
Amongst the forward Souldiers first discend,
Arm'd with his blood-besmeard keene Coutelace.

Who first attempted to excite to Armes
The troopes enraged with the Trumpets sound, 195
Head-long to runne and reck no after harmes,
Where in the flowred Meades dead men were found,
Falling as thick (through warlike crueltie)
As eares of Corne, for want of husbandry,
That (wastfull) shed their graine vppon the ground. 200

O warre, if thou were subiect but to death,
And by desert mightst fall to *Phlegiton*,
The torment that *Ixion* suffereth,
Or his whose soule the Vulter seazeth on,
Were all too little to reward thy wrath: 205
Nor all the plagues that fierie *Pluto* hath
The most outragious sinners layd vpon.

Accursed Catiues, wretches that wee are,
Perceiue we not that for the fatall dombe
The Fates make hast enough, but we (by warre) 210
Must seeke in Hell to haue a haples roome?
Or fast enough doe foolish men not die,
But they (by murther of themselues) must hie,
Hopeles to hide them in a haples tombe?

---

202 mighst *Qq.*

All sad and desolate our Citty lyes,   215
And for faire Corne-ground are our fields surcloid
With worthles Gorse, that yerely fruitles dyes,
And choakes the good, which els we had enioy'd.
Death dwels within vs, and if gentle Peace
Discend not soone, our sorrowes to surcease,   220
Latium (alreadie quaild) will be destroyd.

ACTVS SECVNDVS.

Cornelia.   Cicero.

⟨*Corn.*⟩ And wil ye needs bedew my dead-grown ioyes,
And nourish sorrow with eternall teares ?
O eyes, and will yee (cause I cannot dry
Your ceaselesse springs) not suffer me to die ?
Then make the blood fro forth my branch-like vaines,   5
Lyke weeping Riuers, trickle by your vaults ;
And spunge my bodies heate of moisture so,
As my displeased soule may shunne my hart.
Heauens, let me dye, and let the Destinies
Admit me passage to th' infernall Lake ;   10
That my poore ghost may rest where powerfull fate
In Deaths sad kingdom hath my husband lodg'd.
Fayne would I die, but darksome vgly Death
With-holds his darte, and in disdaine doth flye me,
Malitiously knowing that hels horror   15
Is mylder then mine endles discontent,
And that, if Death vpon my life should seaze,
The payne supposed would procure mine ease.
But yee, sad Powers, that rule the silent deepes
Of dead-sad Night, where sinnes doe maske vnseene :   20
You that amongst the darksome mansions
Of pyning ghosts, twixt sighes, and sobs, and teares,
Do exercise your mirthlesse Empory :
Yee gods (at whose arbitrament all stand)
Dislodge my soule, and keepe it with your selues,   25
For I am more then halfe your prysoner.

218 choake *Qq.*

My noble husbands (more then noble soules)
Already wander vnder your commaunds.
O then shall wretched I, that am but one,
(Yet once both theyrs) suruiue, now they are gone?   30
Alas, thou shouldst, thou shouldst, *Cornelia,*
Haue broke the sacred thred that tyde thee heere,
When as thy husband *Crassus* (in his flowre)
Did first beare Armes, and bare away my loue :
And not (as thou hast done) goe break the bands   35
By calling *Hymen* once more back againe.
Lesse haples, and more worthily thou might'st
Haue made thine auncesters and thee renound,
If (like a royall Dame) with faith fast kept,
Thou with thy former husbands death hadst slept.   40
But partiall Fortune, and the powerful Fates,
That at their pleasures wield our purposes,
Bewitcht my life, and did beguile my loue.
Pompey, the fame that ranne of thy frayle honors,
Made me thy wife, thy loue, and (like a thiefe)   45
From my first husband stole my faithles griefe.
But if (as some belieue) in heauen or hell
Be heauenly powers, or infernall spirits,
That care to be aueng'd of Louers othes,
Oathes made in marriage, and after broke,   50
Those powers, those spirits (mou'd with my light faith)
Are now displeas'd with *Pompey* and my selfe,
And doe with ciuill discord (furthering it)
Vntye the bands that sacred *Hymen* knyt.
Els onely I am cause of both theyr wraths,   55
And of the sinne that ceeleth vp thine eyes,
O deplorable *Pompey*; I am shee,
I am that plague, that sacks thy house and thee.
For tis not heauen, nor *Crassus* (cause hee sees
That I am thine) in iealosie pursues vs.   60
No, tis a secrete crosse, an vnknowne thing,
That I receiu'd from heauen at my birth,
That I should heape misfortunes on theyr head,
Whom once I had receiu'd in marriage bed.

56, 57 And . . . thine eyes, | Thine eyes, O deplorable . . . shee *Qq.*

Then yee, the noble Romulists that rest,   65
Hence-forth forbeare to seeke my murdring loue,
And let theyr double losse that held me deere,
Byd you beware for feare you be beguild.
Ye may be ritch and great in Fortunes grace,
And all your hopes with hap may be effected,   70
But if yee once be wedded to my loue,
Clowdes of aduersitie will couer you.
So (pestilently) fraught with change of plagues
Is mine infected bosome from my youth,
Like poyson that (once lighting in the body)   75
No sooner tutcheth then it taints the blood—
One while the hart, another while the liuer
(According to th' encountring passages),
Nor spareth it what purely feeds the hart,
More then the most infected filthiest part.   80
Pompey, what holpe it thee, (say, deerest life)
Tell mee what holpe thy warlike valiant minde
T' encounter with the least of my mishaps?
What holpe it thee that vnder thy commaund
Thou saw'st the trembling earth with horror mazed?   85
Or (where the sunne forsakes the Ocean sea,
Or watereth his Coursers in the West)
T' haue made thy name be farre more fam'd and feard
Then Summers thunder to the silly Heard?
What holpe it that thou saw'st, when thou wert young,   90
Thy Helmet deckt with coronets of Bayes?
So many enemies in battaile ranged
Beat backe like flyes before a storme of hayle?
T' haue lookt a-skance, and see so many Kings
To lay their Crownes and Scepters at thy feete;   95
T' embrace thy knees, and, humbled by theyr fate,
T' attend thy mercy in this mornefull state?
Alas, and here-withall what holpe it thee
That euen in all the corners of the earth
Thy wandring glory was so greatly knowne?   100
And that Rome saw thee while thou tryumph'dst thrice
O're three parts of the world that thou hadst yok'd?

86 th' *Qq*.

That *Neptune*, weltring on the windie playnes,
Escapt not free fro thy victorious hands?
Since thy hard hap, since thy fierce destinie   105
(Enuious of all thine honors) gaue thee mee,
By whom the former course of thy faire deeds
Might (with a byting brydle) bee restraind;
By whom the glorie of thy conquests got
Might die disgrac'd with mine vnhappines.   110
O haples wife, thus ominous to all,
Worse than *Megera*, worse than any plague:
What foule infernall, or what stranger hell
Hence-forth wilt thou inhabite, where thy hap
None others hopes with mischiefe may entrap?   115
Cic. What end (O race of *Scipio*) will the Fates
Afford your teares? Will that day neuer come
That your desastrous griefes shall turne to ioy,
And we haue time to burie our annoy?
Corn. Ne're shall I see that day, for Heauen and Time   120
Haue faild in power to calme my passion.
Nor can they (should they pittie my complaints)
Once ease my life, but with the pangs of death.
Cic. 'The wide worlds accidents are apt to change;
'And tickle Fortune staies not in a place,   125
'But (like the Clowdes) continuallie doth range,
'Or like the Sunne that hath the Night in chace.
'Then, as the Heauens (by whom our hopes are guided)
'Doe coast the Earth with an eternall course,
'We must not thinke a miserie betided   130
'Will neuer cease, but still grow worse and worse.
'When Isie Winter's past, then comes the spring,
'Whom Sommers pride (with sultrie heate) pursues,
'To whom mylde Autumne doth earths treasure bring,
'The sweetest season that the wise can chuse.   135
'Heauens influence was nere so constant yet,
'In good or bad as to continue it.
When I was young, I saw against poore *Sylla*
Proud *Cynna*, *Marius*, and *Carbo* flesh'd
So long, till they gan tiranize the Towne,   140
And spilt such store of blood in euery street,
As there were none but dead-men to be seene.

Within a while, I saw how Fortune plaid,
And wound those Tyrants vnderneath her wheele,
Who lost theyr liues, and power at once by one   145
That (to reuenge himselfe) did (with his blade)
Commit more murther then Rome euer made.
Yet *Sylla*, shaking tyrannie aside,
Return'd due honors to our Common-wealth,
Which peaceably retain'd her auncient state,   150
Growne great without the strife of Cittizens,
Till thys ambitious Tyrants time, that toyld
To stoope the world and Rome to his desires.
But flattring Chaunce, that trayn'd his first designes,
May change her lookes, and giue the Tyrant ouer,   155
Leauing our Cittie, where so long agoe
Heauens did theyr fauors lauishly bestow.
Corn. Tis true, the Heauens (at least-wise if they please)
May giue poore Rome her former libertie :
But (though they would) I know they cannot giue   160
A second life to *Pompey* that is slaine.
Cic. Mourne not for *Pompey*: *Pompey* could not die
A better death then for his Countries weale.
For oft he search't amongst the fierce allarms,
But (wishing) could not find so faire an end ;   165
Till, fraught with yeeres and honor both at once,
Hee gaue his bodie (as a Barricade)
For Romes defence, by Tyrants ouer-laide.
Brauely he died, and (haplie) takes it ill
That (enuious) we repine at heauens will.   170
Corn. Alas, my sorrow would be so much lesse,
If he had died, his fauchin in his fist.
Had hee amidst huge troopes of Armed men
Beene wounded by another any waie,
It would haue calmed many of my sighes.   175
For why, t' haue seene his noble Roman blood
Mixt with his enemies, had done him good.
But hee is dead, (O heauens), not dead in fight,
With pike in hand vpon a Forte besieg'd,
Defending of a breach ; but basely slaine,   180
Slaine trayterouslie, without assault in warre.
Yea, slaine he is, and bitter chaunce decreed

To haue me there, to see this bloody deed.
I saw him, I was there, and in mine armes
He almost felt the poygnard when he fell.   185
Whereat my blood stopt in my stragling vaines;
Mine haire grew bristled, like a thornie groue;
My voyce lay hid, halfe dead, within my throate;
My frightfull hart (stund in my stone-cold breast)
Faintlie redoubled eu'ry feeble stroke;   190
My spirite (chained with impatient rage)
Did rauing striue to breake the prison ope;
(Enlarg'd) to drowne the payne it did abide
In solitary *Lethes* sleepie tyde.
Thrice (to absent me from thys hatefull light)   195
I would haue plung'd my body in the Sea;
And thrice detaind, with dolefull shreeks and cryes,
(With armes to heauen uprear'd) I gan exclaime
And bellow forth against the Gods themselues
A bedroll of outragious blasphemies: 200
Till (griefe to heare, and hell for me to speake)
My woes waxt stronger, and my selfe grew weake.
Thus day and night I toyle in discontent,
And sleeping wake, when sleepe it selfe, that rydes
Upon the mysts, scarce moysteneth mine eyes.   205
Sorrow consumes mee, and, in steed of rest,
With folded armes I sadly sitte and weepe;
And if I winck, it is for feare to see
The fearefull dreames effects that trouble mee.
O heauens, what shall I doe? alas, must I,   210
Must I my selfe be murderer of my selfe?
Must I my selfe be forc'd to ope the way
Whereat my soule in wounds may sally forth?
Cic. Madam, you must not thus transpose your selfe;
Wee see your sorrow, but who sorrowes not?   215
The griefe is common. And I muse, besides
The seruitude that causeth all our cares,
Besides the basenes wherein we are yoked,
Besides the losse of good men dead and gone,
What one he is that in this broile hath bin,   220

---

196 plund'd *Qq*.   198 uprea'd *Qq*.

And mourneth not for some man of his kin?
Corn. If all the world were in the like distresse,
  My sorrow yet would neuer seeme the lesse.
Cic. 'O, but men beare mis-fortunes with more ease,
  'The more indifferently that they fall ;   225
  'And nothing more (in vprores) men can please
  'Then when they see their woes not worst of all.
Corn. 'Our friendes mis-fortune doth increase our owne.
Cic. 'But ours ·of others will not be acknowne.
Corn. 'Yet one mans sorrow will another tutch.   230
Cic. 'I, when himselfe will entertaine none such.
Corn. 'Anothers teares draw teares fro forth our eyes.
Cic. 'And choyce of streames the greatest Riuer dryes.
Corn. When sand within a Whirl-poole lyes vnwet,
  My teares shall dry, and I my griefe forget.   235
Cic. What boote your teares, or what auailes your sorrow
  Against th' ineuitable dart of Death?
  Thinke you to moue with lamentable plaints
  Persiphone, or *Plutos* gastlie spirits,
  To make him liue that's locked in his tombe,   240
  And wandreth in the Center of the earth?
  'No, no, *Cornelia*, *Caron* takes not paine
  'To ferry those that must be fetcht againe.
Corn. Proserpina indeed neglects my plaints,
  And hell it selfe is deafe to my laments.   245
  Vnprofitably should I waste my teares,
  If ouer *Pompey* I should weepe to death,
  With hope to haue him be reuiu'd by them.
  Weeping auailes not : therefore doe I weepe.
  Great losses greatly are to be deplor'd :   250
  The losse is great that cannot be restor'd.
Cic. 'Nought is immortall vnderneath the Sunne ;
  'All things are subiect to Deaths tiranny :
  'Both Clownes and Kings one self-same course must run,
  'And what-soeuer liues is sure to die.   255
  Then wherefore mourne you for your husband's death,
  Sith, being a man, he was ordain'd to die?
  Sith *Ioues* owne sonnes, retaining humane shape,

---

250 depror'd : *Qq*.

No more then wretched we their death could scape.
Brave *Scipio*, your famous auncestor,   260
That Romes high worth to Affrique did extend ;
And those two *Scipios* (that in person fought,
Before the fearefull Carthagenian walls),
Both brothers, and both warrs fierce lightning fiers—
Are they not dead ? Yes, and their death (our dearth) 265
Hath hid them both embowel'd in the earth.
And those great Cities, whose foundations reacht
From deepest hell, and with their tops tucht heauen ;
Whose loftie Towers (like thorny-pointed speares),
Whose Temples, Pallaces, and walls embost,   270
In power and force, and fiercenes, seem'd to threat
The tyred world, that trembled with their waight ;
In one daies space (to our eternall mones)
Haue we not seene them turn'd to heapes of stones ?
Carthage can witnes, and thou, heauens handwork,   275
Faire Ilium, razed by the conquering Greekes ;
Whose auncient beautie, worth and weapons seem'd
Sufficient t' haue tam'd the Mermidons.
' But whatsoe're hath been begun, must end.
' Death (haply that our willingnes doth see)   280
' With brandisht dart doth make the passage free ;
' And timeles doth our soules to *Pluto* send.
Corn. Would Death had steept his dart in *Lernas* blood ;
That I were drown'd in the Tartarean deepes ;
I am an offring fit for *Acheron*.   285
A match more equall neuer could be made
Then I and *Pompey* in th' Elisian shade.
Cic. ' Death's alwaies ready, and our time is knowne
' To be at heauens dispose, and not our owne.
Corn. Can wee be ouer-hastie to good hap ?   290
Cic. What good expect wee in a fiery gap ?
Corn. To scape the feares that followes Fortunes glaunces.
Cic. ' A noble minde doth neuer feare mischaunces.
Corn. ' A noble minde disdaineth seruitude.
Cic. ' Can bondage true nobility exclude ?   295

Corn. How, if I doe or suffer that I would not?

Cic. 'True noblesse neuer doth the thing it should not.

Corn. Then must I dye.

Cic.　　　　　　　　Yet dying thinke this stil :
'No feare of death should force vs to doe ill.

Corn. If death be such, why is your feare so rife?　　300

Cic. My works will shew I neuer feard my life.

Corn. And yet you will not that (in our distresse)
　We aske Deaths ayde to end lifes wretchednes.

Cic. 'We neither ought to vrge nor aske a thing,
　'Wherein we see so much assuraunce lyes.　　305
　'But if perhaps some fierce, offended King
　'(To fright vs) sette pale death before our eyes,
　'To force vs doe that goes against our hart ;
　'Twere more then base in vs to dread his dart.
　'But when, for feare of an ensuing ill,　　310
　'We seeke to shorten our appointed race,
　'Then tis (for feare) that we our selues doe kill,
　'So fond we are to feare the worlds disgrace.

Corn. Tis not for frailtie or faint cowardize
　That men (to shunne mischaunces) seeke for death ;　315
　But rather he that seeks it showes himselfe
　Of certaine courage gainst incertaine chaunce.
　'He that retyres not at the threats of death,
　'Is not, as are the vulgar, slightly fraied :
　'For heauen it selfe, nor hels infectious breath,　　320
　'The resolute at any time haue stayed,
　'And (sooth to say) why feare we, when we see
　'The thing we feare lesse then the feare to be?
　Then let me die, my libertie to saue ;
　For tis a death to lyue a Tyrants slaue.　　325

Cic. Daughter, beware how you prouoke the heauens,
　Which in our bodies (as a tower of strength)
　Haue plac'd our soules, and fortefide the same ;
　As discreet Princes sette theyr Garrisons
　In strongest places of theyr Prouinces.　　330
　'Now, as it is not lawfull for a man,
　'At such a Kings departure or decease,

---

319 faied: *Qq.*

'To leaue the place, and falsefie his faith ;
'So, in this case, we ought not to surrender
'That deerer part, till heauen it selfe commaund it.   335
'For as they lent vs life to doe vs pleasure,
'So looke they for returne of such a treasure.
Chor. 'What e're the massie Earth hath fraight,
   'Or on her nurse-like backe sustaines,
'Vpon the will of Heauen doth waite,   340
   'And doth no more then it ordaynes.
'All fortunes, all felicities,
   'Vpon their motion doe depend :
'And from the starres doth still arise
   'Both their beginning and their end.   345
'The Monarchies, that couer all
   'This earthly round with Maiestie,
'Haue both theyr rising and theyr fall
   'From heauen and heauens varietie.
'Fraile men, or mans more fraile defence,   350
   'Had neũer power to practise stayes
'Of this celestiall influence,
   'That gouuerneth and guides our dayes.
'No clowde but will be ouer-cast ;
   'And what now florisheth, must fade ;   355
'And that that fades, reuiue at last,
   'To florish as it first was made.
'The formes of things doe neuer die,
   'Because the matter that remaines
'Reformes another thing thereby,   360
   'That still the former shape retaines.
The roundnes of two boules cross-cast
   (So they with equall pace be aim'd)
Showes their beginning by their last,
   Which by old nature is new fram'd.   365
So peopled citties, that of yore
   Were desert fields where none would byde,
Become forsaken as before,
   Yet after are re-edified.
Perceiue we not a petty vaine,   370
   Cut from a spring by chaunce or arte,
Engendreth fountaines, whence againe

Those fountaines doe to floods conuart?
Those floods to waues, those waues to seas,
   That oft exceede their wonted bounds :   375
And yet those seas (as heauens please)
   Returne to springs by vnder-grounds.
Euen so our cittie (in her prime
   Prescribing Princes euery thing)
Is now subdu'de by conquering Time,   380
   And liueth subiect to a king.
And yet perhaps the sun-bright crowne,
   That now the Tyrans head doth deck,
May turne to *Rome* with true renoune,
   If fortune chaunce but once to check.   385
The stately walls that once were rear'd,
   And by a shephards hands erect,
(With haples brothers blood besmear'd)
   Shall show by whom they were infect.
And once more vniust *Tarquins* frowne   390
   (With arrogance and rage enflam'd)
Shall keepe the Romaine valure downe,
   And *Rome* it selfe a while be tam'd.
And chastest *Lucrece* once againe
   (Because her name dishonored stood)   395
Shall by herselfe be carelesse slaine,
   And make a riuer of her blood ;
Scorning her soule a seate should builde
   Within a body, basely seen
By shameles rape to be defilde,   400
   That earst was cleere as heauens Queene.
But, heauens, as tyrannie shall yoke
   Our basterd harts with seruile thrall ;
So grant your plagues (which they prouoke)
   May light vpon them once for all.   405
And let another *Brutus* rise,
   Brauely to fight in *Romes* defence,
To free our Towne from tyrannie,
   And tyrannous proud insolence.

---

409 tyranny's *Hazlitt*

ACTVS TERTIVS.

⟨SCENE I.⟩

Cornelia.   Chorus.

⟨*Corn.*⟩ The cheerefull Cock (the sad nights comforter),
    Wayting vpon the rysing of the Sunne,
    Doth sing to see how *Cynthia* shrinks her horne,
    While *Clitie* takes her progresse to the East ;
    Where, wringing wet with drops of siluer dew,   5
    Her wonted teares of loue she doth renew.
    The wandring Swallow with her broken song.
    The Country-wench vnto her worke awakes ;
    While *Citherea* sighing walkes to seeke
    Her murdred loue trans-form'd into a Rose :   10
    Whom (though she see) to crop she kindly feares ;
    But (kissing) sighes, and dewes hym with her teares :—
    Sweet teares of loue, remembrancers to tyme,
    Tyme past with me that am to teares conuerted ;
    Whose mournfull passions dull the mornings ioyes,   15
    Whose sweeter sleepes are turnd to fearefull dreames,
    And whose first fortunes (fild with all distresse)
    Afford no hope of future happinesse.
    But what disastrous or hard accident
    Hath bath'd your blubbred eyes in bitter teares,   20
    That thus consort me in my myserie ?
    Why doe you beate your brests ? why mourne you so ?
    Say, gentle sisters, tell me, and belieue
    It grieues me that I know not why you grieue.
Chor. O poore *Cornelia*, haue not wee good cause   25
    For former wrongs to furnish vs with teares ?
Corn. O, but I feare that Fortune seekes new flawes,
    And stil (vnsatisfide) more hatred beares.
Chor. Wherein can Fortune further iniure vs,
    Now we have lost our conquered libertie,   30
    Our Common-wealth, our Empyre, and our honors,
    Vnder thys cruell *Tarquins* tyrannie ?

Vnder his outrage now are all our goods,
Where scattered they runne by Land and Sea
(Lyke exil'd vs) from fertill Italy　　　　　　　　　35
To proudest Spayne, or poorest Getulie.
Corn. And will the heauens, that haue so oft defended
Our Romaine walls from fury of fierce kings,
Not (once againe) returne our Senators,
That from the Lybique playnes and Spanish fields,　　40
With feareles harts do guard our Romaine hopes?
Will they not once againe encourage them
To fill our fields with blood of enemies,
And bring from Affrique to our Capitoll,
Vpon theyr helmes, the Empyre that is stole.　　　45
Then, home-borne houshold gods, and ye good spirits,
To whom in doubtfull things we seeke accesse,
By whom our family hath bene adorn'd,
And graced with the name of Affrican,
Doe ye vouchsafe that thys victorious title　　　　50
Be not expired in *Cornelias* blood;
And that my Father now (in th' Affrique wars)
The selfe-same style by conquest may continue.
But wretched that I am, alas, I feare.
Chor. What feare you, Madam?
Corn.　　　　　　　　　　That the frowning heauens　55
Oppose themselues against vs in theyr wrath.
Chor. Our losse (I hope) hath satis-fide theyr ire.
Corn. O no, our losse lyfts Caesars fortunes hyer.
Chor. Fortune is fickle.
Corn.　　　　　　　　　But hath fayld him neuer.
Chor. The more vnlike she should continue euer.　　60
Corn. My fearefull dreames doe my despairs redouble.
Chor. Why suffer you vayne dreames your heade to trouble?
Corn. Who is not troubled with strange visions?
Chor. That of our spirit are but illusions.　　　　64
Corn. God graunt these dreames to good effect bee brought.
Chor. We dreame by night what we by day haue thought.
Corn. The silent Night, that long had soiurned,
Now gan to cast her sable mantle off,

---

33 his *Qq.* : this *Dodsley, Reed, Collier, Hazlitt*

And now the sleepie Waine-man softly droue
His slow-pac'd Teeme, that long had traueled;   70
When (like a slumber, if you tearme it so)
A dulnes, that disposeth vs to rest,
Gan close the windowes of my watchfull eyes,
Already tyerd and loaden with my teares.
And loe (me thought) came glyding by my bed   75
The ghost of *Pompey*, with a ghastly looke,
All pale and brawne-falne, not in tryumph borne
Amongst the conquering Romans, as he vs'de,
When he (enthroniz'd) at his feete beheld
Great Emperors fast bound in chaynes of brasse,   80
But all amaz'd, with fearefull, hollow eyes,
Hys hayre and beard deform'd with blood and sweat,
Casting a thyn course lynsel .ore hys shoulders,
That (torne in peeces) trayl'd vpon the ground;
And (gnashing of his teeth) vnlockt his iawes,   85
(Which slyghtly couer'd with a scarce-seene skyn)
Thys solemne tale he sadly did begin :
Sleep'st thou, *Cornelia*? sleepst thou, gentle wife,
And seest thy Fathers misery and mine?
Wake, deerest sweete, and (ore our Sepulchers)   90
In pitty show thy latest loue to vs.
Such hap (as ours) attendeth on my sonnes,
The selfe-same foe and fortune following them.
Send *Sextus* ouer to some forraine Nation,
Farre from the common hazard of the warrs;   95
That (being yet sau'd) he may attempt no more
To venge the valure that is tryde before.
He sayd. And suddainly a trembling horror,
A chyl-cold shyuering (setled in my vaines)
Brake vp my slumber; when I opte my lyps   100
Three times to cry, but could nor cry, nor speake.
I mou'd mine head, and flonge abroade mine armes
To entertaine him; but his airie spirit
Beguiled mine embrasements, and (vnkind)
Left me embracing nothing but the wind.   105
O valiant soule, when shall this soule of mine

---

78 he] we *Qq. and editors* : *but cf.* tel qu'il souloit estre *Garnier*

Come visite thee in the Elisian shades?
O deerest life, or when shall sweetest death
Dissolue the fatall trouble of my daies,
And blesse me with my *Pompeys* company?   110
But may my father (O extreame mishap)
And such a number of braue regiments,
Made of so many expert Souldiours,
That lou'd our liberty and follow'd him,
Be so discomfited?   O, would it were   115
But an illusion.
Chor.   Madam, neuer feare.
Nor let a senceles Idol of the nyght
Encrease a more then needfull feare in you.
Corn. My feare proceeds not of an idle dreame,
For tis a trueth that hath astonisht me.   120
I saw great *Pompey*, and I heard hym speake;
And, thinking to embrace him, opte mine armes,
When drousy sleep, that wak'd mee at vnwares,
Dyd with hys flight vnclose my feareful eyes
So suddainly, that yet mee thinks I see him.   125
Howbe-it I cannot tuch him, for he slides
More swiftly from mee then the Ocean glydes.
Chor. 'These are vaine thoughts, or melancholie showes,
'That wont to haunt and trace by cloistred tombes:
'Which eaths appeare in sadde and strange disguises   130
'To pensiue mindes (deceiued wyth theyr shadowes);
'They counterfet the dead in voyce and figure,
'Deuining of our future miseries.
'For when our soule the body hath disgaged,
'It seeks the common passage of the dead,   135
'Downe by the fearefull gates of Acheron,
'Where, when it is by *Aeacus* adiudg'd,
'It eyther turneth to the Stygian Lake,
'Or staies for euer in th' Elisian fields,
'And ne're returneth to the Corse interd,   140
'To walke by night, or make the wise afeard.
'None but ineuitable conquering Death
'Descends to hell, with hope to rise againe;

---

108 or] o *Gassner, unnecessarily*   130 eath's *Qq.*

'For ghosts of men are lockt in fiery gates,
'Fast-guarded by a fell remorceles Monster.   145
'And therefore thinke not it was *Pompeys* spryte,
'But some false *Daemon* that beguild your sight.

⟨SCENE II.⟩

Cicero.

Then, O worlds Queene, O towne that didst extend
Thy conquering armes beyond the Ocean,
And throngdst thy conquests from the Lybian shores
Downe to the Scithian swift-foote feareles Porters,
Thou art embas'd ; and at this instant yeeld'st   5
Thy proud necke to a miserable yoke.
Rome, thou art tam'd, and th' earth, dewd with thy bloode,
Doth laugh to see how thou art signiorizd.
The force of heauen exceeds thy former strength :
For thou, that wont'st to tame and conquer all,   10
Art conquer'd now with an eternall fall.
Now shalt thou march (thy hands fast bound behind thee),
Thy head hung downe, thy cheeks with teares besprent,
Before the victor ; Whyle thy rebell sonne,
With crowned front, tryumphing followes thee.   15
Thy brauest Captaines, whose coragious harts
(Ioyn'd with the right) did re-enforce our hopes,
Now murdred lye for Foule to feede vpon.
Petreus, *Cato*, and *Scipio* are slaine,
And *Iuba*, that amongst the Mores did raigne.   20
Nowe you, whom both the gods and Fortunes grace
Hath sau'd from danger in these furious broyles,
Forbeare to tempt the enemy againe,
For feare you feele a third calamitie.
Caesar is like a brightlie flaming blaze   25
That fiercely burnes a house already fired ;
And, ceaseles lanching out on euerie side,
Consumes the more, the more you seeke to quench it,
Still darting sparcles, till it finde a trayne
To seaze vpon, and then it flames amaine.   30
The men, the Ships, wher-with poore Rome affronts him,
All powreles give proud *Caesars* wrath free passage.

Nought can resist him; all the powre we raise
Turnes but to our misfortune and his prayse.
T'is thou (O Rome) that nurc'd his insolence;   35
T'is thou (O Rome) that gau'st him first the sword
Which murdrer-like against thy selfe he drawes,
And violates both God and Natures lawes.
Lyke morall *Esops* mysled Country swaine,
That fownd a Serpent pyning in the snowe,   40
And full of foolish pitty tooke it vp,
And kindly layd it by his houshold fire,
Till (waxen warme) it nimbly gan to styr,
And stung to death the foole that fostred her.
O gods, that once had care of these our walls,   45
And feareles kept vs from th'assault of foes:
Great *Iupiter*, to whom our Capitol
So many Oxen yeerely sacrafiz'd;
Minerua, Stator, and stoute Thracian *Mars*,
Father to good *Quirinus*, our first founder;   50
To what intent haue ye preseru'd our Towne,
This statelie Towne, so often hazarded
Against the Samnites, Sabins, and fierce Latins?
Why from once footing in our Fortresses
Haue yee repeld the lustie warlike Gaules?   55
Why from Molossus and false *Hanibal*
Haue yee reseru'd the noble Romulists?
Or why from *Catlins* lewde conspiracies
Preseru'd yee Rome by my preuention;
To cast so soone a state, so long defended,   60
Into the bondage where (enthrald) we pine?
To serue no stranger, but amongst vs one
That with blind frenzie buildeth vp his throne?
But if in vs be any vigor resting,
If yet our harts retaine one drop of blood,   65
Caesar, thou shalt not vaunt thy conquest long,
Nor longer hold vs in this seruitude,
Nor shalt thou bathe thee longer in our blood.
For I diuine that thou must vomit it,
Like to a Curre that Carrion hath deuour'd,   70

---

57 preseru'd *Gassner. See Note*

And cannot rest, untill his mawe be scour'd.
Think'st thou to signiorize, or be the King
Of such a number nobler then thy selfe?
Or think'st thou Romains beare such bastard harts,
To let thy tyrannie be vnreueng'd?   75
No; for, mee thinks, I see the shame, the griefe,
The rage, the hatred that they have conceiu'd,
And many a Romaine sword already drawne,
T'enlarge the libertie that thou vsurpst,
And thy dismembred body (stab'd and torne)   80
Dragd through the streets, disdained to bee borne.

⟨Scene III.⟩

Phillip.   Cornelia.

⟨*Phil.*⟩ Amongst the rest of mine extreame mishaps,
    I finde my fortune not the least in this,
    That I haue kept my Maister company,
    Both in his life and at hys latest houre:
    Pompey the great, whom I haue honored   5
    With true deuotion, both aliue and dead.
    One selfe-same shyp containd vs, when I saw
    The murdring Egiptians bereaue his lyfe;
    And when the man that had afright the earth,
    Did homage to it with his deerest blood.   10
    O're whom I shed full many a bitter teare,
    And did performe hys obsequies with sighes:
    And on the strond vpon the Riuer side
    (Where to my sighes the waters seem'd to turne)
    I woaue a Coffyn for his corse of Seggs,   15
    That with the winde dyd waue like bannerets,
    And layd his body to be burn'd thereon.
    Which, when it was consum'd, I kindly tooke,
    And sadly cloz'd within an earthen Vrne
    The ashie reliques of his haples bones;   20
    Which, hauing scapt the rage of wind and Sea,
    I bring to faire *Cornelia* to interr
    Within his Elders Tombe that honoured her.
Corn. Ayh-me, what see I?

Phil.   *Pompeys* tender bones
  Which (in extreames) an earthen Vrne containeth.   25
Corn. O sweet, deere, deplorable cynders.
  O myserable woman, lyuing, dying:
  O poore *Cornelia*, borne to be distrest,
  Why liu'st thou toyl'd, that (dead) mightst lye at rest?
  O faithles hands, that vnder cloake of loue   30
  Did entertaine him, to torment him so.
  O barbarous, inhumaine, hatefull traytors,
  Thys your disloyall dealing hath defam'd
  Your King and his inhospitable seate
  Of the extreamest and most odious cryme   35
  That gainst the heauens might bee imagined.
  For yee haue basely broke the Law of Armes,
  And out-rag'd ouer an afflicted soule;
  Murdred a man that did submit himselfe,
  And iniur'd him that euer vs'd you kindly.   40
  For which misdeed be Egipt pestered
  With battaile, famine, and perpetuall plagues.
  Let Aspics, Serpents, Snakes, and Lybian Beares,
  Tygers and Lyons, breed with you for euer.
  And let fayre Nylus (wont to nurse your Corne)   45
  Couer your Land with Toades and Crocadils,
  That may infect, deuoure, and murder you.
  Els earth make way, and hell receiue them quicke,
  A hatefull race, mongst whom there dooth abide
  All treason, luxurie, and homicide.   50
Phil. Cease these laments.
Corn.   I doe but what I ought
  To mourne his death.
Phil.   Alas, that profits nought.
Corn. Will heauen let treason be vnpunished?
Phil. Heauens will performe what they haue promised.
Corn. I feare the heauens will not heare our prayer.   55.
Phil. The plaints of men opprest doe pierce the ayre.
Corn. Yet *Caesar* liueth still.
Phil.   'Due punishment
  ' Succeedes not alwaies after an offence:

---

26 O sweet, o deere, o deplorable cynders *Gassner*   43 Aspies *Qq.*

'For oftentimes tis for our chastisement
'That heauen doth with wicked men dispence,   60
'That, when they list, they may with vsurie
'For all misdeeds pay home the penaltie.
Corn. This is the hope that feeds my haples daies ;
  Els had my life beene long agoe expired.
  I trust the gods, that see our hourely wrongs,   65
  Will fire his shamefull bodie with their flames ;
  Except some man (resolued) shall conclude
  With *Caesars* death to end our seruitude.
  Els (god to fore) my selfe may liue to see
  His tired corse lye toyling in his blood ;   70
  Gor'd with a thousand stabs, and round about
  The wronged people leape for inward ioy.
  And then come, Murder ; then come, vglie Death ;
  Then, *Lethe,* open thine infernall Lake.
  Ile downe with ioy : because, before I died,   75
  Mine eyes haue seene what I in hart desir'd.
  Pompey may not reuiue, and (*Pompey* dead)
  Let me but see the murdrer murdered.
Phil. *Caesar* bewail'd his death.
Corn.   His death hee mournd,
  Whom, while hee lyu'd, to lyue lyke him hee scornd.   80
Phil. Hee punished his murdrers.
Corn.   Who murdred hym,
  But hee that followd Pompey with the sword ?
  He murdred *Pompey* that pursu'd his death,
  And cast the plot to catch him in the trap :
  Hee that of his departure tooke the spoyle,   85
  Whose fell ambition (founded first in blood)
  By nought but Pompeys lyfe could be with-stood.
Phil. *Photis* and false *Achillas* he beheadded.
Corn. That was because that, *Pompey* being theyr freend,
  They had determin'd once of *Caesars* end.   90
Phil. What got he by his death ?
Corn.   Supremacie.
Phil. Yet *Caesar* speakes of *Pompey* honourablie.

---

80 scorne *Qq.*

Corn. Words are but winde, nor meant he what he spoke.
Phil. He will not let his statues be broke.
Cor. By which disguise (what ere he doth pretend)   95
  His owne from beeing broke he doth defend :
  And by the traynes, where-with he vs allures,
  His owne estate more firmely he assures.
Phil. He tooke no pleasure in his death, you see.
Corn. Because hymselfe of life did not bereaue him.   · 100
Phil. Nay, he was mou'd with former amitie.
Corn. He neuer trusted him, but to deceiue him.
  But, had he lou'd him with a loue vnfained,
  Yet had it beene a vaine and trustlesse league ;
  'For there is nothing in the soule of man   105
  'So firmely grounded, as can qualifie
  'Th'inextinguible thyrst of signiorie.
  'Not heauens feare, nor Countries sacred loue,
  'Nor auncient lawes, nor nuptiall chast desire,
  'Respect of blood, or (that which most should moue)   110
  'The inward zeale that Nature doth require :
  'All these, nor anything we can deuise,
  'Can stoope the hart resolu'd to tyrannize.
Phil. I feare your griefes increase with thys discourse.
Corn. My griefes are such, as hardly can be worse.   115
Phil. 'Tyme calmeth all things.
Corn.   No tyme quallifies
  My dolefull spyrits endles myseries.
  My griefe is lyke a Rock, whence (ceaseles) strayne
  Fresh springs of water at my weeping eyes,
  Still fed by thoughts, lyke floods with winters rayne.   120
  For when, to ease th'oppression of my hart,
  I breathe an Autumne forth of fiery sighes,
  Yet herewithall my passion neither dyes,
  Nor dryes the heate the moysture of mine eyes.
Phil. Can nothing then recure these endlesse teares ?   125
Corn. Yes, newes of *Caesars* death that medcyn beares.
Phil. Madam, beware ; for, should hee heare of thys,
  His wrath against you t'will exasperate.
Corn. I neither stand in feare of him nor his.
Phil. T'is pollicie to feare a powrefull hate.   130
Corn. What can he doe?

Phil.   Madam, what cannot men
  That haue the powre to doe what pleaseth them?
Corn. He can doe mee no mischiefe that I dread.
Phil. Yes, cause your death.
Corn.   Thrise happy were I dead.
Phil. With rigorous torments.
Corn.   Let him torture mee,   135
  Pull me in peeces, famish, fire mee vp,
  Fling mee aliue into a Lyons denn:
  There is no death so hard torments mee so,
  As his extreame tryumphing in our woe.
  But if he will torment me, let him then   140
  Depriue me wholy of the hope of death;
  For I had died before the fall of Rome,
  And slept with *Pompey* in the peacefull deepes,
  Saue that I lyue in hope to see ere long
  That *Caesars* death shall satisfie his wrong.   145

Chor. 'Fortune in powre imperious
  'Vs'd ore the world and worldlings thus
                    To tirannize:
  When shee hath heap't her gifts on vs,
                    Away shee flies.   150

  Her feete, more swift then is the winde,
  Are more inconstant in their kinde
                    Then Autumne blasts;
  A womans shape, a womans minde,
                    That sildom lasts.   155

  'One while shee bends her angry browe,
  'And of no labour will allow;
                    Another while
  'She fleres againe, I know not how,
                    Still to beguile.   160

  'Fickle in our aduersities,
  'And fickle when our fortunes rise,
                    Shee scoffs at vs:
  'That (blynd herselfe) can bleare our eyes,
                    To trust her thus.   165

'The Sunne, that lends the earth his light,
'Behelde her neuer ouer night
        Lye calmely downe,
'But, in the morrow following, might
        Perceiue her frowne.   170

'Shee hath not onely power and will
'T'abuse the vulgar wanting skill ;
        But, when shee list,
'To Kings and Clownes doth equall ill
        Without resist.   175

'Mischaunce, that euery man abhors,
'And cares for crowned Emperors
        Shee doth reserue,
'As for the poorest labourers
        That worke or starue.   180

'The Merchant, that for priuate gaine,
'Doth send his Ships to passe the maine,
        Vpon the shore,
'In hope he shall his wish obtaine,
        Doth thee adore.   185

'Vpon the sea, or on the Land,
'Where health or wealth, or vines doe stand,
        Thou canst doe much,
'And often helpst the helples hande :
        Thy power is such.   190

'And many times (dispos'd to iest)
'Gainst one whose power and cause is best
        (Thy power to try)
'To him that ne're put speare in rest
        Giu'st victory.   195

.'For so the Lybian Monarchy,
'That with Ausonian blood did die
        Our warlike field,
'To one that ne're got victorie
        Was vrg'd to yeelde.   200

'So noble *Marius*, *Arpins* friend,
'That dyd the Latin state defend
              From *Cymbrian* rage,
'Did proue thy furie in the end,
              Which nought could swage.   205

'And *Pompey*, whose dayes haply led
'So long thou seem'dst t'haue fauoured,
              In vaine, t'is sayd,
'When the *Pharsalian* field he led,
              Implor'd thine ayde.   210

'Now *Caesar*, swolne with honors heate,
'Sits signiorizing in her seate,
              And will not see
'That Fortune can her hopes defeate,
              What e're they be.   215

'From chaunce is nothing franchized.
'And till the time that they are dead,
              Is no man blest :
'He onely, that no death doth dread,
              Doth liue at rest.   220

ACTVS QVARTVS

⟨Scene I.⟩

Cassius.   Decim⟨us⟩Brutus.

⟨*Cass.*⟩ Accursed Rome, that arm'st against thy selfe
A Tyrants rage, and mak'st a wretch thy King.
For one mans pleasure (O· iniurious Rome)
Thy chyldren gainst thy children thou hast arm'd ;
And thinkst not of the riuers of theyr bloode,   5
That earst was shed to saue thy libertie,
Because thou euer hatedst Monarchie.
Now o're our bodies (tumbled vp on heapes,
Lyke cocks of Hay when Iuly sheares the field)
Thou buildst thy kingdom, and thou seat'st thy King.   10
And to be seruile, (which torments me most)
Employest our liues, and lauishest our blood.
O Rome, accursed Rome, thou murdrest vs,

And massacrest thy selfe in yeelding thus.
Yet are there Gods, yet is there heauen and earth,   15
That seeme to feare a certaine Thunderer.
No, no, there are no Gods; or, if there be,
They leaue to see into the worlds affaires :
They care not for vs, nor account of men,
For what we see is done, is done by chaunce.   20
T'is Fortune rules, for equitie and right
Have neither helpe nor grace in heauens sight.
Scipio hath wrencht a sword into hys brest,
And launc'd hys bleeding wound into the sea.
Vndaunted *Cato* tore his entrails out ;   25
Affranius and *Faustus* murdred dyed ;
Iuba and *Petreus*, fiercely combatting,
Haue each done other equall violence.
Our Army's broken, and the Lybian Beares
Deuoure the bodies of our Cittizens.   30
The conquering Tyrant, high in Fortunes grace,
Doth ryde tryumphing o're our Common-wealth ;
And mournfull we behold him brauely mounted
(With stearne lookes) in his Chariot, where he leades
The conquered honor of the people yok't.   35
So Rome to *Caesar* yeelds both powre and pelfe,
And o're Rome *Caesar* raignes in Rome it selfe.
But, *Brutus*, shall wee dissolutelie sitte,
And see the tyrant liue to tyranize ?
Or shall theyr ghosts, that dide to doe vs good,   40
Plaine in their Tombes of our base cowardise ?
Shall lamed Souldiours, and graue gray-haird men
Poynt at vs in theyr bitter teares, and say :
See where they goe that haue theyr race forgot,
And rather chuse (vnarm'd) to serue with shame,   45
Then (arm'd) to saue their freedom and their fame ?
Brut. I sweare by heauen, th' Immortals highest throne,
Their temples, Altars, and theyr Images,
To see (for one) that *Brutus* suffer not
His ancient liberty to be represt.   50
I freely marcht with *Caesar* in hys warrs,
Not to be subiect, but to ayde his right.
But if (enuenom'd with ambitious thoughts)

He lyft his hand imperiously o're vs;
If he determyn but to raigne in Rome,   55
Or follow'd *Pompey* but to thys effect;
Or if (these ciuill discords now dissolu'd)
He render not the Empyre back to Rome;
Then shall he see that *Brutus* thys day beares
The selfe-same Armes to be aueng'd on hym;   60
And that thys hand (though *Caesar* blood abhor)
Shall toyle in his, which I am sorry for.
I loue, I loue him deerely. ' But the loue
' That men theyr Country and theyr birth-right beare
' Exceeds all loues, and deerer is by farre   65
Our Countries loue then friends or chyldren are.

Cass. If this braue care be nourisht in your blood,
Or if so franck a will your soule possesse,
Why hast we not, euen while these words are uttred,
To sheathe our new-ground swords in *Caesars* throate?   70
Why spend we day-light, and why dies he not,
That by his death we wretches may reuiue?
We stay too-long: I burne till I be there
To see this massacre, and send his ghost
To theyrs, whom (subtilly) he for Monarchie   75
Made fight to death with show of liberty.

Brut. Yet haply he (as *Sylla* whylom dyd),
When he hath rooted ciuill warre from Rome,
Will there-withall discharge the powre he hath.

Cass. Caesar and *Sylla*, *Brutus*, be not like.   80
Sylla (assaulted by the enemie)
Did arme himselfe (but in his owne defence)
Against both *Cynnas* host and *Marius*;
Whom when he had discomfited and chas'd,
And of his safety throughly was assur'd,   85
He layd apart the powre that he had got,
And gaue up rule, for he desier'd it not.
Where *Caesar*, that in silence might haue slept,
Nor vrg'd by ought but his ambition,
Did breake into the hart of Italie,   90
And lyke rude *Brennus* brought his men to field;
Trauers'd the seas, and shortly after (backt
With wintered souldiers vs'd to conquering)

He aym'd at vs, bent to exterminate
Who euer sought to intercept his state.   95
Now, hauing got what he hath gaped for,
(Deere *Brutus*) thinke you *Caesar* such a chyld,
Slightly to part with so great signiorie?
Belieue it not; he bought it deere, you know,
And traueled too farre to leaue it so.   100
Brut. But, *Cassius*, *Caesar* is not yet a King.
Cass. No, but Dictator, in effect as much.
He doth what pleaseth hym (a princely thing),
And wherein differ they whose powre is such?
Brut. Hee is not bloody.
Cass.   But by bloody iarres   105
He hath vnpeopled most part of the earth.
Both Gaule and Affrique perrisht by his warres;
Egypt, Emathia, Italy and Spayne
Are full of dead mens bones by *Caesar* slayne.
Th'infectious plague, and Famins bitternes,   110
Or th' Ocean (whom no pitty can asswage),
Though they containe dead bodies numberles,
Are yet inferior to *Caesars* rage;
Who (monster-like) wyth his ambition
Hath left more Tombes then ground to lay them on.   115
Brut. Souldiers with such reproch should not be blam'd.
Cass. He with his souldiers hath himselfe defam'd.
Brut. Why, then, you thinke there is no praise in war.
Cass. Yes, where the causes reasonable are.
Brut. He hath enrich the Empire with newe states.   120
Cass. Which with ambition now he ruinates.
Brut. He hath reueng'd the Gaules old iniurie,
And made them subiect to our Romaine Lawes.
Cass. The restfull Allmaynes with his crueltie
He rashly styrd against vs without cáuse;   125
And hazarded our Cittie and our selues
Against a harmeles Nation, kindly giuen,
To whom we should do well (for some amends)
To render him, and reconcile old frends.
These Nations did he purposely prouoke,   130
To make an Armie for his after-ayde
Against the Romains, whom in pollicie

He train'd in warre to steale theyr signiorie.
'Like them that (stryuing at th'Olympian sports
'To grace themselues with honor of the game)   135
'Annoynt theyr sinewes fit for wrestling,
'And (ere they enter) vse some exercise.
The Gaules were but a fore-game fecht about
For ciuill discord, wrought by *Caesars* sleights;
Whom (to be King himselfe) he soone remou'd,   140
Teaching a people hating seruitude
To fight for that, that did theyr deaths conclude.
Brut. The warrs once ended, we shall quickly know
Whether he will restore the state or no.
Cass. No, *Brutus*, neuer looke to see that day,   145
For *Caesar* holdeth signiorie too deere.
But know, while *Cassius* hath one drop of blood,
To feede this worthles body that you see,
What reck I death to doe so many good?
In spite of *Caesar*, *Cassius* will be free.   150
Brut. A generous or true enobled spirit
Detests to learne what tasts of seruitude.
Cass. Brutus, I cannot serue nor see Rome yok'd.
No, let me rather dye a thousand deaths.
'The stiffneckt horses champe not on the bit,   155
'Nor meekely beare the rider but by force:
'The sturdie Oxen toyle not at the Plough,
'Nor yeeld vnto the yoke but by constraint.
Shall we then, that are men and Romains borne,
Submit vs to vnurged slauerie?   160
Shall Rome that hath so many ouer-throwne
Now make herselfe a subiect to her owne?
O base indignitie: a beardles youth,
Whom King *Nicomedes* could ouer-reach,
Commaunds the world, and brideleth all the earth,   165
And like a Prince controls the Romulists,
Braue Romaine Souldiers, sterne-borne sons of *Mars*;
And none, not one, that dares to vndertake
The intercepting of his tyrannie.
O, *Brutus*, speake; O say, *Seruilius*,   170

---

155 stiftneckt *Qq.*

Why cry you ayme, and see vs vsed thus?
But *Brutus* liues, and sees, and knowes, and feeles
That there is one that curbs their Countries weale.
Yet (as he were the semblance, not the sonne,
Of noble *Brutus*, hys great Grandfather):   175
As if he wanted hands, sence, sight, or hart,
He doth, deuiseth, sees, nor dareth ought,
That may exstirpe or raze these tyrannies.
Nor ought doth *Brutus* that to *Brute* belongs,
But still increaseth by his negligence   180
His owne disgrace, and *Caesars* violence.
The wrong is great, and ouer-long endur'd :
We should haue practized, conspierd, coniur'd
A thousand waies and weapons to represse,
Or kill out-right, this cause of our distresse.   185

Chor. 'Who prodigally spends his blood,
    'Brauely to doe his country good,
    'And liueth to no other end,
    'But resolutely to attempt
    'What may the innocent defend,   190
    'And bloody Tyrants rage preuent :

    'And he that in his soule assur'd
    'Hath waters force and fire endur'd,
    'And past the pikes of thousand hostes,
    'To free the truth from tyrannie,   195
    'And fearles scowres in danger's coasts,
    'T'enlarge his countries liberty ;

    'Were all the world his foes before,
    'Now shall they loue him euer-more ;
    'His glory, spred abroade by Fame   200
    'On wings of his posteritie,
    'From obscure death shall free his name,
    'To liue in endles memorie.

    'All after ages shall adore,
    'And honor him with hymnes therefore.   205
    'Yeerely the youth for ioy shall bring
    'The fairest flowers that grow in Rome,

---

196 ,danger's *Gassner*: danger *Qq.* : dang'rous *Dodsley, Reed, Collier, Hazlitt*

'And yeerely in the Sommer sing,
'O're his heroique kingly Tombe.

'For so the two Athenians,   210
'That from their fellow cittizens
'Did freely chase vile seruitude,
'Shall liue for valiant prowesse blest;
'No Sepulcher shall ere exclude
'Their glorie equall with the best.   215

'But when the vulgar, mad and rude,
'Repay good with ingratitude,
'Hardly then they them reward
'That to free them fro the hands
'Of a Tyrant, nere regard   220
'In what plight their person stands.

'For high *Ioue* that guideth all,
'When he lets his iust wrath fall,
'To reuenge proud Diadems,
'With huge cares doth crosse kings liues,   225
'Raysing treasons in their Realmes
'By their chyldren, friends, or wiues.

'Therefore he, whom all men feare,
'Feareth all men euery where.
'Feare that doth engender hate   230
'(Hate enforcing them thereto)
'Maketh many vnder-take
'Many things they would not doe.

'O how many mighty Kings
'Liue in feare of petty things.   235
'For when Kings haue sought by warrs
'Stranger Townes to haue o'rethrowne,
'They haue caught deserued skarrs,
'Seeking that was not theyr owne.

'For no Tyrant commonly,   240
'Lyuing ill, can kindly die;
'But eyther trayterously surprizd,
'Doth coward poison quaile their breath,
'Or their people haue deuis'd,
'Or their guarde, to seeke their death.   245

' He onely liues most happilie
' That, free and farre from maiestie,
' Can liue content, although vnknowne :
' He fearing none, none fearing him,
' Medling with nothing but his owne,   250
' While gazing eyes at crownes grow dim.

⟨SCENE II.⟩

Caesar. Mar⟨k⟩ Anthonie.

Caes. O Rome, that with thy pryde dost ouer-peare
    The worthiest Cities of the conquered world ;
    Whose honor, got by famous victories,
    Hath fild heauens fierie vaults with fright-full horror ;
    O lofty towres, O stately battlements,   5
    O glorious temples, O proude Pallaces,
    And you braue walls, bright heauens masonrie,
    Grac'd with a thousand kingly diadems,
    Are yee not styrred with a strange delight,
    To see your *Caesars* matchles victories ?   10
    And how your Empire and your praise begins
    Through fame, which hee of stranger Nations wins ?
    O beautious Tyber, with thine easie streames
    That glide as smothly as a Parthian shaft ;
    Turne not thy crispie tydes, like siluer curle,   15
    Backe to thy grass-greene bancks to welcom vs ;
    And with a gentle murmure hast to tell
    The foming Seas the honour of our fight ?
    Trudge not thy streames to Trytons Mariners,
    To bruite the prayses of our conquests past ?   20
    And make theyr vaunts to old Oceanus
    That hence-forth Tyber shall salute the seas,
    More fam'd then Tyger or fayre Euphrates ?
    Now all the world (wel-nye) doth stoope to Rome :
    The sea, the earth, and all is almost ours.   25
    Be't where the bright Sun with his neyghbor beames
    Doth early light the Pearled Indians,
    Or where his Chariot staies to stop the day,
    Tyll heauen vnlock the darknes of the night :

Be't where the Sea is wrapt in Christall Ise,   30
Or where the Sommer doth but warme the earth :
Or heere, or there, where is not Rome renownd?
There lyues no King, (how great so e're he be)
But trembleth if he once but heare of mee.
Caesar is now earthes fame, and Fortunes terror,   35
And *Caesars* worth hath staynd old souldiers prayses.
Rome, speake no more of eyther *Scipio*,
Nor of the *Fabii*, or *Fabritians* ;
Heere let the *Decii* and theyr glory die.
Caesar hath tam'd more Nations, tane more Townes,   40
And fought more battailes then the best of them.
Caesar doth tryumph ouer all the world,
And all they scarcely conquered a nooke.
The Gauls, that came to Tiber to carouse,
Dyd liue to see my souldiers drinke at Loyre;   45
And those braue Germains, true borne Martialists,
Beheld the swift Rheyn vnder-run mine Ensignes.
The Brittaines (lockt within a watry Realme,
And wald by *Neptune*) stoopt to mee at last.
The faithles Moore, the fierce Numidian,   50
Th'earth that the Euxine sea makes somtymes marsh,
The stony-harted people that inhabite
Where seau'nfold Nilus doth disgorge it selfe,
Haue all been vrg'd to yeeld to my commaund.
Yea, euen this Cittie, that hath almost made   55
An vniuersall conquest of the world,
And that braue warrier, my brother in law,
That (ill aduis'd) repined at my glory—
Pompey, that second *Mars*, whose haught renowne
And noble deeds were greater then his fortunes,   60
Proou'd to his losse, but euen in one assault,
My hand, my hap, my hart exceeded his,
When the Thessalian fields were purpled ore
With eyther Armies murdred souldiers gore ;
When hee (to conquering accustomed)   65
Did (conquered) flie, his troopes discomfited.
Now *Scipio*, that long'd to shew himselfe

---

64 goe *Qq*.   66 discomfited *editors* : discomforted *Qq*.

Discent of Affrican (so fam'd for Armes),
He durst affront me and my warlike bands,
Vpon the Coastes of Lybia, till he lost　　　　70
His scattred Armie: and to shun the scorne
Of being taken captiue, kild himselfe.
Now therefore let vs tryumph, *Anthony*;
And rendring thanks to heauen, as we goe,
For brideling those that dyd maligne our glory,　　　　75
Lets to the Capitoll.

Anth.　　　　Come on, braue Caesar,
And crowne thy head, and mount thy Chariot.
Th'impatient people runne along the streets,
And in a route against thy gates they rushe,
To see theyr *Caesar*, after dangers past,　　　　80
Made Conqueror and Emperor at last.

Caes. I call to witnes heauens great Thunderer,
That gainst my will I haue maintaind this warre,
Nor thirsted I for conquests bought with blood.
I ioy not in the death of Cittizens;　　　　85
But through my selfe-wild enemies despight
And Romains wrong was I constraind to fight.

Anth. They sought t'eclipse thy fame, but destinie
Reuers'd th'effect of theyr ambition;
And *Caesars* prayse increasd by theyr disgrace,　　　　90
That reckt not of his vertuous deeds. But thus
We see it fareth with the enuious.

Caes. I neuer had the thought to iniure them.
Howbeit I neuer meant my greatnes should
By any others greatnes be o're-ruld.　　　　95
For as I am inferior to none,
So can I suffer no Superiors.

Anth. Well, *Caesar*, now they are discomfited,
And Crowes are feasted with theyr carcases.
And yet I feare you haue too kindly sau'd　　　　100
Those that your kindnes hardly will requite.

Caes. Why, *Anthony*, what would you wish mee doe?
Now shall you see that they will pack to Spaine,
And (ioyned with the Exiles there) encamp,
Vntill th'ill spyrit, that doth them defend,　　　　105
Doe bring their treasons to a bloody end.

Anth. I feare not those that to theyr weapons flye,
And keepe theyr state in Spaine, in Spaine to die.
Caes. Whom fear'st thou then, *Mark Anthony*?
Anth.   The hatefull crue
That, wanting powre in fielde to conquer you,   110
Haue in theyr coward soules deuised snares
To murder thee, and take thee at vnwares.
Caes. Will those conspire my death that liue by mee?
Anth. In conquered foes what credite can there be?
Caes. Besides theyr liues, I did theyr goods restore.   115
Anth. O, but theyr Countries good concerns them more.
Caes. What, thinke they mee to be their Countries foe?
Anth. No, but that thou vsurp'st the right they owe.
Caes. To Rome haue I submitted mighty things.
Anth. Yet Rome endures not the commaund of kings.   120
Caes. Who dares to contradict our Emporie?
Anth. Those whom thy rule hath rob'd of liberty.
Caes. I feare them not whose death is but deferd.
Anth. I feare my foe, vntill he be interd.
Caes. A man may make his foe his friend, you know.   125
Anth. A man may easier make his friend his foe.
Caes. Good deeds the cruelst hart to kindnes bring.
Anth. But resolution is a deadly thing.
Caes. If Cittizens my kindnes haue forgot,
Whom shall I then not feare?
Anth.   Those that are not.   130
Caes. What, shall I slay them all that I suspect?
Anth. Els cannot *Caesars* Emporie endure.
Caes. Rather I will my lyfe and all neglect.
Nor labour I my vaine life to assure;
But so to die, as dying I may liue,   135
And leauing off this earthly Tombe of myne,
Ascend to heauen vpon my winged deeds.
And shall I not have liued long enough
That in so short a time am so much fam'd?
Can I too-soone goe taste *Cocytus* flood?   140
No, *Anthony*, Death cannot iniure vs,
'For he liues long that dyes victorious.
Anth. Thy prayses show thy life is long enough,
But for thy friends and Country all too-short.

Should *Caesar* lyue as long as *Nestor* dyd,   145
Yet Rome may wish his life eternized.
Caes. Heauen sets our time; with heauen may nought dispence.
Anth. But we may shorten time with negligence.
Caes. But Fortune and the heauens haue care of vs.
Anth. Fortune is fickle, Heauen imperious.   150
Caes. What shall I then doe?
Anth.   As befits your state,
Maintaine a watchfull guard about your gate.
Caes. What more assurance may our state defend
Then loue of those that doe on vs attend?
Anth. There is no hatred more, if it be mou'd,   155
Then theirs whom we offend, and once belou'd.
Caes. Better it is to die then be suspitious.
Anth. T'is wisdom yet not to be credulous.
Caes. The quiet life, that carelesly is ledd,
Is not alonely happy in this world;   160
But Death it selfe doth sometime pleasure vs.
That death that comes vnsent for or vnseene,
And suddainly doth take vs at vnware,
Mee thinks is sweetest; And, if heauen were pleas'd,
I could desire that I might die so well.   165
The feare of euill doth afflict vs more
Then th'euill it selfe, though it be nere so sore.

                    A Chorus of Caesars friends.

O Faire Sunne, that gentlie smiles
From the Orient-pearled Iles,
Guilding these our gladsome daies   170
With the beautie of thy rayes:

Free fro rage of ciuill strife
Long preserue our *Caesars* life,
That from sable Affrique brings
Conquests whereof Europe rings.   175

And faire *Venus*, thou of whom
The Eneades are come,
Henceforth vary not thy grace
From *Iulus* happy race.

Rather cause thy deerest sonne,   180
By his tryumphs new begun,
To expell fro forth the Land
Firce warrs quenchles fire-brand.

That of care acquitting vs
(Who at last adore him thus),   185
He a peaceful starre appeare,
From our walls all woes to cleere.

And so let his warlike browes
Still be deckt with Lawrel boughes,
And his statues new set   190
With many a fresh-flowrd Coronet.

So, in euery place let be
Feasts, and Masks, and mirthfull glee,
Strewing Roses in the streete,
When their Emperor they meete.   195

He his foes hath conquered,
Neuer leauing till they fled,
And (abhorring blood) at last
Pardon'd all offences past.

'For high *Ioue* the heauens among,   200
'(Their support that suffer wrong)
'Doth oppose himselfe agen
'Bloody minded, cruell men.

'For he short⟨e⟩neth their dayes,
'Or prolongs them with dispraise ;   205
'Or (his greater wrath to show)
'Giues them ouer to their foe.

Caesar, a Cittizen so wrong'd
Of the honor him belong'd,
To defend himselfe from harmes,   210
Was enforc'd to take vp Armes.

For he saw that Enuies dart
(Pricking still their poysoned hart,
For his suddaine glory got)
Made his enuious foe so hote :   215

Wicked Enuie, feeding still
Foolish those that doe thy will.
For thy poysons in them poure
Sundry passions euery houre;

And to choller doth conuart   220
Purest blood about the heart,
Which (ore-flowing of their brest)
Suffreth nothing to digest.

'Other mens prosperitie
'Is their infelicitie;   225
'And their choller then is rais'd,
'When they heare another prais'd.

'Neither *Phoebus* fairest eye,
'Feasts, nor friendly company,
'Mirth, or what so-e're it be,   230
'With their humor can agree.

'Day or night they neuer rest,
'Spightfull hate so pecks their brest,
'Pinching their perplexed lunges
'With her fiery poysoned tongues.   235

'Fire-brands in their brests they beare,
'As if *Tesiphon* were there;
'And their soules are pierc'd as sore
'As *Prometheus* ghost, and more.

'Wretches, they are woe-begone,   240
'For their wound is alwaies one.
'Nor hath *Chyron* powre or skill
'To recure them of their ill.

ACTVS QVINTVS

The Messenger. Cornelia. Chorus.

Mess. Vnhappy man, amongst so many wracks
As I haue suffred both by Land and Sea,
That scorneful destinie denyes my death.
Oft haue I seene the ends of mightier men,

---

242 *Charon Dodsley, Reed, Collier, Hazlitt, wrongly*

L 2

Whose coates of steele base Death hath stolne into ;   5
And in thys direful warre before mine eyes
Beheld theyr corses scattred on the plaines,
And endles numbers falling by my side,
Nor those ignoble, but the noblest Lords.
Mongst whom aboue the rest, that moues me most,   10
Scipio (my deerest Maister) is deceas'd ;
And Death, that sees the Nobles blood so rife,
Full-gorged triumphes, and disdaines my lyfe.

Corn. We are vndone.

Chor.   *Scipio* hath lost the day.
But hope the best, and harken to his newes.   15

Corn. O cruell fortune.

Mess.   These mis-fortunes yet
Must I report to sad *Cornelia*,
Whose ceaseles griefe (which I am sorry for)
Will agrauate my former misery.

Corn. Wretch that I am, why leaue I not the world?   20
Or wherefore am I not already dead?
O world, o wretch.

Chor.   Is this th'vndaunted hart
That is required in extremities?
Be more confirmd. And, Madam, let not griefe
Abuse your wisdom lyke a vulgar wit.   25
Haply the newes is better then the noyse ;
Let's heare him speake.

Corn.   O no, for all is lost.
Farewell, deere Father.

Chor.   Hee is sau'd, perhaps.

Mess. Me thinks, I heare my Maisters daughter speake.
What sighes, what sobs, what plaints, what passions   30
Haue we endurde, *Cornelia*, for your sake?

Corn. Where is thine Emperor?

Mess.   Where our Captaines are.
Where are our Legions? Where our men at Armes?
Or where so many of our Romaine soules?
The earth, the sea, the vultures and the Crowes,   35

---

12 noblest *Hazlitt* : *but cf.* Tant de braues Seigneurs *Garnier*   16 mis-
fortues *Qq*.

Lyons and Beares, are theyr best Sepulchers.
Corn. O miserable.
Chor.   Now I see the heauens
Are heapt with rage and horror gainst this house.
Corn. O earth, why op'st thou not?
Chor.   Why waile you so?
Assure your selfe that *Scipio* brauely dyed;   40
And such a death excels a seruile life.
⟨*Corn.*⟩ Say, Messenger.
⟨*Chor.*⟩   The manner of his end
Will haply comfort this your discontent.
Corn. Discourse the manner of his hard mishap,
And what disastrous accident did breake   45
So many people bent so much to fight.
Mess. Caesar, that wisely knewe his souldiers harts,
And their desire to be approou'd in Armes,
Sought nothing more then to encounter vs.
And therefore (faintly skyrmishing) in craft   50
Lamely they fought, to draw vs further on.
Oft (to prouoke our warie wel-taught troopes)
He would attempt the entrance on our barrs,
Nay, euen our Trenches, to our great disgrace,
And call our souldiers cowards to theyr face.   55
But when he saw his wiles nor bitter words
Could draw our Captaines to endanger vs,
Coasting along and following by the foote,
He thought to tyre and wearie vs fro thence;
And got hys willing hosts to march by night,   60
With heauy Armor on theyr hardned backs,
Downe to the Sea-side; where before faire *Tapsus,*
He made his Pyoners (poore weary soules)
The selfe-same day to dig and cast new Trenches,
And plant strong Barricades; where he (encampt)   65
Resolu'd by force to hold vs hard at work.
Scipio no sooner heard of his designes,
But, being afeard to loose so fit a place,
Marcht on the suddaine to the selfe-same Cittie,
Where few men might doe much, which made him see   70

_____

42 *Corn. and Chor. om. Qq., but in Garnier*

Of what importance such a Towne would be.
The fields are spred, and as a houshold Campe
Of creeping Emmets in a Countrey Farme,
That come to forrage when the cold begins,
Leauing theyr crannyes to goe search about,   75
Couer the earth so thicke, as scarce we tread
But we shall see a thousand of them dead :
Euen so our battails, scattred on the sands,
Dyd scoure the plaines in pursuite of the foe.
One while at *Tapsus* we begin t'entrench,   80
To ease our Army, if it should retyre ;
Another while we softly sally foorth ;
And wakefull *Caesar* that doth watch our being,
(When he perceiues vs marching o're the plaine)
Doth leape for gladnes, and (to murder vow'd)   85
Runnes to the tent, for feare we should be gone,
And quickly claps his rustie Armour on.
For true it is that *Caesar* brought at first
An hoste of men to Affrique meanely Arm'd,
But such as had braue spirits, and (combatting)   90
Had powre and wit to make a wretch a King.
Well, forth to field they marched all at once,
Except some fewe that stayd to guard the Trench.
Them *Caesar* soone and subt'ly sets in ranke,
And euery Regiment warn'd with a worde   95
Brauely to fight for honor of the day.
He showes that auncient souldiers need not feare
Them that they had so oft disordered,
Them that already dream'd of death or flight ;
That tyer'd would nere hold out, if once they see   100
That they o're-layd them in the first assault.
Meane-while our Emperor (at all poynts arm'd),
Whose siluer hayres and honorable front
Were (warlike) lockt within a plumed caske,
In one hand held his Targe of steele embost,   105
And in the other graspt his Coutelas ;
And with a cheerefull looke surueigh'd the Campe,
Exhorting them to charge, and fight like men,
And to endure what ere betyded them.
For now (quoth he) is come that happie day,   110

Wherein our Country shall approue our loue.
Braue Romains, know this is the day and houre,
That we must all liue free, or friendly die.
For my part (being an auncient Senator,
An Emperor and Consul) I disdaine   115
The world should see me to become a slaue.
I'le eyther conquer, or this sword you see
(Which brightly shone) shall make an end of me.
We fight not, we, like thieues, for others wealth:
We fight not, we, t'enlarge our skant confines;   120
To purchase fame to our posterities,
By stuffing of our tropheies in their houses.
But t'is for publique freedom that we fight,
For Rome we fight, and those that fled for feare.
Nay more, we fight for safetie of our lyues,   125
Our goods, our honors, and our auncient lawes.
As for the Empire, and the Romaine state
(Due to the victor) thereon ruminate.
Thinke how this day the honorable Dames,
With blubbred eyes and handes to heauen vprear'd,   130
Sit inuocating for vs to the Gods,
That they will blesse our holy purposes.
Me thinks I see poore Rome in horror clad,
And aged Senators in sad discourse,
Mourne for our sorrowes and theyr seruitude.   135
Me thinks I see them while (lamenting thus)
Theyr harts and eyes lye houering ouer vs.
On then, braue men, my fellowes and Romes friends,
To shew vs worthy of our auncestors:
And let vs fight with courage, and conceite   140
That we may rest the Maisters of the field;
That this braue Tyrant, valiantly beset,
May perrish in the presse before our faces;
And that his troopes (as tucht wyth lightning flames)
May by our horse in heapes be ouer-throwne,   145
And he (blood-thirsting) wallow in his owne.
Thys sayd, his Army crying all at once
With ioyfull tokens did applaude his speeches,
Whose swift shrill noyse did pierce into the clowdes,
Lyke Northern windes that beate the horned Alpes.   150

The clattring Armour, buskling as they paced,
Ronge through the Forrests with a frightfull noyse,
And euery Eccho tooke the Trompets clange :
When (like a tempest rais'd with whirle-winds rage)
They ranne at euer-each other hand and foote ;   155
Where-with the dust, as with a darksome clowde,
Arose, and ouer-shadowed horse and man.
The Darts and Arrowes on theyr Armour glaunced,
And with theyr fall the trembling earth was shaken.
The ayre (that thickned with theyr thundring cryes)   160
With pale, wanne clowdes discoloured the Sunne.
The fire in sparks fro forth theyr Armour flew,
And with a duskish yellow chokt the heauens.
The battels lockt (with bristle-poynted speares)
Doe at the halfe pyke freely charge each other,   165
And dash together like two lustie Bulls,
That (iealous of some Heyfar in the Heard)
Runne head to head, and (sullen) wil not yeeld,
Till, dead or fled, the one forsake the field.
The shyuered Launces (ratling in the ayre)   170
Fly forth as thicke as moates about the Sunne :
When with theyr swords (flesht with the former fight)
They hewe their Armour, and they cleaue their casks,
Till streames of blood like Riuers fill the downes ;
That being infected with the stench thereof   175
Surcloyes the ground, and of a Champant Land
Makes it a Quagmire, where (kneedeepe) they stand.
Blood-thirstie *Discord*, with her snakie hayre,
A fearfull Hagge, with fier-darting eyes,
Runnes crosse the Squadrons with a smokie brand,   180
And with her murdring whip encourageth
The ouer-forward hands to bloode and death.
Bellona, fiered with a quenchles rage,
Runnes vp and downe, and in the thickest throng
Cuts, casts the ground, and madding makes a poole,   185
Which in her rage free passage doth afford
That with our blood she may annoynt her sword.
Now we of our side vrge them to retreate,

154 whire-winds *Qq*.

And nowe before them we retyre as fast.
As on the Alpes the sharpe Nor-North-east wind,   190
Shaking a Pynetree with theyr greatest powre,
One while the top doth almost touch the earth,
And then it riseth with a counterbuffe:
So did the Armies presse and charge each other,
With selfe-same courage, worth, and weapons to;   195
And, prodigall of life for libertie,
With burning hate let each at other flie.
Thryce did the Cornets of the souldiers (cleerd)
Turne to the Standerd to be newe supplyde;
And thrice the best of both was faine to breathe;   200
And thrice recomforted they brauely ranne,
And fought as freshly as they first beganne.
Like two fierce Lyons fighting in a Desart,
To winne the loue of some faire Lyonesse,
When they haue vomited theyr long-growne rage,   205
And proou'd each others force sufficient,
Passant regardant softly they retyre,
Theyr iawbones dy'd with foming froth and blood,
Their lungs like spunges, ramm'd within their sides,
Theyr tongues discouerd, and theyr tailes long trailing: 210
Till iealous rage (engendered with rest)
Returnes them sharper set then at the first;
And makes them couple, when they see theyr prize,
With bristled backs, and fire-sparkling eyes,
Tyll, tyer'd or conquer'd, one submits or flyes.   215
Caesar, whose kinglike lookes, like day bright starrs,
Both comfort and encourage his to fight,
Marcht through the battaile (laying still about him)
And subt'ly markt whose hand was happiest;
Who nicely did but dyp his speare in blood,   220
And who more roughly smear'd it to his fiste;
Who (staggering) fell with euery feeble wound,
And who (more strongly) pac'd it through the thickest;
Him he enflam'd, and spur'd, and fild with horror.
As when *Alecto*, in the lowest hell,   225
Doth breathe new heate within *Orestes* brest,

---

218 laying *Qq.*: **raging** *Gassner*

Till out-ward rage with inward griefe begins
A fresh remembrance of our former sins.
For then (as if prouokt with pricking goades)
Theyr warlike Armies (fast lockt foote to foote),   230
Stooping their heads low bent to tosse theyr staues,
They fiercely open both Battalions,
Cleaue, breake, and raging tempest-like o're turne
What e're makes head to meet them in this humor.
Our men at Armes (in briefe) begin to flye,   235
And neither prayers, intreatie, nor example
Of any of theyr leaders left aliue
Had powre to stay them in this strange carrier:
Stragling, as in the faire Calabrian fields
When Wolues, for hunger ranging fro the wood,   240
Make forth amongst the flock, that scattered flyes
Before the Shepheard, that resistles lyes.
Corn. O cruell fortune.
Mess.   None resisting now,
The field was fild with all confusion
Of murder, death, and direfull massacres.   245
The feeble bands that yet were left entyre
Had more desire to sleepe then seeke for spoyle.
No place was free from sorrow; euery where
Lay Armed men, ore-troden with theyr horses,
Dismembred bodies drowning in theyr blood,   250
And wretched heapes lie mourning of theyr maimes,
Whose blood, as from a spunge, or bunche of Grapes
Crusht in a Wine-presse, gusheth out so fast,
As with the sight doth make the sound agast.
Some should you see that had theyr heads halfe clouen, 255
And on the earth theyr braines lye trembling:
Here one new wounded helps another dying:
Here lay an arme, and there a leg lay shiuer'd:
Here horse and man (o're-turnd) for mercy cryde,
With hands extended to the merciles,   260
That stopt theyr eares, and would not heare a word,
But put them all (remorceles) to the sword.
He that had hap to scape, doth helpe a fresh
To re-enforce the side wheron he seru'd.
But seeing that there the murdring Enemie   265

Pesle-mesle pursued them like a storme of hayle,
They gan retyre, where *Iuba* was encampt;
But there had *Caesar* eftsoones tyranniz'd.
So that, dispayring to defend themselues,
They layd aside theyr Armour, and at last   270
Offred to yeeld vnto the enemy;
Whose stony hart, that nere dyd Romaine good,
Would melt with nothing but theyr deerest blood.

⟨*Corn.*⟩ And Scipio, my Father?
⟨*Mess.*⟩   When he beheld
His people so discomfited and scorn'd;   275
When he perceiu'd the labour profitles
To seeke by new encouraging his men
To come vpon them with a fresh alarme;
And when he saw the enemies pursuite
To beate them downe as fierce as thundring flints,   280
And lay them leuell with the charged earth,
Lyke eares of Corne with rage of windie showres,
Their battailes scattred, and their Ensignes taken;
And (to conclude) his men dismayd to see
The passage choakt with bodies of the dead: 285
Incessantly lamenting th'extreame losse,
And souspirable death of so braue souldiers,
He spurrs his horse, and (breaking through the presse)
Trots to the Hauen, where his ships he finds,
And hopeles trusteth to the trustles windes.   290
Now had he thought to haue ariu'd in Spayne,
To raise newe forces, and returne to field;
But as one mischiefe drawes another on,
A suddaine tempest takes him by the way,
And casts him vp neere to the Coasts of Hyppon,   295
Where th' aduerse Nauie, sent to scoure the seas,
Did hourely keepe their ordinary course;
Where seeing himselfe at anchor, slightly shipt,
Besieg'd, betraide by winde, by land, by sea,
(All raging mad to rig his better Vessels   300
The little while this naual conflict lasted),

---

274 *Corn. and Mess. om. Qq., but in Garnier; hence* thy Father *Dodsley,
Reed, Collier, Hazlitt*

Behold, his owne was fiercely set vpon,
Which being sore beaten, till it brake agen,
Ended the liues of his best fighting men.
There did the remnant of our Romaine nobles,   305
Before the foe and in theyr Captaines presence,
Dye brauely, with their fauchins in their fists.
Then *Scipio* (that saw his ships through-galled,
And by the foe fulfild with fire and blood,
His people put to sword, Sea, Earth, and Hell,   310
And Heauen it selfe coniur'd to iniure him)
Steps to the Poope, and with a princely visage
Looking vpon his weapon, dide with blood,
Sighing he sets it to his brest, and said:
Since all our hopes are by the Gods beguil'd,   315
What refuge now remaines for my distresse,
But thee my deerest, nere-deceiuing sword?
Yea, thee, my latest fortunes firmest hope,
By whom I am assurde this hap to haue,
That, being free borne, I shall not die a slaue.   320
Scarce had he said, but, cruelly resolu'd,
He wrencht it to the pommel through his sides,
That fro the wound the smoky blood ran bubling,
Where-with he staggred; and I stept to him
To haue embrac'd him. But he (beeing afraid   325
T'attend the mercy of his murdring foe
That stil pursued him, and opprest his ships)
Crawld to the Deck, and, lyfe with death to ease,
Headlong he threw himselfe into the seas.
Corn. O cruell Gods, O heauen, O direfull Fates,   330
O radiant Sunne that slightly guildst our dayes,
O night starrs, full of infelicities,
O triple titled *Heccat*, Queene and Goddesse,
Bereaue my lyfe, or lyuing strangle me;
Confound me quick, or let me sinck to hell;   335
Thrust me fro forth the world, that mongst the spirits
Th' infernall Lakes may ring with my laments.
O miserable, desolate, distresful wretch,
Worne with mishaps, yet in mishaps abounding.

302 Beheld *Gassner. See Note*   312 Stepts *Qq.*

What shall I doe, or whether shall I flye   340
To venge this outrage, or reuenge my wrongs?
Come, wrathfull Furies, with your Ebon locks,
And feede your selues with mine enflamed blood.
Ixions torment, *Sysiph's* roling stone,
And th' Eagle tyering on *Prometheus*,   345
Be my eternall tasks, that th' extreame fire
Within my hart may from my hart retyre.
I suffer more, more sorrowes I endure,
Then all the Captiues in th' infernall Court.
O troubled Fate, O fatall misery,   350
That vnprouoked deal'st so partiallie.
Say, freatfull heauens, what fault haue I committed,
Or wherein could mine innocence offend you,
When (being but young) I lost my first loue. *Crassus?*
O wherein did I merrite so much wrong   355
To see my second husband *Pompey* slayne?
But mongst the rest, what horrible offence,
What hatefull thing (vnthought of) haue I done,
That, in the midst of this my mournfull state,
Nought but my Fathers death could expiate?   360
Thy death, deere *Scipio*, Romes eternall losse,
Whose hopefull life preseru'd our happines,
Whose siluer haires encouraged the weake,
Whose resolutions did confirme the rest,
Whose ende, sith it hath ended all my ioyes,   365
O heauens, at least permit of all these plagues
That I may finish the Catastrophe;
Sith in this widdow-hood of all my hopes
I cannot looke for further happines.
For, both my husbands and my Father gone,   370
What haue I els to wreak your wrath vpon?
Now as for happy thee, to whom sweet Death
Hath giuen blessed rest for lifes bereauing,
O enuious *Iulia*, in thy iealous hart
Venge not thy wrong vpon *Cornelia*.   375
But, sacred ghost, appease thine ire, and see
My hard mishap in marrying after thee.
O see mine anguish; haplie seeing it,
T' will moue compassion in thee of my paines,

And vrge thee (if thy hart be not of flynt,   380
Or drunck with rigor) to repent thy selfe,
That thou enflam'dst so cruell a reuenge
In *Caesars* hart vpon so slight a cause,
And mad'st him raise so many mournfull Tombes,
Because thy husband did reuiue the lights   385
Of thy forsaken bed; vnworthely
Opposing of thy freatfull ielosie
Gainst his mishap, as it my helpe had bin,
Or as if second marriage were a sin.

⟨*Chor.*⟩ Was neuer Citty where calamitie   390
Hath soiourn'd with such sorrow as in this:
Was neuer state wherein the people stood
So careles of their conquered libertie,
And careful of anothers tiranny.

⟨*Corn.*⟩ O Gods, that earst of Carthage tooke some care, 395
Which by our Fathers (pittiles) was spoyl'd;
When thwarting Destinie at Affrique walls
Did topside turuey turne their Common-wealth;
When forcefull weapons fiercely tooke away
Their souldiers (sent to nourish vp those warrs);   400
When (fierd) their golden Pallaces fell downe;
When through the slaughter th' Afrique seas were dide,
And sacred Temples quenchlesly enflam'd:
Now is our haples time of hopes expired.
Then satisfie yourselues with this reuenge,   405
Content to count the ghosts of those great Captains,
Which (conquered) perisht by the Romaine swords,
The Hannons, the Amilcars, Asdrubals,
Especially that proudest *Hanniball,*
That made the fayre Thrasymene so dezart.   410
For euen those fields that mourn'd to beare their bodies,
Now (loaden) groane to feele the Romaine corses.
Theyr earth we purple ore, and on theyr Tombes
We heape our bodies, equalling theyr ruine.
And as a *Scipio* did reuerse theyr powre,   415
They haue a *Scipio* to reuenge them on.

---

390 *Chor. om. Qq., but in Garnier*   391 soiour'd *Qq.*   395 *Corn.*
om. *Qq., but in Garnier*   411 mour'd *Qq.*

⟨*Chor.*⟩ Weepe therefore, Roman Dames, and from henceforth
　Valing your Christall eyes to your faire bosoms,
　Raine showres of greefe vpon your Rose-like cheeks,
　And dewe your selues with springtides of your teares.　　420
　Weepe, Ladies, weepe, and with your reeking sighes
　Thicken the passage of the purest clowdes,
　And presse the ayre with your continuall plaints.
　Beate at your Iuorie breasts, and let your robes
　(Defac'd and rent) be witnes of your sorrowes.　　425
　And let your haire, that wont be wreath'd in tresses,
　Now hang neglectly, dangling downe your sholders,
　Careles of Arte, or rich accoustrements,
　That with the gold and pearle we vs'd before
　Our mournfull habits may be deckt no more.　　430
⟨*Corn.*⟩ Alas, what shall I doe? O deere companions,
　Shall I, O, shall I liue in these laments,
　Widdowed of all my hopes, my haps, my husbands,
　And last, not least, bereft of my best Father,
　And of the ioyes mine auncestors enioy'd,　　435
　When they enioy'd their liues and libertie?
　And must I liue to see great *Pompeys* house
　(A house of honour and antiquitie)
　Vsurpt in wrong by lawlesse *Anthony*?
　Shall I behold the sumptuous ornaments　　440
　(Which both the world and Fortune heapt on him)
　Adorne and grace his graceles Enemy?
　Or see the wealth that *Pompey* gain'd in warre,
　Sold at a pike, and borne away by strangers?
　Dye, rather die, *Cornelia* : and (to spare　　445
　Thy worthles life that yet must one day perish)
　Let not those Captains vainlie lie inter'd,
　Or *Caesar* triumph in thine infamie,
　That wert the wife to th'one, and th'others daughter.
　But if I die, before I haue entomb'd　　450
　My drowned Father in some Sepulcher,
　Who will performe that care in kindnes for me?
　Shall his poore wandring lymbs lie stil tormented,
　Tost with the salte waues of the wasteful Seas?

---

417 *Chor. om. Qq., but in Garnier*　　　431 *Corn. om. Qq., but in Garnier*

No, louely Father and my deerest husband,   455
Cornelia must liue (though life she hateth)
To make your Tombes, and mourne vpon your hearses,
Where (languishing) my fumous, faithful teares
May trickling bathe your generous sweet cynders;
And afterward (both wanting strength and moysture,   460
Fulfilling with my latest sighes and gasps
The happie vessels that enclose your bones)
I will surrender my surcharged life;
And (when my soule Earths pryson shall forgoe)
Encrease the number of the ghosts be-low.   465

   Non prosunt Domino, quae prosunt omnibus, Artes.

                                                    THO. KYD.

---

        458 fumous *Gassner*: famous *Qq. See Note*

THE TRAGEDYE OF
SOLYMAN AND
PERSEDA.

VVherein is laide open, *Loues*
constañcy, Fortunes incon-
stancy, and Deaths
Triumphs.

AT LONDON
Printed by *Edward Allde* for
Edward White, and are to be solde at
the little North doore of Paules
Church, at the signe of
the Gun.

EDITOR'S NOTE

THE text adopted is that of the undated Quarto, of which the only known extant copy is in the British Museum, with press-mark C. 34. b. 44. This Quarto, which has not hitherto been collated, gives the best text. The adoption of a reading from any other source is indicated in the footnotes, where also are given all variants found in the two Quarto editions of 1599. Of one of these editions there is a unique copy in the British Museum, with press-mark 11773. c. 11, which, like the undated Quarto, has not hitherto been collated. Of the other edition of 1599 there are a number of specimens (in the British Museum, the Bodleian, South Kensington), but one of those in the British Museum, with press-mark 161. b. 4, is distinguished by the words *Newly corrected and amended* on the title-page. It is therefore convenient to call this edition 'the amended edition of 1599.' It was from Garrick's copy of this edition that Hawkins printed his text of the play, which Hazlitt reprinted with a few conjectural emendations. But mistakenly thinking that 'there was only one impression which received no fewer than three title-pages,' Hazlitt prefixed to his edition the title-page of the undated Quarto, which there is no sign of his having collated.

I have printed as prose a number of speeches, principally by Piston, the 'fool' of the play, which appear in the Quartos, and in the editions of Hawkins and Hazlitt, in doggerel form. The speeches of Basilisco, however, with their stilted vocabulary, I have retained in their original form, which is apparently intended to be irregularly metrical.

Though the undated Quarto has 'Solyman' on the title-page, it generally substitutes 'Soliman' in stage-directions and the text, and I have therefore kept this, the recognized form, in the title of the play.

References in the notes are as follow :—

Undated Q. = Quarto, undated, British Museum C. 34. b. 44

1599 = Quarto, 1599, British Museum 11773. c. 11

1599 A = Quarto, 1599, British Museum 161. b. 4

Hawkins = T. Hawkins' edition in his *Origin of the British Drama*, vol. ii (1773)

Hazlitt = W. C. Hazlitt's edition in his reissue of *Dodsley's Old Plays*, vol. v (1874)

Since the publication of this volume, it has been brought to my notice that the Quarto of *Soliman aud Perseda* (formerly 11773. c. 11, now C. 57. c. 15, in the British Museum) has recently been shown, on typographical evidence, to be a modern reprint of the genuine edition of 1599. This reprint, marked 1599 in the present volume (cf. p. 162), was so ingenious a forgery as to deceive till lately the bibliographical experts of the Museum. As Lowndes, however, mentions that the play was 'reprinted about 1815 on old paper by Smeeton,' the Quarto is doubtless a copy of this issue, of which, I find, there are a few other extant specimens.

1902   F. S. B.

⟨DRAMATIS PERSONAE [1]

Loue ⎫
Fortune ⎬ In Induction and Chorus.
Death ⎭

Soliman, *Emperor of the Turks.*
Haleb ⎫
Amurath ⎬ *his brothers.*
Brusor, *his general.*
Lord Marshal.

Philippo, *Governor of Rhodes.*
Prince of Cyprus, *his son-in-law.*
Erastus, *a knight of Rhodes.*
Guelpio ⎫
Iulio ⎬ *his friends.*
Piston, *his servant.*
Ferdinando.
Perseda, *beloved of Erastus.*
Lucina, *beloved of Ferdinando.*

Basilisco, *a braggart knight.*
Englishman ⎫
Frenchman ⎬ *knights.*
Spaniard ⎭
A Captain.
A Messenger.
Two Witnesses.

Knights, Ladies, Janissaries, Soldiers.⟩

[1] There is no list of *Dramatis Personae* in the *Qq.* Hawkins drew one up, which has been reproduced by Hazlitt. I have expanded it slightly, and made changes in the grouping.

THE TRAGEDIE

OF

SOLIMAN AND PERSEDA

ACTVS PRIMVS.

⟨SCENE I: INDUCTION.⟩

Enter Loue, Fortune, Death.

Loue. What, *Death* and *Fortune* crosse the way of *Loue*?
Fortune. Why, what is *Loue* but *Fortunes* tenis-ball?
Death. Nay, what are you both, but subiects vnto *Death*?
  And I commaund you to forbeare this place;
  For heere the mouth of sad *Melpomene*   5
  Is wholy bent to tragedies discourse:
  And what are Tragedies but acts of death?
  Here meanes the wrathfull muse, in seas of teares
  And lowd laments, to tell a dismall tale:
  A tale wherein she lately hath bestowed   10
  The huskie humour of her bloudy quill,
  And now for tables takes her to her tung.
Loue. Why, thinkes *Death Loue* knows not the historie
  Of braue *Erastus* and his Rodian Dame?
  Twas I that made their harts consent to loue;   15
  And therefore come I now as fittest person
  To serue for Chorus to this Tragedie:
  Had I not beene, they had not dyed so soone.
Death. Had I not beene, they had not dyed so soone.
Fortune. Nay then, it seemes, you both doo misse the marke. 20

Did not I change long loue to sudden hate;
And then rechange their hatred into loue;
And then from loue deliuer them to death?
Fortune is chorus; *Loue* and *Death* be gone.
Death. I tell thee, *Fortune*, and thee, wanton *Loue*,   25
I will not downe to euerlasting night
Till I haue moralliz'd this Tragedie,
Whose cheefest actor was my sable dart.
Loue. Nor will I vp into the brightsome sphere,
From whence I sprung, till in the chorus place   30
I make it knowne to you and to the world
What interest *Loue* hath in Tragedies.
Fortune. Nay then, though *Fortune* haue delight in change,
Ile stay my flight, and cease to turne my wheele,
Till I haue showne by demonstration   35
What intrest I haue in a Tragedie:
Tush, *Fortune* can doo more then *Loue* or *Death*.
Loue. Why stay we then? Lets giue the Actors leaue,
And, as occasion serues, make our returne.
                                        Exeunt.

⟨SCENE II.⟩

Enter Erastus *and* Perseda.

Erast. Why, when, *Perseda*? wilt thou not assure me?
But shall I, like a mastlesse ship at sea,
Goe euery way, and not the way I would?
My loue hath lasted from mine infancie,
And still increased as I grew my selfe.   5
When did *Perseda* pastime in the streetes,
But her *Erastus* ouer-eied her sporte?
When didst thou, with thy sampler in the Sunne
Sit sowing with thy feres, but I was by,
Marking thy lilly hands dexteritie;   10
Comparing it to twenty gratious things?
When didst thou sing a note that I could heare,
But I haue framde a dittie to the tune,
Figuring *Perseda* twenty kinde of ways?
When didst thou goe to Church on hollidaies,   15
But I haue waited on thee too and fro,
Marking my times as Faulcons watch their flight?

When I haue mist thee, how haue I lamented,
As if my thoughts had been assured true.
Thus in my youth : now, since I grew a man,   20
I haue perseuered to let thee know
The meaning of my true harts constancie.
Then be not nice, *Perseda*, as women woont
To hasty louers whose fancy soone is fled :
My loue is ·of a long continuance,   25
And merites not a strangers recompence.

Per. Enough, *Erastus*, thy *Perseda* knowes ;
     She whom thou wouldst haue thine, *Erastus*, knowes.

Erast. Nay, my *Perseda* knowes, and then tis well.

Per. I, watch you vauntages ? Thine be it then—   30
I haue forgot the rest, but thats the effect ;
Which to effect, accept this carkanet :
My Grandame on her death bed gaue it me,
And there, euen there, I vow'd vnto myselfe
To keepe the same, vntill my wandring eye   35
Should finde a harbour for my hart to dwell.
Euen in thy brest doo I elect my rest ;
Let in my hart to keep thine company.

Erast. And, sweet *Perseda*, accept this ring
To equall it : receiue my hart to boote ;   40
It is no boot, for that was thine before :
And far more welcome is this change to me
Then sunny daies to naked Sauages,
Or newes of pardon to a wretch condemnd
That waiteth for the fearefull stroke of death.   45
As carefull will I be to keepe this chaine,
As doth the mother keepe her children
From water pits, or falling in the fire.
Ouer mine armour will I hang this chaine ;
And, when long combat makes my body faint,   50
The sight of this shall shew *Persedas* name,
And add fresh courage to my fainting limmes.
This day the eger Turke of Tripolis,
The Knight of Malta, honoured for his worth,
And he thats titled by the golden spurre,   55

---

18 I haue *1599* -99 *A*   30 you] your *Hazlitt*

The Moore vpon his hot Barbarian horse,
The fiery Spaniard bearing in his face
The empresse of a noble warriour,
The sudden Frenchman, and the bigbon'd Dane,
And English Archers, hardy men at armes,   60
Eclipped Lyons of the Westerne worlde :
Each one of these approoued combatants,
Assembled from seuerall corners of the world,
Are hither come to try their force in armes,
In honour of the Prince of Cipris nuptials.   65
Amongst these worthies will *Erastus* troupe,
Though like a Gnat amongst a hiue of Bees.
Know me by this thy pretious carkanet ;
And if I thriue in valour, as the glasse
That takes the Sun-beames burning with his force,   70
Ile be the glasse and thou that heauenly Sun,
From whence Ile borrow what I do atchieue :
And, sweet *Perseda*, vnnoted though I be,
Thy beauty yet shall make me knowne ere night.
Per. Yong slippes are neuer graft in windy daies ;   75
Yong schollers neuer entered with the rod.
Ah, my *Erastus*, there are Europes Knights
That carry honour grauen in their helmes,
And they must winne it deere that winne it thence.
Let not my beauty prick thee to thy bane ;   80
Better sit still then rise and ouertane.
Erast. Counsell me not, for my intent is sworne,
And be my fortune as my loue deserues.
Per. So be thy fortune as thy features serues,
And then *Erastus* liues without compare.   85

Enter a Messenger.

Here comes a Messenger to haste me hence.
I know your message ; hath the Princesse sent for me?
Mess. She hath, and desires you to consort her to the triumphes.

Enter Piston.

Pist. Who saw my Master? O sir, are you heere? The

---

59 bigbound *undated Q.*   60 Arthers *undated Q.*   69 *See Note*
77 there] these *Hazlitt*   84 serue *1599 -99 A. See Note*   89-91 *printed*
as doggerel in Qq

Prince and all the outlandish Gentlemen are ready to goe
to the triumphs; they stay for you.   91
Erast. Goe sirra, bid my men bring my horse, and a dosen staues.
Pist. You shall haue your horses and two dosen of staues.

                                                   Exit Piston.
Erast. Wish me good hap, *Perseda,* and Ile winne
 Such glory as no time shall ere race out,   95
 Or end the period of my youth in blood.
Per. Such fortune as the good *Andromache*
 Wisht valiant *Hector* wounded with the Greekes,
 I wish *Erastus* in his maiden warres.
 Orecome with valour these high minded knights   100
 As with thy vertue thou hast conquered me.
 Heauens heare my harty praier, and it effect.

                                                   Exeunt.

⟨SCENE III.⟩

Enter Phillippo, *the* Prince of Cipris, Basilisco, *and all the Knights.*

Phil. Braue Knights of Christendome, and Turkish both,
 Assembled heere in thirsty honors cause,
 To be enrolled in the brass leaued booke
 Of neuer wasting perpetuitie,
 Put Lambe-like mildenes to your Lyons strength,   5
 And be our tilting like two brothers sportes,
 That exercise their war with friendly blowes.
 Braue Prince of Cipris, and our sonne in law,
 Welcome these worthies by their seuerall countries,
 For in thy honor hither are they come,   10
 To grace thy nuptials with their deeds at armes.
Cyp. First, welcome, thrise renowned Englishman,
 Graced by thy country, but ten times more
 By thy approoued valour in the field;
 Vpon the onset of the enemy,   15
 What is thy motto, when thou spurres thy horse?
Englishman. In Scotland was I made a Knight at armes,
 Where for my countries cause I chargde my Launce:
 In France I tooke the Standard from the King,

---

  93 of *om. 1599* 98 wounded] 'rounded *Hazlitt. See Note*

And gained the flower of Gallia in my crest :   20
Against the light foote Irish haue I serued,
And in my skinne bare tokens of their skenes ;
Our word of courage all the world hath heard,
Saint George for England, and Saint George for me.
Cyp. Like welcome vnto thee, faire Knight of Fraunce ;   25
Well famed thou art for discipline in warre :
Vpon the incounter of thine enemy,
What is thy mot, renowned Knight of Fraunce ?
Frenchman. In Italy I put my Knighthood on,
Where in my shirt, but with my single Rapier,   30
I combated a Romane much renownd,
His weapons point impoysoned for my bane ;
And yet my starres did bode my victory.
Saint Denis is for Fraunce, and that for me.
Cyp. Welcome, Castilian, too among the rest,   35
For fame doth sound thy valour with the rest.
Vpon thy first encounter of thy foe,
What is thy word of courage, braue man of Spaine ?
Spaniard. At foureteene yeeres of age was I made Knight,
When twenty thousand Spaniards were in field ;   40
What time a daring Rutter made a challenge
To change a bullet with our swift flight shot ;
And I, with single heed and leuell, hit
The haughtie challenger, and strooke him dead.
The golden Fleece is that we cry vpon,   45
And Iaques, Iaques, is the Spaniards choise.
Cyp. Next, welcome vnto thee, renowned Turke,
Not for thy lay, but for thy worth in armes :
Vpon the first braue of thine enemy,
What is thy noted word of charge, braue Turke ?   50
Bru. Against the Sophy in three pitched fields,
Vnder the conduct of great *Soliman,*
Haue I been chiefe commaunder of an hoast,
And put the flint heart Perseans to the sword ;
⟨And⟩ marcht ⟨a⟩ conquerour through Asia.   55

---

20 gained *ed.* : giue *Qq.*: gaue *Hazlitt*   . 22 skenes] Kerns *Hawkins,*
Hazlitt, wrongly   30 with my] with a *1599*   36 rest] best *Hazlitt*
55 And *and* a *add. ed.*   55–6–7 *transposed thus by ed.* : 56–7–5 *Qq.*
See Note

The desert plaines of Affricke haue I staind
With blood of Moores, and there in three set battles fought:
Along the coasts held by the Portinguize,
Euen to the verge of golde abounding Spaine,
Hath *Brusor* led a valiant troope of Turkes,   60
And made some Christians kneele to *Mahomet*:
Him we adore, and in his name I crie,
Mahomet for me and *Soliman*.

Cyp. Now, Signeur *Basilisco*, you we know,
And therefore giue not you a strangers welcome,   65
You are a Rutter borne in Germanie.
Vpon the first encounter of your foe,
What is your braue vpon the enemy?

Bas. I fight not with my tongue; this is my oratrix.

Laying his hand vpon his sword.

Cyp. Why, Signeur *Basilisco*, is it a she sword?   70

Bas. I, and so are all blades with me: behold my instance;
Perdie, each female is the weaker vessell,
And the vigour of this arme infringeth
The temper of any blade, quoth my assertion;
And thereby gather that this blade,   75
Being approoued weaker than this lim,
May very well beare a feminine Epitheton.

Cyp. Tis well prooued; but whats the word that glories your
Countrey?

Bas. Sooth to say, the earth is my Countrey,
As the aire to the fowle, or the marine moisture   80
To the red guild fish: I repute myself no coward;
For humilitie shall mount. I keep no table
To character my fore-passed conflicts.
As I remember, there happened a sore drought
In some part of Belgia, that the iucie grasse   85
Was seared with the Sunne Gods Element:
I held it pollicie to put the men children
Of that climate to the sword,
That the mothers teares might releeue the pearched earth.

---

59 golde abounding Spaine *ed.*: golde, aboording Spaine *Qq.*: gold,
aboarding Spain *Hawkins, Hazlitt. See Note*   75–7 *printed as prose in Qq.*
82 I . . . table *beg.* 83 *Qq.*

The men died, the women wept, and the grasse grew;   90
Else had my Frize-land horse perished,
Whose losse would haue more grieued me
Than the ruine of that whole countrey.
Vpon a Time in Ireland I fought
On horseback with an hundred Kernes   95
From *Titans* Easterne vprise to his Western downefall;
Insomuch that my Steed began to faint:
, I, coniecturing the cause to be want of water, dismounted;
In which place there was no such Element.
Enraged therefore, with this Semitor,   100
⟨I⟩, all on foote, like an Herculian offspring,
Endured some three or foure howers combat,
In which processe my body distilled such dewy showers of swet
That from the warlike wrinckles of my front
My Palfray coold his thirst.   105
My mercy in conquest is equall with my manhood in fight;
The teare of an infant hath bin the ransome of a conquered citie,
Whereby I purchased the surname of *Pities adomant.*
Rough wordes blowe my choller,
As the wind dooth Mulcibers workehouse.   110
I haue no word, because no countrey:
Each place is my habitation;
Therefore each countries word mine to pronounce.
Princes, what would you?
I have seen much, heard more, but done most.   115
To be briefe, hee that will try me, let him waft me with his arme:
I am his, for some fiue launces.
Although it go against my starres to iest,
Yet to gratulate this benigne Prince,
I will suppresse my condition.   120
Phil. He is beholding to you greatly, sir.
Mount, ye braue Lordings, forwards to the tilt;
Myselfe will censure of your chiualrie,
And with impartiall eyes behold your deedes:
Forward, braue Ladies, place you to behold   125
The faire demeanor of these warlike Knights.
                                    Exeunt.

---

100 with] I with *Hazlitt*   101 I *add. ed.*   103 shower *1599*

Manet Basilisco.

Bas. I am melancholy : an humor of Venus belegereth me.
I haue reiected with contemptable frownes
The sweet glances of many amorous girles, or rather ladies :
But, certes, I am now captiuated with the reflecting eye   130
Of that admirable comet *Perseda.*
I will place her to behold my triumphes,
And do woonders in hir sight.
O heauen, she comes, accompanied with a child
Whose chin beares no impression of manhood,   135
Not an hayre, not an excrement.

Enter Erastus, Perseda, *and* Pyston.

Erast. My sweet *Perseda.*

Exeunt Erastus *and* Perseda.

Bas.   Peace, Infant, thou blasphemest.
Pist. You are deceiued, sir ; he swore not.
Bas. I tell thee, Iester, he did worse ; he cald that Ladie his.
Pist. Iester : *O extempore, O flores.*   140
Bas. O harsh, vn-edicate, illiterate pesant,
Thou abusest the phrase of the Latine.
Pist. By gods fish, friend, take you the Latins part? ile abuse you to.
Bas. What, saunce dread of our indignation?
Pist. Saunce? What languidge is that? I thinke thou art a word
maker by thine occupation.   146
Bas. I, teermest thou me of an occupation ?
Nay then, this fierie humor of choller is
Supprest by the thought of loue.   Faire Ladie—
Pist. Now, by my troth, she is gon.   150
Bas. I, hath the Infant transported her hence?
He saw my anger figured in my brow,
And at his best aduantage stole away.
But I will follow for reuenge.
Pist. Naye, but here you, sir ; I must talke with you before you goe.

Then Piston *gets on his back and puls him downe.*

Bas. O, if thou beest magnanimious, come before me.   156
Pist. Nay, if thou beest a right warrior, get from vnder me.

---

137 Peace . . . blasphemest *sep. line Qq.*   145-6 I . . . occupation *sep·*
line Qq.   149 Supprest *end of* 148 *Qq.*   155 I . . . goe *sep. line Qq.*

Bas. What, wouldst thou haue me a *Typhon*,
   To beare vp *Peleon* or *Ossa*?   159

Pist. Typhon me no *Typhons*, but swear vpon my Dudgin
   dagger, not to go till I giue thee leaue, but stay with me, and
   looke vpon the tilters.

Bas. O, thou seekst thereby to dim my glory.

Pist. I care not for that; wilt thou not swear?

Bas. O, I sweare, I sweare.   165

He sweareth him on his dagger.

Pist. By the contents of this blade—

Bas. By the contents of this blade—

Pist. I, the aforesaid *Basilisco*—

Bas. I, the aforesaid *Basilisco*—Knight, good fellow, Knight, Knight—

Pist. Knaue, good fellow, Knaue, Knaue—Will not offer to go
   from the side of *Piston*—   171

Bas. Will not offer to go from the side of *Piston*—

Pist. Without the leaue of the said *Piston* obtained—

Bas. Without the leaue of the said *Piston* licensed, obtayned,
   and granted.   175

Pist. Inioy thy life and liue; I giue it thee.

Bas. I inioy my life at thy hands, I confesse it.
   I am vp: but that I am religious in mine oath—

Pist. What would you do, sir; what wuld you do? Will you vp
   the ladder, sir, and see the tilting?   180

Then they go vp the ladders and they sound within to the first course.

Bas. Better a Dog fawne on me, then barke.

Pist. Now sir, how likes thou this Course?

Bas. Their Launces were coucht too hie, and their steeds ill borne.

Pist. It may be so, it may be so.

Sound to the second course.

Now, sir, how like you this course?   185

Bas. Prettie, prettie, but not famous;
   Well for a learner, but not for a warriour.

Pist. By my faith, me thought it was excellent.

160-2 *Typhon . . . Typhons* | but . . . dagger | not . . . leaue | but . . . tilters
Qq.   169-71 I . . . *Basilisco* | Knight . . . Knight | Knaue . . . Knaue | Will
. . . *Piston Qq.*   174-5 licensed . . . granted *sep. line Qq.*   179-80 Will . . .
tilting *sep. line Qq.*   182 thou] you *1599*   183 and . . . borne *sep. line Qq.*

Bas. I, in the eye of an infant a Peacocks taile is glorious.

Sound to the third course.

Pist. O, well run.   The baye horse with the blew taile, and the
siluer knight are both downe; by Cock and Pie, and Mouse
foot, the English man is a fine knight.   192
Bas. Now, by the marble face of the Welkin,
He is a braue warriour.
Pist. What an oath is there.   Fie upon thee, extortioner.   195
Bas. Now comes in the infant that courts my mistresse.

Sound to the fourth course.

Oh that my launce were in my rest,
And my Beauer closd for this encounter.
Pist. O, well ran.   My maister hath ouerthrowne the Turke.
Bas. Now fie vpon the Turke.   200
To be dismounted by a Childe it vexeth me.

Sound to the fift course.

Pist. O, well run, Maister.   He hath ouerthrowne the Frenchman.
Bas. It is the fury of his horse, not the strength of his arme.
I would thou wouldst remit my oath,
That I might assaile thy maister.   205
Pist. I giue thee leaue: go to thy destruction.   But, syrra,
wheres thy horse?
Bas. Why, my Page stands holding him by the bridle.
Pist. Well, goe; mount thee, goe.
Bas. I go, and *Fortune* guide my Launce.   210

Exit Basilisco.

Pist. Take the braginst knaue in Christendom with thee.   Truly,
I am sorrie for him : he iust like a knight? heele iustle like
a Iade.   It is a world to heere the foole prate and brag :
he will iet as if it were a Goose on a greene.   He goes
many times supperles to bed, and yet he takes Phisick to
make him leane.   Last night he was bidden to a gentle-
womans to supper, and, because he would not be put to carue,
he wore his hand in a scarfe, and said he was wounded.
. He weares a coloured lath in his scabberd, and when twas

---

190 ran *1599 -99 A*   190-3 O . . . taile | and . . . downe | by . . .
foot | the . . . knight *Qq.*   202 ran *1599 -99 A*   206-7 But . . . horse
sep. line Qq.   208 stands *om. 1599*   211-28 *printed as doggerel in Qq.*
212 iustle] iust *1599 -99 A*

found vpon him, he said he was wrathfull he might not
weare no iron. He weres Ciuet, and, when it was askt him
where he had that muske, he said, all his kindred smelt so :
Is not this a counterfet foole ? Well, ile vp, and see how he
speedes.   224

Sound the sixt course.

Now, by the faith of a squire, he is a very faint knight ;
why, my maister hath ouerthrowne him and his Curtall both
to the ground. I shall haue olde laughing ; it will be better
then the Fox in the hole for me.   228

                                                ⟨*Exit.*⟩

⟨Scene IV.⟩

Sound: Enter Philippo, *the* Prince of Cypris, Erastus, Ferdinando,
Lucina, *and all the Knights.*

Cyp. Braue Gentlemen, by all your free consents,
   This knight vnknowne hath best demeand himself :
   According to the proclimation made,
   The prize and honor of the day is his.—
   But now vnmaske thyselfe, that we may see   5
   What warlike wrinckles time has charectered
   With ages print vpon thy warlike face.
Engl. Accord to his request, braue man at armes,
   And let me see the face that vanquished me.
French. Vnmaske thyself, thou well approoued knight.   10
Turke. I long to see thy face, braue warriour.
Luc. Nay, valiant sir, we may not be denide.
   Faire Ladies should be coye to showe their faces,
   Least that the sun should tan them with his beames :
   Ile be your Page this once, for to disarme you.   15
Pist. Thats the reason that he shall helpe your husband
   to arme his head. Oh, the pollicie of this age is wonder-
   full.
Phil. What, young *Erastus* ? Is it possible ?
Cyp. *Erastus,* be thou honoured for this deed.   20
Engl. So yong, and of such good accomplishment :
   Thriue, faire beginner, as this time doth promise,
   In vertue, valour, and all worthinesse :

---

221 no *om. 1599 -99 A*   16-18 Thats . . . helpe | your . . . head | oh . . .
wonderfull *Qq.*

Giue me thy hand, I vowe myselfe thy friend.

Erast. Thankes, worthie sir, whose fauourable hand   25
Hath entred such a youngling in the warre ;
And thankes vnto you all, braue worthy sirs :
Impose me taske, how I may do you good ;
Erastus will be dutifull in all.

Phil. Leaue protestations now, and let vs hie   30
To tread lauolto, that is womens walke ;
There spend we the remainder of the day.

> *Exeunt. Manet* Ferdinando.

Ferd. Though ouer-borne, and foyled in my course,
Yet haue I partners in mine infamy.
Tis wondrous that so yong a toward warriour   35
Should bide the shock of such approoued knights,
As he this day hath matcht and mated too.
But vertue should not enuie good desert :
Therefore, *Erastus*, happy laude thy fortune.
But my *Lucina*, how she changed her colour,   40
When at the encounter I did loose a stirrop,
Hanging her head as partner of my shame.
Therefore will I now goe visit her,
And please her with this Carcanet of worth
Which by good fortune I haue found to day.   45
When valour failes, then gould must make the way.

> *Enter* Basilisco *riding of a mule.*

Bas. O cursed *Fortune*, enemy to *Fame*,
Thus to disgrace thy honored name,
By ouerthrowing him that far hath spred thy praise,
Beyond the course of *Titans* burning raies.   50

> *Enter* Piston.

Page, set aside the iesture of my enemy ;
Giue him a Fidlers fee, and send him packing.

Pist. Ho, God saue you, sir.   Haue you burst your shin ?

Bas. I, villaine, I haue broke my shin bone,
My back bone, my channell bone, and my thigh bone,   55
Beside two dossen small inferior bones.

---

43 now will I *1599 -99 A*   46 must golde *1599 -99 A*   56 of small
1599 -99 A

Pist. A shrewd losse, by my faith, sir.   But wheres your coursers
taile ?

Bas. He lost the same in seruice.   59

Pist. There was a hot piece of seruise where he lost his taile.
But how chance his nose is slit ?

Bas. For presumption, for couering the Emperors Mare.

Pist. Marry, a foule fault ; but why are his eares cut ?

Bas. For neighing in the Emperours court.

Pist. Why, then, thy Horse hath bin a Colt in his time.   65

Bas. True, thou hast said.

O, touch not the cheeke of my Palphrey,

Least he dismount me while my wounds are greene.

Page, run, bid the surgion bring his incision :

Yet stay, Ile ride along with thee my selfe.   70

Pist. And Ile beare you company.

Piston *getteth vp on his Asse, and rideth with him to the doore, and
meeteth the Cryer.*

Enter the Cryer.

Pist. Come, sirra, let me see how finely youle cry this chaine.

Cry. Why, what was it worth?

Pist. It was worth more then thou and all thy kin are worth.

Cry. It may be so ; but what must he haue that findes it ?

Pist. Why, a hundred Crownes.   76

Cry. When, then, Ile haue ten for the crying it.

Pist. Ten Crownes? And had but sixpence for crying a little
wench of thirty years old and vpwards, that had lost her
selfe betwixt a tauerne and a bawdie house.   80

Cry. I, that was a wench, and this is Golde ; she was poore,
but this is rich.

Pist. Why then, by this reckoning, a Hackney man should
haue ten shillings for horsing a Gentlewoman, where he
hath but ten pence of a begger.   85

Cry. Why, and reason good : let them paie that best may, as
the Lawyers vse their rich Clyents, when they let the poore
goe vnder *Forma pauperis.*

Pist. Why then, I pray thee, crie the chayne for me *Sub forma
pauperis,* for money goes very low with me at this time. 90

57–8 But . . . taile *sep. line Qq.*   61 chance] chanc'd it *Hazlitt*   72–102
printed as doggerel in Qq.   77 of it *1599 -99 A*

Cry. I, sir, but your maister is, though you be not.

Pist. I, but hee must not know that thou cryest the Chaine for
  me. I do but vse thee to saue me a labour, that am to
  make inquirie after it.

Cry. Well, sir, youle see me considered, will you not?   95

Pist. I, marry, will I; why, what lighter paiment can there be then
  consideration?

Cry. O yes.

Enter Erastus.

Erast. How now, sirra, what are you crying?

Cry. A chaine, sir, a chaine, that your man bad me crie.   100

Erast. Get you away, sirra. I aduise you meddle with no
  . chaines of mine.

Exit Cryer.

You paltrie knaue, how durst thou be so bould
To crie the chaine, when I bid thou shouldst not?
Did I not bid thee onely vnderhand   105
Make priuie inquirie for it through the towne,
Least publike rumour might aduertise her
Whose knowledge were to me a second death?

Pist. Why, would you haue me runne vp and downe the towne,
  and my shooes are doone?   110

Erast. What you want in shooes, ile giue ye in blowes.

Pist. I pray you, sir, hold your hands, and, as I am an honest
  man, Ile doe the best I can to finde your chaine.

Exit Piston.

Erast. Ah, treacherous *Fortune*, enemy to *Loue*,
Didst thou aduance me for my greater fall?   115
In dalying war, I lost my chiefest peace;
In hunting after praise, I lost my loue,
And in loues shipwrack will my life miscarrie.
Take thou the honor, and giue me the chaine,
Wherein was linkt the sum of my delight.   120
When she deliuered me the Carkanet,
Keep it, quoth she, as thou wouldst keep my selfe:
I kept it not, and therefore she is lost,
And lost with hir is all my happinesse,

III ye] you *1599-99 A*   112 I . . . hands | and . . . man | Ile . . .
chaine *Qq.*

And losse of happines is worse than death. 125
Come therefore, gentle death, and ease my griefe;
Cut short what malice *Fortune* misintends.
But stay a while, good *Death*, and let me liue;
Time may restore what *Fortune* tooke from me:
Ah no, great losses sildome are restord. 130
What, if my chaine shall neuer be restord?
My innocence shall clear my negligence.
Ah, but my loue is cerimonious,
And lookes for iustice at her louers hand:
Within forst furrowes of her clowding brow, 135
As stormes that fall amid a sun shine day,
I read her iust desires, and my decay.

⟨SCENE V.⟩

Enter Solyman, Haleb, Amurath, *and* Ianesaries.

Sol. I long till *Brusor* be returnde from *Rhodes*,
To know how he hath borne him gainst the Christians
That are assembled there to try their valour;
But more to be well assured by him
How *Rhodes* is fenc'd, and how I best may lay 5
My neuer failing siege to win that plot.
For by the holy Alcaron I sweare
Ile call my Souldiers home from *Persia*,
And let the Sophie breath, and from the Russian broiles
Call home my hardie, dauntlesse Ianisaries, 10
And from the other skirts of Christendome
Call home my Bassowes and my men of war,
And so beleager *Rhodes* by sea and land.
That Key will serue to open all the gates
Through which our passage cannot finde a stop 15
Till it haue prickt the hart of Christendome,
Which now that paltrie Iland keeps from scath.
Say, brother *Amurath*, and *Haleb*, say,
What thinke you of our resolution?
Amur. Great *Soliman*, heauens onely substitute, 20
And earths commander vnder Mahomet,
So counsell I, as thou thyselfe hast said.
Hal. Pardon me, dread Soueraigne, I hold it not

Good pollicie to call your forces home
·From *Persea* and *Polonia*, bending them   25
Vpon a paltrie Ile of small defence.
A common presse of base superfluous Turkes
May soon be leuied for so slight a taske.
Ah, *Soliman*, whose name hath shakt thy foes,
As withered leaues with Autume throwen downe,   30
Fog not thy glory with so fowle eclipse,
Let not thy Souldiers sound a base retire,
Till *Persea* stoope, and thou be conquerour.
What scandall were it to thy mightinesse,
After so many valiant Bassowes slaine,   35
Whose bloud hath bin manured to their earth,
Whose bones hath made their deep waies passable,
To sound a homeward, dull, and harsh retreate,
Without a conquest, or a mean reuenge.
Striue not for *Rhodes* by letting *Persea* slip;   40
The ones a Lyon almost brought to death,
Whose skin will counteruaile the hunters toile:
The other is a Waspe with threatning sting,
Whose Hunny is not worth the taking vp.
Amur. Why, *Haleb*, didst thou not heare our brother sweare
Vpon the Alcaron religiously   46
That he would make an vniuersall Campe
Of all his scattered legions: and darest thou
Infer a reason why it is not meete
After his Highnes sweares it shall be so?   50
Were it not ⟨that⟩ thou art my fathers sonne,
And striuing kindnes wrestled not with ire,
I would not hence till I had let thee know
What twere to thwart a Monarchs holy oath.
Hal. Why, his highnes gaue me leaue to speake my will,   55
And, far from flattery, I spoke my minde,
And did discharge a faithfull subiects loue:
Thou, *Aristippus* like, didst flatter him,
Not like my brother, or a man of worth.
And for his highnesse vowe, I crost it not,   60
But gaue my censure, as his highnesse bad.

---

30 throwne *1599* -99 *A*   42 shall *1599*   51 that *add. ed.*

Now for thy chastisement know, *Amurath*,
I scorne them, as a rechlesse Lion scornes
The humming of a gnat in Summers night.
Amur. I take it, *Haleb*, thou art friend to Rhodes.   65
Hal. Not halfe so much am I a friend to Rhodes
  As thou art enemy to thy Soueraigne.
Amur. I charge thee, say wherein; or else, by Mahomet,
  Ile hazard dutie in my Soueraignes presence.
Hal. Not for thy threats, but for my selfe, I say   70
  It is not meete that one so base as thou
  Shouldst come about the person of a King.
Sol. Must I giue aime to this presumption?
Amur. Your Highnesse knowes I speake in dutious loue.
Hal. Your Highnesse knowes I spake at your command,   75
  And to the purpose, far from flattery.
Amur. Thinks thou I flatter? Now I flatter not.
       Then he kils Haleb.
Sol. What dismall Planets guides this fatall hower?
  Villaine, thy brothers grones do call for thee,
     Then Soliman *kils* Amurath.
To wander with them through eternall night.   80
Amur. O *Soliman*, for louing thee I die.
Sol. No, *Amurath*, for murthering him thou dyest.
  Oh, *Haleb*, how shall I begin to mourne,
  Or how shall I begin to shed salt teares,
  For whom no wordes nor teares can well suffice?   85
  Ah, that my rich imperiall Diadem
  Could satisfie thy cruel destinie:
  Or that a thousand of our Turkish soules,
  Or twenty thousand millions of our foes,
  Could ransome thee from fell deaths tirannie.   90
  To win thy life would *Soliman* be poore,
  And liue in seruile bondage all my dayes.
  Accursed *Amurath*, that for a worthlesse cause
  In blood hath shortned our sweet *Halebs* dayes.
  Ah, what is dearer bond then brotherhood?   95
  Yet, *Amurath*, thou wert my brother too,
  If wilfull folly did not blind mine eyes.

---

74 spake *1599 -99 A*

I, I, and thou as vertuous as *Haleb*,
And I as deare to thee as vnto *Haleb*,
And thou as neere to me as *Haleb* was.   100
Ah, *Amurath*, why wert thou so vnkind
To him for vttering but a thwarting word?
And, *Haleb*, why did not thy harts counsell
Bridle the fond intemperance of thy tongue?
Nay, wretched *Solyman*, why didst not thou   105
Withould thy hand from heaping bloud on bloud?
Might I not better spare one ioy then both?
If loue of *Haleb* forst me on to wrath,
Curst be that wrath that is the way to death.
If iustice forst me on, curst be that iustice   110
That makes the brother Butcher of his brother.
Come, Ianisaries, and helpe me to lament,
And beare my ioyes on either side of me:—
I, late my ioyes, but now my lasting sorrow.
Thus, thus, let *Soliman* passe on his way,   115
Bearing in either hand his hearts decay.

Exeunt.

⟨SCENE VI.⟩

Enter Chorus.

Loue. Now, *Death* and *Fortune*, which of all vs three
    Hath in the Actors showne the greatest power?
    Haue not I taught *Erastus* and *Perseda*
    By mutuall tokens to seal vp their loues?
For. I, but those tokens, the Ring and Carkanet   5
    Were *Fortunes* gifts; *Loue* giues no gould or iewels.
Loue. Why, what is iewels, or what is gould but earth,
    An humor knit together by compression,
    And by the world's bright eye first brought to light,
    Onely to feed mens eyes with vaine delight?   10
    Loues workes are more then of a mortall temper;
    I couple minds together by consent.
    Who gaue Rhodes Princes to the Ciprian Prince, but *Loue*?
For. *Fortune*, that first by chance brought them together;
    For, till by *Fortune* persons meete each other,   15

---

102 to him *end of* 101 *Qq*.   113 of *om. 1599*

Thou canst not teach their eyes to wound their hearts.

Loue. I made those knights, of seuerall sect and countries,
　Each one by armes to honor his beloued.

For. Nay, one alone to honor his beloued :
　The rest, by turning of my tickle wheele,　　　　　　　20
　Came short in reaching of faire honors marke.
　I gaue *Erastus* onely that dayes prize,
　A sweet renowne, but mixt with bitter sorrow ;
　For, in conclusion of his happines,
　I made him loose the pretious Carcanet　　　　　　　25
　Whereon depended all his hope and ioy.

Death. And more then so ; for he that found the chaine,
　Euen for that Chaine shall be depriued of life.

Loue. Besides *Loue* hath inforst a foole,
　The fond Bragardo, to presume to armes.　　　　　　　30

For. I, but thou seest how he was ouerthrowne
　By *Fortunes* high displeasure.

Death.　　　　　　　　　　I, and by *Death*
　Had been surprisd, if Fates had giuen me leaue.
　But what I mist in him and in the rest,
　I did accomplish on *Haleb* and *Amurath*,　　　　　　35
　The worthy brethren of great *Soliman*.
　But, wherefore stay we ? Let the sequele prooue
　Who is ⟨the⟩ greatest, *Fortune*, *Death*, or *Loue*.

　　　　　　　　　　　　　　　　　　　　Exeunt.

⟨ACT II.

SCENE I.⟩

Enter Ferdinando *and* Lucina.

Ferd. As fits the time, so now well fits the place
　To coole affection with our woords and lookes,
　If in our thoughts be semblant simpathie.

Luc. My words, my lookes, my thoughts are all on thee ;
　Ferdinando is *Lucinaes* onely ioy.　　　　　　　5

Ferd. What pledge thereof ?

Luc.　　　　　　　An oath, a hand, a kisse.

32–3 By . . . displeasure | I . . . surprised | If . . . leaue *Qq.*　　38 the *add.*
Hawkins　3 semblant *Hazlitt*: semblance *Qq.*　6 An . . . kisse *sep. line Qq.*

Ferd. O holy oath, faire hand, and sugred kisse :
O neuer may *Ferdinando* lack such blisse.
But say, my deare, when shall the gates of heauen
Stand all wide ope⟨n⟩, for celestiall Gods   10
With gladsome lookes to gase at *Hymens* robes?
When shall the graces, or *Lucinas* hand
With Rosie chaplets deck thy golden tresses,
And *Cupid* bring me to thy nuptiall bed,
Where thou in ioy and pleasure must attend   15
A blisful war with me, thy chiefest friend?
Luc. Full fraught with loue and burning with desire,
I long haue longd for light of *Hymens* lights.
Ferd. Then that same day, whose warme and pleasant sight
Brings in the spring with many gladsome flowers,   20
Be our first day of ioy and perfect peace :
Till when, receiue this precious Carcanet,
In signe that, as the linkes are interlaced,
So both our hearts are still combind in one,
Which neuer can be parted but by death.   25

Enter Basilisco *and* Perseda.

Luc. And, if I liue, this shall not be forgot.
But see, *Ferdinando*, where *Perseda* comes,
Whom women loue for vertue, men for bewty,
All the world loues, none hates but enuie.
Bas. All haile, braue Cauelere. God morrow, Madam,   30
The fairest shine that shall this day be seene
Except *Persedas* beautious excellence,
Shame to loues Queene, and Empresse of my thoughts.
Ferd. Marry, thrise happy is *Persedas* chance,
To haue so braue a champion to hir Squire.   35
Bas. Hir Squire? her Knight—and who so else denies
Shall feele the rigour of my Sword and Launce.
Ferd. O sir, not I.
Luc. Heres none but friends ; yet let me challenge you
For gracing me with a malignant stile,   40
That I was fairest, and yet *Perseda* fairer :
We Ladies stand vpon our beauties much.

Per. Herein, *Lucina*, let me buckler him.

Bas. Not *Mars* himselfe had eare so faire a Buckler.

Per. Loue makes him blinde, and blinde can judge no coulours.

Luc. Why then the mends is made, and we still friends.   46

Per. Still friends? still foes; she weares my Carcanet.

Ah, false *Erastus*, how am I betraid.

Luc. What ailes you, madam, that your colour changes?

Per. A suddaine qualme; I therefore take my leaue.   50

Luc. Weele bring you home.

Per.   No, I shall soone get home.

Luc. Why then, farewell: *Fernando*, lets away.

> *Exeunt* Ferdinando *and* Lucina.

Bas. Say, worlds bright starre, whence springs this suddaine change?

   Is it vnkindnes at the little praise

   I gaue *Lucina* with my glosing stile?   55

Per. No, no; her beautie far surpasseth mine,

   And from my neck her neck hath woone the praise.

Bas. What is it, then? If loue of this my person,

   By fauour and by iustice of the heauens,

   At last haue percst through thy tralucent brest,   60

   And thou misdoubts, perhaps, that ile proue coye;

   O, be assur'd, tis far from noble thoughts

   To tyrannise ouer a yeelding foe.

   Therefore be blithe, sweet loue, abandon feare;

   I will forget thy former crueltie.   65

Per. Ah, false *Erastus*, full of treacherie.

Bas. I alwayes told you that such coward knights

   Were faithlesse swaines and worthie no respect.

   But tell me, sweete loue, what is his offence?

   That I with words and stripes may chastice him,   70

   And bring him bound for thee to tread vpon.

Per. Now must I find the meanes to rid him hence.

   Goe thou foorthwith, arme thee from top to toe,

   And come an houre hence vnto my lodging;

   Then will I tell thee this offence at large,   75

   And thou in my behalfe shalt work reuenge.

Bas. I, thus should men of valour be imployd;

---

45 And ... coulours *sep. line Qq.* : colour *1599 -99 A*   51 No ... home
sep. line Qq.   53 Whence...change *sep. line Qq.*

This is good argument of thy true loue :
I go ; make reconing that *Erastus* dyes,
Vnlesse, forewarnd, the weakling coward flies.   80

                         Exit Basilisco.

Per. Thou foolish coward, flies ?   *Erastus* liues,
The fairest shaped but fowlest minded man
That ere sunne saw within our hemyspheare.
My tongue to tell my woes is all to weake ;
I must vnclaspe me, or my heart will breake :   85
But inward cares are most pent in with greefe ;
Vnclasping, therefore, yeeldes me no releefe.
Ah, that my moyst and cloud compacted braine
Could spend my cares in showers of weeping raine ;
But scalding sighes, like blasts of boisterous windes,   90
Hinder my teares from falling on the ground,
And I must die by closure of my wound.
Ah, false *Erastus*, how had I misdoone,
That thou shouldst quit my loue with such a scorne ?

                     Enter Erastus.

Heere comes the *Synon* to my simple heart :   95
Ile frame my selfe to his dissembling art.
Erast. Desire perswades me on, feare puls me back :
Tush, I will to her ; innocence is bould.
How fares *Perseda*, my sweete second selfe ?
Per. Well, now *Erastus*, my hearts onely ioy,   100
Is come to ioyne both hearts in vnion.
Erast. And till I came whereas my loue did dwell,
My pleasure was but paine, my solace woe.
Per. What loue meanes, my *Erastus*, pray thee tell.
Erast. Matchlesse *Perseda*, she that gaue me strength   105
To win late conquest from many victors hands :
Thy name was conquerour, not my chiualrie,
Thy lookes did arme me, not my coate of steele,
Thy beauty did defend me, not my force,
Thy fauours bore me, not my light foote Steed ;   110
Therefore to thee I owe both loue and life.

---

80 weakling *1599 -99 A* : weakoning *undated Q*.   82 shaped *Hazlitt* :
shape *Qq*.   95 to my simple heart] of my heart *1599 -99 A*

But wherefore makes *Perseda* such a doubt,
As if *Erastus* could forget himselfe?
Which if I doe, all vengeance light on me.
Per. Aye me, how gracelesse are these wicked men: 115
I can no longer hould my patience.
Ah, how thine eyes can forge alluring lookes,
And faine deep oathes to wound poor silly maides.
Are there no honest drops in all thy cheekes,
To check thy fraudfull countenance with a blush?   120
Calst thou me loue, and louest another better?
If heauens were iust, thy teeth would teare thy tongue
For this thy periurde false disloyalty:
If heauens were iust, men should haue open brests,
That we therein might read their guilefull thoughts.   125
If heauens were iust, that power that forceth loue
Would neuer couple Woolues and Lambes together.
Yes, heauens are iust, but thou art so corrupt
That in thee all their influence dooth change,
As in the Spider good things turne to poison.   130
Ah, false *Erastus*, how had I misdone,
That thou shouldst pawne my true affections pledge
To her whose worth will neuer equall mine?
What, is *Lucinaes* wealth exceeding mine?
Yet mine sufficient to encounter thine.   135
Is she more faire then I? Thats not my fault,
Nor her desart: whats beauty but a blast,
Soone cropt with age or with infirmities?
Is she more wise? her yeeres are more then mine.
What ere she be, my loue was more then hers;   140
And for her chastitie let others iudge.
But what talke I of her? the fault is thine:
If I were so disgratious in thine eye
That she must needes inioy my interest,
Why didst thou deck her with my ornament?   145
Could nothing serue her but the Carcanet
Which, as my life, I gaue to thee in charge?
Couldst thou abuse my true simplicitie,
Whose greatest fault was ouer louing thee?
Ile keepe no tokens of thy periury: 150
Heere, giue her this; *Perseda* now is free,

And all my former loue is turnd to hate.

Erast. Ah stay, my sweete *Perseda*; heare me speake.

Per. What are thy words but Syrens guilefull songs,
That please the eare but seeke to spoile the heart ?   155

Erast. Then view my teares that plead for innocence.

Per. What are thy teares but Circes magike seas,
Where none scape wrackt but blindfould Marriners ?

Erast. If words and teares displease, then view my lookes
That plead for mercy at thy rigorous hands.   160

Per. What are thy lookes but like the Cockatrice
That seekes to wound poore silly passengers ?

Erast. If words, nor teares, nor lookes may win remorse,
What then remaines ? for my perplexed heart
Hath no interpreters but wordes, or teares, or lookes.   165

Per. And they are all as false as thou thy‚selfe.

　　　　　　　　　　　　　　　Exit Perseda.

Erast. Hard doome of death, before my case be knowne ;
My iudge vniust, and yet I cannot blame her,
Since Loue and iealousie mislead her thus :
Myselfe in fault, and yet not worthie blame,   170
Because that Fortune made the fault, not Loue.
The ground of her vnkindnes growes, because
I lost the pretious Carcanet she gaue me :
Lucina hath it, as her words import ;
But how she got it, heauen knows, not I.   175
Yet this is some aleauement to my sorrow
That, if I can but get the Chaine againe,
I bouldly then shall let *Perseda* know
That she hath wrongd *Erastus* and her frend.
Ah, Loue, and if thou beest of heauenly power,   180
Inspire me with some present stratagem.
It must be so ; *Lucinas* a franke Gaimster,
And like it is in play sheele hazard it ;
For, if report but blazen her aright,
Shees a franke gaimster, and inclinde to play.   185
Ho, *Piston.*

　　　　　　　　　　Enter Piston.

---

169 misled *1599 -99 A*   172-3 *conj. Hazlitt* : The ground . . . lost |
The pretious Carcanet she gaue to me *Qq.*   176 aleauement *Hawkins* :
alleuement *Hazlitt* : aleagement *Qq.*   186 Ho, *Piston end of* 185 *Qq.*

Pist. Heere, sir, what would you with me?

Erast. Desire *Guelpio* and signior *Iulio* come speake with me,
and bid them bring some store of crownes with them; and,
sirra, prouide me foure Visards, foure Gownes, a boxe, and
a Drumme; for I intend to go in mummery.   191

Pist. I will, sir.

Exit Piston.

Erast. Ah, vertuous Lampes of euer turning heauens,
Incline her minde to play, and mine to win.
Nor do I couet but what is mine owne: 195
Then shall I let *Perseda* vnderstand
How iealousie had armd her tongue with malice.
Ah, were she not *Perseda*, whom my heart
No more can flie then iron can Adamant,
Her late vnkindnes would haue changed my minde.   200

Enter Guelpio, Iulio *and* Piston.

Guelp. How now, *Erastus*, wherein may we pleasure thee?

Erast. Sirs, thus it is; we must in mummerie
Vnto *Lucina*, neither for loue nor hate,
But, if we can, to win the chaine she weares:
For, though I haue some interest therein,   205
Fortune may make me maister of mine owne,
Rather than ile seeke iustice gainst the Dame:
But this assure your selues, it must be mine,
By game, or change, by one deuise or other:
The rest ile tell you when our sport is doone.   210

Iul. Why then lets make vs ready, and about it.

Erast. What store of Crownes haue you brought?

Guelp. Feare not for money, man, ile beare the Boxe.

Iul. I haue some little replie, if neede require.

Pist. I, but heare you, Maister, was not he a foole that went
to shoote, and left his arrowes behinde him?   216

Erast. Yes, but what of that?

Pist. Mary, that you may loose your money, and go without
the chaine, vnlesse you carrie false dice.

Guelp. Mas, the foole sayes true; lets haue some got.   220

188-91 *printed as doggerel Qq.*   202 in] to *1599*   209 *the first* By]
Be *1599 -99 A*   214 replie] relay *Hazlitt. See Note*   215-6 that . . . him
sep. line Qq.   218 and . . . dice *sep. line Qq.*

Pist. Nay, I vse not to go without a paire of false Dice; heere
are tall men and little men.

Iul. Hie men and low men, thou wouldst say.

Erast. Come, sirs, lets go:—Drumsler, play for me, and ile
reward thee:—and, sirra *Piston*, mar not our sport with your
foolery.   226

Pist. I warrant you, sir, they get not one wise word of me.

       Sound vp the Drum to Lucinaes *doore.*

Luc. I, marrie, this showes that *Charleman* is come:
  What, shall we play heere? content,
  Since Signior *Ferdinand* will haue it so.   230

Then they play, and when she hath lost her gold, Erastus *pointed
to her chaine, and then she said:*

  I, were it *Cleopatraes* vnion.

Then Erastus *winneth the Chaine, and looseth his gould, and* Lucina
saies:

  Signior *Fernando*, I am sure tis you;—
  And, Gentlemen, vnmaske ere you depart,
  That I may know to whom my thankes is due
  For this so courteous and vnlookt for sport.   235
  No, wilt not be? then sup with me to-morrow:
  Well, then ile looke for you; till then, farewell.

                    Exit Lucina.

Erast. Gentlemen, each thing hath sorted to our wish;
  Shee tooke me for *Fernando*, markt you that?
  Your gould shall be repaide with double thankes;   240
  And, fellow Drumsler, ile reward you well.

Pist. But is there no reward for my false dice?

Erast. Yes, sir, a garded sute from top to toe.

            Enter Ferdinando.

Ferd. Dasell mine eyes, or ist *Lucinas* chaine?
  False treacher, lay downe the chaine that thou hast stole. 245

Erast. He lewdly lyes that cals me treacherous.

Ferd. That lye my weapon shall put down thy throate.

       Then Erastus *slaies* Ferdinando.

---

221 heere ... men *sep. line Qq.*   224 play *ed.*: pray *Qq.*   224–6 *printed
as doggerel Qq.*   S.D. *pointeth 1599*   240 repaide *1599*: repairde *undated Q.
and 1599 A*

Iul. Flie, *Erastus*, ere the Gouernour haue any newes,
Whose neere alye he was and cheefe delight.
Erast. Nay, Gentlemen, flye you and saue your selues,   250
Least you pertake the hardness of my fortune.

                                Exeunt Guelpio *and* Iulio.

Ah, fickle and blind guidresse of the world,
What pleasure hast thou in my miserie?
Wast not enough when I had lost the Chaine,
Thou didst bereaue me of my dearest loue;   255
But now when I should repossesse the same,
To cross me with this haplesse accedent?
Ah, if but time and place would giue me leaue,
Great ease it were for me to purge my selfe,
And to acuse fell *Fortune*, *Loue*, and *Death*;   260
For all these three conspire my tragedie.
But danger waites vppon my words and steps;
I dare not stay, for if the Gouernour
Surprise me heere, I die by marshall law;
Therefore I go: but whether shall I go?   265
If into any stay adioyning Rhodes,
They will betray me to *Phylippos* hands,
For loue, or gaine, or flatterie.
To Turkie must I goe; the passage short,
The people warlike, and the King renownd   270
For all heroyicall and kingly vertues.
Ah, hard attempt, to tempt a foe for ayde.
Necessitie yet sayes it must be so,
Or suffer death for *Ferdinandos* death,
Whom honors title forst me to misdoe   275
By checking his outragious insolence.
Piston, heere take this chaine, and giue it to *Perseda*,
And let her know what hath befallen me:
When thou hast deliuered it, take ship and follow me,
I will be in Constantinople.—   280
Farewell, my country, dearer then my life;
Farewell, sweete friends, dearer then countrey soyle;
Farewell, *Perseda*, dearest of them all,
Dearer to me then all the world besides.   284

                                         Exit Erastus.

---

281 *the second* my *om. 1599*   282 sweete] deare *1599 -99 A*

Pist. Now am I growing into a doubtful agony, what I were
best to do—to run away with this Chaine, or deliuer it, and
follow my maister. If I deliuer it, and follow my maister,
I shall haue thanks, but they will make me neuer the fatter:
if I run away with it, I may liue vpon credit all the while
I weare this chaine, or dominere with the money when I
haue sold it. Hetherto all goes well; but, if I be taken—
I, marry, sir, then the case is altered, I, and haltered to.
Of all things I doe not loue to preach with a haulter about
my necke. Therefore for this once, ile be honest against my
will; *Perseda* shall haue it, but, before I goe, Ile be so bolde
as to diue into this Gentlemans pocket, for good luck sake,
if he deny me not:—how say you, sir, are you content?—A
plain case: *Qui tacet consitiri videtur.*

Enter Phylippo *and* Iulio.

Iul. See, where his body lyes.

Phil. I, I; I see his body all to soone: 300
What barbarous villaine ist that rifles him?
Ah, *Ferdinand*, the stay of my old age,
And cheefe remainder of our progenie—
Ah, louing cousen, how art thou misdone
By false *Erastus*—ah no, by treacherie,   305
For well thy valour hath been often tride.
But, while I stand and weepe, and spend the time
In fruitlesse plaints, the murtherer will escape
Without reuenge, sole salue for such a sore.—
Say, villaine, wherefore didst thou rifle him?   310

Pist. Faith, sir, for pure good will; seeing he was going towards
heauen, I thought to see if he had a pasport to *S. Nicholas*
or no.

Phil. Some sot he seemes to be; twere pittie to hurt him.
Sirra, canst thou tell who slew this man?   315

Pist. I, sir, very well; it was my maister *Erastus.*

Phil. Thy maister? and whether is he gone now?

Pist. To fetch the Sexten to bury him, I thinke.

Phil. Twere pittie to imprison such a sot.

Pist. Now it fits my wisdome to counterfeit the foole.   320

285–98 *printed as doggerel Qq.*   296 this] the *1599 -99 A*   302 *Ferdinando
1599 -99 A*   311–3 Faith . . . will | Seeing . . . heauen | I . . . no *Qq.*

Phil. Come hether, sirra ; thou knowest me
   For the Gouernour of the cittie, dost thou not ? .
Pist. I, forsooth, sir.
Phil. Thou art a bondman, and wouldst faine be free ?
Pist. I, forsooth, sir.   325
Phil. Then do but this, and I will make thee free,
   And rich withall ; learne where *Erastus* is,
   And bring me word, and Ile reward thee well.
Pist. That I will sir ; I shall finde you at the Castle, shall I not ?
Phil. Yes.   330
Pist. Why, ile be heere, as soone as euer I come again.

                        Exit Piston.

Phil. But for Assurance that he may not scape,
   Weele lay the ports and hauens round about ;
   And let a proclamation straight be made
   That he that can bring foorth the murtherer   335
   Shall haue three thousand Duckets for his paines.
   My selfe will see the body borne from hence,
   And honored with Balme and funerall.

                            Exit.

⟨Scene II.⟩

Enter Piston.

Pist. God sends fortune to fooles. Did you euer see wise man
escape as I have done? I must betraie my maister? I, but
when, can you tell?

Enter Perseda.

See where *Perseda* comes, to saue me a labour.—After my
most hearty commendations, this is to let you 'vnderstand,
that my maister was in good health at the sending hereof.
Yours for euer, and euer, and euer, in most humble wise,
Piston.

    Then he deliuered her the chaine.

Per. This makes me thinke that I haue been to cruell.
   How got he this from of *Lucinas* arme?   10
Pist. Faith, in a mummery, and a pair of false dice. I was one
of the mummers my selfe, simple as I stand here.

---

334 a *om. 1599 -99 A*   336 paine *1599 -99 A*   1 men *1599*
-99 A   1–8 *printed as doggerel Qq.*   6 thereof *1599*   S.D. *deliuereth*
1599   11–2 I . . . here *sep. line Qq.*

Per. I rather thinke it cost him very deare.
Pist. I, so it did, for it cost *Ferdinando* his life.
Per. How so?   15
Pist. After we had got the chaine in mummery,
    And lost our box in counter cambio,
    My maister wore the chaine about his necke;
    Then *Ferdinando* met vs on the way,
    And reuil'd my maister, saying he stole the chaine.   20
    With that they drew, and there *Ferdinando* had the prickado.
Per. And whether fled my poore *Erastus* then?
Pist. To *Constantinople*, whether I must follow him.
    But ere he went, with many sighes and teares
    He deliuered me the chaine, and bad me giue it you   25
    For perfect argument that he was true,
    And you too credulous.
Per. Ah stay, no more; for I can heere no more.
Pist. And I can sing no more.
Per. My heart had arm'd my tongue with iniury,   30
    To wrong my friend whose thoughts were euer true.
    Ah, poore *Erastus*, how thy starres malign.—
    Thou great commander of the swift wingd winds,
    And dreadfull *Neptune*, bring him backe againe:
    But, *Eolus* and *Neptune*, let him go;   35
    For heere is nothing but reuenge and death:
    Then let him go; ile shortly follow him,
    Not with slow sailes, but with loues goulden wings;
    My ship shall be borne with teares, and blowne with sighs;
    So will I soare about the Turkish land,   40
    Vntill I meete *Erastus*, my sweete friend:
    And then and there fall downe amid his armes,
    And in his bosome there power foorth my soule,
    For satisfaction of my trespasse past.

              Enter Basilisco *armde.*

Bas. Faire Loue, according vnto thy commaund,   45
    I seeke *Erastus*, and will combat him.
Per. I, seeke him, finde him, bring him to my sight;
    For, till we meete, my hart shall want delight.

                           Exit Perseda.

---

32 maling *Qq.*

Bas. My petty fellow, where hast thou hid thy maister?

Pist. Marrie, sir, in an Armorours shop, where you had not
　　best go to him.　　　　　　　　　　　　　　　　　　　　51

Bas. Why so? I am in honor bound to combat him.

Pist. I, sir, but he knowing your fierce conditions, hath planted
　　a double cannon in the doore, ready to discharge it vppon
　　you, when you go by. I tell you, for pure good will.　　55

Bas. In Knightly curtesie, I thanke thee :
　　But hopes the coystrell to escape me so?
　　Thinkes he bare cannon shot can keepe me back?
　　Why, wherfore serues my targe of proofe but for the bullet?
　　That once put by, I roughly come vpon him,　　　　　　　60
　　Like to the wings of lightning from aboue ;
　　I with a martiall looke astonish him ;
　　Then fals he downe, poore wretch, vpon his knee,
　　And all to late repents his surquedry.
　　Thus do I take him on my fingers point,　　　　　　　　65
　　And thus I beare him thorough euery streete,
　　To be a laughing stock to all the towne :
　　That done, I lay him at my mistres feete,
　　For her to giue him doome of life or death.　　　　　　69

Pist. I, but heere you, sir ; I am bound, in paine of my maisters
　　displeasure, to haue a bout at cuffes, afore you and I part.

Bas. Ha, ha, ha.
　　Eagles are chalenged by paltry flyes.
　　Thy folly giues thee priuiledge ; begon, begon.

Pist. No, no, sir : I must haue a bout with you, sir, thats flat,
　　least my maister turne me out of seruice.　　　　　　　76

Bas. Why, art thou wearie of thy life?

Pist. No, by my faith, sir.

Bas. Then fetch thy weapons ; and with my single fist
　　Ile combat thee, my body all vnarmd.　　　　　　　　80

Pist. Why, lend me thine, and saue me a labour.

Bas. I tell thee, if *Alcides* liued this day,
　　He could not weild my weapons.

49 petty] pretty *Hawkins and Hazlitt, wrongly ; see* iv. 2. 61　　　50–1
where . . . him *sep. line Qq.*　　　　　53–5 *printed as doggerel Qq.*
66 through *1599*　　　70–1 I . . . bound | ln . . . displeasure | To . . . part
sep. lines Qq.　　71 a bout] about *Qq.*　　72–3 Ha . . . flyes *one line Qq.*
75–6 *Undated Q. inserts* iii. 1. 34 *between these lines. By a printer's blunder it
has been transferred from the top of fol. E* 3 *to the top of fol. E* 2　　83 weapon *1599*

O 2

Pist. Why, wilt thou stay till I come againe?
Bas. I, vpon my honour.   85
Pist. That shall be when I come from Turkey.

Exit Piston.

Bas. Is this little desperate fellow gon?
　Doubtlesse he is a very tall fellow;
　And yet it were a disgrace to all my chiualrie
　To combate one so base: 90
　Ile send some Crane to combate with the Pigmew;
　Not that I feare, but that I scorne to fight.

Exit Basilisco.

⟨SCENE III.⟩

Enter Chorus.

Loue. *Fortune*, thou madest *Fernando* finde the chaine;
　But yet by *Loues* instruction he was taught
　To make a present of it to his Mistris.
For. But *Fortune* would not let her keepe it long.
Loue. Nay, rather, *Loue*, by whose suggested power   5
　Erastus vsde such dice, as, being false,
　Ran not by *Fortune*, but necessitie.
For. Meane time, I brought *Fernando* on the way,
　To see and chalenge what *Lucina* lost.
Death. And by that chalenge I abridgde his life,   10
　And forst *Erastus* into banishment,
　Parting him from his loue, in spight of *Loue*.
Loue. But with my goulden wings ile follow him,
　And giue him aide and succour in distresse.
For. And doubt not to, but *Fortune* will be there,   15
　And crosse him too, and sometimes flatter him,
　And lift him vp, and throw him downe againe.
Death. And heere and there in ambush *Death* will stand,
　To mar what *Loue* or *Fortune* takes in hand.

Exeunt.

10 abridge *1599 A*

⟨Act III.

Scene I.⟩

Enter Solyman *and* Brusor, with Ianisaries.

Sol. How long shall *Soliman* spend his time,
  And waste his dayes in fruitlesse obsequies?
  Perhaps my greefe and long continuall moane
  Ads but a trouble to my brothers ghoasts,
  Which but for me would now haue tooke their rest.   5
  Then, farewell, sorrow; and now, reuenge, draw neere.
  In controuersie touching the Ile of Rhodes
  My brothers dyde; on Rhodes ile be reuengd.
  Now tell me, *Brusor*, whats the newes at Rhodes?
  Hath the young prince of Cipris married   10
  Cornelia, daughter to the Gouernour?
Bru. He hath, my Lord, with the greatest pompe
  That ere I saw at such a festiuall.
Sol. What, greater then at our coronation?
Bru. Inferiour to that onely.   15
Sol. At tilt, who woone the honor of the day?
Bru. A worthie Knight of Rhodes, a matchlesse man,
  His name *Erastus*, not twentie yeares of age,
  Not tall, but well proportioned in his lims:
  I neuer saw, except your excellence,   20
  A man whose presence more delighted me;
  And had he worshipt Mahomet for Christ,
  He might haue borne me through out all the world,
  So well I loued and honoured the man.
Sol. These praises, *Brusor*, touch me to the heart,   25
  And makes me wish that I had beene at Rhodes,
  Vnder the habit of some errant knight,
  Both to haue seene and tride his valour.
Bru. You should haue seene him foile and ouerthrow
  All the Knights that there incountred him.   30
Sol. What ere he be, euen for his vertues sake,
  I wish that fortune of our holy wars
  Would yield him prisoner vnto Soliman;
  That, for retaining one so vertuous,

3, 4 *transposed in undated* Q.   4 ghost *1599* A *and undated* Q.
34 *See note on* ii. 2. 75-6

We may ourselues be famd for vertues.   35
But let him passe : and, *Brusor*, tell me now,
How did the Christians vse our Knights?
Bru. As if that we and they had been one sect.
Sol. What thinkst thou of their valour and demeanor?
Bru. Braue men at armes, and friendly out of armes;   40
Courteous in peace, in battell dangerous;
Kinde to their foes, and liberall to their friends;
And, all in all, their deedes heroicall.
Sol. Then tell me, *Brusor*, how is Rhodes fenst?
For eyther Rhodes shall be braue *Solymàns*,   45
Or cost me more braue Souldiers
Then all that Ile will beare.
Bru.   Their fleete is weake;
Their horse, I deeme them fiftie thousand strong;
Their footemen more, well exercised in war;
And, as it seemes, they want no needful vittaile.   50
Sol. How euer Rhodes be fencd by sea or land,
It eyther shall be mine, or burie me.

                    Enter Erastus.

Whats he that thus bouldly enters in?
His habite argues him a Christian.
Erast. I, worthy Lord, a forlorne Christian.   55
Sol. Tell me, man, what madnes brought thee hether?
Erast. Thy vertuous fame and mine owne miserie.
Sol. What miserie? speake; for, though you Christians
Account our Turkish race but barbarous,
Yet haue we eares to heare a iust complaint   60
And iustice to defend the innocent,
And pitie to such as are in pouertie,
And liberall hands to such as merit bountie.
Bru. My gratious Soueraigne,
As this Knight seemes by greefe tyed to silence,   65
So his deserts binds me to speake for him:
This is *Erastus*, the Rhodian worthie,
The flower of chiualrie and curtesie.
Sol. Is this the man that thou hast so describde?

Stand vp, faire Knight, that what my heart desires,   70
Mine eyes may view with pleasure and delight.
This face of thine shuld harbour no deceit.
Erastus, ile not yet vrge to know the cause
That brought thee hether, least with the discourse
Thou shouldst afflict thy selfe,   75
And cross the fulnes of my ioyful passion.
But ⟨as a token⟩ that we are assurde
Heauens brought thee hether for our benefit,
Know thou that Rhodes, nor all that Rhodes containes,
Shall win thee from the side of *Soliman*,   80
If we but finde thee well inclind to vs.
Erast. If any ignoble or dishonourable thoughts
Should dare attempt, or but creepe neere my heart,
Honour should force disdaine to roote it out:
As ayre bred Eagles, if they once perceiue   85
That any of their broode but close their sight
When they should gase against the glorious Sunne,
They straight way sease vpon him with their talents,
That on the earth it may vntimely die
For looking but a scue at heauens bright eye.   90
Sol. Erastus, to make thee well assurde
How well thy speach and presents liketh vs,
Aske what thou wilt; it shall be graunted thee.
Erast. Then this, my gratious Lord, is all I craue,
That, being banisht from my natiue soile,   95
I may haue libertie to liue a Christian.
Sol. I, that, or any thing thou shalt desire;
Thou shalt be Captaine of our Ianisaries,
And in our Counsell shalt thou sit with vs,
And be great *Solimans* adopted friend.   100
Erast. The least of these surpasse my best desart,
Vnlesse true loyaltie may seeme desart.
Sol. Erastus, now thou hast obtaind thy boone,
Denie not *Soliman* his own request:
A vertuous enuie pricks me with desire   105
To trie thy valour: say, art thou content?
Erast. I, if my Soueraigne say content, I yeeld.

---

74 least . . . discourse *beg.* 75 *Qq.*   77 as a token *add. ed.*   104
his own *1599*: this owne *1599 A and undated Q.*: this one *Hawkins, Hazlitt*

Sol. Then giue vs swordes and Targets :—
　And now, *Erastus*, thinke me thine enemie,
　But euer after thy continuall friend ;　　　　　　110
　And spare me not, for then thou wrongst my honour.

　　　Then they fight, and Erastus *ouercomes* Solyman.

　Nay, nay, *Erastus*, throw not downe thy weapons,
　As if thy force did faile ; it is enough
　That thou hast conquered *Soliman* by strength :
　By curtesie let *Soliman* conquer thee.　　　　　115
　And now from armes to counsell sit thee downe.
　Before thy comming I vowd to conquer Rhodes :
　Say, wilt thou be our Lieutenant there,
　And further vs in manage of these wars ?

Erast. My gracious Soueraigne, without presumption,　120
　If poore *Erastus* may once more intreate,
　Let not great *Solimans* command,
　To whose behest I vowe obedience,
　Inforce me sheath my slaughtering blade
　In the deare bowels of my countrimen :　　　　125
　And were it not that *Soliman* hath sworne,
　My teares should plead for pardon to that place.
　I speake not this to shrinke away for feare,
　Or hide my head in time of dangerous stormes :
　Imploy me else where in thy forraine wars,　　　130
　Against the Persians, or the barbarous Moore,
　Erastus will be formost in the battaile.

Sol. Why fauourst thou thy countrimen so much,
　By whose crueltie thou art exylde ?

Erast. Tis not my countrey, but *Phylippos* wrath　　135
　(It must be' tould), for *Ferdinandos* death,
　Whom I in honours cause haue reft of life.

Sol. Nor suffer this or that to trouble thee :
　Thou shalt not neede *Phylippo* nor his Ile,
　Nor shalt thou war against thy Countrimen :　　140
　I like thy vertue in refusing it,
　But, that our oath may haue his currant course,
　Brusor, goe leuie men ;

---

　108 Targers *1599 -99 A*　　109 me thine] thee mine *1599 -99 A*　　127 to] .
in *1599 -99 A*

Prepare a fleet to assault and conquer Rhodes.
Meane time *Erastus* and I will striue　　　　145
By mutuall kindnes to excell each other,
Brusor, be gon: and see not *Soliman*
Till thou hast brought Rhodes in subiection.

　　　　　　　　　　　　　　　　Exit Brusor.

And now, *Erastus*, come and follow me,
Where thou shalt see what pleasures and what sportes　150
My Minions and my Euenukes can deuise,
To driue away this melancholly moode.

　　　　　　　　　　　　　　　　Exit Soliman.
　　　　　　　　　Enter Piston.

Pist. O, maister, see where I am.
Erast. Say, *Piston*, whats the newes at Rhodes?
Pist. Colde and comfortles for you; will you haue them all
　　at once?　　　　　　　　　　　　　　156
Erast. I.
Pist. Why, the Gouernour will hang you, and he catch you;
　　Ferdinando is buried; your friends commend them to you;
　　Perseda hath the chaine, and is like to die for sorrow.　160
Erast. I, thats the greefe, that we are parted thus.
　　Come, follow me, and I will heare the rest,
　　For now I must attend the Emperour.

　　　　　　　　　　　　　　　　Exeunt.

　　　　　　　　　⟨SCENE II.⟩

　　　　Enter Perseda, Lucina, *and* Basilisco.

Per. Accursed chaine, vnfortunate *Perseda*.
Luc. Accursed chaine, vnfortunate *Lucina*.
　　My friend·is gone, and I am desolate.
Per. My friend is gone, and I am desolate.
　　Returne him back, faire starres, or let me die.　　　5
Luc. Returne him backe, fair heauens, or let me die;
　　For what was he but comfort of my life?
Per. For what was he but comfort of my life?
　　But why was I so carefull of the Chaine?

---

148 *After this line in margin of undated Q. there is a manuscript entry in
a sixteenth or seventeenth century hand* the daunce before Piston enters　155–6
will . . . once *sep. line Qq.*

Luc. But why was I so carelesse of the Chaine?   10
   Had I not lost it, my friend had not been slaine.
Per. Had I not askt it, my friend had not departed,
   His parting is my death.
Luc.   His deaths my liues departing,
   And here my tongue dooth stay with swolne hearts greefe.
Per. And here my swolne harts greef doth stay my tongue. 15
Bas. For whom weepe you?
Luc.   Ah, for *Fernandos* dying.
Bas. For whom mourne you?
Per.   Ah, for *Erastus* flying.
Bas. Why, Lady, is not *Basilisco* here?
   Why, Lady, dooth not *Basilisco* liue?
   Am not I worth both these for whom you mourne?   20
   Then take each one halfe of me, and cease to weepe;
   Or if you gladly would inioy me both,
   Ile serue the one by day, the other by night,
   And I will pay you both your sound delight.
Luc. Ah, how vnpleasant is mirth to melancholy.   25
Per. My heart is full; I cannot laugh at follie.

                        Exeunt Ladies.

Bas. See, see, *Lucina* hates me like a Toade,
   Because that, when *Erastus* spake my name,
   Her loue *Fernando* died at the same;
   So dreadfull is our name to cowardice.   30
   On the other side, *Perseda* takes it vnkindly
   That, ere he went, I brought not bound vnto her
   Erastus, that faint hearted run away.
   Alasse, how could I? for his man no sooner
   Informd him that I sought him vp and downe,   35
   But he was gone in twinckling of an eye.
   But I will after my delitious loue;
   For well I wot, though she desemble thus,
   And cloake affection with hir modestie,
   With loue of me her thoughts are ouer gone,   40
   More then was *Phillis* with her *Demophon.*

                            Exit.

---

16 Ah . . . dying *sep. line Qq.*   17 Ah . . . flying *sep. line Qq.*

⟨Scene III.⟩

Enter Philippo, *the Prince of* Cipris, *with other Souldiours.*

Phil. Braue prince of Cipris, and our sonne in law,
  Now there is little time to stand and talke ;
  The Turkes haue past our Gallies, and are landed :
  You with some men at armes shall take the Tower ;
  I with the rest will downe vnto the strand.   5
  If we be beaten backe, weele come to you ;
  And here, in spight of damned Turkes, weele gaine
  A glorious death or famous victorie.
Cyp. About it then.

             Exeunt.

⟨Scene IV.⟩

Enter Brusor *and his Souldiers.*

Bru. Drum, sound a parle to the Citizens.

   The Prince of Cypres *on the walles.*

Cyp. What parle craues the Turkish at our hands ?
Bru. We come with mightie *Solimans* commaund,
  Monarch and mightie Emperor of the world,
  From East to West, from South to Septentrion.   5
  If you resist, expect what warre affordes,
  Mischiefe, murther, bloud, and extremitie.
  What, wilt thou yeeld, and trie our clemencie ?
  Say I, or no ; for we are peremtorie.
Cyp. Your Lord vsurps in all that he possesseth :   10
  And that great God, which we do truly worship,
  Shall strengthen vs against your insolence.
Bru. Now if thou plead for mercie, tis to late :
  Come, fellow Souldiers ; let vs to the breach
  Thats made already on the other side.   15

        Exeunt to the battel.

   Phylippo *and* Cipris *are both slaine.*

⟨Scene V.⟩

Enter Brusor, *with Souldiers, hauing* Guelpio, Iulio, *and* Basilisco,
   with Perseda *and* Lucina *prisoners.*

Bru. Now Rhodes is yoakt, and stoopes to *Soliman.*
  There lies the Gouernour, and there his Sonne :

---

  5 strand] strane *Qq.* 13 thou] you *1599 -99 A*

Now let their soules
Tell sorrie tidings to their ancestors,
What millions of men, opprest with ruine and scath,   5
The Turkish armies did ⟨oer-throw⟩ in Christendome.
What say these prisoners? will they turne Turke, or no?
Iul. First *Iulio* will die ten thousand deaths.
Guelp. And *Guelpio*, rather then denie his Christ.
Bru. Then stab the slaues, and send their soules to hell.   10

They stab Iulio *and* Guelpio.

Bas. I turne, I turne; oh, saue my life, I turne.
Bru. Forbeare to hurt him : when we land in Turkie,
He shall be circumcised and haue his rites.
Bas. Thinke you I turne Turque
For feare of seruile death, thats but a sport?   15
I faith, sir, no:
Tis for *Perseda*, whom I loue so well
That I would follow her, though she went to hell.
Bru. Now for these Ladies : their liues priuiledge
Hangs on their beautie; they shall be preserued   20
To be presented to great *Soliman*,
The greatest honor Fortune could affoord.
Per. The most dishonour that could ere befall.

Exeunt.

⟨SCENE VI.⟩

Enter Chorus.

Loue. Now, *Fortune*, what hast thou done in this later passage?
For. I plast *Erastus* in the fauour
Of *Solyman*, the Turkish Emperour.
Loue. Nay, that was *Loue*, for I coucht my selfe
In poore *Erastus* eyes, and with a looke   5
Orespred with teares, bewitched *Solyman*.
Beside, I sat on valiant *Brusors* tongue,
To guide the praises of the Rhodian knight.
Then in the Ladies passions I showed my power;
And lastly *Loue* made *Basiliscos* tongue   10
To countercheck his hart by turning Turke,

3-4 *one line Qq.*   5-6 oer-throw *add. ed.   See Note*   8 Rhodian]
herodian *Qq.*

And saue his life, in spite of *Deaths* despight.

Death. How chance it then, that *Loue* and *Fortunes* power
  Could neither saue *Philippo* nor his sonne,
  Nor *Guelpio*, nor signior *Iulio*,   15
  Nor rescue Rhodes from out the hands of *Death*?

For. Why, *Brusors* victorie was *Fortunes* gift.

Death. But had I slept, his conquest had been small.

Loue. Wherfore stay we? thers more behind   19
  Which proues that, though *Loue* winke, *Loues* not starke blinde.

                                        Exeunt.

⟨ACT IV.

Scene I.⟩

Enter Erastus *and* Piston.

Pist. Faith, maister, me thinkes you are vnwise that you weare
  not the high Sugerloafe hat, and the gilded gowne the Emperour
  gaue you.

Erast. Peace, foole, a sable weed fits discontent.
  Away, begone.   5

Pist. Ile go prouide your supper: a shoulder of mutton, and
  neuer a Sallet.

                                        Exit Piston.

Erast. I must confesse that *Solyman* is kinde,
  Past all compare, and more then my desart:
  But what helps gay garments, when the minds oprest?   10
  What pleaseth the eye, when the sence is altered?
  My heart is ouerwhelmd with thousand woes,
  And melancholie leads my soule in triumphe;
  No meruaile then if I haue little minde
  Of rich imbroderie, or costly ornaments,   15
  Of honors titles, or of wealth, or gaine,
  Of musicke, viands, or of dainty dames.
  No, no; my hope full long agoe was lost,
  And Rhodes it selfe is lost, or els destroyde:
  If not destroide, yet bound and captiuate;   20

---

13 chanc'd *Hazlitt*   20 Which proues *end of* 19 *Qq*.   1–3
Faith . . . vnwise | That . . . hat | And . . . you *Qq*.   4 Peace . . . begone
one line Qq.   6–7 a shoulder . . . Sallet *sep. line Qq*.

If captiuate, then forst from holy faith;
If forst from faith, for euer miserable:
For what is misery but want of God?
And God is lost, if faith be ouerthrowne.

Enter Soliman.

Sol. Why, how now, *Erastus*, alwaies in thy dumpes?   25
Still in black habite fitting funerall?
Cannot my loue perswade thee from this moode,
Nor all my faire intreats and blandishments?
Wert thou my friend, thy mind would iumpe with mine;
For what are friends but one minde in two bodies?   30
Perhaps thou doubts my friendships constancie;
Then doost thou wrong the measure of my loue,
Which hath no measure, and shall neuer end.
Come, *Erastus*, sit thee downe by me,
And ile impart to thee our *Brusors* newes,   35
Newes to our honour, and to thy content:
The Gouernour is slaine that sought thy death.
Erast. A worthy man, though not *Erastus* friend.
Sol. The Prince of Cipris to is likewise slaine.
Erast. Faire blossome, likely to haue proued good fruite.   40
Sol. Rhodes is taken, and all the men are slaine,
Except some few that turne to Mahomet.
Erast. I, there it is: now all my friends are slaine,
And faire *Perseda* murthered or deflowerd:
Ah, gratious *Soliman*, now showe thy loue   45
In not denying thy poore supplyant.
Suffer me not to stay here in thy presence,
But by my selfe lament me once for all.
Heere if I stay, I must suppresse my teares,
And teares supprest will but increase my sorrow.   50
Sol. Go, then, go spend thy mournings all at once,
That in thy presence *Soliman* may ioy;
For hetherto haue I reaped little pleasure.

                                        Exit Erastus.

Well, well, *Erastus*, Rhodes may blesse thy birth.
For his sake onely will I spare them more   55
From spoile, pillage, and oppression;

S.D. *Exit* Erastus *after* 52, Qq.

Then *Alexander* spard warlike Thebes
For *Pindarus* : or then *Augustus*
Sparde rich Alexandria for *Arrius* sake.

       Enter Brusor, Perseda, *and* Lucina.

Bru. My gratious Lord, reioyce in happinesse :   60
  All Rhodes is yoakt, and stoopes to *Soliman.*
Sol. First, thanks to heauen ; and next to *Brusors* valour,
  Which ile not guerdon with large promises,
  But straight reward thee with a bounteous largesse :
  But what two Christian Virgins haue we here ?   65
Bru. Part of the spoile of Rhodes, which were preserued
  To be presented to your mightinesse.
Sol. This present pleaseth more then all the rest,
  And were their garments turned from black to white,
  I should haue deemd them *Iunoes* goodly Swannes, 70
  Or *Venus* milke white Doues, so milde they are,
  And so adornd with beauties miracle.
  Heere, *Brusor,* this kinde Turtle shall be thine ;
  Take her and vse her at thy pleasure :
  But this kinde Turtle is for *Soliman,*   75
  That her captiuitie may turne to blisse.
  Faire lockes, resembling *Phoebus* radiant beames ;
  Smooth forhead, like the table of high *Ioue* ;
  Small pensild eye browes, like two glorious rainbowes ;
  Quick lampelike eyes, like heauens two brightest orbes ; 80
  Lips of pure Corall, breathing Ambrosie ;
  Cheekes, where the Rose and Lillie are in combate ;
  Neck, whiter then the snowie Apenines ;
  Brests, like two ouerflowing Fountaines,
  Twixt which a vale leads to the Elisian shades, 85
  Where vnder couert lyes the fount of pleasure
  Which thoughts may gesse, but tongue must not prophane.
  A sweeter creature nature neuer made :
  Loue neuer tainted *Soliman* till now.
  Now, faire Virgin, let me heare thee speake.   90
Per. What can my tongue vtter but griefe and death ?
Sol. The sound is hunnie, but the sence is gall :

---

59 *Arias Qq.*   77 lockes *ed.   See Note* : lookes *Qq.*   79 two
Hawkins, Hazlitt : to *Qq.*

Then, sweeting, blesse me with a cheerefull looke.
Per. How can mine eyes dart forth a pleasant looke,
    When they are stopt with flouds of flowing teares?   95
Sol. If tongue with griefe, and eyes with teares be fild,
    Say, Virgin, how dooth thy heart admit
    The pure affection of great *Soliman*?
Per. My thoughts are like pillers of Adamant,
    Too hard to take an new impression.   100
Sol. Nay, then, I see, my stooping makes her proud;
    She is my vassaile, and I will commaund.
    Coye Virgin, knowest thou what offence it is
    To thwart the will and pleasure of a king?
    Why, thy life is doone, if I but say the word.   105
Per. Why, thats the period that my heart desires.
Sol. And die thou shalt, vnlesse thou change thy minde.
Per. Nay, then, *Perseda* growes resolute:
    Solimans thoughts and mine resemble
    Lines parallel that neuer can be ioyned.   110
Sol. Then kneele thou downe,
    And at my hands receiue the stroake of death,
    Domde to thy selfe by thine owne wilfulnes.
Per. Strike, strike; thy words pierce deeper then thy blows.
Sol. Brusor, hide her, for her lookes withould me.   115

> *Then* Brusor *hides her with a Lawne.*

O *Brusor*, thou hast not hid her lippes;
For there sits *Venus* with *Cupid* on her knee,
And all the Graces smiling round about her,
So crauing pardon that I cannot strike.
Bru. Her face is couerd ouer quite, my Lord.   120
Sol. Why so: O *Brusor*, seest thou not
    Her milke white necke, that Alablaster tower?
    Twill breake the edge of my keene Semitor,
    And peeces flying backe will wound my selfe.
Bru. Now she is all couered, my Lord.   125
Sol. Why now at last she dyes.
Per. O Christ, receiue my soule.
Sol. Harke, *Brusor*, she cals on Christ:

I will not send her to him. Her words are musick,
The self same musick that in auncient daies   130
Brought *Alexander* from warre to banquetting,
And made him fall from skirmishing to kissing.
No, my deare, Loue would not let me kill thee,
Though Maiestie would turne desire to wrath.
There lyes my sword, humbled at thy feete ;   135
And I myselfe, that gouerne many kings,
Intreate a pardon for my rash misdeede.
Per. Now *Soliman* wrongs his imperiall state ;
But, if thou loue me, and haue hope to win,
Graunt ⟨me⟩ one boone that I shall craue of thee.   140
Sol. What ere it be, *Perseda*, I graunt it thee.
Per. Then let me liue a Christian Virgin still,
Vnlesse my state shall alter by my will.
Sol. My word is past, and I recall my passions :
What should he doe with crowne and Emperie   145
That cannot gouerne priuate fond affections ?
Yet giue me leaue in honest sort to court thee,
To ease, though not to cure, my maladie.
Come, sit thee downe vpon my right hand heere ;
This seat I keep voide for another friend.—   150
Goe, Ianisaries, call in your Gouernour,
So shall I ioy betweene two captiue friends,
And yet my selfe be captiue to them both
If friendships yoake were not at libertie :—
See where he comes, my other best beloued.   155

Enter Erastus.

Per. My sweete and best beloued.
Erast. My sweete and best beloued.
Per. For thee, my deare *Erastus*, haue I liued.
Erast. And I for thee, or els I had not liued.
Sol. What words in affection doe I see ?   160
Erast. Ah, pardon me, great *Soliman*, for this is she
For whom I mourned more then for all Rhodes,
And from whose absence I deriued my sorrow.

---

129 Her ... musick *sep. line Qq*.   133 No my deare, Loue would *Qq*. :
No, my deare loue would *Hawkins, Hazlitt. See Note*   140 Graunt me
Hawkins : Graunt *Qq*.   143 by] with *1599*

Per. And pardon me, my Lord; for this is he
    For whom I thwarted *Solimans* intreats,   165
    And for whose exile I lamented thus.
Erast. Euen from my childhood haue I tendered thee;
    Witnesse the heauens of my vnfeined loue.
Sol. By this one accedent I well perceiue
    That heauens and heauenly powers do manage loue.   170
    I loue them both, I know not which the better:
    They loue each other best: what then should follow,
    But that I conquer both by my deserts,
    And ioyne their hands, whose hearts are knit already?
    Erastus and *Perseda*, come you hether,   175
    And both giue me your hands—
    Erastus, none but thou couldst win *Perseda*,
    Perseda, none but thou couldst win *Erastus*,
    From great *Soliman*; so well I loue you both:
    And now, to turne late promises to good effect,   180
    Be thou, *Erastus*, Gouernour of Rhodes:
    By this thou shalt dismisse my garison.
Bru. Must he reape that for which I tooke the toile?
    Come, enuie, then, and sit in friendships seate;
    How can I loue him that inioyes my right?   185
Sol. Giue me a crowne, to crowne the bride withall.

            Then he crownes Perseda.

    Perseda, for my sake weare this crowne.
    Now is she fairer then she was before;
    This title so augments her beautie, as the fire,
    That lay with honours hand rackt up in ashes,   190
    Reuiues againe to flames, the force is such.
    Remooue the cause, and then the effect will die;
    They must depart, or I shall not be quiet.
    Erastus and *Perseda*, meruaile not
    That all in hast I wish you to depart;   195
    There is an vrgent cause, but priuie to my selfe:
    Commaund my shipping for to waft you ouer.
Erast. My gratious Lord, whe⟨n⟩ *Erastus* doth forget this fauor,
    Then let him liue abandond and forlorne.
Per. Nor will *Perseda* slacke euen in her praiers,   200
    But still solicite God for *Soliman*,
    Whose minde hath proued so good and gratious. *Exeunt.*

Sol. Farewell, *Erastus* : *Perseda*, farewell to.
　Me thinks I should not part with two such friends,
　The one so renownd for armes and curtesie,　　　205
　The other so adorned with grace and modestie :
　Yet of the two *Perseda* mooues me most,
　I, and so mooues me, that I now repent
　That ere I gaue away my hearts desire ;
　What was it but abuse of Fortunes gift?　　　210
　And therefore Fortune now will be reuengde :
　What was it but abuse of Loues commaund ?
　And therefore mightie Loue will be reuengd :
　What was it but abuse of heauens that gaue her me ?
　And therefore angrie heauens will be reuengd :　　215
　Heauens, Loue, and Fortune, all three haue decreed
　That I shall loue her still, and lack her still,
　Like euer thirsting, wretched *Tantalus* :
　Foolish *Soliman*, why did I striue
　To do him kindnes, and vndoe my selfe?　　　220
　Well gouernd friends do first regard themselues.
Bru. I, now occasion serues to stumble him
　That thrust his sickle in my haruest corne.
　Pleaseth your Maiestie to heare *Brusor* speake ?
Sol. To one past cure good counsell comes too late ;　　225
　Yet say thy minde.
Bru. With secret letters woe her, and with gifts.
Sol. My lines and gifts will but returne my shame.
Luc. Here me, my Lord : let me go ouer to Rhodes,
　That I may plead in your affections cause ;　　　230
　One woman may do much to win another.
Sol. Indeede, *Lucina*, were her husband from her,
　Shee happely might be woone by thy perswades ;
　But whilst he liues there is no hope in her.
Bru. Why liues he then to greeue great *Soliman* ?　　235
　This onely remaines, that you consider
　In two extreames the least is to be chosen.
　If so your life depend vpon your loue,
　And that her loue depends vpon his life,
　Is it not better that *Erastus* die　　　240
　Ten thousand deaths then *Soliman* should perish ?
Sol. I, saist thou so? why, then it shall be so :

But by what means shall poore *Erastus* dye?
Bru. This shall be the meanes : Ill fetch him backe againe,
  Vnder couler of great consequence ;   245
  No sooner shall he land vpon our shore,
  But witnes shall be ready to accuse him
  Of treason doone against your mightines,
  And then he shall be doomd by marshall law.
Sol. O fine deuise ; *Brusor*, get thee gone :   250
  Come thou againe ; but let the lady stay
  To win *Perseda* to my will : meane while
  Will I prepare the iudge and witnesses ;
  And if this take effect, thou shalt be Viceroy,
  And faire *Lucina* Queene of *Tripolie.*   255
  Brusor, be gone ; for till thou come I languish.

                Exeunt Brusor *and* Lucina.

And now, to ease my troubled thoughts at last,
I will go sit among my learned Euenukes,
And heere them play, and see my minions dance.
For till that *Brusor* bring me my desire,   260
I may asswage, but neuer quench loues fire.

                         Exit.

⟨SCENE II.⟩

Enter Basilisco.

Bas. Since the expugnation of the Rhodian Ile,
  Me thinkes a thousand years are ouerpast,
  More for the lack of my *Persedas* presence
  Then for the losse of Rhodes, that paltry Ile,
  Or for my friends that there were murthered.   5
  My valour euery where shall purchase friends,
  And where a man liues well, there is his countrie.
  Alas, the Christians are but very shallow
  In giuing iudgement of a man at armes,
  A man of my desert and excellence :   10
  The Turkes, whom they account for barbarous,
  Hauing forehard of *Basiliscoes* worth,

---

244 Ill . . . againe *sep. line Qq.*   249 by] my *1599*   261 *After this line there is in the margin of undated Q. a MS. note in a sixteenth or seventeenth century hand :* the songe to be sunge before Basilisco enters.

A number vnder prop me with their shoulders,
And in procession bare me to the Church,
As I had beene a second Mahomet.   15
I, fearing they would adore me for a God,
Wisely informd them that I was but man,
Although in time perhaps I might aspire
To purchase Godhead, as did *Hercules* ;
I meane by doing wonders in the world :   20
Amidst their Church they bound me to a piller,
And to make triall of my valiancie,
They lopt a collop of my tendrest member.
But thinke you *Basilisco* squicht for that?
Euen as a Cow for tickling in the horne.   25
That doone, they set me on a milke white Asse,
Compassing me with goodly ceremonies.
That day, me thought, I sat in *Pompeyes* Chaire,
And viewd the Capitoll, and was Romes greatest glorie. 29

Enter Piston.

Pist. I would my maister had left some other to be his agent
here : faith, I am wearie of the office alreadie. What, Sei-
gniour *Tremomundo*, that rid a pilgrimage to beg cakebread?
Bas. O take me not vnprouided, let me fetch my weapons.
Pist. Why, I meant nothing but a *Basolus manus.*
Bas. No, didst thou not meane to giue me the priuie stab?
Pist. No, by my troth, sir.   36
Bas. Nay, if thou hadst, I had not feard thee, I ;
I tell thee, my skin holds out Pistoll proofe.
Pist. Pistoll proofe? ile trie if it will hold out pin proofe.

Then he pricks him with a pin.

Bas. O shoote no more ; great God, I yield to thee.   40
Pist. I see his skin is but pistol profe from the girdle vpward.
What suddaine agonie was that ?
Bas. Why, sawst thou not how *Cupid*, God of loue,
Not daring looke me in the marshall face,
Came like a coward stealing after me,   45
And with his pointed dart prickt my posteriors ?
Pist. Then here my opinion concerning that point ; the Ladies

---

14 bear *Hazlitt*   30-3 *printed as doggerel Qq.*   41 but pistol
profe from] pistol-proof, but from *Hazlitt*   47-53 *printed as doggerel Qq.*

of Rhodes, hearing that you haue lost a capitoll part of
your Lady ware, haue made their petition to *Cupid* to plague
you aboue all other, as one preiuditiall to their muliebritie.
Now sir, *Cupid*, seeing you alreadie hurt before, thinkes it a
greater punishment to hurt you behind. Therefore I would
wish you to haue an eye to the back dore.

Bas. Sooth thou sayest, I must be fencd behinde ;
Ile hang my target there.   55

Pist. Indeed that will serue to beare of some blowes when
you 'run away in a fraye.

Bas. Sirra, sirra, what art thou, that thus incrochest vpon my
familiaritie without speciall admittance ?

Pist. Why, do you not know me ? I am *Erastus* man.   60

Bas. What, art thou that petty pigmie that chalenged me at
Rhodes, whom I refused to combat for his minoritie ? Where
is *Erastus* ? I owe him chastisement in *Persedas* quarrel.

Pist. Do you not know that they are all friends, and *Erastus*
maryed to *Perseda*, and *Erastus* made gouernour of Rhodes,
and I left heere to be their agent ?   66

Bas. O coelum, O terra, O maria, Neptune.
Did I turne Turke to follow her so far ?

Pist. The more shame for you.

Bas. And is she linkt in liking with my foe ?   70

Pist. Thats because you were out of the way.

Bas. O wicked Turque, for to steale her hence.

Pist. O wicked turne coate, that would haue her stay.

Bas. The truth is, I will be a Turke no more.

Pist. And I feare thou wilt neuer prooue good christian.   75

Bas. I will after to take reuenge.

Pist. And ile stay heere about my maisters busines.

Bas. Farewell, Constantinople ; I will to Rhodes.

Exit.

Pist. Farewell, counterfeit foole.—God send him good shipping.
Tis noisd about that *Brusor* is sent to fetch my maister
back againe ; I cannot be well till I heare the rest of the
newes, therefore ile about it straight.   82

Exit.

56–66 *printed as doggerel Qq.*   74 I will] *Hawkins, Hazlitt* : ile *Qq.*
79–82 *printed as doggerel Qq.*

⟨Scene III.⟩

Enter Chorus.

Loue. Now, *Fortune*, what hast thou done in this latter act?
For. I brought *Perseda* to the presence
    Of *Soliman*, the Turkish Emperour,
    And gaue *Lucina* into *Brusors* hands.
Loue. And first I stunge them with consenting loue,   5
    And made great *Soliman*, sweete beauties thrall,
    Humble himselfe at faire *Persedas* feete,
    And made him praise loue, and ⟨his⟩ captiues beautie:
    Againe I made him to recall his passions,
    And giue *Perseda* to *Erastus* hands,   10
    And after make repentance of the deed.
For. Meane time I fild *Erastus* sailes with winde,
    And brought him home vnto his native land.
Death. And I subornd *Brusor* with enuious rage
    To counsell *Soliman* to slay his friend.   15
    Brusor is sent to fetch him back againe.
    Mark well what followes, for the historie
    Prooues me cheefe actor in this tragedie.

                              Exeunt.

⟨Act V.

Scene I.⟩

Enter Erastus *and* Perseda.

Erast. *Perseda*, these dayes are our dayes of ioy:
    What could I more desire then thee to wife?
    And that I haue: or then to gouerne Rhodes?
    And that I doe, thankes to great *Soliman*.
Per. And thanks to gratious heauens, that so   5
    Brought *Soliman* from worse to better;
    For though I neuer tould it thee till now,
    His heart was purposd once to do thee wrong.
Erast. I, that was before he knew thee to be mine.
    And now, *Perseda*, lets forget oulde greefes,   10
    And let our studies wholie be imploid

---

8 his captiues *ed.*: captiues *Qq.*: captiue *Hazlitt*

To worke each others blisse and hearts delight.

Per. Our present ioyes will be so much the greater,
When as we call to minde forepassed greefes :
So singes the Mariner vpon the shore,   15
When he hath past the dangerous time of stormes :
But if my Loue will haue olde greefes forgot,
They shall lie buried in *Persedas* brest.

Enter Brusor and Lucina.

Erast. Welcome, Lord *Brusor*.
Per.   And, *Lucina*, to.
Bru. Thankes, Lord Gouernour.
Luc.   And thankes to you, Madame.
Erast. What hastie news brings you so soone to Rhodes,   21
Although to me you neuer come to soone?
Bru. So it is, my Lord, that vpon great affaires,
Importuning health and wealth of *Soliman*,
His highnes by me intreateth you,   25
As euer you respect his future loue,
Or haue regard vnto his curtesie,
To come your selfe in person and visit him,
Without inquirie what should be the cause.
Erast. Were there no ships to crosse the Seas withall,   30
My armes should frame mine oares to crosse the seas ;
And should the seas turne tide to force me backe,
Desire should frame me winges to flie to him ;
I go, *Perseda* ; thou must giue me leaue.
Per. Though loth, yet *Solimans* commaund preuailes.   35
Luc. And sweete *Perseda*, I will stay with you,
From *Brusor* my beloued ; and Ile want him
Till he bring backe *Erastus* vnto you.
Erast. Lord *Brusor*, come ; tis time that we were gon.
Bru. *Perseda*, farewell ; be not angrie   40
For that I carry thy beloued from thee ;
We will returne with all speede possible,
And thou, *Lucina*, vse *Perseda* so,
That for my carrying of *Erastus* hence
She curse me not ; and so farewell to both.   45
Per. Come, *Lucina*, lets in ; my heart is full.   *Exeunt.*

---

19 And . . . to *sep. line Qq.*   20 And . . . Madame *sep. line Qq.*
31 mine] me *Hazlitt. See Note*

⟨Scene II.⟩

Enter Soliman, Lord Marshall, the two witnesses, *and* Ianisaries.

Sol. Lord marshall, see you handle it cunningly :
And when *Erastus* comes, our periurd friend,
See ⟨that⟩ he be condemd by marshall law ;
Heere will I stand to see, and not be seene.
Marsh. Come, fellowes, see when this matter comes in question
You stagger not ; and, Ianisaries,   6
See that your strangling cords be ready.
Sol. Ah that *Perseda* were not half so faire,
Or that *Soliman* were not so fond,
Or that *Perseda* had some other loue,   10
Whose death might saue my poore *Erastus* life.

Enter Brusor *and* Erastus.

See where he comes, whome though I deerely loue,
Yet must his bloud be spilt for my behoofe ;
Such is the force of marrow burning loue.
Marsh. *Erastus*, Lord Gouernour of Rhodes, I arrest you in
the Kings name.   16
Erast. What thinks Lord *Brusor* of this strange arrest ?
Hast thou intrapt me to this tretcherie,
Intended, well I wot, without the leaue
Or licence of my Lord, great *Soliman* ?   20
Bru. Why, then appeale to him, when thou shalt know,
And be assured that I betray thee not.
Sol. Yes, thou, and I, and all of vs betray him.
Marsh. No, no ; in this case no appeale shall serue.
Erast. Why then to thee, or vnto any else,   25
I heere protest by heauens vnto you all
That neuer was there man more true or iust,
Or in his deeds more loyall and vpright,
Or more louing, or more innocent,
Than I haue bene to gratious *Soliman*,   30
Since first I set my feet on Turkish land.
Sol. My selfe would be his witnesse, if I durst ;
But bright *Persedaes* beautie stops my tongue.

---

3 that *add. ed.*   15 morrow-burning *undated Q. and 1599 A*   15-6 I . . .
name *sep. line Qq.*

Marsh. Why, sirs, why face to face expresse you not
    The treasons you reueald to *Soliman*?   35
⟨1⟩ *Witn.* That very day *Erastus* went from hence,
    He sent for me into his Cabinet,
    And for that man that is of my profession.
Erast. I neuer saw them, I, vntill this day.
⟨1⟩ *Witn.* His Cabine doore fast shut, he first began   40
    To question vs of all sorts of fire-workes ;
    Wherein, when he had fully resolued him
    What might be done, he, spredding on the boord
    A huge heape of our imperiall coyne,
    All this is yours, quoth he, if you consent   45
    To leaue great *Soliman* and serue in Rhodes.
Marsh. Why, that was treason ; but onwards with the rest.

               Enter Piston.

Pist. What haue we heer ? my maister before the Marshall ?
⟨1⟩ *Witn.* We said not I, nor durst we say him nay,
    Because we were alreadie in his gallyes ;   50
    But seemd content to flie with him to Rhodes :
    With that he purst the gould, and gaue it vs.
    The rest I dare not speake, it is so bad.
Erast. Heauens, heer you this, and drops not vengeance on them?
The other Witn. The rest, and worst will I discourse in briefe. 55
    Will you consent, quoth he, to fire the fleete
    That lyes hard by vs heere in *Bosphoron*?
    For be it spoke in secret heere, quoth he,
    Rhodes must no longer beare the turkish yoake.
    We said the taske might easilie be performd,   60
    But that we lackt such drugs to mixe with powder,
    As were not in his gallyes to be got.
    At this he lept for ioy, swearing and promising
    That our reward should be redoubled.
    We came aland, not minding for to returne,   65
    And, as our duty and aleageance bound vs,
    We made all knowne vnto great *Soliman* ;
    But ere we could summon him a land,
    His ships were past a kenning from the shoare :

---

36 1 *Witn. Hawkins* : *Witnesses Qq.*   47 onward *1599 -99 A*
54 drops] drop *Hazlitt*   55 worse *1599 -99 A*   65 for *om. 1599*
-99 A

Belike he thought we had bewrayd his treasons.   70
Marsh. That all is true that heere you haue declard,
  Both lay your hands vpon the Alcaron.
1 *Witn.* Foule death betide me, if I sweare not true.
2 *Witn.* And mischiefe light on me, if I sweare false.
Sol. Mischiefe and death shall light vpon you both.   75
Marsh. Erastus,
  Thou seest what witnes hath produced against thee.
  What answerest thou vnto their accusations?
Erast. That these are Synons, and my selfe poore Troy.
Marsh. Now it resteth I appoint thy death;   80
  Wherein thou shalt confesse ile fauour thee,
  For that thou wert beloued of *Soliman*:
  Thou shalt foorthwith be bound vnto that post,
  And strangled as our turkish order is.
Pist. Such fauour send all Turkes, I pray God.   85
Erast. I see this traine was plotted ere I came:
  What bootes complaining wheres no remedy?
  Yet giue me leaue, before my life shall end,
  To moane *Perseda*, and accuse my friend.
Sol. O vniust *Soliman*: O wicked time,   90
  Where filthie lust must murther honest loue.
Marsh. Dispatch, for our time limited is past.
Erast. Alas, how can he but be short, whose tongue
  Is fast tide with galling sorrow.
  Farewell, *Perseda*; no more but that for her: 95
  Inconstant *Soliman*; no more but that for him:
  Vnfortunate *Erastus*; no more but that for me:
  Loe, this is all; and thus I leaue to speake.
Then they strangle him.
Pist. Marie, sir, this is a faire warning for me to get me gon.
Exit Piston.
Sol. O saue his life, if it be possible;   100
  I will not loose him for my kingdomes worth.
  Ah, poore *Erastus*, art thou dead already?
  What bould presumer durst be so resolued
  For to bereaue *Erastus* life from him,
  Whose life to me was dearer then mine owne?   105

---

70 bewrayd] betraid *1599 -99 A*   76 Erastus ... thee *one line Qq.*
78 accusation *1599 -99 A*

Wast thou? and thou? Lord Marshall, bring them hether,
And at *Erastus* hand let them receiue
The stroke of death, whom they haue spoild of life.
What, is thy hand to weake? then mine shall helpe
To send them down to euerlasting night,   110
To waite vpon thee through eternall shade;
Thy soule shall not go mourning hence alone:
Thus die, and thus; for thus you murtherd him.

    Then he kils the two Ianisaries, that kild Erastus.

But, soft, me thinkes he is not satisfied:
The breath dooth murmure softly from his lips,   115
And bids me kill those bloudie witnesses
By whose treacherie *Erastus* dyed.
Lord Marshall, hale them to the towers top,
And throw them headlong downe into the valley;
So let their treasons with their liues haue end.   120
1 *Witn.* Your selfe procured us.
2 *Witn.*   Is this our hier?

    Then the Marshall beares them to the tower top.

Sol. Speake not a worde, least in my wrathfull furie
I doome you to ten thousand direfull torments.
And, *Brusor*, see *Erastus* be interd
With honour in a kingly sepulcher.   125
Why, when, Lord marshall? great *Hectors* sonne,
Although his age did plead for innocence,
Was sooner tumbled from the fatall tower
Then are those periurde wicked witnesses.

    Then they are both tumbled downe.

Why, now *Erastus* ghost is satisfied: 130
I, but yet the wicked Iudge suruiues,
By whom *Erastus* was condemnd to die.
Brusor, as thou louest me, stab in the marshall,
Least he detect vs vnto the world,
By making knowne our bloudy practises;   135
And then will thou and I hoist saile to Rhodes,
Where thy *Lucina* and my *Perseda* liues.
Bru. I wil, my lord:—lord Marshal, it is his highnes pleasure

---

133 in] too *Hazlitt*

That you commend him to *Erastus* soule.

Then he kils the Marshall.

Sol. Heere ends my deere *Erastus* tragedie,   140
And now begins my pleasant Comedie;
But if *Perseda* vnderstand these newes,
Our seane will prooue but tragicomicall.

Bru. Feare not, my Lord; *Lucina* plaies her part,
And wooes apace in *Solimans* behalfe.   145

Sol. Then, *Brusor*, come; and with some few men
Lets saile to Rhodes with all conuenient speede:
For till I fould *Perseda* in mine armes,
My troubled eares are deft with loues alarmes.

Exeunt.

⟨SCENĒ III.⟩

Enter Perseda, Lucina, and Basilisco.

Per. Now, signior *Basilisco*, which like you,
The Turkish or our nation best?

Bas. That which your ladyship will haue me like.

Luc. I am deceiued but you were circumcised.

Bas. Indeed I was a little cut in the porpuse.   5

Per. What meanes made you to steale backe to Rhodes?

Bas. The mightie pinky-ey'd, brand bearing God,
To whom I am so long true seruitor,
When he espyde my weeping flouds of teares
For your depart, he bad me follow him: 10
I followed him, he with his fier brand
Parted the seas, and we came ouer drie-shod.

Luc. A matter not vnlikely: but how chance,
Your turkish bonnet is not on your head?

Bas. Because I now am Christian againe,   15
And that by naturall meanes; for as the old Cannon
Saies very pretily: *Nihil est tam naturale,*
Quod eo modo colligatum est:
And so foorth.

---

5 porpuse] prepuce *Hazlitt. See Note*   6 *the first* to *om.* 1599
7 pinky-ey'd *Hazlitt*: pickanyed *1599*: pinckanied *1599 A*: pinckanied
undated Q.: pinck-an-ey'd *Hawkins. See Note*   13 chance] chanceth *Hazlitt*
unnecessarily   16-20 And . . . for as | The old . . . pretily | *Nihil . . .*
colligatum est | And so . . . follow her *Qq.*

So I became a Turke to follow her;   20
To follow her, am now returnd a Christian.

Enter Piston.

Pist. O lady and mistris, weepe and lament, and wring your
hands; for my maister is condemnd and executed.

Luc. Be patient, sweete *Perseda*, the foole but iests.

Per. Ah no; my nightly dreames foretould me this,   25
Which, foolish woman, fondly I neglected.
But say, what death dyed my poore *Erastus*?

Pist. Nay, God be praisd, his death was reasonable;
He was but strangled.

Per. But strangled? ah, double death to me: 30
But say, wherefore was he condemnd to die?

Pist. For nothing but hie treason.

Per. What treason, or by whom was he condemnd?

Pist. Faith, two great Knights of the post swore vpon the
Alcaron that he would haue firde the Turkes Fleete.   35

Per. Was *Brusor* by?

Pist. I.

Per. And *Soliman*?

Pist. No; but I saw where he stood,
To heere and see the matter well conuaid.   40

Per. Accursed *Soliman*, prophane Alcaron:
Lucina, came thy husband to this end,
To leade a Lambe vnto the slaughter-house?
Hast thou for this, in *Solimans* behalfe,
With cunning wordes tempted my chastitie?   45
Thou shalt abie for both your trecheries.
It must be so. *Basilisco*, dooest thou loue me? speake.

Bas. I, more then I loue either life or soule:
What, shall I stab the Emperour for thy sake?

Per. No, but *Lucina*; if thou louest me, kill her.   50

Then Basilisco *takes a dagger and feeles vpon the point of it.*

Bas. The point will marre her skin.

Per. What, darest thou not? giue me the dagger then—
Theres a reward for all thy treasons past.

Then Perseda *kils* Lucina.

22-3 O . . . lament | And . . . maister | Is . . . executed *sep. lines*, *Qq.*
46 abide *1599*

Bas. Yet dare I beare her hence, to do thee good.

Per. No, let her lie, a prey to rauening birds :   55
Nor shall her death alone suffice for his ;
Rhodes now shall be no longer *Solymans* :
Weele fortifie our walles, and keepe the towne,
In spight of proud, insulting *Soliman.*
I know the letcher hopes to haue my loue,   60
And first *Perseda* shall with this hand die
Then yeeld to him, and liue in infamie.

Exeunt.

                    Manet Basilisco.

Bas. I will ruminate : Death, which the poets
Faine to be pale and meager,
Hath depriued *Erastus* trunke from breathing vitalitie,   65
A braue Cauelere, but my aprooued foeman.
Let me see : where is that *Alcides*, surnamed *Hercules,*
The onely Club man of his time ? dead.
Where is the eldest sonne of *Pryam,*
That abraham-coloured Troian ? dead.   70
Where is the leader of the Mirmidons,
That well knit *Accill⟨es⟩* ? dead.
Where is that furious *Aiax*, the sonne of *Telamon,*
Or that fraudfull squire of *Ithaca*, iclipt *Vlisses* ? dead.
Where is tipsie *Alexander*, that great cup conquerour,   75
Or *Pompey* that braue warriour ? dead.
I am my selfe strong, but I confesse death to be stronger :
I am valiant, but mortall ;
I am adorned with natures gifts,
A giddie goddesse that now giueth and anon taketh :   80
I am wise, but quiddits will not answer death :
To conclude in a word : to be captious, vertuous, ingenious,
Are to be nothing when it pleaseth death to be enuious.
The great Turque, whose seat is Constantinople,
Hath beleagred Rhodes, whose chieftaine is a woman :   85
I could take the rule vpon me ;
But the shrub is safe when the Cedar shaketh :
I loue *Perseda*, as one worthie ;
But I loue *Basilisco*, as one I hould more worthy,
My fathers sonne, my mothers solace, my proper selfe.   90

---

61 this] his *1599*   70 Troion *Qq.*   83 Are *Hazlitt* : Or *Qq.*

Faith, he can doe little that cannot speake,
And he can doe lesse that cannot runne away :
Then sith mans life is as a glasse, and a phillip may cracke it,
Mine is no more, and a bullet may pearce it :
Therefore I will play least in sight.   95

Exit.

⟨SCENE IV.⟩

Enter Soliman and Brusor, *with Ianisaries.*

Sol. The gates are shut; which prooues that Rhodes reuolts,
And that *Perseda* is not *Solimans* :
Ah, *Brusor*, see where thy *Lucina* lyes,
Butcherd dispightfullie without the walles.
Bru. Vnkinde *Perseda*, couldst thou vse her so ?   5
And yet we vsd *Perseda* little better.
Sol. Nay, gentle *Brusor*, stay thy teares a while,
Least with thy woes thou spoile my commedie,
And all to soone be turnd to Tragedies.
Go, *Brusor*, beare her to thy priuate tent,   10
Where we at leasure will lament her death,
And with our teares bewaile her obsequies ;
For yet *Perseda* liues for *Soliman.*—
Drum, sound a parle :—were it not for her,
I would sacke the towne, ere I would sound a parle.   15

The Drum soundes a parle. Perseda *comes vpon the walls in mans
apparell.* Basilisco *and* Piston, *vpon the walles.*

Per. At whose intreatie is this parle sounded ?
Sol. At our intreatie; therefore yield the towne.
Per. Why, what art thou that boldlie bids vs yeeld?
Sol. Great *Soliman*, Lord of all the world.
Per. Thou art not Lord of all; Rhodes is not thine.   20
Sol. It was, and shall be, maugre who saies no.
Per. I, that say no, will neuer see it thine.
Sol. Why, what art thou that dares resist my force?
Per. A Gentleman, and thy mortall enemie,
And one that dares thee to the single combate.   25
Sol. First tell me, doth *Perseda* liue or no ?
Per. She liues to see the wrack of *Soliman.*

---

93 as *om. 1599*   9 Tragedie *1599*   12 our] her *1599 A*

Sol. Then I will combate thee, what ere thou art.
Per. And in *Erastus* name ile combat thee;
   And heere I promise thee on my Christian faith,   30
   Then will I yeeld *Perseda* to thy hands,
   If that thy strength shall ouer match my right,
   To vse as to thy liking shall seeme best.
   But ere I come to enter single fight,
   First let˙ my tongue vtter my hearts despight;   35
   And thus my tale begins : thou wicked tirant,
   Thou murtherer, accursed homicide,
   For whome hell gapes, and all the vgly feendes
   Do waite for to receiue thee in their iawes :
   Ah, periur'd and inhumaine *Soliman*,   40
   How could thy heart harbour a wicked thought
   Against the spotlesse life of poore *Erastus* ?
   Was he not true ? would thou hadst been as iust.
   Was he not valiant ? would thou hadst bin as vertuous.
   Was he not loyall ? would thou hadst been as louing.   45
   Ah, wicked tirant, in that one mans death
   Thou hast betrayde the flower of Christendome.
   Dyed he because his worth obscured thine ?
   In slaughtering him thy vertues are defamed :
   Didst thou misdoe him in hope to win *Perseda* ?   50
   Ah, foolish man, therein thou art deceiued ;
   For, though she liue, yet will she neare liue thine ;
   Which to approoue, Ile come to combate thee.
Sol. Iniurious, foule mouthd knight, my wrathfull arme
   Shall chastise and rebuke these iniuries.   55

Then Perseda *comes down to* Soliman, *and* Basilisco *and* Piston.

Pist. I, but heere you, are you so foolish to fight with him ?
Bas. I, sirra ; why not, as long as I stand by ?
Sol. Ile not defend *Erastus* innocence,
   But ⟨die⟩ maintaining of *Persedas* beautie.

            Then they fight, Soliman *kils* Perseda.

Per. I, now I lay *Perseda* at thy feete,   60
   But with thy hand first wounded to the death :

---

28 I will] Ile *Qq*.   32 That if *Qq*. : *transp. ed*.   59 But die maintaining of
emend. ed. : But thee maintaining of *undated Q*. : But thee in maintaining *1599 -99 A*

Now shall the world report that *Soliman*
Slew *Erastus* in hope to win *Perseda*,
And murtherd her for louing of hir husband.

Sol. What, my *Perseda*? ah, what haue I done?   65
Yet kisse me, gentle loue, before thou die.

Per. A kisse I graunt thee, though I hate thee deadlie.

Sol. I loued thee deerelie, and accept thy kisse.
Why didst thou loue *Erastus* more then me?
Or why didst not giue *Soliman* a kisse   70
Ere this vnhappy time? then hadst thou liued.

Bas. Ah, let me kisse thee too, before I dye.

Then Soliman *kils* Basilisco.

Sol. Nay, die thou shalt for thy presumption,
For kissing her whom I do hould so deare.

Pist. I will not kisse her, sir, but giue me leaue   75
To weepe ouer hir; for while she liued,
She loued me deerely, and I loued her.

Sol. If thou didst loue her, villaine, as thou saidst,
Then wait on her thorough eternal night.

Then Soliman *kils* Piston.

Ah, *Perseda*, how shall I mourne for thee?   80
Faire springing Rose, ill pluckt before thy time.
Ah heauens, that hitherto haue smilde on me,
Why doe you vnkindly lowre on *Solyman*?
The losse of halfe my Realmes, nay, crownes decay,
Could not haue prickt so neere vnto my heart   85
As doth the losse of my *Persedaes* life:
And with her life I likewise loose my loue;
And with her loue my hearts felicitie.
Euen for *Erastus* death the heauens haue plagued me.
Ah no, the heauens did neuer more accurse me   90
Then when they made me Butcher of my loue.
Yet iustly how can I condemne my selfe,
When *Brusor* liues that was the cause of all?
Come *Brusor*, helpe to lift her bodie vp.
Is she not faire?   95

Bru. Euen in the houre of death.

---

65 ah, what] all that *1599 -99 A*   70 didst thou not *1599 -99 A*
78 saidst] sayest *Hazlitt, unnecessarily*

Sol. Was she not constant?

Bru. As firme as are the poles whereon heauen lies.

Sol. Was she not chaste?

Bru. As is *Pandora* or *Dianaes* thoughts.   100

Sol. Then tell me, (his treasons set aside)
    What was *Erastus* in thy opinion?

Bru. Faire spoken, wise, courteous, and liberall;
    Kinde, euen to his foes, gentle and affable;
    And, all in all, his deeds heroyaeall.   105

Sol. Ah, was he so?
    How durst thou then, vngratious counseller,
    First cause me murther such a worthy man,
    And after tempt so vertuous a woman?
    Be this, therefore, the last that ere thou speake—   110
    Ianisaries take him straight vnto the block;
    Off with his head, and suffer him not to speake.

                                Exit Brusor.

    And now *Perseda*, heere I lay me downe,
    And on thy beautie ⟨Ile⟩ still contemplate,
    Vntil mine eyes shall surfet by my gasing.   115
    But stay; let me see what paper is this?

     Then he takes vp a paper, and reedes in it as followeth.
    Tyrant, my lips were sawst with deadly poyson,
    To plague thy hart that is so full of poyson.
    What, am I poisoned? then, Ianisaries,
    Let me see Rhodes recouerd ere I die.   120
    Souldiers, assault the towne on every side;
    Spoile all, kill all; let none escape your furie.

          ·   *Sound an alarum to the fight.*

    Say, Captaine, is Rhodes recouered againe?

Capt. It is, my Lord, and stoopes to *Soliman.*

Sol. Yet that alayes the furie of my paine   125
    Before I die, for doubtlesse die I must.
    I, fates, iniurious fates, haue so decreed;
    For now I feele the poyson gins to worke,
    And I am weake euen to the very death:
    Yet some thing more contentedly I die   130
    For that my death was wrought by her deuise,
    Who, liuing, was my ioy, whose death my woe.

    106-7 *one line in Qq.*   114 Ile *add. ed.*

Ah, Ianisaries, now dyes your Emperour,
Before his age hath seene his mellowed yeares.
And if you euer loued your Emperour,   135
Affright me not with sorrowes and laments:
And when my soule from body shall depart,
Trouble me not, but let me passe in peace,
And in your silence let your loue be showne.
My last request, for I commaund no more,   140
Is that my body with *Persedas* be
Interd, where my *Erastus* lyes intombd,
And let one Epitaph containe vs all.
Ah, now I feele the paper tould me true ;
The poison is disperst through euerie vaine,   145
And boyles, like *Etna*, in my frying guts
Forgiue me, deere *Erastus*, my vnkindnes.
I haue reuenged thy death with many deaths :
And, sweet *Perseda*, flie not *Soliman*,
When as my gliding ghost shall follow thee,   150
With eager moode, thorow eternall night.
And now pale Death sits on my panting soule,
And with reuenging ire dooth tyrannise,
And sayes : for *Solimans* too much amisse,
This day shall be the peryod of my blisse.   155

Then Soliman *dyes, and they carry him forth with silence.*

⟨SCENE V.⟩

Enter Chorus.

For. I gaue *Erastus* woe and miserie
    Amidst his greatest ioy and iollitie.
Loue. But I, that haue power in earth and heauen aboue,
    Stung them both with neuer failing loue.
Death. But I bereft them both of loue and life.   5
Loue. Of life, but not of loue ; for euen in death
    Their soules are knit, though bodyes be disioynd :
    Thou didst but wound their flesh, their minds are free ;
    Their bodies buried, yet they honour me.
Death. Hence foolish *Fortune*, and thou wanton *Loue* : 10

---

148 death *1599*: deaths *1599 A and undated Q.*   155 *After this line the*
Qq. print a superfluous Exeunt   S.D. *with*] *in 1599*

Your deedes are trifles, mine of consequence.
For. I giue worlds happines and woes increase.
Loue. By ioyning persons I increase the world.
Death. By wasting all I conquer all the world.
And now, to end our difference at last,   15
In this last act note but the deedes of Death.
Where is *Erastus* now, but in my triumph?
Where are the murtherers, but in my triumph?
Where Iudge and witnesses, but in my triumph?
Wheres falce *Lucina*, but in my triumph?   20
Wheres faire *Perseda*, but in my triumph?
Wheres *Basilisco*, but in my triumph?
Wheres faithfull *Piston*, but in my triumph?
Wheres valiant *Brusor*, but in my triumph?
And wheres great *Soliman*, but in my triumph?   25
Their loues and fortunes ended with their liues,
And they must wait vpon the Carre of Death.
Packe, *Loue* and *Fortune*, play in Commedies;
For powerfull *Death* best fitteth Tragedies.
Loue. I go, yet *Loue* shall neuer yeeld to *Death*.   30

Exit Loue.

Death. But *Fortune* shall; for when I waste the world,
Then times and kingdomes fortunes shall decay.
For. Meane time will *Fortune* gouerne as she may.

Exit Fortune.

Death. I, now will *Death*, in his most haughtie pride,
Fetch his imperiall Carre from deepest hell,   35
And ride in triumph through the wicked world;
Sparing none but sacred *Cynthias* friend,
Whom *Death* did feare before her life began:
For holy fates haue grauen it in their tables
That *Death* shall die, if he attempt her end,   40
Whose life is heauens delight, and *Cynthias* friend.

FINIS.

Imprinted at London for Edward White, and are to be sold at his shop, at the little North doore of S. Paules Church at the signe of the Gunne.

---

14 wastning *Qq.*   19 Where Iudge and witnesses, *1599*: Wheres Iudge and witnesse, *1599 A and undated Q.*   26 fortune *1599 A*

The Housholders

Philofophie.

VVherein is perfectly and profitably defcribed,
the true Oeconomia and forme of
Houfekeeping.

With a Table added thereunto of all the notable
thinges therein contained.

*Firft written in Italian by that excellent Orator and Poet
Signior Torquato Taffo, and now tranflated
by* T. K.

AT LONDON

Printed by J. C. *for Thomas Hacket,*
and are to be fold at his fhop in Lomberd-ftreete,
vnder the figne of the Popes head.
M. D. LXXXVIII.

EDITOR'S NOTE

THIS translation is reprinted here for the first time from the Black-Letter Quarto in the British Museum. In this copy, however, the first line of the title is missing, and above the wood-cut are printed the words, ' Wherevnto is anexed a dairie Booke for | all good huswiues,' though no such ' dairie Booke' appears in the volume. The title-page has, therefore, been reproduced from that of the copy in the Bodleian. I have made some changes in the punctuation, and have introduced quotation marks in the passages of dialogue. I have also expanded in a number of places the abbreviated forms of ' quoth,' ' that,' and ' the.' The marginal notes are added to the translation by T. K., whose identity with Thomas Kyd is discussed in the Introduction. The Index also is his addition, and in reprinting it from the Quarto, I have kept the references to the original paging.

A CATALOGVE OR INDEX

OF THOSE THINGS WORTH THE MEMORY

CONTAINED IN THIS BOOKE

D.

E.

FINIS

THE

HOVSHOLDERS PHILOSOPHIE

It was then about that time of the yeere that the Grape-gatherers were wont to presse their Wines, and that the Trees were seene (in some place) dispoiled of their fruite, when I (in the habitte of an vnknowne Pilgrim) rode betwixt *Nouara* and *Vercellis*; where, seeing the ayre wexe blacke, and enuironed on euery side with 5 clowdes ready to raine, I began to set spurs to my Horse; but the whilst I heard a confused cry of dogs, and turning me about, I beheld a little Kidde surchargd, pursued, and anon ouertaken by two swift Grey-hounds, in so much as it there died at my feete. The vnexpected pleasure of which game stayed me til a youth of 10 eighteene or twenty yeeres of age, tall of stature, of a good aspect, well proportioned, tough sinewed, and of a strong constitution, beating and crying out vpon the doggs, tooke the poore Kidde fro forth their mouthes, and gaue it to a pesaunt attending on him, that laid it on his shoulders, and at a beck of the youth gat him 15 swiftly on before. Whereupon the young man, turning towards me, said: ' Tell me, sir, of courtesie, whither is your iourney?' ' I would to *Vercellis*' (quoth I) ' this euening, if the time would giue me leaue.' 'You might happily get thither' (quoth he) 'were it not that the Riuer that runneth before the Cittie, and that deuid- 20 eth the confines of *Piemount* from those of *Millan*, is so ouerflowen that you can hardlie passe it; so that I would aduise you, if it please you, to lodge with me this euening, for not far hence, neere that Riuer, I haue a little Cottage where you may repose yourselfe with less disease then in any other place nigh there- 25 abouts.'

Whilst he thus spake, I stedfastly beheld him, and me thought
I perceiued in his very countenaunce a kind of gentilitie and grace ;
so that (iudging him to be of no base or meane condicion)
seeing him a foote, giuing my Horse to a hyreling that came
5 with me, I dismounted. 'Thereupon' (quoth he) 'you shall aduise
your selfe yonder on the Ryuerside, whether you were better to
passe on or staie : and thether will I goe before, not to arrogat
anie superioritie, but as your guide, because perhaps you are
not well acquainted with the waie.' 'Fortune' (quoth I) 'doth
10 fauour mee with too noble a conduct.   God graunt in other things
she shewe her selfe as prosperous.' Heere I became silent, and
I folowed him, but he regarded oft, and often ouerlooked, and looked
on me as if he were desirous, it seemd, to vnderstande of whence I
was : so that I preuented his desire, and in some sort to satisfie him,
15 said I was neuer till nowe in this Countrey, but heretofore going
into Fraunce I past by Pyemount ; 'howbeit I repent me not that I
came this waie, for the Countrey is very pleasant, and inhabited of
people passing courteous.'   Here perceiuing that I ministred occasion of speech, he could no longer hide what he desired, but sayd.
20   'Tell me,' I pray you, 'what are you, what Countreyman, and
what good fortune ledde you into these parts ? ' 'I was borne'
(quoth I) 'in Naples, a famous Cittie of Italie, my mother a
Neapolitan, my father of Bergamo, a Cittye situate in Lombardy ;
my name and surname I conceale, for they are so obscure, as if
25 I shoulde report them, yet you coulde not be the more enformed of
my state.   The wrath of Fortune and of mightie me⟨n⟩ I shun,
howbeit I am eftsoones shrowded vnder the estate of Sauoy.'
'Vnder a magnanimous, iust, and gratious Prince you soiourne
then' (quoth he).   But modestlie remembring that I desired to
30 conceale some part of mine estate, he enquired no further of me.
Wee had nowe walked little more then halfe a mile but wee ariued
on the side of the Ryuer, swifter then which neuer ranne arrowe
fro forth the strongest bow of Parthia : and it was swoln so high
as it farre surpast the wonted limmits, neither coulde it be con-
35 tained in the compasse whereunto it was accustomed.   And it
was told me by the Countreymen commorants there that the
Passador woulde not put off from the other side, but that
(vpon what occasio⟨n⟩ they knew not) he had refused to waft ouer
some French Gentlemen that would haue gyuen more then
40 ordinary for their passage.   Whereupon, turning to the youth that

was my guide, I said that necessity now bound me to accept his
courtesie, which not withstanding I had not yet determined
to refuse. 'Albeit' (quoth he) 'I had rather acknowledge this
fauour proceeding from your owne disposition then from Fortune,
it pleaseth me notwithstanding that she hath wrought it in such 5
sort as wee shall haue no neede to doubt of your abode.'

Thus more and more he confirmed mine opinion that he was
neither of ignoble birth nor meane capacitie; wherupon content
to be consorted with so well accomplished an Hoste, 'the sooner'
(quoth I) 'you shall please that I receiue the fauour to be lodged, 10
the more shall I accept of it.' And therewithall he ledde me to
his house that was not far situate from the Riuerside, and it was
as high as on the outside we might easily perceiue it comprehended diuers roomes and stories, one aboue another. Before the
house there was a little Court enuironed with Trees, and there 15
they ascended by double staires which were without the Gate,
eyther of them containing fiue and twentie large and most commodious steps. On the top of the staires we entred into a faire Hall,
four square and of conuenient greatnes, for it had two porthals
on the right, and two on the left side, and as manie in the vpper 20
end. Directly against the Gate whereby wee entred was there
another Gate, and thereby we descended by as manie other steps
into a little Court, about the which were prettie lodgings for
seruaunts, and houses for Corne; and thence we past into
a Garden large enough, and filled with fruitfull Trees, verie 25
orderlie and artificially disposed. The Hall was furnished with
hangings and euery other ornament beseeming the lodging of
a Gentleman. In the midst thereof was the Table couered, and
the Cupboorde charged with curious plates of *Candie*, furnished
with all sorts of daintie fruits. 'Faire and passing well placed' 30
(quoth I) 'is this goodlie house, and it can not be possest but of
some noble Gentleman who, though amongst the woods and in
a Countrey Towne, lets not yet to imitate the delicacy and
neatness of the Cittie: but are you the lord thereof?' 'Not I'
(quoth he), 'my Father is, whom God graunt a long life, neither 35
denie I him to be a Gentleman of the Cittie, or vnexperienced in
Courte or on the worldes conditions, albeit he hath spent the greater
part of his time in the Countrey; hauing a Brother that hath long

---

3 quoth he *add. ed.*   10 (quoth I) the sooner *Q*.

beene a Courtier in *Rome*, and that yet abideth there, highlie
fauoured of the good Cardinall *Vercellis*, whose valour and authoritie in these quarters highly are accou⟨n⟩ted.' 'And in what
part of *Europe* and of *Italie*' (quoth I) 'is that good Cardinall
5 knowne, and not accounted of?'

Thus as we were reasoning, there mette vs another youth of
lesse yeeres, but no lesse gentle spirit, that brought worde of his
Father's comming, who eftsoones was returned from surueighing
his possessions. And anon there came the Father on horsebacke,
10 attended with a footeman and another seruitor that rode before;
who, dismounted, immediately came vp the staires. He was
a man of midle age, yet neerer threescore then fiftie; of countenance verie pleasant myxed with comelie grauitie; and by the
whiteness of his hayre and beard (that only made him seeme old)
15 his dignity was much augmented. I, framing my passage towardes
the good man and maister of the house, saluted him with that
reuerence which I thought fitting both his yeres and such as he
should seeme. And hee, turning to his elder Sonne with
a pleasant countenance, asked him whence I was; 'for I haue
20 neuer seene him hereabouts or elswhere' (quoth he) 'to my
remembraunce.' To whom his Sonne made aunswer thus: 'He
cometh from *Nouara*, and trauails towards *Turyno*'; but making
neerer to his Father, he whispred to him in such sorte that hee
would enquire no further of my state, but saide, 'whence soeuer
25 he be, hee is welcome here a shore, for hee is happened on
a place, where, to our powre, honour and seruice alwaies hath
beene vsed to strangers.' I, thanking him for his courtesie, praid
that, as I willingly receaued thys fauour of him, so in other things
I might shew myselfe mindful and regardant.

30   These things thus discoursed, the seruaunts had prouided water
for our hands, and (hauing washt) we sate as it pleased the good
old Gentleman, who desired to doo me honor, beeing a straunger.
Forthwith was the Table furnished with fruits, as Mellons, Cytrons,
and such like, which, at the end of Supper, were, at a wincke of
35 his, reserued and set vp, and then he began thus: 'The good old
man, *Coricius*, the Gardener, of whom I remember I haue read
in *Virgill*,

Nocte domum dapibus mensas onerabat inemptis.

Hyed home at night and fild his bord with delicats vnbought.

'And in imitation wherof *Petrarch* speaketh, reasoning of his
Plowman :

> *Epoi la mensa ingombra,*
> *Di pouere viuande,*
> *Simili a quelle ghiande* 5
> *Le quai fuggendo tutt' il mondo onora.*

> And then he decks his boord about
> With meats of meane esteeme,
> Like to those Jayes whose flight contents
> The world, cause faire they seeme. 10

'So that you neede not meruaile if, I, after their fashion, fill
your Table with vnbought viands, which, though they bee not such
as you are vsed to taste elsewhere, remember you are in a Country
Town, and lodged in the house of a poore Host.' ' I hold it ' (quoth
I) ' a happy thing to haue no neede to send for necessaries to the 15
Cittie for the supply of good manners, I meane, not of good
meate ; for thereof, sir, me seemes heere wants no store.' ' It
lightlie happeneth not ' (quoth hee) ' that I send to the Cittie for
any thing necessarie or fit for the life of a poore Gentlema⟨n⟩, for
(God be praised) I haue aboundaunce of euery thing ministred 20
vnto me vpon myne owne ground, the which I have deuided into
foure parts or formes, call them what you will. The first and
greatest part I plow and sowe with wheate and all kind of graine.
The second part I leaue for Trees and plants which are also
necessarie either for fire, the vse of Architecture, and other instru- 25
ments of houshold ; as also in those places that are sowne are
manie rewes of Trees, whereupon the Vines, after the manner of
our *petit* Countries, are laid and fostered. The third is Meadowe
ground whereon the Heards and little flocks I haue are wont to
graze. The fourth I have reserued for hearbes, flowers, and rootes, 30
where also are some store of hyues for Bees, because beyond this
Orchard, wherein you see that I haue gryft so many fruitfull Plants,
and which, you see, is somewhat seperat fro⟨m⟩ my possessions
there is an other garden full of all sorts of sallet hearbes and other
rootes.' 'You haue well deuided your lands' (quoth I) 'and it 35
is well seene you are studious of *Varro*, not of *Virgil* onely. But
these Mellons heere that are so sweet, are they also growing vpon
your owne grounde ?' 'Yea' (quoth hee) 'and if they please you,
eate of them and tarry not for me. For if I haue eaten but a little, it

---

6 *tutto 'l mondo honora Q.*

R 2

hath not beene for sparing them, but because I deeme them scarce
wholesome : for, albeit they be sweet of sauour and pleasant to
the tast, neuerthelesse hanging alwaies on the earth and not dis-
couered on al sides to the Sunne, it must needs be that there they
5 soke up the superfluous humours of the earth ; which most commonly being vnpossible to be wel or equallie ripened by the vertue
of the Sunne, which cannot enter into euery part, it happeneth that
there are few good mellons to be found, but that many of them
taste like Goords and Cowgomers which also hang vpon the
10 earth vnripened.'

Here he became silent, and I, to shew that I allowed of that he
spake, said little, knowing that olde men, or they that grow in
yeeres, were euer more desirous of reasoning and talk then any
other thing, for we can not please them better then to harken to
15 their speeches with attention.   But he then, almost at a staie,
said, because his wife was wanting : 'Sir, my wife beeing with-
drawne from your presence happily lookes to be inuited ; therefore, if it please you, I will cause her to bee called.   For albeit I
knowe that modest strangers are more abasht with the company
20 of women than of men, yet not onely the Towne, but the custome
of our Countrey, carieth a certain priuiledge, whereof it will be wel
that you begin to aduise your selfe.'

The Wife, beeing called, came and sat her down at the vpper
end of the Table, in that place that was purposelie left empty for
25 her, and the good man of the house beganne againe : ' Nowe haue
you seene' (quoth he) 'all my deerest thinges, for heauen hath not
graunted me a maiden Child, for which I were to thanke the⟨m⟩
much, were it not but that my wife lamenteth oft for want of one
to beare her company, for my Sonnes are for the most part absent
30 and imployed otherwise ; wherefore I thought good to haue
married myne eldest Sonne, had he not much disliked and intreated to the contrarie.'   'I cannot' (quoth I) 'in anie sort
commend this custome of marrying yong me⟨n⟩ so soone.   For
it standeth not with reason that they should first be getting Chil-
35 dren before themselves were come vnto their groweth, wherunto
me thinks your Sonne heere hath attained : besides, the fathers
ought to exceede their children alwaies eyght and twenty or thirty
yeares at the least, for otherwise they are in the vigor of their
yeeres when the youth of their sonnes begin to flourish, insomuch
40 as their desires are yet vnaccomplished, which, if by none other

meanes, yet by example of their children they might moderate :
and oft it is the cause that such regarde is scarcely had or vsed to
them by their Children as is due to Parents ; for many times they
are companions and brothers in their conuersation, nay, nowe and
then (which is most abhominable) they are ryualls and competitors 5
in loue, where, if they exceeded more in yeres, their Fathers could
not match them in theyr young desires, but (beeing decrepit)
shulde solely expect and approue that ayde and comfort at theyr
hands, which is their due, and nature bindeth children vnto.   And
herein I remember that apt forme of speech vsed by *Lucretius*, 10
Natis munire senectam.   For by nature Chyldren are the fortresse
and defences of their Parents ; neither coulde they be such were
they not of able and sufficient yeeres, whe⟨n⟩ their Parents are
ariued and come vnto their age.   Whereunto your selfe being
eftsoones nigh, mee thinks you ought to hold your selfe no less 15
satisfied of the helpe you haue tha⟨n⟩ of the good conditions of
your Sonne, who, though he cannot yet find in his hart to be married, shall happily conforme him selfe thereunto ten or twelue
yeeres hence, and time inough.'   Whilst I spake thus, I remembred that my argument was more acceptable to the Sonne than 20
the father, and he, according to my remembraunce, said : ' I hunted
not all in vaine to day, for I haue not onely kild, but, more then
I looked for, I haue happened on an honest aduocat to pleade my
cause.'   And thereupon he carued me of the daintiest morsels of
the Kid, and laid it on my trenchour ; whereof some was roste, 25
some was backt after the manner of mynced meate.   With the
Kidde was serued (in seuerall dyshes) some part of a wylde Boare,
drest, after our Countrey fashion, with Larde, and in two other
dyshes two payre of Pygeons, the one roasted, the other boyled.
' This wilde boare ' (quoth the good man) ' was taken by a Gentle- 30
man, a friende and neighbor of ours, who often time participates
the profit of his sports with my Son ; the Pigeons, them I haue
from my owne Douehouse, and with these fewe haue we furnished
a poore Supper ; as for Beefe and such like, I holde it rather
a trouble to the stomack and the Table then a necessarie meate 35
for this contagious weather.'   ' It suffiseth mee ' (quoth I), ' if it
bee not more then needes, to eate of two kinds of wilde flesh : and
me thinks I haue supped with noble men to night, in whose time,
wee reade, there was none other flesh eaten then Beefe, Porke,
and Venizon and such like ; for the banquets of *Agamemnon*, as 40

we read in *Homer* (although, by the opinion of *Lucian*, they might
deserue to haue old *Nestor* at the⟨m⟩ almost as a *Parasite*), were
not furnished with other viands.   And the companions of *Vlisses*
bare not so many mishaps and heates of the Sunne for the desire
of Feisants or Partrich, but to feede vppon Beefe.   *Virgil* likewise 5
inducith *Aeneas* that in *Affrick* slew seauen Harts; where, after
the judgment of some, it shold haue beene some other thing, for
in *Affrick* are no Harts bred; but in hauing regard to the conueni-
encie and custome of Noblemens dyet, he faigned or forgat that
which properlie is vsed and eaten in that prouince.'   10

'And wherefore' (quoth the olde man) 'did the Poets faigne
that Noble men of their time did eate such kinde of flesh?'.
'Because' (quoth I) 'they are of great nourishment, and they
(as those that exercised themselues with much labour) had neede
of great nourishment which Birds cannot yeelde, that are so 15
easilie digested: but the flesh of wild Beasts, although they be
of great nourishment, yet are they wholesome because they be
much exercised and stirring, and theyr fatte is farre more
naturall then that of Swine, or other Beastes that fatneth by
the hande, for it is not so soone puft vp and fattened as those 20
Beasts that commonly are stald and foddered.   Therefore it was
aptly said of *Virgil*, speaking of *Aeneas* soldiours,

> *Implentur veteris Bacchi pinguisque ferina⟨e⟩*

> And they are filled euery one
> With olde wine and fat venison.   25

'For they fedde therof at will without any noisome or superfluous
fulness.'   Heerewithall I held my peace, and the olde man began
thus : 'The discourse that you haue made of Wine, and of the
auncient times of Noble men, makes mee remember that which
I haue hearde obserued of *Homer*, who euermore in praysing 30
Wine called it *Nigrum et dulce*, which two conditions, me thinks,
are not very commendable; and so much the more it seemeth
strange vnto me that he should giue Wine commendations of
that sort, the more I haue obserued that the wines of *Leuant*
which are brought ouer heere to vs are white of collour, as are the 35
Malmeseys and the *Romaine* wyne which I haue tasted of in
Venice; without that, the wines which in the Kingdome of *Naples*
are called *Grecian* wines, because they were made of the Grapes
that grow in *Greece*, bee white, or rather, gold-coloured, as that

Wines of the Eastern parts.

aboue all the rest is wherof we haue spoken. And those wines
are more properlie white that are of the *Rheyne* of *Germanie*, and
those others that growe in colde Countries where the Sunne hath
not so much force as it can rypen Grapes before the time of
5 Grape-gathering, albeit happilie the manner of their making may
also be the cause of their whitnes.'

Heere I aunswered that the Wines were termed sweete of
Homer with that kind of *Metaphor* wherwith al things, either
pleasing to the sences or acceptable to the minde, are required
10 to be sweete. 'Howbeit, I denie not that perhaps he loued
sweete Wines himselfe, which also most contenteth me ; neither
is this sweetnes of Wine vnpleasant or hurtful but at some
seasons: and the *Malmesey* ⟨and⟩ *Greeke* and *Romain* Wines
wherof wee haue made mencion, all of them haue some kind of
15 sweetnes, which is neuerthelesse lost the older the Wine is ;
whereupon we read :

Inger mi calices amariores.

Pray fill with bitter wines
These challices of mine.

20   'This was not because the Poet desired bitter Wyne (for there
is none to whom bitternes is not vnpleasant), but because olde
Wine, loosing the sweetnes, yeeldeth that sharp and heddie taste
which he calleth bitter ; and I would so wishe you to vnderstande
that it is called sweete of *Homer*, as it was called bitter by
25 *Catullus* : afterward *Homer* calleth it black, hauing reference
to some particuler Wine that was then in price as is nowe our
Lachrima, which, though it bee prest from one selfe same Grape Which we
as the Wine of *Greece* is, hath yet a vermillion couller.' Hauing call redde
aunswered thus, I tasted of a cup of delicat white Wine with my Wine.
30 Mellons, and afterward, beeing begun to by him, I pledged him
of a Cup of neate Claret wine, and, vpon interposition of some
words, we ended our merry Supper. For the meate taken awaie,
there was sette on the Table all sorts of fruite in great aboundance,
whereof when the old man had onely tasted, hee began thus to
35 reason.

'I haue many times hearde much quest⟨i⟩oning of the noblesse
and varietie of seasons, and I haue seene two Letters that are
extant to be reade, of *Mutius* the one, and the other of *Tasso*,

─────────────────────────

13 and *add. ed.*

wherein they contende of the woorthines betwixt Winter and
Sommer, but me thinks no time may be compared to *Autumn*.
For the Sommer with extreame heate, and the Winter with
extreame colde, are otherwhile so intollerable, as we can neither
5 temperate the one with fruits nor the other with pastimes: and
they are not onely a hynderaunce to the Mariner, who in the
Winter is enforced to keepe the Hauen, to the trauailer, Souldier,
and huntsman, who in Sommer are constrained to retyre them
from the heate, raynes and tempests vnder the shade of a Tree,
10 or shroude of a Church, whether they first find—but to the housekeeper also, who without many inconueniences cannot haue the
time so much as to surueigh his grounds.   The one season, then,
is full of labour and of sweat, neither enioyeth it the third part
of the fruite it bringeth forth for spoile of weather, wormes
15 and windes.   The other, slothfull and sleepie betwixt idlenes and
eating, vniustly consumeth that which the labour of another time
hath yielded.   Which iniustice is indifferently to be noted by the
difference betwixt the day and night.   For in Winter the daie,
which is most vnworthy, yeeldeth to the night, whereof it is
20 vnreasonable that it should be ouercome, and being short, colde,
and cloudie it giveth not men conuenient time to worke or to
contemplate.   So that our operations and contemplations are
enclozed with darknes and reserued to the night, a time nothing
necessarie for the one nor other.   For the sences that are
25 ministers of vnderstanding cannot so entirely exercise their office
in the night.   In the Summer the daie becomes victor, and
raigneth not like a Lord, but like an extreame Tirant that
vsurpeth more then needes, leauing the night not so much time
as that therein we may sufficiently restore our bodies resolued with
30 the exceeding heate and contagions of the day ; of whose shortnes
not onely the Louers (that would haue it long) were wont to lament,
but the goodwife of the house also, who euen then that shee
woulde nestle in the armes of her Husband, is by him forsaken
and awaked.'   And therwithall hee laughed so hartilie, looking vpon
35 his wife, that she blushing held downe her head, and he proceeded.
'These, if I be not beguiled, are the inconueniences and dis-
comodities of the Winter and Sommer, whereof the Spring and
Autumn are not to be touched, for they are fraught with millions
of delights, and in their times the Sun (like a most indifferent
40 Gouernour) formeth the day and night of such equalitie, as the

one hath little cause to complaine of the other.   But if wee wyll
co⟨m⟩pare *Autumn* and the Spring togeather, we shall soone finde
the springe so farre inferior to *Autumn* as hope is to effects, and
floures to fruits, whereof *Autumn* most aboundeth of all other
seasons.   Besides that, whatsoeuer fruite Sommer hath brought 5
forth endureth euen vntill then, and manie other hath *Autumn*
onely proper to his season, whereof as one especiall is Grape-
gathering for the wine-presse, which is, or ought to bee, one of
the cheefest cares the Housekeeper should haue ; for, if hee be
deceiued by his seruaunts in gathering of his Corne, he thereof 10
onely feeles some losse and discommoditie, but if in making of
his Wines they practise neuer so little falshood, he doth not onely
suffer the losse, but shame, when it happeneth that hauing
honorable guests he cannot commende his Supper with good
Wines, without which *Non solum frigescit Venus*, but all his meats 15
are mard that might be drest by the most excellent Cooke
the Duke hath.   Therefore I conclude that Autumn is the most
noble and best season of the yeere, and that which is indeed
most acceptable to the Housekeeper : and I remember I haue
hearde my Father saie, who (if the troth reported of him may but 20
be beleeued) was for naturall ⟨and⟩ *Morall Philosophie* and
eloquent deuise more then meanelie learned, that in this season
the world began, as indeede wee may assuredlie beleeue it did.'
'That' (quoth I) 'hath beene the opinion of some Doctors of the
Hebrues, and Christians of great account, which notwithstanding, 25
beeing no Article of our beliefe, euery manne may credite as he
list.   I, for my part, am one of them that hold the contrary, and
it seemeth to me more likelie that (the world beginning, as it is
supposed) it the⟨n⟩ began about the Spring, which I will thus
constraine my selfe to prooue.   30
    'You shall vnderstand that Heauen is round, and hath all his
parts so vniforme as in it there can bee perceiued neither beginning
nor ende, ryght nor left, vnder nor ouer, before nor behind, which
are the sixe positions of place, vnlesse it happilie be in respect onely
of the motion, because that is the right side whereof the motion 35
hath his beginning ; but because the motion of the Sunne goes
against the *Primum mobile*, it may bee doubted whether these sixe
differences of place ought chiefely to be taken according to the

---

21 and *add. ed. ; cf.* 'della naturale e morale filosofia.'   *Tasso*

motion of the *Primum mobile*, or according to the motion of the
Sun. Neuerthelesse, forasmuch as all thinges contained in thys our
variable and corruptible world chiefely depende vppon the motion
of the Sunne, which is the cause of generation and of corruption,
5 and is indeede the father of all liuing things, it is requisite that
the motion of the Sunne determine the differences of the place.
According therefore to the motions of the Sun, our Pole is the
higher which, according to the motion of the *Primum mobile*,
shuld be the lower. This beeing thus, if we will seeke in what
10 season it is like the world began, we shal see it is most reasonable that it then began when the Sun remouing foregoes not, but
aprocheth vs. Besides, it beginneth with generation, not with corruption, for according to the custome of nature things are first
ingendred and afterward corrupted : but the Sun remouing out of
15 *Aries*, it approcheth vnto vs, and there giueth beginning to the
generation and engendering of thinges. It is likelye, then, that
when the world began, the Sun was in *Aries*, which without doubt
he shall see is so that diligently considereth what was said in
Platos Tymeus of God the Father to those inferior Gods. True it
20 is that who so taketh the positions of place from the motion of
the *Primum mobile*, it must followe that the Pole Antartick is the
higher by Nature, and that the world began in that season wherein
the Sunne, remouing, approcheth neerer vnto our *Antipodes*, and
beginneth generation in those parts of the other world that are
25 opposite to these : which who so graunteth, it would seeme more
likely that the world began in the *Autumnal æquinoctial* when the
Sunne was in *Libra* ; and yet it would follow that it began in the
Spring, because this that is *Autumn* to vs is their Springtime, in
respect whereof, the beginning of the motion should be taken.
30 But the first opinion, as by naturall reason it is most likelie, so
also may it be most commodiously consorted with perswasions.
For our worlde was dignified with the presence of the true Sonne
of GOD, who made choyse to die in *Ierusalem*, which, according to
the Cosmographicall dyscription of some, is in the midst of our
35 Hemysphere. Moreouer it was his will to dye in the Spring, of
purpose to redeeme our humaine generation in that time wherein
at first he had created it.' And heere I ceased, when the olde
man, mooued with my speeches, beganne earnestlie to looke vpon
me, and said.
40 'I haue entertained a greater guest then I expected, and you'

(quoth he) 'are peraduenture one of those of whom the crye is
come into our Countrey, who vppon some common fault are fallen
into mis-fortunes, whereof you are as worthy to be pardoned (co⟨n⟩-
sidering your offence) as to be praised and admired for your
speeches.' 'Report' (quoth I), 'that coulde not happily blazon 5
mine estimation or sufficiencie whereof you are too courteous
a commender, is now deriu'd from my misfortunes.   But what or
whosoeuer I may bee, I am one that speake more for truth sake
then of hatred, dispraise of others, or superfluous conceit of mine
opinions.' 'If you be such an one ' (quoth he), 'for I will not 10
search or pry into your state, you cannot but be an indifferent
and fit Judge of a matter which my Father (loaden both with
age and with experience) participated vnto me a fewe yeeres before
his death, giuing vp the gouernment of his house and care of his
familie to me.'   And whilst he thus spake, the Seruants tooke 15
away, and the auncient Gentlewoman, giuing thanks, arose, and
was attended by her Sonnes, who after a while returning, I
beganne : 'Syr, it shall be very acceptable vnto mee to heare
the dyscourse your Father made vnto you, as you were in purpose
to haue tolde me, but, because it would bee greeuous vnto me to 20
harken thereunto with the dysease of those that are about vs,
I beseech you commaund your Sons to sitte,' who obeying the
gentle commaunds of their father, the good olde man began thus.

'About that time that *Charles* the fift desposed his Monarchie,
and withdrew himselfe from the worlde, as from a tempest, to 25
contemplation and a quiet life, my good Father, beeing then
threescore and tenne yeeres old, my selfe somewhat more then
thirtie, called mee to him, and began to reason with me thus.
"The deedes of greatest Kings, that turne the eyes of all the
world vpon theyr actions, albeit that for their greatnes and 30
magnificence it seemes they can haue no proportion of comparison with priuat men, neuerthelesse they mooue vs now and
then with the authority of theyr examples to imitate them in such
sort as we behold the prouidence of our almighty God followed by
Nature, not onlie in man, a reasonable creature whose dignity doth 35
come so neere the Angels, but also in the industrie of other little
creatures.   Whereby it should not seeme so strange to vs if now
that *Charles* the fift, that thrise renowmed Emperor, hath thus
deposed and discharged him of the weight of his so famous
Monarchie, I also thinke by his example to disgrade me of this 40

petit gouernment of houshold, which to my priuat personne is no
lesse then is his Empire to his Maiestie.   But first, before I shall
surrender this that rather appertaines to thee then to thy Brother,
as well in that thou art his elder as also more enclind to husban-
5 dry (a thing most needful and appropriate to housekeeping), I will
so instructe thee touching things belonging to good gouernment as
I was taught not long since of my Father, who, sprong of simple
parentage, and heyre of a small patrimonie, with industrie, sparing,
and good husbandry did much augment it, which hath not beene
10 deteriorated since by mee, but twice as much encreased since my
father left it.   Howbeit if I haue not looked to my husbandry
with so great care, nor liued so sparingly as he prescribed, neuerthelesse (let me boldly say thus much to thee, my Son) the
knowledge that I had touching the nature of things, and fellow-
15 ship of the worlde more then he, hath beene the cause that I
with little more expence haue easely accomplisht what he (being
vnlettered and not experimented in the world) did hardly compasse with much sparing, and with exceeding toyle euen of his
owne person.
20   ' " Now, to begin, I say thus : that the care of a good house-
holder is deuided into two thinges, that is his body and hys goods.
In his personne he is to exercise three offices, viz. of a *Father*,
a *Husband*, and a *Maister*.   In his goods two purposes are proposed, *Conseruation* and *Encrease*, touching euery of which I will
25 particularly reason ; and first of hys body rather then hys goods,
because the care of reasonable thinges is more woorth then that of
things vnreasonable.
  ' " The good Housekeeper, then, ought principally to haue care
in choosing of his wife, with whom hee must sustaine the
30 personne of a Husbande, which happily is termed by a tytle more
effectuall, *Consort* : for the Husband and the wyfe ought indeed
to be companions and consorts of one selfe fortune ; all the good
and all the euill incident to life ought by them to be common and
indifferently sustained.   In such sort as the soule communicats
35 her operations with the bodie, and the body with the soule, so that
when any part of the bodie grieueth vs the mind can hardly be
content, and vppon the malcontentment of the minde followes the
infirmities or weakenes of the bodie : so shoulde the Husband
lament the sorrowes of the Wife, and the Wife the troubles of the
40 Husband.   And the like communitie shoulde be in all offices and

all operations. And so much is that coniunction that the man
hath with the Wife like to that which the body hath with the soule,
as not without reason the name of Consort or Felow is to be attributed to the Husband and the Wife, as to the Soule it hath beene
heretofore attributed. Forasmuch as *Petrarch*, reasoning of the 5
soule, saith :

L' errante mia Consorte.

My wandering Companion.

' "In imitation perhaps of *Dante*, who in his *Canzonet of Noblesse*
said that the soule was espoused to the bodie. Albeit, for some 10
other respect, it ought rather to bee resembled to the Husband
then the wife. And euen as after that the bande that tyes the
body and the soule togeather is disseuered, it seemeth not that
the soule can bee conioynd with any other body (wherfore foolish
is that opinion of some that imagined the soule did passe from 15
one vnto another, as dooth the Pilgrim passing from one lodging
to another), so shoulde it seeme conuenient then that woman or
man, that haue beene diuorced by death from that first band of
Matrimonie, ought not to be knit vnto a second. Nor without
great admiration should *Dydo* have continued her vnwillingnes 20
of hauing a second husbande, who speaketh thus in the book of
Virgils Aeneidos :

> *Sed mihi vel tellus optem prius ima dehiscat,*
> *Vel pater omnipotens adigat me fulmine ad vmbras,*
> *Ante, pudor, quam te violem aut tua iura resoluam.* 25
> *Ille meos, primus qui me sibi iunxit, Amores*
> *Abstulit ; ille habeat secum seruetque sepulchro.*

First wold I that the parched earth did riue and raught me in,
Or that th' almightie would with lightning driue me to the deepe ;
Ere I to lose or violate my chastity beginne. 30
He hath my loue that first had me ; (interd) he his shal keepe.

' " Notwithstanding, forasmuch as custome and the Lawes dys-
pence with them in this, the woman, as well as the man, may
without shame vndertake the second Marriage, especially if they
doo it for desire of succession, a desire most naturall in all 35
reasonable creatures ; but happier are they that haue but once in
all theyr life beene tyed with that band.

' " Howe much the greater then and straighter the coniunction

---

23 *dehiscat*] *dehiscens Q.*   25 *resoluam*] *resoluem Q.*

is of the husbande and the Wife, so much the more ought euery
one prouide to be indifferently matched ; and truely this equallity
of marriage is in two speciall things to be considered—Estate
and Age.　For as two Palfreys or two Oxen of vnequall stature
5 cannot be coupled vnder one selfe yoake, so a noble woman matching with a man of base estate, or, contrarily, a Gentleman with
a Begger, cannot be consorted well vnder the bands of wedlock.
But when it happeneth yet that, by some accident of Fortune,
a man marrieth a woman of so high a birth, hee ought (not
10 forgetting that he is her husband) more honor and esteeme of her
then of his equall or of one of nearer parentage, and not only
to account her his companion in loue and in his life, but (in
dyuers actions of publique aparance) holde her his superior.
Which honor is not yet accompanied with reuerence as is that
15 which for manner sake wee are wont to doe to others.　And she
ought to consider that no distinction of nobilitie can be so great
but that the league which Nature hath ordeined betwixt men and
women farre exceedeth it, for by Nature woman was made mans
subiect.　But if a man shal take to wyfe an inferior or meane
20 woman, he also ought to weygh that Matrimonie maketh equall
many differences, and, further, that he hath not taken her for
a slaue or seruaunt, but for a fellow and companion of his life.
And thus touching the estate of man and wife, let this suffice.

'"Nowe passing to the age, I say that the Husband prouide
25 to choose his wife rather yong then olde, not onelie because
a woman is more apt to child-bearing in youth the⟨n⟩ otherwise,
but because (according to the testimony of *Hesiodus*) she can
better receiue and retaine all formes of customes and conditions
wherewith it shall content her Husband to commend her.　And
30 for this, that the life of a woman is conscribd and ordinarily
concluded in lesser tyme then Mans, and sooner waxeth olde, as
one in whom naturall heate is not aportioned vnto superfluous
moisture, the man ought to exceede the woman so many yeeres,
as the beginning of the ones age match not with the others, so
35 that one of them before the other become vnable and vnfit for
generation.　Now if it happen that the Husband take a wife with
these conditions, he shall furthermore easily exercise in her that
superioritie that hath been graunted vnto man by Nature,
where otherwise it often commeth to passe that he shal find her
40 so exceeding waiward, crabbed and disobedient, that where he

thought hee made his choyse of a companion that shold helpe to
lighten and exonerat that ponderous and heauie loade which our
humanity affordeth, he findes he is nowe matcht and fallen into the
handes of a perpetuall enemie, who euermore none otherwise
impugneth and resisteth him then our immoderate desires that 5
in our minds so much oppose themselues to reason : for such is
woman in respecte of man as is desire in comparison of vnderstanding ; and euen as desire (which of it selfe is vnreasonable) is,
by obeying · to vnderstanding, formed and beautified with many
faire and necessary vertues, so a woman that conformes her selfe 10
to her Husband is adorned with those vertues wherof by being
obstinat she continueth vnfurnished. It is then a vertue in a
woman to knowe howe to honor and obey her husband, not as
a Seruant doth his Maister, or the bodye the mind, but ciuilly and
in such sort as we see the Cittizens in wel gouerned Citties obey 15
the Lawes, and reuerence their Magistrates ; or so as in our
soules, wherein as wel the well dysposed powers as the orders
of the Cittizens within their Citties compell affections to be
subiect vnto reason. And heerein it hath beene conueniently
ordeined of Nature ; for being needful that in the felowship of 20
ma⟨n⟩ and wife the offices and dueties should be diuers, and
the operations of the one varying from the others, it is conuenient also that their vertues should be diuers.

'"The vertues proper to man are *Wisedome, Fortitude*, and
Liberalitie : To woman, *Modestie* and *Chastitie* ; wherwith both 25
the one and the other of them may very well perform those
operations that are requisite : but albeit *Chastitie* or *Shamefastnes*
be not properly the vertues of a man, yet ought a good Husband
to offend the league of Matrimonie as little as he possibly may,
and not to be so incontinent as (beeing absent for a season from 30
his wife) he cannot abstaine from pleasures of the flesh ; for if
hee himselfe doo not first violate the bandes by so defiling of the
marriage bedde, he shall doubtles much confirme the womans
chastitie, who by nature libidinous, and no lesse inclined to
venerie then man, onely by shame, loue, or feare may not be 35
withdrawn from breaking of her faith vnto her Husbande.

'"Amongst which three affectio⟨n⟩s *Feare* is as worthy of praise
as blame, where the other two are indeede most commendable.
And therefore not without great reason was it said of *Aristotle*
that *Shamefastnes*, which merits no praise in a man, is most 40

praise worthy in a woman : and his Daughter very excellently
approues that no collour better graceth or adornes a womans
cheekes then that which shamefastnes depainteth ; which increaseth and draweth as earnest loue and desire of others to
them, as happily those other artificiall Oyles and dawbings which 5
they vse decreaseth and with draweth from them, beeing in
deede fitter for vizards, pageants, and poppets then wholesome,
handsome, or toothsome.   And truely as a woman of discretion
will in no wise marre her naturall co⟨m⟩plexion, to recouer it
with slime or artificiall coullered trash, so ought the husband 10
in no sort to be consenting to such follies.   But because it
behoueth the rule and authoritie of the Husband to be moderate
in those things chiefely which appertaine to women, which, for
that they are receiued and kept of custome, can not bee condemnd as arguments of much vnshamefastnes, he can practise no 15
way better to dyswade her from such muddy making faire her
face then with shewing himselfe a hater, contemner, and carelesse of those that are faire with that filthy spunging, proigning,
painting, and pollishing themselues.   As for women desirous to
seeme faire to please others I cannot say ; but of honest women 20
desirous to content their Husbands I may boldly speake, that
at such time as they shall see their tricking vp their selues with
Die and suche like filth pleaseth not their husbands eyes, they,
I know, of modestie and loue will suddainly forbeare it.   Much
more easie to be entreated should the husbande be in graunting 25
her those things whereof her bodie with conuenient ornaments
should be sufficiently apparelled, for albeit superfluous pompe
be fitter for a stage or Theater then the person of an honest
Matron, notwithstanding herein much may be attributed to vse,
neyther should a womans fantasie so sharplie be offended, con- 30
sidering that by nature shee is so desirous to adorne and beautifie
her bodie.   For albeit we see that Nature in other creatures hath
effected that the bodies of the Male be more adorned then the
Females (as the Hart with his fayre and bushie braunched
hornes, the princely Lyon with his proude and feltred locks 35
which the Females neuer haue), and hath embroidered the
Peacocks taile with more variety of collours the⟨n⟩ those of theyr
Hens, neuerthelesse wee may perceiue that in the shape of man

Ouid De med. faciei Certus a- mor mo- ru⟨m⟩ est, formam populabi- tur aetas.

she hath had more regard to the beauty of the Female then the
Male. For the flesh of women, as it is more soft and daintie,
so are they ordinarilie more desired to be gazed on, neyther
are their faces shadowed with beards, which albeit they becom
5 men, beeing proper vnto vs, yet can we not deny but that the
countenaunces of youthes, vppon whose faces hayre neuer came,
are fayrer and farre more louely then those of bearded men.
And *Loue* by the iudiciall figures of antiquitie hath beene
portraied like a Boy; so *Bacchus*, so *Apollo*, who of all the
10 other Gods were most fayre, were deciphered without beards,
but with long curled locks trussed up in tresses; whereupon the
Poets call him *Phoebus* with these *Epythetons* almost co⟨n⟩tinually,
Non tosato o chiomato. But hayre (which is a great orname⟨n⟩t Vnkempt.
of Nature) groweth not so hastilie vppon a man nor so soft
15 and fine as vppon women, who delight in theyr hayre as Trees
doo in theyr leaues; and therefore at the death of theyr
husbands spoyling and disrobing themselues of all theyr other
ornaments, they vse yet in some place of *Italie* to cut away
theyr hayre, which also was an auncient custome, as we read of
20 *Hellen* in *Euripides.* How much the more regard then Nature
hath had to the beauty of women, so much the more conuenient
it is that they account of it, and maintaine the same with comely
ornaments.

‘ “Wherefore when thou shalt take a wife, such an one as I
25 desire thou maist haue, fayre, yong, equall in estate with thee,
modest, discreet, courteous, and brought vp in good discipline
vnder the education of a graue Matron and wise mother, how
much the more she shall content thee, so much the more thou
shouldest contend not to discontent her. Wherein thou oughtest
30 not onely giue consent that she may goe apparelled as others
of her calling doo—not restraining her from going to feasts and
other publique shewes where other honest women and those of
credit doo assemble, nor on the other side to giue her the bridle
of libertie so much that she be forwarde with the first at all
35 dauncings, Comedies, and other such assemblies—but also not
to forbid her those honest recreations and desires which are as
incident to youth as flowrs to the Spring time, least she hate or
feare thee with the dread wherewith base slaues or seruaunts are
kept vnder by theyr Maisters; nor yet to be so easily induced to
40 watch or follow her as she thereby become so bold and hardy that

she lay aside honest shame (a decent thing in honest wome⟨n⟩),
which also is a kind of feare distinguished from seruile base feare,
and is as easily accompanied with loue as seruile feare with hate.
And of this feare, which more properly is tearmed shamefastness
5 or reuerence, spake *Homer*, saying :

O my beloued father in law whom I haue hourely feard.

'"Neither should he onely cause or procure shamefastnes in all
her actions and busines of her life, but also in her entertainment
and embracings, for the Husband commeth not with those pro-
10 phane and superstitious cleppings as the delicate and wanton
Louer doth, which maketh me the lesse to meruaile that the
kysses of *Bell' ingannus* Paramour seemed sweeter to her then
her husbandes : albeit I beleeue that there was neuer greater
sweet in loue then that which moderatly springs of honest
15 Matrimonie.   And I could compare the embracings of the
Husbande and the Wife to the temperate suppers of well dieted
men, wherein they taste no lesse commodity of the meats then
the most incontinent and surfeiting co⟨m⟩panion, but hapely so
much the more by how much more their sences (ruld by reason)
20 are vpright Judges of theyr opposites and indigested contraries.
Neither will I yet desist in this mine enterprise.   For when
Homer faigned that *Iuno*, taking away *Venus* garter, went to
seeke her Husband on the Mount of *Ida*, and hauing enticed
hym with loue and louely termes and amorous games,

25   *Lay doun with him vpo⟨n⟩ the grasse al couered with a clowde.*

he meant none otherwise but this, that she taking vppon her the
person of a Louer, and deposing the habit of a Wife, went to seeke
Iupiter.   For the faire wordes, pleasing fashyons, and daintie
whispering speech, that she had taken wyth the garter from *Venus*,
30 were things more beseeming a Louer then a Wife : wherefore it
was conuenient that, beeing ashamed of her selfe, a Clowde shoulde
bee sent to hide her.   And when he saith *Ioue* had not the⟨n⟩ so
much desire towards her as before when he first tooke her to his
Wife, it giueth vs to vnderstand that married women are not for-
35 bidde for a little while to represent the person of yong Louers ;
which, notwithstanding, she must speedilie reforme, because it is
most vnseemlie in them that (as a Father or Mother, Maister or
Maistres of a house) desire to rule theyr family wyth honest and
enterchaungable loue which ought to bee twixt man and wife,

who are also to liue vnder the lawes of Matrimonie.   For if a man,
hauing an vicious or vnchaste wife, should presently kyll her, or
in some other sort but punish her according to the Lawes, he may
be happily employed better in some other action ; which to es-
5 chew (taking a wyfe of our deciphering) he shall neuer neede to
be aduertised by vs.

'" Now proceeding to the education of Children, the care of them
should be deuided so betweene the Father and the Mother as she
may nurse and he may teache them : for the mother ought not to
10 deny her milke to her owne Children, vnlesse she be preuented or
forbidden by infirmitie, forasmuch as that first and tender age of
infancie, apt to be molded of any fashion, oftentimes with the
milke sucketh the conditions of the Nursse.   Besides, if the mylke
altered not the bodies and consequently the manners of yong
15 sucklings, the Nurses shoulde not be so narrowly forbidde the
often vse of wynes ; but the Nurses beeing ordinary base persons,
it followes that the first nourishment which the little ones receiue
of them cannot be so gentle or so delicate as the Mothers, so that
who so denieth the nursing of her child in some sort denies to be
20 the mother of it, because the Mother is chieflie knowne and commended by the bringing of her children vp.

'" But that first age past ouer that is nourished with milk, the
little ones doo yet continue in their Mothers custodie, who are
vsed to be so kind and tender ouer them as oftentimes they bring
25 them vp too delicatly.   For which the Father is commau⟨n⟩ded
to prouide this reamedy : that, forasmuch as that first age aboundeth in naturall heate, he accustome them to cold ; for restraining
the naturall heate within, and causing that which the Philosophers
call *Antiperistasis*, the complexion of the child becommeth strong *Antiperi-*
30 and lustie.   And it was the manner of some nations, and especially *stasis,*
those of *Aquitan* and thereabouts, as we read in *Aristotle*, to wash *where heate*
their newe borne Children in the Riuers, to indurat and harden *expels cold,*
them against the cold, which custome is by *Virgil* attributed to the *or cold ex-*
Latins, as it is to be noted in these verses : *pulseth*
heate ; it is
applied to
well water,
35 *Durum a stirpe genus, natos ad flumina primum* *which is*
Deferimus, saeuoque gelu duramus et vndis : *therefore*
Venatu inuigilant pueri, syluasque fatigant ; *cold in*
Flectere ludus equos, et spicula tendere cornu. *winter be-*
cause, the

---

35 *stirpe*] *stripe* Q.   37 *syluas*] *syluam* Q.

hygh parts
of the ayre
being cold,
the heate
withdraw-
eth to the
lowerparts.

A painful people by our byrth, for first our babes we bring,
Like vs to be inurd to cold, and plundge them in the spring:
But bigger growne, they tende the chase, and tire the woods, to frame
Their horses fit for seruice and their archery for aime.

' " Which custome as I commende not, because to vs that haue 5
not vsed it it seemes extreame, so yet I thinke good to aduise
thee that, if it shall please God to giue thee Children, thou doo
not bring them vp vnder so soft and easie discipline as they
become such milke sops as were those Phrygians, of whom the
same Poet in that same booke of his *Aeneidos* maketh mention : 10

Vobis picta croco et fulgenti murice vestis. . . .
Et tunicae manicas, et habent redimicula mitrae.
O vere Phrygiae (neque enim Phryges), ite per alta
Dindyma, vbi assuetis biforem dat tibia cantum.
Tympana vos buxusque voca⟨n⟩t Berecynthia matris 15
Idaeae ; sinite arma viris, et cedite ferro.

Your robes are dyed with Saffron and with glistring purple buds,
Your cote hath mittins, and your high Priests hats are made like hoods.
O Phrygia in deede (nor Phrygians yet), scale you high Ida hyl,
Where trumpets eccho clangs to those that of the custome skyll ; 20
Cebiles Berecyntian pypes and Tymberils, you see,
Do call you thence ; leaue armour then to such as Souldiers be.

Whom (me thinks) at this day they of some Cities in *Lombardy*
are like, for if any there be valiant, many of the Phrygians also
were couragious.   Nor would I yet that thou sholdest bring them 25
vp so hardly or seuerely as the Lacedemonians were accustomed,
or as *Achylles* of *Chyro* was.   I would not (I say) that thou
shouldest bring the⟨m⟩ vp so fiercely, for such an education
makes the⟨m⟩ rather wilde and sauadge, which though the
Lacedemonians reputed fitting for a noble man, yet was not 30
Achilles such an one in his conditions as others of our time
need to propose him or his behauiour for theyr example.

' " Thy priuate estate requires that so thou teach and bring vp
thy Children as they may become good members of the Cittie
where thy selfe inhabitest, or they shall dwel, good seruitors and 35
subiects to their Prince, which, in theyr trades if they be Merchaunts, in good letters if they bee learned, and in wares if they
be able, they may shew themselues.   Neither shall thy Children
be vnfurnished of all or one of these professions, if thou see that

---

12 *tunicae*] *tunica* Q.   15 *vocant*] *vocat* Q.

they become not werish and of a womanish, effeminate complexion,
but of a strong and manlie constitution, and that they exercise
themselues in practise of the mind and body, al alike or both
togeather.   But because al this part of education and bringing vp
of Children is, or ought to be, in a manner the care of a Father 5
and good Housekeeper, because it is wholie pollitique that should
prescribe an order to the Father, howe he is to educate and bring
vp his Children, to the ende that the Citties discipline may conforme and be agreeable therewith—I will lay a part this argument, or at least dysioyne it from the rest which I will speake of 10
housekeeping ; and it shall suffise me soly to aduise and counsell
that thou bring them vpp in the feare and loue of God, honor of
their Parents, and in their Princes seruice and obedience, and
that they be continually exercised in those most commendable
practises of mind and body as become them, and may better 15
their estate with praise and honesty.

' " We haue now spoken so much as hath beene conuenient for
thee to doo in the person of a Husband and a Father ; eftsoones
it remaineth that we come to the consideration of the third
person, I meane, that of a Gouernour or Maister, terme it as you 20
list, which soly hath relation to the seruant.   And if we shall giue
credite to antiquities written of housekeeping and gouernment of
families, the Maister ought to holde them satisfied with labor,
victuall, and chastisement, and to keepe them exercised in obedience.   But forasmuch as theyr Seruaunts in olde times were slaues 25
taken in warres, and afterward called seruaunts *a seruando* (for
that they were preserud from death), and are at this day for the
most part manumitted and enfranchized, meethinks this latter
part of *chastisment* might well be left, as nothing requisite for our
times or customes (except percase in those partes where slaues 30
yet serue) ; and in steede thereof the Maister to giue them
admonition, which should not be such neyther, as is vsed by the
father to the son, but compleat and vttered with more austeritie
and signiorising termes ; and if that will not serue, to suffer the
disobedient, stifnecked, and vnprofitable seruant to depart, and 35
to prouide himselfe of one that better may content him.   And
yet one thing hath beene forgotten of those men of elder times,
which was not conuenient for slaues, but not onely fitting, but
most needful for freemen, and this is sallarie or wages.   With
wages, meate, work, and admonition, then, the Housekeeper shall 40

so gouerne hys familie as they shall rest content of him, and he
be satisfied of their labour.   But because (albeit the Lawes and
vsages of men are variable and diuers, as wee see perticulerly in
this of seruaunts, who for the greater number are at thys day free-
5 men) yet forasmuch as the Lawes and dyfferences of Nature are
not chaunged either by alteration of time or variety of customes,
whatsoeuer others saye, thou art thus to vnderstand, that this
distinction of *Soueraigne, Ruler, Gouernour,* or *Maister,* is first
founded vpon Nature, for some are naturally borne to commande,
10 and others to obey.   And hee that is borne to obey, were hee of
the Kings bloode, is neuerthelesse a seruaunt, though he be not
so reputed ; because the people that onely haue regarde to exterior
things iudge none otherwise of the conditions of men then they
doo in Tragedies of him they call the King, who, apparrelled in
15 Purple and glistering all in Golde and precious stones, represents
the person of *Agamemnon, Atreus,* or *Etheocles*; where if he
chaunce to faile in action, co⟨m⟩lines, or vtteraunce, they doe
not yet derrogat from his olde title, but they say *The King hath
not playde his part well.*   Likewise *he that represents the person of*
20 *a nobleman,* or Gentleman, that in this life (which is a Theater of
the world) hath beene deposed or bereft of his dignitie, he shall
neuerthelesse be called the Noble or the Gentleman stil, though
he be happily *Dauus, Syrus,* or *Geta.*   But when it happeneth
that some one is found, not onely seruile in condition and of
25 fortune, but base of mind, grosse of vnderstanding, and, as
Petrarch sayth, *Nudo di iudicio e pouero d' argomento* (*Naked of
iudgment, and poore of argument*), as the greater number are, he
may be properly termed a Seruaunt ; and of him and such like
the good Housekeeper (that woulde haue such persons serue him
30 as he might commaund with reason) may well furnish his house,
seeking no further vertue in them then that they may be capable
of his commaundements, and execute them willingly ; wherein
they differ from Horses, Mules, and other Beastes whom Nature
hath also framed apt to learne, and to be ruled, tamed, and guided
35 by man, for they in the absence of their Maisters record the
things commaunded, which these no longer knowe then they are
learned, or scarce performe euen when they are commaunded.
So that a seruaunt may be called *Animal rationale,* a *Reasonable
Creature,* by participation, euen as the *Moone* and the *Starres*
40 receiue light by participation with the sunne, or as mens appetites

by participation with the light of vnderstanding become reasonable : for as our appetites receyue within themselues the forme of that vertue which reason hath imprinted in them, so doth the seruaunt reserue the forme of those impressions whatsoeuer commaunded or required in him by his Maister, and of them and 5 of theyr Maister sometimes may be sayde as *Petrarch*, speaking of himselfe and *Laura*, reasoneth :

> *Si che son fatto uom ligio*
> *Di lei, ch' alto vestigio*
> *M' impresse al core e fece 'l suo simile.* 10

So that I see I am become hir liege man and hir thrall,
That made impressions in my hart, and printed hyrs withall.

' " And because the authority of *Hesiodus*, that auncient Poet, shall not beguile thee, who, reckoning vp the properties of house-keeping, placed the Oxe insteede of the seruaunt, I wil thou 15 vnderstand more properlie that the manner wherwith seruaunts are gouerned differeth much from that wherwith we gouerne Beasts. For that enstruction or kinde of teaching Beastes is not discipline, but an vse and custome dissonant and segregat from reason, not vnlike as the right hande holdeth and disposeth any sort of weapon 20 better then the left, albeit there is no more reason in it then in the other. But the mind also of Seruaunts is accompanied with reason, and may become discipline, as is that of Children ; wherfore they speake without sence and coniecture vnreasonablie that rob and reaue their Seruaunts of the vse of reason : con- 25 sidering it is no lesse needeful for them then Children but more peraduenture, they hauing alreadye so much temperaunce and strength as not only serueth to defend the⟨m⟩selues, but to rescue many times and assist their Maisters, in the perill of some ciuill broyle or other troubles that may often betide them. And 30 therefore was it well sayde of that Thoscan Poet :

> *Ch' innanzi a buon signor fa seruo forte.*

Before his maister, whom he likes,
The sturdy seruaunt stoutly strikes.

' " And not without cause were *Mylos* seruaunts commended so 35 by *Cicero* in his Oration *pro Milone*, and all those others of whom we reade some memorable matters in *Valerius Maximus*, with

---

8 *uom*] *huomo Q.* 32 *signor*] *signior Q.*

many more, whose examples, if I should but practise to recount,
I should soone forget my purpose—*that Seruaunts are properly
those that are borne to obey*, who therfore are not capable of any
office within the Cittie because they want vertue, whereof they
5 taste but barely so much as onely makes them apt and ready
to obey. But if thou hast perused Histories, and redd of that
moste perillous conflict amongst the *Romains* which they called
Cyuill warre, because it was begunne and stirred vp by seruaunts,
and likewise in our time of the Armies which the *Soldane* gathered
10 of slaues; and at this day of those feareful Hostes which the
great Turke mustereth, and for the most part maketh of the
like: thou shalt then record and bring to mind our plain distinction that absolutely will resolue thee, and discharge the
greatest doubt thou canst imagine—*manie are seruaunts by*
15 *Fortune that are free by Nature.* And it is not to be meruailed
at that many cruell conflicts and daungerous warres are caused
and continued by such as these. Howbeit it is a great argument
of basenes that seruile *fortune* can engender seruile euils in a
gentle mind. And yet, for instance, I remember an example
20 of the Scythians worth while the noting, who hauing assembled
an Armie of me⟨n⟩ against theyr seruants that had then rebelled,
knowing none other meane or policy to pacifie or put the⟨m⟩
down, they aduisde to carry with them to the field (besides their
weapons) many whips and bastonadoes, which (making them
25 remember the strypes and strokes that in theyr seruitude they
had receiued) put them presently to flight.

'"But returning to those Seruaunts whereof a house or familie
in deede should be composed or furnished, I cannot commend
those that are neither fitte for warre in mind nor body, but such
30 as are of strong complexion, fit for labor, countrey busines, and
household exercise. These would I deuide into two formes, the
one vnder the other, as the one of superintendents, surueighors,
or work-maisters, the other of workmen. The first shall be the
stewarde to whom by the Maister of the house should the hous-
35 holde care bee commended. The next, to whom the busines of
the stable and of horses should be gyuen, as in great houses it
hath beene accustomed. The thyrd, the Baylieffe, to whom the
Toun affaires belong and are committed. The others shall bee
such inferiours as shall be controld, and at commaundment of
40 those higher officers.

' " But for asmuch as our fortune hath not gyuen vs that wealth
whereby we should expect to haue our houses so distinguished
and multiplyed with offycers, it shal suffise thee to prouide one
for all, that may be Stewarde, Horsekeeper, and Bailieffe, and him
commaunde the rest, that are thy Hyndes and meaner seruaunts, 5
to obey : gyuing euery one hys sallary or day wages, more or lesse
as in theyr labours they deserue : ordeyring victuall for them, for
as they may rather haue too much then want.   Howbeit yet thou
art to feede thy Seruaunts with some other meate then such as
shall be set vpon thyne owne boorde, where dysdayne not nowe 10
and than to see such grosse or homely kind of fare as according
to the season shall be happilye purueighed or prouided for thy
seruaunts, to the ende that they, seeing thyselfe somtimes
vouchsafe to taste therof, may the more willinglie be satisfied
therw⟨ith⟩ ; amongst which, those relicts and fragme⟨n⟩ts of 15
that finer fare that shall be taken from thy Table may be
serued, still hauing some respect to the estate and desert of
euery one.   But because a family well fedde and truely paid
may with idlenes and ease become pestilent, breeding euill
thoughts, and bringing forth worse works — not vnlike those 20
Pooles and standing waters, which (hauing no recourse) putrifie
the good and engender naughtie Fish — thy cheefe care and the
duetie of thy Steward shall be thys, to keepe eurie one per-
ticulerlie exercised in his perticuler office, and generallie all,
in such busines as thou canst not seuerallie set them to.   For 25
euerie thing that belongs to the keeping of a house cannot
necessarily bee doone by him that hath another charge : the
Stewarde he must purueigh the meates ; the Chamberlaine make
the bedds and brush ; the Horsekeeper rubbe the horses and
clense the stable ; and consequently euery other otherwise be 30
occupied.   The carefull Steward or surueighor of the house
should therefore (wyth dyscretion) dispose the works that are
or cannot be deuided or distributed, nowe to one, nowe to
another ; but, aboue the rest, to haue a speciall care that in
the house, Cortes, Tables, or Coffers, be no vncleanes, filth, 35
or Rubbishe, but that the very walles and pauements, lofts and
sellers, Harnes and implements of housuld, maie bee pollished
and kept so cleane, that (as we terme it) it may shine like Siluer,
or looke as bright as Christall.   For cleanlines is not onelie
pleasing or delightfull to beholde, but adioyneth worth, and 40

bettereth things by Nature base and filthie, as continuallie
beastlines and filth corrupt, disgrace, and spoile thinges otherwise of value and account: besides, Cleanlines increaseth and
preserueth the health, as much as sluttishness annoyeth and
impayreth it. Nay, what more is, euery seruant should per- 5
ticulerlie haue such care of scowring and keeping cleane those
tooles and instruments he works withall, and that belong vnto
his office, as the Souldiour hath to see his weapons to be bright;
for such are, is, or should be euery toole to him that hath the
exercise thereof, as are the weapons which the Souldiour vseth: 10
whereupon *Petrarch*, speaking of the Ploughman, writeth thus:

> *L'auaro Zappator l' armi riprende.*
> The Ploughman takes his weapons once againe.

' "After the imitation of *Virgil*, who, before he had called those
instruments weapons, which the Countreymen did vse, wrote thus: 15

> *Dicendum et quae sint duris agrestibus arma*
> And tel the weapo(n)s wherwithal the sturdy clownes ca(n) work.

' "And where also he termes the Bakers instruments weapons:

<table>
<tr><td>Aeneid,
Lib. 2.</td><td>

> *Tum Cererem corruptam vndis, cerealiaque arma*
> *Expediunt fessi rerum.*
>
> Then run the weary forth to fetch the watrie, rotten Corne,
> And baking weapons, &c.

</td><td>20</td></tr>
</table>

' "But because it sometime happeneth that one is too much
charged with labor, and another hath more day then work, one
should so helpe another as wee see by vse in our owne bodies; 25
when the one leg is weary we can rest it on the other, or when
the right hand is ouer labored, we can ease it wyth the left; and
when entercourse of loue and courtesie entreats not thus amongst
them, then shoulde the Maister himselfe commaund the negligent
and vnprofitable Seruant to help and ease the weary and the well 30
imployed.

' "But aboue all, me thinks, the *Charitie* of Maisters and loue
of Seruants to their fellowes in their sicknes is especiallie to be
vsd and shewn, at which time the sicke are to be seuerally
lodged from the whole, and nourished with more choise and 35
daintie meate: nor shoulde the Maister of the house dysdaine, or
shew himselfe so scornful or vnkind as not to visite them; for if

---

12 *Zappator*] *Zappatore Q.*   *riprende*] *reprende Q.*

bruite beasts reioyce to see their Maisters cheerish them, as we
may dailie see in dogs, how much more may we beleeue that men
and reasonable creatures are comforted therwith? Wherupon it
comes to passe that good seruants, liking and affecting of. their
Maisters, vnderstand the⟨m⟩ at a beck, and obey them at a winck 5
of the eye, or bent of the brow, not as a water-spaniel, but as the
hand is sturred to obey the mind, so prompt and ready is the seruant
to obey his Maister. For as the hand is said to be *The instrument of instruments*, being it (indeede) that serues to feede,
apparrell, and keepe cleane the rest of the limns, which are also 10
called instruments, so is the Seruant said to bee an instrument of
instruments, because he keepeth all the instruments of houshold
occupied not only to liue, but to liue wel, wherin he differeth from
all the other instruments. For where they are *Inanima*, things
without soule, he is *Animatus*, and diuinelie is enriched with 15
a soule; and heerein differeth from the hand for that the hand is
fastned and vnited to the bodie, but he seperate and disioyned
from his Maister, and is also different fro⟨m⟩ Artificers, for
*Artificers are Instruments of those things which properly they call
workmanship*; but the Seruaunt is *Instrument of the action*, which 20
also is distinguished from workmanship. So that the seruaunt,
if you will rightly vnderstand him, is *Animatum actionis et Instru-
mentum seperabile, A liuely and seueral instrument of action*. But
forasmuch as of actions, some are placed in care of families
and housholde busines, some stretch further and extend to ciuil 25
administration, there are some Gentlemen (amongst who⟨m⟩
I wish thee to be numbred) that vse to keepe a youth who
in theyr ciuill gouernment doth seme to write and mannedge
some of their affaires, and him they call theyr Clerke; but these
doo farre differ from the other, considering that for the most part 30
they are or ought to be not of seruile or materiall witt, but
capable of fashions, or apt to studie or contemplat; and betwixt
them and their Maisters can be properly no seruitude or signiory,
but rather that kind of friendship which by *Aristotle* is applied in
the highest. Albeit in those good worldes of the Romaine Com- 35
mon wealth these were taken fro⟨m⟩ that number of other seruants, and such an one was *Terence*, the wryter of Comedie, who
was so familiar with *Lelius* and *Scipio* as it is thought there is
somewhat of theyr dooings in his works. The like was *Tyro* (of
whom are many Letters extant that were written by *Tullie*), who 40

beeing an excellent *Grammarian*, was also a most diligent
obseruer of some little things whereof *Cicero* was rather a dys-
prayser then ignoraunt.   But because that vse of seruice as wee
talkt of is (at this day) vtterly extinguished betwixt Maisters and
5 Seruants of such singularity, those lawes of friendship ought to be
obserued and maintained in more high degree.   And heereupon
was that Treatise of vnder officers (especially) writte⟨n⟩ by *Signior
Giouanni della Casa*, which (for that thou art desirous to peruse
his workes) I knowe must many times be redd and redd again by
10 thee; I will therefore perticularize none, but refer thee to the
booke.

'"And nowe because we haue sufficiently spoken (though not
so much as you desire) touching the regard of the person, for that
our speeche hath reference as well to Maydens as men Seruaunts,
15 and because there hath beene nothing left out that belongeth to
a Husband, a Maister, or a Housekeeper, I thinke it requisite
to come to that which we deuised and deuided for the second
part of our discourse, that is of *Wealth* or *substance*, wherein we
wil effectually make mention of the duetie of a Huswife and of
20 womens busines.   The care of *wealth* or *substance*, as we said
before, is imployed to *Conseruation* and *Encrease*, and is deuided
betwixt the Master and Mistresse, because the encrease is as proper to the Maister as the keeping to the Mistresse; howbeit to
him that perticulerly considereth the care of the encrease it is
25 proper to the Maister, and the other common, whatsoeuer others
heertofore haue spoke⟨n⟩ to this purpose.   But forasmuch as
nothing can be encreased that is not first and wholy kept togeather, the Housekeeper that is desirous to preserue his wealth
should perticulerly know the quallitie and quantity of his reuenues
30 and expences, wherewith he is to keepe his house, and to maintaine his family with credit, and (measuring the manner of his
reuenewes with the issue of his charges) so to liue as his expence
may prooue the least; making that proportion with his comings
in as *foure* to *eight*, or *sixe* at least, for he that spends as much as
35 he receiues of his possessions cannot recouer those losses which
by chaunce or Fortune may betide him (as by fires, tempests,
inundations, and other such) nor supply the necessity of some
expence which (beeing accidentall) cannot be prouided for.
Furthermore (to be certified of his substance and the value of
40 his riches) it behooues that he himself haue seene and measured

his possessions, euen with those compasses which gaue begining
to *Geometry* in *Egypt* : which, though they be diuers according
to the variety of Countreys, is (notwithstanding) no occasion of
substantiall difference. It also behooueth that he knowe that
what he reapes be aunswerable vnto that he sowed, and with 5
what proportion the earth restoreth that which it receiueth : and
as requisit it is that hee take the like notice of all whatsoeuer
els belongeth to husbandry or grazing ; and no lesse to harken
after the prices that are sette by publique Magistrates or by
consent of Marketfolks within the Countrey where he dwelleth, 10
then to be enformed how they buy or sell in *Turyno*, *Myllan*,
Lyons, or *Venice*, wherof beeing well aduertised and instructed
he cannot be deceiued by his Bailieffe, beeing a Husbandman,
or abused by his Factor, beeing a Merchaunt. But forasmuch
as I haue said that he ought to be aduised, both of the quantity 15
and quallitie of that which he possesseth, I call not onely that
Quantitie which is measured by *Geometrie* (as are Fields, Mead-
owes, Woods), or that which is accustomd to be numbred by
Algorisme (as Flocks and Heards), but that which is accounted,
(as gold or siluer coyned), for in the quadering and making euen 20
of the enteries with the expences no quantity is more to be considered then that of money which may bee gathered and receiued
of Rent and such like reuenewes, which is often changing and
incertaine ; for Landes are not alwaies let at one rate, their price
and profits rise and fall as other meane things, or things of more 25
account. In which incertainty and variable state of thinges a good
Husbands iudgment, experience, and dilligence so much preuailes
as not only is sufficient to preserue, but to encrease his substance,
which beeing in the manurance and handling of an ignorant, or
ouerweener, dooth not only decrease but perisheth.   30

' " That call I *Quallity* of substance, then, that is artificiall or
naturall, of liuing things, or things without life : *Arteficiall* are
moueables or houshold implements, and hapely the house it selfe,
and money which was first found out by mans appointment.
Because we may liue without it, as they dyd in the old time 35
wherin exchaunge of things was made with out returne of money :
afterward (by the lawe of man) was money inuented, whereupon
it was called *Numus* of Νωμωσ, which (by the Greeke interpretation)
signifieth *Law*, which, commodiously fitting and making equall
things exchanged, hath made the entercourse of buying and 40

selling very easie, and more certaine then when they onely vsed exchaunge.

'"*Arteficiall* riches may all those things be called wherein the Workmanship of the Maister is rather solde and more esteemed then the matter or the thing made : *Naturall* are those that are produced by Nature, wherof also some are without life, as Lands, Medowes, Mettals, and some with life, as Flocks and Heards, whereof the good Housekeeper (oftentime) receiueth profit. Further it commeth into the consideration of *Quallitie* to know whether the Landes or possessions lye neere or far fro⟨m⟩ any Cittie ; if they ioyne to any standing Lake or Poole, by the exhalation of whose euill vapours the ayre becommeth filthy and infected ; or whether any Springs or Ryuers be adiacent, which by ofte recorse and refluence may gather vertue to refine and purge the ayre ; and whether they be guirt or enuironed with hylles, or lye open to the winds ; whether vppon the bancks to any nauigable water, or in a champant Countrey, whereby the commodities raised thereupon may be transported easily in Carres or other carriages vnto the Cittie ; or whether it lie steepeward downe the hyls, vneasie and painful to be past, so that he must needs be chargde w⟨ith⟩ sompter men ; whether it be neere to any high way or common street through which the Trauailers, *Italian* Merchants, or those of *Germany* or *Fraunce* are vsed to passe ; or far from frequence or resort of Passengers, or such as vse to bartre or exchange ; if aloft, where it lyes in prospect, or below in some valley, where it may be ouerflowne : all which conditions, as they much increase and deminish the price and value of the things possesst, so may they be occasion of sparing in expences and teach thee to conserue and multiply thy Reue-newes, if (like a good husband) thou aduise thee and consider it.

'"But to come somewhat more perticulerly to the care and regard that is (indeede) required, he should so prouide that whatsoeuer is necessarye for the vse of his house in the Cittie be brought from his Ferme or Mannor in the Countrey ; and to leaue his house there furnished of so much as may suffise him and his family when he shall bee disposed to soiourne there, and to sell the rest at such conuenient time as things are deerest ; and with the mony that ariseth thereof to buy those things which his owne possessions yeeld not and yet are necessary for a Gentle-man, now and then when they are better cheape. All which he

may easily doo, if, in sparing that expence he vsed at first, he
reserue some mony ouerplus. Againe he may keepe his mony
by him many times when, by his own coniecture, opinion of
Prognostications, or speech of other mens experience, he heares
5 or feareth any dearth or scarcity; and then to lay it out when
hee perceiues the great aboundaunce of the yere and fruitfulnes
of seasons, remembring that example of *Thales*, who (throgh his
knowledge of naturall things) suddainly became rich with a bar-
gaine that he made for Oyle.   This shall bee the Husbands care.
10 But such things whatsoeuer as are brought into the house, eyther
from the Countrey, or bought about in Markets, shall be wholy
recommended to the wyues charge, who is to keep and set the⟨m⟩
vp in seuerall places according to their natures; for some would
be kept moyst and cold, and some dry; othersome would be one
15 while set in the Sunne, another while in the winde; some wilbe
long kept, othersome a little while: all which a good huswife well
considering, shold cause those that wyll not keepe to be first
eaten, and make store of the rest.   Howbeit, those also that
will not keepe without corruption may be holpen many waies,
20 and made to keep long.   For Salt and Vineger doo not onely
keep flesh long time sweete and seazoned, but fish and fowle,
which will bee suddainly corrupt.   Besides, many sorts of fruits
that will quickly putrefie and perish, if they be sharpe or tarte
(otherwise not) will be long maintaind in Vineger.   Likewise
25 the hanging vp in smoke or baking of some kinds of flesh or fish
and diuers sorts of fruits drawes away theyr moysture (that is
cause of theyr corruption) and maketh that they may bee kept
the longer.

'"Again, there are some things, which (beeing dryed) wold become
30 both hard and naught to eate without some kinde of liquor or
conserues; whereof a good Huswife makying store for her prouision, if it happen that by some mischance or hynderaunce whatsoeuer there can not come sufficient store of meate from the market
for her husbands Table, or that they suddainly are driuen to
35 entertaine a straunger, she may (in a minut) furnish her messe with
those iunckets, and that in such good sort as there shalbe no
misse of any other meats.   She must also haue regard that all her
houshold corne be some ground for bread, and othersome made
fit for drink, and so distribute it indifferentlie with equall measure
40 both to the men and mayd seruants vsed for those purposes, amongst

Thales, one
of the seuen
wise men of
Greece.

whom she shall haue one aboue the rest (as the Maister hath his
Stewarde or *Cashur*) that shall keepe one keye, and she another, and
that, though the Maister or Mistres be abroade, there may be one
to deliuer out such thinges as shall be needful, and to bid a stranger
5 drinke; which custome is not gueason in some houses, where the
Steward or Butler beares the keyes as well of houshold necessaries
as all things els, pleasing the Maister and not vnpleasant to the
appetites of those he entertaineth. Therefore a good Huswife
should so prouide that all things whatsoeuer (if occasion of resort
10 of straungers be not to the contrary) may be sparingly disposed,
for thrift or liberalitie is as needful in a woman as a ma⟨n⟩. Besides
she shold busie herselfe in viewing and surueighing such things
as she charged to be kept, measuring things to be measured, and
keeping iust account of things that are to be accounted : neyther
15 ought her care only extend to the spending of them, or vnto other
things rehearsed, but also to the wynes w⟨hich⟩ the older they
are and the longer they are kept become so much the better.
I speake of choyse wynes which get strength with age ; for the
small wynes, and those of little spirite that quickly lose their
20 strength, should be first dronk or sold if thou haue any quantitie.
But her principall care should be of Lynnen or of wollen weauing,
wherewith she may not onely make prouision necessary and fitt for
the ability and credite of her house, but honestly gaine, which is as
requisite in her as is her Husbands profit gathered by the buying,
25 selling, or exchanging other things. Neither ought a good Huswife
to dysdaine or scorne to set her hand nowe and then to some work—
I mean not in the Kitchin, or other soyled places which may spoile
or ray her garments, because such busines are not to be manedged
and handled by noble Matrons (yet to be seene vnto by such
30 whose state may tollerate such thrift), but in those onely that
without noysomnes or filthines she may be bolde to touch ; and
such are properly the wheeles, lombes, and other instruments that
appertaine to weauing, wherewith a good Huswife may furnish any
sufficie⟨n⟩t house or dwelling, either for her eldest sonne or
35 daughter. And not without reason was this arte first attributed
to *Minerua*, goddesse of wysedome, in so much as it was deriued
first from her, as appeareth by these verses in the Booke of
Virgill:

Inde, vbi prima quies medio iam noctis abactae.
40   *Curriculo expulerat somnum, cum foemina primum,*

Cui tolerare colo vitam tenuique Minerua
Impositum, cinerem et sopitos suscitat ignes,
Noctem addens operi, famulasque ad lumina longo
Exercet penso, castum ut seruare cubile
5   *Coniugis, et possit paruos educere natos.*

The first sleepe ended, after midnight did the woman wake
That liud by spinning, and she gins the ymbers vp to rake,
And adding so vnto her labors some part of the night,
Hard at their distaffe doth she hold her maids by candlelight,
10   To keep her chast, and that her children wel maintaine she mighte.

' " In which verses it appeareth that he spake not of base women,
but of a Mistres of a house which had beene accustomed to be
attended on by many seruants : and so much worth it seemeth
that this arte hath in it, as it hath not only been ascribd or
15 attributed to priuat huswifes, but to princely Ladies, as appeareth
by these verses of *Penelope*, the wyffe of *Vlisses* :

Come la nobil Greca ch' alle tele sue
Scemò la notte, quanto il giorno accrebbe.

As did that noble Grecian dame that bated in the night
20   As much as she had wouen by day, to bleare her sutors sight.

' " And *Virgil* of *Circes*, which was not onely a woman and a
Queene but a Goddesse, wrote thus :

Arguto coniux percurrit pectine telas,
Vpon a wel deuided loome thy wife doth weaue apace.

25   ' " In which example he followed *Homer*, who not onely brought *Homer in*
Penelope and *Circes* in the number of women weauers, but placed *his Odiss.*
the daughter of *Alcinoe*, the King of *Phæaces*, amongst them :
and albeit the *Greekes* obserued not so much *decorum* as was
necessarie, the *Romaines* yet, that were both greater and more
30 curious obseruers of such things, forbad the Mistres of the house
all other works, the Kitchin Cookery and such like, but graunted
they might weaue, and that not without great commendation :
and in this kinde of work was *Lucretia* often found, by *Collatyn*,
by *Brutus*, and *Tarquinius*, when they were enamored of her.

35   ' " But to returne to the Mistres of the house or huswife, who
beeing a fortunat mother of Children, the further off she is from
nobles⟨se⟩ or estate, so much the lesse she may dysdaine to busie
herselfe in such things as carie meaner worth in showe and lesse
workmanship then weauing.   And heerin seemeth it that in some
40 sort she shall aduaunce herselfe, and come into comparison with

---

17 *alle*] *a le* Q.   18 *Scemò*] *Scemio* Q.   37 noblesse *ed.* : nobles *Q*.

her good man, for she not onely gathereth but encreaseth, with
the profitt of those labours.   Neuerthelesse, considering that those
benefits are small, and but of slender reckoning, we shall do well
to say that it belongeth to the wife to keepe, and to the husband
to encrease.   But forasmuch as things preserued may the better 5
be disposed, if they be carefully prouided for and ordered, the
good Huswife ought aboue all things to be diligent heerein.   For
if she reserue not things composedly but seperat and placd in
sonder, according to their quallitie and the opportunitie of vsing
them, she shall alwaies haue them ready and at hand, and euer- 10
more know what she hath and what shee wants : and if there can
be no similitude inferd to this purpose worthie of consideration,
Ars memo- most notable is that of *Memory*, which laying vp, preseruing, and ·
ratina. imprinting in it selfe al the Images and formes of *visible* and
intelligible things, could not vtter them in time conuenient, and 15
dispose them to the tongue and penne, vnlesse it had so ordered
and oftentimes recounted them, as without that the *memory* it selfe
coulde scarce containe them ; of so great efficacye and force is
order, but it hath also no lesse grace and comlines in beautifying
and adorning things, as hee that dooth acquaint his studie with 20
the vse of Poetry verie easilie perceiueth.   For *Poesy* hath neuer
more spirit added to it, with the greatest arte and industrie, then
when it is set forth with wel disposed *Epythetons* and significa⟨n⟩t
As by re- termes, that the one ordered with the other may altogeather con-
petition or sent, or musically aunswer crosse, as hath arteficially beene vsed 25
maintain-
ing of a by orators, which though it be pleasant to the eare, is painfull to
point, as the memorie.   And be it so, as some Philosophers haue saide,
Musitions
terme it. that the forme or fashion of the *World* is none other then an
order, co⟨m⟩paring little things with great we may well report
that the forme of a house is the order, and the reformation of 30
the house or familie none other then a second setting it in order,
wherein I purpose to speake somewhat : which, albeit of it selfe it
beare no great semblance of credit, yet for the order and clenlines
it deserues so much, as hauing seene it without disdayne and
diuerslie admiring it, may without impeach (I hope) bee profit- 35
ablye recounted.

' " Returning from *Paris* and comming by *Beona*, I entred the
Hospitall, wherein, though euery Roome I sawe, me thought, was

---

38 me *ed.*: my *Q.*

worthy commendations, yet was the Kytchen to be wondred at,
which, as it was not vsd continually, so did I find it passing neat
and queintly tricked vp, as if it were the chamber of a new maryed
Bride : therin saw I such a quantitie of necessary implements, not
onely for the vse of the Kitchin but seruice of the Table, so dis- 5
creetly ordered and with such proportion, the Pewter so set vppe,
the Brasse and yron works so bright as (when the Sun shyned on
the wyndowes there vpon) cast such a delicat reflection as it might
(me thought) be well resembled to the Armorie of *Venice*, and of
other places meeter to be spoken of then shewed to straungers : 10
and if *Gnato*, that disposd the household of his glorious *Sig.
Capitano* in manner of an Armie, had but had a sight of this,
I am well assured he would haue compared it to some higher
matter then an Armorie.

'"But returning now from keeping to encreasing, it may be 15
doubted whether this arte of encreasing be housekeeping wholy,
or but a member, part, or Minister thereof. If a Minister, because it ministreth the Instruments, as the Armourer doth the
curasse and the Helmet to the Souldiour : and that ministreth
the subiect or the matter, as the Shipwright that receiues the 20
Tymber of him that fells and seazoneth the wood. It is very
manifest that the art of housekeeping and getting is not all one :
for the one it behooueth to prouide, the other to put in vze the
things prouided : now it rests to be considered, whether to get
be a forme or part of housekeeping, or vtterly disioyned and 25
estraunged from it. The facultie of getting may be *Natural*
and not *Naturall*: *Natural* I call that which getteth the liuing
out of those things that hath beene brought forth by Nature
for mans vse and seruice : and forasmuch as nothing is more
naturall then nourishment, which the Mother giueth to her 30
Childe, most naturall aboue the rest must that gayne needes
be that is had and raised of the fruits of the earth, considering
that the Earth is the naturall and vniuersall Mother of vs all.
Naturall also are the nourishments and foode that we receiue
of Beastes, and of the gayne that may be made of them, which 35
is distinguished according to the distinction of Beastes. For of
Beastes some are tame and compynable, othersome solitary and
vntamed: of those are flocks, Heards, and droues compact, of which
no lesse profit may bee raised : these they make their gaine to hunt,
and manie of them serue for sustentation and succour of the life. 40

' " It also seemes that Nature hath engendred not onely bruite
Beasts for the seruice of Man, but hath framed men, that are
apt to obey, to serue those whom also she hath framed to commaund. So that whatsoeuer is gotten or obtained in the warres
5 beeing iust, the same may also bee tearmed naturall gayne : and
heerein will I not conceale what *Theucidides* hath obserued in the
proem of his Historie, that in the olde time prayeng or robberye
was not to be blamed. Wherupon we reade that one asked
another whether he were a Pyrat or a Rouer, as though it were
10 no iniurie to aske him such a question. To which vse or reason
Virgill hauing regard brought in *Numa* boasting thus :

> *Caniciem galea premimus, semperque recentes*
> *Connectare iuuat praedas et viuere rapto.*

We hide our gray haires with our helmets, liking euermore
15   To liue vpo⟨n⟩ the spoile, and waft our praies fro⟨m⟩ shore to shore.

'"And that may well be called *Naturall* gayne which the Knights
of *Malta* haue against the *Barbarians* and *Turkes*.   Euery of
which naturall gaines it seemeth necessarye that Housekeepers
haue knowledge of, but especiall of Husbandrie : and he that
20 mingleth and exchaungeth the profit of all those things togeather
which he gathereth, shoulde happilie therein do nothing vnworthye
or against the title of good Husbandry.   For that trade or science
is at this day commonlie called Merchandize, which is of many
sorts and to be taken many waies ; but that is the most iust
25 which taketh thence where things superfluously abounde, and
transporteth them thither where is want and scarcity of those
comodities, and in their stedd returneth other things whereof
there is some dearth, because it growes not other-where so
plentiously : and heereof speaketh *Tully* in his Booke of *Offices*,
30 that Merchandize, if they were small, were base and but of vile
account ; if great, not much to be dislyked : but hys wordes in
that place are to be taken as the saying of a Stoyck that too
seuerely speaketh of those matters.   For in other places where
hee argueth like a Cittizen, hee commendeth and defendeth
35 merchaunts and the manner of theyr trade, and calleth that
order of the *Publicans* most honest, who had the whole
reuenewes of the Common wealth in their possessions, besides
those things whereof they exercized trafique, and the trade of
merchandize.   But as that forme of merchandize is iust and
40 honest which traffique their commodities to Countreys where

they want, and thereof maketh their best, so most iniust is
that, which hauing bargained for the commodities of a Countrey,
retaileth them or selleth them againe in the same place, watching
the opportunitie and time whe⟨n⟩ they may vtter them vnto
theyr most aduantage. Howbeit the care of opportunity to sell 5
what is a mans owne, and what he gathereth of his owne Reuenewes, and possessions, and of his flocks, heards, and such like,
seeme not either inconuenient or dishonest in a Husbandman.

   ' "And so much touching naturall gayne necessary for a hous-
keeper, wherin he shall much aduauntage him and hys, if hee be 10
but indifferently instructed not onely of the nature, goodnes,
and value of all things that are vsed to be exchaunged, and are
from place to place transported, but also in what Prouince,
Shyre or Countrey grow the better, and in which the worse, and
where in most aboundaunce, where in lesse, where they are helde 15
deerest, and where best cheape. So should he also be enformed
of the fashions, sleights, and difficulties of transporting them, and
of the times and seazons wher in they be carryed or recarried
most conueniently, and of the league and traffique that one Cittie
hath with another, one Prouince or Countrey with another, and of 20
the times wherein such merchandize are solde, which for the most
part are called Fayres or Marts.

   ' "Notwithstanding the Housekeeper ought to handle these
things like a Husbandman, and not like a Merchaunt ; for where
the Merchant preposeth for his principall intent the encrease 25
and multiplying of his stock, which is doone by traffique and
exchaunge (by meanes wherof he many times forgets his house,
his Children, and his Wife, and trauails into forren Countreys,
leauing the care of them to Factors, Friends, and Seruaunts), the
care of the Husbandman or Housekeeper doth reape his profite 30
of exchaunge by a second obiect directed vnto household gouernment, and so much time and labour onely hee bestoweth as his
chiefe and principall care may not thereby be anoyd or hyndered.
Moreouer, euen as euery arte dooth infinitly seeke the end it pur-
poseth, as the honest Phisitian will heale as much as hee can, the 35
Architect erect and builde with as much exelency and perfection
as he can, so the Merchant seemes to make his benefit of things
vnto their vttermost. But the Housekeeper hath his desires of
riches certaine and determinat, for riches are none other then
a multitude of Instruments that appertaine vnto familiar or 40

publique cares ; but the instruments of some arts are not infinit
either in number or in greatnes, for, if they were infinit in
number, the Artificer could not know them, for as much as this
word infinit, as touching the infinitiue, is not comprehended in
5 our vnderstanding, vnlesse it be in things that cannot well be
handled, managed, or lifted for their greatnes.

' " And as in euery arte the instruments should be proportioned
and fit as well for him that worketh, as the thing that shall be
wrought withall (for in a shyppe the Rudder ought to be no lesse
10 then may suffise to direct hys course, nor greater then the
Mariner can guide, and in grauing or cutting the Chizzel should
not be so ponderous and heauie as the Mason may not lift, nor
so light as hee cannot with much a doe pierce the out side of the
Marble), euen so should riches be proportioned and limitted vnto
15 the Housekeeper and the family that he is charged withall, that
he may inherite and possesse so much and no more then shall
suffise not onely for hys liuing but hys liuing well, according to
his estate, condition of time, and customes of the Citty wher he
liueth and inhabiteth.   And where *Crassus* sayd he was not rych
20 that was not able to maintaine an Armie, he happely had reference vnto those ryches which are needfull for a Prince or Ruler
within the Cittie of *Rome*, which were too too much and immoderate
for any one in *Praeneste* or in *Nola*, little Tounes in *Italie*, and
happely superfluous for many men in *Rome*.   For to muster and
25 maintaine Armies becommeth Kings, Tyrants, and other absolute
Princes, and is not necessary or fitting for a Cittizen inhabiting
a place of liberty, who indeede ought not to exceede the rest in
any such condition as may interrupt or spoyle that good proportion that is requisit and meet in the vniting of free men.   For as
30 the nose vppon some mans face, growing by disorder or disdyet
more then Nature made it, may become so grosse and large in
time as it may be no more resembled or reputed for a Nose, so
a Cittizen of any Cittie whatsoeuer, exceeding others in his riches,
either miserably gotten or encreased by wrong, is no more a
35 Cittizen, be hee what or who hee will, for riches are to be considered alwaies in respect of him that doth possesse them.   Nor
can wee well prescribe howe much they ought to be, but this we
may soly and safelie say that they ought to be apportioned to
him that hath them, who ought so much and no more to encrease
40 them then may be afterwards deuided and bequeathed amongst

his Children, to liue well and ciuilly with all. Neither resteth
anie more for me to say conserning this naturall gaine conuenient
for a Housekeeper, which may as properly bee taken and deriued from the Earth, Heards, and Flocks, as by the trade of
merchandize, warre, or hunting : wherfore we may call to mind 5
that there were many *Romains* called from the Plough and Carte
to be Magistrates, and mightie men in Princes Courts, and afterwards, disrobed of their Purple, returned to the Plough.   But
because the Husbandman and carefull housekeeper should haue
regarde vnto his health, not as a Phisition but as a father of a 10
familie, he ought most willingly to apply himselfe vnto that kind
of gayne which most preserueth health.   Wherein he shall also
exercise himselfe, and see his familie and seruaunts busied in those
exercises of the bodie which, not defiling or defacing him, are
great helps to health ; wherunto Idlenes and superfluous ease are 15
enemies profest.   Let him therfore loue to hunt, and to make
more reckoning of those gaines which are gotte and followed with
paine and sweat then those that through deceit, and vnconsorted
with some labor, haue beene and yet are vsed to be gotten.

' " But sithence we haue reasoned of that manner of gayne that is 20
naturall, it shall not bee vnnecessary that wee somewhat manifest
the other which is vnnaturall, although it be impertinent to Husbandry and housekeeping.   This wee deuide into two formes or
kindes.   The one is called *Exchaunge*, the other *Vsurie*, and it is
not naturall, because it doth peruert the proper vse, forasmuch 25
as money was founde out and vsed (a while) to make equall the
inequality of things exchangd, and to estimat and measure prices,
not for that it ought to be exchangd ; for of mony (as touching
the mettall) we haue no neede, neither receiue we any benefit
thereof in our priuat or our ciuil life, but in respect of making 30
eue⟨n⟩ inequalities, and iustly measuring the worth and value of
each thing, it is thought both necessary and commodious.   When
mony, then, is changed with mony, not directed and imployed to
some other vse, it is vsed beyond the proper vse, and so abused.   In
which exchange Nature is not imitated, for as well may exchaunge 35
that doth multiply or accumulat infinite and excessiue profits be
said to haue no end or absolute determination as Vsurie ; but
Nature alwaies worketh to a certaine set and determinat ende, and
to a certaine ende doo all those meanes and members work that
are ordaind to be stirrers vp of Nature.   40

' " I haue told you then that Exchange may multiply in profits
infinitly, because *Number* as touching *Number*, not aplied to
materiall things, groweth to be infinit, and in exchange is not
considered to be otherwise applied. But for thy better vnder-
5 standing what we say, know that *Number* is reputed either
according to the formall or materiall beeing. *Formall number* is
a collection of a summe, not applied to things numbred; *Materiall
number* is a summarie collection of things numbred. *Formall
number* may infinitly encrease, but the *Materiall* cannot multiply
10 so much ; for albeit in respect of the partition or deuision it
seeme that it may multiply in effect, notwithstanding, since
deuision hath no place in that we speake of, we may saie it
cannot infinitlie encrease, because things of all kinds that cannot
be deuided are of number certaine. This deuision being thus
15 considered, much more may riches multiply that consist in bare
money then that which consisteth in thinges measured and
numbred from money : for albeit the number of mony bee not
formall, as that which is applyed to Gold and Siluer, more easily
may a great quantity of mony be heaped vp and gathered togeather
20 then anie other thing, and so by couetous desire to become
infinit. Yet betwixt *Exchange* and *Vsury* there is some difference.
Exchange may be retained, not only for the custome it hath
taken and obtained in many famous Citties, but for the force of
reason that it seemes to beare. For exchange is vsed in steede
25 of our transporting and conueighing Coyne from place to place,
which beeing hardlie to be doone without great discomoditie and
perill, it is reason that the party that exchaungeth may haue
some sufficient gaine allowed. Besides the value of mony of
some Country coyne beeing variable and often to be changd, as
30 wel by the Lawes and institutions as for the sundry worth, weight,
and fineness of the Golde and Syluer, the Reall exchange of
mony might bee in some sort reduced vnto naturall industrie :
wherewith Vsury can neuer be acquainted, beeing an arteficiall
gayne, a corrupter of a Common wealth, a disobeyer of the Lawes
35 of God, a Rebell and resister of all humaine orders, iniurious to
manie, the spoile of those that most vphold it, onely profitable
to it selfe, more infectious than the pestilence, and consorted
with so many perilous euils as are hard or neuer to be cured.

---

25 Coyne *emend. ed.*: Corne *Q.* : *cf.* del danaro *Tasso.*

Euery or either of which hauuing not onely beene condemned by *Leuit-*
Aristotle, but vtterly inhibited by the olde and new Law, who so ⟨*icus*⟩:
considereth not, let him read what verdict *Dante* hath giuen of *Pecuniam*
it in these verses, who to proue Vsury a sinne cyteth a sentence *tuam non*
5 put by *Aristotle* in his booke *de Phisicis*. *dabis fratri*
tuo ad vsu-

       E se tu ben la tua fisica note, *ram et*
       Tu trouerai non dopo molte carte *frugum su-*
       Che l' arte vostra quella, quanto puote, *perabun-*
       Segue, come 'l maestro fa il discente ; *dantia⟨m⟩*
10   *Si che vostr' arte a Dio quasi è Nipote.* *non exiges.*
       Da questi due, se tu ti rechi a mente *Dauid. :*
       Lo Genesi, dal principio, conuiene *Qui habita-*
       Prender sua vita & auanzar la gente. *bit, &c. qui*
       E perchè l' vsuriere⟨e⟩ altra via tiene, *pecuniam*
15   *Per sè natura & per la sua seguace* *non dederit*
       Dispregia, poichè in altro pon la spene. *ad vsuram.*
Luk :
Date mu-
If Aristotles phisicks thou peruse, *tuum nec*
Not turning many leaues thou there shalt finde *inde sper-*
That arte doth Nature imitate and vse *antes.*
20 As pupils pleasing of their Tutors minde,
So that our arte is Neipce to God by kind.
Of this and that, if thou remember it,
In Genesis euen God himselfe doth say,
    Quod ab initio oportuit
25 *Humanum genus vitam sumere*
    Et vnum alium excedere
    Per artem et naturam. Now because
The Vsurers doo wander otherwise
Without regard of God or Godly lawes
30 Nature and arte (her follower) they despise,
For in their Gold their hope beguiled lies.

  ' " It is also said by *Aristotle* that God is *animal sempiternum* et
optimum, of whom both heauen and Nature doe depend ; which
nature is imitated of our arte as much as may be, for arte de-
35 pending vpon Nature, shee is as it were her Chylde, and *per*
consequence Gods Neipce. So that offending Nature we immediatly offende God, and he that offendeth arte offendeth God touching the hurt or annoyaunce of Nature ; but the Vsurer offendeth
Nature, for it is not naturall that money should beget or bring
40 forth money without corruption, since Nature willeth that the
corruption of one bee the generation of another ; and it offendeth
God because it doth not exercise the arte according as God

---

  6 *se tu ben*] *setuben* Q.   8 *puote*] *pote* Q.   10 *vostr'*] *vostra* Q.
12 *Lo*] *Le* Q.   14 *vsuriere*] *vsurier* Q. *tiene*] *tene* Q.

commaunded the first man, when he saide, in the sweate of thy
face thou shalt eate thy bread; and it is not artificiall that money
shoulde bring forth money, as the Vsurers wold haue it, which
putteth the vse in the thing.   With those verses, therefore, mee
5 thinkes not onely our discourse of naturall and not naturall gaine
may be concluded and determined, but whatsoeuer els we
purposed at first concerning Husbandry and Keeping of a house,
which you haue now seene howe it turneth and returneth to the
wife, how to the children, how to the seruaunts, and howe to the
10 conuerting and imploying as also the encrease of whatsoeuer sub-
staunce or possession; which were indeede those Fiue especial
points whereof we promised to speake and to entreate perticulerly.

'"But for it is my chiefe desire that thou record effectually
those things whereof I haue aduised thee, and that in so precise
15 a sort as thou heereafter not forget them, I will bestowe them
and bequeath thee them in writing, that by often reading and
perusing them thou maist not onely learne them but throughly
resolue to imitate and practise them, for practise is in the end im-
posed to all instructions of humaine life."

20 'This was my Father's discourse, gathered by him into a little
Booke which I so often red and studiously obserued as you neede
not meruaile that I haue so perfectly reported and repeated them.
Now would I be silent, to the ende that my discourse should not
be made in vaine, for if anie thing be said that in your opinion
25 may be bettered, let it not, I praye, seeme troublesome vnto you
thereof to certefie mee and amend it.'

'Sir' (quoth I), 'for anie thing that I can see, your father hath
not onely well and learnedly instructed you in all hys institutions,
but you (it seemes) haue exercised them as industriously.   This
30 onely could I wish that somewhat more might be annext to that
which he hath vttered, and that perticulerly is this : *Whether
houshold care or housholde gouernment be all one ; if more then one,
then, being more then one, whether then they be the Knowledge and the
labor of one or more ?'*   'You say true' (quoth hee), 'and heerein
35 onely fayled his discourse, for the gouernment of priuate houses
and of Princes Courtes are different, but I can tell you why hee
spake not of it, because the care of Princes Halles belongeth not
to priuate men.'

'Trust me, Sir,' (quoth I) 'you are of swifter vnderstanding and
40 more eloquent deuise then I expected.   But since wee found

that there is difference in houshold gouernments, it rests that
we consider whether they be discrepant in forme or greatnes.
Forasmuch as if they onely differ in the greatnes, then euen as
the consideration of the forme of a Princes Pallace and a poore
5 mans Cottage appertaines to one and the selfesame Mason,
Carpenter, or Architect, so shoulde the care of either hous-
keeping be one.' But therunto he aunswered thus : 'Though
I were swift of conceit at first, yet now (I doubt) I shall not be so
prompt to find, or so iudicial as to censure that which you propose.
10 Howbeit, I can tell you this, that if my hart or happe would giue
me leaue to keepe a great, yet priuate house (I meane not a little
Court), I beleeue that priuate house of mine should farre surpasse
that Pallace for a Prince, which onely differeth from the other in
the pompe and greatnes.'
15 'You are in the right' (quoth I), 'for as a Prince is still to be
distinguished from a priuate man, by forme ; and as the forme of
their commaundements is distinguished, so are the gouernments
of Princes and of priuate men distinguished ; for when it happeneth that, in comparison of number, the houshold of a poore
20 Prince is as little as a rich mans familie, yet are they to be
gouerned diuersly : neuerthelesse, if that be true which is
approued by *Socrates* to *Aristophanes* in *Conuiuio Platonis,*
*that to compose or wryte a Tragedie and Comedie bee bothe
the worke of one,* albeit they onely differ not in form, but are
25 opposit and contrarie, it should consequentlie be as true that
a good Steward knoweth as well how to gouerne a Princes houshold as a priuate familie, for the manner and facultie of eyther is
alike : and I haue red in a pamphilet that is dedicated to *Aristotle*
that their gouernments or dispensations of a house are deuided
30 into foure parts, *Kingly, Lordly, Ciuill* and *Priuate, Regia, Satra-
picia, Ciuilis and priuata,* which distinction I reprooue not. For
albeit wee differ farre from those of elder times, yet I see the
gouernments of those houses of the Viceroyes of *Naples, Sicilie,*
and the Gouernour of *Mylain,* are as correspondent for proportion
35 to those Royall houses as were of olde that custome of the Dukes
and other noble men : which proportion also may be found
amongst the houses of the Dukes of *Sauoy, Ferrara,* and *Mantua,*
and those Gouernours of *Asti, Vercellis, Modona, Reggio,* and

Reggio a
Cittie in
Lomberdy.

---

38 *Modona*] *Madona Q.*

There is
Modone and
Modona.
Modone a
Cittie in
Greece.
Modona a
Cittie in
Italie.

Monteferrato.   But I cannot see yet how the gouernment of a ciuill and a priuate house doo differ, vnlesse he call his gouernment Ciuill that is busied and employed in office for the honours of Commonwealth, and that mans priuate that is segregat and not called to office, so that wholy hee applies him to his housholde 5 care.   And that this is his distinction may wee gather by the wordes that he hath written : *That priuate gouernment is the least, and yet rayseth profit of those things which are despised and dispraysed of the others, which others are to bee intended those ciuill Gouernours or officers that, being vsd and exercised in affaires of* 10 *more estate, dislike of manie things which neuerthelesse are enter-taind and praised of priuate men.*   But for it may percase come so to passe that some of your sonnes, following the example of theyr Uncle, may endeuour and apply themselues to serue in Court, I could wysh that somewhat might be said concerning that 15 so necessary care of gouerning a Princes house, but nowe it is so late, and we haue set so long, that time and good manners will hardly giue vs leaue, albeit somethings vnspoken of might be reuiued and produced, whereof hee shall haue time and ease to learne and to collect enough, part out of *Aristotles* Bookes and the 20 rest by his owne experience in Court.'

Therewithall the Gentleman seeming to be satisfied with my speeches, arose and accompanied me vnworthy to the Chamber that the while had beene prouided for me, and there in a very soft bed I bequeathed my bones to rest.
                                                                                    25

Me mea, sic tua te ; caetera mortis erunt.

                                                            T. K.

The trueth of the most wicked and secret
murthering of *Iohn Brewen*, *Goldsmith of*
London , committed by his owne wife,
through the prouocation of one Iohn Parker
whom she loued : for which fact she was burned,
and he hanged in Smithfield, on wednesday, the 28 of Iune, 1592. two yeares after the murther was committed.

Imprinted at London for Iohn Kid, and are to be sold
by Edward White, dwelling at the little North doore
of Paules , at the sign : of the Gun. 1592.

Tho. Kyd

EDITOR'S NOTE

THIS Pamphlet is reprinted from the unique copy in Lambeth Palace Library. J. P. Collier included it in his *Illustrations of Early English Popular Literature*, vol. i (1863). I have made some changes in the punctuation, and have introduced quotation marks in the passages of dialogue.

On reconsideration of the MS. signature on the title-page of *The Mvrder of Iohn Brewen*, I interpret it as that of the printer, John Kyd, and not as that of the author, Thomas, which is appended at the end of the pamphlet.

1902   F. S. B.

THE MVRDER OF IOHN BREWEN, GOLD-

smith of London, who through the entise-
ment of Iohn Parker, was poysoned of his owne
wife in eating a measse of Sugersops.

How hatefull a thing the sinne of murder hath beene before
the sight of the eternall God the holy Scriptures doe manifest ;
yet from the beginning we may euidently see how busie the diuell
hath beene to prouoke men thereunto, in so much that when there
was but two brethren liuing in the world, the onelye sonnes of the 5
first man, *Adam,* hee prouoked the one most vnnaturally to murther the other.   And albeit there was none in the world to accuse
Caine for so fowle a fact, so that in his owne conceit hee might
haue walked securely and without blame, yet the blood of the iust
Abel cried most shrill in the eares of the righteous God for ven- 10
geance and reuenge on the murderer.   The Lord therefore or-
dayned a Lawe that the cruel and vniust blood-sheader should
haue his blood iustly shed again : of which law, although no man
is ignorant, and that we see it put in execution daylie before our
eyes, yet doth the Diuell so worke in the hearts of a number that, 15
without respect either of the feare of God, or extreame punishment in this world, they doe notwithstanding committe most
haynous and grieuous offences to the great hazard of their soules
and the destructions of their bodies on earth, onely through
Sathans suggestions, as by this example following may euidently 20
be proued.

There was of late dwelling in *London* a proper young woman
named *Anne Welles,* which, for her fauour and comely personage,
as also in regard of her good behauiour and other commendable
qualities, was beloued of diuers young men, especially of two 25

Goldsmithes, which were Batchelers, of good friends, and well
esteemed for fine workmanship in their trade.   The one of them
was called *Iohn Brewen*, and the other *Iohn Parker*, who, although
hee was better beloued, yet least deserued it (as the sequell here-
5 after will shewe).   But as the truest louers are commonly least
regarded, and the plaine meaning man most scorned of vndiscreete
maidens, so came it to passe by *Brewen*, who, not withstanding
his long and earnest suite, the gifts and fauours which she
receiued, was still disdained and cast off, albeit he had the good will
10 and fauour of al her friends and kinsfolk : but no man was so
high in her books as *Parker*: he had her fauours whosoeuer had
her frowns ; he sate and smiled, when others sobbed, and tryum-
phant in the teares of the dispossessed.   It came to passe that
this nice maiden had, vpon a promise between them, receaued of
15 *Brewen* both golde and iewels, which he willingly bestowed vpon
her, esteeming her the mistris and commaundres of his life ; but
when he saw his suite despised, and his goodwill nothing regarded,
and seeing no hope of her good will and fauour, he determined
that, seeing his suite took no effect, to demaund his golde and
20 iewels againe.   And vpon a time comming vnto her, requested
that he might haue his gifts againe, to whom disdainfully she
made answere that he should stay for it, and the young man
hauing been thus driuen off longer than hee thought good of,
made no more adoe but arested her for the iewels.

25   The stout damsel, that had neuer before been in the like
daunger, was so astonished and dismayed that she concluded,
on condition he would let his Action fal, and not to think euer
the worse of her afterward, to marrie him by a certain day, and to
make him her husba⟨n⟩d ; and this before good witnes she vowed
30 to performè.   *Brewen* was hereof very ioyfull, and released his
prisoner on his owne perill, being not a little glad of his good
successè.   And thereupon so soone as might be, made preparation
for their marriage, albeit it proued the worst bargain that euer he
made in his life.   Now when *Parker* vnderstood of this thing, he
35 was grieuously vexed, and as one hauing deepe intrest in the possession of her person, stormed most outragiously, and with bitter
speeches so taunted and checkt her that she repented the
promise she made to *Brewen*, although she could not any way

---

38 promised *Q*.

amend it; neuerthelesse it kindled such a hatred in her heart
against her new made choyce, that at length it turned to *Brewens*
death and destruction.   And this accursed *Parker*, although he
was not as then in estate to marrie (notwithstanding he ere then
had lien with her and gotten her with child) would neuer let her 5
rest, but continually vrged her to make him away by one meanes
or other.   Diuers and sundry times had they talke together of that
matter, and although she often refused to work his death, yet at
length, the grace of God being taken from her, she consented by
his direction to poyson *Brewen*: after which deede done, *Parker* 10
promised to marrie her so soone as possibly he could.

Now she had not been maried to *Brewen* aboue three dayes,
whe⟨n⟩ she put in practise to poyson him.   And although the
honest young man loued hir tenderly, yet had she conceiued such
deadly hatred against him, that she lay not with him after the 15
first night of her marriage; neither could she abide to be called
after his name, but still to be termed *Anne Welles* as she was
before: and to excuse her from his bed, she sayd she had vowed
neuer to lie by him more till he had gotten her a better house.
And the more to shadow her trecherie, and to shew the discon- 20
tent she had of his dwelling, she lodged neuer a night but the first
in his house, but prouided her a lodging neere to the place where
this graceles *Parker* dwelt.   By this meanes the villaine had free
accesse to practise with her about the murther, who was so importunate and hastie to haue it done that the Wednesday after she 25
was married she wickedly went to effect it, euen according as
Parker had before giuen direction: which was in this sorte.   The
varlet had bought a strong deadly poyson whose working was to
make speedy haste to the heart, without any swelling of the body,
or other signe of outward confection.   This poyson the wicked 30
woman secretly caried with her to her husbands house, with
a mery pleasaunt countenance, and very kindly shee asked her
husband how he did, giuing him the good morrow in most courteous manner, and asked if he would haue that colde morning
a measse of suger soppes (for it was the weeke before shrouetide). 35
'I, mary, with a good will, wife' (quoth he), 'and I take it verie
kindly that you will doe so much for me.'   'Alas, husband'
(quoth she), 'if I could not find in my heart to doe so small

---

a matter for you (especially being so lately married), you might
iustly iudge me vnkinde'; and therewithall went to make ready
his last meat. The thing being done, shee powred out a measse
for him, and strewed secretly therein part of the poyson; and hauing
5 set the porringer doune beside her, while she put the posnet on
the fire againe, with her rising vp from the fire her coat cast
downe that measse which for her husband she had prepared.
'Out, alasse,' quoth she, 'I haue spilt a measse of as good sugur
sops as euer I made in my life.' 'Why,' quoth her husband, 'is
10 there no more?' 'Yes,' quoth she, 'that there is, two as good as
they, or I will make them as good; but it greeues me that any
good thing should so vnluckily be cast away.' 'What, woman,'
quoth he, 'vex not at the matter, your ill lucke goe with them.'
'Mary, Amen,' quoth she, speaking, God knowes, with a wicked
15 thought, though the well meaning man thought on no euill.

'But, I pray you, *Iohn*' (said she), 'shall I intreate you to fetch
mee a penny worth of red herrings, for I haue an earnest desire to
eat some?' 'That I will,' quoth he, 'with a good will.' This sly
shift she deuised to haue his absence, that she might the better
20 performe hir wicked intent; and by the time he came againe she
had made ready a messe of suger sops for him, one for herselfe,
and another for a little boye which she brought with her; but her
husbands she had poysoned as before. When he was come she
gaue her husband his messe, and she and the childe fell also to
25 eating of theirs. Within a pretty while after hee had eaten his,
hee began to waxe very ill about the stomack, feeling also a grieuous
griping of his inward partes, wherupon he tould his wife he felt
himselfe not well. 'How so,' quoth she, 'you were well before you
went forth, were you not?' 'Yes, indeed was I,' said he; then he
30 demaunded if she were well; she answered 'I'; so likewise said the
childe. 'Ah,' quoth her husband, 'now I feele my selfe sicke at
the very heart,' and immediatlie after he began to vomet exceedingly, with such straines as if his lungs would burst in pieces; then
he requested her to haue him to bed, neuer mystrusting the trecherie
35 wrought against him. Now, when it drew some what late, she
tould her husband she must needs goe home to her lodging, and
when he requested her to stay with him, she said she could not, nor
would not. And so vnnaturally left the poysoned man all alone
that whole night longe, without either comfort or companie. All
40 that night was he extreame sicke, worse and worse, neuer ceasing

vomiting till his intrailes were all shrunke and broken within him
(as is since supposed). The next morning she came to him
againe, hauing been once or twice sent for, but made little semblance of sorrow ; and when he quibd her with vnkindnes for not
staying with him one night, she asked him if he would haue her 5
forsworne. 'Did I not,' quoth she, 'sweare I would not stay in
the house one night, till you had gotten another ?' 'Well, *Anne*,'
quoth hee, 'stay with mee now, for I am not long to continue in
this world.' 'Now, God forbid' (quoth she), and with that she
made a shewe of great heauines and sorrow, and then made him 10
a caudle with suger and other spices. And so on the Thursday,
immediatly after he had eaten it, he dyed ; and on the Friday he
was buried, no person as then suspecting any manner of euil
done to him by his wife, but esteemed her a very honest woman,
although through her youth she knew not as then how to behaue 15
her selfe to her husband so kindely as she ought, which they im-
puted to her ignorance rather then to any malice conceaued
against her husband. Now you shall vnderstand that, within a
small space after her husband was dead, she was knowne with
child, and safely deliuered, euery neighbour thinking it had been 20
her husbands, although she since confessed it was not ; but that
child liued not long, but dyed.

The murder lying thus vnespyed, who was so lusty as *Parker*
with the Widdow, being a continuall resorter to her house, whose
welcome was answerable to his desier ? And so bould in the end 25
he grew with her that she durst not denie him anything he requested, and became so ielious that, had shee lookt but merely
vpon a man, shee should haue knowne the price thereof, and
haue bought her merrement deerely. And yet was he not married
vnto her : yea, to ⟨such⟩ slauerie and subiection did he bring her 30
that she must runne or goe wheresoeuer he pleased to appoint her,
held hee vp but his finger at any time ; if she denied him either
money or whatsoeuer else he liked to request, he wold so haule
and pull her as was pittie to behold ; yea, and threaten to stabbe
and thrust her through with his dagger, did she not as he would 35
haue her in all things. So that he had her at commandement
whensoeuer hee would, and yet could she scant please him with
her diligence. In this miserable case hee kept her vnmarried for

---

30 such *add*. Collier

U 2

the space of two yeares after her husband was dead ; at length he
got her with child againe, which, when the woman knew, she was
carefull for the sauing of her credit to keepe it vnspied so long as
she could, in so much that she would not goe forth of her doores
5 for feare her neighbours should perceaue her great bellie.   In the
meane space *Parker* comming vnto her, she was vpon one day aboue
the rest most earnest with him to marrie her.   'You see' (quoth
shee) 'in what case I am, and if you wil not for your owne credit,
yet for my credits sake, marrie me, and suffer mee not to be
10 a poynting marke for others, and a shame among my neighbours.'
The varlet, hearing the great mone shee made vnto him, was
nothing moued therewith, but churlishly answered, shee should not
appoint him when to marrie ; 'but if I were so minded' (quoth he),
'I would be twice aduised how I did wed with such a strumpet as
15 thy selfe,' and then reuiled her most shamefully.   Whereunto shee
answered shee had neuer been strumpet but for him ; 'and wo
worth thee' (quoth she) 'that euer I knewe thee, it is thou and no
man else that can triumph in my spoyle, and yet now thou refusest
to make amends for thy fault : my loue to thee thou hast sufficiently
20 tried, although I neuer found any by thee.'   'Out, arrant queane'
(quoth he), 'thou wouldst marry me to the end thou mightest
poyson me, as thou didst thy husband ; but for that cause I
meane to keepe me as long out of thy fingers as I can ; and
accurst be I, if I trust thee or hazard my life in thy hands.'
25 'Why, thou arrant beast' (quoth shee), 'what did I then which
thou didst not prouoke me to doo ; if my husband were poysoned,
thou knowest (shameles as thou art) it had neuer been done but
for thee ; thou gauest me the poyson, and after thy direction I
did minister it vnto him ; and, woe is mee, it was for thy sake
30 I did so cursed a deede.'   These speeches thus spoken betweene
them in vehemencie of spirite was ouer heard of some that reuealed
it to the maiestrates ; whereupon the woman was carried before
Alderman *Howard* to be examined, and the man before Iustice
Younge, who stoode in the denial thereof very stoutly ; neither would
35 the woman confesse anything till in the ende shee was made to
beleeue that *Parker* had bewrayed the matter, whereupon she
co⟨n⟩fessed the fact in order, as I haue declared.   Then was she
carried into the countrey to be deliuered of her childe, and after
brought back to prison.   And then shee and *Parker* were both
40 araigned and condemned for the murder at the sessions hall nere

newgate; and the woman had iudgement to be burned in *Smyth-field*, and the man to be hanged in the same place before her eyes. This was accordingly performed, and they were executed on Wednesday last, being the 28 of June 1592, two yeares and a halfe after the murder was committed.   The Lord giue all men grace by their example to shunne the hatefull sinne of murder, for be it kept neuer so close, and done neuer so secret, yet at length the Lorde will bring it out; for bloud is an vnceassant crier in the eares of the Lord, and he will not leaue so vilde a thing vnpunished.

THO. KYDD[1].

FINIS.

---

[1] Added in a contemporary hand.

FRAGMENTS

Of lost Poems or Plays by Kyd, preserved in Robert Allott's Miscellany, *England's Parnassus*, 1600.

1. *Time.*

Time is a bondslaue to eternitie.

2. *Tyrannie.*

It is an hell in hatefull vassalage,
Vnder a tyrant, to consume ones age,
A selfe-shauen *Dennis*, or an *Nero* fell,
Whose cursed Courts with bloud and incest swell :
An Owle that flyes the light of Parliaments
And state assemblies, iealous of th' intents
Of Priuate tongues, who for a pastime sets
His Péeres at oddes, and on their furie whets,
Who neither fayth, honour, nor right respects.

3. *Vertue.*

Honour indeede, and all things yeeld to death,
(Vertue excepted) which alone suruiues,
And liuing toyleth in an earthlie gaile,
At last to be extol'd in heauens high ioyes.

THE
FIRST PART

of Ieronimo.

With the Warres of Portugall, and the
life and death of Don
Andræa.

Printed at London for Thomas Pauyer, and are
to be folde at his fhop, at the entrance
into the Exchange 1605.

EDITOR'S NOTE

THE text is based on that of the Black-Letter Quarto of 1605, the only extant early edition, of which a considerable number of copies have been preserved. It was reprinted by Reed in his edition of Dodsley's *Old Plays*, 1780 (vol. iii), and afterwards by Collier, 1825 (vol. iii), and Hazlitt, 1874 (vol. iv). The Quarto is carelessly printed, especially as far as the correct arrangement of the lines is concerned. In many cases the index furnished by the rhyme is ignored. Reed emended a number of passages, but left others untouched, and neither Collier nor Hazlitt added in any considerable degree to Reed's work. I have aimed at as thorough a restoration of the text as possible, and at thus, for the first time, presenting the play with an approach to exactness, I have in the stage-directions substituted *Exeunt* for *Exit* where grammatically necessary, and have preserved uniformity in the spelling of the proper names, which the Quarto sometimes mutilates. Otherwise I have reproduced the curious spelling of the original text. To facilitate reference I have divided the play into three Acts with subdivisions into Scenes.

⟨DRAMATIS PERSONAE [1]

King of Spain.
Duke of Castile, *his brother.*
Lorenzo, *the Duke's son.*
Bellimperia, *Lorenzo's sister.*
Pedringano, *Bellimperia's servant.*

King of Portugal.
Don Pedro, *his brother.*
Balthezer, *the King's son.*

Ieronimo, *Marshal of Spain.*
Isabella, *his wife.*
Horatio, *their son.*

Duke Medina.
Alcario, *his son.*
Andrea ⎫
Rogero ⎬ *Spanish Courtiers.*
Lazarotto ⎭
Spanish Ambassador.
Spanish Lord General.
Spanish Captain.
Portuguese Lord General.
Vollupo ⎫ *Portuguese Noblemen.*
Alexandro ⎭
Messenger.

Ghost of Andrea.
Revenge.
Charon.

Nobles, Soldiers, Attendants, Mourners.⟩

[1] No list of the *Dramatis Personae* is contained in the Quarto, or in any of the later editions

THE FIRST PART OF IERONIMO

⟨ACT I.

SCENE I.⟩

Sound a signate, and passe ouer the stage. Enter at one dore the
King of Spaine, Duke of Castile, Duke Medina, Lorenzo, *and*
Rogero: *at another doore,* Andrea, Horatio, and Ieronimo. Ieronimo
kneeles downe, and the King *creates him Marshall of Spaine :* Lorenzo
putes on his spurres, and Andrea *his sword. The* King *goes along with*
Ieronimo *to his house. After a long signate is sounded, enter all the*
nobles, with couerd dishes, to the banquet. Exeunt Omnes. That done,
enter all agen as before.

King. Frolick, *Ieronimo*; thou art now confirmd
    Marshall of Spaine, by all the dewe
    And customary rights vnto thy office.
Ier. My knee sings thanks vnto your highnes bountie;
    Come hether, boy *Horatio*; fould thy ioynts;   5
    Kneele by thy fathers loynes, and thank my leedge
    For honering me, thy Mother, and thy selfe
    With this high staffe of office.
Hor.   O my leedge,
    I haue a hart thrice stronger then my years,
    And that shall answere gratefully for me.   10
    Let not my youthfull blush impare my vallor :
    If euer you haue foes, or red field scars,
    Ile empty all my vaines to serue your wars :
    Ile bleed for you ; and more, what speech afords,
    Ile speake` in drops, when I do faile in words.   15
Ier. Well spoke, my boy ; and on thy fathers side.
    My leedge, how like you Don *Horatios* spirit ?
    What, doth it not promise faire ?

---

2 dewe *ed.* : dewes *Q.*   7 For *ed.* : by *Q.*   8 O my leedge *beg. of* 9
Qq.   18 not *om. Reed, Collier, Hazlitt*

King. I, and no doubt his merit will purchase more.
  Knight Marshall, rise, and still rise   20
  Higher and greater in thy Soueraines eies.
Ier. O fortunate houre, blessed mynuit, happy day,
  Able to rauish euen my sence away.
  Now I remember too (O sweet rememberance)
  This day my years strike fiftie, and in Rome   25
  They call the fifty year the year of *Iubily*,
  The merry yeare, the peacefull yeere, ⟨the⟩ Iocond yeare,
  A yeare of ioy, of pleasure, and delight.
  This shalbe my yeare of *Iubily,* for tis my fifty.
  Age vshers honor; tis no shame ; confesse,   30
  Beard, thou art fifty full, not a haire lesse.

Enter an Embassador.

King. How now, what news for Spain? tribute returned?
Amb. Tribute in words, my leedge, but not in coine.
King. Ha : dare he still procrastinate with Spaine?
  Not tribute paied, not three years payed?   35
  Tis not at his coine,
  But his slack homage, that we most repine.
Ier. My leedge, if my opinion might stand firme
  Within your highnes thoughts—
King. Marshall, our kingdome calles thee father :   40
  Therefore speake free.
  Thy counsell Ile imbrace as I do thee.
Ier. I thanke your highnes. Then, my Gracious leedge,
  I hold it meete, by way of Embassage,
  To demaund his mind and the neglect of tribute.   45
  But, my leedge,
  Heere must be kind words which doth oft besiedge
  The eares of rough heawn tyrants more then blowes :
  Oh, a polyticke speech beguiles the eares of foes.
  Mary, my leedge, mistake me not, I pray ;   50
  If friendly phraises, honied speech, bewitching accent,
  Well tuned mellody, and all sweet guifts of nature,
  Cannot auaile or win him to it,
  Then let him raise his gall vp to his toong,

27 the *add. Hazlitt*   32 for *Collier, Hazlitt*: from *Q.   See Note*
46–8 But . . . words | Which . . . rough | Heawn . . . blowes *Q.*

And be as bitter as physitions drugs,   55
Stretch his mouth wider with big swolne phrases.
Oh, heeres a Lad of mettle, stout Don *Andrea*,
Mettle to the crowne,
Would shake the Kings hie court three handfuls downe.

King. And well pickt out, knight Marshall; speech well strung;
Ide rather choose *Horatio* were he not so young.   61

Hor. I humbly thanke your highnes,
In placing me next vnto his royall bosome.

King. How stand ye, Lords, to this election?

Omnes. Right pleasing, our dread Soueraigne.   65

Med. Only, with pardon, mighty Soueraigne,
I should haue chose⟨n⟩ Don *Lorenzo*.

Cast. I, Don *Rogero*.

Rog.   O no; not me, my Lords;
I am wars Champion, and my fees are swords;
Pray, king, pray, peeres, let it be Don *Andrea*;   70
Hees a worthy lim
Loues wars and Souldiers; therefore I loue him.

Iero. And I loue him, and thee, valiant *Rogero*;
Noble spyrits, gallant bloods,
You are no wise insinuating Lords,   75
You ha no tricks, you ha none of all their slights.

Lor. So, so, *Andrea* must be sent imbassador?
Lorenzo is not thought vpon : good,
Ile wake the Court, or startle out some bloud.

King. How stand you, Lords, to this election?   80
Omnes. Right pleasing, our dread Soueraigne.

King. Then, Don *Andrea*—
And.   My aproued leedge—

King. We make thee our Lord hie imbassador.

And. Your highnes cirkels me with honors boundes.
I will discharg the waight of your command   85
With best respect ; if friendly tempred phraise
Cannot effect the vertue of your charge,
I will be hard like thunder, and as rough

---

63 In] on *Reed, Collier*   68 *Cast.* wrongly *prefixed to* 67 *Q. ; hence previous
editors assign* 67 *to* Castile, *and first half of* 68 I . . . *Rogero (which has
no prefix in Q.) to* Medina   75 You are] Your *Q.*   85 will *ed.* : still *Q.* :
shall *Hazlitt*   87 effect *ed.* : affect *Q.*

As Northerne tempests, or the vexed bowels
Of too insulting waues, who at one blow　　　　　　90
Fiue marchants wealths into the deepe doth throw.
Ile threaten crimson wars.

Rog.　　　　　　　　　　I, I, thats good;
Let them keep coine, pay tribute with their blood.

King. Farwell then, Don *Andrea*; to thy chargde;
Lordes, let vs in : ioy shalbe now our guest;　　　95
Lets in to celebrate our second feast.

　　　　　　　　　　　　　　　　Exeunt.

　　　　　Manet Lorenzo *solus.*

Lor. Andreas gone embassador;
Lorenzo is not drempt on in this age;
Hard fate,
When villaines sit not in the highest state.　　　100
Ambitions plumes, that florisht in our court,
Seuere authority has dasht with iustice;
And pollicy and pride walke like two exiles,
Giuing attendance, that were once attended,
And we reiected that were once high honored.　　105
I hate *Andrea*, cause he aimes at honor,
When my purest thoughts work in a pitchy vale,
Which are as different as heauen and hell.
One peeres for day, the other gappes for night,
That yawning Beldam with her Iettie skin;　　　110
Tis she I hug as mine effeminate bride,
For such complexions best appease my pride.
I haue a lad in pikell of this stamp,
A melancholy, discontented courtier,
Whose famisht iawes look like the chap of death;　115
Vpon whose eie browes hangs damnation;
Whose hands are washt in rape, and murders bould.
Him with a goulden baite will I allure
(For Courtiers wil doe any thing for gould)
To be *Andreas* death at his retourne :　　　120
Hee loues my sister; that shall cost his life;
So she a husband, he shall lose a wife.
O sweete, sweete pollicie, I hugg thee; good :
Andreas Himens draught shall be in bloud.　　*Exit.*

---

89 vext *Q.*　　　95 let vs] letes *Q.*　　116 hangs *Hazlitt*: hang *Q.*

⟨SCENE II.⟩

Enter Horatio *at one doore,* Andrea *at an other.*

Hor. Whether in such hast, my second selfe?

And. I faith, my deare bosome, to take solemne leaue
Of a most weeping creature.

Hor.   Thats a woman.

Enter Bellimperia.

And. Thats *Bellimperia.*

Hor.   See, see, she meetes you heere :
And what it is to loue, and be loued deere.   5

Bel. I haue hard of your honor, gentle brest ;
I do not like it now so well, me thinkes.

And. What, not to haue honor bestowed on me?

Bel. O yes : but not a wandring honor, deere ;
I could afford ⟨it⟩ well, didst thou stay here.   10
Could honor melt it selfe into thy vaines,
And thou the fountaine, I could wish it so,
If thou wouldst remaine heere with me, and not go.

And. Tis but to Portugale.

Hor. But to demand the tribute, Ladie.

Bel.   Trybute?   15
Alas, that Spaine cannot of peace forbeare
A little coine, the Indies being so neere.
And yet this is not all : I know you are to hot,
To full of spleene for an imbassador,
And will leane much to honor.   20

And. Push.

Bel. Nay, heare me, deere :
I know you will be rough and violent,
And Portingale hath a tempestus son,
Stampt with the marke of fury, and you too.   25

And. Sweet *Bellimperia.*

Bel.   Youle meete like thunder,
Eatch imperious ouer others spleen ;

---

5 it is] is it *Reed, Collier, Hazlitt*   10 it *add. ed.*   15–7 But . . .
Ladie | Trybute . . . peace | Forbeare . . . neere *Q.*   21 Pish *Hazlitt*   22–4
Nay . . . rough | And . . . son *Q.*   26–30 Sweet *Bellimperia* | Weele . . .
ouer | Others . . . will | Striue . . . strike | Out . . . forfend *Q.*   26 Youle
Reed, Collier, Hazlitt : Weele *Q.*

You haue both proud spirits and both will striue to aspire ;
When two vext Clouds iustle they strike out fire ;
And you, I feare me, war, which peace forfend.   30
O deere *Andrea*, pray, lets haue no wars.
First let them pay the souldiers that were maimde
In the last battaile, ere more wretches fall,
Or walke on stilts to timelesse Funerall.

And. Respectiue deere, O my liues happines,   35
The ioy of all my being, do not shape
Frightful conceit beyond the intent of act.
I know thy loue is vigilant ore my bloud,
And fears ill fate which heauen hath yet withstood.
But be of comfort, sweet ; *Horatio* knowes   40
I go to knit friends, not to kindle foes.

Hor. True, Madam *Bellimperia*, thats his taske :
The phraise he vseth must be gently stylde,
The king hath warned him to be smooth and mild.

Bel. But will you indeed, *Andrea* ?   45

And. By this, and by this lip blushing kisse.

Hor. O, you sweare sweetly.

Bel. Ile keepe your oth for you, till you returne.
Then ile be sure you shall not be forsworne.

Enter Pedringano.

And. Ho, *Pedringano*.   50

Ped. Signioro.

And. Are all things abord ?

Ped. They are, my good Lord.

And. Then, *Bellimperia*, I take leaue : *Horatio*,
Be in my absence my deare selfe, chast selfe.   55
What, playing the woman, *Bellimperia* ?
Nay, then you loue me not ; or, at the least,
You drowne my honores in those flowing watters.
Beleeue it, *Bellimperia*, tis as common
To weepe at parting as to be a woman.   60
Loue me more valliant ; play not this moyst prize ;
Be woman in all partes, saue in thy eies.

---

46 *And.* By this | *And.* By this lip blushing kisse *Q.* ; *the second ' And' is
wrongly printed as if it were a contraction for Andrea ; hence previous editors
have wrongly emended, And.* By this | *Bel.* And this lip blushing kiss

And so I leaue thee.

Bel.   Farwell, my Lord:

Be mindfull of my loue, and of your word.

And. Tis fixed vpon my hart; adew, soules friend.   65

Hor. All honor on *Andreas* steps attende.

Bel. Yet he is in sight, and yet—but now hees vanisht.

> *Exit* Andrea.

Hor. Nay, Lady, if you stoope so much to passion,

Ile call him back againe.

Bel.   O, good *Horatio*, no:

It is for honor; prethee let him goe.   70

Hor. Then, Madam, be composd, as you weare wont,

To musick and delight: the time being Commick will

Seeme short and pleasant till his returne

From Portingale: and, madam, in this circle

Let your hart moue;   75

Honord promotion is the sap of loue.

> *Exeunt omnes.*

⟨SCENE III.⟩

Enter Lorenzo *and* Lazarotto, *a discontented Courtier.*

Lor. Come, my soules spaniell, my lifes ietty substance,

Whats thy name?

Laz. My names an honest name, a Courtiers name:

Tis *Lazarotto.*

Lor.   What, *Lazarotto* ?

Laz. Or rather rotting in this lazy age,   5

That yeelds me no imployments; I haue mischiefe

Within my breast, more then my bulke can hold:

I want a midwiue to deliuer it.

Lor. Ile be the hee one then, and rid thee soone

Of this dull, leaden, and tormenting elfe.   10

Thou knowst the loue

Betwixt *Bellimperia* and *Andreas* bosome?

Laz. I, I do.

Lor. How might I crosse it, my sweet mischiefe?

Hunny damnation, how?

---

66 on] one *Q.*   68 Nay . . . againe *one line Q.*   69 O . . . goe *one line Q.*   3 *second* name *beg. of* 4 *Q.*   6 That *end of* 5 *Q.*   11-2 Thou . . . and | *Andreas* bosome *Q.*

Laz.   Well :   15
  As many waies as there are paths to hell,
  And thats enow, ifaith : from vserers doores
  There goes one pathe : from friers that nurse whores
  There goes another path : from brokers stals,
  From rich that die and build no hospitals,   20
  Two other paths : from farmers that crack barns
  With stuffing corne, yet starue the needy swarmes,
  Another path : from drinking schooles one : ⟨one⟩
  From dicing houses : but from the court, none, none.
Lor. Heere is a slaue iust a the stampe I wish,   25
  Whose Incke-soules blacker then his name,
  Though it stand painted with a Rauens quill.
  But, *Lazarotto*, crosse my Sisters loue,
  And ile raine showers of Duckets in thy palme.
Laz. Oh Duckets, dainty ducks : for, giue me duckets,   30
  Ile fetch you duck inough ; for gold and chinck
  Makes the punck wanton and the bawd to winke.
Lor. Discharg, discharg, good *Lazarotto*, how
  We may crose my Sisters louing hopes.
Laz.   Nay now,
  Ile tell you—   35
Lor. Thou knowest *Andreas* gone embassador.
Laz. The better ther is oppertunity :
  Now list to me.

    Enter Ieronimo, *and* Horatio, *and ouer heare their talke.*

  Alcario, the Duke *Medinas* sonne,
  Dotes on your Sister, *Bellimperia* ;   40
  Him in her priuate gallery you shall place,
  To court her ; let his protestations be
  Fashoned with rich Iewels, for in loue
  Great gifts and gold haue the best toong to moue.
  Let him not spare an oath without a iewell   45

---

15 Well *beg. of* 16 Q.   17 doores *ed.* : doore Q.   18 whores
beg. of 19 Q.   19 stals *beg. of* 20 Q.   23 *second* one *add. ed.*   23-4
Another ... from | Dicing ... none Q.   29 And ile *end of* 28 Q.
of Reed, Collier, Hazlitt : and Q.   30-2 Oh ... forgiue me | Duckets
... gold | And ... winke Q. ; *previous editors, misled by the misprint* forgiue,
have made the passage meaningless   33-5 Discharg ... we | May ...
hopes | Nay ... you Q.   37 ther is] thers Q.   37-8 *one line* Q.
S.D. *heare*] heares Q.   44 great *end of* 43 Q.

To bind it fast: Oh, I know womens harts
What stuffe they are made of, my Lord : gifts and giuing
Will melt the chastest seeming female liuing.

Lor. Indeede *Andrea* is but poore, though honorable ;
His bounty amongst souldiers sokes him dry,   50
And therefore great gifts may bewitch her eie.

Ier. Heeres no fine villainie, no damn⟨e⟩d brother.

Lor. But, say she should deny his gifts, be all
Composd of hate, as my mind giues me that she wooll :
What then ?   55

Laz. Then thus : at his returne to Spaine,
Ile murder Don *Andrea*.

Lor.   Darst thou, sperit ?

Laz. What dares not hee do that neer hopes to inherit ?

Hor. Hee dares bee damnd like thee.

Laz.   Dare I ? Ha, ha,
I haue no hope of euerlasting height ;   60
My souls a Moore, you know, saluations white.
What dare not I enact, then ? tush, he dies.
I will make way to *Bellimperias* eies.

Lor. To weepe, I feare, but not to tender loue.

Laz. Why, is she not a woman ? she must weepe   65
A while, as widdowes vse, till their first sleepe ;
Who in the morrow following will be sould
To newe, before the first are thoroughly cold.
So *Bellimperia* ; for this is common ;
The more she weepes, the more shee plaies the woman. 70

Lor. Come then, how ere it hap, *Andrea* shall be crost.

Laz. Let mee alone ; Ile turne him to a ghoast.

Exeunt Lorenzo *and* Lazarotto. *Mane⟨n⟩t* Ieronimo *and* Horatio.

Ier. Farwell, true brace of villaynes ;
Come hether, boy *Horatio*, didst thou here them ?

Hor. O my true brested father,   75

47–8 What . . . Lord | Gifts . . . chastest | Seeming . . . liuing *Q.*   51
therefore *Reed, Collier* : there ore *Q.* : their o'er *Hazlitt*   54 that she wooll
beg. of 55 *Q.*   57 Ile *end of* 56 *Q.*   57 Darst . . . sperit *sep. line Q.*
58 neer] near *Q.*   59–62 Hee . . . thee | Dare . . . euerlasting | Height . . .
saluations | White . . . dies *Q.*   67–70 Who . . . newe | Before . . . so |
Bellimperia . . . more | She . . . woman *Q.*   S.D. *and* Horatio *after*
Lazarotto *Q.*   75–81 O . . . sukt | In . . . *Andrea* | O . . . reuerend |
Yeares . . . haue | Ponyarded . . . his | Soule . . . *Andrea* | Honest . . . vil-
layns *Q.*

My eares haue sukt in poyson, deadly Poyson.
Murder *Andrea*? O Inhumain practis.
Had not your reuerend yeares beene present heere,
I should haue ponyarded the Villaynes bowels,
And shoued his soule out to Damnation.   80
Murder *Andrea*, honest lord? Impious villayns.

Ier. I like thy true hart, boy ; thou louest thy friend :
It is the greatest argument and sign
That I begot thee, for it showes thou art mine.

Hor. O father, tis a charitable deed   85
To preuent those that would make vertue bleed.
Ile dispatch letters to don *Andrea* ;
Vnfould their hellish practise, damnd intent
Against the vertuous riuers of his life.
Murder *Andrea*?

                    Enter Isabella.

Ier.   Peace : who comes here? Newes,   90
Newes, *Isabella*.

Isa.   What newes, *Ieronimo*?

Ier. Strang newes : *Lorenzo* is becom an honest man.

Isa. Is this your wondrous newes?

Ier.   I, ist not wondrous
To haue honesty in hel? Go, tell it Abrod now ;
But see you put no new aditions to it,   95
As thus—'shal I tell you, gossip? *Lorenzo* is
Become an honnest man :'—Beware, beware ;
For honesty,
Spoken in derision, points out knauery.
O, then, take heed ; that Iest would not be trim ;   100
Hees a great man, therefore we must not knaue him.
In, gentle soule ; Ile not bee long away,
As short my body, short shall be my stay.

                              Exit Isabell⟨a⟩.

Hor. Murder *Andrea*? What bloud sucking slaue
Could choke bright honor in a skabard graue?   105

Ier. What, harping still vpon *Andreas* death?

---

84 That . . . thee *end of* 83 *Q.*   90-1 Murder *Andrea* | Peace . . .
newes | *Isabella* | What . . . *Ieronimo Q.*   93 I, ist *ed.* : I, if *Q.* : Is it *Reed,*
Collier, Hazlitt   93-9 Is . . . newes | I . . . tell | It . . . aditions |
To . . . *Lorenzo* | Is . . . beware | For . . . knauery *Q.*

Haue courage, boy : I shall preuent their plots,
And make them both stand like too politique sots.
Hor. Lorenzo has a reach as far as hell,
To hooke the diuell from his flaming cell.   110
O, sprightly father, heele out rech you then ;
Knaues longer reaches haue then honest men.
Ier. But, boy, feare not, I will out stretch them al ;
My minds a giant, though my bulke be small.

Exeùnt omnes.

⟨ACT II.

SCENE I.⟩

Enter the King of Portingale, Balthezer, Alexandro, Donne Vollupo,
and others : a peale of ordenance within ; a great shout of people.
King. What is the meaning of this lowd report ?
Alex. An embas⟨sador⟩, my Lord, is new ariued from Spaine.
King. Son *Balthezer,* we pray, do you goe meet him,
And do him all the honor that belonges him.
Bal. Father, my best indeuour shall obay you ;—   5
Welcom, worthy lord, Spaines choyse embassador,
Braue, stout *Andrea,* for soe I gesse thee.

Enter Andrea.

And. Portugalles eire, I thanke thee ;
Thou semes no les then what thou art, a prince,
And an heroycke spirit ; Portingalles King,   10
I kisse thy hand, and tender on thy throne
My masters loue, peace, and affection.
King. And we receue them, and thee, worthy *Andrea* ;
Thy masters hy prized loue vnto our hart
Is welcome to his friend, thou to our court.   15
And. Thankes, Portingall. My lordes, I had in charge,
At my depart from Spaine, this embasage,
To put your brest in mind of tribute due
Vnto our masters kingdome these three years
Detained and kept back : and I ⟨am⟩ sent to know   20
Whether neglect, or will, detains it so.
King. Thus much returne vnto thy King, *Andrea* :
We haue with best aduise thought of our state,

---

113 I will] lle *Q.*   114 small *emend. Reed* : full *Q.*   2 embas *Q.* :
embassy *Reed, Collier, Hazlitt*   11 *first* thy *ed.* : my *Q.*   20 am *add. Reed*

And find it much dishonord by base homage.
I not deny but tribute hath bin due to Spaine   25
By our forfathers base captiuitie :
Yet cannot raze ⟨'t⟩ out there successors merit?
Tis sayd we shall not answer at next birth
Our fathers fawltes in heauen ; why then on earth?
Which proues and showes, that which they lost by base Captiuitie,
We may redeeme with honored valiansie.   31
We borow nought ; our kingdome is our owne:
Hee is a base King that payes rent for his throne.

And. Is this thy answer, Portingalle ?
Bal.   I, Spaine ;
A royal answer to, which Ile maintaine.   35
Omnes. And all the peeres of Portugalle the like.
And. Then thus all Spaine, which but three minutes agoe
Was thy full friend, is now returned thy foe.
Bal. An excellent foe ; we shall haue scuffling good.
And. Thou shalt pay trybute, Portugalle, with blood.   40
Bal. Trybute for trybute, then : and foes for foes.
And. I bid you sudden warres.
Bal.   I, sudden blowes,
And thats as good as warres. Don, Ile not bate
An inch of courage nor a haire of fate.
Pay tribute ? I, with strockes.
And.   I, with strockes you shall. 45
Allas, that Spaine should correct Portugal.
Bal. Correct ?
O in that one word such torments do I feele
That I could lash thy ribes with valiant steele.
And. Prince *Balthezer*, shalles meete ?   50
Bal. Meete, Don *Andrea* ? Yes, in the battles Bowels :
Here is my gage, a neuer fayling pawne ;
Twill keepe his day, his houre, nay minute ; twill.
And. Then thine and this posses one qualitie.
Bal. O, let them kis.   55

---

27 't *add. ed.* : *The Q. has* (:) *instead of* (?), *which reverses the meaning.*
29 on] one *Q.*   34 I, Spaine *beg. of* 35 *Q.*   37 agoe *beg. of* 38 *Q.*
42-6 I bid . . . warres | I, sudden . . . warres | Don . . . bate | An . . .
fate | Pay . . . strockes | I . . . shall *Q.*   47-9 Correct . . . do | I
feele . . . steele *Q.*   52 Here is] Heres *Q.*   55-7 O . . . noble | Valliant
. . . thee *Q.*

Did I not vnderstand thee noble, valliant,
And worthy my swordes societie with thee,
For all Spaines wealth Ide not graspe hands.
Meet, Don *Andrea*? I tell thee, noble spirit,
Ide wade up to the knees in bloud,   60
Ide make a bridge of Spanish carkases,
To single thee out of the gasping armye.

And. Woot thou, prince? why euen for that I loue ⟨thee⟩.

Bal. Tut, loue me, man, when we haue drunke
Hot bloud together; woundes will tie   65
An euerlasting setled amity,
And so shall thine.

And.   And thine.

Bal.   What, giue no place?

And. To whome?

Bal.   To me.

And.   To thee? why should my face,
Thats placed aboue my mind, fall vnder it?

Bal. Ile make thee yeeld.

And.   I, when you get me downe;   70
But I stand euen yet, iump crowne to crowne.

Bal. Darst thou?

And.   I dare.

Bal.   I am all vext.

And.   I care not.

Bal. I shall forget the Law.

And.   Do, do.

Bal.   Shall I?

And.   Spare not.

Bal. But thou wilt yeeld first.

And.   No.

Bal.   O, I hug thee fort,
The valianst spirit ere trod the Spanish courte.   75

Alex. My leedge, two nobler spyrits neuer met.

Bal. Heere let the rising of our hot bloud set,
Vntill we meet in purple, when our swords
Shall—

---

63 thee *add. ed.*   76 *and* 77 *transposed,* Q.   79 shall *not in text, but
printed at the bottom of the page in* Q. *as the first word of next page, where,
however, the line which it should begin is wanting*

And. Agreed, right valliant prince.   80
   Then, Portugale, this is thy resolute answere?
King. So returne; its so: we haue bethought vs
   What tribute is; how poore that Monarch shoes
   Who for his throne a yeerely penshion owes:
   And what our predesessors lost to Spaine   85
   We haue fresh sperits that can renew it againe.
And. Then I vnclaspe the purple leaues of war:
   Many a new wound must gaspe through an old scar.
   So, Portugale, I leaue thee.
King.   Our selfe in person
   Will see thee safe aboord.   Come, son, come, Lords,   90
   In steade of tribute we must pay our swords.
Bal. Remember, Don *Andrea*, that we meet—
And. Vp hether sayling in a crimson fleete.

                                       Exeunt omnes.

⟨Scene II.⟩

Enter Lorenzo *and* Alcario.

Lor. Do you affect my sister?
Alc. Affect? aboue affection, for her breast
   Is my liues treasure; O entire
   Is the condition of my hot desire.
Lor. Then this must be your plot.   5
   You know *Andreas* gone embassador,
   On whom my Sister *Bellimperia*
   Casts her affection.
   You are in stature like him, speech alike;
   And had you but his vestment on your backe,   10
   Thers no one liuing but would sweare twere he:
   Therefore, sly policy must be youre guide.
   I haue a suit iust of *Andreas* cullers,
   Proportiond in all parts—nay, twins his own:
   This suit within my closet shall you weare,   15
   And so disguisd, woe, sue, and then at last—

---

   83 what *end of* 82 *Q*.   89-90 So . . . thee | Our . . . aboord | Come
. . . lords *Q*.   8 her *emend. Reed*: his *Q*.   8–16 Casts . . . him
| Speech . . . vestment | On . . . would | Sweare . . . must | Be . . . iust | Of . . .
parts | Nay . . . closet | Shall . . . and | Then . . . last *Q*.

Alc. What?

Lor. Obtaine thy loue.

Alc. This fals out rare ; in this disguise I may
    Both wed, bed, and boord her?   20

Lor. You may, you may.
    Besids, within these few daies heele returne.

Alc. Till this be acted I in passion burne.

Lor. All fals out for the purpose : all hits iumpe ;
    The date of his embassage nighe expired   25
    Giues strength vnto our plot.

Alc. True, true ; all to the purpose.

Lor. Moreouer, I will buze *Andreas* landing,
    Which, once but crept into the vulger mouthes,
    Is hurryed heer and there, and sworne for troth ;   30
    Thinke, tis your loue makes me create this guise,
    And willing hope to see your vertue rise.

Alc. Lorenzoes bounty I do more enfould
    Then the greatest mine of Indians brightest gold.

Lor. Come, let vs in ; the next time you shall show   35
    All Don *Andrea*, not *Alcario*.

                              Exeunt omnes.

⟨SCENE III.⟩

Enter Ieronimo *trussing of his points*, Horatio *with pen and incke.*

Ier. Come, pull the table this way ; so, tis well :
    Come, write, *Horatio*, write :
    This speedy letter must away to night.

          Horatio *foulds the paper the contrary way.*

    What, fold paper that way to a noble man?
    To Don *Andrea*, Spaines embassador?   5
    Fie : I am a shamed to see it.
    Hast thou worne gownes in the Uniuersity,
    Tost logick, suckt Philosophy,
    Eate Cues, drunk Cees, and cannot giue a letter
    The right Courtiers crest? O thers a kind of state   10
    In euery thing, saue in a Cuckolds pate.

---

    18 thy *emend. Reed*: my *Q.*   19–22 This . . . rare | In . . . her | You . . .
daies | Heele returne *Q.*   34 mine] mind *Q.*   Indians] India's *Reed,*
Collier, Hazlitt   9–10 Eate . . . cannot | Giue . . . crest | O . . . state *Q.*

Fie, fie, *Horatio*: what, is your pen foule?

Hor. No, Father, cleaner then *Lorenzoes* soule;
  Thats dipt in inck made of an enuious gall;
  Elce had my pen no cause to write at all.   15

Ier. 'Signeor *Andrea*,' say.

Hor. 'Signeor *Andrea*.'

Ier. 'Tis a villainus age this.'

Hor. 'Tis a villainus age this.'   19

Ier. 'That a nobleman should be a Knaue as well as an Ostler.'

Hor. 'That a nobleman should be a Knaue as well as an Ostler.'

Ier. 'Or a seriant.'

Hor. 'Or a seriant.'

Ier. 'Or a Broker.'

Hor. 'Or a Broker.'   25

Ier. 'Yet I speake not this of *Lorenzo*, for hees an honest Lord.'

Hor. 'S foot, Father, ile not write him 'honest Lord.'

Ier. Take vp thy pen, or ile take vp thee.

Hor. What, write him 'honest Lord'? ile not agree.

Ier. Youle take it vp, Sir.   30

Hor. Well, well.

Ier. What went before? Thou hast put me out:
  Beshrow thy impudence or insolence.

Hor. '*Lorenzoes* an honest Lord.'

Ier. Well, Sir;—'and has hired one to murder you.'   35

Hor. O, I cry you mercy, Father, ment you so?

Ier. Art thou a scholler, Don *Horatio*,
  And canst not aime at Figuratiue speech?

Hor. I pray you, pardon me; twas but youths hasty error.

Ier. Come, read then.   40

Hor. 'And has hired one to murder you.'

Ier. 'He meanes to send you to heauen, when you returne
  from Portugale.'

Hor. 'From Portugale.'

Ier. 'Yet hees an honest dukes son.'   45

Hor. 'Yet hees an'—

Ier. 'But not the honest son of a Duke.'

Hor. 'But not the honest'—

Ier. 'O, that villainy should be found in the great Chamber.'

---

27 's foot *emend. Reed*: s oot *Q*.   29 write] right *Q*.

Hor. 'O that villainy'—   50
Ier. 'And honesty in the bottome of a seller.'
Hor. 'And honesty'—
Ier. 'If youle be murdered, you may.'
Hor. 'If youle be'—
Ier. 'If you be not, thanke God and *Ieronimo*.'   55
Hor. 'If you be not'—
Ier. 'If you be, thank the diuell and *Lorenzo*.'
Hor. 'If you be, thank'—
Ier. 'Thus hoping you will not be murdred, and you can choose.'
Hor. 'Thus hoping you will'—   60
Ier. 'Especially being warned before hand.'
Hor. 'Especially'—
Ier. 'I take my leaue,'—boy *Horatio*, write 'leaue' bending in
    the hams like an old Courtier—'Thy assured friend,' say,
    'gainst *Lorenzo* and the diuell, little *Ieronimo*, Marshall.'   65
Hor. '*Ieronimo*, Marshall.'
Ier. So, now read it ore.
Hor. 'Signeor *Andrea*, tis a villainus age this, that a Nobleman
    should be a Knaue as well as an Ostler, or a Seriant, or a
    broker; yet I speake not this of *Lorenzo*: hees an honest
    Lord, and has hired one to murder you, when you returne
    from Portugale: yet hees an honest Dukes sonne, but not
    the honest son of a Duke. O that villainy should be found
    in the great chamber, and honesty in the bottome of a seller.'
Ier. True, boy: thers a morall in that; as much to say, knauery
    in the Court and honesty in a cheese house.   76
Hor. 'If youle be murdred, you may: if you be not, thanke
    God and *Ieronimo*: if you be, thanke the diuell and *Lorenzo*.
    Thus hoping you will not be murdered, and you can choose,
    especially being warnd beforehand, I take my leaue.'   80
Ier. *Horatio*, hast thou written 'leaue' bending in the hams
    enough, like a Gentleman usher? 'S foote, no, *Horatio*; thou
    hast made him straddle too much like a Frenchman: for
    shame, put his legs closer, though it be painefull.
Hor. So: tis done, tis done—'Thy assured friend gainst *Lorenzo*
    and the diuell, little *Ieronimo*, Marshall.'   86

_____

63 *Q., followed by previous editors, prints* (,) *wrongly after, instead of before*
boy   63-5 *printed in doggerel Q.*   68-86 *printed in doggerel Q.*

Enter Lorenzo *and* Isabella.

Isa. Yonder he is, my Lord; pray you speake to him.

Ier. Wax, wax, *Horatio* : I had neede wax too;
Our foes will stride else ouer me and you.

Isa. Hees writing a loue letter to some Spanish Lady,   90
And now he calls for wax to seale it.

Lor. God saue you, good knight Marshall.

Ier. Whose˙ this? my Lord *Lorenzo*? welcom, welcom;
Your the last man I thought on, saue the diuell :
Much doth your presence grace our homely roofe.   95

Lor. O *Ieronimo*,
Your wife condemns you of a vncurtesie,
And ouer passing wrong; and more she names
Loue letters which you send to Spanish Dames.

Ier. Do you accuse me so, kind *Isabella*?   100

Isa. Vnkind *Ieronimo*.

Lor. And, for my instance, this in your hand is one.

Ier. In sooth, my Lord, there is no written name
Of any Lady, then no Spanish dame.

Lor. If it were not so, you would not be afeard   105
To read or show the waxt letter :
Pray you, let me behold it.

Ier. I pray you, pardon me :
I must confes, my Lord, it treats of loue,
Loue to *Andrea*, I, euen to his very bosome.   110

Lor. What newes, my Lord, heare you from Portugale?

Ier. Who, I? before your grace it must not be ;
The Badger feeds not till the Lyons serued :
Nor fits it newes so soone kisse subiects ⟨ears⟩
As the faire cheeke of high authority.   115
Ieronimo liues much absent from the Court,
And being absent there, liues from report.

Lor. Farwell, *Ieronimo*.

                    Exeunt Lorenzo *and* Isabella.

Isa. Welcome, my Lord *Lorenzo*.

Ier. Boy,   120
Thy mothers iealious of my loue to her.

Hor. O she plaid vs a wise part ; now, ten to one

He had not ouer heard the letter read,
Iust as he entered.

Ier.   Though it had happend euill,
He should haue hard his name yokt with the diuell.   125
Heere, seale the letter with a louing knot;
Send it with speede, *Horatio*, linger not,
That Don *Andrea* may preuent his death,
And know his enemy by his enuious breath.

Exeunt omnes.

⟨SCENE IV.⟩

Enter Lorenzo, *and* Alcario *disguised like* Andrea.

Lor. Now, by the honor of Casteels true house,
You are as like *Andrea*, part for part,
As he is like himselfe : did I ⟨not⟩ know you,
By my crosse I sweare, I could not think you but
Andreas selfe, so legd, so facst, so speecht,   5
So all in all : methinks I should salute
Your quick returne and speedy hast from Portugale :
Welcome, faire Lord, worthy embassador,
Braue Don *Andrea.*—O, I laugh to see
How we shall iest at her mistaking thee.   10

Alc. What, haue you giuen it out *Andrea* is returnd?

Lor. Tis all about the court in euery eare,
And my inuention brought to me for newes
Last night at supper; and which the more to couer,
I tooke a boule and quaft a health to him,   15
When it would scarce go downe for extreame laughter
To thinke how soone report had scatterd it.

Alc. But is the villaine *Lazarotto*
Acquainted with our drift?

Lor.   Not for Spains wealth;
Though he be secret, yet suspect the worst,   20
For confidence confounds the stratagem.
The fewer in a plot of iealousie
Build a foundation surest, when multitudes

123–4 He . . . entered *one line Q.*   3 not *add. Reed*   4 but *beg. of*
5 *Q.*   5 speecht *beg. of* 6 *Q.*   18–9 But . . . drift *one line Q.*
20 suspect *ed.:* suspects *Q.*

Make it confused ere it come to head.

Be secret, then; trust not the open aire,   25

For aire is breath, and breath-blown words raise care.

Alc. This is the gallery where she most frequents;

Within this walke haue I beheld her dally

With my shapes substance. O, immortall powers,

Lend your assistance; clap a siluer tongue   30

Within this pallat, that, when I approach.

Within the presence of this demy Goddesse,

I may possess an adimanticke power,

And so bewitch her with my honied speech;

Haue euery sillable a musick stop,   35

That, when I pause, the mellody may moue

And hem perswasion tweene her snowy paps,

That her hart hearing may relent and yeeld.

Lor. Breake of, my Lord: see, where she makes approch.

Enter Bellimperia.

Alc. Then fall into your former vaine of termes.   40

Lor. Welcome, my Lord;

Welcome, braue Don *Andrea*, Spaines best of sperit.

What newes from Portugale? tribute or war?

But see, my Sister *Bellimperia* comes:

I will defer it till some other time,   45

For company hinders loues conference.

Exit Lorenzo.

Bel. Welcom, my lifes selfe forme, deere Don *Andrea*.

Alc. My words iterated giues thee as much:

Welcome, my selfe of selfe.

Bel. What newes, *Andrea*? treats it peace or war?   50

Alc. At first they cried all war, as men resolued

To loose both life and honor at one cast:

At which I thundered words all clad in profe

Which strooke amazement to their pauled speeche,

And tribute presently was yeelded vp.   55

---

24 Make *Reed and later eds.*: Makes *Q.*   27 *Alc. om. Q.* : *wrongly placed by Reed and later eds. before* 28   31 Within *end of* 30 *Q.*   40 vaines *Q.*   41-3 Welcome ... *Don* | *Andrea* ... newes | From ... war *Q.* 48 giues *Q* : giue *Reed and later eds.*

But, maddam *Bellimperia*, leaue we this,
And talke of former suites and quests of loue.

          They whisper. Enter Lazarotto.

Laz. Tis all about the Court *Andreas* come :
    Would I might greete him ; and I wonder much
    My Lord *Lorenzo* is so slack in murder   60
    Not to afford me notice all this while.
    Gold, I am true ;
    I had my hier, and thou shalt haue thy due.
    Wast possible to misse him so ? soft, soft,
    This gallery leads to *Bellimperias* lodging ;   65
    There he is, sure, or wil be, sure; Ile stay :
    The euening to begins to slubber day ;
    Sweet, oportunefull season ; heere ile leane
    Like a court hound that liks fat trenchers cleane.
Bel. But has the King pertooke your embassy ?   70
Alc. That till tomorrow shall be now deferd.
Bel. Nay, then you loue me not :
    Let that be first dispatcht ;
    Till when receiue this token.

          She kisses him. Exit Bellimperia.

Alc. I to the King with this vnfaithfull hart ?   75
    It must not be ; I play to falce a part.
Laz. Vp, *Lazarotto* ; yonder comes thy prize :
    Now liues *Andrea*, now *Andrea* dies.

          Lazarotto *kils him.*

Alc. That villaine *Lazarotto* has kild me
    In stead of *Andrea*.   80

        Enter Andrea, *and* Rogero, *and other⟨s⟩*.

Rog. Welcome home, Lord embassador.
Alc. Oh, oh, oh.
And. Whose grone was that ? What frightfull villaines this,
    His sword vnshethed ? Whom hast thou murdred, slaue ?
Laz. Why, Don, Don *Andrea*.   85
And. No, conterfeiting villaine.
    He ses, my Lord, that he hath murdered me.
Laz. I, Don *Andrea*, or else Don the deuill.

    62–3 Gold . . . hier | And . . . due *Q.*   S.D. *after l.* 73 *Q.*   86 con-
terfelting *Q.*

And. Lay hands on him; ⟨and⟩ some
    Reare vp the bleeding body to the light.   90
Rog. My Lord, I think tis you; were you not heere,
    A man might sweare twere you.
And. His garments, ha, like mine; his face made like.
    An omynous horror all my vaines doth strike.
    Sure, this pretends my death; this misery   95
    Aymes at some fatall pointed tragedy.
            Enter Ieronimo *and* Horatio.
Ier. Son *Horatio,* see *Andrea* slaine.
Hor. Andrea slaine? then, weapon, clyng my brest.
And. Liue, truest friend, for euer loued and blest.
Hor. Liues Don *Andrea*?
And.   I; but slaine in thought   100
    To see so strang a likenes forged and wrought.
    Lords, cannot you yet discry
    Who is the owner of this red, melting body?
Rog. My Lord,
    It is *Alcario,* Duke *Medinas* son;   105
    I know him by this mould vpon his brest.
Laz.. Alcario slaine? hast thou beguild me, sword?
    Arme, hast thou slaine thy bountifull, kind lord?
    Why then rot off, and drop vpon the ground,
    Strew all the galleries with gobbits round.   110
            Enter Lorenzo.
Lor. Who names *Alcario* slaine? it is *Alcario.*
    O cursed deed:
    Couldst thou not see, but make the wrong man bleed?
Laz. S foot, twas yur fault, my lord; you brought noe word.
Lor. Peace; no words; ile get thy pardon.   115
    Why, mum then.
            Enter Bellimperia.
Bel. Who names *Andrea* slaine? O, tis *Andrea*:
    O, I swound, I die.
Lor. Looke to my Sister, *Bellimperia.*
And. Raise vp my deere loue, *Bellimperia.*   120

---

89 on] one *Q.*   and *add. ed.*   89–90 Lay ... bleeding | Body ... light
Q.   95 pretends *Q.*: portends *Reed and later eds.*   104–5 My ... son
one line Q.   106 mould] 'mole *Reed and later eds.*   112–3 O ... see |
But ... bleed *Q.*   118 swound *ed.* : sound *Q.* : swoon *Reed, Collier, Hazlitt*

O, be of comfort, sweet, call in thy sperits;
Andrea liues: O let not death beguile thee.
Bel. Are you *Andrea*?
And.   Doe not forget
That was *Alcario*, my shapes counterfet.
Lor. Why speaks not this accursed, damned villaine?   125
Laz. O, good words, my Lords, for those are courtiers vailes.
The King must heare; why should I make two tailes,
For to be found in two? before the King
· I will resolue you all this strange, strang thing:
I hot, yet mist; twas I mistooke my part.   130
Hor. I, villiane, for thou aym⟨ed⟩st at this true hart.
Ier. Horatio, twas well, as fortune stands,
This letter came not to *Andreas* hands.
Hor. Twas happines indeed.
Bel. Was it not you, *Andrea*, questioned me?   135
Bout loue?
And.   No, *Bellimperia*;
Belike twas false *Andrea*, for the first
Obiect mine eies met was that most accurst;
Which, I much feare me, by all signes pretends
Most doubtfull wars and dangerous pointed ends   140
To light vpon my bloud.
Bel. Angels of heauen forefend it.
And. Some take vp the bodie; others take charg
Of that accursed villaine.
Lor. My Lord, leaue that to me; ile looke to him.   145
Ier. Mark, mark, *Horatio*: a villaine guard a villaine.
And. The King may thinke my newes is a bad guest,
When the first obiect is a bleeding brest.

                                        Exeunt omnes.

⟨SCENE V.⟩

Enter King *of Spaine*, Castile, Medina, Rogero, *and others; a dead
                        martch within.*
King. My Lords,
What heauy sounds are these, neerer, and neerer?

123-4 Are . . . *Andrea* | Doe . . . *Alcario* | My . . . counterfet *Q.*   127-30
The . . . make | Two . . . two | Before . . . all | This . . . mist | Twas . . . part
Q.   135-8 Was . . . loue | No . . . *Andrea* | For . . . met | Was . . . accurst
Q.   139 which] witch *Q.*   pretend *Q.*   1-4 My . . . these |
Neerer . . . runner | Of . . . Spaines | Ineuitable ill *Q.*

Ha, *Andrea*, the foore runner of these newes?
Nay, then I feare Spaines ineuitable ill.
Ha, *Andrea*, speake; what newes from Portugale?   5
What, is tribute paid? ⟨ist⟩ peace or wars?
And. Wars, my dread leedge.
King.   Why then, that bleeding obiect
Doth presage what shall hereafter follow:
Whats he that lies there slaine, or hurt, or both?
Speake.   10
And. My leedge, *Alcario*, Duke *Medinas* son;
And by that slaue this purple act was done.
Med. Who names *Alcario* slaine? aie me, tis he:
Art thou that villaine?
Laz.   How didst know my name?
I see an excellent villaine hath his fame   15
As well as a great courtier.
Med. Speake, villain: wherefore didst thou this accursed deed?
Laz. Because I was an asse, a villainus asse;
For had I hot it right,
Andrea had line there, he walkt vpright;   20
This ominus mistake, this damned error,
Breeds in my soule an euerlasting terror.
King. Say, slaue, how came this accursed euill?
Laz. Faith, by my selfe, my short sword, and the deuill.
To tell you all without a tedious toong,   25
Ile cut them downe, my words shall not be hong.
That haples, bleeding Lord *Alcario*,
Which this hand slew, pox ont, was a huge dotar
On *Bellimperias* beautye, who replide
In scorne, and his hot suite denide;   30
For her affections were all firmly planted
In Don *Andreas* bosome; yet vnwise
He still pursued it with blind louers eies.
Then hired he me with gold—O fate, thou elfe—
To kill *Andrea*, which hire kild himselfe;   35
For not content to stay the time of murder,

---

6 ist *add. ed.*   9 or both *beg. of* 10 *Q.*   19–22 For . . . there | He
. . . mistake | This . . . soule | An . . . terror *Q.*   26 be hong *ed.*: hang
Q. : hang long *Reed, Collier, Hazlitt. See Note*   30 in scorne *end of* 29 *Q.*
35 hire] here *Reed and later eds. wrongly*

He tooke *Andreas* shape vnknowne to me,
And in all parts disguised, as there you see,
Intending, as it seemed, by that sly shift,
To steale away her troth : short tale to tell,   40
I tooke him for *Andrea*, downe he fell.
King. O impious deede,
    To make the heire of honor melt and bleede.
    Beare him away to execution.
Laz. Nay, Lord *Lorenzo*, whers the pardon?   45
    S foot, ile peach else.
Lor. Peace, *Lazarotto*, ile get it of the King.
Laz. Doot quickly then, or ile spred villainy.
Lor. My Lord, he is the most notorious rogue
    That euer·breathd.   *In his eare.*   50
King. Away with him.
Lor. Your highnes may doe well to barre his speech;
    Tis able to infect a vertuous eare.
King. Away with him, I will not heare him speake.
Laz. My Lord *Lorenzo* is a—   55
            They stop his mouth and beare him in.
Ier. Is not this a monstrous courtier?
Hor. He is the court tode, father.
King. Trybute denide vs, ha?
And. It is, my leedge, and that with no meane words :
    He will redeeme his honor lost with swordes.   60
King. So daring, ha, so Peremptory?·
    Can you remember the words he spake?
And. Word for word, my gratious soueraine,
    And these they were :—' Thus much returne to Spaine :
    Say that our setled Iudgment hath aduised vs   65
    What tribute is, how poore that Monarch shewes
    Who for his throne a yearely pension owes ;
    And what our predecesors lost to Spaine
    We haue fresh spirites that can renew it againe.'
King. Ha, soe peremptory, daring, stout?   70
And. Then, my leedge,
    According ⟨to⟩ your gratious, dread Comand,

42–4 O . . . honor | Melt . . . execution *Q.*   71–2 *one line Q.*   72 to
add. Reed

I bad defiance with a vengfull hand.

King. He intertained it?

And. I, and returned it with menasing browes: 75
 Prince *Baltheser,* his son,
 Grew Violent, and wished the fight begune.

Enter Lorenzo.

Lor. So, so, I haue sent my slaue to hell:
 Tho he blab there, the diueles will not tell.

A Tucket within.

King. How now, what means this trumpets sound?   80

Enter a Messenger.

Mess. My leedge, the Portugalles
 Are vp in armes, glittering in steel.

King. Wheres our lord generall, *Lorenzo,* stout *Andrea,*
 With whome I rancke spritely *Horatio?*
 What, for shame, shall the Portugalles   85
 Trample the fields before you?

Gen.   No, my leedge,
 Thers time enough to let out bloud enough,
 Tribute shall flow
 Out of their bowels, and be tendered so.

King. Farwell, braue Lords; my wishes are bequeathd;   90
 A nobler ranke of sperits neuer breathd.

Exeunt King and Nobles.

Ier. O, my sweet boy, heauen shield thee still from care;
 O, be as fortunate as thou art faire.

Hor. And heauen blesse you, my father, in this fight,
 That I may see your Gray head crownd in white.   95

Exeunt omnes.

⟨SCENE VI.⟩

Enter Andrea, and Bellimperia.

Bel. You came but now, ⟨and⟩ must you part agen?
 You told me that your sperit should put on peace;
 But see, war followes war.

And.   Nay, sweet loue, cease,

S.D. *Enter a messenger, after* 81 *Q.*   81 *Mess. prefixed to* 82 *Q.*
86-8 Trample . . . you | No . . . enough | To . . flow *Q.* 93 thou] thee *Q.*
1 and *add. Hazlitt* 2-3 You . . . sperit | Should . . . war | Nay . . . cease *Q.*

Y 2

To be denide our honor, why, twere base
To breath and liue; and wars in such a case   5
Is euen as necessary as our bloud.
Swordes are in season then when rightes withstood.
Deny vs tribute that so many yeeres
We haue in peace tould out? why it would raise
Spleene in the host of Angels: twere enough   10
To make ⟨the⟩ tranquile saints of angry stuffe.
Bel. You haue ore wrought the chiding of my brest;
And by that argument you firmly proue
Honor to sore aboue the pitch of loue.
Lend me thy louing and thy warlicke arme,   15
On which I knit this softe and silken charme
Tyed with an amorous knot: O, may it proue
Inchaunted armour being charmed by loue;
That when it mounts vp to thy warlick crest,
It may put by the sword, and so be blest.   20
And. O what deuinity proceeds from loue.
What happier fortune, then, my selfe can moue?
Harke, the drum beckens me; sweet deere, farwell.
This scarfe shall be my charme gainst foes and hell.
Bel. O, let me kisse thee first.
And.   The drum agen.   25
Bel. Hath that more power then I?
And.   Doot quickly then:
Farwell.
                                        Exit Andrea.
Bel.   Farwell.   O cruell part;
Andreas bosome bears away my hart.
                                        Exit Bellimperia.

⟨ACT III.
SCENE I.⟩

Enter Balthezer, Alexandro, Vollupo, Don Pedro, *with soldiers, drum
and coullers.*

Bal. Come, valliant sperits, you Peeres of Portugale,
That owe your liues, your faiths, and seruices,
To seet you free from base captiuity:

---

5 wars] war *Reed and later eds.*   9-10 We ... out | Why ... host | Of
... enough *Q.*   11 the *add. ed.*: our *Reed, Collier, Hazlitt*   22 then *Q.* :
than *Hazlitt*

O, let our fathers scandall nere be seene
As a base blush vpon your free borne cheeks;   5
Let all the tribute that proud Spaine receaud
Of all those captiue Portugales deceased
Turne into chafe, and choke their insolence.
Methinks no moyetie, not one little thought
Of them whose seruile acts liue in their graues   10
But should raise spleens big as a cannon bullet
Within your bosomes: O, for honor,
Your countries reputation, your liues freedome,
Indeed your all that may be termed reueng,
Now let your blouds be liberall as the sea;   15
And all those wounds that you receiue of Spaine,
Let thers be equall to quit yours againe.
Speake, Portugales: are you resolued as I,
To liue like captiues, or as free borne die?

Voll. Prince *Balthezer*, as you say, so say we—   20
To die with honor, scorne captiuity.

Bal. Why, spoke⟨n⟩ like true Portugales indeed;
I am asured of your forwardnes.
Now, Spaine, sit firme; ile make thy towers shake,
And all that gold thou hadst from Portugale,   25
Which makes thy court melt in Luxuriousnes,
I vow to haue it treble at thy hands.
Hark, Portugales: I heare their Spanish drum.
March on, and meet them; this must be the day
That all they haue receaued they back must pay.   30

The Portugales martch about.

Enter Ieronimo, Andrea, Horatio, Lorenzo, Lord Generall, Rogero, and
attendants with drum and Coullers.

Ier. What, are you brauing vs before we come?
Weele be as shrill as you: strike a larum, drum.

They sound a flourish a both sides.

Bal. Thou ynch of Spaine;
Thou man, from thy hose downe ward, scarse so much;
Thou very little longer then thy beard;   35
Speake not such big words;
Thaile throw thee downe, little *Ieronimo*;

---

7 all those] those all *Q.*   16 receiv'd *Hazlitt*   33-6 Thou . . . downe
ward | Scarse . . . then | Thy . . . words *Q.*

Words greater then thy selfe, it must not ⟨be⟩.

Ier. And, thou long thing of Portugale, why not?

Thou, that art full as tall   40

As an English gallows, vper beam and all;

Deuourer of apparell, thou huge swallower,

My hose will scarse make thee a standing coller.

What, haue I almost quited you?

And. Haue doone, impatiant Marshall.

Bal.   Spanish combatants,   45

What, do you set a little pygmire Marshall

To question with a Prince?

And.   No, Prince *Balthezer,*

I haue desired him peace, that we might war.

What, is the tribute mony tendred yet?

Bal. Trybute, ha, ha; what elles? wherefore meete our drums

But ⟨for⟩ to tender and receiue the somes   51

Of many a bleeding hart, which, eare Sunne fall,

Shall pay deere trybute, euen there liues and all.

And. Prince *Balthezer,* I know your valiant sperit,

I know your curage to be trid and good;   55

Yet, O prince, be not confirmed in blud.

Not that I tast of feare or cowerdyse,

But of religion, pietye, and loue

To many bosomes that yet firmely moue

Without disturbed spleenes. O, in thy hart,   60

Waigh the deere dropes of many a purple part

That must be acted on the feeldes greene stage,

Before the euening deawes quench the sunnes rage.

Let trybute be apeased and so stayed,

And let not wonted fealty be denayed   65

To our desart full kingdome.   Portugales,

Keepe your forfathers Othes; that vertue craues;

Let them not ly forsworne now in their graues,

To make their ashes periorde and uniust,

For heauen can be reuenged on their dust.   70

They swore to Spaine, both for themselues and you,

---

38 it must not be *Hazlitt*: it must not *Q.*: it must be *Reed, Collier*   45-9 Haue
... Marshall | Spanish ... little | Pygmire ... Prince | No ... peace | That
... tribute | Mony ... yet *Q.*   50 Drums *beg. of* 51 *Q.*   51 for *add. ed.*   56
Yet] And yet *Reed and later eds. unnecessarily*   63 sunnes] sonnes *Q.*
65 denayed *Reed*: denied *Q.*

And will posterity proue their sires vntrue?
This should not be mong men of vertuous sprit.
Pay trybute thou, and receiue peace and writ.
Bal. O vertuous coward.
Hor.   O ignoble sperit,   75
To terme him coward for his vertuous merit.
And. Coward? nay then, relentles rib of steele,
What vertue cannot, thou shalt make him feele.
Lor. Proud *Alexandro*, thou art mine.
Alex.   Agreed.
Rog. And thou, *Vullupo*, mine.
Voll.   Ile make thee bleed.   80
Hor. And thou, Don *Pedro*, mine.
Ped.   I care not whose,
Or thine, or thine, or all at once.
Bal. I bind thee, Don *Andrea*, by thy honer,
Thy valiansie, and all that thou holdst great,
To meete me single in the battailes heat,   85
Where ile set downe, in caractors on thy flesh,
Foure precious lines, spoke by our fathers mouth,
When first thou camst embassador; these they are:
' Tis said we shall not answere at next birth
Our Fathers faults in heauen, why then on earth?   90
Which proues and showes that what they lost by base Captiuity,
We may redeeme with wonted Valliansie.'
And to this crimson end our Coullers spred;
Our courages are new borne, our vallors bred.
Therefore, *Andrea*, as thou tenderst fame,   95
Wars, reputation, and a Souldiers name,
Meete me.
And.   I will.
Bal.   Single me out.
And.   I shall.
Alex. Do you the like.
Lor.   And you all, and we.
And. Can we be foes, and all so well agreed?
Bal. Why, man, in war thers bleeding amity;   100

81–2 I . . . once *Q.*   84 thy valiansie *end of* 83 *Q.*   86 on] upon *Q.*
91 Which . . . what | They . . . captiuity *Q.*   94 courage *Q.*

And he this day giues me the deepest wound,
Ile call him brother.
And.   Then, prince, call me so ;
To gaine that name, ile giue the deepest blowe.
Ier. Nay, then, if brother-hood by strokes come dewe,
I hope, boy, thou wilt gaine a brother too.   105
Hor. Father, I doubt it not.
And.   Lord General,
Breath like your name, a Generall defiance
Gainst Portugale.
Gen.   Defiance to the Portugales.
Bal. The like breath our Lord General gainst the Spaniards.
Gen. Defiance to the Spaniards.
And.   Now cease words ;   110
I long to heare the musick of clashed swords.
Bal. Why, thou shalt heare it presently.

                    They offer to fight.
And.   Quickly then.
Bal. Why now.
Gen.   O stay, my Lords,
This will but breede a muteny in the campe.
Bal. I am all fire, *Andrea.*
And.   Art thou ? good :   115
Why, then, ile quench thee, prince, with thy own bloud.

                                        Exit Balthezer.
Bal. Adew.
And.   Adew.
Bal.   Lets meete.
And.   Tis meete we did.

                                        Exeunt Portugales.
Lor. Alexandro.
Alex. Lorenzo.
Rog. Vollupo.   120
Voll. Rogero.
Hor. Don *Pedro.*
Ped. Horatio.
Ier. I, I, Don *Pedro*, my boy shall meete thee.
Come, valliant sperits of Spaine,   125

---

102 Then *emend. Reed* : the Q.   106 I *om. Reed, Collier, Hazlitt*   106-8
Father . . . not | Lord . . . name | A . . . portugale | Defiance . . . Portugales Q.

Valliant *Andrea*, fortunate *Lorenzo*,
Worthy *Rogero*, sprightly *Horatio*—
O let me dwell a little on that name,—
Be all as fortunate as heauens blest host,
But blame me not, Ide haue *Horatio* most.   130
Ride ⟨home⟩ all Conquerours, when the fight is done,
Especially ride thee home so, my son.
So now kisse and imbrace : come, come,
I am wars tuter ; strike a larum, drum.

Exeunt omnes.

⟨SCENE II.⟩

After a long alarum, the Portugales *and* Spaniards *meete. The
Portugales are put to the worst.*

Enter Ieronimo *solus.*

Ier. O valiant boy ; stroake with a Giants arme
His sword so fals vpon the Portugales,
As he would slise them out like Orenges,
And squeese their blouds out. O aboundant ioy,
Neuer had father a more happier boy.   5

Exit Ieronimo.

Enter Balthezer *and a* Souldier.

Bal. Can you not finde ⟨me⟩ Don *Andrea* forth ?
O for a voise shriller then all the trumpets,
To pierce Andreas ears throgh the hot army.
Go, search agen ; bring him, or neare returne.

Exit souldier.

Valliant *Andrea*, by thy worthy bloud,   10
Thy honored faith, which thow pawnedst to mine,
By all that thou holdst deere vpon this earth,
Sweat now to find me in the hight of bloud.
Now death doth heap his goods vp all at once,
And crams his store house to the top with bloud ;   15
Might I now and *Andrea* in one fight

126–8 Valliant . . . *Rogero* | Sprightly . . . name *Q.*   131 home *add. ed.*
1 *Reed and later eds.* put (;) *after* arme, *thus wrongly making* stroake . . . arme
qualify boy, *instead of* sword   3 As *Hazlitt* : as if *Q.*   6 me *add. ed.*
8 pierce *emend. Reed* : prince *Q.*   11 pawnst *Q.*   14 his] hir *Q.*

Make vp thy wardroope richer by a Knight.
Bal. Whose that? *Andrea?*

Enter Rogero.

Rog. Ha, *Vullupo?*
Bal. No; but a better.   20
Rog. Pox ont.
Bal. Pies ont,
  What luck is this: but, Sir, you part not so;
  What ere you be, ile haue a bout with you.
Rog. Content: this is ⟨a⟩ ioy mixed with spight,   25
  To misse a Lord, and meete a prince in fight.
Bal. Come, meete me, Sir.
Rog. Iust halfe way; ile meete it with my sword.

They fight. Balthezer *beats in* Rogero.

Enter Andrea *with a* Captaine.

And. Where might I find this vallorous *Balthezer*,
  This fierce, couragious Prince, a noble worthy,   30
  Made of the ribs of Mars and fortitude?
  He promissed to meete faire, and single me
  Out of the mistie battaile. Did you search
  The left wing for him? speake:
Cap.   We did, my Lord.
And. And could he not be found.
Cap.   Not in that wing, my Lord.
And. Why, this would vex   36
  The resolution of a suffering spleene.
  Prince *Balthezer*, Portugals valliant heire,
  The glory of our foe, the hart of courage,
  The very soule of true nobility.   40
  I call thee by thy right name, answere me.
  Go, Captaine, passe the leaft wing squadron; hie.
  Mingle your selfe againe amidst the army;
  Pray sweat to find him out.

Exit Captaine.

This place ile keepe:
Now wounds are wide, and bloud is very deepe: 45

---

18 Whose that? *Andrea? om. Reed and later eds.*   22–4 Pies . . . Sir |
You . . . haue | A bout . . you *Q.*   25 a *add. ed.*   36–8 Why . . .
resolution | of . . . *Balthezer* | Portugals . . . heire *Q.*

Tis now about the heauy dread of battaile ;
Souldiers drop doune as thick as if death mowed them ;
As sithmen trim the long haird Ruffian fields,
So fast they fall, so fast to fate life yeelds.

Enter Balthezer.

Bal. I haue sweat much, yet cannot find him.—*Andrea.*　50
And. Prince *Balthezer* :
　O lucky minute.
Bal.　　　　　　　O long wished for houre.
　Are you remembred, Don, of a daring message,
　And a proud attempt ?
　You braued me, Don, within my Fathers court.　　55
And. I think I did.
Bal.　　　　　　　This sword shall lash you for 't.
And. Alas ;
　War knows I am to proud a scholler grown,
　Now to be lashed with steele ; had I not knowne
　My strength and courage, it had bin easie then　　60
　To haue me borne vpon the backs of men.
　But now (I am sorry, Prince) you come to late ;
　That were proude steele, yfaith, that should do that.
Bal. I can hold no longer :
　Come, come, lets see which of our strengths is stronger.　65
And. Mine, for a wager.
Bal.　　　　　　　Thine ? what wager, say ?
And. I hold three wounds to one.
Bal.　　　　　　　　Content : a lay ;
　But you shall keepe stakes then.
And.　　　　　　　　Nay, ile trust you,
　For your a prince ; I know youle pay your dew.
Bal. Ile pay it you soundly.
And.　　　　　　　　Prince, you might haue paid　70
　Tribute as well ; then battailes had bin staid.
Bal. Heers tribute for you.
And.　　　　　　　Ile receaue it of you,

---

46 dread *Q. perhaps wrongly* : tread *Hazlitt. See Note*　　50 yet] and *Reed
and later eds*.　　51–8 Prince . . . minute | O . . . houre | Are . . . message |
And . . . Don | Within . . . court | I . . . did | This . . . for it | Alas . . . growne *Q.*
63 were] weare *Q.*　　67 a lay] I lay *Reed and later eds*.　　67–8 I . . .
one | Content . . . then | Nay . . . you *Q.*

And giue you acquittance with a wound or two.

They fight. Balthezer hath Andrea downe.

Enter Ieronimo and Horatio. Horatio beats away Balthezer.

And. Thou art a wondrous friend, a happy sperit ;
 I owe thee now my life. Couldst thou inherit   75
 Within my bosome, all I haue is thine ;
 For by this act I hold thy arm deuine.
Hor. Are you not wounded ? let me search and see.
And. No, my deere selfe, for I was blest by thee.
 Else his vnpitying sword had cleft my hart,   80
 Had not Horatio plaid some Angels part.
 Come, happy mortall, let me ranke by thee,
 Then I am sure no star will threaten me.
Hor. Lets to the battaile once more ; we may meete
 This haughtie prince, and wound him at our feete. 85

Exeunt omnes.

Enter Rogero and Alexandro in their shirts, with Pollaxes.

Rog. Art thou true valliant ? hast thou no cote of proofe
 Girt to thy loines ? Art thou true loyall ?
Alex.   Why looke :
Witnes the naked truth vpon my breast.
Come lets meete, lets meete,
And break our haughty sculs downe to our feete. 90

They fight. Alexandro beats in Rogero.

Enter Lorenzo and Don Pedro at one dore, and Alexandro and
Rogero at another dore. Lorenzo kils Don Pedro, and Alexandro kils
Rogero. Enter at one doore Andrea, at another doore Balthezer.

And. O me, ill stead, valliant Rogero slaine.
Bal. O my sad fates, Don Pedro weltring in his gore.
 O could I meete Andrea, now my blouds
 A tiptoe, this hand and sword should melt him :
 Valliant Don Pedro.   95
And. Worthy Rogero, sure twas multitudes
 That made thee stoope to death ; one Portugale
 Could neare orewhelme thee in such crimson streames :

---

80 vnpiting Q. 86–90 Art . . . no | Cote . . . loines | Art . . . loyall |
Why . . . truth | Vpon . . . meete | Lets . . . sculs | Downe . . . feete Q. 94
A tiptoe end of 93 Q. 97–100 That . . . death | One . . . thee | In . . .
streames | And . . . it | Balthezer . . . Balthezer | Andrea . . . now Q.

And no meane bloud shall quit it.   *Balthezer,*
Prince *Balthezer.*

Bal.   *Andrea,* we meete in bloud now.   100
And. I, in valliant bloud of Don *Rogeroes* sheding,
And each drop worth a thousand Portugales.
Bal. Ile top thy head for that ambitious word.
And. You cannot, prince : see, a reuengfull sword
Waues ore my head.
Bal.   Another ouer mine :   105
Let them both meete in crimson tinctures shine.

They fight, and Andrea *hath* Balthezer *downe.   Enter* Portugales
and releiue Balthezer *and kil* Andrea.

And. O, I am slaine ; helpe me, *Horatio.*
My foes are base, and slay me cowardly ;
Farewell deere, dearest *Bellimperia.*
Yet heerein ioy is mingled with sad death :   110
I keepe her fauer longer then my breath.

He dies.

Sound Alarum, Andrea *slain, and Prince* Balthezer *vanting on him.*
Enter Ieronimo, Horatio *and* Lord Generall.

Hor. My other soule, my bosome, my harts friend,
O my *Andrea* slaine.   Ile haue the price
Of him in princely bloud, Prince *Balthezer.*
My sword shall strike true straines,   115
And fetch *Andreas* ransome fourth thy vaines.
Lord Generall, driue them hence while I make war.
Bal. Hath war made thee so impudent and young ?
My sword shall giue correction to thy toong.
Ier. Correct thy rascals, Prince ; thou correct him ?   120
Lug with him, boy ; honors in bloud best swim.

They fight and breath afresh.

Bal. So young and vallerus ; this arme neare met
So strong a courage of so greene a set.
Hor. If thou beest valliant, cease these idle words,
And let reuenge hang on our glittering swords,   125
With this proud prince, the haughty *Balthezer.*

---

102 worth *ed.*: is worth *Q.*   110 death] breath *Reed and later eds.*   113 O
my] My O *Q.*   Ile *Q.*: I *Reed, wrongly : hence* I('ll) *Hazlitt*   123 of]
in *Reed and later eds.*

Horatio *has Prince* Balthezer *downe ; then enter* Lorenzo *and seizes his weapon.*

Hor. Hand off, *Lorenzo* ; touch not my prisoner.
Lor. Hees my prisoner ; I seizd his weapons first.
Hor. O base renowne,
   Tis easie to seize those were first laid downe.   130
Lor. My lance first threw him from his warlicke steede.
Ier. Thy Lance, *Lorenzo*? now, by my beard, you lie.
Hor. Well, my Lord,
   To you a while I tender my whole prisoner.
Lor. Horatio,   135
   You tender me part of mine own, you kno.
Hor. Well, peace ; with my bloud dispence,
   Vntill my leedge shall end the difference.
Ier. Lorenzo, thou doost boast of base renowne ;
   Why, I could whip al these, were there hose downe.   140
Hor. Speake, prince, to whether doost thou yeeld?
Bal. The vanquisht yeilds to both, to you ⟨the⟩ first.
Hor. O abiect prince, what, doost thou yeild to two?
Ier. Content thee, boy ; thou shalt sustaine no wrong.
   Ile to the King before, and let him know   145
   The sum of victory, and his ouerthrow.

                                              Exit Ieronimo.

Lor. Andrea slaine, thanks to the stars aboue.
   Ile choose my Sister out her second loue.

                                  Exeunt Lorenzo *and* Balthezer.

Hor. Come, noble rib of honor, valliant carcasse,
   I loued thee so entirely, when thou breathedst,   150
   That I could die, wert but to bleed with thee,
   And wish me wounds, euen for society.
   Heauen and this arme once saued thee from thy foe,
   When his all wrathfull sword did basely point
   At the rich circle of thy labouring hart,   155
   Thou groueling vnder indignation
   Of sword and ruth. O then stept heauen and I
   Betweene the stroke, but now alack must die :

---

127 off] of *Q.*   130 were first *ed.* : were forst *Q.*: were forced *Reed, whence Hazlitt's conjecture* whom force   129–30 O . . . those | Were . . . downe *Q.*   133–6 Well . . . my | Whole prisoner | *Horatio* . . . kno *Q.*   142 the *add. Hazlitt*   150 breathest *Q.*

Since so the powers aboue haue writ it downe
In marble leaues that death is mortall crowne.   160
Come then, my friend, in purple I will beare
Thee to my priuate tent, and then prepare
For honord Funerall for thy melting corse.

He takes his scarfe and ties it about his arme.

This scarfe ile weare in memorie of our soules,
And of our muteall loues; heere, heere, ile wind it,   165
And full as often as I thinke one thee,
Ile kisse this little ensigne, this soft banner,
Smeard with foes bloud, all for the maisters honer.
Alas, I pitty *Bellimperias* eies;
Iust at this instant her hart sincks and dies.   170

Exit Horatio *carying* Andrea *on his back.   Enter* Ieronimo *solus.*

Ier. My boy ads treble comfort to my age;
His share is greatest in this victory.
The Portugales are slaine and put to flight,
By Spaniards force, most by *Horatioes* might.
Ile to the Spanish tents to see my sonne,   175
Giue him my blessing, and then all is done.

⟨SCENE III.⟩

Enter two, dragging of ensignes; then the funerall of Andrea: *next*
    Horatio, *and* Lorenzo, *leading prince* Balthezer *captiue; then the*
    Lord General *with others mourning.   A great cry within* ' Caron,
    a boat, a boat.'   Then enter Charon *and the ghoast of* Andrea, ⟨*and*
    Reuenge.⟩

Hor. O, my Lords,
    See, Don *Andreas* ghoast salutes me, see, embraces me.
Lor. It is your loue that shapes this apprehention.
Hor. Do you not see him plainly, Lords?
    Now he would kisse my cheeke. O my pale friende,   5
    Wert thou anything but a ghoast, I could loue thee.
    See, he points at his owne hearse—mark, all—
    As if he did reioyce at funerall.
And. Reueng, giue my toong freedom to paint her part,
    To thank *Horatio*, and commend his hart.   10

---

163 *first* For] An *Hazlitt*   course *Q.*   S.D. *and* Reuenge *add. ed.*
9 my *om. Hazlitt*

Reuenge. No, youle blab secrets then.

And. By *Charons* boat, I will not.

Reuenge. Nay, you shall not : therefore passe ;
Secrets in hell are lockt with doores of brasse :
Vse action, if you will, but not in voice ;   15
Your friend conceiues in signes how you reioyce.

Hor. See, see, he points to haue vs goe forward on.
I prethee, rest ; it shall be done, sweet Don.
O now hees vanisht.

Sound trumpets, and a peale of ordenance.

And.   I am a happy Ghost ;
Reueng, my passage now cannot be crost.   20
Come, *Charon* ; come, hels Sculler, waft me ore
Yon sable streams, which looke like moulten pitche ;
My Funerall rights are made, my herse hung rich.

Exeunt Ghost and Reueng. A great noise within.

Within. *Charon*, a bote ; *Charon*, *Charon*.

Charon. Who cals so loud on *Charon* ?   25
Indeed tis such a time, the truth to tell,
I neuer want a fare to passe to hell.

Exeunt omnes.

⟨SCENE IV.⟩

Sound a florish. *Enter marching* Horatio *and* Lorenzo, *leading prince* Balthezer ; *Lord Generall,* Phillippo, *and* Cassimero, *with followers.*

Hor. These honord rights and worthy duties spent
Vpon the Funerall of *Andreas* dust,
Those once his valliant ashes— march we now
Homeward with victory to crowne Spaines brow.

Gen. The day is ours and ioy yeelds happy treasure ;   5
Set on to Spaine in most triumphant measure.

Exeunt omnes.

Enter Ieronimo *Solus.*

Ier. Foregod, I haue iust mist them : ha,
Soft, *Ieronimo* ; thou hast more friends

---

17 vs *Reed* : his Q.   goe *om. Hazlitt*   22 yon *ed.* : you Q. : your *Reed and later eds.*

To take thy leaue of. Looke well about thee,
Imbrace them, and take friendly leaue. My armes 10
Are of the shortest; let your loues peece them out.
Your welcome, all, as I am a Gentleman;
For my sons sake, greant me a man at least,
At least I am. So good night, kind gentles,
For I hope thers neuer a Iew among you all; 15
And so I leaue you.

Exit.

10–1 Imbrace... leaue | My ... shortest | Let ... out *Q*.

FINIS.

APPENDIX I

VERSES OF PRAYSE AND IOYE

WRITTEN VPON HER MAIESTIES PRESERVATION

WHEREVNTO IS ANNEXED TYCHBORNES LAMENTATION
WRITTEN IN THE TOWRE WITH HIS OWNE HAND
AND AN AVNSWERE TO THE SAME

LONDON
PRINTED BY IOHN WOLFE
1586

VERSES OF PRAISE AND IOY[1]

WRITTEN VPON HER MAIESTIE, AFTER THE APPREHENSION AND
EXECVTION OF BABINGTON, TYCHBORNE, SALISBVRIE,
AND THE REST

Mongst spyny cares sprong vp now at the last,
 sprowt higher then the hautiest of their heads:
That with thy Roselike, Royal peace (O Prince)
 all other princes thou must ouer-peere.
Thee and thy Realme opprest it happ'ly pleasd   5
 our highest God in safety to preserue.
For this, thy people publikely applaude,
 and euerywhere aboundeth godly loue.
Good fortune and an euerlasting fame
 attend on thee in all thine actions.   10
This makes thy friends, this makes thy foes admire,
 and daily hold thy name in reuerence.
Honour'd art, Princely behauiour, zeale to good,
 and, with thee rest, a Royall maiestie.

---

[1] On the question of Kyd's authorship of these Verses see *Introduction* § 1.

These foure faire giftes (O Prince, of right renound)   15
  thy Princely mind most Princely Enterteignes.
Liue, Soueraigne Ladie, Liue, Elizabeth,
  health of thy Countrey, helpe to all our harmes.
Seeld seen, thou Reign'st a maiden and a Queene:
  Long maist thou liue, and heauen be thy home.   20

TYCHBORNES ELEGIE

Written with his owne hand in the Tower before his execvtion

My prime of youth is but a frost of cares,
  my feast of ioy is but a dish of paine:
My crop of corne is but a field of tares,
  and al my good is but vaine hope of gaine.
The day is past, and yet I saw no sunne;   5
And now I liue, and now my life is done.

My tale was heard, and yet it was not told,
  my fruite is falne, and yet my leaues are greene:
My youth is spent, and yet I am not old,
  I saw the world, and yet I was not seene.   10
My thred is cut, and yet it is not spunne;
And now I liue, and now my life is done.

I sought my death, and founde it in my wombe,
  I lookt for life and saw it was a shade:
I trod the earth, and knew it was my tombe,   15
  and now I die, and now I was but made.
My glasse is full, and now my glasse is runne;
And now I liue, and now my life is done.

HENDECASYLLABON

T. K. in Cygneam Cantionem Chidiochi Tychborne

Thy prime of youth is frozen with thy faults,
  thy feast of ioy is finisht with thy fall:
Thy crop of corne is tares auailing naughts,
  thy good God knowes thy hope, thy hap and all.
Short were thy daies, and shadowed was thy sun,   5
T' obscure thy light vnluckelie begun.

Time trieth trueth, and trueth hath treason tript;
  thy faith bare fruit as thou hadst faithles beene:
Thy ill spent youth thine after yeares hath nipt;
  and God that saw thee hath preserude our Queene.   10
Her thred still holds, thine perisht though vnspun,
And she shall liue when traitors liues are done.

Thou soughtst thy death, and found it in desert,
  thou look'dst for life, yet lewdlie forc'd it fade:
Thou trodst the earth, and now on earth thou art,   15
  As men may wish thou neuer hadst beene made.
Thy glorie and thy glasse are timeles runne;
And this, O *Tychborne*, hath thy treason done.

IN NEFARIAM BABINGTONI CAETERORVMQVE
CONIVRATIQNEM HEXASTICON

Quid non Papa ruens spondet, modo iussa capessas?
  en, diadema tibi, sceptraque, pactus Hymen.
Dissimilem votis mercedem nacta, sed ausis
  et sceleri retulit turba nefanda parem.
Successere rogi regno, coruique coronae,   5
  pro sceptro laqueus, pro thalamo tumulus.

THE SAME IN ENGLISH

The Pope, to prop his minions state,
  doth golden proffers make:
Crowne, scepter, roiall marriage bed,
  to those his part that take.
The traytrous crew late reapt reward,   5
  not fitting their desire:
But, as their purpose bloody was,
  so shamefull was their hire.
For chaire of state, a stage of shame,
  and crows for crownes they haue: 10
Their scepter to a halter changde,
  their bed become their graue.

AD SERENISSIMAM REGINAM ELIZABETHAM,
APOSTROPHE

Regna, viue, vale, mundi, patriae, atque tuorum,
  splendida, sola, vigens, gloria, vita, salus.
In te speramus, per te spiramus ouantes:
  det spirare tibi saecula multa Deus.
Pro te dulce mori, nisi pro te viuere durum: 5
  at sine te mors est viuere, vita mori.

THE SAME IN ENGLISH

Raigne, liue, and blisfull dayes enioy,
  thou shining lampe of th' earth:

The only life of countries state,
  thy subiects health and mirth.
On thee we ground our hope, through thee   5
  we draw our breath with ioy: .
God graunt thee long amongst vs breathe,
  God shield thee from annoy.
To die for thee were sweete; to liue
  were wretched but for thee: 10
Without thee, death a second life,
  life double death should be.

APPENDIX II

THE SPANISH TRAGEDY[1]

Containing the lamentable Mvrders of Horatio and
Bellimperia with the pittifvl Death of
old Hieronimo

To the tune of Qveene Dido

You that haue lost your former ioyes,
And now in woe your liues doe leade,
Feeding on nought but dire annoyes,
Thinking your griefes all griefes exceede,
    Assure yourselues it is not so: 5
    Loe, here a sight of greater woe.

Hapless *Hieronimo* was my name,
On whom fond fortune smiled long:
And now her flattering smiles I blame;
Her flattering smiles hath done me wrong.   10
    Would I had dyed in tender yeares:
    Then had not beene this cause of teares.

I Marshall was in prime of yeares,
And wonne great honour in the fielde:
Vntill that age with siluered haires   15
My aged head had ouerspred. ·
    Then left I warre, and stayde at home,
    And gaue my honour to my sonne.

Horatio, my sweet onely childe,
Prickt forth by fames aspiring wings,   20
Did so behaue him in the fielde
That he Prince *Baltazer* Captiue brings;
    And with great honour did present
    Him to the King incontinent.

---

[1] Reprinted, with changes in punctuation, from the *Roxburghe Ballads*,
1. 364-5.

The Duke of *Castyles* Daughter then   25
Desir'd *Horatio* to relate
The death of her beloued friend,
Her loue *Andreas* woofull fate.
    But when she knew who had him slaine,
    She vow'd she would reuenge the same.   30

Then more to vexe Prince *Baltazer*,
Because he slewe her chiefest friend,
She chose my sonne for her chiefe flower,
Thereby meaning to worke reuenge.
    But marke what then did straight befall,   35
    To turne my sweete to bitter gall.

Lorenzo then, to finde the cause
Why that his sister was vnkinde,
At last he found, within a pause,
Howe he might sound her secret minde :   40
    Which for to bring well to effect,
    To fetch her man he doth direct.

Who being come into his sight,
He threatneth for to rid his life,
Except straightwayes he should recite   45
His sister's loue, the cause of strife :
    Compell'd therefore to vnfold his mind,
    Sayd with *Horatio* shee's combinde.

The Villaine then, for hope of gaine,
Did straight conuaye them to the place,   50
Where these too louers did remaine,
Ioying in sight of others face;
    And to their foes they did impart
    The place where they should ioy their heart.

Prince *Baltazer* with his compeeres   55
Enters my bower all in the night,
And there my sonne slayne they vpreare,
The more to worke my greater spight.
    But as I laye and toke repose,
    A voyce I hard, whereat I rose.   60

And finding then his senslesse form,
The murtherers I sought to finde,
But missing them I stood forlorne,
As one amased in his minde,
    And rent and puld my siluered haire,   65
    And curs'd and bann'd each thing was there.

And that I would reuenge the same,
I dipt a napkin in his blood,

Swearing to worke their woefull baine
That so had spoyl'd my chiefest good ;   70
 And that I would not it forget,
 It allwayes at my hart I kept.

THE SECOND PART

TO THE SAME TVNE

Then *Isabella*, my deare wyfe,
Finding her sonne bereau'd of breath,
And louing him dearer then life,
Her owne hand straight doth worke her death.
 And now their deaths doth meet in one,   5
 My griefes are come, my Ioyes are gone.

Then frantickly I ran about,
Filling the ayre with mournefull groanes,
Because I had not yet found out
The murtherers, to ease my mones.   10
 I rent and tore each thing I got,
 And sayd, and did, I knew not what.

Thus as I past the streets, hard by
The Duke of *Castiles* house, as then
A Letter there I did espy,   15
Which show'd *Horatios* wofull end:
 Which *Bellimperia* foorth had flung
 From prison where they kept her strong.

Then to the Court forthwith I went,
And of the King did Iustice craue ;   20
But by *Lorenzos* bad intent
I hindred was, which made me raue.
 Then, vexed more, I stamp'd and frown'd,
 And with my ponyard ript the ground.

But false *Lorenzo* put mee out,   25
And tolde the King then by and by
That frantickly I ran about,
And of my sonne did alwayes cry ;
 And say'd 't were good I should resigne
 My Marshallship, which grieu'd my mind.   30

The Duke of *Castyle*, hearing then
How I did grudge still at his sonne,
Did send for me to make vs friends,
To stay the rumour then begone.
 Whereto I straightway gaue consent,   35
 Although in heart I neuer meant.

Sweete *Bellimperia* comes to me,
Thinking my sonne I had forgot,
To see me with his foes agree,
The which I neuer meant, God wot :   40
    But when wee knew each others mind,
    To worke reuenge a meanes I find.

When Bloody *Baltazar* enters in,
Entreating me to show some sport
Vnto his Father and the King,   45
That to his nuptiall did resort.
    Which gladly I prepar'd to show,
    Because I knew twould worke their woe,

And from the Chronicles of *Spaine*
I did record *Erastus* life,   50
And how the *Turke* had him so slayne,
And straight reuenge wrought by his wife.
    Then for to act this Tragedy,
    I gaue their parts Immediatly.

Sweete *Bellimperia Baltazar* killes,   55
Because he slew her dearest friend,
And I *Lorenzos* blood did spill,
And eke his soule to hell did send.
    Then dyed my foes by dint of knife,
    But *Bellimperia* ends her life.   60

Then for to specifie my wronges,
With weeping eyes and mournefull hart,
I shew'd my sonne with bloody wounds,
And eke the murtherers did impart ;
    And sayd my sonne was as deare to me   65
    As thine, or thine, though Kinges you be.

But when they did behold this thing,
How I had slayne their onely sonnes,
The Duke, the Viceroy, and the King
Vppon me all they straight did run.   70
    To torture me they doe prepare,
    Vnlesse I shuld it straight declare.

But that I would not tell it then,
Euen with my teeth I bit my tongue,
And in despite did giue it them,   75
That me with torments sought to wrong :
    Thus when in age I sought to rest,
    Nothing but sorrowes me opprest.

They knowing well that I could write,
Vnto my hand a pen did reach,   80

Meaning thereby I shuld recite
The authors of this bloody fetch.
    Then fained I my pen was naught,
    And by strange signes a knife I sought.

But when to me they gaue the knife,   85
I kill'd the Duke then standing by,
And eke my selfe bereau'd of life,
For I to see my sonne did hye.
    The Kinges, that scorn'd my griefes before,
    With nought can they theire Ioyes restore.   90

Here haue you heard my Tragicke tale,
Which on *Horatios* death depends,
Whose death I could anew bewayle,
But that in it the murtherers ends.
    For murther God will bring to light,   95
    Though long it be hid from man's sight.

Printed at London for H. Gosson.

FINIS.

APPENDIX III

TRAGEDIA VON DEM GRIEGISCHEN KEYSER ZU CONSTANTINOPEL

EDITOR'S NOTE

THIS adaptation of *The Spanish Tragedie* by Jacob Ayrer of Nürnberg forms the eleventh play in his *Opus Theatricum*, 1618, published thirteen years after his death. The *Opus Theatricum* has been reprinted in five volumes in the *Bibliothek des Litterarischen Vereins*, in Stuttgart, 1865, under the editorship of Adelbert von Keller. In this issue the adaptation forms part of the second volume. It is also reprinted in Tieck's *Altdeutsches Theater*, vol. i.

In the present reprint I have made some slight changes in the stage-directions. I have placed the list of *Die Personen in das Spiel* before instead of after the play, and have similarly transferred the titles of each of the Acts to the beginning instead of the end. I have omitted the abbreviation *S.* or *v. S.* (i.e. *Sagt* or *vnd Sagt*) which is prefixed to every speech in the original; and to the speeches of Amurates and Malignus I have uniformly prefixed their names, for which Ayrer sometimes substitutes their titles.

TRAGEDIA, VON DEM GRIEGISCHEN KEYSER ZU CONSTANTINOPEL VNND SEINER TOCHTER PELIMPERIA MIT DEM GEHENGTEN HORATIO

Mit 18 Personen, hat 6 Actus.

DIE PERSONEN IN DAS SPIEL:

1. Amurates, *der König.*
2. Malignus, *der Hofmarschalt.*
3. Laurentzius, *dess Königs Sohn.*
4. Ernestus, *der Hauptman.*
5. Horatius, *dess Marchalts Sohn.*
6. Pelimperia, *dess Königs Tochter.*
7. Philomena, *die Hofjungfrau.*
8. Herr Balthasar, *der gefangen Fürst auss Portugall.*
9. Petrian, *der Mehrletrager.*
10. Famulus, *der Jung, so auff Herr Lorentz wart.*
11. Jahn, *der Narr oder Hencker.*
12. Gangolffus, *der Portugallisch Gesandt.*
13. Nicolaus, *dess Herr Balthasars Knecht.*
14. Horolt, } *zwen Wächter.*
15. Morolt, }
16. Primus, }
17. Secundus, } *drey Supplicanten.*
18. Tertius, }

ACTUS PRIMUS.

Kompt Jahn, *der Narr, weynt vnd schreyt laut:*

O, es wird war; o, es wird war!
O, es fehlt mir nit vmb ein Har.
Dann heynt, wie es sich hat zutragen,
Hat die Vhr eben viere gschlagen.
O secht drauff! was gelts? ich wils gwinnen: 5
Sie wird noch gar kommen von sinnen,
Wenn man jhr wird die Zeitung sagn,
Wie Andreas sey worn erschlagen.
Ja fürwar, es ist für jhn schad.
Kein solcher Kerls ist in der Statt.   10
Ey, ey! er reuht mich, auff mein Eyd,
Vnd ist mir für jhn hertzlich leyd.

Er greynt, geht hin vnd wider.   *Kompt* Pelimperia *mit* Philomena,
jrer Jungfrauen, sicht sich vmb.

Pel. Philomena, geht nicht dort der Jahn?
  Es wird jhm etwas ligen an,
  Dann sonst wird er nicht also weynen.
  Ich will jhn fragen, wie ers thu meinen ;   15
  Dann er greint gwis vergebens nit.

  Sie geht zu jhm.

  Hör, Jahn, sag mir (das ist mein bitt) !
  Was ist dir, das du weinst also ?

Jahn (ziecht sein Hut ab, knapt). Ich wust nit, das jhr ward alldo,
  Sunst hett ich etwan vielleicht gelacht.   21

  Er sicht auff die ander seiten.

  Ja, hört jhr, heint, da ich erwacht,
  Freylich ja, ich kans für wahr sagen,
  Er ist gester worden erschlagen.
  Dass ist ein böse klägliche sach.   25

Pel. Jahn, sag mirs ! nicht viel vmbstend mach !
  Was meinstu ? das ich es auch wiss !

Jahn (schlegt in die Händ). Ja, auff mein Eyd, es ist gewiss.
  Was gelts ? jhr werds noch selber sagen.

Pel. Was ists dann vnd wer ist erschlagen ?   30
  Sag mirs, das ich es kan verstehn !

Jahn. Im Krieg thuts nicht anderst zugehn.
  Wer nur den andern übermag,
  Macht, das der schwechste vnter lag.
  Also es auch da gangen ist.   35

Pel. Ey, ein rechter halbnarr du bist ;
  Wiltu mirs sagen, so sag her !

Jahn. Ja wol ! was ists denn aber mehr ?
  Ich sey gleich ein halbnarr oder nit,
  So hat er gnommen sein abschid.   40
  Der gut Herr Andres ist schon hin.

Pel. Von hertzen ich erschrocken bin.
  Wer ist hin ? thu mirs doch recht sagen !

Jahn. Eur Andres ist worn erschlagen,
  Dann es hat mir heint traumt davon.   45

Pel. (sinckt nider). Ach jetzt thu mir mein traum aussgahn.
  Ach weh des Jammers ! weh der not !
  Komm vnd erwürg mich, grimmer todt ! -

  Jahn *vnd* Philomena *erhalten sie vnd setzen sie nieder.*

Phil. Du stocknarr, weist sonst nichts zu sagen ?
  Thust den Leuten dein traum fürtragen,   50
  Alss seint sie war vnd müssen geschehen.

Jahn. Ey nun, was gelts ? jhr werds fein sehen.

  Er geht weg.

Phil. Gnedigss Fräulein, seit wolgemut!
 Der Fantast eben reden thut,
 Wie er die sach weiss vnd versteht,   55
 Vnd ich hett nicht glaubt, das jhr hett
 Auff des Narrn traum was gehalten.
Pel. Ach weh, das es sein Gott muss walten!
 Ich weiss des Narrn sinn gar wol.
 Er stecket des war sagens voll   60
 Vnd solchs nur als auss den geschichten.
 Darnach hab ich mich gwiss zurichten.
 Ach weh, weh, aller liebster mein!
 Soll ich dein schon beraubet sein,
 Wie dann heint eben selber mir   65
 In dem gesicht ist kommen für?
 So klag ichs Gott in seinem Reich.
Phil. Königlichs Fräulein, was kümmert jhr euch
 Von wegen eines traums gesicht,
 Auff die man doch sol glauben nicht?   70
 Dann sie gantz falsch vnd trüglich sein,
 Fallen eim im schlaf also ein
 Auss gschichten, den man bey dem tag
 Etwan zu gar hart dencket nach.
 Drumb seit getrost vnd kommt mit mir! 75
 Da will ich euch was lesen für.

   Sie gehen ab. Kompt Amurates, *der König, mit* Maligno, *dem*
         Marschalt, setzt sich.

Amur. Die zeitung gibt, es hab ein Schlacht
 Vnser Volck vor wenig tagen verbracht
 Vnd hab die Portugalischen gschlagen.
Mal. (neigt sich). Ja, man hat auch das wollen sagn, 80
 Dess Königs Son sey wordn gefangen.
Amur. Vns thut warhafftig sehr verlangen,
 Zu erwarten, wenn sie herkommen.
Mal. Herr König, ich hör pfeiffen vnd Drommen.
 Vnser Kriegsvolck das ziecht herein.   85
Amur. Irer zukunfft wir erfreut sein.
 Geht jhn entgagen! sagt dem Hauptman,
 Dass er sie auff den weiden plan
 Lass fürziehen, das wir sie sehen!
Mal. Gnedigster Herr, das sol geschehen!   90

      Er geht ab.

Amur. Der zeitung sind wir hoch erfreut,
 Dass wider kommen vnser Kriegsleut.
 Die wollen wir mit ehrn empfangen.
Mal. (geht mit dem Frauenzimmer ein). Grossmechtiger König, jetzt
 kommt gegangen

Der Feldt Hauptman mit seim gsind her;   95
Die tragen all jhr waffen vnd wehr.

Jetzt kompt Ernestus, *der Hauptman, geht vor, als denn* Lorentz, *dess Königs
Son, dann* Balthasar, *der gefangen Fürst von Portugall, als dann*
Horatius, Nicolaus, Famulus, Petrian *vnd so vil man jhr haben kan;
die gehen zu einer Thür ein. alle für den König, neigen sich vnd zu
der andern Thür wider hinauss.*

Amur. Herr Hauptman, kompt vnd zeigt vns an!
   Wer war, der hinder vnserm Son
   In solchen stattlichen Kleidern gieng?
Ern. Es ist der Jung Printz, den man fieng.   100
Amur. Wer war der, so nach jhm thet gahn?
Mal. Gnedigster Herr, das ward mein Son,
   Welcher hat den Printzen gfangen.
Amur. Sie seind vns zu geschwind abgangen.
   Drumb, Hauptman, last sie widerumben   105
   Wie zuvor auff den Platz herkommen!

*Der Hauptman geht geschwind ab, kompt mit dem Kriegsvolck wider, vnd
als der Printz zu jm kompt, steht er auff.*

Ern. Seit jhr der Printz auss Portugall?
Bal. Ich bins gewest vor dem einmal;
   Jetzt bin ich ein gefangener Mann.
Amur. Es sol euch niemand nichts böss than.   110
   Lorentz, sag, wer hat gfangen jhn?
Lor. Herr König, derselbig Mann ich bin,
   Der den Printzen thet erlangen.
Hor. Nein, Herr König, ich hab jhn gfangen;
   Derhalb hab den ruhm billich ich.   115
Mal. Der König wöll bedencken sich,
   Das meim Son nicht vnrecht geschech!
Amur. Wir wollen schon finden ein Weg.
   Der jung Printz soll vns zeygen an
   Was sie beyd bey der Schlacht gethan,   120
   Vnd welcher jhn gefangen hab.
Bal. Dem Horatio ich mich ergab.
   Der ist, der mich hat gfangen gnommen.
   Darnach ist jhr Lieb darzu kommen,
   Vnd mich gerissen von dem Pferdt,   125
   Mir auch gnommen mein scharpffes Schwert,
   Vnd ander Waffen die ich het.
Amur. Weil euch Horatius fangen thet,
   So gebürt jhm die Rantion;
   Aber dir Lorentz, vnserm Sohn,   130
   Gebürt das Pferdt, Harnisch vnd Wehr.
Hor. (neygt sich). Grossmächtiger König, dieser Ehr
   Bedanck ich mich all mein Lebtag,

Vnd wills verdienen, wo ich mag,
Vnd ferrners wagen Leib vnd Blut.   135

Amur. Mann soll dem, der das beste thut,
Im Krieg allzeit danckbar lohnen.
Balthasar, der Printz, soll bey dir wohnen,
Den halt, dass er nur hab kein klag,
Biss sich sein Vatter mit vns vertrag,   140
Vnd biss er zalt sein Rantzion !

Lor. Ja, Herr König, das will ich than ;
Gut gelegenheit er hie bey mir hat.

Bal. Ich danck euer Majestatt der Gnad,
Biss dass ichs wider kan beschulden.   145

Amur. Ihr müst euch eine weil gedulden,
Biss jhr ein wenig gwonen thut ;
So wird euch schon leichter eur muht.

> Der König *geht ab mit* Maligno *vnd* Horatio.

Lor. (*gibt* Bal. *die Händ*). Weil jhr bey mir seyt einlosirt,
Sich nun für anderst nicht gebürt,   150
Als dass wir treulich zusamm setzen,
Vns mit einander alls Leidts ergötzen,
Weil jhr auch seyt ein Königs Sohn.
Villeicht sichs noch zutragen kan,
Dass jhr bekompt die Schwester mein.   155

Bal. Ja wol ; warumb soll dass nit sein ?
Darzu bin ich in eurn Händen.
Gott helff es als zum besten wenden !

> Sie gehen mit einander ab. Kompt Horatius vnd mit jhm Pelimperia
> vnd Philomena.

Pel. Ach, mein Horati, küner Ritter,
Wie steck ich in Hertzenleydt so bitter !   160
Ich bitt, jhr wolt mir zeigen an
Wer doch das übel hat gethan,
Vnd mein lieben Andream erschlagen.

Hor. Ins vertrauen will ichs euch sagen :
Eur Bruder Lorentz das than hat.   165

Pel. Dess Straff jhn Gott mit vngenad !
Mein Bruder soll er nimmer sein,
Weil er mich bringt in Leid vnd pein.
Ach Andreas, du liebster Schatz,
Hat dich dann mein Bruder auss tratz   170
Vmbgebracht von meinet wegen,
So wöll der liebe Gott dein pflegen
Vnd mir auffs ehst helffen zu dir,
Weil du hie nicht kanst werden mir,
Dass ich doch dort mög bey dir sein !   175

Hor. Seyd getrost, gnedigs Fräuelein !

KYD : BOAS   A a

Bekümmert euch nit mit den dingen
Die man je nit kan widerbringen,
Weil es ist ohn euer schuld geschehen !
Gott wird euch wol wider versehen,   180
Beschern ein Gmahl eurs gleichen,
Ein Adelichen, schönen, reichen.
Das wünsch ich euch von grund meins hertzen.

Er gibt jhr die Händ, neigt sich vnd geht ab.

Pel. Ach weh des jammers, angst vnd schmertzen !
Jetzt denck ich an des Jahnnen traum,   185
Dem du wolst geben gar kein raum,
Vnd sprachst, es wer betrüglichs ding,
Dass man zu achten hett gering
Vnd dass er wer zuschlagen auss.
Kompts mir jetzt nicht als sambt zu hauss,   190
Dass ich mich lang besorget han ?

Phil. Königlichs Fräulein, wie soll man jhm than ?
Gott, der alle ding hat versehen,
Der hatt es gwolt ; drumb ist es gschehen.
Dem könn wir je nicht widerstreben,   195
Müssen vns seim willen ergeben,
Wöll wir anderst recht Christen sein.
Darumb schlagt auss klag, leid vnd pein !
Gott wirds nicht vngerochen lahn ;
Euch wol beschern ein andern Man,   200
Der euch so lieb wird sein als der.

Pel. Ja, es sind wol der Männer mehr,
So wol als etwan der Jungfrauen,
Die sich Person halb lassen schauen.
Aber da fallen stets hinderung ein.   205
Auch glaub ich nicht, das müglich sein
Das mir ein Mensch auff diser Erdn
So lieb als der vorig kan werdn.
Dess steh ich in gross not vnd klag.

Phil. Morgen kompt schon ein anderer tag,   210
Vber morgen ein andere zeit ;
Die bringen balt gross vnterscheid.
Dess Menschen hertz ist wandelbar.
Gnedigs Fräulein, über ein halbs Jar
Habt jhr ein andern mut vnd sin.   215

Pel. Meinstu, das ich gesinnet bin
Heut schwartz vnd morgen weiss zu reden ?
Ich weiss wol was mir ist von nöten,
Vnd was ich drinnen muss bedencken.
Aber meim Bruder wil ichs nit schencken,   220
Oder will mich selber erhencken.

Abgang.

ACTUS SECUNDUS.

Kompt Lorentz, *dess Königs Son, mit* Balthasar.

Lor. Herr Balthasar, wie gfellts allhie eur liebt?
  Mich dunckt das jhr hart seit betrübt.
  Geht euch was ab, so thut mirs sagen!
Bal. Ich hab hie nichts anderst zu klagen
  Als das ich muss gefangen sein,   5
  Vnd das mich der Herr Vatter mein
  Nicht ausslöst vnd bringt Rantion.
  Sonst ich gar nichtes klagen kan.
  Mir gefellts hie so wol als zu hauss.
Lor. Wolt jhr mit auff das Jäid hinauss,   10
  Oder ein weil zum ringlein rennen,
  Oder sehen schöns Feurwerck brennen,
  Vnd wie die Falckner mit Falcken beisen,
  Oder ein weil spatzirn reisen
  Zu dem Wiltgarten in dem holtz,   15
  Oder wolt schiesen mit dem poltz,
  Oder der Büchsen zu der Scheiben,
  Oder wolt sonst die zeit vertreiben
  Mit spiel durch Würffl oder Karten,
  Oder wollen in den Lustgarten   20
  Den Balm schlagen, Tantzen vnd springen,
  Hören Seitenspiel oder Singen,
  Oder was sonst die glegenheit geyt,
  Dardurch vergeht die lange zeit
  Die euch möcht in dem gmach beschwern?   25
Bal. (*seufftzt*). Ach Gott, wann ich was dörfft begern,
  So wehr mir all mein leyd vergangen;
  Wolt gern allhie bleiben gefangen.
  Ach, lieber Gott, ich darffs nit wagen.
Lor. Ey, thuts ohn allen scheuen sagen!   30
  Dann es bleibt wol bey mir verborgen.
          Er gibt jhm die Händ.
Bal. Ich wils sagen; doch thu ich sorgen,
  Ich werd bey euch ein fehlbitt than.
Lor. Sey was es wöll, sagts kecklich an!
  Dann ich euch gar gern helffen thu.   35
Bal. Ach Gott, die Lieb lest mir kein ruh,
  Die ich thu tragen zu eurer Schwester;
  Die peinigt mich je lenger vnd vester,
  Dass ich sorg ich wer trostloss sterben.
Lor. O die will ich euch wol erwerben.   40
          Er gibt jm die Händ.
  Schweigt nur still vnd gebt euch zu ruh!

Mein Schwester ich euch geben thu.

Sie gehn mit einander hin vnd wider, stehn je still, denn sagen sie etwas in die ohrn zusammen. Horatius *kompt, sicht die Königs Sön.*

Hor. Potz, ich seh die zwen Königs Sön
   Auff dem Sal hin vnd wider gehn;
   Es wird gewiss was heimlichs bedeuten.   45
   Ich will mich drehen auff die seiten,
   Dann sie sind mir gewiss nicht gut,
   Weils Balthasar verdriessen thut
   Dass ich jhn hab Rancionirt
   Vnd auss der Schlacht gfangen hergführt.   50
   Der Lorentz aber henckt das maul,
   Dass er nur die Rüstung vnd Gaul
   Auss dem Krieg hat zur Beud genommen,
   Vnd ich den grösten preiss bekommen.

In dem geht die Pelimeria *mit* Philomena *ein, vnd als er abgehen will vnd für sie geht, thut er jr reverentz; so lest sie ein Händschuch fallen, den hebt er auff, neigt sich, küst den, vnd gibt jhr jhn wider :*

   Gnedigs Fräulein, der händschuch gehört euch.   55
Pel. (gibt jhm den andern auch). Da nemmt auch den andern zugleich
   Vnd behaltet sie von wegen mein!
Hor. (thut jr Reverentz). Dass soll mir gar ein lieb gschenck sein.

   Horatius *geht ab.*   Balthasar *hats mit den Händschuch als gesehen.*

Bal. Ach Gott, jetzund ich gsehen han,
   Horatius bringt das best davon.   60

Pelimeria *geht mit der* Philomena *herumb, reden gemächlich zusammen, vnd fechten mit den Händen.*

Lor. Ey, schweigt nur vnd last mich drumb sorgen!
   Er müst an einem strick erworgen
   Ehe er mein Schwester solte kriegen.
   Wir wöllen vns hin zu jhr fügen
   Vnd jhr ein wenig sprechen zu;   65
   So hör wir was sie sagen thu.

   Sie gehn mit einander zu jhr, thun jr Reverentz, geben jr die Händ.

Lor. Hertzliebe Schwester, glaub, weil ich
   Auff dem Sal hab gesehen dich,
   Hab ich dir wollen zusprechen.
   Ich weiss es nit ausszurechen   70
   Dass du vnd auch die Jungfrau dein
   Also heimlich redet allein.
   Ist es dir zu thun vmb einen Mann,
   Weiss ich ein rechten für dich schon;
   Den wolt ich gar balt nennen dir.   75
Pel. Was wolst für ein Mann geben mir?

Deins gebens ich mir wenig acht.
Du hast mein liebsten mir vmbbracht,
Versprichst mir Brüderliche treu,
Der ich mich aber gar nicht freu.   80
Will wol ein Mann bekommen ohn dich.

    Sie geht mit jrer Jungfrau ab. Balthasar *kratzt sich im Kopff.*

Bal. Ach weh! ach sie verachtet mich!
Der Horatius ist jhr lieb.
Zu sterben ich mich schon ergib.
Lor. Ey, schweigt vnd seit nur nit so weich!   85
Es fellt kein Baum von einem streich.
Nemmt ein hertz! vns soll noch wol gelingen.
Ich will sie euch zu wegen bringen.
Gschichts nit mit gutem willen balt,
So muss geschehen mit eim gewalt.   90

    Sie gehn ab. Kompt Horatius.

Hor. Gott lob, mein sach steht trefflich wol.
So ist auch mein hertz freuden vol
Von wegen dreyerley genad
Die mir mein Gott erzeyget hat.
Die erst gnad ist, dass ich im Krieg   95
Gefangen hab mit Glück vnd Sieg
Dess Königs Sohn auss Portugall;
Der gibt mir Gelts ein grosse Zahl
Für zugesprochne Rantion,
Davon ich lang wol leben kan.   100
Die ander Gnad, die mir Gott gab,
Ist dass ich gnad beym König hab.
Aber die dritt gnad ist die best,
Besser als ich zu wünschen west;
Das ist dess Königs Tochter gunst.   105
Die liebet mich in heysser brunst.
Dieselb hat mich hieher bescheiden.
Der wart ich mit hertzlichen Freuden.
Dargegen aber kümmert mich
Dass sich hart setzet wider mich   110
Dess Königs Sohn, Laurentius,
Vor dem ich mich befahren muss.
Er zieh mir ein reiss übern weg,
Sintemal dieweil er gern sech,
Dass sie den Printz Balthasarn nemb.   115
Zum andern förcht ich mich vor dem,
Dass er geb die Heyrat nit nach,
Weil ich nur bin eins Grafen Sohn.
Wie aber dem? was soll ich than?
Hie erwart ich der liebsten mein,   120

Die kompt gleich eben gangen rein.

Kompt Pelimeria *mit* Philomena, *beut jm die Händ.*

Pel. Fürwar, ich hab mich kümmert hart.
Ihr werd lang haben auff mich gwart.
Ich hab zu den vorgehenden Sachen
Vor all ding richtig müssen machen.   125
Heint vmb sechs Vhr in eurm Garten,
Da will ich euer allein erwarten,
Mit euch beschliessen alle ding,
Wie ich den König darzu bring
Dass er mich euch zum Gmahel lass.   130

Hor. Gar wol hab ich verstanden das;
Will mich einstelln zu rechter Zeit,
Weil die Nacht leichtlich schrecken geyt
Den Weibspersonen, wo die sein
Dess Nachts auss jhrem Gmach allein.   135
Gott lass vns bede frisch vnd gsund
Erleben die glückselig stund!
Vnd dass man vns nicht sehe hie stehn,
Will ich auff dissmal von euch gehn.

Er druckt sie vnd geht ab.   Sie sicht jhm nach.

Pel. Vnd wenn der König nit haben wolt   140
Dass ich Horatium nemen sollt,
So wolt ich mir selbst thun den Todt.

Phil. Gnedigs Fräulein, darfür sey Gott!
Wie lang ists (denckt eur Gnad nit dran?),
Da jhr wolt nemen gar kein Mann?   145
Doch habt jhr euch eins andern bsunnen,
Zwar kein vnfletigen lieb gewunnen,
Sonder euch nach eim schön vmbgsehen.

Pel. Weist nicht? man thet vor Alters jehen,
Wenn einer etwas kauffen wolt,   150
Dass er etwas guts nemen solt,
Wenn ers schon desto theurer nem.
Als dass ich nur jetzt überkäm
Dess Königs Consens vnd vergunst,
Wolt ich mir nichts mehr wünschen sunst,   155
Oder es kost mir Leib vnd Leben.

Phil. Hat der König das vorig nachgeben,
So hab ich gar kein zweiffl dran,
Dass ers da nicht noch eh werd than.
Nun kompt! der Tag der neigt sich jmmer.   160
Wir wölln nein ins Frauenzimmer.

Sie gehn ab.   Kompt Balthasar *vnd* Lorentz.

Bal. (*kläglich*). Ach Gott, ich lig hie vergebens
Vnd hab all Hoffnung meines Lebens

Mir gäntzlich auss dem Sinn gesetzt,
Vnd muss dess dings sterben zu letzt,   165
Weil das Königlich Fräuelein
So gantz vnd gar nicht achtet mein,
Will sich auch an eur Lieb nit kehrn.
Lor. Ich will jhr den Hochmut fein wehrn.
Eur Lieb mir nur zusehen thu!   170
Was ich schaff, da helfft mir darzu!
Petrian, balt komm herein zu mir!

> Petrian, *ein junger Kerl, laufft ein.*

Pet. Gnedigster Herr, was wolt doch jhr?
Zu eurem dienst bin ich bereidt.
Lor. Mein Petrian, mich bescheidt!   175
Ich wolt dich gern etwas fragen,
Wann du mir wolst die warheit sagen,
Vnd du solst es vmb sonst nit than.
Pet. Ja wenn ich der sach wissens han,
So will ich sagen die warheit.   180
Lor. Weistu nicht wen jetziger zeit
Mein Schwester an dem Hof hat lieb?
Pet. Ey, darauff ich kein achtung gib;
So will es mir auch nicht gebürn.
Lor. (*ziecht vom Leder, setzt jms Rapier ans hertz*). So mustu dein
Leben verliern.   185
Weil dus nit wilt in guten than,
Ich dich villeicht wol zwingen kan
Dass dus mit bösen sagen must.
Pet. O verschont! ich wils sagen sust.
Die Jungfrau liebt Horatium,   190
Vnd wie ich heint heimlich vernumm,
So will er in seins Vatters Garten
Irer heint auff den Abend warten;
Da werdens haben ein gesprech.
Doch bitt ich das jhr in keim weg   195
Was ich gesagt hab wolt vermelten;
Müsts sonst all mein tag entgelten
Bey jhr vnd andern Höflingen.
Lor. Meinst, das ich sag von disen dingen?

> *Er greifft in Sack.*

Sich, da hab dir ein schenck zu lohn!   200
Erfehrst du mehr, so zeig mirs an!
So gib ich dir noch ein verehrung.
Bal. (*gibt jm. auch gelt*). Sich! da hab dir ein ritterzehrung!
Vnd halt die sach still vnd verschwiegen,
Du solst noch anderst von vns kriegen.   205

> *Er nimmts vnd geht ab.*

Lor. Wolt der Lecker mein Schwester erwerben?
Nein zwar, er muss die nacht noch sterben.
Doch vnvermerckt, das sies nicht weiss!
Wir wölln jhm auffwarten mit fleiss,
Vnd wölln jhm geben seinen lohn,   210
Dass ers hinfort nit mehr soll thon.

     Sie gehn ab. *Kompt* Horatius *mit* Petrian.

Hor. Alhie steh, vnd wart vor der Thür!
Du weist wen du solst lassen zu mir.
Wenn du aber hörst frembde Leut,
So schau das mir das werd bedeut,   215
Damit ich eine warnung nem!

Pet. Ja, ich wil recht nachkommen dem.

     Er geht auff die ander seiten.

Ich will es gehn dem Fürsten sagen.
Dass wird mir gwiss ein Tranckgelt tragen.

     Er geht ab. Horatius *geht auff vnd nider.*

Hor. Nun hat die gegenwertig nacht   220
Mit jhren schwartzen flügn gmacht
Die Himel Wolcken dunckel zwar,
Auch Mond vnd Stern verfinstert gar,
Den schönen tag von hinnen trieben.
Doch wenn sie mich bringt zu der lieben,   225
Bistu mir lieber als der tag;
Dann bey dir ich gelangen mag
Zu dem darnach ich lang hab gstrebt;
Kein frölichere zeit noch nie erlebt.

     Pelimeria *geht ein, beut* Horatio *die Händ.*

Pel. Ach hertzenallerliebstes Lieb,   230
Euch ich mich gar zu eygen gib,
Will auch von euch nicht setzen wider.
Doch bitt ich, setzt euch zu mir nider!
Mein hertz ist mir traurig vnd schwer.
Wenn nur kein gfahr vorhanden wer,   235
Darvon wir kämen in ein Schaden.

     Sie setzen sich zusammen.

Hor. Weibsbilder sind mit Forcht beladen,
Förchten sich, wo es nicht bedarff,
Haben Gedancken schwer vnd scharff.
Aber, Hertzlieb, schlaget die auss!   240
Könn wir doch nauff ins Sommerhauss,
Das ist verwahret nach dem besten
Mit Schlossen, Rigeln der allervesten.
Dasselbig könd wir sperren zu.

Darumb, bitt ich, gebt euch zu ruh!   245
Allhie sind wir ohn alle gfahr.
Pel. O hertzenlieb, fürwar, fürwar,
Fürwar die Sach die ist nit gut;
Dann wenn mich etwas anden thut,
So geht es mir gwiss in die Händ.   250
Hor. Ich hoff all Vnglück hab ein End,
Vnd bin frölich vnd freuden voll.

Jetzt lauffen die zwen Fürsten ein, sind vermumbt.

Pel. (laufft davon vnd schreyt). Ach Gott, das hat mich geandet wol.
O Herr Marschalt! O Herr Marschalt!
Köndt jhr vns helffen, so kompt baldt!   255

Horatius *greifft nach der Wehr. Die zwen Fürsten drucken jhn zu boden,
stossen jhm den Dolchen in Leib.*

Hor. Ihr Bösswicht, wie kompt jhr herein?
Was Mörderey soll das doch sein?

Sie schweigen still, binden jhn an vnd hencken jhn.

Lor. Sich, also hast du deinen lohn.
Ein todter Hund nicht beissen kan.

Sie gehen eyllend ab. Kompt der Marschalt *in einer Nachtschauben, hat ein
Hemmet über die Kleider an, ein schlaffhauben auff, mit einer blossen Wehr.*

Mal. Ach wer hat mich so hart erschreckt,   260
Mit seim Geschrey auss dem schlaff erweckt,
Vnd mich bey meinem Ampt genennt,
Dass ich soll kommen vnd helffen bhend?
Wer bist du, der so gschryen hat?

Er steht still.

Wenn nur niemand wer gschehen schad!   265
Ich muss mich ein wenig vmbsehen.

Er kompt, wo sein Sohn hengt.

Ach weh, weh! was ist dem geschehen?

*Er schneid jhn ab, legt jhn für sich, so ists sein Sohn; er zicht ein blutigs
Tüchlein rauss, rüttelt jhn, zicht jhn bey der Nasen vnd sagt kläglich:*

Ach weh! Ach Horati, mein Sohn!
Ach Horati, wer hat dir than?
Ach weh, du mein einiges Kind,   270
Dass ich dich solcher gstalt hie find
Mit einem so durchstochnen Hertzen!
O weh meins schmertzen über all schmertzen!
Weh meiner pein über all pein!
Ach wer müssen die Mörder sein?   275
Dass ich mich nur an jhn künd rechen!
Ach weh! mein Hertz will mir zerbrechen,
Meine Sinn wollen mir vergehn.

Was soll ich in der klag hie stehn ?
Ich will mich gehn selbst bringen vmb,   280
Dass ich nur auss dem Hertzleyd kumm.

Er kehrt die Wehr über sich, will sich erstechen, besinnt sich doch vnd würfft
sie wider weg.

Ach nein, es ist die zeitlich Pein
Gegen der Höll gar schlecht vnd klein.
Drumb will ich nicht Händ an mich legen,
Sonder geflissen sein dargegen,   285
Dass ich erforsch die Feinde mein ;
Dann das hat thun keiner allein.
Erfahr ich wer sind die Bösswicht,
So schon ich selbst meins Lebens nicht,
Sonder will jhn geben den Lohn,   290
Wie sie dir, mein Sohn, haben than.
Nun will ich jhn tragen ins Hauss,
Vnd will jhn lassen wäydnen auss,
Vnd jhn auff das best balsamirn,
Stett sehnlich klag über jhn führn,   295
So lang biss ich mich grochen hab.
Als dann ich jhn leg in ein Grab ;
Will jhn auch lassen mahlen ab.

Er küst sein Sohn offt vnd tregt jhn ab.

ACTUS TERTIUS.

Lorentz geht ein mit Balthasar *in jren Fürstlichen Kleidern.*

Lor. Der Sach ist nun ein anfang gmacht.
Auch so hab ich nechten zu Nacht
Ergriffen auch die Schwester mein ;
Die hab ich lassen legen ein,
Vnd soll nicht eh kommen an Tag
Biss dass sie euch die Eh zusag.   5
Was gilts, ich wöll sie dultig machen ?
Bal. Wir haben gross Gfahr bey der Sachen,
Vnd ich werd von meim Gewissen
Gar hart genaget vnd gebissen,
Dass ich mein Händ geleget an   10
Horatium, der mir nichts than.
Solt dann die Mordthat erst aussbrechen,
Wie hart wür man die an vns rechen !
Fürwar das übl thut mich reuhen.   15
Lor. Ey schweigt still ! jhr dörfft bey mein treuen
Euch nicht fürchten, dass mans erfahr,
Oder die That werd offenbar.
Doch müss wir Niclaus vnd Petrian

Auch eben wie Horatio than,   20
Denn wenn einer von mir nimbt gelt
Vnd mir einen verräht vnd melt,
So nimbt er Gott, verräht auch mich.
Aber dass jhm das wehre ich,
Vnd dass sie dahin nicht mehr dencken,   25
Woll wir jhn allen beyden schencken,
Vnd darzu geben gute Wort.
Morgen müssen sie bede fort,
So bleiben wir bede vnvermehrt.
Bal. Ich will als thun was jhr begert,   30
Dass nur die Sach verschwigen bleib,
Vnd ich die Jungfrau krieg zum Weib.

In dem kompt Niclaus, *geht zu* Balthasar.

Nic. Gnediger Herr, ich hab die Kleider
Widerumb tragen zu dem Schneider,
Der will sie machen nach eurem beger.   35
Lor. Hört, mein Nicolaus! kompt doch hieher!
Ein guten Dienst habt jhr vns than;
Darumb gebürt euch was zu lohn.

Er gibt jm ein Ketten.

So nemet dise Ketten hin!
Auch sollt jhr das gnissen forthin   40
Bey eurm Herrn so wol als mir.
Bal. Ich will ein neus Kleid kauffen dir.
Doch schweig still vnd sag nichts davon,
Vnd heiss vns rein den Petrian!
Dem haben wir was zuvermelten.   45
Nic. Gott wöll euch diss reichlich vergelten!
Petrian will ich schaffen kommen.
Lor. Niclaus, wir haben vns fürgenommen
Die Nacht zu üben ein Kurtzweil.
Darzu dörff wir eur hilff zum Theil.   50
Das soll heint gschehen vmb siben Vhr.
Da solt jhr auff dem Kirchhof nur
Warten biss wir bed zu euch stossen.
Nic. Ja ich will mich da finden lassen
Vmb dieselb Zeit; das glaubt nur gwiss!   55
Lor. Wir werden vns verlassen auff diss.

Nicolaus *geht ab.   Kompt* Petrian.

Pet. Ir gnedige Herrn, der Nicolaus
Der hat mich gheissen zu euch herauss.
Lor. (*gibt* Petrian *auch ein Ketten*). Du bist ein guter Petrian,
Vnd hast vns grossen Dienst gethan: 60
Darumb so nimb zu Lohn die Ketten!

Er gibt jhm die Ketten.

Noch mehr wir dir zusagen hetten.
Der Niclaus der ist dir nicht gut,
Böss Karten er ausswerffen thut,
Dass ich förcht er möcht vns verrahten ;   65
Dardurch kömbstu am meinsten zu schaden,
Weil vns ein alts Sprichwort vergwist :
Wo der Zaun an dem nidersten ist,
Da steigt man an dem meinsten drüber.
Vns zwen möcht man wol tragen nüber ;   70
Aber wo bleibst du ? drumb wöll wir
Ein sehr guten raht geben dir,
Dem Niclaus das Maul zu verbinden.
Heint wirst du jhn auff dem Kirchhof finden,
Sobald die Vhr thut siben schlagen.   75
Wann du nun wolst ein Kunststück wagen,
Vnd jhm schiessen ein Kugl in Leib,
Dass vnser Sach verschwigen bleib
So wolten wir dir ehrlich lohnen.
Pet. Thet ich Horatii nit schonen,   80
Hab jhm bracht den strick an die Kehln,
Will ich dess Niclaus auch nit fehln.
Das glob ich euch bey Treu vnd Ehr.
Morgen frü lebt er schon nicht mehr.
                   Er geht ab.
Lor. Secht nur ! wie fein schickt sich all sach !   85
Jetzund will ich bestellen die Wach,
Dass sie beym Kirchhof haben acht.
So bald ein Püxen knalt vnd kracht,
Sollen sie lauffen von stund an
Vnd den, der den Schuss hat gethan,   90
Sollen sie gfangen setzen ein.
Der Galg soll auch sein Kirchhof sein.
Dardurch machen wir vns allbeyd
Vor jhnen gute sicherheit.
Balthasar *schüttelt den Kopff, vnd gehn ab.   Kommen* Horolt *vnd* Morolt, *die*
    zwen Scharwächter, haben mit sich noch etliche stumme Personen.
Horolt. Nun hört mir zu, jhr lieben Gesellen !   95
Weiln wir die Wach versehen söllen,
So wolt fein dapffer zsamen halten,
Wie vns herkam von den alten !
Sanct Marx will ich euch zum Loss geben ;
Das soll ein jeder mercken eben,   100
Wenn er gfragt wird was das Loss sey,
Auff dass man jhn erkenn darbey ;
Dann welcher das nicht mercken thet,
Sein Leib vnd Leben verwickelt hett,
Oder dass man jhn zu boden schlüg.   105

Morolt. Ey, jhr dörfft kein sorg haben für mich.
   Ich bin dess vnterrichtet gnug.
   Thet eins mals in Vngern ein Zug,
   Da hett ich auch dess Loss vergessen;
   Da thet mir der Wachmeister messen   110
   Mit seim Federspiess meine Ohrn.
   Davon bin ich so witzig worn
   Dass ichs forthin vergiss nit mehr.
Horolt. Still, still! es gehn Leut dorten her.
   Da müss wir sehen wer sie sein.   115
   Seinds nicht richtig, so führ wirs ein.

         Kompt Lorentz *mit* Balthasar.

Lor. Glück zu, jhr Wächter! wie steht all sach?
Horolt. Ey, gnediger Herr, also gemach!
   Wir sind gleich allererst auffzogen.
Lor. Hört zu, was mich hat jetzt bewogen   120
   Euch ein Befelch zu zeigen an!
   Es finden sich etlich Person,
   Die haben böse Practick vor,
   Halten sich vor Sanct Affra Thor,
   Finden sich gmeiniglich vmb siben Vhr,   125
   Damit man fürkomm der Auffruhr.
   So gebeut ich euch bey der Pflicht
   Vnd dass jhrs vnterlasset nicht,
   Wen jhr der orten thut erlangen,
   Sey wer da wöll, die thut all fangen,   130
   Werns schon vnser Diener vnd Knecht!
Horolt. Den Sachen weiss ich zuthun recht.
   Eur Fürstlich Gnad kein zweiffl trag!
   Ich will sie kriegen, eh es wird Tag.

         Sie bede gehn ab.

   So habt gut acht, wie ist vermelt!   135
   Es tregt ein ein gülden fangGelt.
   Da können wir ein Trunck drumb than.
Morolt. Das Gelt wir balt verdienet han.
   Wir wollen vns bey der Kirchecken
   Hinder eim grossen Pfeiler verstecken,   140
   Daselbst vns Keiner mag empflihen,
   Vnd wollen jetzt alsbalt auffziehen.

      Sie gehen ab. Kompt Petrian, *hat ein gespandte Püxen.*

Pet. Die bede Fürsten sind kostfrey,
   Geben mir guten trost dabey,
   Dass sie mich hoch erheben wöllen.   145
   Ich soll jhn zgfallen mein Gsellén,
   Wenn er jetzt balt wird fürgehn müssen,

Mit einer Kugel zu Todt schiessen.
Dass will ich than ohn all mein Schaden,
Mein Büxen hab ich doppelt gladen.   150
Kompt er, so schiess ich jhn behend,
Dass ers weiss in dem Kopff vmbwend.
Schau, schau! dort schleicht er auss eim Hauss.
Ich will jhm machen sein garauss.

Nicolaus geht ein.

Nic. Mich reut warlich Horatius.   155
Jetzund ich in forchten sein muss
Dass solches übel komm an Tag,
Vnd folg ernstliche Straff hernach.

Petrian schiest.

Auweh! wer hat geschossen mich?
Pet. Dasselb will dir nicht sagen ich.   160

Wenn der Petrian *mit trucknem Papier den* Nicolaus *schiest, hat er innwendig
ein kleines Sprützlein voll Prsillich; das druckt er, als griff er an die
Wunden, sprützt die Prisill durch ein löchlein auss dem Wammes, wie
Blut; so turckelt er vmb, biss er stirbt, vnd lests folgends auslauffen.*
Horolt, Morolt *vnd die andern Wächter lauffen herfür, fallen auff* Petrian.

Horolt. Du Lecker, baldt gib dich gfangen!
Solst an Galgen werden ghangen,
Dass du hie in der Statt loss schiest!
Pet. Zu frieden jhr mich lassen müst,
Ich bin dess jungen Printzen knecht.   165
Horolt. Ey, schad nichts; du bist vns der recht.
Man schiest nicht in dess Königs Statt.
Morolt. Secht! da er ein erschossen hat.
Den will ich legen in ein Ecken.

Morolt schleifft Nicolaus *ab.*

Horolt. So will ich den ins loch nein stecken: 170
Darumb geh nur balt fort dein Strassen!

Petrian geht mit.

Pet. Ihr müst mich wol wider rauss lassen.

Sie führn jn ab.   Kompt Lorentz *vnd* Balthasar.

Lor. Ich hab mein Jungen aussgesand,
Zu sehen was die Wächter hand
Nächten die Nacht wol aussgericht.   175
Ich meint, ja, es sollt fehlen nicht,
Wie wir gester haben beschlossen.
Bal. Es gehn vns noch wol an die possen;
Aber das Spil ist noch nicht auss.
Gott geb dass nichts böss folg darauss,   180
Denn mir ist mein Hertz gar zu schwer.
Wolt dass ich in Portugall wer.

Famulus, der Jung, geht ein.

Fam. Gnedige Herrn, der Petrian
   Lest euch vmb eur Hilff ruffen an ;
   Der ligt dort in eim Thurn tieff,   185
   Vnd hat mir geben disen Brieff.

        Lorentz *liest den Brieff, lacht vnd gibt jn dem* Balthasar.

Lor. Herr, eur Lieb wollen den Brieff lesen !

       Zu dem Famulo *sagt er, vnd gibt jhm Gelt :*

Zu jhm sprich, du seist bey mir gwesen,
Er soll haben ein gutes hertz !
Wenn man jhn auch schon führt auffwertz   190
Zum Galgen, als wolt man jhn hencken,
Sol er doch jhm nichts böss gedencken,
Dann ich wöll jhn ohn als beschedigen,
Von aller schand vnd schmach erledigen.
Zeig jhm die Büchsen ! doch schau drauff,   195
Das du die machst bey leib nit auff !
Sag, des Königs Brieff seind darinnen,
Die jhn bald ledig machen können !
Da gib jhm jetzt die zwantzig Kronen !
Sag jhm, er dörff keins Gelts nicht schonen,   200
Er soll jhm kauffen was er beger !
Gibt er das auss, schick ich jhm mehr.

             Der Jung geht ab.

Lor. Meister Jahn ! Jahn ! komm doch herfür !

       Jahn *geht ein, hat ein Henckers Schwert an.*

Jahn. Ey, gnedigste Herrn, was wollet jhr ?
Lor. Ich meint zwar, du könst selbst wol dencken ; 205
   Morgen solstu Petrian hencken.
Jahn (besinnt sich). Petrian hencken ? Hencken Petrian ?
   Ey, was hat der gut Kerll gethan,
   Vnd das ich jhn auffhencken sol ?
Bal. Ey, du wirst es erfahren wol.   210
Jahn (geht hinzu vnd mist mit seim spiess an Lor.). Ey ja, ein Galg ist
   wol so hoch als jhr.
Lor. (gibt jm ein mauldaschen). Wolstu den Galgen messen an mir ?
   Gehin ! mess jhn an deines gleichen !
   (Zu Bal.). Wir zwen wollen zu Hauss heimschleichen.

            Sie gehen ab.

Jahn. Den Printzen hett ich gehencket gern.   215
   Solt mir ein solcher zu theil wern,
   Ich wolt mit allem lust jhn hencken,
   Vnd jhm das schlagen wol eindrencken.

       Er geht ab. Kompt Famulus.

Fam. Wenn man mir hat verbotten schon,

Dass ich die Büchssn nit sol auffthon,   220
So kan ichs jedoch lassen nicht,
Vnd mir gleich wie den Weibern gschicht.
Wenn man denselben was verbeut,
Gwinnens darzu begierligkeit.
Darumb so mach ich auff die Büchsen.   225

Er thut sie auff, lacht.

Da find ich auff der Welt gar nichsen ;
Vnd man hat mirs verbotten so hart.
Nun mach ich mich bald auff die fahrt,
Vnd richt Petrian botschafft auss,
Trag darnach die lehr Büchsen zu hauss.   230

Abgang. Kompt Malignus *mit* Ernesto, *dem Hauptman, setzt sich.*

Mal. Dieweil der gfangen bey der nacht
Hat ein Soldaten vmbgebracht,
Vnd solche Mordthat klar bekennt,
So hat das Königlich Regiment
Jn drauff verdampt zu stranguliern ;   235
Vnd wir beyd solln, zu exequiern,
Meister Jahnnen das anzeigen,
Vnd jhm den Theter machen eygen.

Ern. Gstrenger Herr Marschalt, weil er bekend
Dass er mit seiner eygen hend   240
Hat vmbgebracht Nicolaum,
So hencket man jhn billich drum.

Jahn kompt, führt Petrian *an eim strick.*

Mal. Du bekenst doch noch die mordthat !
Pet. Was mein maul einmal geredt hat
Vnd was mein Hand einmal hat than,   245
Da wird ich nimmer weichen von.
Gott geb, was jhr, Herr Marschalt, sagt !
Ich bin nit so blöd vnd verzagt
Dass ich mich förchte für dem Todt.

Mal. So raht ich dir, befilch dich Gott,   250
Dann das Königlich Regiment
Hat dich des Strangs wirdig erkennt.
Drumb, Jahn, geh hin vnd knüpff jhn an !
Doch solst jhn todt wider rab than,
Vnd jhn begraben in ein grab.   255

Der Marschalt *vnd* Hauptman *gehn ab.*

Jahn. Ich thu wessen ich befelch hab.
Komm her ! ich will dich hübsch anstricken.
Pet. Ey schweig ! es wird dich nit hart drücken.
Jahn. Ey nun, so drück es aber dich !
Pet. Du solst den Tag nicht hencken mich,   260
Vnd wenn du auch werst noch so klug.

Jahn. Ey, ich will dir sein gscheid genug
  Vnd dich hoch nauff an Galgen binden;
  Du wollst mir dann vntern händn verschwinden.

> *Sie kommen zum Galgen.* Jahn *steigt hinauff.*

  Nun bet (da sichst dein Kirchhof du),   265
  Ehe dass ich zeich die Schlingen zu!
  Als dann wird es dir sein zu spet.
Pet. Ich hab noch wol zeit, dass ich bet.
  Du wirst balt hören andere mehr.
Jahn. Auff dich zu warten ich nit beger.   270
  Wiltu beten, so magst dus than.
  Ich hab dich angebunden schon,
  Vnd stoss dich über die Läyttern ab.
Pet. Noch zeit gnug ich zu beten hab.

> Jahn *würfft jhn hinunter.*

  Der Schelm will kein guts Wort aussgeben.   275
  Schad wers doch dass man jhn liess leben.
  Nun will ich jhn vor ziehen auss,
  Sein Kleider mit mir tragen zu Hauss,
  Ihn werffen in ein Gruben drauss.

> *Er schneid jhn ab, zicht jhn auss vnd tregt jhn ab.*

ACTUS QUARTUS.

> *Kompt* Malignus, *der Marschalt, allein vnd sagt*

Ach wie thuts mir so schmertzlich weh!
Wo ich in meim Hauss steh vnd geh,
So kompt mir stetigs für mein Sohn
Vnd thut mich gleichsam manen dran
Sein vnschuldigen Todt zurechen.   5
So weiss ich nicht, wer sein die Frechen
Die jhn erwürgt in meinem Garten.
Erfahr ichs, so müssen sie gwarten
Was sie meinem Sohn haben than.
Vnd weil ichs nicht erfahrn kan,   10
So macht ein schmertz den andern schmertzen,
Die mir ligen an meinem Hertzen.
Schau! dort kompt gleich der Famulus rein.
Was wird nun neuss vorhanden sein?

> Famulus *geht ein, tregt ein Brieff, gibt jhn dem Marschalt.*

Fam. Gestrenger Herr, nembt disen Brieff!   15
  Als ich von der Gfengnuss her lieff,
  Pelimperia mir den gab.
Mal. Mein lieber Junger, gross danck du hab!
  Du darffst warten auff kein antwort.

Darumb geh deines wegs nur fort!   20
   Famulus *geht ab.* *Er bricht den Brieff auff, verwundert sich.*
Ach der Brieff ist geschrieben mit Blut.
Sein innhalt also lauten thut:
Zuvor mein Ehrn gebürlichen gruss!
Eurnthalb ich mich wundern muss,
Vnd kan nicht wissen was es macht   25
Dass jhr eurs Sohns so wenig acht,
• *Den die zwen Printzen haben erstochen.*
Vnd wenn jhr das last vngerochen,
Weil ich jhn hab zur Ehe genommen,
Hett er wol hoch können ankommen,
Dass jhm die Mörder abgeraubt.   30
Vnd ich will nicht sanfft legen mein Haubt,
Hilfft mir Gott auss der Gfängknuss wider,
Biss ich auch leg zur Erden nider
Die zwen Printzen, ich arme Mäydt;
Des schwer ich hiemit einen Eyd.   35
Thut jhr was dabey, so ists gut.
Den Brieff schrib ich mit meinem Blut.
Ach Gott! Ach Gott! was sold das sein?
Soll dann die eygen Herrschafft mein,
Der ich so lang wol dienet han,   40
Mir geben so ein bösen Lohn,
Vnd mir mein einigen Sohn vmbbringen?
Ich kans nicht rechen mit der Klingen:
Sie sind mir beyd zu hoch geborn.
Klag ich dann schon, so is verlorn: 45
Ich kan kein recht desshalb gewinnen. •
Dess muss ich noch kommen von sinnen.
Der Richter ist verdächtlich mir.
O grechter Richter, ich klag es dir.
Lass leuchten die Sonn der Grechtigkeit!   50
Mein Sohn noch in meim Hauss todt leit;
Den will ich nicht lassen begraben
Biss sie allbeyd bezahlet haben
Mit jhrem Blut den Sohne mein.
        Jetzt geht Jahn *ein, tregt ein Brieff, greynt.*   55

Jahn. Ey, ey, ey! der schmertzlichen Peyn!
Den Brieff hab ich in Hosen vnden
In dess Petrians Sack gefunden,
Darauss ich gar wol spüren kan
Dass man jhm hat vnrecht gethan.
Nun meinthalb! ich kan nichts darfür.   60
Mal. (*sicht sich vmb*). Sich, Halbnarr, wie schreyst? was ist dir?
Vnd was hast du da für ein Brieff?

Jahn (weynt). Inn Petrians sack ich jhn ergriff,
 Darauss ich gar wol mercken kan   65
 Dass man jhm vnrecht hat gethan.
 Desshalb thut er mich gar sehr reuhen.
Mal. (list den Brieff also): Mein Petrian, bey meinen treuen,
 So will ich dir genedig sein;
 Darumb du in dem Gfengnuss dein   70
 Solst dich mit gedult wol gehaben.
 Mit grosser Freud will ich dich laben.
 Halt du nur verschwigen die Sach!
 Vom Galgen ich dich ledig mach,
 Solst du schon sein gebunden an,   75
 Dann ich hab Brieff vom König schon.
                          Datum. Lorentz.
Jahn (kläglich). Da hörns ja selber, eur Gnad,
 Dass jhn der König loss gesprochen hat;
 Aber jhr hiest jhn hencken mich.   80
 Kein schuld will daran tragen ich.
 Secht jhr, wie jhr es verantwort!

            Er schnupfft, als greyn er.

Mal. Pack du dich deines Wegs nur fort,
 Vnd lass dir wachssen kein grabs Har!

          Jahn *kratzt sich im kopff vnd geht ab.*

 Durch den Brieff wird mir offenbar   85
 Dass diser gehenckt Petrian
 Mir hat helffen ermördn mein Sohn
 Vnd dass der jung Printz Herr Lorentz
 (Gott geb jhm Peuln vnd Pestilentz!)
 Den Petrian angelernt hat   90
 Dass er verbracht hat die Mordthat,
 Auff dass die, so gewisset drumb,
 Alle bede sind kommen vmb.
 Seiner Schwester in der hafft dahinden
 Will er das Maul auch damit binden,   95
 Dass niemand mehr verhanden wer
 Der drumb west, wie Balthasar vnd er.
 So schwer ich warlich Gott gesprochen,
 Dass ichs nicht lass an jhm vngrochen,
 So baldt vnd ich hab glegenheit,   100
 Ich will sie noch vmbbringen beyd.

*Er zuckt sein Schwert, denn auch den Dolchen, haut vnd sticht vmb sich, wird
                          vnsinnig.*

 Ach, mir vergeht gleich all mein sinn.
 O mein Horati, wo komst hin?
 Schau! dort laufft er, sicht wie ein mauss.
                          B b 2

Hört Horati! nein, er will da nauss.   105
Er laufft von einer seiten zu der andern.

Den Hasen hett ich bald befangen.
Hör, Päurla, von wann bistu gangen?
Ja, der König sitzt über der Malzeit.
Herr Balthasar, wolt jhr auffs gejäydt?
Schau, schau! dort reit auch Lorentz her,   110
Springt in mein Garten mit seim Pfer.
Wenn wir denn heint die Birn blaten,
Lieber thut mir im Grass kein schaden!
Dass Sommerhauss hab ich erst baut.
Secht! da kompt meins Horati Braut.   115
O Horati, mein lieber Son!
Wart! ich lass dich noch nit davon.

Er laufft vnsinniger weiss mit bloser Wehr vnd Dolchen ab.   Kompt König
Amurates *mit* Laurentio, Balthasar *vnd* Ernesto, *dem Hauptman, vnd*
Gangolffo, *dem Portugalischen Gsandèn, der tregt zwen seck mit Gelt.* Der
Marschalt *gehet auch ein vmb den König herumb, sicht sie alle nach einander*
an, thut gar nerrisch.

Amur. (liest ein Brieff). Königlicher Gsander von Portugal,
Wir lesen eur Credentz zumal.
Darinn finden geschrieben wir,   120
Was jhr vns bringet mündlich für;
Dem sollen wir glauben zustellen,
Vnd jhre Lieb auch halten wöllen
Alles was jhr vns werd zusagen,
Daran wir auch kein zweiffel tragen.   125
Darauff möcht jhr eur sach fürbringen.
Gangolff (neigt sich). Gnedigster Herr, vor allen dingen
Ich jhr Majestat anzeigen muss
Meins Gnedigsten Herrn freundlichen gruss,
Vnd sein willige dienst dabey;   130
Vnd weil sein Son gefangen sey
Vmb ettlichs Gelt Rancionirt,
Hab ich dasselb mit mir hergfürt,
Vnd ist mein hohe bitt darneben,
Den jungen Printzen ledig zugeben.   135
Dass übrig eur Majestat begern,
Ob es wol thut mein Herrn bschwern,
So will er doch das alls eingehn,
In ewiger bündnuss bey euch stehn,
Nicht thun wider euch vnd die eurn.   140
Dass soll ich mit meim Eyd beteurn,
Vnd aller diser Red begrieff
Verfertigen mit Sigll vnd Brieff,
Dass es nun forthin dabey bleib.

Amur. Dass man dise ding all beschreib,   145
   Befelch man in der Cantzeley!
   Vnd jhr solt selbst auch sein dabey,
   Dass man vor als collationir,
   Deutlich beschreibe nach gebür.
   Darauff drück wir auch vnser Secret,   150
   Vnd wöllens halten vest vnd steht.
   Aber das Rancionirgelt,
   Davon jhr auch besonders gemelt,
   Dass gehört vnserm Hof Marschalt.
Mal. (*spricht thöricht vnd fellt zu fuss*). Ja es ist mir mein hertz
   erkalt.   155
   O Gerechtigkeit, Gerechtigkeit!
Lor. (*stöst jhn weg*). Eur fürbringen sich jetzt nit leid!
   Ir secht, der König hat zuthan.
Mal. Ja mir ist auch gelegen dran.
Amur. Was ist dem Marschalt widerfahrn,   160
   Dass er thut so seltzam gebarn?
   Wir seinds an jhm nit gwohnet vor.
Lor. (*sagt dem König in ein Ohr*): Herr König, der Geltgeytzig thor
   Hat ghört das der Gesand vermelt,
   Er bring das Rancionir Gelt;   165
   Darauff ist er also gesessen,
   Hat sorg, das man werd sein vergessen,
   Vnd wer jhm das nit folgen lahn.
Amur. Ey, was wir euch zugsaget han,
   Das soll euch werden; nempt das Gelt hin!   170

Man gibt jhm das Gelt, er würffts zum Eingang hinein, geht alle weil ab.

Mal. Damit ich nicht zufrieden bin.
   Ich wolt das Gelt wer nie gemacht,
   Dann es hat mir mein Sohn vmbbracht.

      Balthasar *stöst* Lorentzen. Lorentz *sagt jm etwas in ein Ohr.*

Amur. Herr Balthasar, jhr seyt glöset auss.
   Wenn nun eur Lieb will heim zu Hauss,   175
   So soll es Ihr vergünnet sein;
   Denn alle Claussel gross vnd klein,
   Die wir haben mündlich bedingt,
   Vnd was vns Feind- vnd freundschafft bringt,
   Dass alls wir zu halten begern.   180
Lor. Herr König, wolts euch nicht beschwern,
   Dass ich eur Majestat fall ein!
   Printz Balthasar, der gliebste mein,·
   Hatt sich gegen mir also erklert
   Dass er jetzt noch nicht heim begert,   185
   Sonder wann ers erhalten künd,
   Sein Hertz vnd Gmüt jhm darzu stünd

Dass er eur Tochter nemen wolt.
Wenns nur eur Majestatt will sein sollt,
Wolt er vor Hochzeit halten mit jhr.   190
Amur. Wenns von euch selber hören wir,
So wöll wir euch gut antwort geben.
Bal. Sie liebet mir für Leib vnd Leben.
Wenn sie mich liebet, wie ich sie,
Wird sie mirs nicht abschlagen je.   195
Vnd wenn ich sie nur sollt erwerben,
So wollt ich desto lieber sterben,
Vnd mich achten den seligsten Mann.
Amur. (gibt jhm die Händ). Vnsern Willen den habt jr schon.
Doch vnser Tochter woll wir fragen,   200
Die wir nicht sahen in etlich Tagen.
Darauff sollt jhr balt antwort wissen.
Lor. Pelimperia wir sagen lissen,
Dass sie sich innen halten sollt,
Eur Gnaden will erwarten wollt.   205
Die soll noch dises Tages spatt
Gstellt werden für eur Majestatt.

Malignus *geht ein, ist wider thöricht.*

Mal. O königliche Majestatt!
Lor. (treibt jhn zurück). Dieselbig jetzund zuthun hat.
Kompt etwan wider ein ander mal!   210
Mal. So komm ich in noch grösser Qual.
Mein Hertz im Leib will sich vmbkehrn,
Dass man mich nicht ein Wort will hörn.
Amur. Vns deucht, du vnd der Marschalt beyd
Mit einander vneinig seyd.   215
Das wolten wir nicht gern hörn.
Lor. Grossmächtiger König, nein, bey mein Ehrn,
Der Marschalt ist ein frommer Mann,
Vnd mir niemals kein Leid gethan.
Dass ich jhn aber nicht wolt für lassen,   220
Ist seine sach gschaffen der massen
Dass sie die Würdigkeit nicht hat
Zubringen für eur Majestat,
Wie ich der will anzeigen bald.
Amur. Hat dann die Sach ein solche Gstallt,   225
So haben wirs bedenckens klein.
Drumb kompt all zu der Tafel reyn!
Thut mit dem Gsandten lustig sein!

Abgang jhr aller.

ACTUS QUINTUS.

Kompt der Marschalt, hat ein Buch vnd list:

Wer königlicher Dienst will geniessen,
Der muss auch bey sich selbst beschliessen
Dass er Vnbilligkeit woll tragen,
Vn wenn jm was gschicht, nichts wöll sagen.

Er schlegt ins Buch.

Ja freylich gehts mir auch also.   5

Er list weiter.

Noch ferrners find ich geschriben do :
Gleich wie die war gerechtigheit
Drucket den vngerechten allzeit,
Also auch die bossheit begert
Dass der gerechte werd beschwerd.   10
Also thut auch Herr Lorentz mir ;
Der will mich gar nicht lassen für,
Dass mein beschwerung komm an tag,
Dass ich dir, Gott von Himel, klag.

Er liest wider im Buch gemächlich, ficht mit den Händen, schüttelt den Kopff
vnd ist vngeduldig. Kompt Primus, Secundus, Tertius, drey Supplicanten ;
hat ein jeder ein Supplication.

Primus. Ach, wie gehts zu im Regiment?   15
Die Königs Räthe schuldig send
Die armen zu hören, wie die reichen,
Von dem rechten nicht abzuweichen,
Sonder ein gleiches vrthel zusprechen,
Guts belohnen, das böss zurechen,   20
Wittwen vnd Wäisen zuverthäydigen,
Die betrübten nit zubeleydigen,
Ir beschwerung gern anzuhörn.
So will es sich jetzt alls vmbkehrn ;
Dann ich je kein bekommen kan   25
Der nur mein Supplicatz nem an,
Dass sie im Raht verlesen wür.
Man lest mich sten rauss vor der Thür,
Alss wenn ich wer ein armer hund.

Secundus. Gott spar vns den Marschalt lang gsund !   30
Derselbig hört die armen gern,
Vnd wo sie etwan hilff begern
In jhrn guten gerechten sachen,
Hilfft er es alles richtig machen
Vnd schneid ab all weitläufftigkeit.   35

Tertius. Weil es sich dann also begeit
Dass er dort steht, liest in eim Buch,

Was kans schaden, das mans versuch
Dass wir jhm vnser Bittschrifft geben,
Vnd beten jhn fleissig darneben,   40
Dass er vns die thet bringen für?

Mal. (sicht sich vmb). Ihr guten Leut, wolt jhr zu mir?

Sie zichen alle die Hüt ab.

Primus. Gestrenger Herr, versteht mich recht!
Am Hoff ist ein Einspenniger Knecht,
Hat mir abkaufft vor dem ein Pferdt   45
Vmb 20 Gülden, ward es wol werth;
Hat sich verschrieben vnd versprochen
Mich zu bezahlen in vier Wochen,
Wie das zeyget sein Handschrifft an.
Jetzt ich nichts von jhm bringen kan,   50
Vnd trohet mir noch sehr darzu.

Mal. (sicht die Verschreibung). Mein lieber Freund, gebt euch zuruh!
Er muss euch zahln in acht tagen,
Oder ich will jhn vom Hof weg jagen.

Zum andern sagt er :

Was halt jhr dann für eine Klag?   55

Secundus (gibt jhm die Supplication). Ich hab mir ein Hauss kaufft
die Tag,
Vnd hab schon mein Gelt drumb aussgeben:
So will der nechst Nachbaur darneben
Mich abtreiben von solchem Kauff,
Vnd sagt, er hab den Vorkauff drauff.   60
Das fellt mir schwer über all massen.

Mal. Ich will es die Räht lesen lassen.
Darumb·kompt wider nach Mittag,
Dass ich als dann den Bscheyd euch sag!
Nun was habt jhr dann? das zeygt an!   65

Tertius (gibt jhm ein Supplication vnd sagt kläglich): Ach Gott!
mein allerliebster Sohn
Ist mir die Tag worden gfangen,
Vnd vnschuldig an Galgen ghangen;
Der ist gewest mein Trost vnd Schatz,
Wie jhr find in der Supplicatz.   70

Mal. (list vnd sagt): Ach jetzt find ich, wie es ist gangen,
Dass Horatius ist wordn erhangen,
Vnd hat dein sohn gholffen darzu.

Er wird vnsinnig.

So back dich nauss an Galgen, du!
O Horati, du küner Heldt!   75
Hat man die Buben auff dich bestellt?

Er zerreist die Schrifften alle zu stücken. Die Supplicanten lauffen alle zu.

Primus. O Herr Marschalt, meine Handschrifft,
  Die dess Einspänniger Schuldt betrifft!

Sie wollen jhm die Brieff nemen. Er gibt jedem ein Dötschkappen, zerreist die
      Brieff zu klein stücken vnd geht ab.

Secundus. Ach Gott, was fang wir jetzund an?
Tertius. Also ich kein Hülff kriegen kan.   80
  Ach weh, dass es Gott muss erbarmen!
  Wie gehts allhie so hart den Armen,
  Vnd werden noch darzu geschlagen!
  Was thun wir nun?' wem woll wirs klagen?

Sie gehn traurig ab. Kompt Lorentz, Balthasar *vnd mit jhm* der Famulus.

Lor. Famule, geh ind Gfängnuss nein,   85
  Vnd lass kommen mein Schwester rein!

      Famulus *neygt sich vnd geht ab.*

  Herr Balthasar, jetzt wöllen wir
  Meiner Schwester hie halten für,
  Dass sie euch soll zum Gmahl krigen,
  Dardurch wir sie bereden mügen,   90
  Wenn sie anredt der Vatter mein,
  Dass sie sich willig geb darein,
  Vnd dass alle Sach richtig sey.
Bal. Dises Fürschlags ich mich hoch frey,
  Dann durch das mittel wird fürkommen   95
  Dass aller Argwohn von vns gnommen,
  Der auff vns schier wolt beissen ein.

      Pelimperia *kompt mit* dem Famulo.

Lor. (*zu dem Famulo*). Gehe du dieweil ins Gmach hinein!
  Ich will auch balt kommen hinach.

      Geht zu seiner Schwester, gibt jhr die Händ.

  Schwester, Gott geb dir ein guten Tag!   100
  Wie sichst mich an so streng vnd bitter?
Pel. Meynst, ich zürn nicht billich mitter,
  Dass du mich so lang sperrest ein?
  Soll das Brüderlich ghandelt sein?
  Was Leidts hab ich dir thun mein Tag?   105
Lor. Hör, Schwester, ich sag dirs darnach
  Warumb das alls geschehen sey.
  Du wirst mir dancken der Lieb vnd Treu
  Dass ich dirs hab zum besten than.
  Schau, da sieh Printz Balthasar an!   110
  Hast du dardurch zum Gmahl bekommen.
  Der König wird dich fragen darumben,
  Ob du auch sein begerst zur Ehe.
Pel. Ach Gott, soll mir das thun nicht wehe,
  Dass mein gar allerärgster Feind   115

Mich zum Gmahl zuhaben vermeynt?
Das nimbt mich wunder über wunder.
Bal. (führt Lorentz auff die seyten). Ach Gott, ich habs ghört jetzunder
Dass sie mich gar nicht haben will.
Lor. Ach, mein Herr Balthasar, schweiget still !   120
Weibsbilder sind Wanckelmuts voll,
Vnd sind doch zu bereden vol,
Dass sie thun was sie lang verreden.

Sie kehrn wider. Balthasar *gibt jhr die Händ.*

Bal. Eurenthalb wolt ich mich lassen tödten,
Vnd jhr stellt euch gegen mir so wilt
Das mir mein junges Leben gilt,   125
Wenn jhr mich list thun ein fehlbitt.
Pel. Fürst Balthasar, weiss warlich nit ;
Doch weils der König bewilligt hat,
Will ich jhn vor halten zu Raht ;   130
Vnd wenn er das für rahtsam find,
Ir bessere antwort kriegen künd.
Bal. (gibt jhr die Händ). Der Bscheid mir gute Hoffnung geyt.
Dem lieben Gott befohlen seyt !

Zu Lorentz *sagt er, vnd geht alle weil ab:*

Ich hoff, sie soll noch werden gut.   135
Lor. Darumb schweigt vnd seyt nur wolgemuth !
Ich bin schon gar wol Informirt
Wie sie zuvermögen sein wird
Euch anzunemen mit gutem danck.
Bal. Gschicht das nicht balt, so wer ich kranck.   140

Sie bede gehn ab.

Pel. Ich wolt mich in mein Hertz nein schemen,
Soll ich meins liebsten Mörder nemen,
Den er mir an der seytn erstach,
Dess ich nimmer vergessen mag.
Darff doch vor schand auch nichtes sagen.   145
Allein will ichs dem Marschalt klagen,
Vnd jhm mit Worten hart zu sprechen,
Biss er sein Sohn an jhm thut rechen.
Schau ! dorten geht er gleich hereyn.

Malignus *geht ein.*

Mal. O Horati, lieber Sohn mein,   150
Dein Todt reut mich je lenger, je mehr !
Pel. Ach Gott, wie reut er mich so sehr !
Der mir vor hat mein Hertz erfreut,
Der bringt mir jetzt gross Hertzenleidt.
O Freud, wie bald hast dich verkehrt !   155
Mal. Ich hab das Königlich Fräulein ghört.

Er geht zu jhr, beut jhr die Händ.

Ach Gott, wo seyt jhr so lang gwesen?
Eurn kläglichen Brieff hab ich glesen.
Doch versteh ich nicht recht die Gschicht;
Drumb bitt ich euch, mich vnterricht!   160
Wie ist Horatius vmbkommen?
Pel. Wir zwey haben einander gnommen,
Vnd als wir wolten rahtschlagen
Wie ichs meim Vatter liss fürtragen,
Verzielt er mich in eurn Garten   165
Mein in dem Sommerhauss zu warten.
Petrian, derselb Verrähter,
Der Mordstiffter vnd Vbelthäter,
Der von der Sachen hat gewist,
Von meim Bruder dahin bracht ist,   170
Dass ers jhm vnd Balthasar gsagt,
Die zuvor haben gemacht ein packt,
Dass ich Balthazar nemen sollt.
Als ich aber das nit thun wolt,
Sonder behalten Horatium,   175
Schwuren sie jhn zubringen vmb.
Derhalb vnd als wir beyde sein
Kaum kommen in den Garten rein,
Vnd vns allererst nidergesetzt,
Noch nit mit gutem Gspräch ergötzt,   180
Sind sie vermumbt kommen geloffen,
(Dann die Thür hat jhn glassen offen
Der arg Verrähter Petrian,)
Vnd mein liebsten erstochen han,
Vnd jhn gehangen an ein strick: 185
Da entran ich zu all meim Glück.
Doch legten sie mich gfänglich ein.
Wolt jhr den Mord lassen gut sein,
Vnd euch an jhn beden nit rechen,
So wolt vnd müst ich von euch sprechen   190
Dass jhr keins ehrlichen Manns seyd werht.
Mal. Mein Hertz hat stetigs Rach begert,
Das mir oft drob mein Witz entgangen;
Hett nie Zeyt die Rach anzufangen.
Darzu so hab ich nie gewist   195
Wie es alles zugangen ist.
Ietzt aber, so ich hab den bscheidt,
Darzu die zeit vnd glegenheit,
So wil ich schon recht thun den Sachen,
Euch vom Balthazar ledig machen.   200
Doch muss sich eur genaden stellen
Als ob sie Balthazar nemen wöllen.
So will ich freundlich stellen mich.

Dann werden sie erfreuen sich,
Meinen es sey vergessen schon.
Denn fang ich ein Tragedi an   205
Mit jhnen vor dem König agirn ;
Dareyn wolt euch auch lassen ziern !
Die Gschicht bring ich also herumb
Dass jhr leicht bringt Balthazar vmb ;
So will ich den Lorentz erstechen.   210
Vnd will es schon der König rechen,
So stich ich mein Dolchen in mich.
Pel. Ja, desgleichen so thu auch ich,
Dann wenn ich jhm sein Lohn hab geben,
Beger ich lenger nit zu leben.   215
Ich gehe dahin, es bleib dabey !
Doch also dass verschwigen sey !

*Pelimperia geht ab. Der Marschalt geht hin vnd schüttelt den Kopf, ficht mit
jhm selbst, kompt der König mit Ernesto, dem Hauptman, Lorentz vnd
Balthasar, Pelimperia vnd Philomena, Gangolffo, dem Gesanaten.*

Amur. Sohn Lorentzo, nun sag vns balt !
Was hast du doch mit dem Marschalt ?
Wir mercken dass er zornig ist.   220
Lor. (*neigt sich*). Allergrossmächtiger König, so wist
Dass ich mein Tag vor, wie jetzund,
Mit jhm gezürnt hab kein stund.
Zürnt er mit mir, so weiss ichs nit.
Amur. Wir woltens ja gern sehen nit.   225
Herr Marschalt, trett zu vns herbey,
Vnd zeiget vns an was euch sey !
Habt jhr ein Zorn zu jhn zweyen ?
Mal. Nein, Herr König, bey mein treuen.   230
Sie sind beyd mein Gnedige Herrn ;
Beger jhn guts zu thun, so ferrn
Ich das an Leib vnd gut vermag.
Lor. (*gibt jhm die Händ*). Darfür ich euch grossen danck sag.
Dagegen sollt jhr das auch wissen,   235
Wo jhr könd meiner dienst geniessen,
So will ich sparn gar keinen fleiss.
Bal. (*gibt jm auch die Händ*). Weil ich dann auch kein Vrsach weiss
Darumb ich zürnen sollt mit euch,
So bin ich vrbietig dergleich   240
Euch auch zu dienen, wo ich kan.
Mal. (*gibt jhm die Händ*). Zu vnterthenigem danck nimm ichs an,
Vnd will danckbar erfunden wern.
Amur. Frid vnd Einigkeit hab wir gern.
Nun komm du, Pelimperia,   245
Siechst du den jungen Printzen da,

Dess Königs Sohn aus Portugall?
Den geb wir dir zu einem Gmahl.
Das wirst du zu Danck nemen an.
Pel. (*neygt sich*). Was Euer Maiestatt will han,   250
    Darzu will ich gehorsam sein.
Amur. (*steht auff, gibt* Bal. *die Händ*). Ietzt seyd jhr der lieb Eyden mein.
    Vnd Gott wöll euch zu disem stück
    Geben vil Wolfart, Heyl, vnd Glück,
    Vnd dass jhr langs Leben mögt haben.   255
Bal. Weil mich eur Majestatt begabn
    Mit dem höchsten Schatz auff der Welt,
    Der besser ist als gut vnd Gelt,
    So danck ich der demütig drumb.
    (*Zu* Pel.) Vnd jhr, Hertzlieb getreu vnd fromm,   260
    Jhr seyt die alleredelst Gab,
    Die ich für all Königreich lieb hab,
    Die mir mein Hertz vnd Seel erfreut.
Amur. Dass man ein köstlichs Mahl bereyt
    Zu Ehrn dem königlichen Gsanden,   265
    Dass er daheim in seinen Landen
    Kan seinem König zeygen an
    Dass man jhm hab gross Ehr gethan!
    Auch wöll wir Gsandte schicken mit,
    Dass man jhn auff die Hochzeit bitt,   270
    Vnd geb auch sein Consens darein.
Mal. All ding vor wol bestellet sein.
    Von essen, trincken vnd Confect,
    Kasten, Küchen vnd Keller voll steckt,
    Dass das wenigst nicht mangeln soll.   275
    Vnd gfellt es auch dem König wol,
    So wöllen wir, wie bey den Alten,
    Ein gar Herrlich Tragedi halten, -
    Die ich mir vor lengst hab erlesen;
    Zeigt an von schönen künen Wesen,   280
    Vnd schickt sich wol für Manns Person.
    Ich selbst will mich drein legen an,
    Denn nur vier Person gehörn drein.
    Die zwo können bed Fürsten sein,
    Vnd Pelimperia das Weibsbild.   285
Amur. Man hat dergleich hie lang nicht gspilt.
    Schau, Lorentz, dass es angricht werd!
    Vnd machs, wies der Marschallt begert!
    So schauen wir mit Freuden zu.
Lor. Eur Majestatt befelch ich thu.   290

Der König *geht mit seinen Leuten ab.* Pelimperia *bleibt mit* Philomena *zurück.*

Pel. Hier muss ich auff den Marschalt warten.

Phil. Das Spil thut sich gar seltzam karten,
  Dass jhr den Printzen nemen solt,
  Von dem jhr vor nichts wissen wolt,
  Vnd der euch hat eur Lieb erschlagen.   295
Pel. Ey, schweig still vnd thu nichts davon sagen,
  Wenn du behalten willt mein Hult,
  Sonder nimb dir ein wenig gedult!
  Es ist das Spil noch nicht gar auss.
  Dort kompt auch gleich der Marschalt rauss.   300

  Der Marschalt geht ein, gibt der Pelimperia ein Zettel.

Mal. Den Zettel thut ausswendig lehrn!
  Thut allen Zorn gantz abwertz kehrn,
  Biss wir vnsern Feinden nachmals
  Den strick haben bracht an den Halss!
  So wöllen wir jhn zucken die Schlingen,   305
  Vnd all vnsere Feind vmbbringen.
  Gott geb, dass vns nicht thu misslingen!

  Sie geben die Händ einander vnd gehn ab.

ACTUS SEXTUS.

*Malignus, der Marschalt, geht ein, thut als schlag er Töppicht auff, butzt es alles
  zu der Comedi sauber; so kommen zu ihm Lorentz vnd Balthasar.*

Lor. Herr Marschalt, jhr thut euch bemühen.
  Werden wir denn so bald auffzihen,
  So wöll wir vnser Person staffirn.
Mal. Vns Comedianten wills gebürn
  Dass wir zeitlich gnug sind bereyt.   5
  Wenn der König sitzt an der Mahlzeit,
  So zihen wir dann auff alsbald.
Bal. Ich bitt, verzeicht mir, Herr Marschalt!·
  Mich deucht, ein Comedi macht Freud,
  Ein Tragedi nur Traurigkeit;   10
  Vnd weil wir sind in Freud erquickt,
  So hett sich für vns bass geschickt
  Ein fein posierlichs glächter Spil.
Mal. Davon halten die Weiber vil,
  Die gern tantzen, lachen vnd singen;   15
  Dargegen soll man von ernstlichen dingen
  Den Männern sagen vnd agirn.
Lor. Machts halt, wie es sich will gebürn!
  Wir wöllen gehn vns richten zu,
  Dass man alsbald auffzihen thu.   20

*Sie gehn alle ab, kompt der König mit seinen Leuten, als dem Ernesto, et-
  lichen Trabanten, vnd was er haben kan, setzt sich.*

Amur. Der Marschalt hats alls wol zugricht.
So spilt er auch ein schöne Gschicht,
Die wir haben gelesen schon.
Ernest. Mit der sach er wol vmbgehn kan.
Das machts, er hat sie offt getrieben,   25
Hat vil gelesen vnd geschrieben,
Auch selbst vil in der That erfahrn,
Hofdiener gwest vor langen Jahrn;
Dessgleichen ich nicht kenn im Reich.
Ich mercks, er will anfangen gleich.   30

Jetzt trumblt man, vnd zichen die Comedianten auff, vnd ist Balthasar *der*
Türckisch Soldan, Lorentz *ein Ritter von Rodis,* Pelimperia *die Liebhabent*
Jungkfrau, dess Soldans Schwester, Marschalt *der König auss Babylon; gehn*
vmb; alsdann gehen sie alle wider ab.   Kompt Balthazar, *in gestallt dess*
Türckischen Soldan, mit seiner Schwester, welche die Pelimperia *vertritt.*

Bal. *Hör, Schwester, es kompt mir jetzt für,*
Es streb der König von Babl nach dir,
Vnd du wollst jhn zum Gemahl han.
Nun ist er schier ein alter Mann
Vnd du bist ein junge Jungfrau.   35
Darumb dich eben wol fürschau!
Alt Männer vnd Junge Weiber
Haben zweyerley vngleich Leiber.
Solt dir dann dein freyen vmbschlagen,
Vnd du wollst kommen vnd mirs klagen,   40
Wenn du wollst handeln ohn mein raht,
So magst du dir haben den Schad,
Zu sampt dem aussglächter vnd hohn.
Pel. (in gestallt dess Soldans Schwester). *Ich hat gut Heyraht gehabt*
schon,
Vnd hat vnter denselben allen   45
Eur Lieb noch nie keiner gefallen.
Einer war euch nicht reich genung,
Einer zu alt, der ander zu jung,
Einer war nicht von Königlichem Gschlecht.
Wo nem ich ein, der euch wer recht?   50
Ihr thut mir alle Heyraht wehrn.
Wenn könd ich so kommen zu ehrn,
Ich wolt wol hie bey euch verligen
Dass ich nimmer kein Mann köndt kriegen.
Dasselb ich nicht erwarten will,   55
Vnd euch vertrauen in dem Spil,
Wenn jhr mir schlagt die Heyraht ab,
Dass ich ein Ordens Ritter hab,
Der will mich mit sich führen hin.
Vnd ich gäntzlich dess Willens bin   60

Mich mit demselben wegk zu begeben,
Vnd bey jhm zu sterben vnd leben.

Bal. (im Namen dess Soldans). *Ey, Schwester, thu ein wenig gmach!*
Lass mich nachdencken bass der Sach,
Vnd geh du in dein Gmach hinein!   65
Ich will von studan bey dir sein.

Die Jungfrau geht ab.

Meiner Schwestr Heyraht bringt mir leiden.
Ich muss sehen, wie ichs kön scheiden,
Vnd will dem König sagen frey
Dass mein Schwester nicht redlich sey,   70
Vnd dass sie an dem Ritter henck,
Damit er jhr nicht mehr nachdenck.
Auch so will ich dencken darneben,
Wie ich sie alle bring vmbs Leben.
Ich mag die Heyraht nicht nachgeben.   75

Er geht ab. Kompt Malignus *in gestallt dess Königs auss Babylonia.*

Mal. *Ach, sollt das Königlich Fräulein*
Mir zu der Ehe versprochen sein
Von jhrem Bruder, wie von jhr,
So wer alls leid benommen mir.
Aber wie ich mir lass sagen,   80
Thut er jhr andre Leut antragen
Vnd buhl vmb sie ein Ritter gwiss
Dess Ritters Orden von Rodis;
Vnd der thu darauff practicirn,
Dass er sie wöll mit gwalt weg führn.   85
Dieser wann er mir nur auffstiess,
Vnd sich dergleich vernemen liess,
So wolt ich jhm ohn allen schmertz
Den Stilet stossen durch sein Hertz,
Vnd die Jungfrauen retten mit.   90
Dort kompt, die meim Hertz machet frid.

Kompt Pelimperia *in Namen dess Soldans Schwester.*

Seyt mir willkom zu tausentmal!
Ach, wie leyd ich gross noth vnd qual
Von wegen eurer Lieb allein!

Pel. *Aber Soldan, der Bruder min,*   95
Thut mir das hefftig widerrahten,
Vnd zwar jhm selbst vnd mir zu schaden.
Dann lest er nicht die Heyrat zu,
Ich jhm zu schand vnd schmach was thu
Das ich zuvor nicht hett im Sinn;   100
Vnd köndt ich dann vmbbringen jhn,
Solt er mirs beichten keinem Pfaffen.

Mal. *Er hat euch zu gebieten noch schaffen,*
  Vnd bin so wol könig als er.
  Auch müst mir leid sein dass ich wer   105
  Nicht so mächtig, reich, vnd so gut,
  Nicht so wehrhafft an Hertz vnd Muht,
  Als er vnd eben seins gleichen.
  Drumb thut nicht von vns abweichen!
  Dann wir begern euch zu ehrn.   110
  Von dem Ritter thut euch abkehrn,
  Der euch mit gewalt wolt wegk führn!
Pel. *Ich will thun was sich will gebürn,*
  Vnd schwer damit, bey Eyd vnd Ehr,
  Wenn mich mein Bruder hindert mehr   115
  Wenn er mir bissher hat gethan,
  Vnd ich mich an jhm rechen kan,
  Dass ich will keinen fleiss nicht sparn
  Mein Lieb eur Lieb zuoffenbarn,
  Will ich dieselben haben vor andern.   120
Mal. *Königlichs Fräulein, ich muss jetzt wandern.*
  Doch habt gedult! ich komm bald wider,
  Vnd stich den Ritter zu boden nider,
  Der euch mit Gwalt wegführen wolt!
Pel. *Ach Gott, wenn das geschehen sollt,*   125
  Vnd ich könd eur Majestatt erwerben,
  So muss mein Bruder durch mich sterben,.
  Wenn jhr mir ein wenig wolt beystehn.
Mal. *Ja, ich fürcht sie nicht alle zwen.*
  Thun sie euch böss, schwer ich ein Eyd,   130
  Sie müssen sterben alle beyd.

                 Sie gehen ab.

Amur. Die Tragedi vns wol gefellt;
  Der Marschalt hats wŏl angestellt.
  Wie sie aber zu end wird gehn,
  Das gibt der Aussgang zuverstehn.   135

    Jetzt kompt Lorentz *in gestallt des Ritters auss Rodis.*

Lor. *Die Lieb wird in mir wie ein Feur.*
  Kein Pein vnd Straff, wie vngeheur
  Man mir die nur fürmahlen kan,
  Sollt mich nicht abtreiben davon
  Dass ich nicht absteh von meim ohrn.   140
  Gott geb, Gott grüss, was ich hab geschworn!
  Dess Königs Schwester muss mein sein,
  Oder will leyden Todes peyn.

Jetzt geht Pelimperia *in gestallt des Soldans Schwester ein.* Lorentz *in gestallt*
               dess Ritters geht zu jhr.

Königlichs Fräulein, krafft meins Hertzens,
Ein Heylerin alls Leyds vnd Schmertzens,   145
Ein Widerbringerin meins Lebens,
Last mein Hoffnung nicht sein vergebens!
Dann sollt ich euch nicht überkommen,
So wer mir all mein Trost benommen.
Darumb bitt ich, thut mich gewern!   150
Sicht es schon eur Bruder vngern,
Wöll wir wol an ein Ort davon,
Da er vns kein leid nicht mag than.
So will ich euch also versehen
Dass euch kein abbruch soll geschehen   155
An eurem Königlichen Stand.
Wollt jhr das thun, gebt mir eur Hand!
Pel. *Dasselb aber ist mir nicht eben,*
Dass ich euch meine Händ soll geben.
Ich verheyrat mich solcher Gstallt   160
Ausser meins Standts noch nicht so balt,
Auch nicht wider meins Bruders willen.

    Kompt der Marschalt *in gestallt dess Königs auss Babylon.*

Mal. *Halt! ich will dir dein hochmut stillen;*
Die Jungfrau steht mir zuversprechen.
Mein Stilet will ich in dich stechen.   165

    Er sticht den Lorentz *in gestallt dess Ritters, dass er stirbt.*

Amur. (*oben auff der Zinen*). Wenn das nur thut spillweiss geschehen,
   So ist gar lustig zuzusehen.

    Kompt Balthazar *in gestallt dess Soldans.*

Pel. *O gebt bald euren Dolchen mir,*
Dass ich mein Bruder im Zorn schwir,
Denselben auch stoss in sein Leib,   170
Ich vnd jhr vor jhm sicher bleib!

    Er schleicht jhr den Dolchen zu.

Bal. *Was habt jhr da für ein Blutbad?*
Vnd sagt, wer euch bestellet hat
Allein zu seyn bey meiner Schwester?
Ich hab dirs erst verbotten gester,   175
Du sollst der Mannsbild müssig stahn.

    Pelimperia *in gestallt seiner Schwester stöst jhm den Dolchen in Leib*

Pel. *Von deint wegen will ichs nicht lohn.*

    Er fellt vmb vnd stirbt.

Also sind vnser Feind gerochen,
Vnd die zwen Ehrendieb erstochen.
Jedoch seind wir in grosser gfahr;   180

Dass ein end nem mein traurn gar,
Vnd ich mich nicht mehr förchten darff
Meins Vatters straff, ernstlich vnd scharff,
Vnd komm zu eurem Sohn dest neher.
So gseng euch Gott, hertzlieber Schwehr!   185
Meins bleibens ist allhie nicht mehr.

Sie ersticht sich auch.

Amur. Wir glauben, bey königlicher Ehr,
Dass sie allsand gestorben sind.
Darunter sind drey KönigsKind,
Ein Sohn, ein Tochter, vnd ein Eyden.   190
Mal. (reist die Larffen weg). Der König lass sich dess bescheiden,
Dass auch den gringen Leuten sind
Gleich so lieb vnd wehrt jhre Kind
Als sie sind eurer Majestatt.
Die Tragedi den ernst hat,   195
Dass wir vnser Feind gar erstechen,
An dem wir vns begern zu rechen.

Er geht geschwind, zeicht sein Todten Sohn vnter dem aussgang aller mit Blut
am Leib gezeichnet herfür.

Secht doch die traurig Tragedi an!
Das hat eur Sohn gethan meim Sohn.
Das hat meim Vätterlichen Hertzen   200
Gebracht solch jammer, noht vnd schmertzen
Dass mirs kein Mensch auff Erden glaubt.
Dardurch ich ward der Sinn beraubt.
Nun weil wir vns gerochen haben,
So will ich dich lassen begraben,   205
Mein Hertzenallerliebsten Sohn,
Vnd will mir vor den Todt auch than.

Er tregt sein Sohn wider zu ruck, bringt ein strick vnd ein blosen Dolchen.

Nun will ich mich an den strick hencken.

Der König laufft mit seinem Gesind ein, nimpt jhm den Strick.

Amur. Ey, Gsell, das thu dir nur nicht dencken!

Sie reissen jhm Strick vnd Dolchen auss den Händen.

Du must ein ander Straff aussstehn.   210
Drumb sag bald, wie thets alls zugehn,
Dass du so vil mord hast gestifft?

Malignus *erwischt ein messer, schneit jhm die Zungen ab, wirfft sie wegk, vnd*
helt ein blutigs Tüchlein fürs Maul.

Schau doch einer zu dem Bösswicht!
Eh er vnss der Warheit bericht,
Eh schneyd er jhm selbst ab die Zungen,   215

Dass er darzu nicht werd gezwungen,
Doch solls nicht vnverschwigen bleiben.
Bringt ein Schreibzeug! so muss ers schreiben.

Es laufft einer ab, bringt ein Schreibzeug.

Auff dass wir dessen wissens han,
Wie dises übel sein Vrsprung gwan.   220

Er setzt sich vnd schreibt, schüttelt den kopff, er könn mit der Federn nicht
schreiben, man soll jhm ein Messerlein geben, er wöll die feder anderst
schneiden. Man gibt jhm eins, er stösts in den König, der fellt vnd stirbt,
alsdann ersticht er sich selbst.

Ernestus, *der Hauptman, beschleust:*

Ach ist das nit ein grosse Klag,
Dass so vil gross Leud auff ein Tag,
Nur von geschöpffter missgunst wegen,
Sind ermörd worden vnd erlegen!
Dann erstlich gwan Lorentz verdruss,   225
Dass der kühn Heldt Horatius
In dem krieg erlanget den Preiss,
Dass er auff jhn leget mit fleiss
Mit Verrähterey jhn vmbzubringen,
Vnd sein Schwester dahin zu zwingen,   230
Dass sie Balthazar nemb zur Ehe.
Dess must er sterben in Hertzen wehe.
Das stifftet als der böss Feind an.
Als man aber den Mord hett than,
So machet er gar gross die Gfahr,   235
Dass der Mord nicht würd offenbar,
Dass er vnd auch sind Helffer liessen
Ihren eignen Diener erschiessen,
Den andern aber an Galgen hencken,
Dass man dess übels nicht solt dencken.   240
Die Schwester liess er setzen ein.
Doch wards alls offenbaret fein,
Wie sich der erst Mord hett zutragen.
Darauss erfolgt gross weh vnd klagen,
Biss endlich die Mordthat war gerochen,   245
Den Authorn jhr Practick zerbrochen,
Dass sie in jren Sünden sturben,
Bedes an Seel vnd Leib verdurben.
Darauss man hat zu mercken schon,
Dass die Arbeit hat gleichen Lohn,   250
Dass auch keiner dem andern wehr
Was derselb hat mit Recht vnd Ehr,
Meyd böse Nachred hinder rück,
Den Gottsfürchtigen nicht vnterdrück,
Bey Leib aber begehe kein Mord,   255

Die weil Gott verbeut durch sein Wort,
Dass man ja niemand tödten soll !
Dann straffts die Oberkeit schon wol
Auff anruffen so balden nicht,
Sonder etwan durch die Finger sicht,   260
So thut doch Gott dat nicht vergessen,
Vnd lest eim solchen wider messen
Wie er andern gemessen hat ;
Vnd das offt auss eim kleinen schad
Kompt eines gantzen Lands verderben,   265
Dass siben vmb eins willen sterben.
Wie hie die Rädleinsführer beyd,
Der König, der die Grechtigkeit
Auff anruffen nicht liess ergehn,
Müssen schröckliche Straff aussstehn,   270
Von hinn scheiden ohn Reu vnd Beicht
Darauss man hat zu glauben leicht
Wie sie seind auss dem Leben gfahrn.
Gott wöll vns vor der gleich bewahrn,
Vnd zu dem ewigen Leben sparn !   275

Abgang.

NOTES

NOTES

THE SPANISH TRAGEDIE

ACT I.

SCENE I.

THIS Induction was probably suggested by the opening Scene of Seneca's *Thyestes*, where the Ghost of Tantalus appears in the company of a Fury.

1–5. Few passages in Elizabethan literature were so often quoted and caricatured as these lines. Cf. Heywood's *The Fair Maid of the West, Part I*, v. i:

> 'It is not now as when Andrea liv'd
> Or rather Andrew, our elder Journeyman !
> What, Drawers become Courtiers ? Now may I speake,
> With the old ghost in *Ieronimo*:
> "When this eternall substance of my soule
> Did live imprisoned in this wanton flesh,
> I was a Courtier in the Court of Fesse." '

And Fletcher's *Knight of the Burning Pestle*, v. iii, where Ralph enters with a forked arrow through his head, and cries:

> 'When I was mortal, this my costive corps
> Did lay up figs and raisins in the Strand:
> Where sitting, I espied a lovely dame,
> Whose master wrought with lingel and with awl.'

See too Shirley's *The Bird in a Cage*, iii. 1, where Bonamico, who is supposed to have died, reappears among his friends, and after quoting ll. 1–2, 'and so forth,' asks them, 'And how d'ye like *Don Andrea*, gentlemen?' For other parodies in *Wily Beguiled*, Tomkis' *Albumazar*, and Rawlins' *The Rebellion*, see *Introduction*, pp. xciv–xcviii.

10. *In secret*. These words are of importance. The love of Andrea and the high-born Bel-imperia was clandestine, and Pedringano, a servant in the Duke of Castile's household, had acted as go-between. The affair was, however, discovered, and had led to a violent display of anger on the Duke's part. This we learn from

several references in later parts of the play. Thus in Act ii. 1. 45-50, Lorenzo, Bel-imperia's brother, reminds Pedringano :

> 'It is not long, thou knowst,
> Since I did shield thee from my fathers wrath,
> For thy conueiance in *Andreas* loue,
> For which thou wert adiudg'd to punishment :
> I stood betwixt thee and thy punishment,
> And since, thou knowest how I haue fauoured thee.

Similarly Lorenzo (iii. 10. 54-5) recalls to Bel-imperia

> 'that olde disgrace,
> Which you for *Don Andrea* had indurde.'

and tells her (iii. 10. 70) that her melancholy since the news of Andrea's death

> 'My Fathers olde wrath hath exasperate.'

The Duke himself refers to the episode (iii. 14. 108-12) :

> 'How now, girle ?
> Why commest thou sadly to salute vs thus ?
> Content thy selfe, for I am satisfied :
> It is not now as when *Andrea* liu'd ;
> We haue forgotten and forgiuen that.'

For the bearing of these passages on the questions of the source of the play and the authenticity of *The First Part of Ieronimo*, see *Introduction*, pp. xxxi and xlii.

15. *the late conflict with Portingale.* See *Introduction*, pp. xxx-xxxi.

18-85. This narrative of the descent of Andrea's Ghost into Hell is skilfully modelled on Virgil's account of Aeneas' visit to the under-world in the *Aeneid*, Bk. vi. With 20-2 cf. *Aen.* vi. 326-8, and with 30-1 cf. *Aen.* vi. 417-25, 'honied speech' being substituted for the *melle soporatam et medicatis frugibus offam* of the original. With 32-37 cf. *Aen.* vi. 430-2; with 41-4 cf. *Aen.* vi. 440-4; with 47 cf. *Aen.* vi. 477-8 ; and with 57-8 cf. *Aen.* vi. 625-7. Similarly 59-64 and 72-3 follow *Aen.* vi. 540-3, but with one noteworthy modification. Virgil writes :

> '*Hic locus est partes ubi se via findit in ambas.*
> *Dextera, quae Ditis magni sub moenia tendit;*
> *Hac iter Elysium nobis; at laeva malorum*
> *Exercet poenas, et ad impia Tartara mittit.*'

But Kyd substitutes 'three waies,' because Aeneas, to whom Deiphobus gives this description, has already in his descent passed the 'fieldes of loue' and the 'Martiall fields,' while Andrea has only hitherto heard them mentioned by 'Eacus' and 'Rhadamant.' He has therefore to include them in his picture of the regions through which he descends after his passport is drawn, and thus we have the triple division with 'the foresaid fields' on the right, 'deepest hell' on the left, and the

'Elizian greene' in the middle. The punishments of hell, 65–71, are
adapted from *Aen.* vi. 570–1, 601, 608–713, and 616–7 ; and 'the gates
of Horn,' 82–3, are taken from *Aen.* vi. 893.

46. *Martialist.* Used by Greene, Beaumont and Fletcher, and
Dekker, but not by Shakespeare.

81. *rounded*, whispered. Cf. *Winter's Tale*, i. 2. 217–8 :

> 'They're here with me already, whisp'ring, rounding :
> "Sicilia is a so-forth."'

SCENE II.

12–14. Adapted from Claudian's *De Tertio Consulatu Honorii*, 96–98 :

> '*O nimium dilecte Deo, cui fundit ab antris*
> *Aeolus armatas hyemes; cui militat aether,*
> *Et coniurati veniunt ad classica venti.*'

41. *Cornet*, a troop of cavalry ; so called from the standard at its
head. Cf. Peele's *Battle of Alcazar*, Act i :

> 'Take a cornet of our horse,
> As many argolets and armed pikes.'

52–4. Cf. *Corn.* v. 170–1 and 183–4.

55–6. Partly taken from Statius, *Thebais*, viii. 399 :

> '*Ense minax ensis, pede pes, et cuspide cuspis;*'

partly (as Schick suggests) formed on the analogy of such passages as
Aeneid x. 361 :

> '*haeret pede pes, densusque viro vir.*'

and *Curtius*, iii. 2. 13 :

> '*vir viro, armis arma, conserta sunt.*'

59. *scindred.* A unique spelling ; possibly a misprint.

70. *Heere–hence*, from henceforth. Cf. Chapman, *Hymn to Hermes*, 59 :

> 'But Hermes herehence having his content
> Cared for no more.'

92. *their Vice-roy.* See *Introduction*, p. xxx.
Stage-direction *tucket*, a flourish of trumpets.

139. *controlde*, overmastered, held in check.

143. *corsiue*, corrosive, annoyance. Seldom used in this metaphorical
sense.

160. *whether.* Here used in its early pronominal sense, 'which of
the two.' This use is not found in Shakespeare, but it occurs in A. V.
St. Matthew, xxi. 31, 'whether of them twain did the will of his
father ?'

164. *wan.* This M.E. form of the preterite is found in Qq. of 1 *Henry IV*,
iii. 2. 59, but Ff. read 'won.'

172. Cf. *King John*, ii. 1. 137 :

> 'You are the Hare, of whom the Proverb goes,
> Whose valour plucks dead Lyons by the beard.'

Scene III.

5. Cf. for a repetition of this violent *oxymoron* Act iii. 13. 29, and iv. 2. 31 :

> 'But let her rest in her vnrest awhile.'

and *Richard III*, iv. 4. 29 :

> 'Rest thy vnrest on England's lawfull earth.'

7. Schick suggests that the line is a paraphrase of Seneca's *Phaedra*, 607 :

> '*Curae leves loquuntur, ingentes stupent.*'

15-7. Probably another case of ·adaptation. Schick notes that John Webster, the writer of the pamphlet *Academiarum Examen* (1654), quotes in his introductory *Epistle to the Reader* the line :

> '*Qui cadit in terram, non habet vnde cadat.*'

Similarly Thomas Andrewe, in *The Vnmasking of a Feminine Machiavell* (1604) fol. B3b, quotes in the margin :

> '*Qui iacet in terram* ⟨sic⟩ *non habet vnde cadat.*'

On Andrewe's poem, see further *Introduction*, p. xcvi.

74. *Where then became*, what became of. A good instance of the transition from the more restricted meaning of 'become,' as a verb of motion, to its wider and vaguer use.

82. *Terseraes Lord.* Alexandro was apparently *Capitão Donatario* of Tersera or Terceira, one of the islands belonging to the Azores group. This title was bestowed upon the original discoverers and colonizers of countries annexed to the Portuguese crown, and gave its holder almost despotic sway. The privileges of the post were hereditary, and descended to the lineal successors of those to whom they were granted. See *Introduction*, p. xxix, for the bearing of this passage upon the date of the play.

Scene IV.

7. *nill.* Not used by Shakespeare, except twice in the proverbial form 'will he, nill he,' 'will you, nill you.'

20. Cf. *Aeneid*, ii. 615-6 :

> '*Iam summas arces Tritonia* (*respice*) *Pallas*
> *Insedit, nimbo effulgens et Gorgone saeva.*'

22. *pauncht*, stabbed in the belly. Cf. *Tempest*, iii. 2. 101 :

> ' Batter his skull, or paunch him with a stake.'

Shakespeare, by putting it into the mouth of Caliban, indicates that it is a coarse phrase.

dingd, knocked down. Another curiously blunt phrase in its connexion here.

27. *remorce*, regret, pity.

35. *welding*, carrying. An unusual sense of the word, developed from the meaning 'to possess, make use of.' The retention of the M.E. form by Kyd is noticeable.

53-4. *will not slacke . . . to serue.* For this uncommon use of 'slack,' followed by an infinitive, cf. *Deut.* xxiii. 21 : 'When thou shalt vow a vow unto the Lord thy God, thou shalt not slack to pay it.'

90. *ambages*, round-about phrases.

97. *translucent.* Cf. *Soliman and Perseda*, ii. 1. 60, where the variant 'tralucent' is used.

98. *words of course*, obligatory, ceremonial phrases. Cf. Steele, *Tatler*, 109 : 'Their congratulations and condolences are equally words of course.'

105. *humerous*, capricious, variable.

Scene V.

22. *pompous*, splendid, stately; without any disparaging connotation. Cf. Coryat, *Crudities*, i. 36 : 'I will make relation of those pompous ceremonies that were publiquely solemnized.'

26-31. Kyd's history is here curiously inaccurate. There is no reason to suppose that Robert of Gloucester was ever in Portugal. But the capture of 'Sarasin' Lisbon in 1147 was effected partly by the help of a body of Englishmen. Affonso Henriques, the Portuguese hero-king, was fortunate in securing for this hazardous enterprise the assistance of a fleet of crusaders who had put in at Oporto on their way to the Holy Land. The bulk of those on board were English, and a letter written by one of them is still extant, mentioning among the leaders Hervey Glanvill, constable of the men of Norfolk and Suffolk, Simon of Dover, constable of all the ships of Kent, and Andrew of London. Robert of Gloucester, as it happens, died of fever in England, on Oct. 31, in this year, exactly a week after the capture of Lisbon.

36-42. Kyd's history is here not quite so wild as before, for Edmund Langley, Earl of Kent, fifth son of Edward III, did make an expedition to Portugal during his brother Richard II's reign. With this exception, however, his account is ludicrously wrong. Edmund set sail from England in July, 1381, to help the King of Portugal against the Spaniards. But through inaction very little was effected, and the King made peace secretly with his enemies. When his treachery was discovered, Edmund would have attacked him had he felt strong enough, but, as it was, he had no choice except to return to England in October, 1382. In 1385 he took part in the expedition to Scotland, and for his services was rewarded by a grant of £1000, and the title Duke of York. (See *Dictionary of National Biography*, Article *Edmund de Langley*.)

47-52. Kyd's history is still mainly fanciful. John of Gaunt made an expedition to Spain in 1367, under the Black Prince, to support

Pedro the Cruel against Henry of Trastamare, but the allusion is here more probably to his later expedition of 1386-7, when he claimed the throne of Castile. He met with success at first, but sickness broke out among his troops, and he was forced to retire from Spain and fall back upon Bayonne. Negotiations, however, followed, which resulted in the marriage of his daughter, Catharine, to the heir to the Castilian throne.

ACT II.

SCENE I.

1-10. Modelled, especially 3-6 and 9-10, on the opening lines of Sonnet 47, in Watson's *Hecatompathia*:

> 'In time the Bull is brought to weare the yoake ;
> In time all haggred Haukes will stoope to Lures ;
> In time small wedge will cleaue the sturdiest Oake ;
> In time the marble weares with weakest shewres.
> More fierce is my sweete loue, more hard withall
> Then Beaste or Birde, then Tree or stony wall.'

Watson's lines are an adaptation of the opening lines of Serafino's 103rd Sonnet :

> '*Col tempo el Vilanello al giogo mena*
> *El Tor, si fiero e si crudo animale;*
> *Col tempo el Falcon s'usa a menar l' ale,*
> *E ritornare à te chiamando à pena.*'

On the significance of the passage in helping to date the play see *Introduction*, pp. xxiv and xxix. Further parallels may be found in *Euphues*, e.g.: 'The softe droppes of raine pearce the hard marble, many strokes ouerthrow the tallest oke.' Line 3 is quoted in *Much Ado about Nothing*, i. 1. 271, but as it is a proverbial expression, we cannot be certain, though it is highly probable, that Shakespeare is referring to the present Scene. In *The Poëtaster*, Act iii. 1, at Tucca's command to recite 'in an amorous vein,' the 1st Pyrgus declaims ll. 9-10, 25-26, 21-22, 27-28 of Balthazar's speech. An amusing parody of the Scene occurs in Nathaniel Field's *A Woman is a Weathercock*, Act i. 2 :

> '*Sir Abr. Ninny.* O no, she laughs at me and scorns my suit :
> For she is wilder and more hard withal,
> Than beast or bird, or tree, or stony wall.
> *Kate.* Ha! God-a-mercy, old Hieronimo.
> *Abr.* Yet might she love me for my lovely eyes.
> *Count Fred.* Ay, but perhaps your nose she doth despise.
> *Abr.* Yet might she love me for my dimpled chin.
> *Pendant.* Ay, but she sees your beard is very thin.
> *Abr.* Yet might she love me for my proper body.
> *Strange.* Ay, but she thinks you are an arrant noddy...
> *Abr.* Yet might she love me in despite of all.
> *Lucida.* Ay, but indeed I cannot love at all.'

20. *I, but.* On Kyd's use of this and other distinctively Euphuistic constructions, see *Introduction*, p. xxiv.

45-50. See note on i. 1. 10.

47. *conueiance,* cunning, secret agency.

58. *If case.* For this construction cf. 3 *Henry VI*, v. 4. 34:

> 'If case some one of you would flye from us.'

67-75. These lines, with the omission of 75-6, and with slight verbal changes in 69 and 72, are recited by the two Pyrgi in the Scene from *The Poetaster* referred to in the Note on 1-10 above.

87. *this cross.* 92 proves that the 'cross' was the hilt of Lorenzo's sword.

107. *tam armis quam ingenio.* A well-known motto of which *tam Marti quam Mercurio* is a variant.

SCENE II.

S.D. Balthazar *and* Lorenzo *aboue.* The reading of the earlier Qq. *aboue* is right, for Balthazar and Lorenzo overhear the dialogue between the lovers from a raised platform at the back of the stage, probably identical with the 'gallerie' from which later the Court views Hieronimo's play, cf. iv. 3. 12. In *The Tempest*, iii. 3. 19 ff., Prospero, while surveying the invitation of his enemies to the enchanted banquet by strange shapes, is described in the Ff. stage-directions as, 'on the top.'

37. *counterchecke.* In using this phrase Bel-imperia is keeping up the metaphor of a 'war' between herself and her lover; she will meet his loving strategy with a kindred countermove.

46. *trauellers,* labourers, in which sense the spelling of Qq. 1623-33 'trauailers' is now usual.

50. *the prickle at her breast.* An allusion to the common legend that the nightingale sings with a 'prickle' or 'thorn' at her breast, in order to keep awake.

SCENE III.

3. *coy it,* affect shyness. Cf. Massinger, *A New Way to Pay Old Debts*, iii. 2:

> 'When he comes to woo you, see you do not coy it.'

9-21. On the probable semi-historical references here, see *Introduction*, p. xxx.

SCENE IV.

7. *controles,* is at issue with, conflicts with the promptings of.

28. *record,* repeat their songs. Cf. Ben Jonson, *Penates*:

> 'Sweet robin, linnet, thrush,
> Record from every bush.'

44-5. Quoted, with slight verbal variations, by Gullio in *The Returne from Pernassus*, iii. 1. 1025-6, whereupon Ingenioso comments, 'Faith, gentleman! you're reading is wonderfull in our English poetts.' Sarrazin (p. 43) quotes from *The Historie of Soliman and Perseda* in Wotton's *Courtlie Controuersie* a passage which he thinks Kyd may have had in mind: 'And with their bodies likewise encreased and augmented their new conceiued loue, like vnto the yong Vine, which embraceth the tender Elme, wherunto it is so firmly vnited by their mutuall growth, as in fine they are incorporate togither.' The resemblance, however, may be accidental, and it is certainly a far-fetched suggestion that Shakespeare had Kyd's lines in his memory when he wrote, *Comedy of Errors*, ii. 2. 176:

> 'Thou art an Elme, my husband, I a Vine,
> Whose weaknesse married to thy stronger state
> Makes me with thy strength to communicate.'

SCENE V.

1-12. There is abundant testimony to the enduring impression created by the tragic situation at the close of Scene iv and here. The Quartos from 1615 onwards have a woodcut illustrating the episode, which was doubtless singled out for this honour on account of its popularity. Imitations and caricatures of it were incessant for half a century. It suggested, as shown in *Introduction*, pp. lxxxix-xc, a striking passage in *Arden of Feversham*, iii. 2; and in *The Returne from Pernassus*, iv. 3, Studioso gives proof of his theatrical powers by reciting part of Hieronimo's speech. Generally, however, the episode is ridiculed by other dramatists. In *The Poetaster*, iii. 1, it is thus parodied:

> '*Tuc.* Now thunder, sirrah, you, the rumbling player.
> 2 *Pyr.* Ay, but somebody must cry "Murder," then, in a small voice.
> *Tuc.* Your fellow-sharer there shall do 't; cry, sirrah, cry.
> 1 *Pyr.* Murder! Murder!
> 2 *Pyr.* Who calls out murder, lady, was it you?
> *Hist.* O admirable good, I protest.'

For other burlesques in Ludowick Barry's *Ram Alley*, v. 1, and Rawlins' *Rebellion*, v. 1, see *Introduction*, pp. xci and xcvii-xcviii. The opening line of Hieronimo's speech, in particular, became a regular byword. Shakespeare uses the phrase 'naked bed' in *Venus and Adonis*, 397:

> 'Who sees his true love in her naked bed';

and he has a jest at this line and at iii. 12. 31 in *The Taming of the Shrew*, Induction, l. 9: 'Go by, S. Ieronimie, goe to thy cold bed, and warm thee.' The same words, except 'Go by, S. Ieronimie,' are repeated by Edgar in *King Lear*, iii. 4. 48. In Thomas Randolph's *Conceited Pedlar* (printed 1630) occurs the statement: 'If your laughter give my embryon jests but safe deliverance, I dare maintain it in the

throat of Europe, Jeronimo rising from his naked bed was not so good
a midwife.' Fletcher in *The Chances*, Act v. 3 (quoted by Fleischer),
puts the line, in garbled form, 'Who calls Jeronimo from his naked
bed?' into the mouth of Don John.

29. *leese*. This M.E. form had not died out entirely in Elizabethan
English. It is found in Shakespeare, *Sonnet* v :

> 'But flowers distill'd, though they with winter meet,
> Leese but their show, their substance still lives sweet.'

and in Ben Jonson, *Every man out of his Humour*, v. 1 : 'Take heed
you leese it not, signior, ere you come there.'

40-1. Sarrazin compares *Hamlet*, iv. 7. (Quarto 1):

> 'Reuenge it is must yeeld this heart releefe ;
> For woe begets woe, and griefe hangs on griefe.'

55-6. Cf. i. 5. 15.

91. *infective*, infectious.

46. *sweet louely Rose*. Used of Richard II by Hotspur, 1 *Henry IV*,
i. 3. 175.

49. *the glasses of his sight*. Cf. *Coriolanus*, iii. 2. 117 :

> 'And Schooleboyes Teares take up
> The Glasses of my sight.'

67-80. A *pastiche*, in Kyd's singular fashion, of tags from classical
poetry, and lines of his own composition. Dr. Traube of Munich
(quoted by Schick) has pointed out the probable source of 72-3 in
Tibullus, ii. 4. 55 ff. :

> '*Quidquid habet Circe, quidquid Medea veneni,*
> *Quidquid et herbarum Thessala terra gerit....*
> *Si modo me placido videat Nemesis mea vultu,*
> *Mille alias herbas misceat illa, bibam.*'

The latter part of 78: '*sic, sic iuuat ire sub umbras*' is from *Aeneid*, iv. 660.

ACT III.

SCENE I.

1-11. An adaptation of Seneca's *Agamemnon*, 57-73.

> '*O regnorum magnis fallax*
> *Fortuna bonis, in praecipiti*
> *Dubioque locas excelsa nimis.*
> *Nunquam placidam sceptra quietem*
> *Certumve sui tenuere diem ;*
> *Alia ex alia cura fatigat*
> *Vexatque animos nova tempestas.*
> *Non sic Libycis Syrtibus aequor*
> *Furit alternos volvere fluctus,*

> *Non Euxini turget ab imis*
> *Commota vadis unda, nivali*
> *Vicina polo,*
> *Ubi, caeruleis immunis aquis,*
> *Lucida versat plaustra Bootes,*
> *Ut praecipites regum casus*
> *Fortuna rotat.*
> *Metui cupiunt, metuique timent.'*

8. *striueth ... the waues.* This use of a singular verb, followed by a subject in the plural is, of course, frequent in Elizabethan English.

19. *traine*, deceitful expression, guile. Cf. iii. 2. 38, where the word is used in the sense of 'trap' or 'snare.'

21. *consorted*, consorted with, accompanied. This transitive use of the verb is somewhat rare. Shakespeare uses it metaphorically, *Love's Labour's Lost*, ii. 1. 178:

> 'Sweet health and faire desires consort your grace.'

The noun occurs in Kyd's letter to Puckering: 'of whose consent if I had been, no question but I shold also haue been of their consort.'

23. *coastes*, keeps close to. Cf. Fletcher and Rowley's *Maid in the Mill*, i. 1:

'Who are these that coast us? You told me the walk was private.'

43. Sarrazin notes the parallelism between this and 1 *Tamburlaine*, i. 1:

> 'But this it is that doth excruciate
> The verie substance of my vexed soule.'

47. *when*, an expression of impatience. Cf. Prospero's exclamation to Caliban, *Tempest*, i. 2. 316: 'Come, thou tortoise, when?' Dodsley, ignorant of this Elizabethan use of 'when,' changed it wrongly to 'with him.'

52. *malisde*. The use of this verb without an accusative following is very rare.

79. *quitall*, requital.

98. *meane*, moderate.

SCENE II.

1-4. On Jonson's ironical praise of these 'fine speeches' in *Everyman in his Humour*, i. 4, and on the parody of them in Tomkis' *Albumazar*, see *Introduction*, pp. lxxxiii–lxxxiv and xcv–xcvi.

2. There seems an echo of this line in *Romeo and Juliet*, iv. 5. 58:

> 'O loue! o life! not life, but loue in death!'

12. *secretary to my mones*, the confidant to whom my moans are uttered.

13. *wake.* I have retained the reading of Qq., as though there is a singular subject 'night,' the verb is probably attracted in to the plural by the preceding word 'visions.' In 15 'solicite' is probably similarly attracted by 'wounds,' and 21 'driue' by 'dreames.'

24-5. Quoted (with change of 'Whats here?' into 'Whats this?') in Field's *A Woman is a Weathercock*, i. 1, when Nevill finds Scudamore reading a letter from Bellafront.

38. *traine*, snare, trap. Cf. iii. 1. 19.

48. *circumstances*, round-about, indirect methods. Cf. Shakespeare, *Merchant of Venice*, i. 1. 154:

> 'You . . . herein spend but time,
> To winde about my loue with circumstance.'

83. *S. Luigis*. Schick's plausible conjecture for the '*S. Luigis*' of the earlier Qq. *Luigi*, as he says 'is at any rate Italian, if not Spanish.'

94. *Che le Ieron*. An unintelligible exclamation, possibly a corruption of the page's name.

SCENE III.

15. *suspect*, suspicion.

S.D. *Shootes the Dagge*. A 'dagge' or 'dag' is a heavy pistol. Reed quotes, among other illustrations, three instances of the word from *Arden of Feversham*, iii. 6.

37. *Ile be his Priest*. A euphemism for ' I'll murder him,' the priest being the attendant at a man's death. Fleischer compares 2 *Henry VI*, iii. 1 :

> 'And to preserve my Soveraigne from his foe,
> Say but the word, and I will be his Priest.'

SCENE IV.

3. *mistrust*, suspect.

24. *the fact*, the criminal deed. Cf. *Murder of Iohn Brewen*, p. 287, l. 8.

35. *hardly shall deny*, shall with difficulty resist my pleadings.

36. It seems strange that Balthazar, still technically a prisoner of war, should claim the right to interfere with judicial proceedings in Spain.

42. *limde*, ensnared.

45. *holpe*. For this form of the strong past part. of. *Tempest*, i. 2. 62-3:

> 'Were we . . . blessedly holpe hither.'

46. *fatch*, contrivance, stratagem.

56. *to stand good Lord*, to act as a good lord to him.

69. *turned off*, hanged.

78. *tickle*, critical, touch-and-go.

79. *ends . . . doubts*. Cf. Note on iii. 1. 8.

83. *pretence*, intention.

SCENE VI.

16. Hieronimo probably refers to the handkerchief dipped in Horatio's blood (cf. ii. 5. 51) which lies concealed near his heart.

23. *geere*, business.

44-5. *thou wouldst . . . my habit.* An allusion to the custom of the hangman obtaining the clothes of those whom he executed.

48. *without boot,* except it be to my advantage (which it will not be).

67. *companion,* low fellow. Cf. *2 Henry IV,* ii. 4. 132 : 'I scorne you, scuruie companion.'

94. *That . . . hapines,* that bar it from reaching happiness. Here the singular verb 'intercepts' comes after a plural subject. The construction is more frequent when the verb precedes the subject.

Scene VII.

8. Kyd repeats these striking, if overstrained, figures of speech, in *Cornelia,* i. 40 :

> 'And with their blood made marsh the parched plaines.'

And v. 420 :

> 'And dewe yourselues with springtides of your teares.'

16. *countermurde,* strongly fenced in. A 'countemure' is a wall built within, or outside of, another wall for additional defence. The use of the verb is rare.

65. *band,* cursed.

Scene VIII.

Here Hawkins, followed by the later English Editors, begins a new Act. But there is no warrant for this division in the Quartos. Kyd evidently wrote the play in four Acts, each closing with the appearance of The Ghost and Revenge as Chorus. Schick notices appositely that the Elizabethan versions of Seneca's *Thebais* and *Octavia* are divided into four Acts.

5. *recure* combines here its original meaning of 'heal' with a suggestion of 'recover,' 'bring back,' due to its confusion with M.E. recouren = recoveren.

8. *outrage,* outcry.

11. *whipstalke,* the handle of a whip.

Scene IX.

13. *apply me,* conform myself.

Scene X.

19. *soothe me vp,* confirm what I say. Schick compares O.E. gesôðian = to prove the truth of, bear witness. Cf. Massinger, *Duke of Milan,* v. i :

> 'Sooth me in all I say:
> There's a main end in it.'

20. *stand on tearmes with,* make conditions with, stands on her rights.

21. Lorenzo's jaunty and laconic allusion to Horatio's murder and Bel-imperia's secret detention is highly characteristic.

28. *With extreames abuse my company*, use fatal violence to my companion.

54-5, and 68-70. See Note on i. 1. 10.

102-3. Another piece of classical patchwork, of which the meaning is obscure.

SCENE XI.

8. *ballace.* An Elizabethan variant of 'ballast.' Cf. Induction to *Every man in his Humour* : 'When his belly is well ballaced, and his brain rigged little, he sails away withal.'

17. *Bacon.* Very rarely used, as here, of a live pig.

23. *vnsquard, vnbeuelled*, uneven and unpolished.

39. *Tooke him vnto mercy.* This simple emendation gives a satisfactory sense. 'Him '= Balthazar, with, 'that valiant but ignoble Portugal in apposition.' It would appear, however, from Balthazar's words, i. 2. 161-5, that Horatio would have killed him, but for Lorenzo's intervention.

43. *And things called whippes.* This phrase comes probably from the old *Hamlet.* Cf. Armin's *Nest of Ninnies*, p. 55 (1608) : 'Ther are, as Hamlet saies, things cald whips in store.' It is used also in 2 *Henry VI*, ii. 1. 136: 'Have you not Beadles in your Towne, and things call'd Whippes?'

13-25. Sarrazin (*Thomas Kyd*, &c., p. 53) has pointed out some similarities of phrase between this passage and Spenser's description of the Cave of Despair, *Faerie Queene*, i. 9. 33 and 34. Cf. especially 19, 20 with :

> ' Ere long they come, where that same wicked wight
> His dwelling has, low in an hollow cave
> Far underneath a craggy cliff ypight.'

But the parallelism is probably only accidental.

SCENE XII.

1. S.D. *Enter* Hieronimo *with a Ponyard in one hand and a Rope in the other.* Hieronimo appears with the stock 'properties' of a would-be suicide. Schröer (*Über Titus Andronicus*, pp. 77, 78) compares the scene in Greene and Lodge's *Looking Glass for London*, where the repentant usurer enters similarly provided. In the *Faerie Queene*, i. 9. 29, Despair, when persuading Sir Trevisan and Sir Teruin to die, offers the one a ' rope,' the other ' a rusty knife.' So in Skelton's *Magnyfycence*, l. 2312 ff., Despair offers Magnyfycence a knife and a rope.

3. *seld seene*, unusual, curious.

14, 15. *this path . . . or this*, i. e. the rope or the poniard.

16-9. Schick points out that the sequence of ideas here is exactly the same as in Hieronimo's Latin hexameters, ii. v. 78-80.

22. *I'll be with thee to bring*, I'll chastise you, bring you to reason. Cf. *Troilus and Cressida*, i. 2. 305 :

> '*Pand.* I'll be with you niece, by-and-by.
> *Cress.* To bring, uncle ?'

24. *there goes the hare away.* A proverbial phrase, meaning 'here the matter ends.' Schick, however, quoting Gosson's *Schole of Abuse*, p. 70: '*Hic labor, hoc opus est,* there goeth the hare away,' interprets the phrase here, 'there is the game I want to hunt ; that's where the game lies !'

31. *Hieronimo beware ; goe by, goe by.* Perhaps no single passage in Elizabethan drama became so notorious as this. It is quoted over and over again as the stock phrase to imply impatience of anything disagreeable, inconvenient, or old-fashioned. Thus Sly in the Induction to *The Taming of the Shrew* (ll. 7-10), in answer to the Hostess' question : 'You will not pay for the glasses you haue burst ?' retorts, ' No, not a deniere. Go by, S. Ieronimo, goe to thy cold bed and warme thee.' (Cf. Note on ii. 5. 1-12.) In Dekker's *Shoemaker's Holiday* (1600), Sibil, when bidding Rose disregard Rowland Lacy, says: 'If I were as you, I de cry, go by Ieronimo, go by.' In Dekker's *Satiromastix* (1602), when Blunt offers Horace money if he will write an ode, Tucca cries, ' Goe by Ieronimo, goe by.' In Dekker and Webster's *Westward Hoe*, ii. 3 (c. 1604), Mistress Birdlime describes a woman as, 'like a play ; if new, very good company, very good company ; but if stale, like old Ieronimo, go by, go by.' In Middleton's *Blurt, Master Constable*, iv. i. (1602), Simperina, wishing to get rid of the old courtier Curvetto, cries, 'Go from my window go, go away ; go by, old Ieronimo.' In *A new Dittie in prayse of Money*, contained in a collection issued by T. Delaney (1607), and quoted by Koeppel (*Engl. Studien*, xviii. 133), the proverbial character of the phrase is still more clearly shown :

> 'When thou hast money, then friendes thou hast many,
> When it is wasted, their friendship is cold.
> Goe by, Ieronimo ; no man then will thee know.'

Similar, though even more striking, is the use of the phrase quoted by Dyce from Taylor's *Superbiae Flagellum* (1630) :

> 'For as a cart-wheele in the way goes round,
> The spoake that's high'st is quickly at the Ground,
> So Enuy or iust cause, or misconceit,
> In Princes Courts continually do waite,
> That he that is this day Magnifico
> To-morrow may goe by Ieronimo.'

Dyce further (*Remarks on Collier's and Knight's editions of Shakespeare*) quotes a use of it as a nickname from Fletcher's *The Captain*, iii. 5, where Jacomo is told that he will be called :

> ' Bloody-bones, and Spade, and Spit-fire,
> And Gaffer Madman, and Go-by-Ieronimo,
> And Will-with-a-whisp, &c.'

61. It is evident from the King's words here, and from the dialogue that follows between him and Lorenzo, 83 ff., that he is still ignorant of Horatio's murder. There is a want of plausibility in this, for Hieronimo has no object in concealing the fact from the King, though he may hesitate to denounce the powerful Lorenzo as the murderer.

71. *Ile rip the bowels oj the earth.* Cf. *Jew of Malta*, i. 1:

'Ripping the bowels of the earth for them.'

where the present passage is probably imitated.

79. *outrage.* See Note on iii. 8. 8.

101. *our selfe will exempt ⟨him⟩ the place.* The emendation here proposed is simpler than that adopted by Hazlitt and Schick. Moreover it is natural to speak of exempting a man from a place involving duties; not of holding the place itself exempt. Again, the use of the emphatic pronoun 'our selfe' is thus explained. Lorenzo has urged that Hieronimo should be made to resign his office. The King answers that, as this would increase the Marshal's melancholy, he, of his own accord, will excuse him from his duties, without demanding his resignation, till the matter can be fully investigated. Collier's emendation 'execute' is not given in his edition of Dodsley, but in his Introduction to *The Murder of Iohn Brewen*. It may possibly be right, as the Marshal's duties are chiefly judicial (cf. iii. 4. 36, and iii. 6. 11, 12 and 35, 36), and could be temporarily discharged by the King.

XII A.

30. *Then we burne day light.* A proverbial expression, meaning ' we waste time.'

36. *agglots*, ornamental tags; 'aglots' and 'aglets' are variants of this word, but 'aggots,' the earlier reading, = 'agates.'

101. *reaued*, robbed of; the weak form of the past participle is uncommon.

109. *tree.* Hieronimo is anticipating his more emphatic request in 121, 122; but it is possible that 'teare,' the reading of 1602 A, is right.

114. *matted*, apparently means ' set in a mat or mount, i. e. a piece of thick paper or cardboard used to protect or set off a picture.' Schick, who gives 'dull' as the meaning, evidently looks on 'matted' as a variant of 'mat' or 'matt' = faint or dull in colour.

123. *seemingly*, in semblance. The Painter can show on his canvas the symbol of a cry.

130. *beardes . . . of Iudas his owne collour*, red beards. Reed quotes, among other illustrations, Middleton's *Chaste Maid in Cheapside*, iii. 2: 'What has he given her? ... Two great 'postle spoons, one of them gilt. Sure that was Judas with the red beard.' He refers to Leland's *Collectanea* and Plot's *Oxfordshire* as authorities for the statement that painters constantly represented Judas with red hair. There may be an allusion also to the ' make-up ' of Judas in the Miracle Plays.

131. iuttie ouer, hang over, project.

140. ierring. Rare variant of 'iarring,' i.e. being marked off by the vibrations of the pendulum.

SCENE XIII.

1. *Vindicta mihi.* From Seneca's *Octavia* :

> '*Vindicta debetur mihi.*'

The exclamation '*Vindicta*' is ridiculed in *The Poetaster*, iii. 1, and in the Induction to *A Warning for Faire Women*, but the reference may not be to this passage. See *Introduction*, p. xc.

5. An inexact form of Seneca's *Agamemnon*, 115 :

> '*Per scelera semper sceleribus tutum est iter.*'

With this quotation Hieronimo begins a new train of thought. Instead of attending on the will of heaven, he reflects that one crime opens the way for another, 'euils vnto ils conductors be,' and that therefore he should repay violence with violence. In any case 'death's the worst of resolution,' i. e. resolute action can at worst end in death. Even the man who imagines that by patient endurance he will attain to a calm existence is likely to have his life cut short.

13, 14. From Seneca's *Troades*, 511, 512. In the next four lines Kyd freely translates the verses.

19. A rendering of Lucan's *Pharsalia*, vii. 819 :

> '*Caelo tegitur, qui non habet urnam.*'

22. *With open but ineuitable ills.* The reading of all Quartos, but the sense is not satisfactory. We should expect a contrast between the open and therefore by no means 'ineuitable ills' employed by vulgar wits, and the secret yet certain method which Hieronimo contemplates.

24. *kindeship,* kindness; a M.E. form.

29. See Note on i. 3. 5.

35. An expansion of Seneca's *Oedipus*, 515 :

> '*Iners malorum remedium ignorantia.*'

The corrupt reading of 1633 Q. was adopted till Sarrazin traced the source of the quotation.

45. *coile,* disturbance, tumult.

58. *Corrigidor.* A Spanish magistrate, 'the chief Justicer or gouernour of a towne.' Kyd, however, seems here to consider a ' Corrigidor ' an advocate, not a judicial functionary.

61. *an action of the Case.* 'An action for redress of wrongs not specially provided against by law, in which the whole cause of complaint was set out in the writ.'

62. *Eiectione firmae.* A writ which lay to eject a tenant from his holding.

72. *Corsicke rockes.* Cf. Seneca's *Octavia*, 382:

> '*Remotus inter Corsici rupes maris.*'

Reed, not understanding the allusion, thought 'corsick' (as he spelt it) a variant of 'corsy,' which he explained as 'large, huge, great.'

103. *ore turnest then.* Neither this nor *oerturned then*, the reading of the three latest Qq., gives satisfactory sense. If *ore turnest* is kept, the simplest emendation is *thou* for *then*; and lines 102–7 might then be interpreted: 'Hieronimo, when, like a raging sea tossed with wind and tide, thou rollest wave after wave (of passion) in constant succession on the surface, whilst in the depths too there is tumult though less obvious, art thou not ashamed to neglect the sweet revenge of thy Horatio?' Fleischer in his 'Bemerkungen' retains the original reading, but this leaves *ore turnest* without a subject. His interpretation is ingenious, though, I think, over-subtle. He supposes Hieronimo to reproach himself because like a storm-tossed sea he sets only the upper waves in motion while leaving the depths in comparative calm, i.e. he utters his grief in words, but does not show himself stirred to the depths by taking revenge. The four Editors who read *o'erturneth then* do not comment on the passage. Schick keeps *o'erturnest then* in his text, but in a note favours an emendation proposed by Mr. Gollancz, *oreturneth thee*, the two following lines to be taken as an exclamation. If either of the readings with the emendation *oreturneth* be adopted, *when as* in 102 should preferably be written *whenas* = 'when.'

118. *canst.* Used here in its early sense, 'hast knowledge of, skill in'; cf. Lovelace's lines:

> 'Yet can I music too: but such
> As is beyond all voice and touch.'

125. *rent*, a variant of 'rend.' Cf. *Euphues*, 'renting his clothes and tearing his haire.'

151. *fauour*, appearance.

SCENE XIV.

6, 7. Another of Kyd's historical blunders. The Portuguese were never 'Kings and commanders of the westerne Indies.' The lines may be a confused reference to the capture of the Azores by the Spanish fleet in 1582.

11. A sea-voyage between the capitals of Portugal and Spain is only to be paralleled by Valentine's similar sea-voyage from Verona to Milan (*Two Gentlemen of Verona*, i. 1. 171).

17. *condiscent*, consent. This somewhat rare word, with its legal flavour, is suited to an official pronouncement by the King.

25. The Viceroy's deliberations with his Council upon the King of Spain's 'articles' (cf. iii. 1. 105–7) had evidently ended in their unanimous acceptance.

37. *extremities*, unrestrained expression of emotion.

111-3. See Note on i. 1. 10.

117. *tro.* An unusual variant of 'trow,' which, when added at the end of a question, expresses contemptuous wonder. Cf. *Much Ado about Nothing*, iii. 4. 59 : 'What means the fool, trow?'

118. *Pocas palabras*, few words. This Spanish phrase, from its use here, became a stock jest. Shakespeare puts it in mangled form into Sly's mouth, *Taming of the Shrew*, Induction, 5 : "Therefore *paucas pallabris*; let the world slide.'

130. *No; would he had.* An 'aside,' though possibly the opening word, 'No,' is addressed to Hieronimo.

156. *I marry ... and shall.* For this elliptical phrase cf. 1 *Henry IV*, v. 2. 32 : 'Marry, and shall, and verie willingly.'

168, 169. Schick, who quotes Dunlop (*History of Prose Fiction*, ii. 310), states that the more correct form of this quotation seems to be :

> '*Chi mi fa più carrezze che non suole*
> *O mi ha ingannato o ingannar mi vuole.*'

Dunlop assigns the lines to Ariosto, without, however, specifying the context.

SCENE XV.

3. *Erichtho.* Hazlitt substitutes *Alecto*, but Fleischer suggests that Kyd may have been misled by Ovid's epithet *furialis* applied to *Erichtho*, the Thessalian witch (*Heroides*, xv. 139) into taking her for one of the Furies.

2-6. A corrupt passage. I have adopted Schick's emendation which is satisfactory from a metrical point of view, though 'O'er-ferried' in 5 is a doubtful conjecture. The penultimate syllables in *Acheron* and *Erebus* may, however, have been elided, and the passage have run originally as follows :

> 'Solicite *Pluto*, gentle *Proserpine*,
> To combate *Acheron* and *Erebus* in hell.
> For neere by *Stix* and *Phlegeton* ⟨were known⟩,
> Nor ferried *Caron*, &c.'

Hazlitt wrongly modernizes 'neere' as 'near' instead of 'ne'er.'

10. I have restored, with emended punctuation, the reading of the earlier texts, which means 'to let pass unnoticed, while thou art asleep, the events that thou art warned to watch.' Dodsley's reading, based on Q. of 1633, has been wrongly adopted by later editors.

29. *boare.* As the present tense is used in the rest of the description of the 'dumme shew,' Fleischer conjectures *beare*, but the torch-bearers have probably passed across the stage before *Reuenge* begins to speak.

ACT IV.

⟨SCENE I.⟩

20. *thus careles should be lost.* A pleonastic and irregular clause, as if the preceding words had run, 'But monstrous Fathers to permit that those, &c.'

32. *heaven applies our drift.* Schick rightly, I think, interprets: 'Heaven furthers our drifting plans, brings them to a definite goal.' Collier follows the Qq. in his edition of the play, but in his Introduction to *The Murder of Iohn Brewen* he suggests 'applauds our drift' as the right reading.

46. *I will consent, conceale.* Cf. First Q. *Hamlet*, iii. 4 :

'I will conceale, consent, and doe my best.'

70-9. On the question of autobiographical references here see *Introduction*, pp. xvii, xxii, and lvi.

86-8. It is through Heywood's quotation of these lines in his *Apology for Actors* (1612) that Kyd's authorship of *The Spanish Tragedie* is established. He is describing the Roman custom of choosing prisoners condemned to death to act on the stage 'such parts as were to be kil'd. . . These were Tragedies naturally performed. And such Caius Caligula, Claudius Nero . . . and other Emperours of Rome vpon their festivals and holy daies of greatest consecration vsed to act. Therefore M⟨r⟩ Kid in *The Spanish Tragedie*, vpon occasion presenting itselfe, thus writes.' Then follow the three lines.

105. *as it is our Countrey maner.* Though Balthazar is the speaker, the reference, of course, is not to Portuguese, but English stage-custom. It was usual before the performance of a play for its 'argument' or plot to be communicated to the audience. Before 'the play within the play' in *Hamlet*, a dumb-show is performed which, in Ophelia's words, 'imports the argument of the play' (iii. 2. 150). In *A Midsummer-Night's Dream*, v. i. 129 ff., the interlude of Pyramus and Thisbe is prefaced by a dumb-show, after which the 'Prologue' expounds the plot. In the case of Hieronimo's play this preliminary exposition was peculiarly necessary, as it was played 'in vnknowne languages'; cf. 171-7. The 'argument' having been recited here, nominally for the benefit of the 'Kingly troupe,' but really for the instruction of the audience in the theatre, Kyd cleverly avoids a repetition of it before the performance, by making Hieronimo present the King with a copy of the play (iv. 3. 6) in which the 'argument' is set down. No doubt such a copy was often presented to illustrious spectators.

107-29. On the relation of this version of the story to Wotton's novel and to the play of *Soliman and Perseda*, see *Introduction*, pp. lvi-lvii.

117. *Bashawes*, Pachas ; the earlier English form of the Turkish title, derived indirectly through the Italian *bassa*.

140. *seueral abstracts*, separate copies of the individual parts.

147. *the huntresse*, Diana.

163-5. A company of Italian players performed before the Queen at Windsor in 1577. Whetstone in his *Heptameron of Civil Discourses* (1582) mentions comedians of Ravenna, who were not 'tied to any written device,' but who had 'certain grounds or principles' (i. e. outlines of performance) 'of their own.' These improvised comedies were known as *commedie dell' arte*, and it is to the performances of this company that Kyd is probably alluding.

166–7. See *Introduction*, p. xx.

184, 185. The later texts evidently give the lines in right order, as Hieronimo's 'shew' behind the curtain is the body of Horatio which he afterwards uncovers, 4. 89.

SCENE II.

13. *complot* apparently has the meaning of 'part-plotter, part-agent,' but I can find no other instance of such a use of the word, which elsewhere signifies 'plot' or 'conspiracy.' In his desire for a pun, Kyd has probably extended the meaning of the word.

16. *vnmanur'd*, uncultivated.

29. *to hold excusde*, to make excuses for. Cf. *Two Gentlemen of Verona*, iv. 1. 53, 54:

> 'We cite our faults,
> That they may hold excus'd our lawlesse liues.'

Hazlitt's emendation therefore is not needed.

SCENE III.

S.D. *he knocks up the curtaine*. It is behind this 'curtaine' that during the performance of Hieronimo's play Horatio's body is concealed. Cf. iv. 1. 185.

12. *the gallerie*. The actor-spectators were seated probably on the same raised platform from which Lorenzo and Balthazar had overheard the dialogue between Horatio and Bel-imperia, ii. 2. 7 ff.

17. *the Title*, a board or playbill giving the name of the piece, and the scene. Collier compares *Wily Beguiled*:

> '*Prologue.* How now, my honest rogue, what play shall we have here to-night?
>
> *Player.* Sir, you may look upon the title.'

Malone in his 'Historical Account of the English Stage' in his edition of Shakespeare (1821), iii. 108, quotes the mangled form of the line in the Q. of 1610.

SCENE IV.

80. A play, *Aiax and Vlysses*, was produced in 1571. Among the 'Romaine peeres' who had been made the subjects of dramas were *Quintus Fabius* (1574), *Mutius Scevola* (1577), and *Cipio Africanus* (1580). Stephen Gosson in the *Schoole of Abuse*, p. 40 (1579), mentions that he had himself written a piece called *Catilins Conspiracies*.

84. Cf. *Jew of Malta*, i. 2:

> 'The hopelesse daughter of a haplesse Jew.'

and *Cornelia*, i. 214:

> 'Hopeles to hide them in a haples tombe.'

86. A usual function of the speaker of the Epilogue. Cf. Epilogue to 2 *Henry IV*: 'I was lately heere in the end of a displeasing Play, to pray your patience for it, and to promise you a better: I did meane (indeede) to pay you with this, which if (like an ill venture) it come vn-luckily home, I breake, and you, my gentle Creditors, lose.'

103. *sorted*, chosen, sought out.

110. *soonest*. Cf. *Henry V*, iii. 6. 120:

> 'The gentle gamester is the soonest winner.'

and *Antony and Cleopatra*, iii. 4. 27:

> 'Make your soonest haste.'

112. *Through girt*, pierced. 'Girt' is here the past participle of 'gird' = 'strike,' which is to be distinguished from 'gird' = to encircle.

118. *Marcht in a net*. A proverbial phrase to denote a transparent attempt at deceit. In *Henry V*, i. 2. 93-4, the Archbishop of Canterbury, after showing that the Kings of France, while denying Henry's claim in virtue of the Salic Law, themselves inherit through the female line, taunts them with rather choosing:

> 'To hide them in a Net
> Than amply to imbarre their crooked titles.'

122-8. See ii. 5. 51-2.

S.D. *He runs to hange himselfe*. Cf. iv. 1. 129.

156. *Breake ope the doores*, i.e. of the 'gallerie,' whence the King and Viceroy and their suite were watching the play, and the key of which Hieronimo had secured. Cf. iv. 3. 12-3.

186-7. It is difficult to see what secret Hieronimo is so determined to guard after the comprehensive revelation contained in his long speech.

175. *secure*, careless, unconcerned.

180. Adapted from *Dr. Faustus*, Scene iii. 303:

> 'Had I as many souls as there be stars.'

S.D. *He bites out his tongue*. This superfluous horror is probably suggested by classical precedents. Schick quotes aptly from *Euphues*, p. 146: 'Zeno, because he would not be enforced to reveal anything against his will by torments, bit off his tongue, and spit it in the face of the tyrant.' Cf. *Titus Andronicus*, iii. 1. 131.

SCENE V.

15. *consort*. See Note on iii. 1. 21.

17-24 and 31-44. Echoes of the Virgilian imitations in the Induction. Cf. Note on i. 1. 18-85.

18. *inurde*, put into operation, carried on.

28. *bugs*, bugbears, objects of terror.

NOTES

TO

CORNELIA

⟨WHERE the quotations from G., i. e. Garnier's *Cornelie*, correspond to one or more complete lines of Kyd's translation only a numerical reference to the latter is given.⟩

The Argument.

24. *Pompey's faction* : 'les enfans de Pompee.' G.

27. *assaulted* : 'inuesti.' G.

29. *his so mighty enemy* : 'son ennemy.' G.

32. *the Townes and places thereabouts* : 'toutes les villes du pays.' G.

34. *this most faire and miserable Ladie* : 'la miserable Cornelie.' G.

36. *vnderstanding . . . Affrique* : 'entendant comme de surcrois le nouueau desastre d'Afrique.'

38. Garnier adds the following words, which Kyd has not translated : 'Vous verrez ce Discours amplement traitté en Plutarque és vies de Pompee, de Cesar, et de Caton d'Vtique : En Hirtius cinquiesme liure des Commentaires de Cesar : Au cinquiesme liure des guerres ciuiles d'Appian, et quarante-troisiesme de Dion.'

ACT I.

5, 6. 'Vous choisissez au moins les plus coupables testes,
     Et le reste sauuant, les broyez de tempestes.' G.

It is doubtful if Kyd understood fully 'les broyez de tempestes,' i. e. 'overwhelm them (les plus coupables) with storms.'

18. *are returnd from Stix.* G. has simply 'revienne.'

19. 'armez pour nostre Capitole.' G.

25. 'Tu nous trames ces maux,' G., i. e. 'thou hatchest such evils against us.'

26. 'Tu renuerses nos loix, mortelle Conuoitise.' G. Kyd makes 'couetize' an attribute of 'Ambition' in 24, instead of an independent

Personification. Reed quotes examples of this archaic synonym of 'covetousness' from Ben Jonson's *Catiline* and *Alchemist*, and Nash's *Pierce Penilesse*.

28–9. 'Nos peres t'ont trouuee au pied des premiers murs,
      Et mourant delaissee à leur nepueux futurs.' G.

'mourant' qualifies 'peres,' but is mistakenly applied by Kyd to 'conuoitise.' Hence the introduction in 30 of 'reuiuing,' which represents nothing in the original.

31. *out-lanched*, spilt. A rare compound, involving an inaccurate use of 'lanch,' which means 'cut' or 'pierce,' and cannot strictly govern 'blood.'

32. *hongst*. Originally a North-Midland form of the past tense of the causal verb *heng*. Not found after early seventeenth century.

32. *O Hell*: 'ô crime.' G.

34–7. A paraphrase rather than a translation of :

      ' Il n'ÿ a foy qui dure entre ceux qui commandent
      Egaux en quelque lieu, tousiours ils se debandent,
      Ils se rompent tousiours, et n'a jamais esté
      Entre rois compagnons ferme societé.'

'Ils se debandent'='they become disunited.'

38. *the father and the sonne*: 'le Gendre et le Beau-pere.' G.

40. *made marsh*. Cf. *Spanish Tragedie*, iii. 7. 8.

55. *signorize*, have dominion. A rare word, used by Fairfax transitively, 'He that signiorizeth Hell' (*Translation of Tasso*, iv. 46). Cf. Act iii. 2. 8.

59–63. For a similar list of nationalities cf. *Soliman and Perseda*, i. 2. 53–61.

59. *the flaxen-haird high Dutch* : 'les blons Germains.' G.

60. *madding after*, madly eager for. A rare use of the verb. Chaucer has 'in armes for to madde' (*Troilus and Criseyde*, i. 479).

61. 'Ny le Gaulois ardent.' G.

62.   'Le More qui erre
      Aux Libyques sablons, renommé de Didon.' G.

'erre aux'='wanders over' not 'travels to.' Kyd's omission of the reference to Dido is curious.

72. 'L'Aquilon, le Midy, le Couchant, le Matin.' G. Kyd has misunderstood the line, which means, 'The North, the South, the West, the East.' But Gassner is not therefore justified in substituting 'North' for 'Morne.'

75. *thy posteritie*: 'tes enfants.' G.

83. *topside-turuey*. One of the many variants of 'topsy-turvy.' As topsy-tervy (1528) is the first recorded form, the probable derivation is top+so+tervy from M.E. *terven*=to throw ; 'topside' is thus an incorrect form, due to a mistaken association with 'side.'

84. *thy maine-saile torne* : 'tes voiles abatus.' G.

85. 'Tes costez entrouuerts de rames deuestus.' G.

92. 'Tu te vantes en vain de tes nobles ayeux.' G. Kyd has introduced an antithesis between this and the following line which does not exist in the original.

100–1. An obscure rendering of:

'Aussi que peu souuent en temps calme nous chaut
De tenir la raison pour bride comme il faut.'

100. *sild.* Rare variant of 'seld'='seldom.'

102–5. Expanded from the original, and more emphatic:

'Nous sommes insolens des presens de Fortune,
Comme s'elle deuoit nous estre tousiours vne,
Tousiours ferme et durable, et qu'elle n'eust les piez,
Comme elle a, sur le haut d'vne boule pliez.' ·

124. 'Exemple aux orgueilleux de l'inconstance humaine.' G.

133. *from the Carte and plough*: 'de grands-peres champestres.' G. Cf. *The Housholders Philosophie*, p. 279, l. 6, and *Introduction*, p. lxiii.

140. G. has simply 'qui ne nous doiuent rien.' The addition of 'but reuenge for wrongs' is characteristic of Kyd.
ought, owed.

144. *to heauen*: 'Aux Dieux, peres communs de tous.' G.

149–50. 'Tenir toute la terre à nostre main sujette,
Et voir sous mesme ioug l'Ethiope et le Gete.' G.

150. *what lyke vs best*, what pleases us most.

151–4. 'Celuy commande plus, qui vit du sien contant,
Et qui va ses desirs par la raison domtant:
Qui bourreau de soymesme apres l'or ne soupire,
Qui ne conuoite point vn outrageux Empire.' G.

158. *for stayning*, i. e. 'to prevent it stayning.'

159–221. Kyd's rendering of the chorus departs in so many points from the original that for purposes of comparison I give the latter fully:

'Sur ton dos chargé de miseres
Des Dieux la colereuse main
Venge les crimes que tes Peres
Ont commis, ô peuple Romain:
Et si pour destourner l'orage
Qui pend sur tes murs menacez,
Les Dieux n'appaises courroucez,
Ton malheur croistra d'auantage.

"L'ire des bons Dieux excitee
"Est parasseuse à nous punir:
"Souuent la peine meritee
"Se garde aux races à venir:

"Mais d'autant qu'ils l'ont retenue,
"Prompts à pardonner nos pechez,
"D'autant plus se monstrent faschez
"Quand nostre offense continue.

"Lors ils tirent de sa cauerne
"La noire Peste, pour soufler
"Un venin puisé dans l'Auerne,
"Et le souflant corrompent l'air:
"Ou la Famine chagrineuse
"Aux membres foibles de maigreur:
"Ou la Guerre pleine d'horreur,
"Plus que toutes deux outrageuse.

La guerre, par qui l'Ausonie
A tant engressé de guerets
En la belliqueuse Emonie
Grosse de soldars enterrez,
Qui pour nous saccager encore
Va pousser des Thessales champs
La meutre et les discords mechans
Jusques dans la campagne More.

De celuy brusloyent les entrailles
D'ire, de rage et de rancoeur,
Qui fist des premieres batailles
Herisser vn camp belliqueur :
Qui sur les montagnes de Thrace
Fist le premier descendre Mars,
Horriblant parmy les soldars
D'vne sanglante coutelace.

Qui de trompettes éclatantes
Osa le premier eschauffer
Les troupes d'horreurfremissantes,
Pour les precipiter au fer :
Qui par les campagnes herbues
Fist tomber nos crops tronçonnez
Comme quand les bleds moissonez
Tombent en iauelles barbuës.

A celuy rué dans les gouffres
Qui bouillonnent en Phlegethon,
La peine, Ixion, que tu souffres,
De Promethé l'oiseau glouton
N'est digne peine de son crime :
De son crime iuste loyer
Pluton y deuroit employer
Tous les tourmens de son abysme.

Las miserables que nous sommes,
Assez tost en dueil eternel
La Parque ne pousse les hommes
Deuant le iuge criminel !
Assez tost nostre corps ne tombe
Dans le ventre obscur des tombeaux
Si nous de nous mesmes bourreaux
Ne nous apprestons nostre tombe !

Nos Citez languissent desertes,
Les plaines au lieu de moissons
Arment leurs espaules couuertes
De larges espineux buissons.
La mort en nos terres habite,
Et si l'alme Paix ne descend
Dessur nous peuple perissant,
La race Latine est destruitte.'

Kyd mistranslates lines 174, 176, 180, and 184-6. He also gives an unintelligible version of stanzas 6 to 8, through failing to recognize that ' celuy ' in the first line of stanza 6 does not refer back to ' la guerre ' in stanza 5, but introduces a new subject, namely *the man*,

> ' Qui fist des premieres batailles
> Herisser vn camp belliqueur,'

and whose misdeeds and proper punishment are the theme of this and the two following stanzas.

181. *Emonye*, Haemonia or Thessaly, in which Pharsalia is situated.

193. *Coutelace*. A rare variant of 'cutlass,' showing clearly its French origin.

216. *surcloid*, choked up with ; a rare intensitive of cloy.

221. *quailed*, subdued.

ACT II.

8. *shunne* : 'abandonne.' G.

10. ' Me face trauerser l'infernale riuiere.' G.

12. *my husband* : 'mes espoux.' G.

20. *where sinnes doe maske unseene*: 'ou les trespassez vont.' G. Kyd misinterprets, 'les trespassez,' i.e. 'the dead,' as 'trespasses.' In 30 however he renders 'apres le trespas d'eux ' correctly.

23. *Empory.* Rare variant of 'Empery' =dominion.

34. 'Rmporté de Bellonne, emporta tes amours.' G. Kyd completely mistakes the sense. The reference is not to Crassus' first appearance in arms, but to his death in battle.

35. *goe break the bands* : 'en violant les Manes.' G.

39, 40. *with faith . . . slept* :

'Qui sa foy loyale
Veut rendre à son espoux en l'onde stygiale.' G.

47. *as some belieue* : 'Comme certe il faut croire.' G.

50. *and after broke.* Condensed from :

'Quand l'vn ou l'autre atteint d'inconstance pariure
Faulse l'amour promis apres la sepulture.' G.

56. 'Et du trespas cruel qui te sille les yeux.' G. Kyd again misinterprets *trespas.*

79, 80. 'Et n'espargne non plus ce mal contagieux.
Vn membre qui est sain qu' vn membre carieux.' G.

89. *Heard,* herdsman, rustic : ' des paisans.' G.

93. ' Renuersez comme espics de gresle saccagez,' G., i.e. 'overthrown, like ears of corn beaten down by hail.'

94. ' D'auoir veu les yeux bas tant de grands Rois barbares
Apporter,' &c. G.
Kyd applies 'les yeux bas' to Pompey instead of to the barbarian Kings.

124-7. ' Les accidens humains sur nostre teste tournent,
‹ Et iamais attachez en vn lieu seiournent,
' Non plus que ce grand ciel, que nous voyons tousiours
' D'vn train infatigable entretenir ses tours.' G.

125. *tickle,* uncertain, volatile.

129. *Coast,* skirt, move round about. Cf. *Gaw. and Gr. Knt.* 1696 : ' Þe sunne . . . costez þe clowdes of þe welkyn.'

132-5. An expansion of :

'Apres l'Hyuer glacé le beau Printemps fleuronne,
L'Esté chaud vient apres, apres l'Esté Autonne.'
On 135 see *Introduction,* pp. lxii–lxiii.

139. *flesh'd,* violently enraged. Cf. *Tragedy of Barnavelt,* iv. 3 : ' There can be no attonement . . . Vandort is flesh'd upon me.'

147. *then Rome* : ' qu' aucun.' G.

156. *Leauing* : 'deliurant.' G.

171-7. A paraphrase of :

'Las ! mon dueil seroit moindre, et les larmes fecondes,
Qui tombent de mes yeux comme de larges bondes,
Se pourroyent estancher, si entre les combas
Il eust le fer au poing acquis vn beau trepas,
Couché sur vn monceau de hasardeux gendarmes,
Ouuert d'vne grand' playe au trauers de ses armes,
Dans le flanc, dans la gorge, et degouttant parmy
Son heroique sang, du sang de l'ennemy.'

172. *fauchin.* An unusual variant of 'falchion,' akin to M.E. *fauchoun.*

186. ' Lors le sang me gela dans mes errantes veines.' G.

187. *like a thornie groue* : 'Comme espics dans les pleines.' G.

191-2.   ' L'esprit qui se gesnoit de rage impatiente
            S'efforca de briser sa prison violente.' G.

Kyd apparently takes 'rage impatiente'.as equivalent to ' sa prison '
in the following line. But 'de rage impatiente' is an adverbial clause,
and ' sa prison violente' means the body.

197-8.   ' Et trois fois retenuë auec larmes et cris,
            Auec force de bras, à plaindre ie me pris.'

Kyd mistakes the sense. Cornelia is speaking of the means by which
her companions restrained her from suicide

200. *A bedroll . . . blasphemies* : 'Mille outrageux blasphémes.' G.
' Bedroll ' or ' beadroll,' originally a list of those to be specially prayed
for ; hence any lists or series.

201-5.   ' Depuis, ô Ciceron, mon corps s'est affoibly,
            Mais non pas ma douleur, qui ne sent point d'oubly.
            Ie trespasse viuante, et quoy que le iour sorte
            De sa couche moiteuse, ou que la nuict l'emporte,
            Soit que Phebus gallope, ou soit que retiré,
            Le ciel soit brunement de sa sœur esclairé,
            Ie suis tousiours veillante, et le somne qui rampe,
            De son pauot mouillé mes paupieres ne trempe.' G.

Here Kyd condenses the third to the sixth lines into the single
verse 424 ; the last two lines are badly mistranslated, the meaning
being, ' I am always awake, and creeping slumber with its moist
poppy does not steep my eye-lids.'

208. *winck*, shut my eyes in sleep. Cf. *Babies Book*, p. 50: ' Go to
bedde bi tyme, and wynke.'

219. *dead and gone* : ' morts ou chassez.' G.

225. *indifferently*, impartially.

229.   ' Nostre propre malheur reprend souci d'vn autre.'
Acknowne, past participle of 'acknowe,' O.E. *oncnawan*, to recognize.

233. A curious metaphorical paraphrase of ' Nos pleurs parmi les
pleurs communément tarissent.'

234-5. A mistranslation of :

            ' Les miennes tariront, quand cendre en vn cercueil
            Ie ne sentirai plus ny tristesse ny dueil.'

i. e. ' My tears will be dried, when, ashes in a coffin, I shall feel no
more sadness nor mourning.'

250-1.   ' Ie pleure inconsolable, ayant vn bien perdu
            Helas ! qui ne pourra m'estre iamais rendu.' G.

258. 'Et que les fils des Dieux, nez sur terre,' G., i.e. 'godlike heroes,'
like Scipio, mentioned in 260.

269. *Towers like thorny-pointed speares* : 'tours en pointes herissees.' G.

273. *to our eternall mones.* Added by Kyd.

275. *handwork.* Elizabethan form of O. E. *handweorc*, and almost obsolete in Kyd's time. 'Handiwork' is modern form of O. E. *hand-geweorc*.

276. *razed* : 'embrase,' i.e. 'burnt.' G.

280. A mistranslation of 'Possible que la mort nous mire en deuisant,' i.e. 'haply Death aims at us while we talk.'

283. *in Lernas blood.* This rendering of 'sang Lernean' suggests that Kyd did not understand that the allusion is to the blood of the Lernaean hydra, slain by Hercules.

291. *in a fiery gap* : 'dans une fosse ombreuse.' G.

292. 'De sortir d'vn malheur qui iour et nuit m' étreint.' G.

293. 'Nul humain accident ne domte vn grand courage.' G.

301. 'D'elle (i.e. la mort) ie n'eus iamais ny crainte ny souci.' G.

304-5. An expansion of : 'Il ne faut l'appeller ny recourir à elle.'

318-23. A paraphrase of :

'Quiconques ne fremist aux menaces de mort,
'N'est suiect comme vn peuple aux iniures du Sort.
'L'eau, la flamme, le fer, le ciel, et Jupin mesme
'Ne sçauroyent de frayeur luy faire le front blesme.
'Que peut-il redouter, quand ce qui est la peur,
'Quand la mort que lon craint, luy asseure le cœur?'

The last two lines are mistranslated ; they mean, 'of what can he be afraid, when that which is the very object of fear, when death dreaded by the world, gives boldness to his heart?'

319. *slightly fraied,* easily frightened.

332. *At such a Kings departure or decease.* A mistranslation of 'au desceu de son Roy,' i.e. 'without the knowledge of his King.'

336-7.   'On l' iroit offensant (i.e. Dieu) luy qui veut bien qu' ainsi
        Qu' il nous preste la vie, il la retire aussi.' G.

338-409. For purposes of comparison I again give the Chorus in the original.

'" Tout ce que la massiue terre
" Soutient de son dos nourricier
" Est suiet au ciel qui l'enserre,
" Et à son branle iournalier :
" Les felicitez, les desastres
" Despendent de ce mouuement,
" Et chaque chose prend des astres
" Sa fin, et son commencement.

" Les Empires, qui redoubtables
" Couurent la terrestre rondeur,
" De ces tournemens variables
" Ont leur ruine et leur grandeur :

" Et les hommes, foible puissance,
" Ne sçauroyent arrester le cours
" De ceste celeste influence
" Qui domine dessur nos iours.

" Rien ne durable ne seiourne,
" Toute chose naist pour perir,
" Et tout ce qui perist retourne
" Pour vne autre fois refleurir.

" Les formes des choses ne meurent
" Par leurs domestiques discors
" Que les matieres qui demeurent
" Ne refacent vn autre corps.

"La rondeur des boules mouuantes,
"Tournoyant d'vn egal chemin,
"Couple des natures naissantes
"Le commencement à leur fin.
"Ainsi les Citez populeuses
"Qui furent champs inhabitez
"Eecherront en plaines poudreuses,
"Puis retourneront en Citez.

Ne voit-on pas commes les veines
Des rochers dressez en coupeaux
Enfantent les belles fontaines,
Et les fontaines les ruisseaux,
Les ruisseaux les grosses rivieres,
Les rivieres aux flots chenus
Se vuident aux eaux marinieres,
Et la mer aux rochers veinus?

Comme nostre ville maitresse
Des Princes a senty les loix,
La suitte des temps vainqueresse
L'assuiettira sous les Rois:
Et la couronne blondoyante,
Qui cendoit des Tyrans le chef
De mille gemmes rayonnante,
Le viendra ceindre de rechef.

Encor les murailles leuees
Par vne pastourale main,
Dans le sang fraternel lauees,
Rougiront de meurtre inhumain.
Et encor l'iniuste arrogance
D'vn Tarquin ardant de fureur
Tiendra la Romaine vaillance
En espouuentable terreur.

Encor d'vne chaste Lucrece
L'honneur coniugal outragé
Sera par sa main vengeresse
Dessur son propre sang vengé:
Dedaignant son ame pudique
Supporter le seiour d'vn corps
Qu'aura l'audace tyrannique
Souillé d'impudiques efforts.

Mais ainsi que la Tyrannie
Vaincra nos cœurs abastardis,
Aduienne qu'elle soit punie
Aussi bien qu'elle fut iadis:
Et qu'vn Brute puisse renaistre
Courageusement excité,
Qui des insolences d'vn maistre
Redeliure nostre Cité.'

Kyd's version of this Chorus, applying the Platonic doctrine of a circular movement throughout nature to the history of Rome, is, in the main, spirited and lucid. But it contains several obscurities, and one or two serious mistakes. In 340–1 the rendering of the concrete statement—

'Est suiet au ciel qui l'enserre,
Et à son branle iournalier'

by an abstract generalization deprives the passage of much of its definiteness; 354, *No clowde but will be ouer-cast*, suggests an entirely different idea from *Rien de durable ne seiourne*; in 362–5 the image of the 'boules' coupling in their circular movement beginnings and endings is obscurely expressed; and 370–1 are an inaccurate version of

'Ne voit-on pas comme les veines
Des rochers dressez en coupeaux.'

But it is in 378–89 that Kyd goes completely astray, his version giving no hint of the meaning of the original that Rome, which was once under kings, will by the revolution of time again be subjected to them, and that her walls will again be stained with fratricidal bloodshed.

338. *fraight.* Variant of 'freight,' contracted form of pa. part.; here apparently used in a passive sense = 'been freighted or laden with.'

350–1. *practise stayes of,* put a check on, bring to a standstill. The use of the plural ' stayes ' in this active sense is rare.

373. *conuart.* Unusual variant of ' conuert ' in the sense of ' change, turn into '; cf. *Macb.* iv. 3. 229 :

' Let griefe

Conuert to anger.'

385. *check,* show herself recalcitrant (to Caesar) ; a metaphor from falconry.

389. *infect.* For this form cf. *Sp. Tr.* iii. 1. 36.

ACT III.

SCENE I.

1–18. Added by Kyd. Cf. *Introd.* p. lxxv.

3–6. A somewhat obscure allusion to the legend of Clytie, daughter of Oceanus, who when deserted by her lover Apollo pined away and was changed into a sunflower, which always turned its face to the sun-god. Cf. Ovid, *Metamorph.* iv. 256 ff.

7. *broken song.* Shakespeare uses the phrase ' broken music ' in *Henry V,* v. 2. 231, *A. Y. L. I.* i. 2. 150, and *Tr. and Cress.* iii. 1. 52 in the sense of ' concerted music ' or ' part-music.' Kyd has evidently this technical meaning of ' broken ' in his mind, though its application to the song of the swallow is obscure.

10. According to the usual version of the legend Adonis was transformed not into a rose, but an anemone.

13. *remembrancers.* A metaphorical use of the title of certain Exchequer officials, employed in recording documents.

20. *blubbred eyes.* Cf. *Cambyses (Dods.* iv. 208) : ' With blubbred eyes into my arms I will thee take.'

21. *consort*: cf. *Sp. Tr.* iii. 1. 21, Note.

27. *flawes,* sudden attacks. Cf. *Faer. Qu.* v. 5. 6.

33.   ' Et presque tous les bons
Sont tombez sous sa rage.' G.

Kyd misinterprets *les bons,* i.e. ' good men,' as neuter.

36. *Getulie,* Gaetulia, a district in Northern Africa.

40. *from the Lybique playnes*: ' aux Libyques plaines,' G.; i.e. ' in the Libyan plains,' but Kyd's phrase may mean ' with the Lybique plains as their base.'

51. An obscure rendering of ' Du sang Cornelien ne soit point esloigné.'

68. ' Tournoit plus loing du soir que de l'Aube du iour.' G.

72. *dulnes,* drowsiness ; cf. *Temp.* i. 2. 185 : ' Thou art inclinde to sleepe : 'tis a good dulnesse.'

77. *brawne-falne,* shrunken in flesh, thin ; cf. Lyly, *Euph.* (p. 127 *Arb.*): ' His armes brawne-fallen for want of wrastling,' and Chapman, *Gent. Ush.* i. 288 : ' Leane and brawn-falne : I, and scarsly sound.'

82. *lynsel,* a cloth of wool and linen mixed.

106-7.   'Chere Ame, quand viendra la seuere Clothon
             Despecer de mes iours le fatal peloton?' G.

i.e. 'untie the fatal knot of my days.'

128-9. This rendering of 'Ce sont fantômes vains et larues soli-
taires' obscures the sense.

129. *trace*, wander.   For this intrans. use cf. *Faer. Qu.* vi. 3. 29:

             'Not wont on foot with heavy arms to trace.'

130. *eaths*, easily.   'Eath,' in this sense, is often found in M.E.,
but the form here used, with the addition of a genit. 's,' is rare, if not
unique.

134. *disgaged*, disengaged, set free ; a rare word.

141. *or make the wise afeard.*   Added by Kyd.

142-3. A mistranslation of :

             'Personne, que la Mort ineuitable domte,
             En ce monde laissé des Enfers ne remonte.'

SCENE II.

4. G. has simply 'aux Scythes porte-trousses,' an allusion, probably
misunderstood by Kyd, to the Scythians carrying their belongings
everywhere with them.

5. *embas'd*, dishonoured.

7. *signiorizd.*   Cf. note on i. 55.

18. Kyd omits the second line of the couplet :

             'Sont morts atterrassez, pasture des oiseaux,
             Pasture des poissons qui rament sous les eaux.'

29-30. A mistranslation of :

             'Il s'enflamme, il s'asprit de l'aduersaire effort
             Tant qu'il trouue où se prendre, et puis il tombe mort.'

31. *affronts*, confronts, opposes.

38. 'Violant de Nature et des hommes la loi.'   G.

39-44. Substituted for the following lines :

             'Comme vn simple paisant qui de fortune trouue
             Des loueaux en vn bois an desceu de la Louue,
             Les massacre soudain, fors vn tant seulement,
             Qu'il emporte et nourrist pour son esbatement,
             Auecques ses aigneaux aux pastis il le meine,
             Il l'estable auecque eux comme vne beste humaine,
             Le traitte tendrement : mais luy grand deuenu,
             Au lieu d'auoir le bien du Berger recognu,
             Vne nuict qu'il s'auise, estrangle insatiable
             Tout le foible troupeau, puis s'enfuit de l'estable.'

49. *Minerua, Stator*: 'Feretrien, Stateur,' G.   Kyd does not
understand that these are epithets of Jupiter in 47.   He was surnamed *Feretrius* from the *feretrum* or litter on which the trophies of

vanquished foes were borne to his temple. Why Kyd should have thought Minerva was meant, I cannot conjecture.

57. *reseru'd*, preserved; a common Eliz. meaning of the word. Hence Gassner's emendation is needless.

80-1.   'Et ton corps déchiré de cent poignars aigus
       Immoler à nos chefs par ta force vaincus.'

SCENE III.

9. *affright*. Very rarely used, as here, as pa. part. of active verb 'affright.'

10. 'En vn moment decheu, tomba mort à l'enuers.' G.

15-6. A mistranslation of :

      'Vn buscher ie dressay de petites aiselles
       Esparses çà et là, demeurant de nasselles,'

i.e. 'I made a pile of small anchors, scattered here and there, remaining from the ships.'

15. *Seggs*, sedges. This M.E. form was still common in Eliz. English.

21. After this Kyd omits the line :

    'Des Syrtes et des rocs esprouuez si souuent.'

23. *that honoured her.* Added by Kyd.

26-29. Abridged from :

    'O douce et chere cendre, ô cendre deplorable,
    Qu'auecques vous ne suis-ie ! ô femme miserable,
    O pauure Cornelie, hé n'aura iamais fin
    Le cours de ceste vie où me tient le destin ?
    Ne seray-ie iamais auecques vous, ô cendre !
    N'est-il temps qu'on me face au sepulchre descendre ?'

37. *the Law of Armes*: 'le deuoir d'hostelage.' G.

43. *Aspics, Serpents, Snakes*: 'Les serpens de Cyrene.' G.

48. 'Ou que la terre s'ouure et referme sur vous.' G.

56. After this Kyd omits the following lines :

  '*Corn.* Nos suppliantes voix leurs courages n'emeuuent?
  Phil. De nulles passions emouuoir ne se peuuent.
  Corn. Ne font iustice à ceux qui la vont demandant?
  Phil. Or qu'on ne la demande, ils nous la vont rendant.'

60. *heauen doth with wicked men dispence*, i.e. 'does not interfere with, lets go unpunished'; 'les grands dieux gardent expressément,' G.

69. *god to fore*, God going before, assisting. For the older form of the phrase 'God to-forn' cf. Chaucer, *Tr. and Cr.* i. 1049, and *Rom. of Rose*, 7198. Shakespeare uses the modernized form 'God before'; cf. *Henry V*, i. 2. 307-8 :   'For, God before,
    We'll chide this dauphin at his father's door.'

84. 'Et qui pour le meurtrir a mis tout son effort.' G. With Kyd's line cf. *Sp. Tr.* iii. 4. 40-1.

88. *Photis,* 'Photin,' G., i.e. Photinus, the minister of Ptolemy of Egypt, who advised his master to have Pompey put to death.

93. A paraphrase of:

'Tout le bien qu'il en dit n'est que deguisement.'

99-100. '*Phil.* Il n'eust voulu voir mort celuy qui fut son gendre.
 Corn. Si eust, puisqu'il vouloit la liberté defendre.' G.

Kyd entirely mistranslates the second line.

107. *inextinguible.* A variant of 'inextinguishable,' from late Lat. *inextinguibilis* through French.

 signiorie, dominion, rule. Cf. note on i. 55.

108. *Not heauens feare* : 'Non la crainte des Dieux et du grondant tonnerre.' G.

110-1. Garnier is more explicit :

'Non le respect du sang, non l'amour ordinaire
 Du pere à ses enfans, des enfans à leur pere.'

113. After this Kyd omits two lines :

'*Phil.* Laissez cela, Madame.
 Corn.   Il faut que ie le laisse,
 Attendant des grands Dieux la faueur vengeresse.'

stoope. For this trans. use cf. 2 *Henry IV*, v. 2. 120 :

'I will stoop and humble my intents
 To your well-practised wise direction.'

117. After this Kyd omits four lines :

'Plustot dedans la mer les animaux paistront,
 Et les poissons flottans sur la terre naistront :
 Plustot le clair Soleil ne luira plus au monde,
 Que mon mal se relâche, et ma peine feconde.'

118-124. A paraphrase of :

'Ma tristesse est vn roc, qui durant les chaleurs
 Produist comme en hyuer vne source de pleurs,
 Qui ne s'epuise point : car bien qu'à grand' secousse
 Vn Auton de soupirs de l'estomac ie pousse,
 Ardant comme vne braise, encor' ce chaud venteux
 Ne sçauroit desecher mes yeux tousiours moiteux.'

In 122 *Auton*, i.e. 'South-wind,' is mistranslated 'Autumne.'

125. *recure.* Cf. note on *Sp. Tr.* iii. 8. 5.

136. *fire mee vp* : 'Qu'il m'applique le feu.' G. A very rare instance of 'fire,' in the sense of 'set fire to,' having a personal object.

146-220. This chorus is rendered by Kyd more faithfully than those in Acts I and II. He does not completely distort the meaning in important passages ; but he diverges in details so widely from the original that I give Garnier's lines in full.

'Fortune, qui ceste rondeur
Assuiettist à sa grandeur,
Inconstante Deesse,
Nous embrasse et nous comble
  d'heur,
Puis tout soudain nous laisse.

Ses pieds plus legers que le vent
Elle deplace plus souuent,
Que des Autons l'haleine
N'esboule le sable mouuant
De la cuite Cyrene.

Ore elle nous monstre le front
De mille liesses fecond,
Ore elle se retourne,
Et de son œil au change prompt
Sa faueur ne seiourne.

Instable en nos prosperitez,
Instable en nos aduersitez,
De nous elle se ioüe,
Qui tournons sans cesse agitez
Au branle de sa roüe.

Iamais au soir le blond Soleil
Ne luy veit tombant au sommeil
Vne face benine,
Qu'au matin des qu'il ouure l'œil
Ne la trouue chagrine.

Elle n'a seulement pouuoir
Sur vn peuple à le deceuoir,
Mais sa dextre volage
Peut vn grand empire mouuoir,
Comme vn simple mesnage.

Et donne les mesmes terreurs
Aux couronnes des Empereurs
Tremblans à sa menace,
Qu'à la moisson des Laboureurs
Qui depend de sa grace.

Le marchand qui fait escumer
Pour le proffit l'auare mer,
Craintif sur le riuage,
Te vient deesse reclamer
Pour faire bon voyage.

Tu peux sur les flots mariniers,
Tu peux sur les sillons blatiers,
Sur les vignes fertiles,
Et tu peux sur tous les mestiers
Qui s'exercent aux villes.

Mais sur tout se monstre ton
  bras
Puissant au hasard des combas,
Où plus qu'en autres choses
Qui se conduisent icy bas
Arbitre tu disposes.

Tel a par ton pouuoir mocqueur
Toute sa vie esté vaincueur,
Qui au fort de sa gloire
Perd contre vn ieune belliqueur
Sa vie et la victoire.

Ainsi l'Empereur Libyen
Qui du beau sang Ausonien
Enyura nostre plaine
Fut vaincu vaincueur ancien
D'vn ieune Capitaine.

Ainsi Maire l'honneur d'Arpin,
Qui defendit le nom Latin
De la Cimbroise rage,
Esprouua de ton cœur mutin
L'ineuitable outrage.

Et Pompé, de qui les beaux iours
Tu as fauorisé tousiours
De gloire liberale,
En vain implora ton secours
Aux plaines de Pharsale.

Ore Cesar, qui gros d'honneur
Se voit de la terre seigneur,
Presomptueux n'y pense,
Ne preuoyant de son bon-heur
La constante inconstance.

Rien ne vit affranchi du Sort :
Personne deuant qu'estre mort
Heureux on ne peut dire.
A celuy seul qu'esteint la mort
Fortune ne peut nuire.'

153. *then Autumne blasts* : 'Autons' mistranslated as in 122.
159. *fleres*, smiles flatteringly. Rarely used in this sense, unless

followed by 'on' and the object. Cf. *Chester Plays*, ii. 51 : 'Though he flyer, flatter, and flicker.'

164. *bleare our eyes*, dim our sight ; hence, 'blind, deceive.'

187. *where health or wealth*. The sense here is obscure. Kyd probably did not understand the meaning of 'les sillons blatiers,' i. e. 'furrows full of corn.'

190. After this Kyd omits the tenth stanza in Garnier's chorus.

196. *the Lybian Monarchy* : 'l'Empereur Libyen,' G., i. e. Hannibal. Kyd, however, may not have understood the allusion, as the description of Scipio Africanus as 'one that ne're got victorie' is most inapt.

201. *Arpins friend* : 'l'honneur d'Arpin.' Kyd is apparently unaware that 'Arpin'=Arpinum, and is the name, not of a man, but of a place.

212. *signiorizing*. Cf. note on i. 55.

219-20. A curious perversion of Garnier's statement that only the dead are secure from Fortune's assaults.

ACT IV.

SCENE I.

5. *the riuers of theyr bloode*. A favourite image of Kyd.   Cf. *Sp. Tr.* iv. 4. 124.

18. *They leaue to see into*, they have ceased to regard.

24. 'Et sanglant eslance dedans la mer voisine.' G.

36. *powre and pelfe* : 'un pouuoir supreme.' G.

42-3. An expansion of :

> 'Et que les Peres vieux voisent disant de nous.'

61-2. A mistranslation of :

> 'Il verra que ma dextre au sang haineur soüillee
> Sera, quoy qu'il m'en fasche, au sien propre moüillee.'

71.   'Il m'est à tard de voir le beau iour esclairer,
>   Qu'il meure.' G.

spend . . . daylight, waste time ; a variant of the proverbial phrase 'to burn daylight.' Cf. *Sp. Tr.* iii. 12 A. *30*.

88-9. An expansion of :
>   'et Cesar au contraire
> Sans auoir ennemy.'

91. *brought his men to field* : 'dans le champ de Mars . . . a conduit ses soldars.' G. Kyd misinterprets the allusion to the *Campus Martius*.

103-4. 'Il peut tout, il fait tout, bref il est Roy, sinon
>   Qu'il ne porte d'vn Roy la couronne et le nom.' G.

109. *Spayne*. Abridged from :
>   'Le bord
> De l'Espagne esloignee, où le Soleil s'endort.'

116–7. '*Brut.* Il ne le faut blasmer de ceux qu'emporte Mars.
Cass. Il en est l'homicide auecques ses soldars.' G.

124–9. An expansion of :

'Il a mis en danger par sa temerité,
Contre vn peuple innocent, nous et nostre Cité.
On le deuoit liurer pour expier la ville,
D'auoir sans cause esmeu l'Alemagne tranquille.'

132. *whom.* Refers to 'these Nations' in 130.

138–42. 'Les Gaules à Cesar estoyent vn auant-ieu
Du discord citoyen, qu'il a depuis esmeu
Pour se faire monarque, apprenant à combatre
Vn peuple qui ne veut au seruage s'abatre.'

Kyd takes the relatival clause 'qu'il a depuis esmeu' as referring to
'Les Gaules' instead of 'discord citoyen,' and translates 'esmeu' as
'remov'd' instead of 'stirred up.' 'apprenant à combatre vn peuple'
is also misunderstood, the meaning being 'learning to fight a nation.'
The obscure ending of 142 is added by Kyd.

149–150. 'Il (i.e. Cassius) fuira le seruage ostant la tyrannie,
Ou l'ame de son corps il chassera bannie.' G.

170–1. 'O Brute, ô Seruilie,
Qu'ores vous nous laissez vne race auilie.' G.

Cassius is apostrophizing the early Republican heroes, not, as Kyd's
version suggests, his own contemporaries.

cry you ayme, encourage, abet (the tyrant). It originally meant 'to
encourage the archers by crying out "Aim" when they were about to
shoot.'—Nares. The phrase occurs in *King John* ii. 1. 196.

186–251. The Chorus runs thus in the original :

'Celuy qui d'vn courage franc
Prodigue vaillament son sang
Pour le salut de la Patrie,
Qui sa vie entretient exprés
Pour meurtrir les Tyrans pourprés
Sans crainte qu'elle soit meurtrie :

Et qui au trauers des cousteaux,
Des flammes, et des gouffres d'eaux
Asseuré dans son ame brave,
Les va tuer entre les dars
De mille escadres de soldars
Deliurant la franchise esclaue,

Comme vn Peuple ne tombe pas,
De la mort gloute le repas :
Son renom porté par la gloire

Sur l'aile des siecles futurs
Franchira les tombeaux obscurs
D'vne perdurable memoire.

Les peuples qui viendront aprez
Luy feront des honneurs sacrez,
Et chaque an la ieunesse tendre
Ira le chef de fleurs orné
Chanter au beau iour retourné
Dessur son heroïque cendre.

Ainsi les deux Atheniens
Qui du col de leurs citoyens
Ont la seruitude arrachee
Viuront tousiours entre les preux,
Et iamais au sepulchre creux
Ne sera leur gloire cachee.

Le peuple, qui ne satisfait
Que d'ingratitude au bienfaict
De ceux le merite guerdonne,
Qui pour le deliurer des mains
De quelques tyrans inhumains
Mettent en danger leur personne,

Et Iupiter pere de tous,
Vomissant son iuste courroux
Sur les superbes diadémes,
Fait à fin de les malheurer
Encontre eux souuent coniurer
Leur enfans,et leur femmes mesmes.

Ne dois-tu pas craindre vn chacun,
Toy qui te fais craindre au com-
    mun ?
La crainte, qui la haine engendre,
Importune nous poursuiuant,
A beaucoup d'hommes fait souuent
Beaucoup de choses entreprendre.

O combien les Rois sont couuerts
Tous les iours de hazards diuers !
Qu'au sort est suiette leur vie !
Pressant vne pauure Cité
En estroitte captiuité,
Qui ne leur doit estre asseruie.

Peu de Tyrans selon le cours
De nature ferment leurs iours :
Plustot par les poisons couardes
Ils meurent traistrement surpris,
Plustost par les peuples aigris,
Et plustost par leurs propres gardes.

Celuy vit bien plus seurement,
Qui loin de tout gouuernement
Caché dessous vn toict de chaume,
Sans rien craindre et sans estre
    craint,
Incogneu, n'a l'esprit atteint
Des troubles sanglans du Royaume.'

This Chorus is, as a whole, correctly and forcibly rendered, but in a few passages Kyd diverges from the original. Thus 198–9 mean 'as a Nation does not perish, devoured by gluttonous Death.' In 208 *in the Sommer* is a mistranslation of ' au beau iour retourné,' i.e. 'at the return of the glorious day when he performed his deed.' 216-21 pervert the original meaning that the people, though ungrateful for benefits, yet rewards the merits of those who at personal risk free them from tyrants. In 231, *enforcing them thereto* should qualify 'Feare,' not 'Hate,' as the stanza emphasizes the reflex effect of the fear which a Tyrant inspires. 234-39 describe, with reference to Caesar and Rome, the dangers run by a Tyrant trying to enslave a free city, not by a king attacking 'stranger towns.'

196. *scowres*, roves ; der. from L. *excurrere.* Cf. *Paston Letters*, iii. 185, ' In plesurys new your hert doth score and raunge.'

241. *kindly.* Here used, as comparison with the French text shows, in the sense of 'according to Nature's course.'

243. *quaile*, overpower, bring to an end. Cf. i. 221, where, as here, the word is used transitively, though it is derived from O. E. *cwellan*, to die. The proper causative is ' quell.'

SCENE II.

7. *bright heauens masonrie*: 'que les dieux ont maçonnez eux-mesmes.' G.

13-6. An expansion of :

> ' O beau Tybre et tes flots de grand' aise ronflans,
> Ne doublent-ils leur crespes à tes verdureux flancs,
> Joyeux de ma venue ? '

15. *crispie*, rippled.

19. *Trytons Mariners*: 'Tritons mariniers.' G.

28-9. A mistranslation of:

> 'Soit où son char lassé de la course du iour
> Le ciel quitte à la nuict qui commence son tour.'

45. *at Loyre*: 'dans le Loire.' G. Kyd apparently takes Loire to be the name of a town.

51. 'Ceux que l'Euxin ondoye,' i. e. 'those who are washed by the Euxine's waves.' For the phrase 'makes marsh' cf. i. 40 and *Sp. Tr.* iii. 7. 8.

57. *my brother in law*: 'mon gendre.' G. Kyd evidently did not know that Pompey was married to Caesar's daughter Julia.

59. *haught*, high; 'orig. *haut, hault*, from contemporary French; corrupted late in 16th cent. to *haught* after words like *caught, taught*, &c., in which *gh* had become mute; perh. influenced by *high, height*.'— *N.E.D.*

68. *Discent of*, descended from; a rare form of the pa. part.

69. *affront*. Cf. note on iii. 2. 31.

118. *owe*, own.

119. *mighty things*: 'tant de riches provinces.' G.

123. ' Je ne crains point ceux-là qui restent de la guerre.' G.

128. ' On ne sçauroit flechir les resolus courages.' G.

136. 'Ains que laissant la tombe à mon terrestre faix,' G., i.e. 'leaving the tomb to my earthly frame.'

147. 'Nos iours sont limitez qu'on ne sçauroit estendre.' G.

150. 'Sur l'attente des Dieux ne se faut hasarder.' G.

155-6. Substituted for 'Il n'est telle rancueur qu'elle est de citoyens.'

160. *alonely*, solely, exclusively; orig. form 'all only.'

168-243. The Chorus runs thus in the original:

'O Beau Soleil qui viens riant
Des bords perleux de l'Oriant,
Dorant ceste iournee
De clairté rayonee :

Garde de ciuile fureur
Le chef de ce grand Empereur,
Qui de l'Afrique noire
Apporte la victoire.

Et toy de qui, douce Venus,
Les Eneades sont venus,
Ta faueur ne recule
De la race d'Iule.

Ains fay que luy ton cher enfant
Entre son peuple trionfant
Repousse de la terre
Les tisons de la guerre,

Que bien tard quittant le souci
De nous qui l'adorons icy
Nouuel astre il esclaire
A nos murs salutaire.

Io que son grand front guerrier
Soit tousiours orné de laurier,
Et ses belles statues
De lauriers reuestues.

Io que par tous les cantons
On n'apperçoiue que festons,
Qu'à pleines mains on rue
Des fleurs parmi la rue.

Il a vaincu ses ennemis,
Il les a tous en route mis,
Puis sans meurtrir personne
A chacun il pardonne.

Aussi les bons Dieux, le support
De tous ceux à qui lon fait tort,
Sont tousiours aduersaires
Des hommes sanguinaires.

Iamais ils n'allongent leurs iours,
Ains les accourcissent tousiours,
Et font tomber leur vie
En la main ennemie.

Cesar priué par ses haineurs,
Citoyen, des communs honneurs,
Contraint de se defendre
Alla les armes prendre.

La seule enuieuse rancueur,
Qui leur espoinçonnoit le cueur
Pour sa gloire soudaine,
Alluma ceste haine.

Mechante Enuie, hé que tu fais
D'encombre à ceux que tu repais !
Que ton poison leur verse
Vne langueur diverse.

Il tourne le sang de leur cueur
En vne iaunastre liqueur,

Qui par tuyaux chemine
Le long de leur poitrine.

L'estrangere prosperité
Leur est vne infelicité :
La tristesse les mange
Au son d'vne loüange.

Ny de Phebus l'œil radieux,
Ny le repas delicieux,
Ny le somme amiable
Ne leur est agreable.

Ils ne reposent iour ne nuict,
Tousiours ce bourreau les poursuit
Qui leur mord les entrailles
De pinçantes tenailles.

Ils portent les flambeaux ardans
D'vne Tisiphone au dedans,
Leur ame est becquetee
Comme d'vn Promethee.

La playe ne se ferme point :
Elle est tousiours en mesme poinct :
De Chiron la science
N'y a point de puissance.'

Kyd's translation is in the main accurate, but he misunderstands the fifth stanza (184-7), which means : 'And quitting, as late as possible, the care of us who adore him here, may he shine a new star in heaven, beneficent to our walls.' The reference is not to Caesar in his lifetime, but to his future apotheosis.

202. *agen.* Variant of 'again' in its meaning of 'against.' A mixed form between Southern *ayen* and Northern *again*, showing the common literary pronunciation even when *again* was written. Cf. *N.E.D.*

ACT V.

1-2. Abridged from :

'Malheureux que ie suis! entre mille dangers
De fer, de feu, de sang, et de flots estrangers,
Entre mille trespas, entre mille trauerses,
Que i'ay souffert sur terre, et sur les ondes perses !'

22. *O world, o wretch* : 'O dolente ! ô chetiue !' G.
24. *confirmd*, self-controlled, resolute.
26. 'Possible que la route est moindre que le bruit.' G.
31. 'Suffiront, Cornelie, à plaindre vos malheurs.' G.
39. *O earth, why op'st thou not* : 'Venez me prendre, ô Parque.' G.
50-1. 'Tâchoit escarmouchant de nous tirer du fort.' G.

52. *warie wel-taught troopes*: 'bandes casanieres.'

53. *barrs*, barriers.   Cf. 'Holborn bars.'

58. *Coasting along*, hanging close upon us; for a trans. use of the verb 'cf. ii. 129.

63. *his Pyoners (poore weary soules)*: ' Ses gens lassez.' G. 'Pyoners' are the soldiers who clear the way before an army, by digging and cutting; derived from Fr. 'pionnier,' an extension of 'pion,' a footsoldier.

66. *to hold us hard at work*: 'l'enleuer des mains de l'aduersaire,' G., i. e. ' to capture it (Thapsus) from the enemy.'

70-1. A mistranslation of :

'Cognoissant de combien importoit telle ville,
Et qu'auec peu de gens y commandoit Virgile.'

72. *The fields are spred*: ' Tout s'epand par les champs.'   G.

78. *battails*: 'bataillons.'   G.

80. *One while at Tapsus*: ' Or de Tapse approchans.'   G.

89. *meanely Arm'd.*   Abridged from :

' Qui n'auoyent rien que la targue et la pique,
Le fer dessur le dos.'

91. *to make a wretch a King*: 'faire vn Colonnel vaincueur.'   G.

101. *o're-layd them*, pressed them sore.

111. *approue*, put to the test.

124. ' Pour le peuple Romain par la crainte escarte.'   G.

127-8.   'Ores le bien, l'Empire, et l'estat des Romains
(Le vray prix du vaincueur) balance entre nos mains.'   G.

130. *blubbred.*   Cf. note on iii. 1. 20.

142. *valiantly beset*: 'percé de part en part.'   G.

143. *before our faces*: 'au pied de son rampart.'

146. Added by Kyd.

147-52. 'Ainsi dist : et ses gens criant tous à la fois
De parole et de mains approuuerent sa voix.
Le bruit monta leger iusques dedans les nuës :
Comme quand l'Aquilon souffle aux Alpes cornuës,
Les chesnes esbranlez, l' vn à l'autre battant,
Dans l'espesse forest font vn son esclatant.'   G.

The noise of the shouting army is not compared by Garnier to that of northern winds, but of oaks swayed by those winds.   Kyd, however, strangely mistakes 'chesnes esbranlez' for 'the clattering armour' of Scipio's troops.

151. *buskling*; here apparently ='shaking.'   The word (which is apparently a frequentative of ' busk,' to prepare or get ready) is used in this sense transitively in Studley's *Trans. of Herc. Oet.* 189, 'He buskling up his burning mane, doth dry the dropping south.'

155. *euer-each other*, one another; 'euer-each'= M. E. *everyche*, i. e. each ; the combination with ' other ' is rare.

160-4. An expansion of:

> ' L'air resonne de cris, le Soleil appallist,
> Le feu sort des harnois, et dans le ciel iaillist.'

165. 'Se choquent furieux de longues piques iointes.' G.

167-9. A paraphrase of:

> ' Ialoux de commander l'vn et l'autre aux troupeaux
> Courent impetueux si tost qu'ils s'entre-aduisent
> Et de corne et de front le test ils s'entre-brisent.'

170. Cf. *Sp. Tr.* i. 2. 54.

171. *as moates about the Sunne*: 'comme festus,' i.e. 'like straws.'

174-7. A paraphrase of:

> ' Le sang decoule à terre, et ia par gros bouillons
> Court enflé par la plaine entre les bataillons.
> La terre se poitrist, et toute la campagne,
> Qui volloit en poussiere, au sang Romain se bagne :
> Deuient grasse et visqueuse, et fond dessous les pieds,
> Comme un limon fangeux qui les retient liez.'

176. *Champant.* A variant of champaign, i.e. 'level, open.'

183-5. Cf. *Sp. Tr.* i. 2. 52.

185. *casts the ground*, throws the earth into mounds.

190-3. An inaccurate version of the original, which compares the struggle to the motion of a Pine shaken by two contending winds :

> 'Comme aux Alpes on voit quand la Bize et le Nort
> Contre-soufflent vn Pin de leur plus grand effort,
> Ore de ce costé son chef à terre prendre,
> Ore de cestuy-là contrairement descendre.'

198. *the Cornets of the souldiers* (*cleerd*) : 'les bataillons esclaircis de soldars,' G., i.e. 'the battalions with their ranks thinned.' For 'Cornet' in the sense of a 'troop of cavalry'. cf. *Sp. Tr.* i. 2. 41.

207. *Passant regardant softly they retyre* : 'à trois pas se retirent.' G. 'Passant regardant,' an heraldic term used of a beast in a bearing, walking, but with his head turned behind him.

210. *discouerd*, disclosed to view.

215. 'Tant que l'vn des deux meure.' G.

216-224. Modelled, as Steevens has pointed out, on Lucan's *Pharsalia*, vii. 557-64 :

> ' *Hic Caesar rabies populis stimulusque furorum,*
> *Ne qua parte sui pereat scelus, agmina circum*
> *It vagus, atque animis ignes flagrantibus addit ;*
> *Inspicit et gladios, qui toti sanguine manent,*
> *Qui niteant primo tantum mucrone cruenti,*

Quae presso tremat ense manus, quis languida tela,
Quis contenta ferat, quis praestet bella iubenti
Quem pugnare iuvet.'

219-21. A paraphrase of:

'Voyoit de qui la dextre
Se monstroit au carnage ou plus ou moins adextre :
Voyoit de qui les dars ne rougissoyent q'au bout,
Et ceux qui degoutoyent ensanglantez du tout.'

223. A mistranslation of 'Et ceux qui trespassoyent estendus dans la presse.' Kyd wrongly interprets *trespassoyent*, i.e. 'died,' as 'pac'd it through.'

227-8. A perversion of :

'et qu'une torche ardante
Luy (i.e. Oreste) rallume au dedans sa coulpe renaissante.'

If 'our' be the right reading, 228 is almost unintelligible, but perhaps it is a mistake for 'his.'

231-2. 'Vont la teste baissee, et fermes sur leur piques
Ouurent de grands efforts les phalanges Libyques.'

'Both Battalions' is meaningless here.

242. 'Aux yeux de leurs bergers, qui hardis les defendent.'

246-7. A mistranslation of:

'et les bandes entieres
Trebuchoyent plus espois que iauelles blatieres,'

i.e. 'and whole companies lay stretched on the ground thicker than sheaves of corn.'

254. Added by Kyd, and, apparently, meaning 'that the sight terrifies those who are unhurt.'

255-9. Cf. *Sp. Tr.* i. 2. 59-62.

257. A mistranslation of:

'Les vns percez à iour, les autres soustenoyent
De leurs mourantes mains leurs boyaux qui trainoyent,'

i.e. 'Some pierced through and through, others holding with dying hands their trailing entrails.'

258. After this Kyd omits the line, 'Ou se tiroyent du corps vne fleche pointue.'

263-4. 'Ce qui peut eschaper en fuyant, print parti
De regagner le camp dont il estoit parti.' G.

268. 'Mais las ! desia Çesar de malheur l'occupoit.' G. *eftsoones* may be used by Kyd incorrectly in the sense of 'already,' or it may mean 'forthwith.'

280. *as thundring flints* : 'comme vn tonnerre.' G.

281-2. Added by Kyd.

287. *souspirable*, lamentable ; adopted from Garnier, and probably a unique use.

295. *Hyppon*, Hippo Regius, on the coast of Numidia.

298-300. 'Qui [i.e. la flotte adversaire] le [i.e. Scipion] voyant à
l'ancre avec peu de vaisseaux,
Assiegé de la terre, et du vent, et des eaux,
L'inuestit de furie enfonçant en peu d'heures,
Que dura le combat, ses nauires meilleures.'

By referring *qui* to Scipio instead of to the enemy's fleet Kyd completely misinterprets the meaning, which is, ' Who seeing him at anchor,
with few vessels, assaulted by land, wind, and water, attacked him
furiously, sinking in the few hours that the fight lasted his best
ships.'

298. *slightly shipt*. For 'shipt' = furnished with a ship or ships, cf.
Oth. ii. 1. 47 : ' Is he well shipp'd ?'

302. *Behold*. Gassner's change to ' Beheld' is wrong; the word is
merely an exclamation.

303. *brake agen*, broke up completely. For the form 'agen' cf. note
on iv. 2. 202, and for the intensive use, cf. *Merch. of Ven.* iii. 2. 205 :
' Wooing heere until I swet againe.'

307. *their fauchins in their fists*. Cf. ii. 172, and note.

308. *through-galled* : ' entr'ouvert,' G. = pierced in every quarter. A
rare compound of ' gall,' which is used specially of arrows or shot.

311. *coniured*, united in a conspiracy.

328. *Crawld to the Deck* : ' S'auance sur le bord.' G.

345. *tyering*. Variant of 'tiring,' i.e. 'preying'; cf. *3 Henry VI*, i.
1. 268 :
'And like an empty eagle
Tire on the flesh of me and of my son.'

361-5. Added by Kyd.

374. *Iulia*, Pompey's former wife, the daughter of Caesar.

380-3. A paraphrase of :
'Et te repentiras (si tu n'as bien le cœur
Plus que d'vne Tigresse enyuré de rigueur)
D'auoir ton Adrastee attisé si cruelle
Au cœur de ton Cesar pour vne faute telle.'

381. *rigor*. The abstract English word scarcely gives the sense of
rigueur, i.e. ' pitiless rage.'

387-9. An expansion of :
' indignement ialouse
Contre l'heur vsurpé d'vne seconde espouse.'

393. ' Si desireux d'vn maistre.' G.

397. ' Quand le destin contraire aux phalanges d'Afrique.' G.

398. *topside turuey*. Cf. note on i. 83.

400.   ' Ses guerriers nourriçons enuoyez au trespas.' G.

i.e. ' Its soldiers, the state's life-blood, sent to death.'

404-7. 'Ore Dieux Afriquains, ore est venu le temps
 Que de nous reuengez deuez estre contans,
 Et contans les esprits de ces vieux Capitaines
 Qui vaincus ont passé par les armes Romaines.' G.

Kyd makes nonsense of the passage by interpreting 'contans' in 406 as 'counting,' depending on 'Dieux Afriquains' and governing 'les esprits de ces vieux Capitaines.'

410. *so dezart* : 'si roux.' G. Kyd's rendering suggests that he was unaware that Thrasymene was a lake.

419-20. An expansion of :

'Pleurons, ô troupe aimee, et qu'à iamais nos yeux
 En nostre sein mourant decoulent larmoyeux.'

418. *Valing*, casting down ; rarely used, as here, without the connotation of submission to a superior.

420. *springtides of your teares.* Cf. *Sp. Tr.* iii. 7. 8.

427. *neglectly*, negligently ; very rare, possibly unique use of the word.

428. *accoustrements.* This form is used by Shakespeare in *A. Y. L. I.* iii. 2. 402 : 'You are rather point deuice in your accoustrements.'

433. Garnier has simply 'Veufue de mes Espoux.'

444. *Sold at a pike* : 'Vendre sous vn pique,' G., i.e. 'venalis sub hasta.' Kyd probably did not understand the allusion.

458. *fumous* : 'fumeuses,' G., i.e. 'vaporous.' Hence Gassner's emendation is probably right, and I have adopted it. But Kyd may have misunderstood the meaning of the French word and translated it by 'famous.'

463-4. An expansion of the line, 'Ie vomiray ma vie, et tombant legere Ombre.' With 464 cf. the two opening lines of *Sp. Tr.*

NOTES

SOLIMAN AND PERSEDA

ACT I.

SCENE I.

10-11. From the contrast between the 'bloody quill' of Melpomene in 11 and her 'tung' in 12 the reference here seems to be to a non-dramatic version of the story, probably Wotton's translation of Yver's tale in *A Courtlie Controuersie.*

17. Cf. *Sp. Tr.* i. 1. 91.

26. *to euerlasting night.* Cf. *Sp. Tr.* ii. 2. 57, 'into eternal night,' and *Ard. of Fev.* iii. 2. 9, 'And Arden sent to everlasting night.'

27. *moralliz'd,* shown the moral of.

29. *brightsome.* For a similar formation cf. 'gladsome,' ii. 1. 11.

SCENE II.

2-3. For an elaborated form of this simile cf. *Corn.* i. 79-87.

6. *pastime.* Rarely used as a verb. Cf. Latimer, *Sermon of the Plough*: 'They pastime in their prelacies with gallant gentlemen.'

9. *feres,* companions.

13. *dittie.* Used in its strict sense of the words to a tune. Cf. *A.Y.L.I.* v. 3. 36: 'There was no great matter in the dittie, yet the note was very vntunable.'

23. *nice,* coy.

30. *I, watch you vauntages?* 'Are you on the look out to get the better of me?'

36. For an elaboration of this metaphor cf. *Sp. Tr.* ii. 2. 7-9.

39. *this ring.* In Wotton's tale (p. 36) Erastus gives Persida (as the name is there spelt) 'a jewell wherein was a Diamante and an Emeralde.'

41. *boot,* additional gift, profit.

53-61. Cf. the similar lists of nationalities in *Corn.* i. 59-63, and iv. 2. 44-50 ; see *Introd.* p. lvii.

59. *sudden,* hasty, passionate. Cf. *Macb.* iv. 3. 59:

> 'Sudden, malicious, smacking of every sin
> That has a name.'

61. *Eclipped.* A singular, and etymologically indefensible, variant of *Yclipped.*

62. *approoued*, tested.

69. *And if I thriue in valour, as the glasse.* The Qq. punctuate, 'thriue, in valour as the glasse.' If this is right then 'valour' means 'worth, efficacy.' But the punctuation adopted in the text is probably correct.

81. *and ouertane*, and be overcome. The omission of the auxiliary verb before the participle is frequent in Eliz. English.

88. *triumphs*, ceremonies, shows.

90. *outlandish*, foreign.

98. *wounded with the Greekes.* For this use of 'with' to indicate the agent, cf. *W.'s Tale*, v. 2. 68 : 'He was torn to pieces with a bear.' Hazlitt needlessly adopts ''rounded,' the marginal MS. emendation in one of the 1599A Qq.

Scene III.

22. *skenes*, Irish daggers, usually of bronze, double-edged, and more or less leaf-shaped ; Gaelic *sgian*, a knife. Hawkins, followed by Hazlitt, wrongly reads 'Kerns.' Cf. l. 95.

41. *Rutter*, a trooper, or dragoon ; Dutch *ruiter*. Cf. *Dr. Faustus*, i. 1. 103 : 'Like Almain rutters with their horsemen's staves.'

48. *lay*, faith, creed. For an instance of this rare use of the word cf. Chaucer, *Man of Lawe's Tale*, 278 :

> 'She . . . seyde him she wold reneye her lay,
> And cristendom of preestes handes fonge.'

49. *braue*, cry of bravado.

51. *the Sophy*, the Shah of Persia.

55-7. The text is corrupt, but the transposition of 55, thus making Brusor's march through Asia follow his defeat of the Persians, is a plausible emendation, especially as his passage from the plains of Africa to the 'coasts held by the Portinguize' (58) would also be in natural sequence.

59. *golde abounding.* The simplest emendation of the Q. reading, where the comma between 'golde' and 'aboarding' is a printer's error. Hawkins and Hazlitt, however, read 'aboarding,' i.e. 'landing on the coast of,' which apparently refers to Brusor. But this leaves 'Euen to the verge of golde' unexplained.

77. *Epitheton*, appellation; uncommon, but used by Foxe, Holinshed, and in the Douay Bible. Cf. *The Hous. Phil.* p. 257, 12 and 274, 23.

95. *Kernes*, light-armed foot-soldiers ; Irish *Ceatharnach.*

108. *Pities adomant*, the loadstone of pity.

140. *O extempore, O flores.* A corruption, of course, of *O tempora, O mores.*

143. *By Gods fish.* An oath, apparently, of Piston's coining.

146-7. *occupation*, trade, especially of a mechanical kind. Hence Basilisco's indignation.

160-1. *Dudgin dagger*, a dagger with a hilt made of 'dudgin,' a particular kind of wood, probably boxwood.

169-71. Alluded to in *King John*, i. 1. 243-4:

'*Lady Faulc.* What means this scorn, thou most untoward knave?
Bast. Knight, Knight, good mother, Basilisco-like.'

191-2. *By Cock and Pie, and Mouse foot.* In the colloquial oath, 'By Cock and Pie,' the word 'Cock' is a corruption (with intermediate form 'Gock') of God; 'Pie' is the ordinal of the Roman Catholic Church. For the coupling of the expression with 'Mouse-foot,' cf. Dent's *Pathway to Heaven* (1601): 'I know a man that will neuer sweare but by Cocke or Pie or Mousefoot. I hope you will not say they be oathes.'

212. *iustle.* Unusual variant of 'iostle.'

214. *iet,* 'strut.'

227. *olde,* great; a frequent Eliz. use of the word.

228. *the Fox in the hole,* a game played by boys, who hopped on one leg, and beat one another with pieces of leather.

SCENE IV.

15. In Wotton's tale (pp. 39-40) it is the Prince of Cyprus who, 'seazing vpon the hinder skirt of his helmet with an ardent boldness, drew it so rudely, or rather happily towards him, as the latchets and buckles slipping, he openly discovered the bare head of our Rhodian Erastus.' In so doing he cut the chain (p. 43) 'with the gorget of Erastus' armoure,' and it slipped from him without his perceiving it.

31. *lauolto,* a lively round dance of Italian origin. Cf. *Hen. V,* iii. 5. 33: 'lavoltas high, and swift corantos.'

37. *mated,* overcome.

52. *a Fidlers fee.* A proverbial phrase for a scanty wage. Cf. 1st Pt. *Returne fr. Parnass.* i. 1. 380: 'He .. gave me fidler's wages and dismist me.'

55. *channell bone,* collar bone; 'channel(l)' and 'cannel' are often found in M.E. and in Eliz. Engl. = 'neck'; cf. Part II *Tamb.* i. 3. 102: 'and cleaue him to the channel with my sword.'

68. *dismount.* Rarely used, as here, of a horse throwing its rider.

97. *consideration.* Used here, probably, in its technical legal sense. If so, it is one of the earliest examples of such a use, as the *N.E.D.* gives no instance of it, with this specific meaning, before 1592.

116. *In dalying war,* in playing at war, in spending time in warlike sports; a rare meaning of 'dally,' which, when followed by an object, usually means 'to delay, put off.'

127. *misintends,* is malignantly planning; a rare word, used by Spenser, *Sonnet* xvi, in the sense of 'aim badly.'

130. Cf. *Corn.* ii. 250-1.

SCENE V.

12. *Bassowes.* An uncommon variant of 'Bashawes,' i.e. 'Pachas.'

36. *hath bin manured to,* has been spilt like manure on; probably a unique construction.

39. *mean*, moderate, partial.

49. *Infer*, bring forward.

58. *Aristippus-like.* A reference to Aristippus, who in R. Edwardes' *Damon and Pithias* (Hazlitt, Dodsley's *Old Plays*, iv. p. 16) plays the part of the typical flatterer :

> 'I professe now the courtly philosophie,
> To crouche, to speake fayre ; myselfe I applie
> To feede the kinge's humour with pleasant deuises.'

63. *rechlesse.* Assibilated form of ' reckless.'

73. *giue aime to this presumption,* direct these presumptuous speeches to their mark ; a metaphor from archery. Cf. *Corn.* iv. 1. 172 : 'cry you ayme,' and Note.

SCENE VI.

20. *tickle*, unstable, inconstant.

30. *Bragardo.* A unique variant of ' bragard ' or ' braggart.'

ACT II.
SCENE I.

2-3. Cf. *Sp. Tr.* ii. 2. 3-4.

3. *semblant*, resembling, similar.

15-16. Cf. *Sp. Tr.* ii. 2. 32, and ii. 4. 36.

45. *And blinde can iudge no colours.* A proverbial phrase.

50. In Wotton's tale (p. 45) Persida ' in excuse of hir departure sayde, that the streyghtnesse of hir gown greued hir so sore as she was very ill at ease therwith.'

60. *tralucent brest.* Cf. *Sp. Tr.* i. 4. 97.

85. In Wotton's tale, Persida, after complaining of the ' streyghtnesse ' of her gown, ' the better to counterfeite the matter caused Agatha to vnclaspe hir bodie : but alas she was griped with an other claspe more vneasye to be loosed.'

99. *my sweet second selfe.* Cf. *Sp. Tr.* ii. 4. 9.

110. *light foote*, swift, cf. ii. 3. 21, and *Faerie Queene*, iii. 4. 7 :

> 'There she alighted from her light-foot beast.'

130. Cf. *Euphues*, p. 100 (Arber) : ' Is not poyson taken out of the Honnysuckle by the Spider ? '

137. *blast.* Strictly ' a blasted or withered blossom,' but here ' a blossom that withers quickly.'

163. *remorse*, pity.

176. *aleauement*, alleviation. The emendation is, however, perhaps unnecessary, as *aleagement*, the reading of the Qq., may be a unique formation, from *aleage* a variant of M.E. *allege*=' lighten, allay.' Spenser uses the verb in *Shep.'s Cal.* March :

> 'The ioyous time now nigheth fast,
> That shall alegge this bitter blast.'

214. *replie*, supply.

221. *a paire*, a set; cf. ' a pair of cards,' i. e. ' a pack of cards.'

223. *Hie men and low men.* A slang phrase for false dice, so called because loaded in such a way as to turn up respectively high or low numbers. Cf. W. Cartwright, *Ordinary*, ii. 3 :

> ' your high
> And low men are but trifles : your pois'd dye
> That's ballasted with quicksilver and gold.'

224. *Drumsler*, ' drummer'; a rare form, a corruption of 'Drum-slayer' or 'Drumslade.'

228. *Charleman is come.* An obscure allusion. Hazlitt's suggestion that Lucina calls Ferdinand Charleman in sport is not very plausible.

231. *vnion*, a large pearl.

232. Suggested by Wotton's words (p. 51), 'Lucina who had receyued the Carquenet in exchaunge of hir Chayne, knew his chapman, other-wise she would hardly haue departed from the Iewell.'

238. *sorted*, turned out, happened.

243. *garded*, ornamented with a border of lace.   Cf. *Merch. of Ven.* ii. 2. 170 :

> ' Give him a livery
> More guarded than his fellows.'

244. *Dasell mine eyes.* For the intransitive use of the verb, cf. Webster, *Duch. of Malfi*, iv. 2 :

> ' Cover her face : mine eyes dazzle : she died young.'

266. *stay*, place of sojourn.

290. *dominere*, live riotously. Cf. Jonson, *Ev. Man. in Hum.* ii. 1 :
' Let him spend, and spend, and domineere.'

SCENE II.

11. *a pair of false dice.* Cf. note on ii. 1. 221.

17. *counter-cambio*, exchange ; a unique adaptation of Italian *con-tracambio.*

21. *prickado.* A burlesque phrase formed on the analogy of *passado*, the technical term for a forward thrust in fencing.

57. *coystrell*, varlet ; originally, a groom or servant to a Knight.

64. *surquedry*, arrogance, presumption; cf. Chaucer, *Persones Tale*, 403 : ' Presumption is when a man undertaketh an emprise that him ought not to do, or elles that he may not do ; and this is called surquidrie.'

91. *Pigmew.*   Rare variant of ' Pygmy.'

ACT   III.

SCENE I.

18. *not twentie yeares of age.* Wotton represents Erastus as being about sixteen years old. When Persida gave him the chain he had attained the age of fifteen, and he had ' enioyed this iewell' for ten months before the Tournament, when he lost it (pp. 35 and 37).

38. *sect*, troop, company ; not used in its distinctively ecclesiastical sense.

53. *Whats he.* Hazlitt's emendation may be right, but the Qq. reading throws the metrical stress on the emphatic word 'he,' and 'bouldly' may have had a trisyllabic pronunciation.

85-90. Cf. 3 *Henry VI*, ii. 1. 91-2.

> 'Nay, if thou be that princely eagle's bird,
>   Show thy descent by gazing 'gainst the sun.'

88. *talents.* Archaic form of 'talons.'

92. *presents*, presence.

SCENE II.

41. Demophon, the son of Theseus, was beloved by Phyllis, who, on being abandoned by him, committed suicide. The story is told by Ovid, *Heroides*, ii. 1.

SCENE V.

5-6. The text is partly corrupt, but the suggested emendation in 6 probably represents the original meaning.

SCENE VI.

11. *countercheck*, act in opposition to. The word is used, with a slightly different significance, in *Sp. Tr.* ii. 2. 37.

ACT IV.
SCENE I.

2. *Sugerloafe hat*, a hat of a conical shape, which is sometimes called 'a sugarloafe' alone.

25. *thy dumps.* The phrase, which is not found before the sixteenth century, has not here the modern colloquial association ; the use of 'dumps' with a poss. pronoun is rare.

55-7. Cf. Wotton, (p. 55): 'Euen as Alexander the greate pardoned Thebes for the loue of Pindarus, and Stagirius (*sic*) for the good will he bare to Aristotle: or as the fortunate Augustus entreated rebellious Alexandria at the requeste of Arrius.'

77-83. On the possible debt of this description to Watson's *Hecatompathia*, Son. 21, cf. *Introd.*, pp. xxiv and lix, note.

77. *lockes.* Evidently a right emendation, as Soliman is describing Perseda's beauties in detail.

133. The Qq. rightly put a comma between 'my deare,' addressed to Perseda, and 'Loue,' which is a personification contrasted with 'Maiestie' in 134.

145-6. Suggested by Erastus' words to Soliman, Wotton (p. 60): 'I humbly thanke the Heauens whyche haue planted a hearte so noble and vertuous in the breaste of my soueraigne King, to haue power to brydle his will, the which is vnto you a Trophee more glorious, than if you had conquered the Occidente Empire.'

176. The joining of Erastus and Perseda's hands by Soliman apparently constitutes a marriage. Wotton alludes (p. 60) to a more formal ceremony: 'Immediately the marriage was celebrated with great solemnitie and magnificence, whyche the Emperour honoured in person wyth his whole Courte.'

222. *stumble*, trip up, defeat; this metaphorical trans. use is infrequent.

233. *perswades*, persuasions; a rare form.

245. *Vnder couler of great consequence*, under pretence of matters of great moment.

SCENE II.

1. *expugnation*, taking by storm, conquest; not uncommon in sixteenth and seventeenth century writers.

12. *forehard*, heard before; an unusual compound.

23. *collop*, a slice; usually, a slice of bacon or meat for frying.

24. *squicht*. A unique use of the word, which is of onomatopoeic formation, and means 'shrieked, squealed.'

32. *Tremomundo*. A corruption perhaps of Spanish *Tremebundo*.
    cakebread, bread made in flattened cakes.

34. *Basolus manus*. Piston's corruption of the Spanish salutation, *Beso las manos*, 'I kiss your hands.' The phrase is fairly frequent in Eliz. literature. Cf. Puttenham, *Arte of English Poesie*, p. 292: 'With vs the wemen giue their mouth to be kissed, in other places their cheek, in many places their hand, or in steed of an offer to the hand, to say these words *Bezo los manos*'; and Gabriel Harvey's *Letters*, p. 136: 'I like not those same congyes by *Bezo las Manos*.'

43-6. Probably a parody of Tamburlaine's words, Part II *Tamburlaine*, v. 3:

> 'See, where my slave, the ugly monster, Death
> Shaking and quivering, pale and wan for fear,
> Stands aiming at me with his murdering dart,
> Who flies away at every glance I give,
> And when I look away, comes stealing on.'

50. *muliebritie*, womanhood; rarely used.

62. *minoritie*. Used here apparently in the sense of 'lowness of stature.'

ACT V.

SCENE I.

13-7. For the thought and imagery here, cf. *Sp. Tr.* ii. 2. 7-17.

24. *Importuning*, importing, having a bearing on; for a similar confusion of 'importune' and 'import,' cf. *Faer. Qu.* iii. 1. 16:

> 'But the sage wisard tells, as he has redd,
>   That it importunes death.'

wealth, well-being.

31. *mine*. Hazlitt reads 'me' on the analogy of 33, but 'frame' here = 'be used as,' and is naturally followed by the possessive pronoun, while in 33 'frame' = 'fashion' and is followed by the ethical dative.

37. *Ile want him*, I will do without him.

Scene II.

4. Soliman hides behind a partition or curtain (cf. *Sp. Tr.* iv. 3. 1, S.D.), and the rest of his speeches till after Erastus' execution are 'asides.'

36. Wotton (p.66) briefly relates that Erastus was accused by false witnesses of treason and rebellion, 'for that he had consented (sayd they) to deliuer the Ile of Rhodes into the possession of the Christians.'

48. Piston remains on the stage unseen. Thus we have an unusually complicated grouping here: (1) In the centre of the stage Erastus, the Marshall, the Witnesses, and the Janissaries, (2) Soliman, (3) Piston.

65. *minding*, intending.

69. *a kenning*. A verbal substantive from 'ken' in its sense of 'descry'; used sometimes, possibly here, to denote a marine measure of about twenty miles.

84. In Wotton's tale (p. 66) Erastus is beheaded.

87. Cf. the almost identical line, *Sp. Tr.* i. 4. 92.

92. *limited*, appointed.

118. *the tower's top*. Represented probably by the gallery at the back of the stage; cf. *Sp. Tr.* iv. 3. 12.

126. *when*. An expression of impatience; cf. *Sp. Tr.* iii. 1. 47.

126–8. Cf. Ovid, *Metam.* xiii. 415:

> '*Mittitur Astyanax illis de turribus unde*
> *Pugnantem pro se, proavitaque regna tuentem,*
> *Saepe videre patrem monstratum a matre solebat.*'

134. *detect*, expose.

149. *deft*, deafened; this pa. part. of the verb 'deaf' is rarely used.

Scene III.

5. *porpuse*. A corruption by Basilisco of 'prepuce' = foreskin.

7. *pinky-ey'd*, small-eyed; to 'wink and pink' with the eyes means 'to contract them and peep out of the lids.' Cf. Holland's *Pliny*, Bk. xi: 'Also them that were pink-eyed and had very small eies, they termed *ocellae*'; also *Ant. and Cleop.* ii. 7. 121:

> 'Plumpy Bacchus, with pink eyne.'

16. *the old Cannon*. I have been unable to trace the source of Basilisco's quotation.

25. Cf. the almost identical line, *Sp. Tr.* i. 3. 76.

34. *Knights of the post*, witnesses ready to swear falsely for a bribe;

so called from being always found waiting at the posts set up outside the sheriff's doors.

40. *conuaid*, carried out; cf. *K. Lear*, i. 2. 109: 'I will ... conuey the businesse as I shall find meanes.'

70. *Abraham-coloured*, with auburn-coloured hair. 'Abraham' is a corruption of 'auburn,' of which 'abern' and 'abron' are variants. Cf. *Coriol*. ii. 3. 21 : 'Our heads are some browne, some blacke, some Abram,' which the fol. of 1685 alters to 'auburn.'

81. *quiddits*, captious, subtle arguments.

82. *captious*. Probably here='crafty, clever.'

87. A proverbial expression.

93. *phillip*. Variant of 'fillip'='a blow.'

SCENE IV.

10. Cf. *Sp. Tr.* i. 4. 35.

S. D. *in mans apparell*. Wotton (p. 67) speaks of Persida, 'buckling vnto her body the armour which sometime pertained vnto hir friend, I meane the greene armour.'

54. *Iniurious*, insulting. ·

59. A partly corrupt line, of which no entirely satisfactory emendation can be suggested.

S. D. *Soliman kils Perseda*. In Wotton's tale (p. 67) Persida is killed, not in single combat, but by 'a volue of shot' from the Turkish army, 'among the which two bullets sent from a Musket stroke hir through the stomack.'

81. Cf. the almost identical line, *Sp. Tr.* ii. 5. 46. Wotton (p. 68) also compares the stricken Persida to a rose, but to one 'which by age hath lost ye red liuely hue.'

146. *boyles like Etna*. For the simile cf. *Sp. Tr.* iii. 10. 75.

154. *amisse*, fault ; a substantival use of the adverb, found chiefly in Eliz. English.

S. D. *Then Soliman dyes*. In Wotton's tale (pp. 69–72) Soliman is not poisoned, but survives the lovers, whom he buries in a gorgeous tomb.

SCENE V.

37. *Cynthias friend*, Queen Elizabeth.

NOTES

THE HOVSHOLDERS PHILOSOPHIE

Page 239, 4. *Betwixt* Novara *and* Vercellis. Tasso's journey took place in October 1578, when he was fleeing in disguise for safety from the Court of Urbino to that of the Prince of Savoy.

10. *The unexpected pleasure of which game stayed me.* T. has simply 'poco stante.'

23-4. *not far hence, neere that Riuer*: 'di quà dal fiume,' T., i. e. on this side of the river.

25. *disease*, discomfort.

P. 240, 5-7. *Thereupon . . . staie.* Kyd, apparently through a grammatical blunder, has transferred these words to the 'giovinetto.' T. puts them into his own mouth: 'e gli dissi che sulla ripa del fiume prenderei consiglio secondo il suo parere di passar oltre, o di fermarmi.'

14. *preuented*, anticipated.

15-6. *but heretofore, going into* Fraunce, *I past by* Pyemount. A mistranslation of T., who states that he passed through 'Piemonte' before, but by a different road: 'perciocchè altra fiata, che andando in Francia passai per lo Piemonte, non feci questo cammino.'

27. *shrowded*, sheltered.

36. *commorants*, residents. The word is not uncommon as an adjective, but is very rarely used, as here, as a substantive, except in the technical sense of 'members of the Cambridge Senate resident in the town (commorantes in villa) who were no longer members of their colleges.' Cf. *N. E. D. sub voce.*

37. *Passador*: 'passatore,' T.; here used in the sense of a 'ferriman.'

38. *upon what occasio⟨n⟩ they knew not.* Added by Kyd.

P. 241, 11. *ledde me to*: 'mi additò,' T., i. e. 'pointed out.'

12-3. *and it was as high.* Before these words Kyd omits 'Ella era di nuovo fabbricata.'

19. *porthals*: 'appartamenti di stanze.' T.

20-1. *and as manie in the vpper end*: 'ed altrettanti appartamenti conosceva, ch' erano nella parte della casa superiore.' T.

29. *curious plates of* Candie: 'candidissimi piatti di creta.' T.

P. 242, 7. *Spirit*: 'aspetto.' T.

8. *eftsoones*. Apparently means here 'just then,' though this is unusual.

28. *in other things*: 'in altra occasione.' T.

29. *regardant*. Rarely used, as here, without reference to sight.

39. From *Georgics* IV. 133.

P. 243, 3–6. From Petrarch, *Canzone IX*, 21–4; the two last lines are completely mistranslated in 9–10, as Kyd confuses *ghiande* = 'acorns' with *ghiandaje* = 'jays.'

15–7. *necessaries ... for the supply of good manners, I meane, not of good meate*: 'cose necessarie al bel vivere, non che al vivere.' T.

27. *rewes*. A M.E. variant of 'rows'; cf. Chaucer, *Knight's Tale*, 2007–8:

'To hakke and hewe
The okes old and leye hem on a rewe.'

31. *some store of hyues for Bees*: 'molti alberi d'api.' T.

32. *gryft*. Very rare variant of 'graft' used as pt. part.

P. 244, 9. *Cowgomers*. A very rare, probably unique, variant of 'cowcombers' or 'cucumbers.'

15–6. *But he then ... was wanting*. An inaccurate rendering of 'Ma egli, quasi pure allora avveduto che la moglie vi mancasse, disse.'

38. *otherwise*: 'di meno eccedendoli,' T.; this mistranslation partly causes the confused rendering in 245, 6–9.

40—**245**, 1. *which if ... moderate*: 'le quali, se non per altro, almeno per esempio de' figliuoli, debbono moderare.' T.

P. 245, 6–9. *where, if they exceeded ... children vnto*. Completely mistranslated. T. draws two pictures of the evils which occur respectively when a father is too young or too old. The first extends from 244, 38 to 245, 6; the second then proceeds: 'ma se di molto maggior numero di anni eccedessero, non potrebbero i padri ammaestrare i figliuoli, sarebbero vicini alla decrepità, quando i figliuoli fossero ancora nell' infanzia, o nella prima fanciullezza, nè da loro potrebbero quell' ajuto attendere, e quella gratitudine, che tanto dalla natura è desiderata.'

11. *Natis munire senectam*. From Lucretius, iv. 1249.

15–7. *no less satisfied ... your Sonne*: 'non meno dell' età che dell' altre condizioni de' vostri figliuoli dobbiate esser soddisfato'; the wrong rendering of 'dell' età' destroys the sequence of the argument.

21. *according to my remembrance*: 'del mio accorgere accorgendosi.' T.

34–5. *as for Beefe and such like ... and the Table*: 'perchè il bue si porta piuttosto per un cotal riempimento delle mense.' T.

38. *with noble men*: 'con gli Eroi'; the specialized use of the phrase in Greek mythology is not understood.

P. 246, 3–5. *And the companions ... uppon Beefe*. A mistranslation, showing that Kyd was ignorant of the Homeric story of Odysseus and the horses of the Sun: 'Ed i compagni di Ulisse non per cupidità di fagiani, o di pernici, ma per mangiare i buoi del Sole, sopportarono tante sciagure.'

6. *inducith*, introduceth.

6-7. *where, after the judgment of some, it shold haue beene some other thing*: 'ove per altro [i. e. nevertheless] non di cervi, ma di alcuna sorte di uccelli dovea far preda.'

8-9. *but in hauing regard . . . Noblemen's dyet.* Kyd again misunderstands *Eroi*: 'ma mentre egli volle aver riguardo alla convenevolezza ed al costume degli Eroi.'

20-1. *those Beasts that commonly are stald and foddered.* T. has simply 'animali domestici.'

22. *speaking of* Aeneas *soldiours.* Added by Kyd, who thus shows his acquaintance with the passage, *Aen.* i. 215.

31. *Nigrum et dulce*: 'nero et dolce,' T.; the use of the Latin epithets here is curious.

P. 247, 17. From *Catullus*, 27, 2.

P. 248, 2. *but me thinks no time may be compared to* Autumn. Cf. *Corn.* ii. 135, and see *Introduction*, pp. lxii–lxiii.

4. *otherwhile*: 'altrui.' T.

5. *with pastimes*: 'Co' giuochi e con gli spettacoli.' T.

8. *who in Sommer*: 'che ora,' i. e. 'in these seasons' (not Summer only), as the following words clearly show.

10. *whether they first find.* A mistranslation of 'che sopraggiungono all' improviso,' i. e. 'which ⟨raynes and tempests⟩ unexpectedly occur.'

13. *the third part*: 'se non in picciola parte.' T.

14. *for spoile of weather, wormes, and windes.* Added by Kyd.

23. *are enclozed with darknes and reserued to the night.* T. has simply 'sono nella notte riserbate.'

23-4. *nothing necessarie*: 'poco opportuno.' T.

27. *a Lord*: 'giusto signore.' T.

30. *and contagions*: 'ed afflitti dalle fatiche.' T.

39-40. *a most indifferent Gouernour*: 'giustissimo signore.' T.

P. 249, 7-8. *whereof as one especiall is Grape-gathering for the wine-presse.* An awkward rendering of 'della quale ⟨stagione⟩ è propria ancora la vendemmia.'

11-2. *if in making . . . falshood.* An inaccurate rendering of 's'egli nel fare i vini usa trascuraggine alcuna,' i. e. 'if he shows any carelessness in making his wines.'

15. *Non solum frigescit Venus*: 'non sol Venere è fredda,' T.; an allusion to Terence, *Eun.* iv. 5, 6, '*Sine Cerere et Libero friget Venus*,' which Kyd partly quotes, though inaccurately.

20. *my Father saie.* After this Kyd omits 'dal quale ancora alcune delle cose dette udii dire.'

22-3. *that in this season . . . beleeue it did*: 'che in questa stagione ebbe principio il mondo, se in alcuna ebbe principio, come per fede certissimamente tener debbiamo, che avesse.' T.

P. 250, 11. *foregoes*, goes away from.

12-3. *Besides, it beginneth with generation, not with corruption*:
‘ e comincia ⟨i.e. il Sole⟩ la generazione, e non la corruzione.’ T.

19-20. *what was said in* Platos Tymeus ... *inferior Gods.* The
reference is to *Tymaeus*, 41, but the passage lends no support to the
argument here.

22. *the world*: ‘ il moto.’ T.

P. 251, 1-2. *are peraduenture one of those of whom the crye is come*:
‘ e voi siete uno per aventura del quale alcun grido.’ T.

3-5. *whereof you are as worthy* . . . *your speeches*: ‘il quale è
altrettanto degno di perdono per la cagione del suo fallire, quanto per
altro di lode e di maraviglia.’ T.

9-10. *superfluous conceit of mine opinions*: ‘per soverchia ani-
mosità di opinioni.’ T.

16. *giuing thanks.* Added by Kyd.

17. *by her Sonnes.* After this T. adds, ‘ e ritirossi alle sue stanze.’

21. *dysease*, inconvenience, discomfort.

24. Charles V ‘ *desposed his Monarchie*’ in 1554.

40. *disgrade.* Very rarely used, as here, to mean ‘ deprive, un-
burden,’ without a punitive sense.

P. 252, 9. *good husbandry*: ‘ con tutte l’ arti di lodato padre di
famiglia.’ T.

15-6. *with little more expence*: ‘con maggiore spesa,’ T., i.e.
‘ though my expenditure has been greater.’

17. *experimented*, experienced ; a common sixteenth century
use.

28-9. *to haue care in choosing of his wife.* T. has simply ‘ aver
cura della moglie.’

P. 253, 21-2. *in the book of* Virgils Aeneidos. Added by Kyd.

23-7. From *Aeneid*, iv. 25-9.

28. *rought.* M. E. pret. of ‘ reach,’ here used with ‘ in ’ in the
unusual sense of ‘ swallow up.’

P. 254, 7. *a Begger*: ‘ donna ignobile.’ T.

14-5. *Which honor* . . . *to others*: ‘i quali ⟨atti⟩ da niuna
esistenza sono accompagnati, quali son quegli onori, che per buona
creanza si sogliono fare altrui.’ T.

17-8. *but that the league* . . . *farre exceedeth it.* An ambiguous
version of ‘ che maggiore non quella ⟨differenza⟩, che la natura ha posta
fra gli uomini e le donne.’

P. 255, 2. *exonerat.* Usually has as object the person or thing
relieved, not, as here, the load.

16-8. *or so as in our soules* . . . *vnto reason*: ‘ O nell’ anima
nostra, nella quale così ordinate le potenze, come nelle città gli ordini
de’ cittadini, la parte affetuosa suole alla ragionevole ubbidire.’ T.

31-3. *for if hee himselfe* . . . *the marriage bedde.* T. has simply
‘ se non violerà egli le leggi maritali.’

39. *was it said of* Aristotle. The remark here attributed to

Aristotle does not occur in his discussion of αἰδώς (*Nich. Eth.* iv. 9), where he says that shame is commendable in the young.

P. 256, 3–8. *which increaseth . . . or toothsome.* An expansion of 'il quale tanto alle donne accresce di vaghezza, quanto loro per- avventura ne tolgono quei colori artificiali, de' quali quasi maschere, o scene, si sogliono colorare.' The illustrative quotation in the margin is from Ovid, *De medicamine faciei*, 45.

7. *poppets.* Variant of 'puppets.'

8. *toothsome*, agreeable. Applied usually to edibles.

10. *with slime or artificiall coullered trash* : 'con gli artificiali imbellettamenti.' T.

15–8. *he can practise . . . pollishing themselues.* An expansion of 'Con niun' altra maniera potrà meglio il marito fare che non s'imbelletti, che col mostrarsi schivo de' belletti e de' liscii.'

18. *proigning.* An earlier form of 'pruning'='trimming, adorn- ing'; rarely used, as here, in this sense, without reference to a bird's trimming of its wings.

22–3. *their tricking vp . . . filth.* T. has simply 'così lisciata.'

24. *of modestie and loue.* Added by Kyd.

35. *proude and feltred* : 'superbe,' T.; 'feltred' = tangled, matted. Cf. Tuberville's *Tr. of Ovid's Eps.* 16 b, 'Heavy helmet on thy head and feltred lockes to beare.'

38. *in the shape of man* : 'nella specie dell' uomo.' T.

P. 257, 9. *like a Boy* : 'non barbato, ma senza barba.' T.

10. *deciphered*, delineated.

11. *with long . . . tresses.* T. has simply 'con lunghissime chiome.'

12–3. *call him* Phoebus . . . chiomato : 'chiamano Febo con aggiunto quasi perpetuo, non tosato o chiomato,' T., i.e. 'call Phoebus by the constant epithets of "Non tosato o chiomato."' It is singular that Kyd should leave the epithets untranslated in his text, as if T. were speaking of Italian instead of Classical poets. Nor is his marginal rendering 'vnkempt' accurate.

14. *so hastilie* : 'tanto.' T.

29. *not to discontent her* : 'non solo di piacere a lei, ma di com- piacerla.' T.

31. *as others of her calling doo.* After this Kyd omits 'e di quel, che porti l'uso della nostra città.'

34. *be forwarde with the first* : 'sia fra le prime veduta e va- gheggiata.'

P. 258, 6. T. quotes the line in an Italian version, 'O da me ognor temuto, e paventato, suocero caro.'

9–10. *with those prophane . . . Louer doth.* T. has simply 'in quel modo stesse, che viene l'amante.'

12. Bell' ingannus *Paramour* : 'Catelda.' T.

20. *of theyr opposites and indigested contraries* : 'degli oggetti.' T.

21–2. *Neither will I . . . when* Homer. A mistranslation of 'Nè

voglio a questo proposito tacere, che quando Omero,' i. e. ' Nor in discussing this subject will I refrain from mentioning that when Homer.'

24. *with loue, and louely termes, and amorous games*. T. has
simply ' nel suo amore.'

25. A verse-rendering of T.'s prose, 'con lui si colca nell' erba,
ricoperta da una nuvola maravigliosa.'

32–4. *And when he saith . . . his Wife*. A mistranslation of ' bene
è vero, che dicendole Giove, che non avea avuto egual desiderio di lei
da quel dì che prima la prese per moglie,' i.e. ' It is true that when
Jove says that he had not had equal desire for her since the day when
he first took her to wife.'

36–259,1. *because it is . . . loues of Matrimonie*. Kyd here condenses
two separate statements, ' perciocchè è inconvenientissimo a coloro che
come padre, o madre di famiglia, vogliono con onestà e con amore
maritale regger la casa : nè altro mi sovviene che dire del vicendevole
amore, che dee essere tra il marito e la moglie, e delle leggi del matri-
monio.'

P. 259, 1–7. *For if a man . . . aduertised by vs*. A confused version
of ' perciocchè, se il considerare, se il marito dee uccidere la moglie
impudica, o in altro modo secondo le leggi punirla, è considerazione,
che peravventura può più opportunamente in altro proposito essere
avuta ; e se tale la prenderai, quale figurata l' abbiamo, non dei
temere che mai ti venga occasione, per la quale di essere da me stato
intorno a ciò consigliato, debba desiderare.'

29. *Antiperistasis*. For a metaphorical use of this phrase, explained by Kyd in his marginal note, cf. Burkitt on 2 *Cor*. iv. 16
(quoted in *N.E.D.*) : ' The cold blasts of persecution . . . did, by
a spiritual antiperistasis, increase the heat of grace within.'

complexion, constitution.

31. *those of* Aguitan *and thereabouts* : ' dei Celti.' T.

36–9. From *Aen*. ix. 603–6.

P. 260, 5–6. *Which custome . . . extreame* : ' E benchè io quel costume non vitupero.' T.

10. *in that same booke of his* Aeneidos. Added by Kyd. The lines
are from *Aen*. ix. 614–20, omitting 615.

17–22. This version of the Virgilian passage contains several mistakes. In 17 ' purple buds' does not represent *murex*, and in 18
' your high Priests hats are made like hoods ' is an incorrect rendering
of *habent redimicula mitrae*. In 19 the point of the contrast between
the feminine *Phrygiae* and the masculine *Phryges* is missed, and
' scale you high Ida hyl ' is an inaccurate version of *ite per alta
Dindyma*.

23. *some Citties* : ' alcuna città.' T.

28–32. *for such . . . theyr example*. A confused version, due
partly to the misunderstanding of *Eroi*, as in P. 245, 34–5, and P. 246,
8–9 : ' perchè quella educazione rende gli uomini fieri, come de'
Lacedemoni fu giudicato, et quando ella pur fosse conveniente agli

Eroi, benchè tale non fu Achille ne' costumi, che alcuno Eroe se lo
debba proporre per esempio.'

P. 261, I. *werish*, weak, puny ; also used in sense of insipid. Cf.
Palsgrave, p. 328 : ' *werysshe*, as meate is that is not well tastye.'

5-9. *is, or ought to be . . . agreeable therewith.* A confused version
of ' è cura in guisa del padre di famiglia che ella insieme è del politico,
il quale dovrebbe prescrivere a' padri il modo, col quale dovessero i
figliuoli allevare, acciocchè la disciplina della città riuscisse uniforme.'

13-4. *and in their Princes seruice and obedience.* Added by Kyd.

14-6. *and that they . . . and honesty.* An expansion of ' egualmente
nell' arti lodevoli dell' animo e del corpo esercitati.'

27-8. *and are at this day . . . enfranchized.* A mistranslation of
' ed oggi sono per lo più uomini liberi,' i.e. ' and in these days servants
are for the most part freemen.'

34. *signiorising termes* : ' e di più severo imperio ' ; ' signiorise ' is
a favourite phrase of Kyd. Cf. *Corn.* i. 55.

P. 262, 16-7. *if he chaunce . . . or vtteraunce.* T. has simply ' se
avviene che egli ben non rappresenti la persona, della quale si è vestito.'

19-21. *Likewise he that . . . dignitie.* A wrong rendering of ' Simil-
mente chi non ben sostiene la persona di Principe, o di gentiluomo
che in questa vita (che è quasi teatro del mondo) dalla fortuna gli è
stata imposta.'

25-7. *and, as* Petrarch *sayth . . . the greater number are.* Added
by Kyd.

35. *record*, remember.

36-7. *which these . . . are commaunded.* T. has simply ' il che
delle bestie non avviene.'

P. 263, 4. *the forme of those impressions whatsoeuer* : ' le forme
delle virtù.' T.

22-3. *the mind . . . with reason* : ' la docilità de' servi è con
ragione.'

P. 264, 8. *Cyuill warre* : ' Guerra Servile.' T.

17-20. *Howbeit it is . . . worth while the noting.* A confused expansion of ' Tuttavolta grande argomento della viltà che la fortuna servile suole negli animi generare è l'esempio degli Sciti.'

23-4. *besides their weapons many whips and bastonadoes.* T. has
simply ' le sferze.'

28-9. *I cannot commend . . . nor body.* The insertion of ' neither
. . . nor' reverses the meaning of ' questi non loderei che fossero e di
animo e di corpo atti alla guerra.'

33. *The first* : ' nella prima,' T., i.e. ' in the first of the two formes '
or classes just mentioned.

35. *The next* : ' e quello,' T., continuing the enumeration of the
servants in the first class. Similarly in 37 *The thyrd* is substituted
for ' ed.'

38. *the Toun affaires* : ' le cose di villa tutte.' T.

The others : ' nell' altra,' T , i.e. ' in the second class.'

P. 265, 21. *which (hauing no recourse)*: 'che non si muovono.' T. For this use of 'recourse,' to denote the flowing movement of water, cf. *Tr. and Cress.* v. 3. 55 : 'Their eyes o'ergalled with recourse of tears.'

22. *naughtie*, bad, worthless.

35-6. *no vncleanes, filth, or Rubbishe.* T. has simply 'niuna bruttura.'

38-9. *it may shine . . . as Christall*: 'risplendano a guisa di specchi.' T.

P. 266, 12. From Petrarch, *Canz.* ix. 18.

16. From *Georg.* i. 160.

19-20. From *Aen.* i. 177-8. The marginal reference to '*Aeneid*, Lib. 2,' which is not given by Tasso, is wrong.

29. *the Maister himselfe*: 'il maestro di casa (i.e. the steward) o il padrone stesso.' T.

34-5. *are to be seuerally lodged from the whole*: 'in letti più morbidi ed agiati debbono esser posti a giacere.' T.

P. 267, 6. *bent of the brow.* Cf. *Ant. and Cleop.* i. 3. 36 :

> 'Eternity was in our Lippes and Eyes,
> Blisse in our browes bent.'

14-6. *they are* Inanima . . . *with a soule.* Expanded from 'ove gli altri sono inanimi, il servo è animato.'

22. *if you will rightly vnderstand him*: 'se tu vuoi avere di lui perfetta cognizione.' T.

25. *some stretch further*: 'alcune escono fuori.' T.

29. *Clerke*: 'Cancelliere.' T.

32. *capable of fashions*: 'atto alle azioni.' T.

34-5. *is applied in the highest*: 'è detta in eccellenza.' T.

35. *in those good worldes*: 'ne' buoni secoli.' T.

39-40. *The like was* Tyro . . . *written by* Tullie. An ambiguous rendering of 'Tale anche fu Tirone, al quale sono scritte molte lettere di Marco Tullio.' Tullius Tiro, the freedman of Cicero, and a distinguished grammarian, was one of his chief correspondents. *Ad Fam.*, Bk. XVI, is entirely addressed to him.

P. 269, 1. *those compasses*: 'quelle misure.' T.

8-12. *and no lesse* . . . Venice. A paraphrase of 'nè minore ⟨notizia⟩ averla dee de' prezzi che alle cose sono imposti, o da' pubblici magistrati, o dal consenso degli uomini ; nè meno essere informato, come le cose si vendano o si comprino in Turino, in Milano, in Lione o in Venezia, che come nella sua patria sian vendute o comprate.'

17. *Fields*: 'i campi e le vigne,' T.

18-9. *numbred by* Algorisme: 'misurata da' numeri aritmetici.' T. 'Algorisme'='the Arabic or decimal system of numeration,' hence 'arithmetic' generally; 'fr. Arab. *al-Khowārazmī*, the *native of Khwārazm (Khiva)*, surname of the Arab mathematician Abu Ja'far Mohammed Ben Musa, who flourished early in the 9th c. and through the translation of whose work on Algebra the Arabic numerals became generally known in Europe' (*N.E.D.*).

P. 269,19–20. *that which ... coyned*: 'quella ancora che del danaro è misurata.' T.

20. *quadering*, orig. 'making square'; hence 'making foursquare with,' 'matching.' For the use of this rare verb intransitively cf. Kyd's *Letter to Puckering*: 'Nor wold indeed the forme of devyne praiers used duelie in his Lordships house haue quadred with such reprobates.'

24–5. *for Landes ... more account*: 'conciosiachè le terre non sono sempre ñel medesimo preggio, e molto meno i frutti loro, e il danaro, non che altro suol crescere, o calare.' T.

29. *manurance*. Used here in its original sense of 'handling,' without the connotation of 'cultivating,' either literally or metaphorically.

ouerweener. For this rare subst. cf. Massinger, *Parl. of Love*, ii. 1: 'A flatterer of myself, or overweener.'

31–2. *That call I ... without life*. A perversion of 'Qualità chiamo poi delle facoltà ch' elle siano o artificiali o naturali, o animate o inanimate.'

P. 270, 14. *by ofte recorse and refluence*, by frequent flow and ebb. Cf. P. 265, l. 21.

17. *in a champant Countrey*, in a flat, open district. Cf. *Corn.* v. 176–7:
'of a Champant Land
Makes it a Quagmire.'

19. *steepeward*. A very rare, if not unique form.

22–4. *the Trauailers ... to passe*. An inaccurate rendering of 'i peregrini, e i mercanti d' Italia in Germania o in Francia sogliono trapassare.'

25–6. *if aloft ... ouerflowne*: 'se in colle che signoreggi, che goda di bella veduta, o in valle humile che ne sia priua.' T.

40. *they are better cheape*, they are lower in price.

P. 271, 2–7. *Againe he may keepe ... of seasons*. An expansion of 'Potrà anco trattenere alcuna volta l' entrate secondo i pronostici, e i giudicii, che si fanno della carestia, e dell' abbondanza degli anni, e delle stagioni.'

26. *diuers sorts of fruits*: 'dall' uve e da' fichi e da altri frutti.' T.

35–6. *furnish her messe with those iunckets*: 'arricchire la mensa.' T.

37–9. *that all her houshold ... drink*: 'che tutti i frumenti, che in casa sono, si macinino, e se ne faccia il pane.' T.

P. 272, 5. *which custome is not gueason in some houses*. A mistranslation of 'chè strana usanza è certo quella d' alcune case,' i.e. 'but strange certainly is the custom of some houses.' 'Gueason' is a rare variant of 'geason'='scarce, uncommon.'

8. *Therefore*: 'nondimeno,' T; the change destroys the logical connexion.

11. *for thrift ... as a ma⟨n⟩*. A mistranslation of 'perchè la parsimonia è virtù così propria di lei, come dell' uomo la liberalità.'

21. *of Lynnen or of wollen weauing*: 'de' lini, e delle tele, e delle sete.' T.

28. *ray*, cover with dirt, defile.   Cf. *T. of Sh.* iv. 1, 3, 'Was euer man so beaten ? Was euer man so rayed?'

29-30. *yet to be seene . . . such thrift.*   Added by Kyd.

33-5. *may furnish . . . sonne or daughter*: 'può fare alla figliuola ricco ed orrevol mobile.' T.

37-8. *these verses in the Booke of* Virgill.   From *Aen.* viii. 407-13.

P. 273, 9. *by candlelight.*   A mistranslation of *ad lumina*, i. e. 'till dawn.'

15-6. *as appeareth . . .* Vlisses: 'come di Penelope si legge.' T.

20. *to bleare*, to dim.   Hence to 'blear the sight of' a person = to 'blind,' 'hoodwink' him.

23. From *Georg.* i. 294.

26-7. *but placed . . . amongst them*: 'ma la figliuola del Re Alcinoo pone fra le lavatrici.' T.   Kyd's mistranslation shows that he had not read the story of Nausicaa.

P. 274, 18-25. *of so great efficacye . . . aunswer crosse.*   A paraphrase of 'Di tanta virtù è l' ordine quanta detta abbiamo, ma è di non minor bellezza, il che di leggiero potrà comprendere, chi leggerà i Poeti, i quali con niun altro artificio aggiungono più di vaghezza a' versi loro, che con ordinare le parole in guisa, che l' vna coll' altra, o come simile, o come pari si accordi, o come contraria risponda.'

35. *without impeach*, without bringing disparagement upon myself.

P. 275, 2-3. *passing neat and queintly tricked vp.*   T. has simply 'così pulita.'

10. *meeter to be spoken of, then shewed to straungers*: 'che a' forestieri sogliono esser dimostrate.' T.

21. *that fells and seazoneth*: 'che taglia.' T.

21-2. *It is very manifest.*   Before these words Kyd omits 'E cominciando a risolvere i dubbii.'

37. *compynable*, a variant of 'companable,' which has been replaced since the seventeenth century by 'companionable.'

39. *no lesse profit*: 'non picciola vtilità.' T.   The use of the comparative is confusing.

P. 276, 8. *Wherupon we reade*: 'onde si legge ne' Poeti.' T.

11. Virgill . . . *brought in* Numa *boasting thus.*   The two lines which follow are from *Aen.* vii. 748-9, with '*caniciem galea premimus*' wrongly substituted for '*armati terram exercent.*'   Virgil is referring to Ufens and his people, not to Numanus, wrongly called Numa by Kyd.

18. *Barbarians and Turkes.*   T. has simply 'Barbari.'

28-9. *because it growes not other-where so plentiously.*   Added by Kyd.

36-9. *who had the whole . . . trade of merchandize*: 'il quale avea in mano l'entrate della Repubblica, e da' quali la mercanzia era esercitata.' T.

P. 277, 14. *Shyre or Countrey.* Added by Kyd.

16. *best cheape,* at the lowest price. Cf. P. 270, l. 40.

29–32. *the care . . . houshold gouernment.* A confused rendering of 'il padre di famiglia ha l'acquisto della trasmutazione per obietto secondo, e dirizzato al governo della casa.'

38—**P. 278,** 6. *But the Housekeeper . . . for their greatnes*: 'ma il padre di famiglia ha il desiderio delle ricchezze terminato, perciocchè le richezze altro non sono, che moltitudine di instrumenti appartenenti alla cura famigliare e pubblica ; ma gl' instrumenti in alcun' arte non sono infiniti, nè di numero, nè di grandezza : chè se infiniti fossero di numero, non potrebbe l' artefice avere di loro cognizione, conciossia-cosachè l' infinito, in quanto infinito, non è compreso dal nostro intelletto : se di grandezza, non potrebbero esser maneggiati ; oltrechè non si concede corpo d' infinita grandezza.' Here the correspondence between 'il padre di famiglia' and 'alla cura famigliare' is obscured by translating the former 'Housekeeper' (38) and the latter 'familiar cares ' (40); ' certaine and determinat ' (39) is an inaccurate rendering of ' terminato,' i. e. ' limited ' ; the substitution of ' some arts' (P. 278, l. 1) for ' alcun' arte,' i. e. 'any art,' invalidates the argument, and in the remainder of the passage Kyd goes entirely astray.

P. 278, 14–7. *euen so should riches . . . shall suffise.* An inaccurate rendering of ' così parimente le ricchezze debbono esser proporzionate al padre di famiglia ed alla famiglia, ch' egli sostiene, e che di quelle dee esser erede, tanto e non più quanto bastino.'

21–2. *which are needfull . . .* Rome : ' ch' era convenevole ad un Principe cittadino di Roma.' T.

22. *too too much.* Perhaps the repetition of 'too' is a misprint, but 'too much' may be treated as equivalent to a single epithet qualified by 'too.'

23, *little Tounes in* Italie. Added by Kyd.

24. *for many men in* Rome : 'anco in uomo Romano.' T.

33–4. *exceeding others . . . wrong.* T. has simply 'che tanto si avanzi.'

P. 279, 6. *from the Plough and Carte*: 'dall' aratro.' T. Cf. *Cornelia,* i. 133, and *Introduction* p. lxiii.

7. *and mightie men in Princes Courts.* Added by Kyd, and curiously inapplicable to Roman Republicans.

39–40. *doo all those meanes . . . Nature.* Perversion of 'operano tutte quelle arti, che della natura sono imitatrici.'

P. 280, 7. *is a collection of a summe*: 'è una ragunanza di unità.' T.

13–4. *because things . . . of number certaine*: 'perchè gl' individui in ciascuna specie sono di numero finito.' T.

33–8. *wherewith Vsury . . . neuer to be cured.* Substituted for T.'s unimpassioned statement, 'alla quale l' usura non si può ridurre, che è scompagnata da ogni pericolo.'

P. 281, 2–5. *who so considereth . . .* de Phisicis. T. has simply 'e di lei ragionando Dante, disse.'

6-16. From *Inferno*, xi. 104-14.

21. *Neipce to God by Kind*, grandchild to God by relationship.

32—**P. 282,** 4. *It is . . . the thing.* Added by Kyd.

P. 282, 23. *Now would I be silent*: ' ora rimarrebbe solo,' T., i.e. ' now it would only remain.'

P. 283, 5-6. *Mason, Carpenter, or Architect.* T. has simply ' archi-tetto.'

12-4. *I beleeue . . . and greatnes.* A mistranslation of ' posso credere, che la casa del privato da quella del Principe, per altro che per grandezza sola, sia differente.'

22. In conuiuio Platonis. Cf. *Sympos.* 223.

28. *dedicated*: ' attribuito.' T. The use of ' dedicate ' in this sense is apparently unique.

35-6. *as were of olde . . . noble men*: ' come anticamente quello de' Satrapi.' T.

NOTES

THE MVRDER OF IOHN BREWEN

Page 287, 8. *fact*, criminal deed. Cf. *Sp. Tr.* iii. 4. 24.

22. *proper*, handsome.

23. *fauour*, appearance. Cf. *Sp. Tr.* iii. 13. 151.

P. 288, 14. *nice*, fastidious, capricious.

37. *checkt*, reviled, taunted.

P. 289, 20. *shadow*, screen, disguise.

30. *confection*, poisoning, corruption. The use of 'a confection' in the sense of a poison or potion is common, but this extension of the meaning is rare.

35. *suger-soppes*, sugar-plums.

P. 290, 5. *posnet*, a small basin.

34. *mystrusting*, suspecting.

P. 291, 4. *quibd*, reproached ; a rare verb.

P. 293, 4-8. *the hateful sinne . . . vnpunished.* Cf. with this passage *Sp. Tr.* ii. 5. 57-9, iii. 6. 95-6, and iii. 13. 2-3.

NOTES

TO

THE FIRST PART OF IERONIMO

ACT I.

SCENE I.

S.D. *Signate*. A variant of *Sennet*, a particular set of tones on a trumpet or cornet. Cf. Dekker, *Satirom.* : 'Drums sound a flourish, and then a Sennet.'

11. *impare*, discredit.

32. *for Spain*. This emendation gives a metrically correct line; otherwise 'from Portingale' would be preferable.

115. *chap*, jaw.

SCENE II.

21. *Push*. An exclamation of impatience. Cf. Middleton, *Your Five Gallants*, ii. 1 : 'Push, I take't vnkindly, faith.' Hence Hazlitt's emendation is needless.

35. *Respectiue*, careful, anxious.

61. *play not this moyst prize*. To 'play prizes' is 'to contend publicly for a prize,' hence 'to contend only for show'; thus to 'play a moyst prize' is 'to make an ostentatious display of weeping.'

SCENE III.

7. *bulke*, body.

42-8. Reed compares *Two Gent. of Verona*, iii. 1. 89-91 :

'Win her with gifts if she respect not words;
Dumb jewels often, in their silent kind,
More than quick words do move a woman's mind.'

103. *As short my body*. An allusion probably to the part being played by a boy. Cf. 114 below; also ii. 3. 65, and 88-9, iii. 1. 33-8, and *Introduction* p. lxii.

105. *skabard*. Apparently a variant of 'scabbed' in the sense of 'vile,' 'loathsome.'

ACT II.

Scene I.

60-1. Cf. *Tamb.* Part II. i. 4:

'And I would striue to swim through pooles of blood,
Or make a bridge of murthered Carcases.'

71. *iumpe*, exactly.

Scene III.

8. *Tost logic*, bandied words in logical disputations.

9. *Eate Cues, drunk Cees.* 'Cue' is a University term for a certain small quantity of bread. Cf. *Patient Grissil*, p. 9 : 'Eight to a neck of mutton—is not that your commons?—and a cue of bread.' The term originally meant half a farthing, formerly denoted in College accounts by the letter *q* for *quadrans*. 'Cee' similarly meant $\frac{1}{16}$ of a penny, and came to denote in University parlance a small quantity of beer. Cf. Earle's *Microcosmographie*, p. 38 : 'Hee ⟨an old College butler⟩ domineers over Freshmen . . . and puzzles them with strange language of Cues and Cees, and some broken Latine.'

29. *ile take vp thee*, I will rebuke thee, quarrel with thee.

121. *iealious*, suspicious.

Scene IV.

4. *by my crosse*, the cross formed by the hilt of Lorenzo's sword. Cf. *Sp. Tr.* ii. 1. 87.

29. *my shapes substance*, i.e. the real Andrea.

33. *adimanticke*, natural to adamant or loadstone ; a very rare word.

67. *to slubber day*, to obscure day. Reed compares *Oth.* i. 3. 223 : 'You must, therefore, be content to slubber the gloss of your new fortunes.'

95. *pretends*, portends.

98. *clyng*, probably 'cleave fast to,' hence 'cleave,' 'pierce.' Reed suggests, wrongly, I think, that 'Horatio means that his weapon shall *cling to him*, or *not leave* him, until he has gratified his revenge for his friend's murder.'

118. *swound*, swoon.

128. *found*, found out.

139. *pretends*. Cf. note on 95.

Scene V.

20. *he*, i.e. Alcario.

26. A pun upon 'cut downe,' in its senses of 'shorten' and of 'cutting down a body from the gallows.' Reed's emendation may be right, but I think that Lazarotto intends a contrast between his 'words' and his own approaching fate.

63. *Word for word*. A comparison of 64-5 with ii. 1. 83 shows that Andrea does not report the King of Portugal's speech absolutely 'word for word.'

S.D. *A Tucket*, a flourish of trumpets.

SCENE VI.

27. *part*, parting.

ACT III.

SCENE I.

33-8. Cf. note on i. 3. 103.

89-92. Repeated from ii. 1. 28-31, with substitution of 'that what' for 'that which' in 91.

SCENE II.

22. *Pies.* A variant of 'pize,' a mild form of oath.

46. *the heauy dread of battaile.* A possible emendation is 'the heauy dead of battaile,' on the analogy of 'the dead of night.'

67. *a lay*, a wager. Cf. 2 *Hen. VI*, v. 2. 27:

'*Clif.* My soul and body on the action both?
York. A dreadful lay!—address thee instantly.'

103. *top*, slice off.

141. *whether.* Cf. note on *Sp. Tr.* i. 2. 160.

SCENE III.

S.D. Phillippo *and* Cassimero. On the introduction here of these hitherto unmentioned characters cf. *Introduction* p. xliv. note.

INDEX TO THE INTRODUCTION

INDEX TO NOTES

ABBREVIATIONS USED

Sp. Tr.	= The Spanish Tragedie.
C.	= Cornelia.
S. and P.	= Soliman and Perseda.
H. P.	= The Housholders Philosophie.
M. I. B.	= The Murder of Iohn Brewen.
F. P. I.	= The First Part of Ieronimo.